TRAINING & REFERENCE

murach's
ASP.NET 4.6
web programming
with C# 2015

Mary Delamater

Anne Boehm

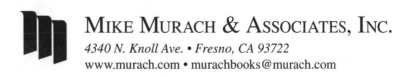
MIKE MURACH & ASSOCIATES, INC.

4340 N. Knoll Ave. • Fresno, CA 93722

www.murach.com • murachbooks@murach.com

Authors:	Mary Delamater
	Anne Boehm
Editor:	Mike Murach
Production:	Maria Spera

Books for .NET developers

Murach's C# 2015

Murach's ADO.NET Database Programming with C#

Murach's Visual Basic 2015

Murach's ASP.NET 4.5 Web Programming with VB 2012

Books for web developers

Murach's HTML5 and CSS3 (3rd Ed.)

Murach's JavaScript and jQuery (3rd Ed.)

Murach's PHP and MySQL (3rd Ed.)

Books for Java and Python programmers

Murach's Python Programming

Murach's Beginning Java with Eclipse

Murach's Java Programming (5th Ed.)

Murach's Java Servlets and JSP (3rd Ed.)

Murach's Android Programming (2nd Ed.)

Books for database programmers

Murach's SQL Server 2016 for Developers

Murach's MySQL (2nd Ed.)

Murach's Oracle SQL and PL/SQL for developers (2nd Ed.)

For more on Murach books, please visit us at www.murach.com

Printed in the United States of America

10 9 8 7 6 5 4 3
ISBN: 978-1-890774-95-0

Contents

Expanded contents

Chapter 5   How to test and debug ASP.NET applications

Section 2   ASP.NET essentials

Chapter 6   How to use the standard server controls

Chapter 18   How to use model binding and the Entity Framework

Section 4   Finishing an ASP.NET application

Chapter 19   How to secure a web application

Chapter 20   How to authenticate and authorize users

Chapter 21   How to use email, custom error pages, and back-button control

Introduction

ASP.NET is one of the primary technologies for developing web applications today. Together with Microsoft's Visual Studio, it provides a host of productivity features that let you quickly build professional e-commerce applications.

Because this book assumes that you already know the basics of C#, it gets you off to a fast start with ASP.NET. In fact, by the end of chapter 5, you'll know how to use ASP.NET and Visual Studio to develop and test multi-page database applications. You'll also know how to integrate HTML5 and CSS3 into your ASP.NET applications and how to use Bootstrap for responsive web design.

But this is much more than a beginning book. By the time you're done, you'll have all the skills you need for developing e-commerce web applications at a professional level. You'll also find that this book does double duty as the best on-the-job reference book that money can buy.

What this book does

To be more specific about what this book presents, here is a brief description of each of its sections:

- Section 1 is designed to get you off to a fast start. It shows you how to use Visual Studio and ASP.NET to develop both one-page and multi-page Web Forms applications that get data from a database. It shows you how to integrate HTML5, CSS, and Bootstrap into your web applications. It even shows you how to test and debug your web applications, a part of the job that many books treat too lightly or too late. At that point, you're ready for rapid progress in the sections that follow.

- Section 2 presents the other skills that you're likely to use in every ASP.NET application that you develop. That includes how to use the server controls and validation controls, as well as how to use state, cookies, and URL encoding to control the operation of an application. It also includes how to use master pages, Bootstrap classes and components, and friendly URLs to create user-friendly web applications.

- In section 3, you'll learn how to use the data access features of ASP.NET. That includes using SQL data sources, which reduce the amount of data access code that you need to write for an application. It includes bound controls that are designed to work with data sources, including the GridView, DetailsView, FormView, ListView, and DataPager controls. It includes object data sources, which make it easier to build 3-layer applications that separate the presentation code from the data access code. And it includes model binding, which lets you bind directly to data controls.

- Section 4 presents the skills that you need for finishing an e-commerce application. Here, you'll learn how to secure data transmissions between client and server, how to authenticate and authorize users with ASP.NET Identity, how to use email, how to prevent problems caused by Back button refreshes, and how to deploy your applications. At this point, you've learned everything you need to know to develop and deploy e-commerce web applications.

- Then, section 5 shows you how to take your applications to another level. First, you'll learn how to use ASP.NET Ajax to build rich Internet applications (RIAs). Then, you'll learn how to create and consume WCF and Web API services. Last, you'll be introduced to ASP.NET MVC, which is completely different than developing web applications with Web Forms, but does a better job of separating the presentation, business, and database code.

To get the most from this book, we recommend that you start by reading the first section from start to finish. But after that, you can skip to any of the other sections to get the information that you need, whenever you need it. Since this book has been carefully designed to work that way, you won't miss anything by skipping around.

Why you'll learn faster and better with this book

Like all our books, this one has features that you won't find in competing books. That's why we believe you'll learn faster and better with our book than with any other. Here are some of those features.

- Because section 1 presents a complete subset of ASP.NET in just 5 chapters, you're ready for productive work much faster than you are when you use competing books. This section also uses a self-paced approach that lets experienced programmers move more quickly and beginners work at a pace that's right for them.

- Because the next 3 sections present all of the other skills that you need for developing e-commerce web applications, you can go from beginner to professional in a single book.

- If you page through this book, you'll see that all of the information is presented in "paired pages," with the essential syntax, guidelines, and examples on the right page and the perspective and extra explanation on the left page. This helps you learn faster by reading less...and this is the ideal reference format when you need to refresh your memory about how to do something.

- To make sure that you learn ASP.NET as thoroughly as possible, all of its features are presented in the context of complete applications. These applications include the web forms, the aspx code, and the C# code. As we see it, the best way to learn ASP.NET is to study applications like these, even though you won't find them in most competing books.

What software you need

To develop ASP.NET applications, you can use any of the full editions of Visual Studio 2015. These editions come with everything you need, including Visual Studio, C#, a built-in web server called IIS Express that's ideal for testing ASP.NET applications on your own computer, and a scaled-back version of SQL Server called SQL Server Express LocalDB.

For a no-cost alternative to the commercial packages, you can download Visual Studio 2015 Community Edition from Microsoft's website. It too provides all of the items listed above, it's a terrific product for learning how to develop ASP.NET applications, and both the applications and the skills that you develop with it will work with any of the full editions of Visual Studio. For information about installing these products, please refer to appendix A.

How our downloadable files can help you learn

If you go to our website at www.murach.com, you can download all the files that you need for getting the most from this book. These files include:

- all of the applications in this book
- the starting code for the exercises at the ends of the chapters
- the solutions to the chapter exercises

These files let you test, review, and copy the application code. In addition, if you have any problems with the exercises, the solutions are there to help you over the learning blocks. Even when you've come up with a solution that works, our solution may show you another way to handle a problem. Here again, appendix A shows you how to download and install these files.

3 companion books for ASP.NET programmers

As you read this book, you may discover that your C# skills aren't as strong as they ought to be. In that case, we recommend that you get a copy of *Murach's C# 2015*. It will get you up-to-speed with the language. It will show you how to work with the most useful .NET classes. And as a bonus, it will show you how to develop Windows Forms applications.

The second companion is *Murach's SQL Server 2016 for Developers*. To start, it shows you how to write SQL statements in all their variations so you can code the right statements for your data sources. This often gives you the option of having Microsoft SQL Server do more, which simplifies your application code. Beyond that, this book shows you how to design and implement databases and how to use features like stored procedures.

Another book that we recommend is *Murach's ADO.NET 4 Database Programming with C#*. This book shows you how to write the ADO.NET code that you need for using object data sources in your applications. It gives you insight into what ADO.NET is doing as you use SQL data sources. And it shows you how to work with XML, create reports, and use LINQ and the Entity Framework.

3 books for every web developer

Although chapter 3 presents a subset of the HTML and CSS skills that you need for ASP.NET programming, every web developer should have a full set of these skills. For that, we recommend *Murach's HTML5 and CSS3 (3rd Edition)*. Beyond that, every web programmer should know how to use JavaScript and jQuery for client-side programming. For that, we recommend *Murach's JavaScript (2nd Edition)* and *Murach's jQuery (2nd Edition)*.

If you're new to these subjects, these books will get you started fast. If you have experience with these subjects, these books make it easy for you to learn new skills whenever you need them. And after you've used these books for training, they become the best on-the-job references you've ever used.

Support materials for trainers and instructors

If you're a corporate trainer or a college instructor who would like to use this book for a course, we offer an Instructor's CD that includes: (1) a complete set of PowerPoint slides that you can use to review and reinforce the content of the book; (2) instructional objectives that describe the skills a student should have upon completion of each chapter; (3) test banks that test mastery of those skills; (4) extra chapter exercises and projects that prove mastery; and (5) solutions to the extra exercises and projects.

To learn more about this Instructor's CD and to find out how to get it, please go to our website at www.murach.com and click on the Trainers or Instructors link. Or, if you prefer, you can call Kelly at 1-800-221-5528 or send an email to kelly@murach.com.

Please let us know how this book works for you

This is the sixth edition of our ASP.NET book. For each edition, we've added the new features of ASP.NET, but we've also tried to improve both the technical excellence and educational effectiveness of every chapter in this book.

Now that we're done, we hope that we've succeeded in making this edition our best one ever. So, if you have any comments, we would appreciate hearing from you. If you like our book, please tell a friend. And good luck with your web programming.

Anne Boehm, Author
anne@murach.com

Mary Delamater, Author
maryd@techknowsolve.com

Section 1

The essence of ASP.NET programming

This section presents the essential skills for designing, coding, and testing ASP.NET web applications. After chapter 1 introduces you to the concepts and terms that you need to know for ASP.NET programming, chapter 2 shows you how to develop a one-page web application with ASP.NET. That includes designing the form for the application and writing the C# code that makes it work, and that gets you off to a fast start.

Next, chapter 3 shows you the right way to use HTML5, CSS3, and Bootstrap with an ASP.NET application, and chapter 4 shows you how to develop a two-page Shopping Cart application that gets product data from a database. At that point, you'll know how to build multi-page applications. Then, chapter 5 shows you how test and debug ASP.NET applications.

When you finish all five chapters, you'll be able to develop real-world applications of your own. You'll have a solid understanding of how ASP.NET works. You'll be ready for rapid progress as you read any of the other sections of the book...and you can read those sections in whatever sequence you prefer.

1

An introduction to ASP.NET programming

This chapter introduces you to the basic concepts of web programming and ASP.NET. Here, you'll learn how web applications work and what software you need for developing ASP.NET web applications. You'll also see how the HTML code for a web form is coordinated with the C# code that makes the web form work the way you want it to. When you finish this chapter, you'll have the background that you need for learning how to develop ASP.NET web applications with Visual Studio 2015.

An introduction to web applications

A *web application* consists of a set of *web pages* that are generated in response to user requests. The Internet has many different types of web applications, such as search engines, online stores, auctions, news sites, social sites, and games.

Two pages of a Shopping Cart application

Figure 1-1 shows two pages of an ASP.NET web application. In this case, the application is for an online store that lets users purchase Halloween products, including costumes, masks, and decorations. In chapter 4, you'll learn how to build this application.

The first web page in this figure is used to display information about the products that are available from the Halloween store. To select a product, you use the drop-down list that's below the banner at the top of the page. Then, the page displays information about the product including a photo, short and long descriptions, and the product's price. The application gets the data for these pages from a database.

If you enter a quantity in the text box near the bottom of the page and click the Add to Cart button, the second page in this figure is displayed. This page lists the contents of your shopping cart and provides several buttons that let you remove items from the cart, clear the cart, return to the previous page to continue shopping, or proceed to a checkout page.

Of course, the complete Halloween Superstore application also contains other pages. For example, if you click the Check Out button in the second page, you're taken to a page that lets you enter the information for completing the order. As you go through this book, you'll learn how to add other pages to this application.

The Order page of a Shopping Cart application

The Cart page of a Shopping Cart application

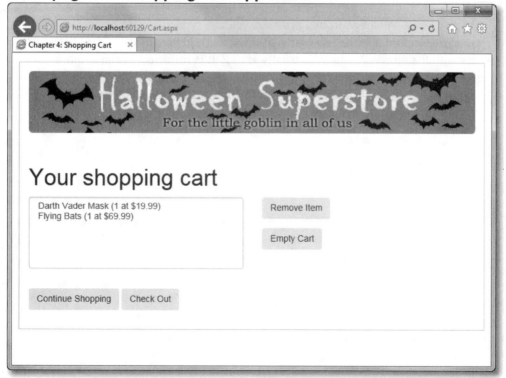

Figure 1-1   Two pages of a Shopping Cart application

The components of a web application

The diagram in figure 1-2 shows that web applications consist of *clients* and a *web server.* The clients are the computers, tablets, and mobile devices that use the web applications. They access the web pages through programs known as *web browsers.* The web server holds the files that make up the pages of a web application.

A *network* is a system that allows clients and servers to communicate. The *Internet* is a large network that consists of many smaller networks. In a diagram like the one in this figure, the "cloud" represents the network or Internet that connects the clients and servers.

Networks can be categorized by size. A *local area network* (*LAN*) is a small network of computers that are near each other and can communicate with each other over short distances. Computers in a LAN are typically in the same building or adjacent buildings. This type of network is often called an *intranet*, and it can run web applications that are used throughout a company.

In contrast, a *wide area network* (*WAN*) consists of multiple LANs that have been connected. To pass information from one client to another, a router determines which network is closest to the destination and sends the information over that network. A WAN can be owned privately by one company or it can be shared by multiple companies.

An *Internet service provider* (*ISP*) is a company that owns a WAN that is connected to the Internet. An ISP leases access to its network to companies that need to be connected to the Internet. When you develop production web applications, you will often implement them through an ISP.

To access a web page from a browser, you can type a *URL* (*Uniform Resource Locator*) into the browser's address area and press Enter. The URL starts with the *protocol*, which is usually HTTP. It is followed by the *domain name* and the folder or directory *path* to the file that is requested. If the file name is omitted in the URL, the web server looks for a default file in the specified directory. The default files usually include index.html, index.htm, default.html, and default.htm.

The components of a web application

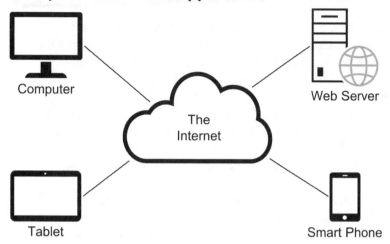

The components of an HTTP URL

Description

- A web application consists of clients, a web server, and a network.

- The *clients* use programs known as *web browsers* to request web pages from the web server. Today, the clients can be computers, smart phones, or tablets.

- The *web server* returns the pages that are requested to the browser.

- A *network* connects the clients to the web server.

- To request a page from a web server, the user can type the address of a web page, called a *URL*, or *Uniform Resource Locator*, into the browser's address area and then press the Enter key.

- A URL consists of the *protocol* (usually, HTTP), *domain name*, *path*, and file name. If you omit the protocol, HTTP is assumed. If you omit the file name, the web server will look for a file named index.html, index.htm, default.html, or default.htm.

- An *intranet* is a *local area network* (or *LAN*) that connects computers that are near each other, usually within the same building.

- The *Internet* is a network that consists of many *wide area networks* (*WANs*), and each of those consists of two or more LANs. Today, the Internet is often referred to as "the Cloud", which implies that you don't have to understand how it works.

- An *Internet service provider* (*ISP*) owns a WAN that is connected to the Internet.

Figure 1-2   The components of a web application

How static web pages are processed

A *static web page* like the one in figure 1-3 is a web page that doesn't change each time it is requested. This type of web page is sent directly from the web server to the web browser when the browser requests it. You can spot static pages in a web browser by looking at the extension in the address bar. If the extension is .htm or .html, the page is probably a static web page.

The diagram in this figure shows how a web server processes a request for a static web page. This process begins when a client requests a web page in a web browser. To do that, the user can either enter the URL of the page in the browser's address bar or click a link in the current page that specifies the next page to load.

In either case, the web browser builds a request for the web page and sends it to the web server. This request, known as an *HTTP request*, is formatted using the *HyperText Transfer Protocol* (HTTP), which lets the web server know which file is being requested.

When the web server receives the HTTP request, it retrieves the requested file from the disk drive. This file contains the *HTML (HyperText Markup Language)* for the requested page. Then, the web server sends the HTML back to the browser as part of an *HTTP response*.

When the browser receives the HTTP response, it *renders* (translates) the HTML into a web page that is displayed in the browser. Then, the user can view the content. If the user requests another page, either by clicking a link or entering another URL into the browser's address bar, the process begins again.

A static web page

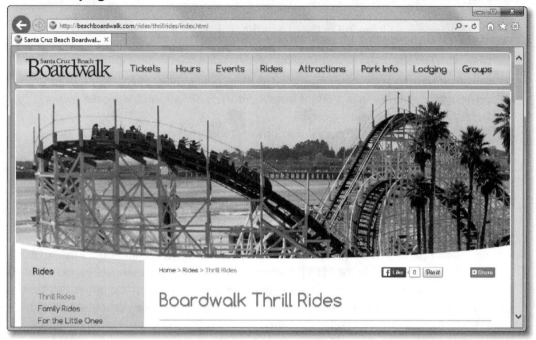

How a web server processes a static web page

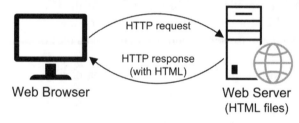

Web Browser   Web Server
                               (HTML files)

Description

- *Hypertext Markup Language* (*HTML*) is used to design the pages of a web application.

- A *static web page* is built from an *HTML document* that's stored on the web server and doesn't change. The file names for static web pages usually have .htm or .html extensions.

- When the user requests a static web page, the browser sends an *HTTP request* to the web server that includes the name of the file that's being requested.

- When the web server receives the request, it retrieves the HTML for the web page and sends it back to the browser as part of an *HTTP response*.

- When the browser receives the HTTP response, it *renders* the HTML into a web page that is displayed in the browser.

Figure 1-3   How static web pages are processed

How dynamic web pages are processed

A *dynamic web page* like the one in figure 1-4 is a page that's created by a program on an *application server*. This program uses the data that's sent with the HTTP request to generate the HTML that's returned to the server. In this example, the HTTP request included the product code. Then, the program retrieved the data for that product from a *database server*, including the path to the photo for the product.

The diagram in this figure shows how a web server processes a dynamic web page. The process begins when the user requests a page in a web browser. To do that, the user can click a link that specifies the dynamic page to load or click a button that submits a form that contains the data that the dynamic page should process.

In either case, the web browser builds an HTTP request and sends it to the web server. This request includes whatever data the application needs for processing the request. If, for example, the user has entered data into a form, that data will be included in the HTTP request.

When the web server receives the HTTP request, the server examines the file extension of the requested web page to identify the application server that should process the request. The web server then forwards the request to that application server.

Next, the application server retrieves the appropriate program. It also loads any form data that the user submitted. Then, it executes the program. As the program executes, it generates the HTML for the web page. If necessary, the program will also request data from a database server and use that data as part of the web page it is generating.

When the program is finished, the application server sends the dynamically generated HTML back to the web server. Then, the web server sends the HTML back to the browser in an HTTP response.

When the web browser receives the HTTP response, it renders the HTML and displays the web page. Note, however, that the web browser has no way to tell whether the HTML in the HTTP response was for a static page or a dynamic page. It just renders the HTML.

When the page is displayed, the user can view the content. Then, when the user requests another page, the process begins again. The process that begins with the user requesting a web page and ends with the server sending a response back to the client is called a *round trip*.

When you build ASP.NET applications, *Internet Information Services* (*IIS*) is used for the web server, and ASP.NET is used for the application server. You're also likely to use Microsoft's SQL Server for the *DBMS* (*database management system*).

A dynamic web page

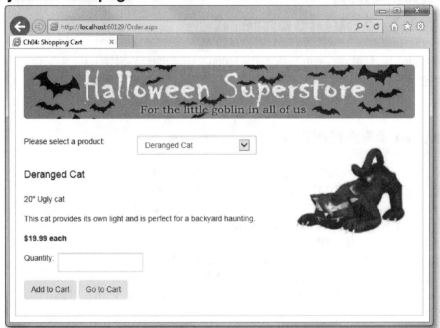

How a web server processes a dynamic web page

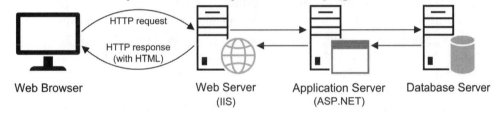

Description

- A *dynamic web page* is a web page that's generated by a program running on a server.

- When a web server receives a request for a dynamic web page, it looks up the extension of the requested file and passes the request to the appropriate *application server* for processing.

- When the application server receives the request, it runs the appropriate program. Often, this program uses data that's sent in the HTTP request to get related data from a *database management system* (*DBMS*) running on a *database server*.

- When the application server finishes processing the data, it generates the HTML for a web page and returns it to the web server. Then, the web server returns the HTML to the web browser as part of an HTTP response.

- The process that starts when a client requests a page and ends when the page is returned to the browser is called a *round trip*.

- When you build ASP.NET applications, *Internet Information Services* (*IIS*) is used for the web server and ASP.NET is used for the application server.

Figure 1-4   How dynamic web pages are processed

An introduction to ASP.NET development

In the topics that follow, you'll be introduced to the main ASP.NET technologies and the differences between them, the three types of development environments you can work in, and more.

The two main ASP.NET technologies

Figure 1-5 summarizes the two main ASP.NET technologies. ASP.NET *Web Forms* were introduced in 2002 as a replacement for *ASP (Active Server Pages)*, which is now called *Classic ASP*. In contrast to ASP, ASP.NET Web Forms let you work with a design model like the one for Windows Forms.

The primary focus of ASP.NET Web Forms is *Rapid Application Development (RAD)*. It accomplishes this by letting web developers work with server controls on a design surface. Then, ASP.NET converts the server controls to HTML. In this book, you'll learn to develop web applications with ASP.NET Web Forms.

In recent years, Microsoft added ASP.NET MVC to its web development offerings. It provides a way to implement the *Model-View-Controller* (*MVC*) pattern that offers separation of concerns and unit testing.

Separation of concerns refers to breaking an application into components so each one deals with a single concern. For example, one component can be responsible for communicating with the database, another for presenting information to users, and so on. *Unit testing* refers to code that tests whether other code does what it's supposed to do.

Because the benefits of ASP.NET MVC are compelling, new ASP.NET web development is often done with MVC. That's why the last chapter of this book presents an introduction to MVC. On the other hand, Web Forms development is easier than MVC development and may be more appropriate for smaller projects that need to be done quickly.

The two main types of Web Forms projects

In the web development world, the terms *web site*, *web application*, and *web project* are often used interchangeably. When you use Visual Studio 2015, though, these terms have specific meanings.

In ASP.NET Web Forms, a *web project* is either an *ASP.NET Web Forms Site* (or *web site*) or an *ASP.NET Web Forms Application* (or *web application*). The difference between the two is in how the projects are configured, compiled, and deployed, as indicated in figure 1-5.

Although there are pros and cons to each project type, Microsoft recommends that you use web application projects for new development, since they plan to focus their development efforts on that project type. Because of that, the projects for this book are all web application projects.

The two main ASP.NET technologies
- ASP.NET Web Forms
- ASP.NET MVC

The differences between the technologies

Technology	Description
ASP.NET Web Forms	A development environment similar to Windows Forms, with controls on a design surface. Its focus is on Rapid Application Development (RAD).
ASP.NET MVC	A development environment similar to PHP or classic ASP. It uses the Model-View-Controller (MVC) design pattern and the Razor templating engine for in-line data binding. Its focus is on separation of concerns and unit testing, and it gives the developer complete control over the HTML.

The two main types of ASP.NET Web Forms projects
- Web application projects
- Web site projects

The differences between the project types

Project type	Description
Web application	A project file stores information about the application, and the application files are compiled into a single assembly. This assembly is then deployed to the web server. A few of the newest ASP.NET features are only available to web applications.
Web site	There is no project file. Rather, all the files that are in the root directory are included in the web site. The files are individually deployed to the web server, and the site is dynamically compiled the first time the web site is requested.

Description
- Microsoft has developed several ASP.NET technologies over the years. The two most popular are ASP.NET Web Forms and ASP.NET MVC.
- *Web Forms* is the oldest and most established technology. It provides for *RAD* (*Rapid Application Development*) by letting developers build web pages by working with controls on a design surface.
- *MVC* (*Model-View-Controller*) is relatively new to the .NET family. It addresses perceived weaknesses in Web Forms, such as inadequate *separation of concerns* and the difficulty of *unit testing*. Since ASP.NET MVC is becoming increasingly popular, the last chapter in this book provides an introduction to it.
- When you work with Web Forms, you can create either a *web application project* or a *web site project*. Microsoft recommends that new development be done using web application projects, and some new functionality is only available with this type of project.

Figure 1-5   ASP.NET technologies and Web Forms project types

Three environments for developing ASP.NET applications

Figure 1-6 shows three development environments for ASP.NET applications. In a standalone environment, a single computer serves as both the client and the server. In an intranet environment, the clients are connected to the server over an intranet. And in an Internet environment, the clients are connected to the server over the Internet.

In all three environments, the clients need an operating system like Windows 7, 8, or 10 that supports ASP.NET 4.6 development, the .NET Framework 4.5.2 or 4.6, and Visual Studio 2015. Since the .NET Framework comes with Windows 7, 8, and 10, and also with Visual Studio 2015, you don't need to install it separately.

For the server, you need to install IIS as the application server and a database management system like SQL Server. In a standalone environment, you're likely to use IIS Express and SQL Server Express LocalDB, which come with Visual Studio 2015. But in an intranet or Internet environment, you're likely to use a full version of IIS and SQL Server.

In an intranet environment, the server also uses *WebDAV (Web-based Distributed Authoring and Versioning)*. WebDAV provides the services that Visual Studio 2015 uses to communicate with the web application on the server. Normally, though, you don't have to worry about this because the network manager sets this up.

In an Internet environment, the server also requires an *FTP server*, which is used to copy the files in a web application between the client computer and the server. The FTP server uses *File Transfer Protocol (FTP)* to perform the copy operations, and IIS can be configured to act as an FTP server as well as a web server. Here again, you usually don't have to worry about this because the server manager sets this up.

The table in this figure shows that Visual Studio 2015 is available in three editions. Most professional developers will work with the Professional edition, but large development teams may use the Enterprise edition, which includes features that provide for specialized development roles such as architects, developers, and testers.

A free alternative is Visual Studio Community Edition. This edition is designed for individual developers, students, and hobbyists, and everything that you'll learn in this book will work with the Community edition.

If you're learning on your own, you will most likely work in a standalone environment using Visual Studio 2015 Community Edition, IIS Express, and SQL Server Express LocalDB, which are all free. If you're working in a computer lab for a course, you will most likely work in an intranet environment, but it could also be an Internet environment. To install the client software that you'll need for any of these environments, you can follow the procedures in appendix A.

Standalone development

Windows 7 or later
.NET Framework 4.6 Visual
Studio 2015
IIS Express
SQL Server Express LocalDB

Intranet development

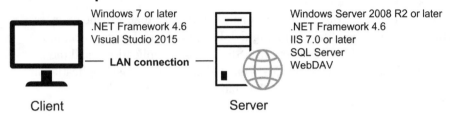

Windows 7 or later
.NET Framework 4.6
Visual Studio 2015

— **LAN connection** —

Windows Server 2008 R2 or later
.NET Framework 4.6
IIS 7.0 or later
SQL Server
WebDAV

Client   Server

Internet development

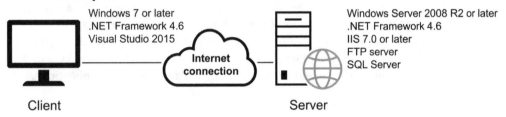

Windows 7 or later
.NET Framework 4.6
Visual Studio 2015

Internet connection

Windows Server 2008 R2 or later
.NET Framework 4.6
IIS 7.0 or later
FTP server
SQL Server

Client   Server

The three editions of Visual Studio 2015

Edition	Description
Visual Studio Community 2015	Free edition for Windows, web, and mobile apps.
Visual Studio Professional 2015	For individuals or small teams, it includes basic tools for testing, database deployment, and change and lifecycle management.
Visual Studio Enterprise 2015	For teams, it includes full testing, modeling, database, and lifecycle management tools.

Description

- When you use standalone development, a single computer serves as client and server.

- When you use intranet development, a client communicates with a server over a *local area network* (*LAN*). For this, the server uses *WebDAV* (*Web-based Distributed Authoring and Versioning*).

- When you use Internet development, a client communicates with a server over the Internet. For this, the server requires an *FTP server*. The FTP server uses *File Transfer Protocol* (*FTP*) to transfer files between the client computer and the server.

Figure 1-6   Three environments for developing ASP.NET applications

The components of the .NET Framework

Because you should have a basic understanding of what the *.NET Framework* does as you develop applications, figure 1-7 summarizes its major components. As you can see, this framework is divided into two main components, the .NET Framework Class Library and the Common Language Runtime, and these components provide a common set of services for applications written in .NET languages like Visual Basic or C#.

The *.NET Framework Class Library* consists of *classes* that provide many of the functions that you need for developing .NET applications. For instance, the ASP.NET classes are used for developing ASP.NET web applications, and the Windows Forms classes are used for developing standard Windows applications. The other .NET classes let you work with databases, manage security, access files, and perform many other functions.

The *Common Language Runtime*, or *CLR*, provides the services that are needed for executing any application that's developed with one of the .NET languages. This is possible because all of the .NET languages *compile* to a common *Intermediate Language* (or *IL*), which is stored in an *assembly*.

The CLR also provides the Common Type System that defines the data types that are used by all the .NET languages. That way, you can use the same data types no matter which .NET language you're using to develop your applications.

The .NET Framework

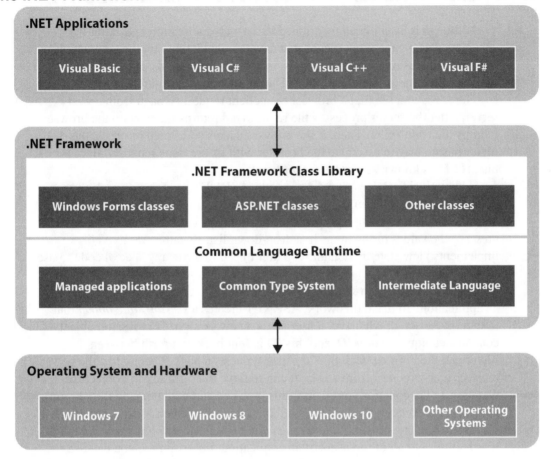

Description

- .NET applications work by using services of the *.NET Framework*. The .NET Framework, in turn, accesses the operating system and computer hardware.

- The .NET Framework consists of two main components: the .NET Framework Class Library and the Common Language Runtime.

- The *.NET Framework Class Library* provides pre-written code in the form of classes that are available to all of the .NET programming languages.

- The *Common Language Runtime*, or *CLR*, manages the execution of .NET programs by coordinating essential functions such as memory management and security.

- The Common Type System is a component of the CLR that ensures that all .NET applications use the same data types regardless of what programming languages are used.

- All .NET programs are *compiled* into *Microsoft Intermediate Language* (*MSIL*) or just *Intermediate Language* (*IL*), which is stored in an *assembly*. This assembly is then run by the CLR.

Figure 1-7   The components of the .NET Framework

How state is handled in ASP.NET applications

Although it hasn't been mentioned yet, a web application ends after it generates a web page. That means that any data maintained by the application, such as variables or control properties, is lost. In other words, HTTP doesn't maintain the *state* of the application. This is illustrated in figure 1-8.

Here, you can see that a browser on a client requests a page from a web server. After the server processes the request and returns the page to the browser, it drops the connection. Then, if the browser makes additional requests, the server has no way to associate the browser with its previous requests. Because of that, HTTP is known as a *stateless protocol*.

Although HTTP doesn't maintain state, ASP.NET provides several ways to do that, as summarized in this figure. First, you can use *view state* to maintain the values of server control properties. For example, you can use view state to preserve the values of the items in a drop-down list. Because ASP.NET implements view state by default, you don't need to write any special code to use it.

Second, you can use *session state* to maintain data between executions of an application. To make this work, ASP.NET creates a *session state object* that is kept on the server whenever a user starts a new session. This session object contains a unique *session ID*, and this ID is sent back and forth between the server and the browser each time the user requests a page. Then, when the server receives a new request from a user, it can retrieve the right session object for that user. In the code for your web forms, you can add data items to the session object so their previous values are available each time a web form is executed.

Third, you can use an *application state object* to save *application state* data, which applies to all of the users of an application. For example, you can use application state to maintain global counters or to maintain a list of the users who are currently logged on to an application.

Fourth, you can use *server-side caching* to save data. This is similar to application state in that the data saved in the cache applies to all users of an application. However, caching is more flexible than application state because you have control over how long the data is retained.

Last, you can use the individual user accounts of ASP.NET to keep track of user data. Although this is similar to session state, the data persists between user sessions because it is stored in a database.

Why state is difficult to track in a web application

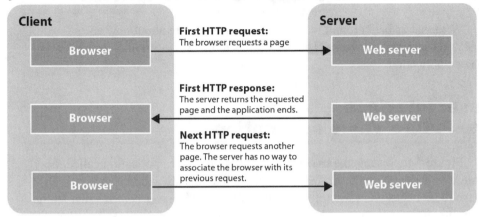

Concepts

- *State* refers to the current status of the properties, variables, and other data maintained by an application for a single user. The application must maintain a separate state for each user currently accessing the application.

- HTTP is a *stateless protocol*. That means that it doesn't keep track of state between round trips. Once a browser makes a request and receives a response, the application terminates and its state is lost.

Five ASP.NET features for maintaining state

Feature	Description
View state	Implemented by default, so no special coding is required. See chapter 2.
Session state	Uses a session state object that is created when a user starts a new session. The values in this object are available until the session ends. See chapter 4.
Application state	Uses an application state object that is created when an application starts. The values of this object are available to all users of the application until the application ends. See chapter 8.
Server-side caching	Like application state, the values in a server-side cache can be shared across an application. Unlike application state, a cache item is maintained only until its expiration time is reached. See chapter 8.
Individual user accounts	One account can be maintained for each user of an application. The data in an account is stored in a database and maintained from one user session to another. See chapter 20.

Description

- ASP.NET provides five ways to deal with the stateless protocol of a web application. The two that you'll use the most are *view state* and *session state*.

Figure 1-8   How state is handled in ASP.NET applications

How an ASP.NET application works

With that as background, you're ready to learn more about how an ASP.NET application works. That's why this topic presents a one-page Future Value application.

The user interface
for the Future Value application

Figure 1-9 presents the user interface for a one-page application called the Future Value application. In ASP.NET, pages like this are called *web forms*. To make these pages work, each form contains ASP.NET *server controls* that let the user interact with the page. For instance, this page contains these server controls: a drop-down list, two text boxes, a label that displays the future value, and two buttons. It also uses validation controls that check the user entries for validity.

To use the Future Value application, the user selects a monthly investment amount from the drop-down list, enters data into the two text boxes, and clicks the Calculate button. Then, if the data is valid, the future value is displayed. Otherwise, error messages are displayed below the buttons. To clear the controls, the user can click the Clear button.

The processing for the Calculate and Clear buttons is done on the server. That means that when either button is clicked, the form is submitted to the server, the C# code on the server processes the data in the form, and the form is returned to the browser. In other words, clicking either button leads to a round trip.

For example, when the Calculate button is clicked, the C# code on the server calculates the future value, and the form is returned to the browser with the future value displayed. That's a round trip. Similarly, when the Clear button is clicked, the C# code on the server resets the value in the drop-down list to 50 and clears the text boxes and the Future Value label. Then, the form is returned to the browser. That's also a round trip.

In some cases, though, the form isn't submitted to the browser when the Calculate button is clicked. That happens when JavaScript is enabled in the user's browser and one or more entries are invalid. Then, the JavaScript code that has been generated from the validation controls runs in the browser, detects the invalid entries, and displays appropriate error messages...without submitting the form to the server. That saves a round trip.

What if JavaScript isn't enabled in the user's browser? Then, the form is submitted to the server, and the server checks the entries for validity. That too is done by the code that's generated by the validation controls. In this example, that means a round trip occurs each time the user clicks the Calculate button if JavaScript is disabled. Fortunately, though, most browsers have JavaScript enabled.

The Future Value application after the user clicks the Calculate button

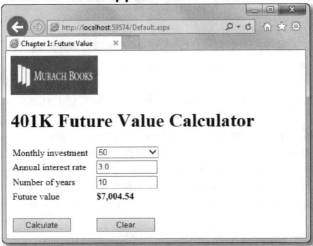

The Future Value application with error messages displayed

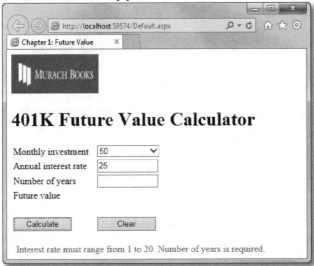

Description

- To calculate the Future Value of a monthly investment, the user selects a value in the drop-down list, enters values into the two text boxes, and clicks the Calculate button.

- If JavaScript is enabled in the browser, it is used to check the user's entries. If the entries are valid, the form is submitted to the server, the future value is calculated, and the page is returned to the browser with the future value displayed. If the entries are invalid, error messages are displayed by the JavaScript and the form isn't submitted. If JavaScript isn't enabled, the form is submitted to the server and the validation is done there.

- If the user clicks on the Clear button, the form is submitted to the server, the drop-down list is reset to 50, the text boxes are cleared, and the page is returned to the browser.

Figure 1-9   The Future Value application

The files used by the Future Value application

Figure 1-10 presents the Future Value form as it appears in the Web Forms Designer that you use when you develop web forms with Visual Studio 2015. In chapter 2, you'll learn how to use this Designer, but for now just try to get the big picture of how this form works.

If you look closely at the Designer window in the middle of Visual Studio, you can see the table that's used for this form. You can also see the server controls: the drop-down list that's used to select a monthly investment amount, text boxes for interest rate and number of years, a label for displaying the result of the future value calculation, and Calculate and Clear buttons.

If you look at the Solution Explorer to the right of the Designer window, you can see the folders and files that this application requires. These are summarized in the table in this figure.

The first three files in the table are for the web form. The file with aspx as the extension (Default.aspx) contains the code that represents the design of the form. This code consists of standard HTML code plus asp tags that define the server controls. This is called *aspx code*, because the file that contains the code has the aspx extension.

The file with aspx.cs as the extension (Default.aspx.cs) contains the C# code that controls the operation of the form. The cs file extension indicates that it is a C# file. This is called a *code-behind file* because it provides the code behind the web form.

The file with aspx.designer.cs as the extension (Default.aspx.designer.cs) contains the C# code that's generated by Visual Studio when you add server controls to the form. This is called a *designer file* because it provides code that Visual Studio uses to work with server controls in the Web Forms Designer. You should never need to make changes to this file, but it can be interesting to see what's in it.

The fourth and fifth files in the table in this figure are the configuration files. The Web.config file contains configuration information like which version of the .NET Framework is being used. The packages.config file contains information about the NuGet packages the application is using. You'll learn about NuGet packages in chapter 2.

The sixth file is the jpg file for the logo that's displayed at the top of the form. This file is in the Images folder that's shown in the Solution Explorer.

These files and the Images folder are all that this one-page application requires. However, two other folders are often used for Web Forms applications. A Models folder is used for user classes, and an App_Data folder is used for databases or data files. You'll see these used in the Shopping Cart application in chapter 4.

The Future Value form in Design view of Visual Studio 2015

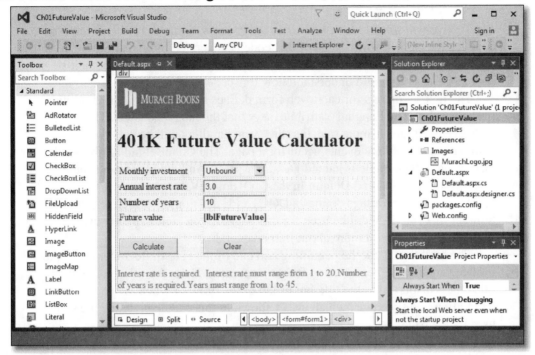

Some of the files in the Future Value application

Folder	File	Description
(root)	Default.aspx	The aspx file for the default page.
(root)	Default.aspx.cs	The code-behind file for the default page.
(root)	Default.aspx.designer.cs	The generated code for the default page.
(root)	Web.config, packages.config	XML files that contain configuration data.
Images	MurachLogo.jpg	The logo image for the form.

Description

- For each web form in a web application, ASP.NET 4.6 keeps three files. The file with the aspx extension holds the HTML code and the asp tags for the server controls. The file with the aspx.cs extension is the *code-behind file* that contains the C# code for the form. And the file with the aspx.designer.cs extension contains code generated by Visual Studio when you add server controls to the aspx file.

- Every ASP.NET application also includes a Web.config file with configuration data, and most applications include a packages.config file that contains information about NuGet packages used by the application.

- The Future Value application also contains a folder named Images that contains the jpg file for the logo that's displayed at the top of the page.

- Two other folders that you'll find in many ASP.NET web applications are a Models folder for user classes, and an App_Data folder for databases or data files.

Figure 1-10   The Future Value application in Visual Studio 2015

The aspx code for the Default form

To give you some idea of how aspx code works, figure 1-11 shows the aspx code for the Default form. Most of this code is generated by Visual Studio as you use the Web Forms Designer to design a form, so you don't have to code it all yourself. But you should understand how this code works.

The first set of tags for each web form defines a *page directive* that provides four attributes. The Language attribute says that the language is C#. The AutoEventWireup attribute says that the event handlers will be called automatically when the events occur for a page. The CodeBehind attribute says that the code-behind file is named Default.aspx.cs. And the Inherits attribute specifies the class named Default in the Ch01FutureValue namespace.

The second set of tags defines a DOCTYPE declaration, which tells the browser that HTML5 will be used for this page. If you aren't already using HTML5, you can learn more about it in chapter 3.

The html tags mark the beginning and end of the HTML document, and the head tags define the head section for the document. Here, the title tags define the title that is displayed in the title bar or tab of the browser when the page is run. In addition, the style tags, which aren't shown in this example, define the styles used by the page.

The content of the web page itself is defined within the div tags, which are within the body and form tags. Notice that the first form tag includes a Runat attribute that's assigned a value of "server." That indicates that the form will be processed on the server by ASP.NET. This attribute is required for all ASP.NET web forms and all ASP.NET server controls.

The asp tags within the div tags define the server controls that appear on the page. Since these controls include the Runat attribute with a value of "server," they will be processed on the server by ASP.NET. The last phase of this processing is generating the HTML for the controls so the page can be displayed by a browser.

The aspx code for the Calculate and Clear buttons includes an OnClick attribute. This attribute names the event handler that's executed when the user clicks the button and the form is posted back to the server.

The aspx code for the Clear button includes a CausesValidation attribute. This attribute tells the page whether to fire the validation event used by the validation controls. Setting this attribute to False for the Clear button means that the data validation controls will do their work when you click Calculate, but not when you click Clear.

Within the form, an HTML table is used to format the server controls. Here, the first four rows include the server controls that accept the user entries and display the future value. The fifth row provides vertical spacing. And the last row includes the Calculate and Clear button controls.

After the table are four field validator controls that aren't shown. These are server controls that provide validity checking, both in the browser with JavaScript and on the server with C#, and they cause error messages to be displayed when an error occurs. In the next chapter, you'll learn how to build this web form with its controls.

The aspx file for the Default form (Default.aspx)

```aspx
<%@ Page Language="C#" AutoEventWireup="true" CodeBehind="Default.aspx.cs"
Inherits="Ch01FutureValue.Default" %>

<!DOCTYPE html>

<html xmlns="http://www.w3.org/1999/xhtml">
<head id="Head1" runat="server">
    <title>Chapter 1: Future Value</title>
    <style type="text/css"><!-- CSS code for the generated styles --></style>
</head>
<body>
    <form id="form1" runat="server">
    <div>
        <img alt="Murach" class="style1" src="Images/MurachLogo.jpg"  /><br />
        <h1>401K Future Value Calculator</h1>
        <table class="style2">
            <tr>
                <td class="style3">Monthly investment</td>
                <td><asp:DropDownList ID="ddlMonthlyInvestment"
                    runat="server" Width="106px"></asp:DropDownList></td>
            </tr>
            <tr>
                <td class="style3">Annual interest rate</td>
                <td><asp:TextBox ID="txtInterestRate" runat="server"
                    Width="100px">3.0</asp:TextBox></td>
            </tr>
            <tr>
                <td class="style3">Number of years</td>
                <td><asp:TextBox ID="txtYears" runat="server"
                    Width="100px">10</asp:TextBox></td>
            </tr>
            <tr>
                <td class="style3">Future value</td>
                <td><asp:Label ID="lblFutureValue" runat="server"
                    Font-Bold="True"></asp:Label></td>
            </tr>
            <tr>
                <td class="style3"> </td>
                <td> </td>
            </tr>
            <tr>
                <td class="style3"><asp:Button ID="btnCalculate"
                    runat="server" Text="Calculate" Width="100px"
                    OnClick="btnCalculate_Click" /></td>
                <td><asp:Button ID="btnClear" runat="server"
                    Text="Clear" Width="100px" OnClick="btnClear_Click"
                    CausesValidation="False" /></td>
            </tr>
        </table>
        <br />
        <!-- aspx code for the field validators -->
    </div>
    </form>
</body>
</html>
```

Figure 1-11   The aspx code for the Default form of the Future Value application

The C# code for the Default form

To give you some idea of how the C# code for a form works, figure 1-12 presents the code-behind file for the Default form. Here, I've highlighted the most important code.

The first two highlighted lines are generated by Visual Studio. The first line is a namespace declaration and has the same name as the project. The second line is a class declaration and has the same name as the form.

Because the class declaration uses the partial keyword, this is a partial class that must be combined with another partial class when it's compiled. In fact, the code in this partial C# class is combined with the compiled code in its aspx file and designer file. The rest of this class declaration indicates that this class inherits the System.Web.UI.Page class, which is the .NET class that provides the basic functionality of ASP.NET pages.

Each time this web form is requested, ASP.NET initializes it and raises the Load event, which is handled by the Page_Load method. You will often see a page property called IsPostBack used in the Page_Load method to determine whether or not a page is being posted back. If the value is false, the page is being loaded for the first time.

For this application, if the page is being loaded for the first time, the code executes a loop that puts a range of dollar amounts into the drop-down list for monthly investment. Otherwise, nothing is done by this method.

Another page property that you will often use is called IsValid. This property indicates whether the page's validation controls detect invalid data in the server controls when the Calculate button is clicked. This property is used in the btnCalculate_Click method that is executed when the user clicks on the Calculate button, which starts a postback.

If the IsValid property indicates that the data is valid, this method retrieves the values from the server controls, converts them to the proper data types, and sends them to the CalculateFutureValue method for processing. When that method returns the future value, the btnCalculate_Click method formats the result as currency and puts it in the future value label. Then, the form is returned to the browser.

The btnClear_Click method is executed when the user clicks on the Clear button. This too starts a postback. Then, after the Page_Load method is executed, the btnClear_Click method clears the server controls by setting the index of the drop-down list to 0 and setting the text box and label properties to empty strings.

Since this book assumes that you already know how to use C#, you should be able to follow the C# code in this figure. The new points to note are (1) the Page_Load method is executed each time the page is requested, (2) the IsPostBack property tells whether a page is being requested for the first time, and (3) the IsValid property tells whether the validator controls have detected invalid data.

The code-behind file for the Default form (Default.aspx.cs)

```csharp
using System;
using System.Web;
using System.Web.UI;
using System.Web.UI.WebControls;
// the rest of the default using directives

namespace Ch01FutureValue
{
    public partial class Default : System.Web.UI.Page
    {
        protected void Page_Load(object sender, EventArgs e)
        {
            if (!IsPostBack)
                for (int i = 50; i <= 500; i += 50)
                    ddlMonthlyInvestment.Items.Add(i.ToString());
        }

        protected void btnCalculate_Click(object sender, EventArgs e)
        {
            if (IsValid) {
                int monthlyInvestment =
                    Convert.ToInt32(ddlMonthlyInvestment.SelectedValue);
                decimal yearlyInterestRate =
                    Convert.ToDecimal(txtInterestRate.Text);
                int years = Convert.ToInt32(txtYears.Text);
                decimal futureValue = this.CalculateFutureValue(
                    monthlyInvestment, yearlyInterestRate, years);
                lblFutureValue.Text = futureValue.ToString("c");
            }
        }

        protected decimal CalculateFutureValue(int monthlyInvestment,
        decimal yearlyInterestRate, int years)
        {
            int months = years * 12;
            decimal monthlyInterestRate = yearlyInterestRate / 12 / 100;
            decimal futureValue = 0;

            for (int i = 0; i < months; i++)
            {
                futureValue = (futureValue + monthlyInvestment)
                    * (1 + monthlyInterestRate);
            }
            return futureValue;
        }

        protected void btnClear_Click(object sender, EventArgs e)
        {
            ddlMonthlyInvestment.SelectedIndex = 0;
            txtInterestRate.Text = "";
            txtYears.Text = "";
            lblFutureValue.Text = "";
        }
    } // end class
} // end namespace
```

Figure 1-12   The C# code for the Default form of the Future Value application

Perspective

Now that you've read this chapter, you should have a general understanding of how ASP.NET applications work and what software you need for developing these applications. With that as background, you're ready to learn how to develop ASP.NET applications of your own. You'll start that process in the next chapter.

Terms

web application
web page
client
web browser
web server
network
intranet
LAN (local area network)
Internet
WAN (wide area network)
ISP (Internet service provider)
URL (Uniform Resource Locator)
protocol
domain name
path
static web page
HTML (Hypertext Markup Language)
HTTP request
HTTP (HyperText Transfer Protocol)
HTTP response
render HTML in the browser
dynamic web page
application server
database server
DBMS (database management system)
round trip
IIS (Internet Information Services)
Web Forms

ASP (Active Server Pages)
classic ASP
RAD (Rapid Application Development)
MVC (Model-View-Controller)
separation of concerns
unit testing
web application project
web site project
WebDAV (Web-based Distributed Authoring and Viewing)
FTP server
FTP (File Transfer Protocol)
.NET Framework
.NET Framework Class Library
CLR (Common Language Runtime)
IL (Intermediate Language)
compile
assembly
state
stateless protocol
view state
session state
web form
server control
aspx code
code-behind file
designer file
page directive

Summary

- A *web application* consists of a set of *web pages* that are run by clients, a web server, and a network. *Clients* use *web browsers* to request web pages from the web server. The *web server* returns the requested pages.

- A *local area network* (*LAN*), or *intranet*, connects computers that are near each other. By contrast, the *Internet* consists of many *wide area networks* (*WANs*).

- One way to access a web page is to type a *URL* (*Uniform Resource Locator*) into the address area of a browser and press Enter. A URL consists of the *protocol* (usually, HTTP), *domain name*, *path*, and file name.

- To request a web page, the web browser sends an *HTTP request* to the web server. Then, the web server gets the HTML for the requested page and sends it back to the browser in an *HTTP response*. Last, the browser *renders* the HTML into a web page.

- A *static web page* is a page that is the same each time it's retrieved. In contrast, the HTML for a *dynamic web page* is generated by a server-side program, so its HTML can change from one request to another. Either way, HTML is returned to the browser.

- For ASP.NET applications, the web server is usually *Internet Information Services* (*IIS*) and ASP.NET is the application server. The web server may also use a *database management system* (*DBMS*) like SQL Server.

- One way to develop ASP.NET applications is to use *Web Forms*. This is similar to using Windows Forms and encourages *Rapid Application Development* (*RAD*).

- Another way to develop ASP.NET applications is to use ASP.NET *MVC* (*Model-View-Controller*). It provides better *separation of concerns* and *unit testing*.

- To develop ASP.NET applications on your own computer, you need Windows 7 or later, Microsoft .NET Framework 4.5.2 or 4.6, Visual Studio 2015, IIS Express, a DBMS like SQL Server Express LocalDB, and one or more browsers.

- The *.NET Framework* provides the services that ASP.NET applications use to access the operating system and computer hardware. Its main components are the *Class Library* and the *Common Language Runtime* (*CLR*).

- HTTP is called a *stateless protocol* because it doesn't keep track of the data (state) between *round trips*. However, ASP.NET provides five ways to keep track of state including *view state* and *session state*.

- The pages in an ASP.NET application are called *web forms*. They contain *server controls* like drop-down lists, text boxes, labels, and buttons.

- Each page in an ASP.NET application consists of an aspx file for the HTML and server controls, an aspx.cs file for the C# in the *code-behind file*, and an aspx.designer.cs file for the generated C# code in the *designer file*.

- Before a web form can be run, its aspx and C# files are compiled into an *assembly* that consists of *Intermediate Language* (*IL*) that is run by the CLR.

Before you do the exercises for this book...

Before you do the exercises for this book, you should install the software that's required for this book as well as the downloadable applications for this book. Appendix A shows how to do that.

Exercise 1-1   Use Visual Studio to run the Future Value application

In this exercise, you'll run the Future Value application. This will test whether you've successfully installed the software and applications for this book.

Start Visual Studio and open the Future Value application

1. Start Visual Studio.

2. Use the File→Open→Project/Solution command. In the dialog box that's displayed, navigate to this folder:

   `C:\aspnet46_cs\Ex01FutureValue`

   Then, select the Ch01FutureValue.sln file and click the Open button.

Run the Future Value application

3. Press F5 to run the application. That should display the Future Value form in Visual Studio's default web browser.

4. Without changing the values that are displayed, click the Calculate button. This starts a postback that returns the page with the result of the calculation.

5. Click the Clear button to clear the values from the text box controls.

6. Click the Calculate button again. Then, note the error messages that are displayed. These messages were generated by the validation controls.

7. Click the Clear button again. Note that the error messages go away. That's because the Clear button has its CausesValidation attribute set to False.

8. Select an investment amount from the drop-down list, enter an annual interest rate greater than 20 and a number of years greater than 45. Then, click the Calculate button to see the error messages that are displayed.

9. Change the interest rate to 5 and the number of years to 30. Then, Click the Calculate button to see that the future value is displayed, which means the entries were valid.

10. Experiment on your own if you like. When you're through, close the browser and then use the File→Close Solution command to close the web application. Then, close Visual Studio.

2

How to develop a one-page web application

In the last chapter, you were introduced to the basic concepts of web programming and ASP.NET. Now, this chapter shows you how to use Visual Studio to develop the Future Value application that you reviewed in the last chapter. If you've used Visual Studio to develop Windows applications, you'll see that you develop ASP.NET web applications in much the same way. As a result, you should be able to move quickly through this chapter.

How to work with ASP.NET web application projects

This chapter starts by presenting some basic skills for working with ASP.NET web application projects. Once you're comfortable with those skills, you'll be ready to learn how to build your first ASP.NET web application.

How to start a new web application

To start a new web application, you use the New Project dialog box shown in figure 2-1. This dialog box lets you select the type of project you want to create by choosing a *template*. To create an ASP.NET web application, for example, you choose the ASP.NET Web Application template.

The New Project dialog box also lets you specify the name for the project, and it lets you identify the folder in which it will be stored. By default, projects are stored in the Visual Studio 2015\Projects folder under the My Documents folder, but you can change the default folder if you want to. To do that, display the Options dialog box (Tools→Options). Then, expand the Projects and Solutions group, select the General category, and enter the folder you want to use in the Projects Location text box.

If you want to change the location that's shown in the New Project dialog box, you can click the Browse button to select a different location; display the Location drop-down list to select a location you've used recently; or type a path directly. If you specify a path that doesn't exist, Visual Studio will create the necessary folders for you.

When you click the OK button, Visual Studio automatically creates a new folder for the project using the project name you specify. In the dialog box in this figure, for example, Ch02FutureValue is the project name and C:\aspnet46_cs is the location. By default, Visual Studio also creates a new folder for the solution using the same name as the project. As a result, Visual Studio will create one folder for the solution, and a subfolder for the project. It also creates an application on the IIS Express web server.

When you create a new web application, Visual Studio 2015 also lets you choose a *target framework*. The target framework determines the features that are available to an application. By default, the target framework for a web application is .NET Framework 4.5.2, even though the most recent version of the .NET Framework is 4.6. That's because version 4.5.2 has been widely deployed, while version 4.6 has not as of this writing. Fortunately, everything in this book will work with the 4.5.2 version of the framework.

The New Project dialog box

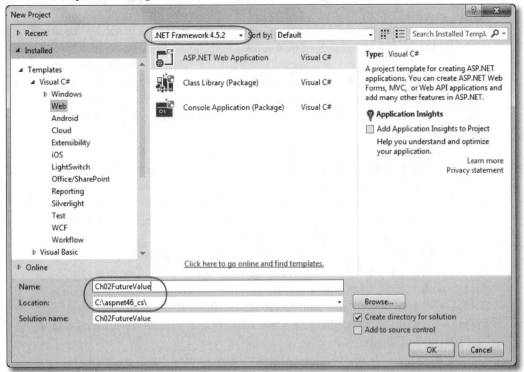

How to start a new web application

- Use the File→New→Project command or click on the "New Project…" link on the Start Page to open the New Project dialog box.

- Choose Web from the Installed→Templates→Visual C# category, and choose the ASP.NET Web Application template.

- Enter a name for the project, which will enter the same name for the solution. Then, enter the location (folder) for the project (and solution).

- Click the OK button to display the New ASP.NET Project dialog box shown in the next figure.

Description

- If the Create Directory For Solution box is checked, Visual Studio creates a folder for the solution and a subfolder for the project. Otherwise, these files are stored in the same folder.

- In addition to the solution folder and file that are created in the location you specify, Visual Studio creates a web application on the IIS Express web server.

- By default, new web applications use .NET Framework 4.5.2, even though the most recent version is 4.6. If you want to change the version, you can use the drop-down list at the top of the dialog box.

Figure 2-1   How to start a new web application

How to work with the web application templates

After you complete the New Project dialog box described in the last figure, the New ASP.NET Project dialog box shown in figure 2-2 is displayed. This dialog box lets you choose the specific template for your web application. The template you choose determines the files and folders that Visual Studio adds to the project when it creates your web application. The four templates you'll work with in this book for ASP.NET 4.5.2 and ASP.NET 4.6 are described in the table in this figure.

The Empty template creates just two configuration files: the Web.config and packages.config files that you learned about in chapter 1. However, if you check the Web Forms checkbox in the Add Folders And Core References For section, App_Data and Models folders will also be added, along with a Global.asax file. Most of the applications in this book use the Empty template, often with the core references and folders for Web Forms added.

The Web Forms template, sometimes called the *default template*, adds numerous files and folders that provide various functionality. For example, this template includes an authentication system, a URL routing system, and a Bootstrap theme. If you ever want to use any of these features, this template is a good source of sample code. You'll see some of the code from this template in later chapters of this book.

The MVC template sets up the directory and routing structure used by ASP.NET MVC. You'll learn how to use this template in chapter 25 when you're introduced to MVC. Note that this template uses MVC5, which is the current release of MVC.

The Web API template sets up the directory and routing structure used to create a REST based web service. You'll learn how to create web services using this template in chapter 24.

Although you won't learn how to use any of the other templates in this book, you might want to experiment with them. For example, the Single Page Application template uses HTML5, jQuery, KnockoutJS, and Bootstrap to create a single page that communicates with the server and updates portions of itself with JavaScript. That way, after the page loads, it never does a full round trip and page refresh, which makes it seem more like a desktop application. This kind of application, known as a SPA, is widely used for mobile applications.

The Azure templates use Microsoft's Azure cloud platform and Web API to create backend services for web and mobile applications. And the ASP.NET 5 template lets you get the ASP.NET 5 Release Candidate (RC). This version of ASP.NET, also called ASP.NET Core 1, is still under development. You can use it to create MVC-based web applications, but it won't include Web Forms.

Before you go on, you should notice the Host In The Cloud check box near the lower right of the New ASP.NET Project dialog box. Before you click the OK button to create a project, you should be sure this check box isn't selected since you'll be storing your applications on a local drive and not in the Cloud.

The New ASP.NET Project dialog box

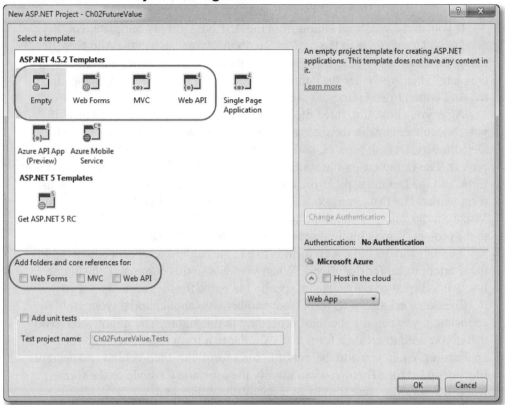

The ASP.NET 4.5.2 / ASP.NET 4.6 templates you'll use in this book

Template	Contains...
Empty	Two configuration files but no other files or folders.
Empty/Web Forms option	Two configuration files, empty App_Data and Models folders, and a Global.asax file with an empty Application_Start method.
Web Forms	Numerous files and folders for various functionality (see chapter 20).
MVC	Basic files and folders for an MVC application (see chapter 25).
Web API	Basic files and folders for a Web API web service (see chapter 24).

Description

- The first group of templates are labeled ASP.NET 4.5.2 or ASP.NET 4.6, depending on which version of the .NET Framework you chose in the New Project dialog box.

- ASP.NET provides several project templates. This book uses the Empty template, although often with the core references for Web Forms added.

- The Web Forms template, sometimes called the *default template*, includes functionality for authentication, URL routing, and Bootstrap. You'll see the Web Forms, MVC, and Web API templates later in this book.

- The ASP.NET 5 template lets you get the ASP.NET 5 release candidate, which isn't addressed in this book.

Figure 2-2   How to work with the web application templates

How to add a web form to a web application

If you start a web application from the ASP.NET Empty template, you'll need to add a *web form* to the project. To do that, you can use the Add New Item dialog box shown in figure 2-3. From this dialog box, you select the Web Form template. Then, you enter the name you want to use for the new form and click the Add button to add it to your web application.

After you click Add, three files are added to your project. For instance, if you change the name in the dialog in this figure to Default, then files named Default.aspx, Default.aspx.cs, and Default.aspx.designer.cs will be added to the project. The Default.aspx file contains the HTML and ASP code that defines the form, and the Default.aspx.cs file contains the C# code that determines how the form works. The Default.aspx.designer.cs file contains generated code used by Visual Studio, and you shouldn't need to edit this file. After these files are added to the project, Visual Studio displays the aspx file for the web form.

Another way to add a web form is to use the Add→Web Form command in the shortcut menu for the project. When you choose this command, the dialog box that's displayed only lets you specify the name for the form.

To add an existing web form from another web application to your web application, you can use the third procedure in this figure. You might want to do that if you need to create a form that's similar to a form in another web application. When you add the aspx file for a form, the code-behind and designer files are added too. Then, you can modify the aspx and C# code so the form works the way you want it to in your new web application.

When you add an existing web form in this way, you should know that the form will retain the name of the project it came from as the namespace name. Although the application will run correctly, the different namespace name might be confusing. Because of that, you should consider changing the name in the namespace declaration for the code-behind and in the Inherits attribute of the Page directive for the aspx file so they match the name of the current project.

The Add New Item dialog box for adding a new web form

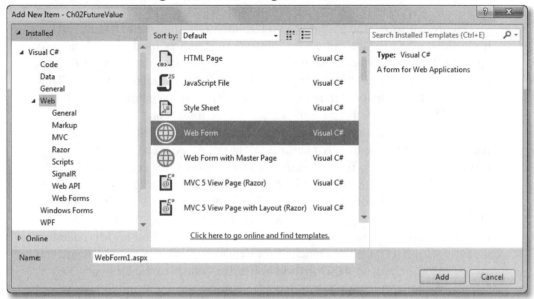

Two ways to open the Add New Item dialog box

- Right-click the project in the Solution Explorer, and choose Add→Add New Item from the shortcut menu.

- Click on the project in the Solution Explorer to select it, and then choose the Project→Add New Item command.

How to add a new web form to a project

- In the Add New Item dialog box, select the Web Form template, enter a name for the form, and click the Add button.

- Choose Add→Web Form from the shortcut menu for the project. Then, enter a name for the form in the dialog box that's displayed and click the OK button.

How to add an existing web form to a project

- In the Solution Explorer, right-click the project and choose Add→Add Existing Item. Then, locate the form you want to add, select its .aspx file, and click the Add button.

Description

- If there's a *web form* in another application that's like what you need, you can copy that form into your application. That copies the aspx, code-behind, and designer files. Then, you can modify the aspx code and C# code so the form works the way you want it to.

- The drop-down list above the list of templates lets you change their order. The two buttons let you choose whether the templates are displayed as small or medium icons.

Figure 2-3   How to add a web form to a web application

How to work with the Visual Studio IDE

Figure 2-4 shows the Visual Studio IDE after a form named Default has been added to the Future Value web application. If you've used Visual Studio for building Windows applications, you should already be familiar with the *Toolbox*, *Solution Explorer*, and *Properties window*, as well as the Standard toolbar. They work much the same for web applications as they do for Windows applications.

For instance, the Solution Explorer shows the folders and files of the web application. In the example in this figure, the Solution Explorer shows the Images folder with the logo banner image, the collapsed web form, and the two configuration files. To expand the web form and see the code-behind and designer files, you click on the arrowhead to the left of the web form.

To design a web form, you use the *Web Forms Designer* that's in the center of Visual Studio. When you add a new web form to a web application, this Designer is displayed in *Source view*, which shows the starting HTML code for the form. However, you'll do much of the design in *Design view*, which you can switch to by clicking on the Design button at the bottom of the Designer. You can also work in *Split view*, which includes both Source view and Design view.

As you work in the Designer, you'll notice that different toolbars are enabled depending on what view you're working in. In Source view, for example, the Standard and HTML Source Editing toolbars are enabled. In Design view, the Standard and Formatting toolbars are enabled. This is typical of the way Visual Studio works.

As you build a web application, you can close, hide, or size the windows that are displayed. You'll see some examples of this as you progress through this chapter, and this figure presents several techniques that you can use for working with the windows.

After you've designed a web form, you'll need to switch to the Code Editor, which will replace the Designer in the center of the screen. Then, you can write the C# code in the code-behind file for the form. One way to switch to the Code Editor is to double-click on the code-behind file in the Solution Explorer. You'll learn more about that in a moment.

The Solution Explorer also contains Properties and References items. When you double-click on Properties, a tab displaying the properties of the application opens in the center of the screen. You can also see these properties in code by expanding the Properties item and then double-clicking on the AssemblyInfo.cs file. When you expand the References item, you'll see a list of the assemblies for the namespaces that the application can use. These namespaces contain the classes that the project requires, and most of them are included when the project is created.

As you work with Visual Studio, you'll see that it often provides several ways to do the same task. Some, of course, are more efficient than others, and we'll try to show you the best techniques as you progress through this book. Often, though, how you work is a matter of personal preference, so we encourage you to review and experiment with the toolbar buttons, the buttons at the top of the Solution Explorer, the tabs at the top of the Web Forms Designer or Code Editor, the shortcut menus that you get by right-clicking on an object, and so on.

Visual Studio with the Designer in Source view and three other windows

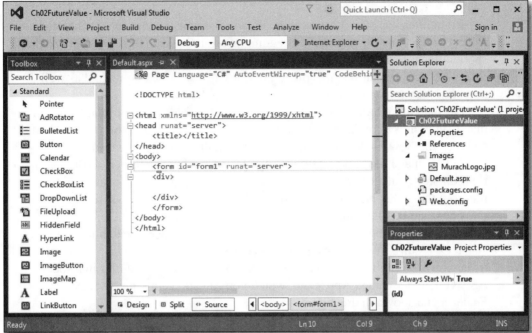

How to work with views and windows

- To change the Web Forms Designer from one view to another, click on the Design, Split, or Source button at the bottom of the Designer window.

- To hide a window, click on its Auto Hide button, which is a pin icon. Then, the window is shown as a tab at the side of the screen. To display the window again, move the mouse pointer over the tab or click on it. To restore the window, display it and click on the Auto Hide button.

- To size a window, place the mouse pointer over one of its boundaries and drag it.

- To close a window, click on the close button in its upper right corner. To redisplay it, select it from the View menu.

- To add line numbers to a window, use the Tools→Options command to display the Options dialog box, then expand Text Editor and All Languages, click on General, check the Line Numbers check box, and click OK.

Description

- The primary window for designing web forms with Visual Studio is the *Web Forms Designer*, or just *Designer*, that's in the middle of the IDE.

- The three supporting windows are the *Toolbox*, the *Solution Explorer*, and the *Properties window*.

- Visual Studio often provides several different ways to do the same task. In this book, we'll try to show you the techniques that work the best.

Figure 2-4   How to work with the Visual Studio IDE

How to add folders and files to a web application

Right after you start a new web application, it makes sense to add any other folders or files that the application is going to require. To do that, you can use the shortcut menus for the project or its folders in the Solution Explorer as shown in figure 2-5. As you can see, this menu provides a New Folder command as well as an Existing Item command.

For the Future Value application, I first added a folder named Images. To do that, I right-clicked on the project at the top of the Solution Explorer, chose Add and then the New Folder command, and entered the name for the folder. Then, I added an image file named MurachLogo.jpg to the Images folder. To do that, I right-clicked on the folder, chose Add and then Existing Item, and selected the file from the dialog box that was displayed.

Those are the only other folders and files that are needed for the Future Value application, but often you'll need others. For instance, the application in chapter 4 requires three existing business classes, a database, and a number of image files. As you'll see in that chapter, you store the database files in a special ASP.NET folder named App_Data, which you can add using the Add ASP.NET Folder menu shown in this figure.

The Future Value project as a new folder is being added

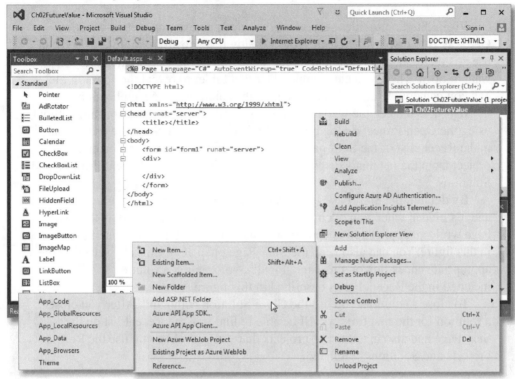

How to add a folder to a web application

- To add a standard folder, right-click on the project or folder you want to add the folder to in the Solution Explorer and choose Add→New Folder. Then, type a name for the folder in the dialog box that's displayed and press Enter.

- To add a special ASP.NET folder, right-click on the project in the Solution Explorer and choose Add→Add ASP.NET Folder. Then, select the folder from the list that's displayed.

How to add an existing item to a web application

- In the Solution Explorer, right-click on the project or folder that you want to add an existing item to. Then, select Add→Existing Item and respond to the dialog box.

Description

- When you create a new web form, Visual Studio generates the starting HTML for the form and displays it in Source view of the Web Forms Designer.

- Before you start designing the first web form of the application, you can use the Solution Explorer to add any other folders or files to the web application.

Figure 2-5   How to add folders and files to a web application

How to open and close a web application

Visual Studio provides several ways to open an existing web application. One way is to display the Open Project dialog box shown in figure 2-6. You can use this dialog box to locate the folder that contains the web application you want to open. Then, you can double-click this folder to reveal the solution file, and you can double-click this file to open the solution for the application.

If you've opened the web application recently, you can open it again without using the Open Project dialog box. To do that, you can click on the project name in the Recent list of the Start page, also shown in this figure. Or, you can select a project from the list that's displayed when you choose File→Recent Projects and Solutions.

By default, the Start Page is displayed each time you open Visual Studio, and it's hidden when you open an application. If you want to display the Start Page while an application is open, you can do that using the command shown in this figure. You can also keep the Start Page open at all times by selecting the appropriate check box on this page. Finally, you can pin a solution so it's always included in the Recent list as described in this figure.

To close a solution, you use the Close Solution command. After you close a solution for the first time, you'll be able to find it in the Recent list on the Start Page and also in the list of projects that you see when you use the Recent Projects and Solutions command.

The Visual Studio Start Page and the Open Project dialog box

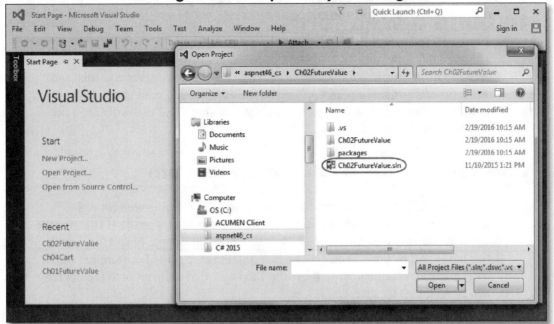

How to use the Open Project dialog box to open a web application

- Use the File→Open→Project/Solution command or click the "Open Project…" link in the Start section of the Start page to display this dialog box.
- Locate the folder that contains the web application and double-click it to display the solution file. Then, double-click the solution file or select it and click the Open button.

Other ways to open a web application

- Click on the project name in the Recent list of the Visual Studio Start Page.
- Click on the project name in the File→Recent Projects and Solutions menu.

How to close a web application

- Use the File→Close Solution command.

How to work with the Start Page

- To open the Start Page, select View→Start Page.
- To keep the Start Page open after you open an application, select the appropriate check box in the lower left corner of the Start Page.
- To pin a project so it always appears in the Recent list, hover your mouse over the solution name and click on the horizontal pin icon that appears. To unpin a solution, click its pin icon again.

Description

- You use a web application's solution file to open it. This file has an .sln file extension.

Figure 2-6   How to open and close a web application

How to use Visual Studio to build a web form

Now that you know how to start, open, and close a web application, you're ready to learn how to build a web page with HTML, web server controls, and validation controls. If any of this seems confusing as you read about it, the exercise at the end of this chapter will show you that all of the skills are quite manageable.

How to enter the HTML for a web form

Figure 2-7 presents the primary ways to add HTML to a web form. For many HTML elements, the easiest way to add them is to type the HTML for the elements directly into the source code, taking full advantage of *IntelliSense*. In this figure, for example, you can see how IntelliSense provides a *snippet* for an h1 element. Just remember to press the Tab key twice to insert both the opening and closing tags for an element.

For some elements, though, it's better to insert a snippet using the second technique in this figure. To do that, you move the insertion point to where you want the snippet, right-click to display a menu, select Insert Snippet, select HTML, and select the HTML element that you want to insert. If, for example, you insert the snippet for an img element, the HTML includes the src and alt attributes.

This figure also shows how you can add an img element to the HTML by dragging the image from the Solution Explorer and dropping it wherever you want it. If you drop it in Design view, the Accessibility Properties dialog box is displayed. And that makes it easy to enter the Alternate Text property, which gets converted to an alt attribute in the HTML.

Whether or not you use the Accessibility Properties dialog box, the alt attribute should always be coded for an img element because it improves accessibility. Specifically, this attribute is used by screen readers to describe an image for the visually impaired. If an image is used for decorative purposes only, the value of this attribute should be an empty string ("").

In contrast, the Long Description property in the Accessibility Properties dialog box gets converted to the longdesc attribute. Since that attribute isn't supported by HTML5 or any modern browser, though, you should leave it blank.

Usually, you'll want to make a few adjustments and additions to the HTML right after the form is added to the application. For instance, you'll want to enter a title for the form in the title element that's in the head section. That's the title that's displayed in the title bar or tab of the browser when the form is run. You'll also want to add an h1 element to the form that describes what the page does.

After making the HTML entries, you can use either Source view or Design view to add web server controls to the form. If you work in Design view, though, you'll want to switch back to Source view from time to time. That way, you can review the source code that has been added, make sure the code is in the right location, and make adjustments to the source code.

The Future Value form in Split view after an img element has been added

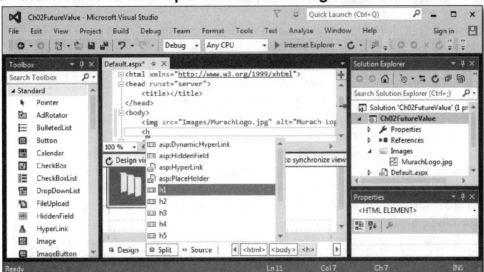

How to add HTML elements to a form

- Enter the code for the element in Source view. As you work, Visual Studio's *IntelliSense* will help you enter *snippets*, tags, attributes, etc. To add a snippet, press the Tab key twice.

- To insert a snippet for an HTML element in Source view without using IntelliSense, move the insertion point to where you want the snippet. Then, right-click, select Insert Snippet, select HTML, and select the element that you want inserted.

Two ways to add an img element to a form

- Insert a snippet for the element. That includes the src and alt attributes, but you have to add the values.

- Drag the image from the Solution Explorer to the Designer. This inserts an img element with a valid src attribute. In Design view, the Accessibility Properties dialog box is also displayed.

How to add and remove comments

- To add a comment at the insertion point, click the Comment button in the HTML Source Editing toolbar, or press Ctrl+K and then Ctrl+C. If you select lines of code before you do this, the lines will be *commented out*.

- To remove a comment, move the insertion point into it and click the Uncomment button, or press Ctrl+K and then Ctrl+U. If you select lines of code that have been commented out before you do this, they will be uncommented.

How to synchronize the views when you're working in Split view

- Save the file or click on the message that's displayed between the views.

Figure 2-7   How to enter the HTML for a web form

How to add a table to a form

By default, forms use *flow layout*. This means that the text and controls you add to a form are positioned from left to right and from top to bottom. Because of that, the position of the controls can change when the form is displayed depending on the size of the browser window and the resolution of the display.

Usually, though, you will want more control than flow layout provides. One way to get that control is to use a table, which you'll learn about now. Another way is to use CSS, which you'll learn about in the next chapter.

Figure 2-8 shows how to add a table to a form in Design view. In this case, a table of six rows and two columns has already been added to the form, but the Insert Table dialog box is displayed to show what the settings are for that table. Usually, you can keep the dialog box entries that simple, because you can easily adjust the table once it's on the form.

The easiest way to resize a row or column is to drag it by its border. To change the width of a column, drag it by its right border. To change the height of a row, drag it by its bottom border. You can also change the height and width of the entire table by selecting the table and then dragging it by its handles.

You can also format a table in Design view by selecting one or more rows or columns and then using the commands in the Table menu or the shortcut menu that's displayed when you right-click the selection. These commands let you add, delete, or resize rows or columns. They also let you merge the cells in a row or column. If, for example, you want a control in one row to span two columns, you can merge the cells in that row.

Note that when you make some of these changes, Visual Studio adds classes to the HTML elements as well as a style element in the head section of the form that contains the rule sets for the classes. You'll see this when you review the aspx code for the Future Value form.

How to add text to the cells of a table

In figure 2-8, you can see that text has been entered into the cells in the first four rows of the first column of the table. To do that, you just type the text into the cells. Then, you can format the text by selecting it and using the controls in the Formatting toolbar or the commands in the Format menu. If, for example, you want to bold the four text entries, you can select the four cells that contain the text and click on the Bold button in the Formatting toolbar.

The Future Value form with a table that has been inserted into it

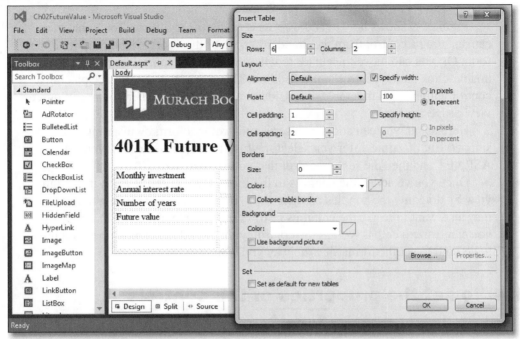

How to add a table to a form

- Use the Table→Insert Table command to display the Insert Table dialog box. Then, set the number of rows and columns that you want in the table, set any other options that you want, and click OK.

How to format a table after it has been added to a form

- To resize a row, drag it by its bottom border. To resize a column, drag it by its right border. To resize the entire table, select the table and then drag one of its handles.
- To select rows, columns, or cells, drag the mouse over them or hold the Ctrl key down as you click on the cells. To add, delete, size, or merge selected rows or columns, use the commands in the Table menu or the shortcut menu.

How to add text to a table and format it

- To add text to a table, type the text into the cells of the table.
- To format the text, select it and use the controls in the Formatting toolbar or the commands in the Format menu.

Description

- To control the alignment of the text and controls on a web form, you can use tables.
- Some of the formatting that you apply to tables, rows, and columns is saved in CSS rule sets in a style element in the head section of the HTML. You'll learn more about CSS in the next chapter.

Figure 2-8   How to add a table to a form and add text to the table's cells

How to add web server controls to a form

Figure 2-9 shows how to add *web server controls* to a form. To do that, you can just drag a control from the Standard group of the Toolbox and drop it on the form. Or, you can move the cursor to where you want a control inserted and then double-click on the control in the Toolbox. This works whether you're placing a control within a cell of a table or outside of a table, and whether you're in Source view or Design view.

Here again, you can add a web server control to a form by inserting a snippet. But this time, after you select the Insert Snippet command, you select ASP.NET and then the server control that you want to add.

Once you've added the controls to the form, you can resize them in Design view by dragging the handles on their sides. If the controls are in a table, you may also want to resize the columns or rows of the table. But keep in mind that you can resize a cell as well as the control within a cell, and sometimes you have to do both to get the formatting the way you want it.

How to set the properties of the controls

After you have placed the controls on a form, you need to set each control's *properties* so the control looks and works the way you want it to. To set those properties, you can work in the Properties window as shown in this figure. To display the properties for a control, just click on it in Design or Source view.

In the Properties window, you select a property by clicking it. Then, a brief description of that property is displayed at the bottom of the window. To change a property setting, you change the entry to the right of the property name by typing a new value or choosing a new value from a drop-down list. In some cases, a button with an ellipsis (…) will appear when you click on a property. Then, you can click the button to display a dialog box that sets the property.

Some properties are displayed in groups. In that case, a + symbol appears next to the group name. To expand the properties in the group, just click the + symbol, which then changes to a – symbol.

To display properties alphabetically or by category, you can click the appropriate button at the top of the Properties window. At first, you may want to display the properties by category so you can see what the different properties do. Once you become more familiar with the properties, though, you may be able to find the ones you're looking for faster if you display them alphabetically.

Another way to set properties for some controls is to use the control's *smart tag menu*. In this figure, for example, you can see the smart tag menu for the drop-down list. Because smart tag menus help you set common properties, they're displayed automatically when you drag a control to a form in Design view. Later, you can display the smart tag menu of a control by hovering the mouse pointer over it until its smart tag appears and then clicking on that tag.

As you work with properties, you'll find that many are set the way you want by default. In addition, some properties such as Height and Width are set as you size and position the controls in Design view. As a result, you usually only need to change a few properties for each control.

The Future Value form after six server controls have been added to it

How to add a web server control to a web form

- Drag the control from the Standard group in the Toolbox to the form or to a cell in a table on the form. Or, move the cursor to where you want the control in either Source or Design view, and double-click on the control in the Toolbox to place it there.

- To insert a snippet for a server control in Source view, move the insertion point to where you want the snippet. Then, right-click, select Insert Snippet, select ASP.NET, and select the control that you want inserted.

How to set the properties for a control

- Select a control by clicking on it, and all of its properties are displayed in the Properties window. Then, you can select a property in this window and set its value.

- To change the Height and Width properties, drag one of the handles on a control. This also changes the Height and Width in the Properties window.

- To sort the properties in the Properties window by category or alphabetically, click on one of the buttons at the top of the window. To expand or collapse the list of properties in a group, click on the + or – symbol for the group.

- To display a smart tag menu for a control in Design view, select the control and click the Smart Tag icon on the right of the control. In Source view, click in the aspx code for the control and hover over the line that appears under the <asp> tag to reveal the smart tag icon and then click on it.

Description

- Many *web server controls* have *smart tag menus* that provide options for performing common tasks and setting common *properties*.

Figure 2-9   How to add web server controls to a form and set their properties

Common properties for web server controls

The first table in figure 2-10 presents the properties for web server controls that you're most likely to use as you develop web forms. If you've worked with Windows controls, you'll notice that many of the properties of the web server controls provide similar functionality. For example, you use the ID property to identify a control that you need to refer to in your C# code, and you can use the Text property to set what's displayed in or on the control.

In contrast, the AutoPostBack, CausesValidation, EnableViewState, and Runat properties are unique to web server controls. As you should already know, the Runat property just indicates that the control must be processed by the web server. The other three properties are more interesting.

The AutoPostBack property determines whether the page is posted back to the server when the user changes the value of the control. Note that this property is only available with certain controls, such as drop-down lists, check boxes, and radio buttons. Also note that this property isn't available with button controls. That's because button controls always either post a page back to the server or display another page.

The CausesValidation property is available for button controls and determines whether the validation controls are activated when the user clicks the button. This lets the browser check for valid data before the page is posted back to the server. You'll learn more about validation controls in a moment.

The EnableViewState property determines whether a server control retains its property settings from one posting to the next. For that to happen, the EnableViewState property for both the form and the control must be set to True. Since that's normally the way you want this property set, True is the default.

The second table in this figure lists four more properties that are commonly used with drop-down lists and list boxes. For instance, you can use the Items collection to add, insert, and remove ListItem objects, and you can use the SelectedValue property to retrieve the value of the currently selected item. Although you can set these properties at design time, they are often set by the C# code in the code-behind file. You'll learn more about these properties when you review the code-behind file for the Future Value form.

Common web server control properties

Property	Description
AutoPostBack	Determines whether the page is posted back to the server when the value of the control changes. Available with controls like check boxes, text boxes, and lists. The default value is False.
CausesValidation	Determines whether the validation specified by the validation controls is done when a button control is clicked. The default value is True.
EnableViewState	Determines whether the control maintains its view state between HTTP requests. The default value is True.
Enabled	Determines whether the control is functional. The default value is True.
Height	The height of the control.
ID	The name that's used to refer to the control.
Runat	Indicates that the control will be processed on the server by ASP.NET.
TabIndex	Determines the order in which the controls on the form receive the focus when the Tab key is pressed. A value of -1 means the control isn't included in the tab order.
Text	The text that's displayed in the control.
ToolTip	The text that's displayed when the user hovers the mouse over the control.
Visible	Determines whether a control is displayed or hidden.
Width	The width of the control.

Common properties of drop-down list and list box controls

Property	Description
Items	The collection of ListItem objects that represents the items in the control. Although you can set the values for these list items at design time, you normally use code to add, insert, and remove the items in a drop-down list or list box.
SelectedItem	The ListItem object for the currently selected item.
SelectedIndex	The index of the currently selected item starting from zero. If no item is selected in a list box, the value of this property is -1.
SelectedValue	The value of the currently selected item.

Note

- When buttons are clicked, they always post back to the server or display other pages. That's why they don't have AutoPostBack properties.

Figure 2-10   Common properties for web server controls

How to add validation controls to a form

A *validation control* is a type of ASP.NET control that's used to validate input data. The topics that follow introduce you to the validation controls and show you how to use two of them. Then, in chapter 7, you can learn how to use all of these controls.

An introduction to the validation controls

Figure 2-11 shows the Validation group in the Toolbox. It offers five controls that can be called *validators*. These are the controls that you use to check that the user has entered valid data. You can use the last control in this group, the validation summary control, to display all the errors that have been detected by the validators on the form.

To add a validation control to a web form, you can use the same techniques that you use to add a server control. Before you can access the validation controls in the Toolbox, though, you need to open the Validation group by clicking on the arrowhead to its left. You can also add a validation control to a form by inserting a snippet.

In this example, four validators have been added to the form: two required field validators and two range validators. In this case, the controls have been added below the table so ASP.NET will use flow layout to position the controls. However, these controls could have been added to a third column of the table. Although these controls don't show when the form is displayed, the messages in their ErrorMessage properties are displayed if errors are detected.

In most cases, client-side validation is done when the focus leaves an input control that has validators associated with it. That can happen when the user presses the Tab key to move to the next control or clicks another control to move the focus to that control. Validation is also done when the user clicks on a button that has its CausesValidation property set to True.

To perform client-side validation, a browser must have JavaScript enabled. Because most browsers enable it, validation is usually done on the client. That way, a round trip to the server isn't required to display error messages if invalid data is detected. However, validation is always done on the server too when a page is submitted. ASP.NET does this validation after it initializes the page.

When ASP.NET performs the validation tests on the server, it sets the IsValid property of each validator to indicate whether the test was successful. Then, after all the validators are tested, it sets the IsValid property of the page to indicate whether all the tests were valid. This is the property that's usually tested by the C# code when the page is posted to the server. You'll see how this works when you review the code-behind file for this form.

The validation controls on the Future Value form

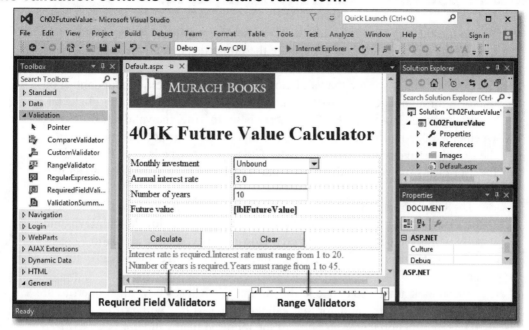

How to add a validator to a web form

- In either Design or Source view, move the insertion point to where you want the validator and double-click on the validator in the Validation group in the Toolbox. Or, drag the validator from the Toolbox to where you want it.

- In Source view, right-click, select Insert Snippet, select ASP.NET, and select the validation control that you want to insert.

How to set the properties for a validation control

- In either Design or Source view, use the Properties window.

- In Source view, enter the properties for the validator with help from IntelliSense.

Description

- You can use *validation controls* to test user entries and produce error messages. The validation is typically done when the focus leaves the control that's being validated and also when the user clicks on a button that has its CausesValidation property set to True.

- Each validation control is associated with a specific server control, but you can associate more than one validation control with the same server control.

- If the user's browser has JavaScript enabled, the validation controls work by running JavaScript in the browser. Then, if the validation fails, the page isn't posted back to the server, which saves a round trip. If the browser doesn't have JavaScript enabled, the validation is done on the server.

Figure 2-11   An introduction to the validation controls

How to use the required field validator

To use the *required field validator*, you set the properties shown in the table at the top of figure 2-12. These are the properties that are used by all the validators.

To start, you associate the validation control with a specific input control on the form through its ControlToValidate property. Then, when the user clicks on a button whose CausesValidation property is set to True, the validator checks whether a value has been entered into the input control. If not, the message in the ErrorMessage property is displayed. The error message is also displayed if the user clears the value in the input control and then moves the focus to another control.

The Display property of the validation control determines how the message in the ErrorMessage property is displayed. When you use flow layout, Dynamic usually works the best for this property. However, if you use a validation summary control as explained in chapter 7, you can change this property to None.

If you look at the aspx code in this figure, you can see how the properties are set for a required field validator that validates the text box with txtInterestRate as its ID. Here, the ForeColor property of the required field validator is set to "Red" so the error message will be displayed in that color. In the next chapter, you'll learn how to use CSS to get the same result.

How to use the range validator

The *range validator* lets you set the valid range for an input value. To use this control, you set the properties in the first table in this figure, plus the properties in the second table. In particular, you set the minimum and maximum values for an input value.

The aspx code in this figure also shows how the properties are set for the range validator for the text box with txtInterestRate as its ID. For this to work correctly, you must set the Type property to the type of data that you're testing. Because the interest rate entry can have decimal positions, for example, the Type property for its range validator is set to Double. In contrast, because a year entry should be a whole number, the Type property for its range validator should be set to Integer.

Common validation control properties

Property	Description
ControlToValidate	The ID of the control to be validated.
Display	Determines how an error message is displayed. Specify Static to allocate space for the message in the page layout, Dynamic to have the space allocated when an error occurs, or None to display the errors in a validation summary control.
ErrorMessage	The message that's displayed in the validation control when the validation fails.

Additional properties of a range validator

Property	Description
MaximumValue	The maximum value that the control can contain.
MinimumValue	The minimum value that the control can contain.
Type	The data type to use for range checking (String, Integer, Double, Date, or Currency).

The aspx code for a RequiredFieldValidator control

```
<asp:RequiredFieldValidator ID="RequiredFieldValidator1" runat="server"
    ControlToValidate="txtInterestRate" Display="Dynamic"
    ErrorMessage="Interest rate is required." ForeColor="Red">
</asp:RequiredFieldValidator>
```

The aspx code for a RangeValidator control

```
<asp:RangeValidator ID="RangeValidator1" runat="server"
    ControlToValidate="txtInterestRate" Display="Dynamic"
    ErrorMessage="Interest rate must range from 1 to 20."
    MaximumValue="20" MinimumValue="1" Type="Double" ForeColor="Red">
</asp:RangeValidator>
```

Description

- The *required field validator* is typically used with text box controls, but can also be used with list controls.
- The *range validator* tests whether a user entry falls within a valid range.
- If the user doesn't enter a value into a control that a range validator is associated with, the range validation test passes. Because of that, you should also provide a required field validator if a value is required.

Figure 2-12   How to use the required field and range validators

How to work with unobtrusive validation

ASP.NET 4.5 and later have a feature called *unobtrusive validation* that you need to be aware of. This feature controls how the client-side validation of the validation controls is done. Figure 2-13 shows the two settings for unobtrusive validation that a web application can have.

A setting of Webforms means that unobtrusive validation is enabled and ASP.NET will use jQuery for validation. *jQuery* is a JavaScript library that provides for cross-browser compatibility and reduces the amount of JavaScript that an ASP.NET application requires. A setting of None means that unobtrusive validation is disabled and ASP.NET will do the validation the way it was done in versions prior to 4.5, which is to use script elements within the HTML to supply the JavaScript for the validation.

The benefit of using unobtrusive validation is that it reduces the amount of JavaScript that has to be generated. That's why unobtrusive validation is enabled by default.

The problem with this is that if you start a web application from the Empty template, unobtrusive validation is enabled but the jQuery library and configuration needed to use it aren't there. This means that if you try to use a validation control, you'll get an error. There are two ways to fix this.

One fix is to add the components that are required by unobtrusive validation. To do that, you can use NuGet, which is a Visual Studio feature that makes it easy to add third-party and open-source packages to an application. You'll learn more about NuGet later, but this figure shows how to use NuGet to install the package that provides everything you need to make unobtrusive validation work in your web application.

The other fix is to disable unobtrusive validation. To do that for one page, you can set the UnobtrusiveValidationMode property to None in the Load event handler for the page, as shown in this figure. To do that for all pages in a web application, you can add an appSettings element like the one in this figure to the Web.config file.

Two values for the UnobtrusiveValidationMode setting

Value	Description
Webforms	Uses the jQuery library for the validation that's done by the validation controls.
None	Uses the older method of generating the JavaScript code for the validation controls and including it within script elements in the HTML for the page.

The NuGet Package Manager page

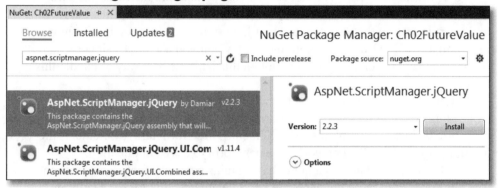

How to install the NuGet package for jQuery validation

- Right-click on the project in the Solution Explorer and select Manage NuGet Packages.

- In the page that appears, click "Browse" and type "aspnet.scriptmanager.jquery" in the search box.

- Select the package in the left pane and click on the Install button in the right pane.

A Load event handler that turns off unobtrusive validation for a page

```
protected void Page_Load(object sender, EventArgs e) {
    UnobtrusiveValidationMode = UnobtrusiveValidationMode.None;
}
```

A Web.config setting that turns off unobtrusive validation
for an application

```
<appSettings>
    <add key="ValidationSettings:UnobtrusiveValidationMode" value="None"/>
</appSettings>
```

Description

- ASP.NET provides a feature called *unobtrusive validation*. When it's enabled, a JavaScript library named *jQuery* is used to do the validation that's specified.

- Unobtrusive validation is on by default when you start a new web application from the Empty template. So if you're using the validation controls, you either need to turn unobtrusive validation off or install the NuGet package for jQuery validation.

Figure 2-13   How to work with unobtrusive validation

The aspx code for the Future Value form

Figure 2-14 presents the aspx code for the Future Value form. To help you see how the code relates to the form in the browser, this figure starts with the form displayed in Internet Explorer. Here, you can see that the title in the browser tab is the same as the title in the title element in the head section of the HTML.

After the title element, you can see a style element that includes two CSS rule sets. You can also see class attributes in the table and td elements that refer to these rule sets. In the next chapter, you'll learn how this works, but for now realize that ASP.NET does this automatically when you use the Designer to format the elements on a page, even though this isn't the best way to handle this formatting.

Within the body element, the first two elements are for the image and the h1 heading. You can see how these are rendered in the browser. This is followed by a form element that contains a div element. These form and div elements are generated by ASP.NET when you add a new form to a web application.

Within the div element is a table that contains six tr elements, one for each row. Within each of these elements are two td elements, one for each column. That's the way the HTML for a table works. In the first td element for each of the first four rows, you can see the text that has been entered. In the second td element for each of these rows, a server control has been added. For instance, the control in the first row is a drop-down list, and the control in the second row is a text box. You can see how this table is rendered in the browser.

For each control, the ID property is used to give the control an identifier that's easy to refer to. Here, ddl is used as a prefix for a drop-down list and txt is used as a prefix for a text box. That makes it easy to tell what type of control an identifier refers to. These identifiers are followed by names that clearly identify the controls. Within those names, the first letter of each word is capitalized, which makes the names easier to read. This is the naming convention that's used throughout this book and the one that we recommend for your own use.

The design of the Future Value form

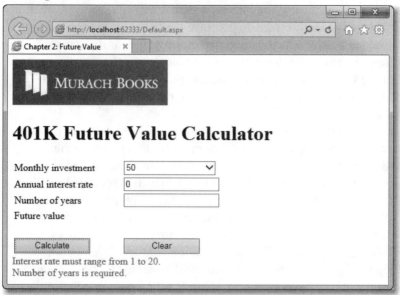

The aspx code for the Future Value form

```
<%@ Page Language="C#" AutoEventWireup="true" CodeFile="Default.aspx.cs"
Inherits="Ch02FutureValue.Default" %>

<!DOCTYPE html>

<html xmlns="http://www.w3.org/1999/xhtml">
<head runat="server">
    <title>Chapter 2: Future Value</title>
    <style type="text/css">
        .auto-style1 {
            width: 100%;
        }
        .auto-style2 {
            width: 172px;
        }
    </style>
</head>
<body>
    <img src="Images/MurachLogo.jpg" alt="Murach Logo"/>
    <h1>401K Future Value Calculator</h1>
    <form id="form1" runat="server">
    <div>
        <table class="auto-style1">
            <tr>
                <td class="auto-style2">Monthly investment</td>
                <td><asp:DropDownList ID="ddlMonthlyInvestment"
                        runat="server" Height="22px" Width="147px">
                    </asp:DropDownList></td>
            </tr>
```

Figure 2-14   The aspx code for the Future Value form (part 1 of 2)

In the code for the first text box control, you can see that the Text property has been set to a value of 3.0. That is the interest rate that will be displayed when the form is first displayed in the browser. In contrast, the value for the second text box control is coded between the opening and closing tags for the control. These are two different ways to set the starting value for a control.

In the code for the fifth row of the table, you can see that ASP.NET has put a non-breaking space ( ) in the cell for each column. It does that for all of the empty cells in a table.

In the sixth row, you can see the aspx code for the Calculate and Clear buttons. Here, each of the buttons has an OnClick property that points to the C# code in the code-behind file that will be run when the button is clicked. The Clear button also contains a CausesValidation property, which is set to False. This property tells the page not to do validation when the button is clicked. Because the default value of the CausesValidation property is True for buttons, this property doesn't need to be set for the Calculate button.

This table is followed by the code for the validation controls. Because these controls are outside the table, their placement will be determined by flow layout. To have some control over this layout, a break element (<br />) is coded after the two interest rate validators. That means the error messages for the interest rate will be displayed on one line, and the messages for the years will be on another line. However, the Display property for these validators has been set to Dynamic, which means that space will be allocated for them only when it is needed.

The aspx code for the Future Value form (continued)

```
        <tr>
            <td class="auto-style2">Annual interest rate</td>
            <td><asp:TextBox ID="txtInterestRate" runat="server"
                Text="3.0"></asp:TextBox></td>
        </tr>
        <tr>
            <td class="auto-style2">Number of years</td>
            <td>
                <asp:TextBox ID="txtYears" runat="server">10
                </asp:TextBox></td>
        </tr>
        <tr>
            <td>Future value</td>
            <td><asp:Label ID="lblFutureValue" runat="server"
                Font-Bold="True"></asp:Label></td>
        </tr>
        <tr>
            <td class="auto-style2"> </td>
            <td> </td>
        </tr>
        <tr>
            <td class="auto-style2">
                <asp:Button ID="btnCalculate" runat="server"
                    Text="Calculate" Width="122px"
                    OnClick="btnCalculate_Click" /></td>
            <td>
                <asp:Button ID="btnClear" runat="server" Text="Clear"
                    Width="122px" CausesValidation="False"
                    OnClick="btnClear_Click" /></td>
        </tr>
    </table>
    <asp:RequiredFieldValidator ID="RequiredFieldValidator1"
        runat="server" ErrorMessage="Interest rate is required."
        ControlToValidate="txtInterestRate" Display="Dynamic"
        ForeColor="Red">
    </asp:RequiredFieldValidator>
    <asp:RangeValidator ID="RangeValidator1" runat="server"
        ErrorMessage="Interest rate must range from 1 to 20."
        ControlToValidate="txtInterestRate"
        Display="Dynamic" ForeColor="Red" Type="Double"
        MaximumValue="20" MinimumValue="1">
    </asp:RangeValidator><br />
    <asp:RequiredFieldValidator ID="RequiredFieldValidator2"
        runat="server" ErrorMessage="Number of years is required."
        ControlToValidate="txtYears" Display="Dynamic" ForeColor="Red">
    </asp:RequiredFieldValidator>
    <asp:RangeValidator ID="RangeValidator2" runat="server"
        ErrorMessage="Years must range from 1 to 45."
        ControlToValidate="txtYears" Type="Integer" Display="Dynamic"
        ForeColor="Red" MaximumValue="45" MinimumValue="1">
    </asp:RangeValidator>
    </div>
    </form>
</body>
</html>
```

Figure 2-14   The aspx code for the Future Value form (part 2 of 2)

How to add C# code to a form

To add the functionality required by a web form, you add C# code to its code-behind file. This code responds to the events that the user initiates on the form. This code also responds to events that occur as a form is processed.

How to use the Code Editor

Figure 2-15 shows how to use the *Code Editor* to enter and edit C# code, starting with two ways to start an event handler. If, for example, you double-click a control, an event handler for the default event of the control is started. If you double-click on a button control, for example, an event handler for the Click event of that control is created. Then, you can enter the code that you want to be executed within the braces of the event handler.

To create event handlers for other control events, you can use the Events button at the top of the Properties window. When you click this button, a list of all the events for the control that's currently selected is displayed. Then, you can double-click on any event to generate an event handler for that event.

When Visual Studio generates an event handler for a control, it also adds the appropriate event property to the aspx code for that control. In the aspx code, for example, you saw the OnClick event properties that were generated for the Calculate and Clear buttons on the Future Value form. This is how events are wired to event handlers in ASP.NET.

When you add a web form to an application, Visual Studio automatically starts the Page_Load event handler. Then, you can add the code you need to this handler. An easy way to display this handler is to double-click outside the body of the form in Design view.

You can also code methods other than event handlers by entering the code for the method directly into the Code Editor window. Then, you can call those methods from the event handlers for the form.

As you enter C# code, be sure to take advantage of the snippets that the Code Editor offers. If, for example, you insert the snippet for a for loop, all of the code that you need for that structure is inserted into the code-behind file. Then, you can modify that code to suit your requirements. As you work, the Code Editor also provides IntelliSense that makes it easier to enter code.

Another useful feature of the Code Editor is the Quick Actions light bulb icon. When errors occur in your code, they're underlined with a wavy line. If Visual Studio has suggestions for how to fix the error, this light bulb icon appears when you hover your mouse over the wavy line. Then, you can use the technique described in this figure to see and apply the suggested fixes.

Sometimes you'll notice the light bulb icon at the beginning of a line of code even though there aren't errors. That means that the Code Editor has identified something in that line of code that can be improved. Then, you can use the same technique you use to fix an error to get and apply the suggested improvements if you choose to.

When you test a web form, you may want to *comment out* portions of code by putting those portions of code within C# comments. Then, because comments

The Code Editor for a web form

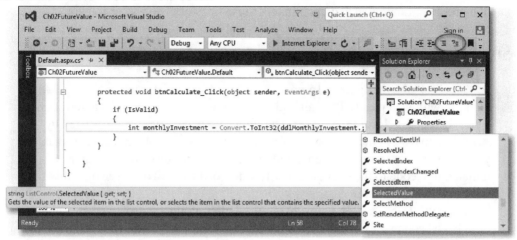

Two ways to start an event handler

- Double-click on a control in the Designer to start an event handler for the default event of that control.

- Select a control in the Designer, click the Events button in the Properties window (the button with the lightning bolt), and double-click the event you want.

How to insert a code snippet

- Move the insertion point to where you want the snippet. Right-click, select Insert Snippet, select Visual C#, and select the snippet.

How to use the Quick Actions light bulb feature

- If errors are detected, they are underlined with a wavy line. Hover your mouse over the error to see an explanation. If a light bulb icon appears, click the down arrow next to it for a list of possible fixes for the error. Then, click on a fix to apply it.

How to comment out a portion of code

- Select the lines of code, then click on the Comment button in the Text Editor toolbar. To uncomment the lines, select them and click the Uncomment button.

Description

- An *event handler* is a C# method that is executed when an event occurs, and Visual Studio will generate the starting code for an event handler.

- The *Code Editor* includes editing features such as IntelliSense, automatic indentation, snippets, syntax checking, and Quick Actions light bulbs.

- When you add a web form to a project, Visual Studio automatically adds a Load event handler for the page. You can double-click outside the body of the form in Design view to display this event handler.

- To enter a method other than an event handler, you type the method from scratch.

Figure 2-15   How to use the Code Editor to enter and edit C# code are ignored, you can test the form to see whether those statements were the cause of a problem. Later, you can uncomment those lines of code and test again.

How to use page and control events

The first table in figure 2-16 presents some of the common events for working with web pages. The Init and Load events of a page occur whenever a page is requested from the server. The Init event occurs first, and it's used by ASP.NET to restore the view state of the page and its controls. Because of that, you don't usually create an event handler for this event. Instead, you add any initialization code to the event handler for the Load event. You'll see how this works in the next figure.

In contrast, the PreRender event is raised after all the control events for the page have been processed. It's the last event to occur before a page is rendered to HTML. In section 2, you'll see how this event can be useful when working with data in session state.

The second table in this figure lists some of the common events for web server controls. When the user clicks a button, for example, the Click event of that control is raised. Then, the page is posted back to the server, the event handlers for the Init and Load events of the page are executed, followed by the event handler for the Click event of the button that was clicked.

The TextChanged event occurs when the user changes the value in a text box. In contrast, the CheckedChanged event occurs when the user clicks a radio button or check box, and the SelectedIndexChanged event occurs when the user selects an item from a list.

If you want the event handler for one of these events to be executed immediately when the event occurs, you can set the AutoPostBack property of the control to True. Then, the event handler will be executed after the Init and Load event handlers for the page. If you don't set the AutoPostBack property to True, the event is still raised, but the event handler isn't executed until another user action causes the page to be posted to the server. Then, the event handlers for the Init and Load events of the page are executed, followed by the event handlers for the control events in the order they were raised.

In this figure, you can see the event handler for the Click event of the Clear button on the Future Value form. This event handler resets the value in the drop-down list to the first value in the list by setting the SelectedIndex property of the control to 0. This handler also resets the text boxes and label to empty strings. Note that the name of this event handler is btnClear_Click, which is the ID of the button followed by an underscore and the name of the event. If you look back at the aspx code, you'll see that this is the same name that's in the OnClick event property that ASP.NET adds to the control when it generates the event handler.

Common ASP.NET page events

Event	Method name	Occurs when...
Init	Page_Init	A page is requested from the server. This event is raised before the view state of the page controls has been restored.
Load	Page_Load	A page is requested from the server, after all controls have been initialized and view state has been restored. This is the event you typically use to perform initialization operations such as retrieving data and initializing form controls.
PreRender	Page_PreRender	All the control events for the page have been processed but before the HTML that will be sent back to the browser is generated.

Common ASP.NET control events

Event	Occurs when...
Click	The user clicks a button, link button, or image button control.
TextChanged	The user changes the value in a text box.
CheckedChanged	The user selects a radio button in a group of radio buttons or selects or unselects a check box.
SelectedIndexChanged	The user selects an item from a drop-down list or a list box.

Code for the Click event of the btnClear button

```csharp
protected void btnClear_Click(object sender, EventArgs e)
{
    ddlMonthlyInvestment.SelectedIndex = 0;
    txtInterestRate.Text = "";
    txtYears.Text = "";
    lblFutureValue.Text = "";
}
```

Description

- All of the events handlers for an ASP.NET web page and its server controls are executed on the server. Because of that, a page must be posted back to the server before its events can be handled.

- When a page is posted back to the server, the Init and Load events are always raised so any event handlers for those events are run first. Then, the event handlers for any control events that were raised are executed in the order in which they were raised.

Figure 2-16   How to use page and control events in your C# code

The C# code for the Future Value form

Figure 2-17 presents the C# code for the code-behind file of the Future Value form. It consists of multiple using directives (not all shown here), three event handlers, and a method named CalculateFutureValue. The event handlers handle the Load event for the page, the Click event of the Calculate button, and the Click event of the Clear button. The CalculateFutureValue method is called by the event handler for the Click event of the Calculate button.

In the code in this figure, the highlighted properties are the ones that are commonly tested in the code for web forms. The first one is the IsPostBack property that's used in the Page_Load method. If it is True, it means that the page is being posted back from the user. If it is False, it means that the page is being requested by the user for the first time.

As a result, the statements within the if statement in the Page_Load method are only executed if the page is being requested for the first time. In that case, the values 50 through 500 are added to the drop-down list by using the Add method of the Items collection for the list. For all subsequent requests by that user, the IsPostBack property will be True so the values aren't added to the drop-down list. Instead, the values are restored from view state.

In contrast, the unobtrusive validation mode needs to be set every time the page loads. If it isn't set, an error will occur. That's why the code that sets this mode comes before the if statement in the Page_Load event handler.

The other page property that's commonly tested is the IsValid property. It's useful when the user's browser doesn't support the client-side scripts for the validation controls. In that case, the application has to rely on the validation that's always done on the server. Then, if IsValid is True, it means that all of the input data is valid. But if IsValid is False, it means that one or more controls contain invalid input data so the processing shouldn't be done.

In the btnCalculate_Click method, you can see how the IsValid test is used. If it isn't True, the processing isn't done. But otherwise, this method uses the SelectedValue property of the drop-down list to get the value of the selected item, which represents the investment amount. Then, it uses the Text properties of the text boxes to get the years and interest rate values. After it gets these values, it converts them to their data types (integer and decimal). Last, it calls the CalculateFutureValue method to calculate the future value, uses the ToString method to convert the future value to a string with currency format, and puts the formatted value in the label of the form. When this method ends, the web form is sent back to the user's browser.

Notice that this code doesn't do anything if IsValid is false. That's because it doesn't need to. If the data isn't valid, the validation controls will display the appropriate messages, just like they do when client-side scripts are enabled.

With the exception of the IsPostBack and IsValid properties and the unobtrusive validation setting, this is all standard C# code. Because of that, you shouldn't have any trouble following it. But if you do, you can quickly upgrade your C# skills by getting our latest C# book.

The C# code for the Future Value form

```csharp
using System;
using System.Web;
using System.Web.UI;
// more using directives generated by Visual Studio

namespace Ch02FutureValue
{
    public partial class Default : System.Web.UI.Page
    {
        protected void Page_Load(object sender, EventArgs e)
        {
            UnobtrusiveValidationMode = UnobtrusiveValidationMode.None;
            if (!IsPostBack)
                for (int i = 50; i <= 500; i += 50)
                    ddlMonthlyInvestment.Items.Add(i.ToString());
        }

        protected void btnCalculate_Click(object sender, EventArgs e)
        {
            if (IsValid)
            {
                int monthlyInvestment =
                    Convert.ToInt32(ddlMonthlyInvestment.SelectedValue);
                decimal yearlyInterestRate =
                    Convert.ToDecimal(txtInterestRate.Text);
                int years = Convert.ToInt32(txtYears.Text);
                decimal futureValue = this.CalculateFutureValue(
                    monthlyInvestment, yearlyInterestRate, years);
                lblFutureValue.Text = futureValue.ToString("c");
            }
        }

        protected decimal CalculateFutureValue(int monthlyInvestment,
                        decimal yearlyInterestRate, int years)
        {
            int months = years * 12;
            decimal monthlyInterestRate = yearlyInterestRate / 12 / 100;
            decimal futureValue = 0;
            for (int i = 0; i < months; i++)
            {
                futureValue = (futureValue + monthlyInvestment) *
                            (1 + monthlyInterestRate);
            }
            return futureValue;
        }

        protected void btnClear_Click(object sender, EventArgs e)
        {
            ddlMonthlyInvestment.SelectedIndex = 0;
            txtInterestRate.Text = "";
            txtYears.Text = "";
            lblFutureValue.Text = "";
        }
    }
}
```

Figure 2-17   The C# code for the Future Value form

How to test a web application

After you design the forms and develop the C# code for a web application, you need to test it to be sure it works properly. Then, if you discover any errors, you need to find the errors, correct them, and test again. For now, you'll just learn some basic skills for testing and application. But in chapter 5, you'll learn more about testing and debugging.

How to run a web application

To run a web application, you can use one of the techniques in figure 2-18. Before Visual Studio runs the application, though, it compiles the aspx and C# code for the web forms. Then, if the web forms compile without errors, Visual Studio runs the application using IIS Express and displays the starting page of the application in your default browser. At that point, you can test the application to make sure that it works the way you want it to.

However, if any errors are detected as part of the compilation, Visual Studio opens the Error List window and displays the errors. These can consist of *syntax errors* that have to be corrected as well as warning messages. In this figure, just one error message and no warning messages are displayed.

To fix an error, you can double-click on it in the Error List window. This moves the cursor to the line of code that caused the error in the Code Editor. By moving from the Error List window to the Code Editor for all of the messages, you should be able to find the coding problems and fix them.

Keep in mind, though, that the error may not be in the statement in the line of code that causes the problem. For instance, the message in this example says that futurevalue doesn't exist, but the problem is that this variable was spelled differently when it was declared. To fix that, you need to fix the declaration.

After you fix all of the compilation errors and run the application in the browser, you should be aware that an *exception* may occur. That happens when ASP.NET can't execute one of the statements in the C# code, even though it compiled without error. Then, if the exception isn't handled by the application, ASP.NET switches to the Code Editor window and highlights the statement that caused the exception. At that point, you can stop the application by clicking on the Stop Debugging button in the Debug toolbar or using the Debug→Stop Debugging command. Then, you can fix the problem and test again.

In addition to testing whether the web application runs without error, you should also test to see that it displays correctly in different browsers. Visual Studio makes it easy to change the default browsers for this purpose by providing a drop-down browser list. After you use that list to change the default browser, you can click on the browser name or press F5 to run the web application in that browser.

Visual Studio with the Error List window and browser list displayed

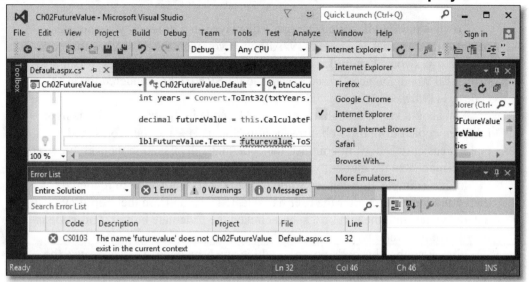

How to run an application

- To run an application in the default browser, press F5 or click on the browser name in the Standard toolbar.
- To change the default browser, select a browser from the drop-down browser list.

How to stop an application

- Click the Close button in the upper right corner of the browser. For some browsers like Internet Explorer, that will stop the application in Visual Studio.
- In Visual Studio, click the Stop Debugging button in the Debug toolbar (the one with the red square on it) or press Shift+F5. This also stops an application when an exception occurs.

How to fix syntax errors and exceptions

- To go to the statement that caused a syntax error, double-click on the error in the Error List window. That will give you a clue to the cause of the error.
- When an exception occurs, the application is interrupted and the statement that caused the error is displayed in Visual Studio. Then, you can stop the application and debug it.

Description

- If any errors are detected when you run an application, a dialog box asks whether you want to continue by running the last successful build. If you click No, the application isn't run and an Error List is displayed.
- If a statement can't be executed when the application is run, even though it compiles successfully, an *exception* will occur. Then, you need to debug the problem.

Figure 2-18   How to run a web application

How to view the HTML that's sent to the browser

To view the HTML for a page that's displayed in a browser, you can use one of the techniques in figure 2-19. Although you won't need to view this code often, it gives you a better idea of what's going on behind the scenes. It can also be helpful when you need to see exactly how ASP.NET has rendered the aspx code to HTML.

You should know, though, that the HTML code in the example in this figure has been copied from the web browser into Notepad++ and then formatted to make it easier to follow. In contrast, the code that's displayed in the web browser isn't formatted so it's harder to review.

In this example, you can see some of the HTML that has been rendered for the Future Value form after the user has selected a value from the drop-down list, entered values into the text boxes, and clicked the Calculate button. This code is instructive in several ways.

First, note that this code doesn't include any aspx code. That's because the aspx has been converted to HTML. For instance, the aspx for the drop-down list in the first row of the table has been converted to an HTML select element that contains one option element for each value in the list.

Second, note that view state data is stored in a hidden input field named _VIEWSTATE. However, the value of this field is encoded so you can't read it. Because the data in view state is passed to and from the browser automatically, you don't have to handle the passing of this data in your code.

Third, note that the values that the user entered are included in the HTML. For instance, the value in the drop-down list is 50, and the value in the first text box is 3.0. This illustrates that you don't need view state to save the information that's entered by the user. Instead, view state is used to maintain the state of properties that have been set by code. For example, it's used to maintain the values that are loaded into the drop-down list the first time the user requests the form.

Fourth, note the script element that comes right after the view state data. Although the JavaScript code that it contained has been replaced with a comment, this is one of several script elements that were generated for this form. They provide the JavaScript code for validating the data in the browser.

Fifth, note that the HTML for a label server control is a span element, not a label element as you might expect. If you were able to scroll down, you would also see that the error messages for the validation controls are displayed in span elements. As you will see in the next chapter, you sometimes need to know how a server control is rendered in HTML if you want to apply CSS formatting to it, and reviewing the source code is one way to find out.

Keep in mind that this HTML is generated automatically by ASP.NET, so you usually don't have to worry about it. You just develop the application by using Visual Studio, and the rest of the work is done for you. Sometimes, though, reviewing the source code can help you solve a debugging problem.

Some of the HTML for the Future Value form after a post back

```
<body>
    <img src="Images/MurachLogo.jpg" alt="Murach Logo"/>
    <h1>401K Future Value Calculator</h1>
    <form method="post" action="./Default.aspx" onsubmit="javascript:return WebForm_OnSubmit();" id="form1">
<div class="aspNetHidden">
<input type="hidden" name="__EVENTTARGET" id="__EVENTTARGET" value="" />
<input type="hidden" name="__EVENTARGUMENT" id="__EVENTARGUMENT" value="" />
<input type="hidden" name="__VIEWSTATE" id="__VIEWSTATE" value="WGkbSuZOa7jU79TqYVNILyVNOCXSKZCU8c1gQur391Bhq
</div>

<script type="text/javascript">
    // One of several script elements that contain JavaScript code
</script>

    <div>
        <table class="auto-style1">
            <tr>
                <td class="auto-style2">Monthly investment</td>
                <td>
                    <select name="ddlMonthlyInvestment" id="ddlMonthlyInvestment" style="height:22px;width:14
                        <option selected="selected" value="50">50</option>
                        <option value="100">100</option>
                        <option value="150">150</option>
                        <option value="200">200</option>
                        <option value="250">250</option>
                        <option value="300">300</option>
                        <option value="350">350</option>
                        <option value="400">400</option>
                        <option value="450">450</option>
                        <option value="500">500</option>

                    </select>
                </td>
            </tr>
            <tr>
                <td class="auto-style2">Annual interest rate</td>
                <td>
                    <input name="txtInterestRate" type="text" value="3.0" id="txtInterestRate" />
                </td>
            </tr>
            <tr>
                <td class="auto-style2">Number of years</td>
                <td>
                    <input name="txtYears" type="text" value="10" id="txtYears" />
                </td>
            </tr>
            <tr>
                <td>Future value</td>
                <td>
                    <span id="lblFutureValue" style="font-weight:bold;">$7,004.54</span>
                </td>
            </tr>
```

Two ways to view the HTML for a page in a browser

- Select the View→Source command from the browser's menu.
- Right-click on the web page and select the View Source command from the shortcut menu.

Description

- When an ASP.NET page is requested by a browser, ASP.NET generates the HTML for the page and returns that HTML to the browser.
- View state data is stored in a hidden input field within the HTML. This data is encoded so you can't read it.
- If the page contains validation controls, the HTML for the page contains script elements that include the JavaScript that does the validation.
- Values that the user enters into a page are returned to the browser as part of the HTML.

Figure 2-19   How to review the HTML that's sent to the browser

Perspective

The purpose of this chapter has been to teach you the basic skills for creating a one-page ASP.NET application with Visual Studio. If you've already used Visual Studio and C# to develop Windows applications, you shouldn't have any trouble mastering these skills. You just need to get used to using the properties and events for web server controls and validation controls.

As you will see in the next chapter, though, you should also have a solid set of HTML and CSS skills. That way, you can separate the content for a web page (the HTML) from its formatting (the CSS), and that makes it easier to develop and maintain the pages of a web application. You'll also learn the basics of using Bootstrap in the next chapter, which makes it easier to develop pages that can be displayed on devices of varying sizes.

Terms

template	snippet
target framework	web server control
default template	smart tag menu
web form	property
Web Forms Designer	validation control
Designer	validator
Toolbox	required field validator
Solution Explorer	range validator
Properties window	unobtrusive validation
Source view	jQuery
Design view	event handler
Split view	Code Editor
IIS Express	syntax error
flow layout	exception
IntelliSense	

Summary

- You create a web application from a *template* that determines the folders and files that Visual Studio adds to the project.

- The *target framework* determines the features that are available to an application. By default, the target framework for a web application is .NET Framework 4.5.2.

- When you use Visual Studio to design *web forms*, the primary window is the *Web Forms Designer* (or just *Designer*). It is supported by the *Toolbox*, the *Solution Explorer*, and the *Properties window*.

- When you use the Designer to build a web form, you can work in *Source view*, *Design view*, or *Split view*.

- In Source view, *IntelliSense* and *snippets* help you enter the tags and attributes for HTML elements and web server controls. In Design view, the Toolbox makes it easy to add web server controls to a form and the Properties window helps you set the *properties* for the controls.

- ASP.NET provides *validation controls* that provide for both client-side and server-side data validation. For client-side validation, JavaScript must be enabled in the user's browser, but most browsers have it enabled.

- When *unobtrusive validation* is used for a web application, ASP.NET will use a JavaScript library called *jQuery* for the validation. That option is on by default when you start a new web application.

- Visual Studio provides a *Code Editor* with IntelliSense and snippets that makes it easier to enter the C# statements for the *event handlers* and other methods that a web application requires.

- Three of the page events that can trigger an event handler are the Init, Load, and PreRender events. The first two are raised each time a page is requested from the server. The last one is raised right before the HTML is generated for a page.

- Four of the server control events that can trigger an event handler are the Click event for a button, the TextChanged event for a text box, the CheckedChanged event for a check box or radio button, and the SelectedIndexChanged event for a list.

- The IsPostBack property of a page can be used to tell whether a page is being posted back from a browser or loaded for the first time. The IsValid property of a page can be used to tell whether the validation controls have found that all of the entries are valid.

- If you try to run a web form that has *syntax errors* in the C# code, Visual Studio stops compiling the assembly and displays the errors in an Error List window.

- An *exception* occurs when ASP.NET can't execute one of the statements in the C# code, even though it compiles without error. Then, you need to stop the application, find the cause of the exception, and fix it.

- If you view the source code while a page is displayed in a browser, you can see the hidden fields that are used for view state, the scripts that are used for data validation, and the HTML that's generated for the server controls.

Before you do the exercises for this book...

If you haven't already done so, you need to install the software that's required for this book as well as the downloadable applications. Appendix A shows how to do that.

Exercise 2-1   Build the Future Value application

This exercise guides you through the development of the Future Value application that's presented in this chapter. This will give you a chance to experiment with the many features that Visual Studio offers.

Start, close, and open the web application

1. Start a web application with the Empty template as shown in figures 2-1 and 2-2. Name the application Ex02FutureValue and store it in the C:\aspnet46_cs directory.

2. Add a web form as shown in figure 2-3 and name it Default.aspx.

3. Add a folder named Images to your project and add the MurachLogo.jpg file to it using the techniques in figure 2-5. The jpg file is in the C:\aspnet46_cs directory.

4. Close the application as shown in figure 2-6, saving changes if you're prompted to. Then, open the application again as shown in this figure.

Use the Web Forms Designer to build the form

5. Open the Default.aspx web form and switch to Source view. Type "Chapter 2: Future Value" in the title element in the head section of the HTML.

6. Move the cursor to the end of the opening body tag and press the Enter key to create a new line. Next, drag the Murach logo file from the Images folder in the Solution Explorer to the new line. That should create an img element with a properly coded src attribute. Now, add an alt attribute to this element with "Murach Logo" as its value, and switch to Design view to see the changes.

7. Switch to Source view, place the insertion point after the img element, and add an h1 element that has "401K Future Value Calculator" as its content.

8. Switch to Design view to see this change. Then, run the form in the default browser by pressing F5. That automatically saves the changes to the Default.aspx file. After your form is displayed in the default browser, close the browser. If your default browser is Internet Explorer, this should stop the application.

9. Return to Visual Studio. If the Toolbox isn't available, that means the web form is still running. So, click the Stop Debugging button in the Debug toolbar to stop the application.

10. In Source view, place the insertion point inside the div tags. Then, in Design view, use the techniques in figure 2-8 to add a table that provides for six rows and two columns. Next, add the text shown in the first four rows to the first column of the table. Then, drag the right boundary of the first column to reduce its width as shown in this figure.

11. Switch to Source view to see the HTML for the table. Note that a style element has been added to the head section and class attributes have been added to the table element and some of the td elements. This was generated when you reduced the width of the first column by dragging its boundary. Note too that non-breaking space characters ( ) have been generated for the empty td elements.

12. Switch to Design view and use the techniques in figure 2-9 to add the drop-down list, text boxes, label, and buttons shown in that figure to the table. Then, adjust the size of the list, text box, and buttons, but not the label, so the table looks the way you want it to.

13. Use the techniques of figure 2-9 and the summary in figure 2-10 to set the ID and Text properties of the controls. For the Clear button, also set the CausesValidation property to False. For the label, delete the value of the Text property.

14. Press F5 to run the application, and check the web form to make sure it looks the way it's supposed to. Then, switch to Visual Studio and click the Stop Debugging button in the Debug toolbar.

Add the validation controls

15. In Source view or Design view, add the validation controls for the text boxes as shown in figures 2-11 and 2-12.

16. In Design view, double-click outside the body of the web form to go to the event handler for the Load event of the page in the code-behind file for the form. Then, turn off unobtrusive validation by adding the statement in the Load event handler shown in figure 2-13. IntelliSense makes this easy.

17. Press F5 to run the application. Then, test the field validators by leaving fields blank or entering invalid data. The validation will be done when the focus leaves a text box or when you click on the Calculate button.

18. Stop the application. Then, if necessary, fix any problems and test again. If, for example, validation is done when you click the Clear button, make sure its CausesValidation property is set to False. Or, if a range validator is behaving strangely, make sure its Type property is set correctly.

Add the C# code and test as you go

19. Double-click outside of the body of the form in Design view to switch to the Code Editor. That will take you to the Load event handler that you started coding earlier.

20. At the top of the Code Editor, note the using directives that Visual Studio generates. Then, add the rest of the code for the Load event handler shown in figure 2-17, taking full advantage of the IntelliSense that's provided. Then, press F5 to compile and test this event handler. If any syntax errors are detected, use the techniques in figure 2-18 to fix them.

21. In the aspx file, in Design view, double-click on the Clear button to start an event handler for the Click event of that button. Then, enter the code for this event handler as shown in figure 2-17, and test again.

22. Enter the code for the CalculateFutureValue method that's shown in figure 2-17. When you're ready to add the for loop, right-click, select Visual C# from the shortcut menu, and select the for snippet. Then, finish the coding for this method.

23. In the aspx file, in Design view, double-click on the Calculate button to start an event handler for the Click event of that button. Next, type "if" and then press the Tab key twice to insert the snippet for the if statement. Then, enter the code for this event handler. This method should call the CalculateFutureValue method as in figure 2-17. Then, test this code.

24. If necessary, fix any design or coding problems that remain. When you're through, the application should work the way you want it to.

Do more testing and experimenting

25. Set the EnableViewState property of the drop-down list to False, and test the application to see what happens. When an exception occurs, stop the application and reset the property.

26. Set the EnableClientScript property for all four validators to False so the validation will only be done on the server. Then, test the application to make sure that the validation still works. When you're through testing, end the application and reset these properties.

27. Run the application again, and use the technique in figure 2-19 to review the HTML that's sent to the browser. There, you can see the HTML that's generated for the web form, the input element with the "hidden" type that's used for view state, and the script elements that contain the JavaScript that's used for client-side validation.

28. When you're through experimenting, close the project. Then, close Visual Studio.

3

How to use HTML5, CSS3, and Bootstrap with ASP.NET

In chapter 2, you learned how to build the Future Value application without worrying about the HTML or CSS that was generated by Visual Studio. But there is a right way to use the HTML and CSS for a web application. Specifically, the HTML should provide the content and structure for a web page, and the CSS should provide the formatting. In addition, a web page should look good on all devices. You'll learn how to do these things in this chapter.

The Future Value application with CSS formatting

Figure 3-1 presents another version of the Future Value application that you learned to develop in the last chapter. This time, a table isn't used to align the labels and server controls. Instead, CSS is used for all of the formatting including the alignment. This separates the formatting (the CSS) from the content (the HTML), and that's a best practice for today's web applications.

The user interface

In this figure, you can see that the user interface doesn't look exactly like the one in the last chapter. Instead, the form is centered on the screen with a black border around it, and the error messages are displayed to the right of the server controls that get the entries. In this example, the user has entered 33 for the annual interest rate, and the error message says the rate must range from 1 to 20.

The HTML that's generated for a new form

When you create a new form with Visual Studio, it generates the code that's shown in the first example in this figure. Then, the second example shows how you can modify the generated code.

Here, the DOCTYPE declaration at the top of the page says that HTML5 will be used for the HTML document (or page). If you're familiar with the declarations for earlier versions of HTML, you know that they were far more complicated than that.

This declaration is followed by the html element that includes all of the other elements for the page. Within its opening tag, you can see the xmlns attribute that was generated by ASP.NET. Although this attribute isn't necessary when you use HTML5, it doesn't hurt anything. So, you can either leave it the way it is or delete it, whichever you prefer.

In the head element, you should code a value in the title element that will be displayed in the browser's title bar or tab when the application is run. In the browser in this figure, you can see the contents of the title element in the tab for the application.

When you use an external style sheet for the CSS that will format a page, you also code a link element within the head element. This link element identifies the external style sheet that will be used. More about that in a moment.

Last, you can usually delete the div tags that are generated by ASP.NET because they aren't needed within a form element. Besides that, you should use the HTML5 semantic elements instead of div elements to show the structure of a document. You'll learn about those elements shortly.

The user interface for the Future Value application

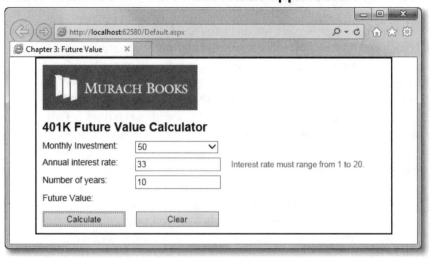

The HTML that's generated for a new form

```
<!DOCTYPE html>
<html xmlns="http://www.w3.org/1999/xhtml">
<head runat="server">
    <title></title>
</head>
<body>
    <form id="form1" runat="server">
    <div>

    </div>
    </form>
</body>
</html>
```

The HTML after it has been modified for this application

```
<!DOCTYPE html>
<html xmlns="http://www.w3.org/1999/xhtml">
<head runat="server">
    <title>Chapter 3: Future Value</title>
    <link href="site.css" rel="stylesheet">
</head>
<body>
    <form id="form1" runat="server">

    </form>
</body>
</html>
```

Description

- The DOCTYPE element indicates that HTML5 will be used for the document.
- The title element specifies the name that will be shown in the browser's title bar or tab.
- The link element references the external style sheet that contains the CSS for the page.

Figure 3-1   The user interface and starting HTML for the Future Value application

The aspx code for the application

Figure 3-2 presents the aspx code for this version of the Future Value application. It includes a header element for the header of the document and a main element for all of the other content of the document. These are HTML5 semantic elements.

The header element contains one standard HTML img element. It displays the logo at the top of the page. The main element starts with a standard HTML h1 element that displays the heading right below the logo.

Within the form element, you can see four standard label elements. They precede and identify the four server controls: the drop-down list, the two text boxes, and the label control that will display the result. The last two server controls are button controls for the Calculate and Clear buttons.

After each of the server controls for the text boxes, you can see two validators. The first is a required field validator, and the second is a range validator. Because these validators come right after the text boxes that they validate, CSS can be used to align them so they are displayed to the right of the boxes that they relate to.

Using the techniques that you learned in the last chapter, you should be able to create a page like this without much trouble. But at that point, the layout of the page will be a mess. Then, you have to create the external style sheet and the styles that will format the page.

As you'll see in a moment, you can select the HTML elements that you want to format with CSS using id or class attributes. That's why the CssClass properties have been added to the code in this figure. For instance, the drop-down list and the two text boxes have been coded with their CssClass properties set to "entry", the four validators have their CssClass properties set to "validator", and the two buttons have their CssClass properties set to "button". Each of the controls also has an ID property that the CSS can use to select that element. Then, when the form is rendered, these properties are converted to HTML id and class attributes that are used for formatting with CSS.

When you start using CSS to format your pages, you may not know which controls need ID or CssClass properties. That's okay, though, because you can switch back and forth between the style sheet and the Designer. Then, after you get more familiar with the use of CSS, you'll have a better idea of how to set the ids and classes before you create the styles in the external style sheet.

The aspx code for the body of the Future Value application

```
<body>
    <header>
        <img id="logo" alt="Murach Logo" src="Images/MurachLogo.jpg" />
    </header>
    <main>
        <h1>401K Future Value Calculator</h1>
        <form id="form1" runat="server">
            <label for="ddlMonthlyInvestment">Monthly investment:</label>
            <asp:DropDownList ID="ddlMonthlyInvestment" runat="server"
                CssClass="entry"></asp:DropDownList><br />
            <label for="txtInterestRate">Annual interest rate:</label>
            <asp:TextBox ID="txtInterestRate" runat="server"
                CssClass="entry">6.0</asp:TextBox>
                <asp:RequiredFieldValidator ID="RequiredFieldValidator1"
                    runat="server" CssClass="validator"
                    ErrorMessage="Interest rate is required."
                    ControlToValidate="txtInterestRate"
                    Display="Dynamic">
                </asp:RequiredFieldValidator>
                <asp:RangeValidator ID="RangeValidator1" runat="server"
                    CssClass="validator"
                    ControlToValidate="txtInterestRate" Display="Dynamic"
                    ErrorMessage="Interest rate must range from 1 to 20."
                    MaximumValue="20" MinimumValue="1"
                    Type="Double">
                </asp:RangeValidator><br />
            <label for="txtYears">Number of years:</label>
            <asp:TextBox ID="txtYears" runat="server"
                CssClass="entry">10</asp:TextBox>
                <asp:RequiredFieldValidator ID="RequiredFieldValidator2"
                    runat="server" CssClass="validator"
                    ControlToValidate="txtYears" Display="Dynamic"
                    ErrorMessage="Number of years is required.">
                </asp:RequiredFieldValidator>
                <asp:RangeValidator ID="RangeValidator2" runat="server"
                    CssClass="validator" ControlToValidate="txtYears"
                    Display="Dynamic"
                    ErrorMessage="Years must range from 1 to 45."
                    MaximumValue="45"
                    MinimumValue="1" Type="Integer">
                </asp:RangeValidator><br />
            <label for="lblFutureValue">Future value:</label>
            <asp:Label ID="lblFutureValue" runat="server" Text="">
            </asp:Label><br />
            <asp:Button ID="btnCalculate" runat="server" Text="Calculate"
                CssClass="button" OnClick="btnCalculate_Click" />
            <asp:Button ID="btnClear" runat="server" Text="Clear"
                CssClass="button" OnClick="btnClear_Click"
                CausesValidation="False" />
        </form>
    </main>
</body>
```

Figure 3-2   The aspx code when CSS is used for the formatting

The CSS style sheet for the application

Figure 3-3 presents the CSS style sheet for the Future Value application. If you're new to *CSS* (*Cascading Style Sheets*), you just need to understand what each of the rule sets in this figure applies to because you're going to learn more about CSS in a moment.

For instance, the first three rule sets apply to the HTML body, h1, and label elements. In this case, the names before the braces { } are just the names of the HTML elements.

The next three rule sets are for the elements with class attributes equal to entry, validator, and button. Note that these names are preceded by dots (periods) to indicate that they are class names.

The last three rules sets are for elements with the id attributes that are specified. For instance, the first rule set is for the element with an id attribute equal to ddlMonthlyInvestment. In the style sheet, the ids are preceded by the pound sign (#) to indicate that they are ids.

As you learn more about CSS, you can refer back to this page to see how the CSS leads to the formatting shown in figure 3-1. For instance, the width property in the rule set for the body says that the body should be 550 pixels wide. The margin property says the body should have no top or bottom margin, but it should be centered horizontally in the browser (auto). And the border property says that the body should have a solid border that's 2 pixels wide. Since no color is specified, the border will have the same color as the text.

The external style sheet for the Future Value application

```css
/* The styles for the elements */
body {
    font-family: Arial, Helvetica, sans-serif;
    font-size: 85%;
    width: 550px;
    margin: 0 auto;
    padding: 10px;
    background-color: white;
    border: 2px solid;
}
h1 {
    font-size: 140%;
    padding: 0;
    margin-bottom: .5em;
}
label {
    float: left;
    width: 10em;
}

/* the styles for classes */
.entry {
    margin-left: 1em;
    margin-bottom: .5em;
    width: 10em;
}
.validator {
    font-size: 95%;
    color: red;
    margin-left: 1em;
}
.button {
    margin-top: 1em;
    width: 10em;
}

/* The styles for the server controls */
#ddlMonthlyInvestment {
    width: 10em;
}
#lblFutureValue {
    font-weight: bold;
    margin-left: 1em;
}
#btnClear {
    margin-left: 1em;
}
```

Figure 3-3   The CSS for the Future Value application

The HTML and CSS skills that you need

Although this book assumes that you're already familiar with HTML and CSS, the next several topics present a quick review of the HTML and CSS skills that you need for developing web applications. If you don't already have these skills, we recommend *Murach's HTML5 and CSS3* as a companion to this book.

How to code HTML elements

Figure 3-4 shows how to code *HTML elements* like those in the table within an *HTML document*. To start, each HTML element is coded within a *tag* that starts with an opening bracket (<) and ends with a closing bracket (>). For example, <h1>, <p>, and <br> are all HTML tags.

Most HTML elements are made up of three parts. The *opening tag* marks the start of the element. It consists of the element name (such as h1) plus one or more optional *attributes* (such as id or class) that provide additional information for the tag. After the opening tag is the *content*, which is the text or other data that makes up the element. After the content is the *closing tag* that marks the end of the element. The closing tag consists of a slash followed by the element's name.

Not all HTML elements have content and closing tags, however. For instance, the <br> and <img> elements don't have closing tags. These can be referred to as *self-closing tags*.

Attributes are coded with an attribute name, an equals sign, and a value in quotation marks, as shown in the second group of examples in this figure. Here, for example, the <a> element has an href attribute that provides the URL that the link should go to when it is clicked, as well as a title attribute that provides text that's displayed when the user points to the link.

You can also code *comments* within an HTML document as shown in the second last example in this figure. That way, you can describe sections of code that might be confusing. You can also use comments to *comment out* a portion of HTML code. That way, the code is ignored when the web page is displayed in a browser. That can be useful when testing a web page.

If you want to code a space within a line that the web browser doesn't ignore, you can use   (for non-breaking space) as shown in the last example in this figure. This is just one of the many *character entities* that you can use to display special characters in HTML, and Visual Studio automatically puts these characters into the empty cells of each row when it generates a table. Note that each character entity starts with an ampersand (&) and ends with a semicolon (;).

In the table at the top of figure 3-4, you can see that some of the elements are *block elements* and some are *inline elements*. The difference is that by default, block elements are displayed on their own lines. In contrast, inline elements flow to the right of preceding elements and don't start new lines.

When you use HTML5, you can use the syntax for either of its predecessors: HTML or XHTML. However, Visual Studio uses the XHTML syntax by default, so that's what's shown in this figure. In addition, we recommend that you use lowercase for all HTML code, even though HTML5 allows mixed cases.

Common HTML elements

Element	Type	Defines
h1	Block	A level-1 heading with content in bold at 200% of the base font size.
h2	Block	A level-2 heading with content in bold at 150% of the base font size.
h3	Block	A level-3 heading with content in bold at 117% of the base font size.
p	Block	A paragraph at 100% of the base font size.
img	Block	An image that will be displayed on the page.
form	Block	A form that can be submitted to the web server for processing.
a	Inline	A link that goes to another page or a location on the current page when clicked.
input	Inline	A control on a form like a text box or button.
label	Inline	A label that identifies a control on a form.
br		A line break that starts a new line.

How to code HTML elements

Two block elements with opening and closing tags

```
<h1>Halloween SuperStore</h1>
<p>Here is a list of links:</p>
```

Two self-closing tags

```
<br />
<img src="logo.gif" alt="Murach Logo" />
```

How to code the attributes for HTML elements

```
<a href="contact.html" title="Click to Contact Us" class="nav_link">
    Contact Us</a>
```

How to code an HTML comment

```
<!-- The text in a comment is ignored -->
```

How to code a character entity for a space

```
<td> </td>
```

Description

- An *HTML document* contains *HTML elements* that specify the content of a web page.
- By default, *block elements* are displayed on new lines, but *inline elements* flow to the right of the elements that precede them.
- An *attribute* consists of an attribute name, an equals sign, and a value in quotation marks.
- *Comments* can be used to describe or *comment out* portions of HTML code.
- *Character entities* provide for special characters, like a non-breaking space ( ).

Figure 3-4   Basic rules for coding HTML elements

Incidentally, you may have noticed in the first two chapters that we refer to HTML elements by the name used in the opening tag. For instance, we refer to h1 and img elements. To prevent misreading, though, we enclose one-letter element names in brackets. As a result, we refer to <a> elements and <p> elements. That will continue throughout this book.

How to use the HTML5 semantic elements

By default, Visual Studio uses HTML5 when you create a new web page, which means you can use the *HTML5 semantic elements* that improve the structure of an HTML page. These elements are presented in figure 3-5. By using them, you improve the *search engine optimization (SEO)* of your web pages, at least in some search engines. So, if you aren't already using them, you should start soon.

Besides SEO improvements, the semantic elements make it easier to apply CSS to these elements because you don't have to code id attributes that are used by the CSS. Instead, you can apply the CSS to the elements themselves. You'll learn more about this in a moment. The semantic elements also improve a website's accessibility, which you'll also learn more about in a moment.

Be aware, however, that older browsers won't recognize the HTML5 semantic elements, which means that you won't be able to use CSS to apply formatting to them. In figure 3-10, you'll learn some techniques for making your CSS work in older browsers.

The primary HTML5 semantic elements

Element	Contents
header	The header for a page.
main	The main content of a page. Can only appear once per page, and cannot be the child of an article, aside, footer, header, or nav element.
section	A generic section of a document that doesn't indicate the type of content.
article	A composition like an article in the paper.
nav	A section of a page that contains links to other pages or placeholders.
aside	A section of a page like a sidebar that is related to the content that's near it.
figure	An image, table, or other component that's treated as a figure.
footer	The footer for a page.

A page that's structured with header, main, and footer elements

```
<body>
    <header>
        <h1>San Joaquin Valley Town Hall</h1>
    </header>
    <main>
        <p>Welcome to San Joaquin Valley Town Hall. We have some
            fascinating speakers for you this season!</p>
    </main>
    <footer>
        <p>&copy; San Joaquin Valley Town Hall.</p>
    </footer>
</body>
```

The page displayed in a web browser

San Joaquin Valley Town Hall

Welcome to San Joaquin Valley Town Hall. We have some fascinating speakers for you this season!

© San Joaquin Valley Town Hall.

Description

- HTML5 provides *semantic elements* that you should use to structure the contents of a web page. Using these elements can be referred to as *HTML5 semantics*.

- All of the HTML5 elements in this figure are supported by the modern browsers. They will also work on older browsers if you use the workarounds in figure 3-10.

- Two benefits that you get from using the semantic elements are (1) simplified HTML and CSS, and (2) improved *search engine optimization (SEO)*.

Figure 3-5   How to use the HTML5 semantic elements

How to use the div and span elements with HTML5

If you've been using HTML for a while, you are certainly familiar with the div element. It has traditionally been used to divide an HTML document into divisions that are identified by id attributes, as shown in the first example of figure 3-6. Then, CSS can use the ids to apply formatting to the divisions.

But now that HTML5 is available, div elements shouldn't be used to structure a document. Instead, they should only be used when the HTML5 semantic elements aren't appropriate and no structure is implied. If, for example, you want to group a series of elements so you can apply CSS to them, you can put them within a div element. But that doesn't affect the structure of the content that's implied by the HTML5 elements.

Note too that div elements are often used in JavaScript applications. If, for example, a section element contains three h2 elements with each followed by a div element, JavaScript can be used to display or hide a div element whenever the heading that precedes it is clicked. And, as you'll see later in this chapter, the div element is used often by Bootstrap. Here again, this doesn't affect the structure of the content that's implied by the HTML5 elements.

Similarly, span elements have historically been used to identify portions of text that can be formatted by CSS. By today's standards, though, it's better to use elements that indicate the contents of the elements, like the cite, code, and <q> elements.

But here again, span elements are often used in JavaScript applications. This is illustrated by the second example in this figure. Here, span elements are used to display the error messages for invalid entries.

Similarly, ASP.NET generates span elements for the messages that are displayed by its validator server controls. ASP.NET also generates span elements for its label server controls. This is illustrated by the third example in this figure, which shows that ASP.NET generated span tags for validator and label controls in the HTML it sent to the browser. Incidentally, you can see in this example that ASP.NET also generated an input tag for a text box control.

The div and span elements

Element	Description
div	A block element that provides a container for other elements.
span	An inline element that lets you identify text that can be formatted with CSS.

The way div elements were used before HTML5

```
<div id="header">
    <h1>San Joaquin Valley Town Hall</h1>
</div>
<div id="main">
    <p>Welcome to San Joaquin Valley Town Hall. We have some
        fascinating speakers for you this season!</p>
</div>
<div id="footer">
    <p>&copy; San Joaquin Valley Town Hall.</p>
</div>
```

Span elements in the HTML for a JavaScript application

```
<label for="email_address1">Email Address:</label>
<input type="text" id="email_address1" name="email_address1">
<span id="email_address1_error">*</span><br>

<label for="email_address2">Re-enter Email Address:</label>
<input type="text" id="email_address2" name="email_address2">
<span id="email_address2_error">*</span><br>
```

Span elements generated by ASP.NET for two validators and a label control

```
<label>Number of years:</label>
<input name="txtYears" type="text" value="10" id="txtYears" class="entry" />
    <span id="RequiredFieldValidator2" class="validator"
        style="display:none;">Number of years is required.</span>
    <span id="RangeValidator2" class="validator"
        style="display:none;">Years must range from 1 to 45.</span><br />
<label>Future value:</label>
<span id="lblFutureValue"></span><br />
```

Description

- Before HTML5, div elements were used to organize the content within the body of a document. Then, the ids for these div elements were used to apply CSS formatting to the elements.

- Today, HTML5 semantic elements should replace most div elements. That makes the structure of a page more apparent. As you'll soon see, though, Bootstrap uses a lot of divs.

- Before HTML5, span elements were used to identify portions of text that you could apply formatting to. Today, a better practice is to use elements that identify the contents, like the cite, code, and <q> elements.

- Be aware, however, that ASP.NET generates span elements for validators and also for label server controls.

Figure 3-6   How to use the div and span elements with HTML5

How to provide CSS styles for an HTML page

Figure 3-7 shows the three ways that CSS styles can be provided for an HTML page. The first way is to code a link element in the head section of an HTML document that specifies a file that contains the CSS for the page. This file is referred to as an *external style sheet*, and it's a best practice to provide styles in this way. That separates the HTML from the CSS.

The second way is to code a style element that contains the CSS for the page in the head section. This can be referred to as *embedded styles*. The benefit of using embedded styles is that you don't have to switch back and forth between HTML and CSS files as you develop a page. Overall, though, it's better to use external style sheets because that makes it easier to use them for more than one web page.

The third way to provide styles is to code style attributes within HTML elements. This can be referred to as *inline styles*. But then, there's no separation between the HTML and the CSS.

When you develop a web page as in chapter 2, Visual Studio generates both embedded and inline styles. But as you've seen in figures 3-2 and 3-3, it's better to put all of the styles for a page in an external style sheet. For some web forms, it also makes sense to use two or more external style sheets for a single page, as illustrated by the last example in this figure.

When you provide external styles, embedded styles, and inline styles, the inline styles override the embedded styles, which override the external styles. If, for example, all three types of styles set the font color for h1 elements, the inline style will be the one that's used. Similarly, if two external style sheets are used for a page, the styles in the second style sheet override the ones in the first sheet.

When you provide the styles for a web page in an external style sheet, you need to *attach* the style sheet to the page. To do that, you code a link element in the head section of the HTML that points to the style sheet, as shown by the examples in this figure. This figure also describes two ways to generate the link element for an external style sheet with Visual Studio.

Three ways to provide styles

Use an external style sheet by coding a link element in the head section

```
<link rel="stylesheet" href="Content/site.css">
```

Embed the styles in the head section

```
<style>
    body {
        font-family: Arial, Helvetica, sans-serif;
        font-size: 87.5%; }
    h1 { font-size: 250%; }
</style>
```

Use the style attribute of an element to provide inline styles

```
<span style="color: red; font-size: 14pt;">Warning!</span>
```

The sequence in which styles are applied

- Styles from an external style sheet
- Embedded styles
- Inline styles

A head element that includes two external style sheets

```
<head>
    <title>The Halloween Store</title>
    <link rel="stylesheet" href="site.css">
    <link rel="stylesheet" href="order.css">
</head>
```

The sequence in which styles are applied

- From the first external style sheet to the last

How to generate a link element for an external style sheet

- To generate a link element in Source view, drag the style sheet from the Solution Explorer into the head element for the page.
- To generate a link element in Design view, choose the Format→Attach Style Sheet command and select the style sheet from the Select Style Sheet dialog box.

Description

- It's a best practice to use *external style sheets* because that leads to better separation of concerns. Specifically, you separate the content for a page (HTML) from its formatting (CSS).
- External style sheets also make it easy to use the same styles for two or more pages. In contrast, if you use *embedded styles* or *inline styles*, you have to copy the styles to other documents before you can use them again.
- If more than one rule for the same property is applied to the same element, the last rule overrides the earlier rules.

Figure 3-7   How to provide CSS styles for an HTML page

How to code the basic CSS selectors

Figure 3-8 shows how to code the basic CSS *selectors* for applying styles to HTML elements. To start, this figure shows the body of an HTML document that contains a main and a footer element. Here, the h1 element is assigned an id of "first_heading", and the two <p> elements in this section have class attributes with the value "blue". Also, the <p> element in the footer has a class attribute with two values: "blue" and "right". This means that this element is assigned to two classes.

The three rule sets in the first group of examples are *type* (or *element*) *selectors*. To code a type selector, you just code the name of the element. As a result, the first rule set in this group selects the body element. The second rule set selects the main element. And the third rule set selects all <p> elements.

In these examples, the first rule set changes the font for the body element, and all of the elements within the body inherit this change. This rule set also sets the width of the body and centers it in the browser. Then, the second rule set puts a border around the main element and puts some padding inside it. Last, the rule set for a paragraph sets the margins for its sides in this sequence: top, right, bottom, and left. That's why the paragraphs in the main element are indented.

The two rule sets in the second group of examples use *class selectors* to select HTML elements by class. To do that, the selector is a period (.) followed by the class name. As a result, the first rule set selects all elements that have been assigned to the "blue" class, which are all three <p> elements. The second rule set selects any elements that have been assigned to the "right" class. That's the paragraph in the footer division. Here, the first rule set sets the color of the font to blue and the second rule set aligns the paragraph on the right.

The rule set in the last example uses an *id selector* to select an element by its id. To do that, the selector is a pound sign (#) followed by the id value that uniquely identifies an element. As a result, this rule set selects the h1 element that has an id of "first_heading" and sets its margins.

A key point here is that a class attribute can have the same value for more than one element on a page. Then, if you code a selector for that class, it will be used to format all the elements in that class. In contrast, since an element's id must be unique, an id selector can only be used to format a single element.

Another key point is that a more specific style overrides a less specific style. For instance, an id selector is more specific than a class selector, and a class selector is more specific than a type selector. That means that a style for an id selector will override the same style for a class selector, which will override the same style for a type selector. Beyond that, the rules in a rule set flow from top to bottom. So, if you've set multiple rules for a property of an element, the last one will override the previous ones.

HTML that can be selected by element type, class, or id

```
<body>
    <main>
        <h1 id="first_heading">The Speaker Lineup</h1>
        <p class="blue">October 19: Jeffrey Toobin</p>
        <p class="blue">November 16: Andrew Ross Sorkin</p>
    </main>
    <footer>
        <p class="blue right">Copyright SJV Town Hall</p>
    </footer>
</body>
```

CSS rule sets that select by element type, class, and id

Three rule sets with type selectors

```
body {
    font-family: Arial, Helvetica, sans-serif;
    width: 410px;
    margin: 1em auto;
}
main {
    border: 2px solid black;
    padding: 1em;
}
p { margin: .25em 0 .25em 3em; }
```

Two rule sets with class selectors

```
.blue { color: blue; }
.right { text-align: right; }
```

One rule set with an id selector

```
#first_heading { margin: 0 1em .25em; }
```

The elements displayed in a browser

The Speaker Lineup

October 19: Jeffrey Toobin
November 16: Andrew Ross Sorkin

Copyright SJV Town Hall

Description

- You code a *type selector* for all elements of a specific type by naming the element.
- You code a *class selector* for an element with a class attribute by coding a period followed by the class name. Then, the rule set applies to all elements with that class name.
- You code an *id selector* for an element with an id attribute by coding a pound sign (#) followed by the id value. Then, the rule set applies to the element with that id.

Figure 3-8   How to code the basic CSS selectors

How to code CSS rule sets and comments

CSS code consists of *rule sets* that are applied to HTML elements by their selectors. This is illustrated by the six rule sets in figure 3-9. As you can see, each rule set consists of a selector, a set of braces { }, and one or more *rules* within the braces. Within each rule, there's the name for a *property*, a colon, the value or values for the property, and an ending semicolon.

Now, to give you a better idea of how CSS works, here's a quick description of the rule sets in this figure. Remember, though, that this book is about ASP.NET, not CSS, so it isn't going to try to teach you how to use the dozens of properties that CSS provides. For that, you'll need our HTML5 and CSS3 book.

The first rule set consists of seven rules. The first rule specifies the font to be used for the body of the document, and all the elements within the body inherit that font. The second rule specifies that the base font for the application should be 85% of the default font size for the user's browser. If you refer back to figure 3-4, you can see that a <p> element will be 100% of that base font size, and an h1 element will be 200% of that size.

The third rule for the body of the document sets its width to 550 pixels. Then, the fourth rule specifies no margin on the top or bottom of the body, and an automatic margin to the left and right of the body. The automatic margins are what centers the body in a browser window.

The fifth rule for the body provides 10 pixels of padding within the body. Then, the last two rules for the body say that the background color should be white and the body should have a solid border around it that's two pixels wide. In figure 3-1, you can see the padding at the top, left, and bottom of the body, and you can see the border around it.

The second rule set is for all h1 elements. It sets the font size to 140% of the base font, the padding to 0, and the bottom margin to .5 em. Since an *em* is a unit of measure that's roughly equal to the width of a capital M in the font that's being used, it varies based on the font size that's used for an element. In this case, that .5 em margin provides the space after the heading that separates it from the labels and controls that follow it.

The third rule set applies to all of the label elements on the page. Here, the first rule floats the labels to the left. That means that the control that follows each label will flow to the right of it. Also, since validators become HTML span elements, they will flow to the right of the controls. Then, the second rule sets the width of each label to 10 ems. That provides the alignment for the four labels and controls without using a table.

The fourth rule set applies to all elements that have their class attributes set to "entry". That includes the drop-down list and the two text boxes. The rules in this rule set provide a left and bottom margin and set the width for those controls.

The fifth rule set is for the control that has ddlMonthlyInvestment as its id attribute, which is the drop-down list. This rule set sets the width of the control to 10.5 ems. But the rule set for the "entry" class has already been applied to that control and set its width to 10 ems. However, since an id selector is more specific than a class selector, the second rule overrides the first and sets the width to 10.5 ems.

Some of the styles in the external style sheet in figure 3-3

```css
/* The styles for the elements */
body {
    font-family: Arial, Helvetica, sans-serif;
    font-size: 85%;
    width: 550px;
    margin: 0 auto;
    padding: 10px;
    background-color: white;
    border: 2px solid;
}
h1 {
    font-size: 140%;
    padding: 0;
    margin-bottom: .5em;
}
label {
    float: left;
    width: 10em;
}

/* the styles for classes */
.entry {
    margin-left: 1em;
    margin-bottom: .5em;
    width: 10em;
}

/* The styles for the server controls */
#ddlMonthlyInvestment {
    width: 10.5em;
}
#lblFutureValue {
    font-weight: bold;
    margin-left: 1em;
}
```

Description

- A CSS *rule set* consists of a selector and one or more rules within braces.
- A CSS *selector* consists of the identifiers that are coded at the beginning of the rule set. If more than one selector is coded for a rule set, the selectors are separated by commas.
- A CSS *rule* consists of a *property*, a colon, a *value*, and a semicolon. Although the semicolon for the last declaration in a block is optional, it's a best practice to code it.
- To make your code easier to read, you can use spaces, indentation, and blank lines within a rule set.
- CSS *comments* begin with the characters /* and end with the characters */. A CSS comment can be coded on a single line, or it can span multiple lines.

Figure 3-9   How to code CSS rule sets and comments

The last rule set is for the control with lblFutureValue as its id. That's the label control that is used to display the Future Value result when the user clicks the Calculate button. This rule set provides a left margin for the label and sets the text in the label to bold.

How to ensure cross-browser compatibility

If you want your web application to be used by as many visitors as possible, you need to make sure that your web pages are compatible with as many browsers as possible. That's known as *cross-browser compatibility*. That means you should test your applications on as many browsers as possible, including the five browsers summarized in figure 3-10. This table shows the variance in the levels of HTML5 compatibility for these browsers, which is significant.

Today, all modern browsers support the HTML5 semantic elements, so you shouldn't have any problems with those browsers. It's the older browsers that you may need to be concerned about, especially IE8 because it still represents a small portion of the market. That's why this figure presents a workaround for making your applications work with older browsers.

This workaround is a *JavaScript shiv* that ensures that the HTML5 elements will work with older browsers. To implement it, you code the first script element shown in this figure within the head element for a page. This shiv loads a JavaScript file into the web page that provides HTML5 compatibility for older browsers.

While you're learning, you won't need to test your web pages on old browsers. That's why the HTML5 shiv isn't used by any of the applications in this book. For production applications, though, you usually do need to provide for compatibility with older browsers. This is particularly true if you need to support IE, as even the newer versions of IE don't support the HTML5 main element.

For this book, you should test all of your applications on Internet Explorer as well as one other browser, like Chrome or Firefox. That will be an adequate test of browser compatibility. In contrast, you should test production applications on all five of the browsers, including the older versions of these browsers that are still in use.

Just so you're aware of it, this figure also shows how to use the normalize.css style sheet to fix minor differences between browsers. To do that, you download the style sheet and include it as the first style sheet for all of your web pages. In this book, though, it isn't used for any of the applications so you might see some occasional variations between browsers. In that case, you may want to try using this style sheet to see whether it resolves the variations.

The current browsers and their HTML5 ratings (perfect score is 555)

Browser	Release	HTML5 Test Rating
Google Chrome	51	521
Opera	31	525
Mozilla Firefox	40	467
Apple Safari	9	400
Internet Explorer	Edge	402

The website for these ratings

`http://www.html5test.com`

The code that includes the JavaScript shiv for HTML5 compatibility

```
<script src="http://html5shiv.googlecode.com/svn/trunk/html5.js"></script>
```

What the HTML5 shiv does

- This JavaScript *shiv* (or *shim*) forces older browsers, like Internet Explorer 8, to recognize the HTML5 semantic elements and lets you apply CSS to these elements.
- The effect of the shiv is to add the HTML5 semantic elements to the DOM in the browser and also to add a CSS rule set that tells the browser to treat the HTML5 elements as block elements instead of inline elements.

The URL for downloading the normalize.css style sheet

`http://necolas.github.io/normalize.css`

What the normalize.css style sheet does

- Normalize.css is a style sheet that makes minor adjustments to browser defaults so all browsers render HTML elements the same way.
- For instance, the normalize.css style sheet sets the margins for the body of the document to zero so there's no space between the body and the edge of the browser window. The normalize.css style sheet also sets the default font family for the document to sans-serif.

Description

- Today, there are still differences in the way that different browsers handle HTML and CSS. As a developer, though, you want your web pages to work on as many different web browsers as possible. This is called *cross-browser compatibility*.
- At this writing, you still need to provide workarounds for IE8, but you shouldn't need to provide for other old browsers. However, you do need to provide for the main element in all current versions of IE. Eventually, all browsers will support HTML5 and CSS3 so the workarounds won't be necessary.
- To provide cross-browser compatibility, you can use the *HTML5 shiv* and the *normalize.css style sheet*. However, neither are used in the applications for this book.

Figure 3-10   How to ensure cross-browser compatibility

Visual Studio features for working with HTML and CSS

In the last chapter, you learned the basic techniques for entering and editing the HTML for a form. Now, you'll learn about the enhanced features that Visual Studio offers for working with HTML.

How to use the features for entering HTML

Figure 3-11 shows some of the advanced IntelliSense features for working with HTML. In particular, *snippets* of code are offered as you enter the start of a tag in Source view of the Designer. For instance, the first example shows that the snippet for the link element is offered when you enter the letter *l*. Then, if you press the Tab key twice, the snippet is added to the source code. In this case, that's a complete link element with the href attribute ready for your entry.

The second example shows how the smart indent feature works. If you press the Enter key when the insertion point is in the content area of an element, the closing tag is dropped down two lines and the cursor is indented in the middle line ready for your content entry.

This figure also summarizes three other features that help you enter the HTML for a form. If you experiment with these features, you'll quickly see what a big help Visual Studio is.

IntelliSense as an HTML element is entered in Source view

IntelliSense options including snippets are displayed as you start a tag

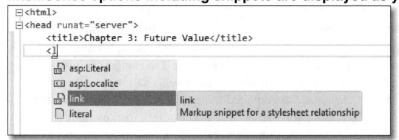

Press the Tab key twice to enter the snippet for the tag

The smart indent feature

If you press the Enter key when the cursor is in the content area...

```
⊟<body>
     <header>|</header>
```

...the closing tag is dropped down two lines
with the cursor where you want it

```
⊟<body>
     <header>

     </header>
```

Other Visual Studio features for entering HTML

- If you change the opening tag for an element, the closing tag will be automatically changed too.

- If you enter the opening bracket followed by the letters that are capitalized in the name of a control, like <cb for the asp:CheckBox control, IntelliSense will list the control.

- When you start the entry of an attribute, IntelliSense lists the attributes that apply to the HTML element.

Description

- Visual Studio provides many features that make it relatively easy to enter HTML code, including IntelliSense and *snippets*.

Figure 3-11   How to use the Visual Studio features for entering HTML

How to add the attributes
for the WAI-ARIA accessibility standards

The *accessibility* of a web application refers to the qualities that make it accessible to as many users as possible, especially disabled users. For instance, visually-impaired users may not be able to read text that's in images, so you need to provide other alternatives for them. Similarly, users with motor disabilities may not be able to use the mouse, so you need to make sure that all of the content and features of your web application can be accessed through the keyboard.

To a large extent, this means that you should develop your applications so the content is still usable if images aren't used and the mouse and JavaScript are disabled. A side benefit of doing that is that your application will also be more accessible to search engines, which rely primarily on the text portions of your pages.

Beyond that, you can adhere to the WAI-ARIA specification for the World Wide Web Consortium (W3C), which makes rich Internet applications even more accessible to the disabled. As figure 3-12 shows, Visual Studio 2015 provides IntelliSense features that support these recommendations. Here, the first example shows how IntelliSense lists the WAI-ARIA values for the role attribute that tells a user what role an HTML element plays on the form. The second example shows how IntelliSense lists the ARIA attributes for an HTML element.

Because this is a book on ASP.NET, not accessibility, these features aren't shown in the applications for this book. For most professional web applications, though, you should provide a high level of accessibility. To help you learn more about accessibility, this figure lists three sources of information.

IntelliSense with a list of WAI-ARIA values for the role attribute

IntelliSense with a list of ARIA attributes for an HTML element

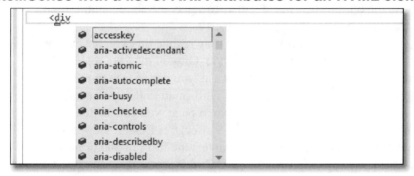

Types of disabilities

- Visual
- Hearing
- Motor
- Cognitive

Information sources

- The WebAIM website provides a good starting point for learning about accessibility at http://www.webaim.org.
- The World Wide Web Consortium (W3C) provides a full set of accessibility guidelines at http://www.w3.org/TR/WCAG.
- W3C also provides a specification called WAI-ARIA (Web Accessibility Initiative—Accessible Rich Internet Applications) that shows how to make rich Internet applications more accessible to the disabled at http://www.w3.org/TR/wai-aria.

Description

- *Accessibility* refers to the qualities that make a web application accessible to users, especially disabled users.
- The IntelliSense for Visual Studio 2015 supports the WAI-ARIA attributes for accessibility.

Figure 3-12   How Visual Studio provides for the WAI-ARIA accessibility standards

How to create and edit an external style sheet

Figure 3-13 starts by showing how to create an external style sheet that is added to the project folder. Then, if you haven't already done so, you can add a link element to the head section of the HTML that points to the external style sheet. To do that, you can use one of the techniques in figure 3-7 or just enter the link element into the aspx source code.

To enter and edit rule sets in the external style sheet, you first open it in the Editor window. Then, you can go to work. As you work, IntelliSense will help you by listing properties, values, and snippets. In this figure, for example, IntelliSense shows the options that make it easy to select the solid value for the second parameter in the rule for the border property.

As you enter the selector for a rule set, you may realize that you haven't set up the id or class attribute that you need for a style. Or, you may not remember the id or class attribute that you used. In either case, you can switch to the aspx code for the form and add the attribute or get the information that you need.

To see the changes that your CSS has made to a page, you can switch to Design view for the page or pages that your CSS affects. If Design view doesn't clearly show the changes that you made, you can test the form in one or more browsers. That's the sure way to know how your CSS is working.

As you work with styles, you may want to add comments or you may want to comment out one or more rule sets or rules. To do that, you can use the techniques in this figure. This makes working with comments much easier, and the keystrokes work the same with HTML code.

Visual Studio also provides *hierarchical indentation* if you code relational selectors, like parent, child, and sibling selectors. If, for example, you provide a rule set for nav elements followed by a rule set for ul elements that are children of nav elements, the second rule set will be indented to show this hierarchical structure. For the applications in this book, though, relational selectors aren't needed so you won't see this indentation.

An external style sheet in Visual Studio

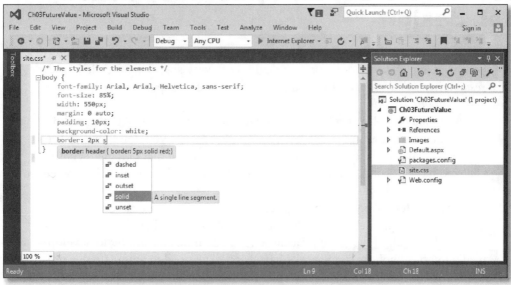

How to create an external style sheet

- Right-click on the project in the Solution Explorer. Then, choose the Add→Style Sheet command, type the name for the new style sheet, and click OK.

How to enter and edit the styles for an external style sheet

- Open the style sheet in the Editor, and enter the styles into the style sheet.
- If necessary, modify the aspx code so it provides the ids and class names that you need for the selectors in the style sheet.
- After you enter a rule set or a series of rule sets, switch to Design view to see whether the styles are working the way you want them to. Or, test the form in a browser.

How to comment out and uncomment one or more rules

- Press Ctrl+K, Ctrl+C to comment out selected rules, or Ctrl+K , Ctrl+U to uncomment them. Or, click the Comment or Uncomment button in the Text Editor toolbar.

Description

- As you enter CSS code, Visual Studio provides IntelliSense and snippets, including support for CSS3 and vendor-specific properties (like -moz- and -webkit- properties).
- By default, if you use relational selectors like parent, child, and sibling selectors, Visual Studio displays the rule sets with *hierarchical indentation*.

Figure 3-13   How to create and edit an external style sheet

How to use Bootstrap for responsive web design

As phones and tablets become more popular, it's important to make sure your web applications look good on devices of every size. This is called *responsive web design*, and web applications that use responsive design are called *mobile friendly*.

An application that uses responsive web design doesn't just look good on phones and tablets, it's easier to use too. That's because you don't have to scroll and resize on a small screen. In fact, this is so important that Google recently changed its search algorithm to make applications that are mobile friendly return higher in search results.

One way to make your web applications responsive is to use CSS3 *media queries*. Media queries let you adjust the layout of a page based on conditions, such as the width of the screen. Because it can be time consuming to develop media queries, though, frameworks have been developed to automate this process.

A *framework* contains general code for common situations and can be customized to meet the needs of individual projects. One popular framework for responsive web design is *Bootstrap*, originally developed by Twitter. Bootstrap uses CSS and JavaScript to make a web page automatically adjust for different screen sizes. In the following topics, you'll learn how to use Bootstrap with your ASP.NET web applications.

The responsive user interface of the Future Value application

Figure 3-14 shows a version of the Future Value application that uses Bootstrap to make it responsive. Here, the first screen corresponds to the width of a desktop browser. As you can see, the page has a large banner section and a border, and the labels, controls, and validation messages are laid out side by side just like they were in the non-responsive version of this application shown in figure 3-1.

The second screen corresponds to the width of a tablet browser. In this screen, the page still has a large banner and a border, but the labels, controls, and validation messages are stacked on top of each other. This narrows the page to match the narrowed screen, and makes it so you don't need to scroll from side to side to see the whole page. The controls also span the width of the screen to make them easier to use on touch screens.

The third screen corresponds to the width of a smart phone browser. In this screen, the border is gone and the banner and its contents have adjusted their positions to accommodate the narrower screen. The labels, controls, and validation messages are still stacked, and they still span the screen so they're easy to use on touch screens. But they've also narrowed to fit in the screen.

The important thing to note is that these changes take place automatically when you narrow or widen the browser window or you display the page on a phone, tablet, or desktop. All you have to do is add Bootstrap to your application and then use the classes it provides.

The responsive Future Value application at different screen widths

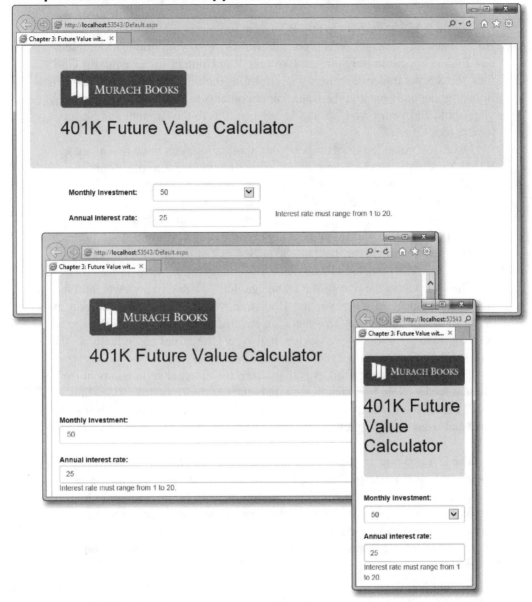

Description

- A web application should adapt to every screen size. This is called *responsive web design*.

- You can use Bootstrap to implement a responsive web design with ASP.NET. Bootstrap uses CSS and JavaScript to adjust the layout of a web page.

Note

- The Web Forms template that you learned about in chapter 2 uses Bootstrap, and it is a good source of sample code. You'll get a chance to review this code in exercise 3-3.

Figure 3-14   The responsive user interface of the Future Value application

How to add Bootstrap to your web application

Figure 3-15 shows how to add Bootstrap to your application using the NuGet Package Manager. When you add Bootstrap to your application, three new folders appear in the Solution Explorer. The Content folder contains CSS files, the Scripts folder contains JavaScript files including the jQuery library that Bootstrap depends on, and the fonts folder contains font files. For consistency, you should add your own CSS and JavaScript files to the Content and Scripts folders too.

Once you've added Bootstrap to your application, you need to add some HTML tags to the head element of any page that you want to use Bootstrap. Usually, that will be every page in your application.

The first tag you need to add is a *meta* tag. A meta tag provides information about your web application to browsers, but these tags aren't displayed to the user. Common meta tags contain keywords and descriptions, the author of the document, or the date the page was last modified. For Bootstrap, you need to add a meta tag whose name attribute is set to "viewport".

The *viewport* is the part of the web page that's visible to a viewer, and its size varies by device. When you use Bootstrap, you should set the viewport meta tag as shown in this figure. This meta tag ensures that the width of the page will correspond to the width of the device. It also sets the initial zoom factor so the browser doesn't scale the page on smaller devices.

The next two tags are link tags that attach the external style sheets in the Content folder. Note here that the tag that attaches the Bootstrap style sheet is coded before the tag that attaches the user style sheet. That way, the user style sheet can override the styles in the Bootstrap style sheet, and it can add new styles.

The last two tags are script tags that attach the JavaScript files for the jQuery library and for Bootstrap. The script tag uses an src attribute to indicate the source, or location, of the JavaScript file. In this case, the files are both located in the Scripts folder. Like the link tags, the script tags must be coded in the correct sequence. Specifically, the script tag for the jQuery library must be coded before the script tag for the Bootstrap file. That's because Bootstrap depends on the jQuery library.

If you look in the Content and Scripts folders, you'll see that they contain many more files than those that are attached in this figure. That's because the download contains files for different situations. For example, both the CSS and JavaScript files come in a minified version and a regular version. You can tell the difference between these versions by their extensions. In most cases, you'll use the minified files as shown in this figure. If you want to examine or debug the code that Bootstrap provides, though, you can use the regular files.

Once you've added these tags to a web form, Visual Studio provides IntelliSense support for the various CSS classes that Bootstrap uses. You'll learn about many of these classes next.

The NuGet Package Manager page

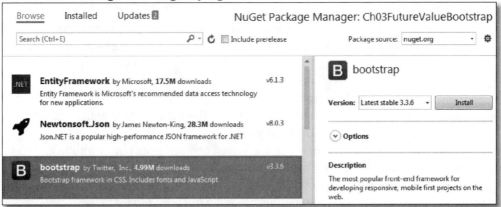

How to add the Bootstrap NuGet package to your web application

1. Right-click on the project in the Solution Explorer and select Manage NuGet Packages.

2. In the page that appears, click "Browse" and make sure that nuget.org is selected in the Package Source drop-down list.

3. Select Bootstrap from the packages that appear in the left pane. (If you don't see this package, type "Bootstrap" in the search box.) Click on the Install button to add both Bootstrap and the jQuery files that Bootstrap needs.

How to add Bootstrap to a web form

```
<head runat="server">
    <title>Chapter 3: Future Value with Bootstrap</title>
    <meta name="viewport" content="width=device-width, initial-scale=1" />
    <link href="Content/bootstrap.min.css" rel="stylesheet" />
    <link href="Content/site.css" rel="stylesheet" />
    <script src="Scripts/jquery-1.9.1.min.js"></script>
    <script src="Scripts/bootstrap.min.js"></script>
</head>
```

Description

- You can use the NuGet Package Manager to add Bootstrap to a web application. Then, you add Bootstrap to a web form by adding the link and script tags shown above to the head element.

- The link tag for the Bootstrap CSS file should be coded before the link tag for your own CSS files. That way, your CSS files can override the Bootstrap styles.

- The script tag for the jQuery JavaScript file should come before the script tag for the Bootstrap JavaScript file, since the Bootstrap file depends on the jQuery file.

- After you've added these tags to your web form, Visual Studio provides IntelliSense for the Bootstrap CSS classes.

- The *viewport* is the part of the page that is visible to viewers. The *viewport meta tag* controls the width of the viewport and the page's initial zoom when it first loads.

Figure 3-15   How to add Bootstrap to your web application

The classes of the Bootstrap grid system

To create responsive web applications, Bootstrap uses a *grid system* that's based on containers, rows, and columns. A container contains one or more rows, and a row can contain up to 12 columns. Bootstrap provides predefined CSS classes to work with its grid system. The most important of these classes are presented in the first table in figure 3-16.

To start, you use the container and container-fluid classes to identify the main content of the page. The difference between them is that an element that uses the container class is centered in the screen and has a specific width in pixels based on the viewport's width. This is sometimes called a *boxed layout*. An element that uses the container-fluid class, by contrast, is always the same width as the viewport. This is sometimes called a *full width layout*.

The main content of a page should be divided into rows using the row class. Then, within each row, you can code elements with one or more of the column classes that control how the content in the row is displayed. Each class specifies one of the screen sizes listed in the second table in this figure, along with the number of columns that the element should span.

To understand how this works, the first example in this figure shows a div element that uses the col-md-4 class. This means that when the element is displayed on a desktop whose width is less than 1200 pixels, it will occupy four of the twelve possible columns. Note that if the element is displayed on a desktop whose width is greater than or equal to 1200 pixels, it will also occupy four columns. That's because if a class isn't specified for a screen size, the column count of the next smallest screen size that is specified will be used.

The second example is similar, except that it specifies a second class for a desktop whose width is greater than or equal to 1200 pixels. In this case, the element will occupy only three columns at that width but four columns at the narrower width.

Notice that neither of these examples includes classes for smaller devices like tablets and phones. Because of that, the element will occupy all twelve columns in these devices, since that's the default.

You can also use CSS classes to move an element to the right a specified number of columns. To do that, you use a class that indicates the screen size and the number of columns that the element should be offset. This is illustrated in the third example in this figure. Here, the element will occupy four columns on a large screen just as in the first two examples. However, the column will be offset one column to the right.

If you've found this hard to visualize, don't worry. The next figure will present an example that demonstrates how the grid system works.

Some of the CSS classes of the Bootstrap grid system

Class	Description
`container`	Contains rows or other content. Centered in the body element, with a specific width based on the viewport size.
`container-fluid`	Contains rows or other content. Set to 100% of the width of the viewport.
`row`	Contains columns inside a container.
`col-`*size*`-`*count*	The number of columns an element should span on the specified screen size. The number of columns in a row should not exceed 12.
`col-`*size*`-offset-`*count*	The number of columns an element should be moved to the right on the specified screen size.

Valid size values

Size	Description
`lg`	A screen with a width greater than or equal to 1200 pixels (e.g. large desktops).
`md`	A screen with a width greater than or equal to 992 pixels (e.g. desktops).
`sm`	A screen with a width greater than or equal to 768 pixels (e.g. tablets).
`xs`	A screen with a width less than 768 pixels (e.g. phones).

An element that spans four columns on medium and large screens

```
<div class="col-md-4">This element spans four columns</div>
```

An element that spans a different number of columns on medium and large screens

```
<div class="col-md-4 col-lg-3">This element spans three or four columns</div>
```

An element that is moved one column to the right on large screens

```
<div class="col-md-4 col-lg-offset-1">This element spans four columns</div>
```

Description

- Bootstrap uses a grid system based on containers, rows, and columns. All rows should be inside a container, and each row must contain no more than 12 columns.

- The default behavior of an element in a row is to span all 12 columns. Because of that, the elements in a row will stack vertically in all screen sizes if you don't assign a column CSS class.

- You can assign a different column class to an element for each screen size to specify the number of columns the element should span at those sizes.

- If you don't assign a column class for a screen size, the class for the next smallest screen size will be used.

Figure 3-16   The classes of the Bootstrap grid system

How the Bootstrap grid system works

To help you understand how the Bootstrap grid system works, figure 3-17 shows an example of a simple grid that contains three rows. Here, the grid is shown as it would appear on a desktop, a tablet, and a phone. As you can see in the HTML that follows the screens, each row is defined by a div element that's assigned the class named "row". In addition, the div elements that define the rows are coded within a main element that's assigned the class named "container".

Each row in the grid contains two div elements that are used to define the columns. Because none of the column classes are assigned to the div elements in the first row, each element spans all twelve columns of the row, or the entire width of the viewport, regardless of the screen size. That causes the columns to be stacked vertically as shown here.

The div elements in the second row are assigned classes for the desktop viewport (md). Here, the first div element specifies a width of four columns and the second element specifies a width of eight columns. As you can see in the first screen, this causes the divs to be displayed side by side at the desktop width. They will also be displayed side by side at the large desktop width, since no classes are specified for that width (lg). In that case, the width of the next smallest screen size (md) will be used.

In contrast, the divs will be stacked at the tablet (sm) and phone (xs) sizes as shown here. That's because no column classes are included for these viewport sizes. In that case, each div element will span all twelve columns.

The div elements in the third row are assigned the same column classes for the desktop viewport as the divs in the second row. In addition, they're assigned column classes for the tablet (sm) viewport. These classes specify a width of six columns for each div element.

That means that on desktop and large desktop devices, these divs will display side by side at the same widths as the divs in the second row. These divs will display side by side on tablet devices as well, but this time at equal widths. If you compare the last row in the first two screens in this figure, you should see how they differ.

Note that, just as in the second row, no classes are assigned to the div elements for the phone size (xs). Because of that, the div elements span all twelve columns and are stacked vertically.

This figure also presents the CSS that augments the Bootstrap CSS classes. This CSS was used to make it easy for you to see the rows and columns in the grid.

A Bootstrap grid on medium, small, and extra small screens

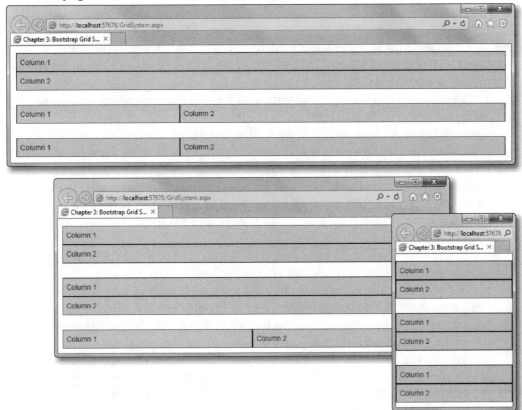

The HTML for the grid example

```
<main class="container">
    <div class="row">
        <div>Column 1</div>
        <div>Column 2</div>
    </div>
    <div class="row">
        <div class="col-md-4">Column 1</div>
        <div class="col-md-8">Column 2</div>
    </div>
    <div class="row">
        <div class="col-md-4 col-sm-6">Column 1</div>
        <div class="col-md-8 col-sm-6">Column 2</div>
    </div>
</main>
```

The CSS that augments the Bootstrap CSS classes

```
.container { padding-top: 1em; }
.row { margin-bottom: 2em; }
.row div {
    border: 1px solid black;
    padding: 0.5em;
    background-color: lightgrey; }
```

Figure 3-17   How the Bootstrap grid system works

How to work with the Bootstrap CSS classes for forms

Bootstrap also provides some predefined CSS classes for working with the labels and controls of a form. The table in figure 3-18 presents some of the most important of these classes.

To start, you can use the form-vertical or form-horizontal class to determine the layout of the labels and controls on the form. With a vertical layout, the labels and controls stack on top of each other and the controls span the width of the viewport, as shown in the first example in this figure. With a horizontal layout, you use the grid system that you learned about in the last topic to align labels and controls horizontally, as shown in the second example in this figure. Notice in the HTML for the form with the vertical layout that the form element doesn't use the form-vertical class. That's because this is the default layout for form elements.

You use the form-group class with both vertical and horizontal layouts. This class groups labels and controls that go together, and it determines the spacing for those controls. You can see how this class is used in both of the examples in this figure. Note that this class is assigned to a div element that contains the label and control that go together. Also note that when you use this class, it defines a row in the grid. Because of that, you don't have to use the row class.

You use the form-control class to apply styling to input, textarea, and select HTML elements. The styling this class applies not only makes these elements more attractive, but more useful on mobile devices. For example, it makes them taller than unstyled HTML elements. It also makes them span the width of the viewport in a vertical layout or the width of the column span in a horizontal layout. This makes the controls easier to use on touch screens.

As I mentioned, you use the grid system to align the controls in a horizontal layout. In the HTML for the horizontal layout shown in this figure, for example, you can see that the label elements use the col-sm-2 class. In addition, the input elements that define the text boxes are coded within div elements that use the col-sm-10 class. That way, the labels will each span two columns on tablets, desktops, and large desktops, and the controls will each span ten columns. Because a column class isn't assigned for phones, however, the labels and controls will be stacked when displayed on a phone. In other words, since the layout uses the grid system, it is responsive.

You use the last class, control-label, to apply styling to a label that's grouped with a control. In most cases, you'll only use this class with the horizontal layout.

Some of the Bootstrap CSS classes for working with forms

Class	Description
form-vertical	The form labels and controls stack vertically. This is the default for forms.
form-horizontal	Used with the grid system to align labels and controls in a horizontal layout.
form-group	Applies spacing to labels and controls that go together. Behaves as a grid row, so you don't need to use the row class.
form-control	Applies styling to input, textarea, or select controls in a form.
control-label	Applies styling to a control's label. Used with the form-horizontal class.

A form with two text boxes in vertical layout

Email:

Password:

The HTML for the form

```
<form id="form1" runat="server">
    <div class="form-group">
        <label for="email">Email:</label>
        <input type="email" class="form-control" id="email" />
    </div>
    <div class="form-group">
        <label for="pwd">Password:</label>
        <input type="password" class="form-control" id="pwd" />
    </div>
</form>
```

A form with two text boxes in horizontal layout

Email:

Password:

The HTML for the form

```
<form id="form1" runat="server" class="form-horizontal">
    <div class="form-group">
        <label class="control-label col-sm-2" for="email">Email:</label>
        <div class="col-sm-10">
            <input type="email" class="form-control" id="email" />
        </div>
    </div>
    <div class="form-group">
        <label class="control-label col-sm-2" for="pwd">Password:</label>
        <div class="col-sm-10">
            <input type="password" class="form-control" id="pwd" />
        </div>
    </div>
</form>
```

Figure 3-18   How to work with the Bootstrap CSS classes for forms

How to work with the Bootstrap CSS classes for other HTML elements

The grid and form classes that you learned about in the last two topics allow you to set the basic structure of a web page and control the layout for different viewport sizes. Bootstrap also provides many CSS classes for styling individual elements and components. You'll learn more about these classes in chapter 10. For now, figure 3-19 presents some of the most common classes, like those for styling buttons and images.

The example in this figure shows how some of these classes work. Here, the HTML starts with a div element that uses the container class. This centers the page and adjusts its size based on the size of the viewport. Then, the header element uses the jumbotron class, which makes the header appear as a large grey box with rounded corners. It also gives the text in the h1 element within the header element a larger font.

Two additional classes are used to style the image within the header. First, the img-rounded class causes the image to be displayed with rounded corners, even though the original image doesn't have rounded corners. Note that this won't work in older versions of Internet Explorer. Second, the img-responsive class causes the size of the image to be adjusted as the size of the viewport changes. That way, the entire image is always visible in the viewport.

Next, this example uses the form-vertical class by default, which, along with the form-group class, provides appropriate spacing and styling for the elements in the form. Note that the elements in the form aren't full screen and vertically stacked like they were in the vertical form example of the last figure. That's because the form elements in this example don't use the form-control class. This shows that, even though the form CSS classes are designed to go together, sometimes you might not use all of them to get the look you want.

Within the form group, the example in the figure uses the text-info class to make the text in the span element blue. Then, it uses some of the button classes to style the Yes and No buttons. The btn class provides the basic size and rounded corners. The btn-default class makes the No button white with a border. And the btn-primary class adds emphasis to the Yes button by making it blue with white text.

Some of the Bootstrap CSS classes for working with buttons

Class	Description
btn	Produces a simple grey button with dark text and rounded corners.
btn-default	Changes the background color to white and adds a border.
btn-primary	Adds emphasis by changing the background color to blue and the text to white.

Some of the Bootstrap CSS classes for working with images

Class	Description
img-rounded	Adds rounded corners to an image. Doesn't work in older versions of IE.
img-responsive	Makes the image automatically adjust to fit the size of the viewport.

Some other common Bootstrap CSS classes

Class	Description
jumbotron	A large grey box with rounded corners and large font.
text-*context*	Classes that use color for emphasis. Includes text-danger (red), text-warning (yellow), and text-info (blue).

A form with a jumbotron, an image, and two buttons

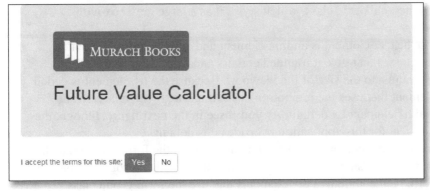

The HTML for the form

```
<div class="container">
    <header class="jumbotron">
        <img id="logo" alt="Murach logo" src="Images/MurachLogo.jpg"
             class="img-rounded img-responsive"/>
        <h1>Future Value Calculator</h1>
    </header>
    <main><form id="form1" runat="server">
        <div class="form-group">
            <span class="text-info">I accept the terms for this site:</span>
            <button id="btnYes" runat="server"
                class="btn btn-primary">Yes</button>
            <button id="btnNo" runat="server"
                class="btn btn-default">No</button>
        </div>
    </form></main>
</div>
```

Figure 3-19   How to work with the Bootstrap CSS classes for other HTML elements

The Bootstrap version of the Future Value application

Now that you understand how the basic Bootstrap classes work, you're ready to see the aspx code and the custom CSS for the responsive version of the Future Value application that you saw in figure 3-14.

The aspx code for the application

Figure 3-20 shows the aspx code for the Bootstrap version of the Future Value application. The head element of the page starts with a viewport meta tag, which is followed by link tags for the Bootstrap style sheet and the custom style sheet (site.css). Because the link tag for the custom style sheet is coded after the link tag for the Bootstrap style sheet, its styles can override or augment the styles in the Bootstrap style sheet.

Next, the two script tags include the JavaScript files for the jQuery library and for Bootstrap. Because Bootstrap uses the jQuery library, its script tag is coded after the script tag for the jQuery library.

The body element of the page contains a div element that uses the container class so the page is centered and its width adjusts to the width of the viewport. This div element contains a header element and a main element. The header element uses the jumbotron class, which styles it as a large grey box with rounded corners.

Inside the header element is an img element and an h1 element. The img element uses classes that give it rounded corners and cause its size to automatically adjust to the size of the viewport. Because the h1 element is coded within an element that uses the jumbotron class, it has text with a larger font than a normal h1 element by default. As you'll see in the next figure, though, the custom style sheet for this application overrides this default.

The main element contains a form element that uses the form-horizontal class. That's what makes the side-by-side layout of the labels and controls possible. Inside the form element are five div elements that use the form-group class.

The first form group contains the monthly investment label and drop-down list. Since this is a horizontal layout, the label uses the control-label class for styling. The label also uses the col-md-3 class so it spans three columns on desktop and large desktop devices. The drop-down list, which uses the form-control class, is coded within a div element that also uses the col-md-3 class. Notice that in this case, only six of the available twelve columns are used. This shows that you don't have to use all twelve columns.

The second and third form groups are for the interest rate and number of years. Since the code for these two groups is almost identical, only the interest rate group is shown here. It starts with a label and a div element that contains a text box, each of which span three columns. Then, the div element with the text box is followed by another div element that contains a required field validator and a range validator. This div element spans six columns. Note that the text boxes use the form-control class, and the validators use the text-danger class so the messages are red.

The aspx code for the head and body of the Future Value application

```
<head runat="server">
    <title>Chapter 3: Future Value with Bootstrap</title>
    <meta name="viewport" content="width=device-width, initial-scale=1" />
    <link href="Content/bootstrap.min.css" rel="stylesheet" />
    <link href="Content/site.css" rel="stylesheet" />
    <script src="Scripts/jquery-1.9.1.min.js"></script>
    <script src="Scripts/bootstrap.min.js"></script>
</head>
<body>
<div class="container">
    <header class="jumbotron">
        <img id="logo" alt="Murach logo" src="Images/MurachLogo.jpg"
            class="img-rounded img-responsive"/>
        <h1>401K Future Value Calculator</h1>
    </header>
    <main><form id="form1" runat="server" class="form-horizontal">
        <div class="form-group">
            <label for="ddlMonthlyInvestment" class="control-label col-md-3">
                Monthly Investment:</label>
            <div class="col-md-3">
                <asp:DropDownList ID="ddlMonthlyInvestment" runat="server"
                    CssClass="form-control"></asp:DropDownList ></div>
        </div>
        <div class="form-group">
            <label for="txtInterestRate" class="control-label col-md-3">
                Annual interest rate:</label>
            <div class="col-md-3">
                <asp:TextBox ID="txtInterestRate" runat="server"
                    CssClass="form-control">3.0</asp:TextBox></div>
            <div class="col-md-6">
                <asp:RequiredFieldValidator CssClass="text-danger"
                    <!-- rest of validator --> ><asp:RequiredFieldValidator>
                <asp:RangeValidator CssClass="text-danger"
                    <!-- rest of validator --> ></asp:RangeValidator></div>
        </div>
        <div class="form-group">
            <!-- Number of years label, textbox, and validators -->
        </div>
        <div class="form-group">
            <label for="lblfutureValue" class="control-label col-md-3">
                Future Value:</label>
            <div class="col-md-9">
                <asp:Label ID="lblFutureValue" runat="server"
                    CssClass="text-info"></asp:Label></div>
        </div>
        <div class="form-group">
            <div class="col-md-offset-3 col-md-9">
                <asp:Button ID="btnCalculate" runat="server"
                    Text="Calculate" OnClick="btnCalculate_Click"
                    CssClass="btn btn-primary" />
                <asp:Button ID="btnClear" runat="server" Text="Clear"
                    OnClick="btnClear_Click" CssClass="btn btn-primary"
                    CausesValidation="False" /></div>
        </div>
    </form></main>
</div>
</body>
```

Figure 3-20   The aspx code for the Bootstrap version of the Future Value application

The fourth form group contains labels that show the future value calculation. The label element uses the control-label class for styling and spans three columns, while the label server control spans nine columns and uses the text-info class.

The fifth form group contains the Calculate and Clear buttons. Notice that the div element that contains these buttons uses the col-md-offset-3 class as well as the col-md-9 class. The offset class moves the buttons three columns to the right, which lines them up with the controls in the previous rows. Then, the buttons use the btn and btn-primary classes for styling.

Note that no column classes are included for small and extra small devices. This means that on those devices, the form elements will be full screen and stacked vertically as shown in figure 3-14.

The custom CSS for the application

Because the Bootstrap CSS classes are numerous and flexible, they provide most of the styles you need for your web applications. That's why the custom style sheet for this application includes just three rule sets, each with a single rule. The rest of the styling is done by Bootstrap.

The first rule set in this style sheet selects the h1 element within the element that's assigned to the jumbotron class. The one rule within this rule set sets the font size for the h1 element to 250% of the base font size. This overrides the default font size defined by the Bootstrap style sheet and makes it smaller.

The second rule set augments the Bootstrap container class by adding a border to it. In contrast, the third rule set doesn't override or augment a Bootstrap class. Rather, this rule set causes the label element with the id equal to "lblFutureValue" to display with bold text.

The preferred way to customize Bootstrap is to use a separate style sheet like the one shown here. That way, if you later replace the Bootstrap style sheet in order to change the Bootstrap theme, you won't lose your customizations like you would if you applied the changes directly to the Bootstrap style sheet. You'll learn more about Bootstrap themes in chapter 10.

The custom style sheet for the Future Value application

```
.jumbotron h1 {
    font-size: 250%;
}

.container {
    border: 1px solid #cecece;
}

#lblFutureValue {
    font-weight: bold;
}
```

Description

- You can add your own CSS style sheet to override the default Bootstrap styles or add new styles.

- Creating a separate style sheet is the preferred way of making changes to Bootstrap. If you change the Bootstrap style sheet instead, you will lose your changes if you replace the Bootstrap style sheet to change the theme. You'll learn more about Bootstrap themes in chapter 10.

- In the custom style sheet above, the default font size for the h1 element in the jumbotron is overridden, and a border is added to the Bootstrap container class. In addition, the font weight for the label that displays the future value is changed to bold.

Figure 3-21   The custom CSS for the Bootstrap version of the Future Value application

Perspective

Now that you've completed this chapter, you know the right way to use HTML, CSS, and Bootstrap in a Web Forms application. That means using HTML for the content and structure of a page, using CSS in an external style sheet for all of the formatting, and using Bootstrap for responsive web design. That separates the content and structure of each page from its formatting. And that makes it easier to create and maintain a mobile friendly web page.

Because this book is about ASP.NET programming, not HTML and CSS, this chapter has presented only what you need to know about HTML and CSS for this book. As you will see, all of the applications in this book use simple HTML and CSS, and the programming is the same whether the formatting is simple or complex.

Of course, there's a lot more to HTML and CSS than what's presented in this chapter. So if you want to learn more, we recommend *Murach's HTML5 and CSS3*. Its first eight chapters are a crash course in the HTML5 and CSS3 skills that every web developer should have. Then, after you read those chapters, our HTML5 and CSS3 book becomes your best on-the-job reference.

There's also a lot more to Bootstrap than what's presented in this chapter. Because of that, chapter 10 will teach you more about how to work with Bootstrap in ASP.NET.

Terms

CSS (Cascading Style Sheets)	element (or type) selector
HTML document	class selector
HTML element	id selector
tag	rule set
opening tag	rule
attribute	property
content (HTML)	em
closing tag	cross-browser compatibility
self-closing tag	JavaScript shiv
comment	snippet
comment out	accessibility
character entity	hierarchical indentation
block element	responsive web design
inline element	mobile friendly
HTML5 semantic elements	media query
HTML5 semantics	framework
SEO (search engine optimization)	Bootstrap
style sheet	viewport
external style sheet	viewport meta tag
attach a style sheet	grid system
embedded styles	boxed layout
inline style	full width layout
CSS selector	

Summary

- A best practice is to use HTML for the content and structure of a web page and CSS for formatting. To do that, you use *external style sheets* to provide the CSS.

- To *attach* an external style sheet to a web page, you code a link element in the head section of the *HTML document* for the page. That element points to the location of the style sheet.

- By default, *block elements* in HTML are displayed on their own lines in browsers. In contrast, *inline elements* don't start new lines.

- The *HTML5 semantic elements* include the header, main, section, nav, aside, and footer elements. Using them makes it easier to apply CSS and also improves *SEO* (*search engine optimization*) in some search engines.

- ASP.NET generates span elements for validators as well as label controls. These are inline elements that usually flow to the right of preceding inline elements.

- *Embedded styles* are coded in a style element in the head section of an HTML document, which provides some separation between HTML elements and their styles. But *inline styles* are coded as attributes in the HTML elements themselves.

- The basic *CSS selectors* are *type* (or *element*) *selectors*, *class selectors*, and *id selectors*. Those are the ones that are used in the applications for this book.

- When you use CSS, you need to understand the order in which styles override other styles. For instance, more specific styles override less specific styles, and the last style that's applied overrides previous styles.

- A CSS *rule set* consists of one or more *rules*, and each rule consists of a *property* name and values.

- To assure *cross-browser compatibility*, you need to test your web applications in all of the browsers that are likely to access your application. You can also use a *JavaScript shiv* to make your HTML5 work with older browsers.

- Visual Studio provides features for working with HTML and CSS that include IntelliSense and *snippets*. Additionally, it provides HTML support for the WAI-ARIA *accessibility* specification.

- *Responsive web design* helps you create *mobile friendly* web applications that look good and are easy to use on all screen sizes.

- One way to create a responsive web design is to use *media queries*, which let you adjust the layout of a web page based on conditions such as the width of the screen. Another way is to use a framework like *Bootstrap*, which uses CSS and JavaScript to make your web pages automatically adjust to different screen sizes.

- Bootstrap uses a *grid system* based on containers, rows, and columns, and predefined CSS classes for forms, elements, and other components to create responsive web applications.

Exercise 3-1   Work with external style sheets in the Future Value application

In this exercise, you'll develop the Future Value application with an external style sheet used for all formatting. This will make you work with HTML and CSS.

Open the Future Value application and review its external style sheet

1. Open the Ex03FutureValue web application in the C:\aspnet46_cs folder. It already contains a web form named Default.aspx, a code-behind file for the form that's just like the one in chapter 2, a folder named Images that contains an image file named MurachLogo.jpg, and a starting style sheet named site.css.

2. Open the Default.aspx file in Source view and note that the form already contains the labels, controls, and validation controls needed by the Future Value application, but it doesn't contain an HTML table for layout. However, a br element has been added after the drop-down list, each text box, and the label server control so the next element starts on a new line.

3. Now, review the head element to see that it doesn't contain any styling information. Then, view the form in Design view to see how it looks, and notice that the labels and controls are bunched together.

4. Run the application and click on the buttons to see that the application works, even though the formatting needs work.

Attach the existing style sheet and add the required styles

5. Open the site.css file, and notice that it contains styles for the body and h1 elements. Then, using figure 3-7 as a guide, drag the style sheet from the Solution Explorer and drop it into the head section of the HTML for the form. That should generate a link element that attaches the style sheet to the form.

6. Run the form to make sure that the style sheet has been attached properly. If it is, the form should be centered in the browser and have a black border around it, and the h1 element should be smaller and have less space below it.

7. Add another rule set to the site.css file for the label elements. Then, add the two styles shown in figure 3-3 to this rule set.

8. Set the CssClass properties for the drop-down list and the text boxes to "entry". Then, add the rule set for this class shown in figure 3-3. Note the changes in Design view as the formatting starts to take shape.

9. Add the rule set for the button class. Then, use the Designer to set the CssClass properties for the buttons and note that "button" is available from the drop-down list because this class is already in the style sheet. Now, check these changes in Design view.

10. Use the same procedure to create the rule set for the validator class and assign that class to the validators.

11. Test the form in one or more browsers. It should look the way it does in figure 3-1. If it doesn't, fix the problems. Then, close the application.

Exercise 3-2   Work with the Bootstrap classes in the Future Value application

In this exercise, you'll review the Bootstrap files and classes that are used by the responsive version of the Future Value application. Then, you'll modify some of the classes to see how those changes affect the application.

Open the Future Value application and review the Bootstrap files

1. Open the Ex03FutureValueBootstrap web application in the C:\aspnet46_cs folder.

2. Open the Content, fonts, and Scripts folders to see the files that were added by Bootstrap.

3. Use the procedure in figure 3-15 to display the Nuget Package Manager page for Bootstrap. When you're done reviewing this page, close it.

Review and modify the Bootstrap classes

4. Display the Default.aspx file in Source view, and review the Bootstrap classes that are used by this page.

5. Run the application. Click on the Clear button to clear the drop-down list, text boxes, and label server control. Then, click the Calculate button so the validation messages are displayed.

6. Narrow and widen the browser window to see how the layout responds. Pay attention to when the labels and controls change from being displayed side-by-side to being stacked. When you're done, close the browser.

7. Locate the Bootstrap column classes, and change the size from md to sm. Then, repeat steps 5 and 6 to see what affect the changes you've made have on the page.

8. Repeat step 7, this time changing the size used by the column classes from sm to xs. Make the browser as narrow as you can, and see how the page lays out.

9. Repeat step 7, changing the column classes back to sm. When you're done, close the web application, or...

10. If you're feeling adventurous, experiment with adding column classes for the xs viewport. See if you can make it so the elements don't stack vertically but still look good at the narrowest viewport size. When you're done, close the web application.

Exercise 3-3   Review the files and code generated by the Web Forms template

In this exercise, you'll create an application using the Web Forms template. Then, you'll review some of the files and code that's generated by this template.

Create the application and review the folders and files

1. Start a web application named WebFormsTemplate and store it in the C:\aspnet46_cs directory. When the New ASP.NET Project dialog box is displayed, select the Web Forms template.

2. Once the project is created, take some time to review the "Your ASP.NET application" page that's displayed in the internal browser. When you're done, close this page. (If you want to open it again, right-click the Project_Readme.html file in the Solution Explorer, select Browse With→Internal Web Browser, and then click the Browse button.)

3. Click on the Default.aspx file in the Solution Explorer and then press F5 to display the page in the default browser. Use the navigation bar at the top of the page to navigate to the About and Contact pages and then to the Register page. When you're done, close the browser.

4. Use the Solution Explorer to review the other files and folders that were generated for the project.

Review the Bootstrap code for the application

5. Display the Default.aspx file in Source view, and notice that it uses Bootstrap classes. However, it doesn't include the Bootstrap meta, link, and script tags. That's because the Web Forms template uses a master page that includes these elements. You'll learn more about master pages in chapter 9.

6. Press F5 to run the application again. Then, make the browser window as narrow as possible, and watch how the page responds. Now, widen the browser, again watching how the page responds. When you're done, close the browser.

7. Find the Login.aspx file in the Account folder, display it in Source view, and review its Bootstrap code. Then, press F5 to display the page in the default browser, and narrow and widen the page to see what happens.

8. Continue experimenting with other pages of the application. When you're done, close the application.

4

How to develop a multi-page web application

In chapter 2, you learned how to develop a simple, one-page web application. Then, in chapter 3, you learned how to use HTML, CSS, and Bootstrap with any web application. Now, you'll learn how to develop a multi-page web application, which requires several new skills, including how to use session state and how to get the data for a web form from a database.

Introduction to the Shopping Cart application

In this chapter, you'll learn to build two pages of a Shopping Cart application. This application gets product data from a database, stores data in session state, and uses three business classes. So even though this application is simple, you're going to learn a lot about developing web applications with ASP.NET and C#.

The two pages of the Shopping Cart application

Figure 4-1 shows the two pages of the Shopping Cart application. The Order page, named Order.aspx, includes a drop-down list from which the user can select a product. The product names in this list are retrieved from a SQL Server database via a SQLDataSource control, or just data source. Then, since the AutoPostBack property of the drop-down list is set to True, the page is posted back to the server.

On the server, the code-behind file for the Order page gets the data for the selected product from the data source, which has retrieved the data for all of the products from the SQL Server database. Then, the data for the selected product is displayed in several labels, and the ImageUrl property of the Image control on the right of the page is set to the URL for the image.

Once a product is selected, the user can enter a quantity and click the Add to Cart button. However, validation controls make sure that the entry is an integer that ranges from 1 to 500. If the entry is valid, the code-behind file for the Order page updates a list that represents the user's shopping cart. Because this list must be updated each time a product is added to the cart, the list that represents the shopping cart is saved in a session state object so it is available throughout the user's session. Then, the code behind file passes control to the Cart page.

The code-behind file for the Cart page gets the list for the cart from the session state object and displays the page shown in this figure. Then, the user can click the Remove Item button to remove the selected item or the Empty Cart button to remove all of the items. In either case, the code-behind file for the Cart page updates the cart list for the session state object, makes the changes, and redisplays the page.

On the Cart page, the user can also click the Continue Shopping button to return to the Order page or the Check Out button to go to a page that gets the data for completing the purchase. In this case, though, the checkout page hasn't been implemented yet so a message to that effect is displayed when the user clicks the Check Out button.

The Order page

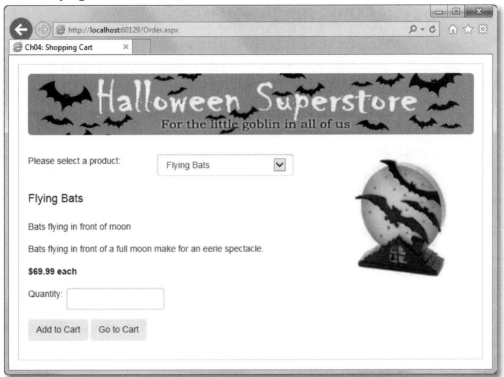

The Cart page

Figure 4-1   The two pages of the Shopping Cart application

The files and folders used by the Shopping Cart application

Figure 4-2 summarizes the files and folders used by the Shopping Cart application. This application was created using the Empty template with folders and core references for web forms. Then, the Bootstrap NuGet package was added.

By default, Visual Studio places new web form files and their code-behind files in the application's root folder. But it also has special folders for other files, some of which it creates for you when you select the core references or use NuGet packages. The first table in this figure lists the folders in the Shopping Cart application. Note that all but one of these folders were added by Visual Studio when the application was created or when the Bootstrap NuGet package was added.

As this table indicates, each of these folders are used for certain types of files. For instance, class files (other than the class files for web pages) are stored in the Models folder, and any database files used by the application are stored in the App_Data folder. Another common folder not shown here is the Bin folder, which is used to store compiled assemblies, such as *class libraries*. And, of course, you can create your own folders. For example, it's common to create an Images folder to store any image files used by the application.

The second table in this figure lists the files that make up the Shopping Cart application, and the folders that contain them. As you can see, the Models folder contains three class files named CartItem.cs, CartItemList.cs, and Product.cs. These files define the CartItem, CartItemList, and Product classes required by the application. And the App_Data folder contains a SQL Server database file named Halloween.mdf.

The Content, font, and Script folders contain the CSS, font, and JavaScript files required by the Bootstrap framework. In addition, the Content folder includes a style sheet named site.css. This CSS file contains custom styles that override or augment the Bootstrap styles or that provide for other custom formatting for the application.

The Images folder includes just one image file, banner.jpg, which provides the banner that's displayed at the top of each page. However, this folder also includes a subfolder named Products, which includes a separate image file for each product in the Products table of the database. Then, because the name of the image file for each product is retrieved from the SQL Server database, the application can display the correct image for each product.

The root folder for the application contains three files for each of the application's web pages: one for the page itself, one for the code-behind file, and one for the designer file. The root folder also contains configuration files that are added automatically when you create an application, as well as a Global.asax file that's added automatically when you select core references for web forms.

The Solution Explorer for the Shopping Cart application

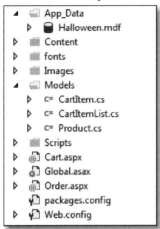

Folders in the Shopping Cart application

Folder	Contains	Added By
App_Data	Database files	Core references for web forms
Content	CSS files	Bootstrap NuGet package
fonts	Font files	Bootstrap NuGet package
Images	Image files	Developer
Models	C# class files	Core references for web forms
Scripts	JavaScript files	Bootstrap NuGet package

Files in the Shopping Cart application

Folder	File	Description
App_Data	Halloween.mdf	The Halloween database file.
Content	(multiple)	The CSS files used to style the web pages.
Images	banner.jpg	An image file that displays at the top of each page.
Images\Products	(multiple)	An image file for each product in the database.
Models	CartItem.cs	A class that represents an item in the shopping cart.
Models	CartItemList.cs	A class that represents the shopping cart.
Models	Product.cs	A class that represents a product.
(root)	Cart.aspx	The aspx file for the Cart page.
(root)	Cart.aspx.cs	The code-behind file for the Cart page.
(root)	Cart.aspx.designer.cs	The designer file for the Cart page.
(root)	Order.aspx	The aspx file for the Order page.
(root)	Order.aspx.cs	The code-behind file for the Order page.
(root)	Order.aspx.designer.cs	The designer file for the Order page.
(root)	Global.asax	A file for working with application objects.
(root)	*.config	The web and packages configuration files.

Figure 4-2   The files and folders used by the Shopping Cart application

How to work with multi-page web applications

To create a multi-page web application, you need to learn some new skills like how to change the starting page for a web application, how to transfer from one form to another, and how to add classes to your project.

How to change the starting page for a web application

If a web application consists of a single form, that form is displayed when you run the application. However, if a web application contains two or more forms, the current form (the one that's selected in the Solution Explorer) is displayed when you run the application. Or, if a form isn't selected, the form named Default.aspx is displayed.

But what if a form isn't selected and the web application doesn't contain a Default.aspx file? Then, the browser displays an error message when the application is run. To make sure that the correct page is displayed when you run an application, then, you should always set the starting page for a multi-page application. Figure 4-3 shows you how to do that.

How to rename or delete folders and files

Figure 4-3 also shows how to rename or delete the folders and files in a web application. Note, however, that when you use the Rename command for a web form, it renames the aspx, code-behind, and designer files for the form, but it doesn't change the class names used in these files. Although the page will still run, the different names can be confusing and lead to errors later on. Because of that, you'll usually want to change the name of the partial class in the code-behind file so it's the same as the new name of the web form. In addition, you'll want to change the class name in the Inherits attribute of the page directive in the aspx file. If you change the class name, be sure you change it in both places or the application won't run.

Most of the time, the Rename and Delete commands are all you'll need. However, if you think that you might need a file or web form later on, you can use the Exclude from Project command instead of the Delete command. That way, you don't actually delete the file, and you can restore it later by using the Include in Project command.

The menu for changing the starting page, renaming files, and deleting files

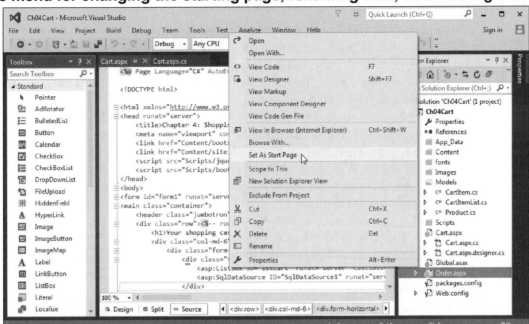

How to change the starting page for a web application

- Right-click on the aspx file and select Set As Start Page from the shortcut menu.

How to rename a single file

- Right-click on the file, select Rename from the shortcut menu, and change the name.

How to rename a web form

- Use the rename procedure described above. Then, open the code-behind file and change the name of the partial class to the new name of the form. Finally, open the aspx file and change the class name in the Inherits property of the page directive.

How to delete a file from the web application

- Right-click on the file and select Delete from the shortcut menu. If the file is an aspx file, that will delete the aspx file and its code-behind and designer files from the application.

- Another alternative is to select Exclude from Project from the shortcut menu for the file.

Description

- By default, ASP.NET will display the page named Default.aspx when you run a web application if the application contains a page with that name. If you want a different page to be displayed, you need to change the starting page.

- When you use the Rename command to rename a web form, the file names are changed, but the class name in the code-behind and designer files and page directive isn't. Although the web page will still run, the different names can be confusing.

Figure 4-3   How to change the starting page and rename or delete folders and files

How to add a class to a web application

If you select the Web Forms option when you create a web application from the Empty template as described in chapter 2, a Models folder is automatically added to the application. Then, you can add your own classes to this folder. Even if you don't select this option, though, it's a best practice to create the Models folder and then add your classes to it.

To add a new class to the Models folder, you use the Add New Item dialog box shown in figure 4-4. From this dialog box, you click on the Code link under the desired language. Then, you select the Class template, enter the name for the class, and click the Add button. When you do, Visual Studio will create a file that contains the declaration for the new class, and you can complete the class by coding its properties and methods.

Note that when you create a class, Visual Studio places its declaration within a namespace. The name of that namespace depends on the names of the project and the folder that contain the class file. In this figure, for example, the class file is being created in the Models folder of a project named Ch04Cart. Because of that, the class is stored in a namespace named Ch04Cart.Models. This refers to a namespace named Models that's nested within a namespace named Ch04Cart. Since this namespace isn't required, you can delete it after the class is created. That's what we've done for all of the business classes in this book so they aren't specific to any application.

To add an existing class to a web application, you use the Add Existing Item command. Then, the class file that you select is copied to your application. If the class contains a namespace declaration, you should change it so the namespace name matches the name used by the other classes in the project. Or, if the other classes don't include a namespace declaration, you can omit the declaration from the new class.

You can also use an existing class that is stored in a *class library*. This is a collection of classes compiled into a single assembly with a .dll file extension. To use the classes in a class library, you add a reference to the library as described in this figure. That will add the library to the Bin folder and make its classes available to your web application.

The dialog box for adding a new class to the Models folder

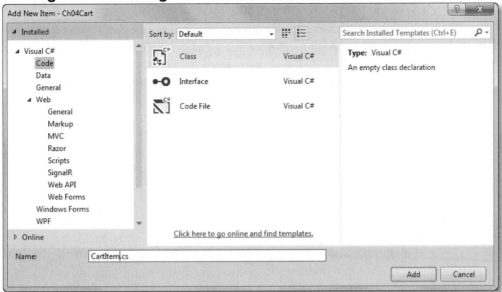

Two ways to open the Add New Item dialog box

- Right-click the Models folder in the Solution Explorer, and then choose Add→New Item from the shortcut menu.
- Click on the Models folder in the Solution Explorer to select it, and then choose the Project→Add New Item command.

How to add a new class to a web application

- From the Add New Item dialog box, click on the Code link under the Visual C# item and select the Class template. Then, enter a name for the class and click the Add button. Visual Studio will create a file with namespace and class declarations.

How to add an existing class to a web application

- To add a class from another project to a web application, right-click the Models folder in the Solution Explorer and select Add→Existing Item. Then, locate the class file you want to add, select it, and click the Add button to copy the file to your project.
- After the class is added, you might need to change its namespace.

How to use a class that's part of a class library

- Right-click the project in the Solution Explorer and select Add Reference from the shortcut menu.
- Click the Browse tab in the dialog box that's displayed, and then locate and select the dll file for the class library you want to use. Visual Studio will add the class library to a project folder named Bin, which is created if it doesn't already exist. To use the classes in the class library without qualification, add a using directive for the class library.

Figure 4-4   How to add a class to a web application

How to redirect or transfer to another page

When you develop an application with two or more pages, you'll need to know how to go from one page to another page. For example, when the user clicks the Add to Cart button on the Order page of the Shopping Cart application, the Cart page should be displayed. Similarly, when the user clicks the Continue Shopping button on the Cart page, the Order page should be displayed. Figure 4-5 presents three ways to do that.

When you use the Transfer method of the HttpServerUtility class, ASP.NET immediately terminates the execution of the current page. Then, it loads and executes the page specified in the Transfer method and returns it to the browser. The drawback to using this method is that when the new page is sent to the browser, the browser has no way of knowing that the application returned a different page. As a result, the URL for the original page is still displayed in the browser's address box. Sometimes that's what you want, but know that this can be confusing to the user and also prevents the user from bookmarking the page.

The Redirect method of the HttpResponse class works somewhat differently. When this method is executed, it sends a special message called an *HTTP redirect message* back to the browser. This message causes the browser to send a new HTTP request to the server to request the new page. Then, the server processes the page and sends it back to the browser. That way, the URL in the browser's address box matches the page being displayed. Although it requires an extra round trip, the user friendliness of this method usually outweighs the small performance gain that you get when you use the Transfer method. Most of the time, then, this is the method you'll use in your applications.

Unlike the Transfer and Redirect methods, the RedirectPermanent method is typically used when a page is physically moved or renamed within a web application. Suppose, for example, that you create a web application that includes a page named Products.aspx that's stored in the project folder. But later, you decide to create a subfolder named Customer, and you move the Products page to this folder. Then, you can use the RedirectPermanent method as in the third example in this figure to redirect to the page. The main advantage of using this method is that search engines will store the new URL. That way, if the page is requested at the old location, it can be displayed from its new location.

The Transfer method of the HttpServerUtility class

Method	Description
`Transfer(URL)`	Terminates the execution of the current page and transfers control to the page at the specified URL.

The Redirect and RedirectPermanent methods of the HttpResponse class

Method	Description
`Redirect(URL)`	Redirects the client to the specified URL and terminates the execution of the current page.
`RedirectPermanent(URL)`	Permanently redirects to the specified URL and terminates the execution of the current page.

Code that transfers control to another page

```
Server.Transfer("Cart.aspx");
```

Code that redirects the client to another page

```
Response.Redirect("Cart.aspx");
```

Code that permanently redirects the client to another page

```
Response.RedirectPermanent("Customer/Products.aspx");
```

Description

- The Transfer method is a member of the HttpServerUtility class, which contains helper methods for processing web requests. To refer to this class, you use the Server property of the page.

- The Redirect and RedirectPermanent methods are members of the HttpResponse class, which contains information about the response. To refer to this class, you use the Response property of the page.

- When you use the Transfer method, the current page is terminated and a new page is processed in its place. This processing is efficient because it takes place on the server, but the URL in the browser's address bar isn't updated.

- When you use the Redirect method, the server sends a special message to the browser called an *HTTP redirect message*. Then, the browser sends an HTTP request to the server that requests the new page. This requires an extra round trip, but the URL for the current page is shown in the browser's address bar.

- If you change the name or location of a page, you can use the RedirectPermanent method to identify the new URL for the page. Then, search engines will store that URL and use it to display the page when they receive a request for the old URL.

Figure 4-5   How to redirect or transfer to another page

How to use cross-page posting

A fourth way to transfer to a different web page is to use *cross-page posting* as described in figure 4-6. To use cross-page posting, you specify the URL of another page in the PostBackUrl property of a button control. Then, when the user clicks the button, an HTTP Post message that contains the URL specified by the PostBackUrl property is sent back to the server. As a result, the page with that URL is loaded and executed instead of the page that was originally displayed.

For example, the Go to Cart button on the Order page uses cross-page posting to go to the Cart page. As a result, the PostBackUrl property of this button is set to Cart.aspx as shown in this figure. Then, when the user clicks the Go to Cart button, ASP.NET loads and executes the Cart.aspx page instead of the Order.aspx page.

Notice that the URL in the PostBackUrl property of this control starts with a tilde (~) operator. This operator is added automatically when you set the PostBackUrl property from the Properties window, and you'll learn more about it in the next topic.

If the user enters data into one or more controls on a page that uses cross-page posting, you can use the PreviousPage property to retrieve the data entered by the user. Usually, you'll do this in the page's Load event handler. As the example in this figure shows, you should first check to make sure that the PreviousPage property refers to a valid object. If it doesn't, it means that either the page isn't being loaded as the result of a cross-page posting, or the request came from another web application. In either case, no previous page is available.

If the PreviousPage property refers to a valid object, there are two ways you can use it to retrieve data from the previous page. First, you can use the FindControl method to find a control on the previous page. Because this method returns an object, you'll need to cast it to the appropriate control before you can work with its properties. For example, the code in this figure finds a text box on the previous page, casts it to a text box, and then uses its Text property to retrieve the data that the text box contains.

The other alternative is to use *custom properties* as in the third example in this figure. This requires code in two more places. First, you must add a custom property in the code-behind file of the previous page. Second, you must add a PreviousPageType directive at the top of the aspx file of the new page, just below the Page directive. Once these two pieces of code are in place, the custom property is available from the PreviousPage object.

Because of the extra programming that's required to retrieve data entered by the user, cross-page posting is best used when no user input needs to be processed. For instance, since no data needs to be processed when the user clicks the Go to Cart button on the Order page, cross-page posting is used instead of the Response.Redirect or Server.Transfer method. However, the Response.Redirect method is used for the Add to Cart button on the Order page so the selected product and the quantity entered by the user can be easily retrieved.

The PostBackUrl property of the Button control

Property	Description
PostBackUrl	Specifies the URL of the page that should be requested when the user clicks the button.

Members of the Page class used with cross-page posting

Property	Description
PreviousPage	Returns a Page object that represents the previous page.
Method	**Description**
FindControl(id)	Returns a Control object with the specified id. You must cast the Control object to a specific control before you can work with it.

The aspx code for a button that posts to a different page

```
<asp:Button ID="btnCart" runat="server" Text="Go to Cart"
    CausesValidation="False" PostBackUrl="~/Cart.aspx" />
```

How to use the FindControl method to get data from another page

```
if (PreviousPage != null) {
    TextBox txtQuantity =
            (TextBox) PreviousPage.FindControl("txtQuantity");
    lblQuantity.Text = txtQuantity.Text;
}
```

How to use a custom property to get data from a previous page

Code that sets a property in the previous page

```
public string QuantityText {
    get { return this.txtQuantity.Text; }
}
```

A PreviousPageType directive in the new page

```
<%@ PreviousPageType VirtualPath="~/Order.aspx" %>
```

Code in the new page that gets the value from the property

```
if (PreviousPage != null)
    lblQuantity.Text = PreviousPage.QuantityText;
```

Description

- *Cross-page posting* lets you use the PostBackUrl property of a button to specify the page that should be requested when the user clicks the button.

- When you post to another page, the previous page is available via the PreviousPage property. Then, you use the FindControl method or custom properties to retrieve data entered by the user.

- If you use *custom properties*, you must set the PreviousPageType directive right below the Page directive at the top of the aspx file.

Figure 4-6   How to use cross-page posting

How to code absolute and relative URLs

In chapter 1, you learned about the basic components of an *absolute URL*, which includes the domain name of the website. When coded within a Transfer or Redirect method, an absolute URL lets you display a page at another website. For example, the first two statements in figure 4-7 display a page at the website with the domain name www.murach.com.

To display a page within the same website, you can use a *relative URL*. This type of URL specifies the location of the page relative to the directory that contains the current page. This is illustrated by the third and fourth statements in this figure. The third statement displays a page that's stored in the same directory as the current page. The fourth statement displays a page in the Login subdirectory of the directory that contains the current page.

The next two statements show how you can use a relative URL to navigate up the directory structure from the current directory. To navigate up one directory, you code two periods followed by a slash as shown in the fifth statement. To navigate up two directories, you code two periods and a slash followed by two more periods and a slash as shown in the sixth statement. To navigate up additional directories, you code two periods and a slash for each directory.

To navigate to the root directory for the host, you code a slash as shown in the seventh statement. You can also navigate to a directory within the root directory by coding the path for that directory after the slash, as shown in the eighth statement.

In addition to coding URLs on Transfer, Redirect, and RedirectPermanent methods, you can code them for the properties of some server controls. This is illustrated by the last two examples in this figure. The next to last example shows how you might set the PostBackUrl property of a button control. And the last example shows how you might set the ImageUrl property of an image control.

Notice that both of these URLs start with a tilde (~) operator. This operator causes the URL to be based on the root directory of the website. For example, the Cart.aspx file in the first URL is located in the root directory, and the banner.jpg file in the second URL is located in the Images subdirectory of the root directory.

Keep in mind, though, that the tilde operator only works on the server. For example, it will work in the Response.Redirect method or in the ImageUrl property of an Image server control, but it won't work in the src property of an HTML img element unless the img element has a runat="server" attribute.

Although you can use relative URLs in examples like these, it's easier to maintain URLs that use the tilde operator when you move pages or files from one folder to another. That's because it's easier to maintain a URL that's relative to the root directory of the website than it is to maintain a URL that's relative to another page. For that reason, you should use the tilde operator whenever you code a URL for a property of a server control.

Examples of absolute and relative URLs

Statements that use absolute URLs
```
Response.Redirect("https://www.murach.com/shop-books/all");
Response.Redirect("https://www.murach.com/search");
```

Statements that use relative URLs that are based on the current directory
```
Response.Redirect("Checkout.aspx");
Response.Redirect("Login/Register.aspx");
```

Statements that use relative URLs that navigate up the directory structure
```
Response.Redirect("../Register.aspx");
Response.Redirect("../../Register.aspx");
Response.Redirect("/Register.aspx");
Response.Redirect("/Login/Register.aspx");
```

Server control properties that use URLs that are based on the root directory of the current web application
```
PostBackUrl="~/Cart.aspx"
ImageUrl="~/Images/banner.jpg"
```

Description

- When you code an *absolute URL*, you code the complete URL including the domain name for the site. Absolute URLs let you display pages at other websites.

- When you code a *relative URL*, you base it on the current directory, which is the directory that contains the current page.

- To go to the root directory for the host, you code a slash. Then, you can code one or more directories after the slash.

- To go up one level from the current directory, you code two periods and a slash. To go up two levels, you code two periods and a slash followed by two more periods and a slash. And so on.

- If you're specifying a URL for the property of a server control, you can use the web application root operator (~) to base the URL on the root of the web application.

Figure 4-7   How to code absolute and relative URLs

How to create and use data sources

To connect to a database and work with its data, you can use an ASP.NET control called a *data source*. To illustrate how this works, the following topics show you how to work with a data source control called SqlDataSource. This control can be used to retrieve data from a SQL database file, such as a Microsoft SQL Server LocalDB database file.

How to create a SQL data source

ASP.NET provides several data source controls in the Data group of the Toolbox, including the SqlDataSource control. Figure 4-8 shows how to create this type of data source.

If you are going to use the SQL data source to connect to a local database file, you must first create a database and add it to the App_Data folder of the web application. For example, the Shopping Cart application for this chapter has a SQL Server database file named Halloween.mdf in the App_Data folder.

Since the data source isn't displayed on the page when the application is run, it doesn't matter where you place it on the page. However, if the data source is going to be bound to a control, it makes sense to place it near that control.

After you add the SQL data source to the page, its smart tag menu is displayed. Then, you can choose the Configure Data Source command to bring up the first page of the Configure Data Source wizard, which is shown in this figure. From this dialog box, you select the database file you want to use for the data source.

Once you've selected the data source, you must configure the data source as described in the next figure. Then, you can bind it to a control such as a drop-down list as described in the figure after that.

The first page of the Configure Data Source wizard

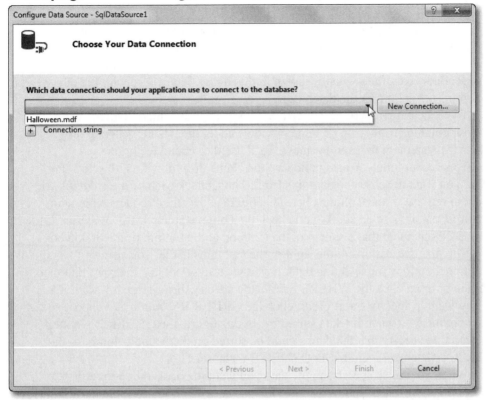

How to create a SQL data source

1. In the Web Forms Designer, open the Data group of the Toolbox and drag the SqlDataSource control to the form in either Design or Source view.

2. Select Configure Data Source from the smart tag menu for the data source, which displays the Configure Data Source dialog box shown above.

3. From the drop-down list, select the database file or connection string that you want to use, and click Next.

4. If this is the first time you're connecting to the database file, a dialog box asks whether you want to save the connection to the application configuration file. Then, leave the Yes box checked, enter a name for the connection, and click Next.

5. Complete the Configure Data Source wizard as described in the next figure.

Description

-   Before you create a *data source* for a local database file, you must add the database file to the App_Data folder.

-   Data source controls are visible in the Designer, but don't show when the web application runs.

Figure 4-8   How to create a SQL data source

How to configure a SQL data source

The previous figure showed you how to complete the first page of the Configure Data Source wizard by selecting the SQL database file to use. Figure 4-9 shows you how to complete the rest of the Configure Data Source wizard. The second page of the wizard, shown in this figure, lets you specify the query that retrieves data from the database.

To create a query, you can code a SQL SELECT statement. Or, you can choose columns from a single table or view and let the wizard generate the SELECT statement for you. For now, we'll use the second technique.

To select columns from a table, use the Name drop-down list to select the table you want to select the columns from. Then, check each of the columns you want to retrieve in the Columns list. This figure shows the Products table with six of its columns selected. As you check the columns, the wizard creates a SQL SELECT statement that's shown in the text box at the bottom of the dialog box.

The first two buttons to the right of the Columns list let you specify additional options for selecting data. If you want to select just the rows that meet certain criteria, click the WHERE button and specify the criteria you want. Or, if you want to specify a sort order, click the ORDER BY button and choose the columns you want the data sorted by. In this figure, the ORDER BY button was used to specify that the data should be sorted on the Name column, so the SELECT statement includes an ORDER BY clause.

When you finish specifying the data you want the data source to retrieve, click Next. This takes you to the last page of the wizard, which includes a Test Query button. If you click this button, the wizard retrieves the data that you have specified. You can then look over this data to make sure it's what you expected. If it isn't, click the Previous button and adjust the query. If it is, click Finish.

The second page of the Configure Data Source wizard

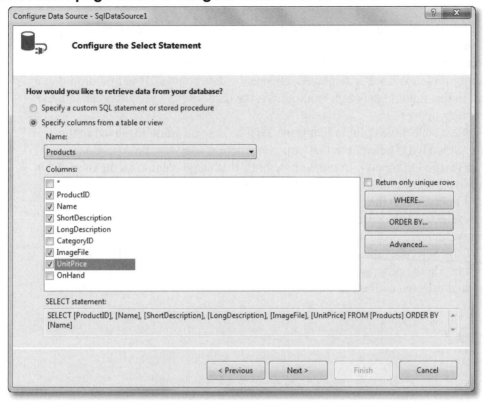

The aspx code for a SQL data source control

```
<asp:SqlDataSource ID="SqlDataSource1" runat="server"
    ConnectionString='<%$ ConnectionStrings:HalloweenConnection %>'
    SelectCommand="SELECT [ProductID], [Name], [ShortDescription],
        [LongDescription], [ImageFile], [UnitPrice]
        FROM [Products] ORDER BY [Name]">
</asp:SqlDataSource>
```

Description

- The Configure Data Source wizard lets you create a query using SQL. You can enter the SELECT statement for the query directly, or you can let the wizard construct the SELECT statement from your selections.

- You can click the WHERE button to specify one or more conditions that will be used to select the records.

- You can click the ORDER BY button to specify a sort order for the records.

- You can click the Advanced button to include Insert, Update, and Delete statements for the data source.

- When you click the Next button, you are asked whether you want to preview the data that's going to be returned by the data source. To do that, click Test Query.

Figure 4-9   How to configure a SQL data source

How to bind a drop-down list to a data source

Once you've created a data source, you can *bind* it to a drop-down list, as shown in figure 4-10. To start, select the Choose Data Source command from the smart tag menu for the drop-down list. Then, when the Data Source Configuration Wizard is displayed, choose the data source in the first drop-down list. In this figure, that's SqlDataSource1, the data source that was created in the previous figures.

Next, select the column that provides the data you want displayed in the drop-down list. The column that you select here is used for the drop-down list's DataTextField property. In this figure, that's the Name column so the drop-down list displays the name of each product in the data source.

Finally, select the column that you want to use as the value of the item selected by the user. The column you select here is used for the list's DataValueField property, and the value of that column can be retrieved by using the list's SelectedValue property. In this figure, that's the ProductID column. As a result, the program can use the SelectedValue property to get the ID of the product selected by the user.

The Data Source Configuration Wizard dialog box

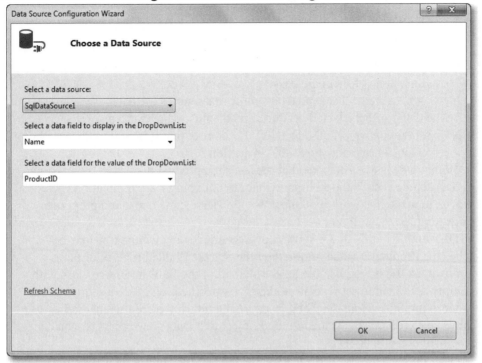

The aspx code for a drop-down list that's bound to a data source

```
<asp:DropDownList ID="ddlProducts" runat="server"
    AutoPostBack="True" DataSourceID="SqlDataSource1"
    DataTextField="Name" DataValueField="ProductID">
</asp:DropDownList>
```

Properties for binding a drop-down list

Property	Description
DataSourceID	The ID of the data source that the drop-down list should be bound to.
DataTextField	The name of the data source field that should be displayed in the drop-down list.
DataValueField	The name of the data source field whose value should be returned by the SelectedValue property of the drop-down list.

Description

- You can *bind* a drop-down list to a data source so the list automatically displays data retrieved by the data source.
- You can use the Data Source Configuration Wizard dialog box to configure the data binding for a drop-down list. To display this dialog box, select the Choose Data Source command from the list's smart tag menu.
- Alternatively, you can use the Properties window or edit the aspx code directly to set the data binding properties for a drop-down list.

Figure 4-10   How to bind a drop-down list to a data source

How to use C# code to get data from a data source

For the Shopping Cart application to work, it must retrieve the data for the product selected by the user from the drop-down list. Although there are several ways to do that, none of them are easy.

One way is to create a second data source that queries the database again to retrieve the data for the selected product, and then use a special type of ASP.NET server control called a DetailsView control that is bound to this second data source. You'll learn how to do that in section 3.

Another way is to write code that retrieves the product data from the existing SQL data source. That's the technique that the Shopping Cart application uses. However, to make this work, you must use the classes, methods, and properties that are summarized in figure 4-11.

The example in this figure shows how to retrieve data from a row that matches the ProductID value returned by the SelectedValue property of the drop-down list. First, you use the Select method of the SqlDataSource class with the Empty argument to retrieve all of the rows specified by the data source from the underlying SQL database. Then, because the return type of this method is IEnumerable, you must cast the returned object to a DataView object so you can use the methods of that class.

Once you have the rows in a DataView object, you can use the RowFilter property to filter the rows so only the row selected by the user is available. To do that, you build a filter expression that lists the column name and value. For example, ProductID='jar01' filters the data view so only the row whose ProductID column contains jar01 is included. The second statement in this figure creates a filter expression for the ID of the product the user selected.

Once you've filtered the DataView object so only the selected row is available, you can use two indexes to retrieve the data for a column. The first index identifies the only row that has been selected, so its value is 0, and this row is returned as a DataRowView object. Then, you can specify the index of the column you want to retrieve from the row, either as a string that provides the column name or as the position of the column. In this example, column names are used for the columns that need to be retrieved. (Although using an column position is slightly more efficient, specifying the column name makes the code more understandable.)

Once you establish the row and column index for each value, all that remains is to cast this value to the appropriate type. In this example, all of the columns except the UnitPrice column are cast to strings using their ToString methods, and the UnitPrice column is cast to a decimal type.

In this example, the values that are retrieved from the data source are stored in local variables. Later in this chapter, though, you'll see similar code that retrieves these values and stores them in a Product object.

The Select method of the SqlDataSource class

Method	Description
`Select(selectOptions)`	Returns an IEnumerable object that contains the rows retrieved from the underlying database. To get all the rows, the selectOptions parameter should be DataSourceSelectArguments.Empty.

Members of the DataView class for retrieving rows

Property	Description
`RowFilter`	A string that is used to filter the rows retrieved from the database.

Indexer	Description
`[index]`	Returns a DataRowView object for the row at the specified index position.

Members of the DataRowView class for retrieving columns

Indexer	Description
`[index]`	Returns the value of the column at the specified index position as an object.
`[name]`	Returns the value of the column with the specified name as an object.

Code that gets product information for the selected product

```
DataView productsTable = (DataView)
    SqlDataSource1.Select(DataSourceSelectArguments.Empty);
productsTable.RowFilter =
    "ProductID = '" + ddlProducts.SelectedValue + "'";
DataRowView row = productsTable[0];

string id = row["ProductID"].ToString();
string name = row["Name"].ToString();
string shortDesc = row["ShortDescription"].ToString();
string longDesc = row["LongDescription"].ToString();
decimal price = (decimal)row["UnitPrice"];
string imgFile = row["ImageFile"].ToString();
```

Description

- The Select method of the SqlDataSource class returns an IEnumerable object that contains the rows retrieved from the database. To work with these rows, you must cast the IEnumerable object to a DataView object.

- The RowFilter property of the DataView class lets you filter rows in the data view based on a criteria string.

- You can use the indexer of the DataView class to return a specific row as a DataRowView object. Then, you can use the indexer of the DataRowView class to return the value of a specified column. The indexer for the column can be an integer that represents the column's position in the row or a string that represents the name of the column.

- The DataView and DataRowView classes are stored in the System.Data namespace.

Figure 4-11   How to use C# code to get data from a data source

How to use session state

In chapter 1, you learned that HTTP is a stateless protocol. You also learned that ASP.NET uses *session state* to keep track of each user session and that you can use session state to maintain program values across executions of an application. Now, you'll learn how to use session state.

How session state works

Figure 4-12 shows how session state solves the problem of state management for ASP.NET applications. As you can see, session state tracks individual user sessions by creating a *session state object* for each user's session. This object contains a *session ID* that uniquely identifies the session. This session ID is passed back to the browser along with the HTTP response. Then, if the browser makes another request, the session ID is included in the request so ASP.NET can identify the session. ASP.NET then matches the session with the session state object that was previously saved.

By default, ASP.NET sends the session ID to the browser as a *cookie*. Then, when the browser sends another request to the server, it automatically includes the cookie that contains the session ID with the request. In section 2, you'll learn more about how cookies work. You'll also learn how to implement session state by including the session ID in the URL for a page instead of in a cookie.

Although ASP.NET automatically uses session state to track user sessions, you can also use it to store your own data across executions of an application. This figure lists three typical reasons for doing that. First, you can use session state to maintain information about the user. After a user logs in to an application, for example, you can use the login information to retrieve information about the user from a file or a database. Then, you can store that information in the session state object so it's available each time the application is executed.

Second, you can use session state to save objects that the user is working with. To illustrate, consider a maintenance application that lets the user change customer records. In that case, you can save the customer record that's currently being modified in the session state object so it's available the next time the application is executed.

Third, you can use session state to keep track of the operation a user is currently performing. For example, if a maintenance application lets the user add or change customer records, you can save an item in the session state object that indicates if the user is currently adding or changing a record. That way, the application can determine how to proceed each time it's executed.

How ASP.NET maintains the state of a session

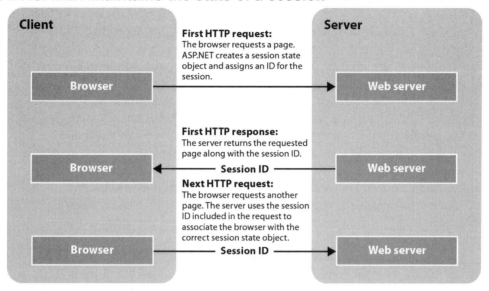

Typical uses for session state

- **To keep information about the user**, such as the user's name or whether the user has registered.
- **To save objects the user is working with**, such as a shopping cart or a customer record.
- **To keep track of pending operations**, such as what steps the user has completed while placing an order.

Description

- ASP.NET uses *session state* to track the state of each user of an application. To do that, it creates a *session state object*.
- The session state object includes a *session ID* that's sent back to the browser as a *cookie*. Then, the browser automatically returns the session ID cookie to the server with each request so the server can associate the browser with an existing session state object.
- If you want your application to work on browsers that don't support cookies, you can configure ASP.NET to encode the session ID in the URL for each page of the application. You'll learn more about this in chapter 8.
- You can use the session state object to store and retrieve items across executions of an application.

Figure 4-12   How session state works

How to work with data in session state

Figure 4-13 shows how you can use the session state object to store application data. To do that, you use the members of this object, which is created from the HttpSessionState class. To access this object from a web form, you use the Session property of the page.

The session state object contains a collection of items that consist of the item names and their values. One way to add an item to this collection is to use the indexer as shown in the first example. Here, an object named cart is assigned to a session state item named Cart. If the Cart item doesn't exist when this statement is executed, it will be created. Otherwise, the value of the Cart item will be updated.

Another way to add an item to the session state collection is to use the Add method, as in the second example. Here again, if the item already exists, it's updated when the Add method is executed. Otherwise, it's added to the collection.

You can also use the indexer to retrieve the value of an item from the session state collection, as in the third example. Here, the value of the Cart item is retrieved and assigned to the cart variable. Since the value of a session state item is stored as an Object type, you typically cast it to the appropriate type. In this example, the value of the Cart item is cast to a SortedList and the cart variable that it's assigned to is defined as a SortedList.

Because the session state object uses valuable server memory, you should avoid using it to store large items. Or, if you must store large items in session state, you should remove the items as soon as you're done with them. To do that, you use the Remove method as in the fourth example in this figure.

The first four examples in this figure use the Session property of the page to access the session state object. Because Session is a property of the System.Web.UI.Page class, however, you can only use this property from a class that inherits the System.Web.UI.Page class. In other words, you can only use it from a code-behind file for a page.

To access session state from a class that doesn't inherit the System.Web.UI.Page class, such as a database or business class, you use the Session property of the HttpContext object for the current request. To get this HttpContext object, you use the Current property of the HttpContext class as illustrated in the last example in this figure.

Common members of the HttpSessionState class

Property	Description
SessionID	The unique ID of the session.
Count	The number of items in the session state collection.

Indexer	Description
[name]	The value of the session state item with the specified name.

Method	Description
Add(name, value)	Adds an item to the session state collection.
Clear()	Removes all items from the session state collection.
Remove(name)	Removes the item with the specified name from the session state collection.

A statement that adds or updates a session state item

```
Session["Cart"] = cart;
```

Another way to add or update a session state item

```
Session.Add("Cart", cart);
```

A statement that retrieves the value of a session state item

```
SortedList cart = (SortedList) Session["Cart"];
```

A statement that removes an item from session state

```
Session.Remove("Cart");
```

A statement that retrieves the value of a session state item from a class that doesn't inherit System.Web.UI.Page

```
SortedList cart = (SortedList) HttpContext.Current.Session["Cart"];
```

Description

- The session state object is created from the HttpSessionState class, which defines a collection of session state items.
- To access the session state object from the code-behind file for a web form, use the Session property of the page.
- To access the session state object from a class other than the code-behind file for a web form, use the Current property of the HttpContext class to get the HttpContext object for the current request. This object contains information about the HTTP request. Then, you can use its Session property to get the session state object.
- By default, session state objects are maintained in server memory. As a result, you should avoid storing large items in session state.

Figure 4-13   How to use session state for storing and retrieving data

The business classes of the Shopping Cart application

Now that you've learned the basic skills for developing a multi-form application, you're ready to see all the aspx and C# code for the Shopping Cart application that's shown in figure 4-1. This starts with the C# code for the business classes.

The members of the three business classes

Figure 4-14 summarizes the members of the three business classes used by the Shopping Cart application. As you can see, the Product class is a simple class that contains only properties. An object created from this kind of class is sometimes referred to as a *Data Transfer Object*, or *DTO*. As its name implies, a DTO is used primarily to store and transfer data. Product objects are used to transfer data between the Order page and the business classes.

The CartItem class contains a Product property, which is a Product object, and a Quantity property, which is an int. It also contains an overloaded constructor, which lets you either create an empty CartItem object or populate its Product and Quantity properties on creation. In contrast to the Product class, the CartItem class contains methods as well as properties. Its first method adds to the Quantity property. Its second method returns a string containing quantity and product information, formatted in a single line. Although a CartItem object is also used to transfer data, it isn't a DTO because it has additional functionality.

The CartItemList class is a container class. In effect, it is the shopping cart. An object created from this class stores and keeps track of CartItem objects. It contains an internal list to store CartItem objects, a read-only property to display the number of CartItem objects it contains, indexers to get a CartItem object by index or product ID, and methods to add and remove CartItem objects and to clear the entire CartItemList object.

The CartItemList class also contains a static method called GetCart that retrieves a CartItemList object from the session state object if one is there. Otherwise, this method creates a CartItemList object and adds it to the session state object.

Members of the Product class

Property	Description
ProductID	Gets and sets the ID of a Product.
Name	Gets and sets the name of a Product.
ShortDescription	Gets and sets the short description of a Product.
LongDescription	Gets and sets the long description of a Product.
UnitPrice	Gets and sets the unit price of a Product.
ImageFile	Gets and sets the name of the image file for a Product.

Members of the CartItem class

Constructor	Description
CartItem()	Creates a CartItem.
CartItem(product, quantity)	Creates a CartItem for the specified product and quantity.

Property	Description
Product	Gets and sets the Product of a CartItem.
Quantity	Gets and sets the quantity of a CartItem.

Method	Description
AddQuantity(quantity)	Adds the quantity that's passed to it to the quantity for a CartItem. Only called when the item is already in the cart.
Display()	Returns a string with CartItem data formatted so it can be displayed in one line of the list box on the Cart page.

Members of the CartItemList class

Constructor	Description
CartItemList()	Creates a CartItemList.

Property	Description
Count	Gets the number of items in the CartItemList.

Indexer	Description
[index]	Gets a CartItem using the index that's passed to it.
[id]	Gets a CartItem using the product ID that's passed to it. If the product isn't found, it returns null.

Method	Description
GetCart()	Gets the CartItemList from or creates it in session state.
AddItem(product, quantity)	Adds a CartItem to the CartItemList.
RemoveAt(index)	Removes the CartItem at the index from the CartItemList.
Clear()	Removes all CartItem objects from the CartItemList.

Figure 4-14   The members of the classes used by the Shopping Cart application

The C# code for the Product class

Now that you have a general idea of what the members of three business classes do, you can study the code for these classes. To start, figure 4-15 shows the C# code for the Product class. This class represents a product that the user can order from the Shopping Cart application. It has a property for each of the columns in the Products table in the SQL Server database except CategoryID and OnHand.

The C# code for the CartItem class

Figure 4-15 also shows the code for the CartItem class, which represents one item in the shopping cart. After the parameterless constructor, the next constructor for this class accepts two parameters that are used to initialize the Product and Quantity properties. These properties hold the Product object and quantity for the cart item.

The CartItem class also includes two methods. The first one, AddQuantity, is used to add the quantity that's passed to it to the cart item. This method is called when the user adds a quantity to the cart for a product that's already in the cart. The second one, Display, returns a string that formats the data in a cart item so it can be displayed in one line of the list box on the Cart page.

There are two features of this C# code worth mentioning. First, the CartItem class and the Product class are defined using auto-implemented properties. This is because the properties don't do anything but store and retrieve the values passed to them. Usually, this is all you'll need when working with properties. Sometimes, though, you'll want to do something with the property value, like run some data validation code or use it in a calculation. When that's the case, you'll need to use private fields that are accessible through standard properties.

Second, the Display method of the CartItem class uses the Format method of the String class to create its return value. Here, the values in the last three parameters of this method are plugged into the literal that's specified by the first parameter. Using the Format method for this type of formatting is recommended over the traditional method of combining string literals and values with plus (+) signs, because it performs better and is less error prone. You could also use the new string interpolation functionality of C# here.

The code for the Product class

```
public class Product
{
    public string ProductID { get; set; }
    public string Name { get; set; }
    public string ShortDescription { get; set; }
    public string LongDescription { get; set; }
    public decimal UnitPrice { get; set; }
    public string ImageFile { get; set; }
}
```

The code for the CartItem class

```
public class CartItem
{
    //constructors that create an empty CartItem object or one with values
    public CartItem() {}
    public CartItem(Product product, int quantity)
    {
        this.Product = product;
        this.Quantity = quantity;
    }

    //public properties for a CartItem object
    public Product Product { get; set; }
    public int Quantity { get; set; }

    //method that adds the quantity to the current quantity
    public void AddQuantity(int quantity)
    {
        this.Quantity += quantity;
    }

    //method that formats an item's name, quantity, and price in one line
    public string Display()
    {
        string displayString = string.Format("{0} ({1} at {2} each)",
            Product.Name,
            Quantity.ToString(),
            Product.UnitPrice.ToString("c"));
        return displayString;
    }
}
```

Description

- The Product class represents a product.
- The CartItem class represents a product that the user has added to the shopping cart plus the quantity ordered.
- The Product and CartItem classes are defined with auto-implemented properties. However, if you need to do more than just store the property values, you need to use private fields that are accessible through standard properties.
- The Display method uses the Format method of the string object to format the item's properties in a single line that can be used in the Cart.

Figure 4-15   The code for the Product and CartItem classes

The C# code for the CartItemList class

Figure 4-16 shows the code for the CartItemList class, which represents a list of CartItem objects. This list is defined in a private field named cartItems at the beginning of the class. Then, the constructor for this class initializes this field with a new List<CartItem> object.

Next, the Count property is a read-only property that returns a count of the items in the list. It's followed by an overloaded read-only indexer. The first indexer gets a cart item in the list using the index that's passed to it. This indexer is used to get the items in the cart when they're displayed in the list box on the Cart page.

The second indexer gets a cart item using the product ID that's passed to it. This indexer is used to determine if a product is already in the cart. If a product with the specified ID isn't found, this indexer returns a null value. This second indexer uses a loop to find the product with the specified ID, but it could just as easily use a LINQ to Objects method with a lambda expression. Since C# functionality isn't our focus here, though, this code uses traditional techniques.

The first method, GetCart, gets the CartItemList object that's stored in a session state item named "Cart". Then, it checks to see if that object is equal to null. If it is, it means that a cart hasn't yet been created for the current user. Then, a new CartItemList object is created and added to session state. Either way, the CartItemList object is returned to the calling program.

You should notice two things about this method. First, it's a static method. That makes sense because it simply retrieves the CartItemList object that's stored in session state. It doesn't work with the current CartItemList object. Second, because this code isn't in a code-behind file, you can't use the Session property of the page to refer to the session state object. Instead, you have to refer to the session state object through the HttpContext object for the current request.

The next method, AddItem, adds a new cart item to the cart item list. It accepts a Product object and quantity as parameters. Then, it creates a CartItem object from these values and adds the cart item to the cart item list.

The last two methods, RemoveAt and Clear, should be easy to understand. The RemoveAt method removes the cart item at the given index from the list of cart items. And the Clear method removes all the cart items from the list.

Notice that the methods that add and remove items from the cart don't refer to session state directly. That's because session state is an object. So when you retrieve the cart from session state, you store it in a reference type variable. Then, when you use that variable to add and remove items from the cart, the session state object is updated automatically. This will make more sense when you see the code for the Order and Cart pages.

The code for the CartItemList class

```
using System;
using System.Collections.Generic;
using System.Web;

public class CartItemList
{
    //internal list of items and the constructor that instantiates it
    private List<CartItem> cartItems;
    public CartItemList() {
        cartItems = new List<CartItem>();
    }

    //read-only property that returns the number of items in the internal list
    public int Count {
        get { return cartItems.Count; }
    }

    //indexers that locate items in the internal list by index or product id
    public CartItem this[int index] {
        get { return cartItems[index]; }
    }
    public CartItem this[string id]    {
        get {
            foreach (CartItem c in cartItems)
                if (c.Product.ProductID == id) return c;
            return null;
        }
    }

    //static method to get the cart object from session state
    public static CartItemList GetCart() {
        CartItemList cart = (CartItemList)HttpContext.Current.Session["Cart"];
        if (cart == null)
            HttpContext.Current.Session["Cart"] = new CartItemList();
        return (CartItemList) HttpContext.Current.Session["Cart"];
    }

    //methods that add, remove, and clear items in the internal list
    public void AddItem(Product product, int quantity) {
        CartItem c = new CartItem(product, quantity);
        cartItems.Add(c);
    }
    public void RemoveAt(int index) {
        cartItems.RemoveAt(index);
    }
    public void Clear() {
        cartItems.Clear();
    }
}
```

Description

- The second indexer uses a foreach loop to find and return the CartItem object with the specified id. If the loop completes without returning an object, the indexer returns null.

Figure 4-16   The code for the CartItemList class

The web forms of the Shopping Cart application

This chapter ends by presenting the aspx and C# code for the Order and Cart pages. If you've followed everything to this point, you shouldn't need much explanation. But the code is described in detail in case you need that.

The aspx code for the Order page

Figure 4-17 shows the aspx code for the Order page shown in figure 4-1. In keeping with the recommendations of chapter 3, this page is formatted using Bootstrap as well as a custom style sheet. As you saw in that chapter, you typically use a lot of div elements with Bootstrap, which can make your HTML harder to read. Because of that, you may want to include comments that describe the layout as shown here. That can help other developers understand your code.

Remember too that some of the Bootstrap CSS classes are designed to work together, and if you don't use them together it can throw off your formatting. If you don't use column classes inside a form group, for example, the elements in that group will have different padding than the elements in a form group that does use column classes. Because of that, you should always use column classes, even if there's only one item in the form group. That's why the code shown here includes several form groups with just one element in a column that spans all 12 columns.

The first div element in this code uses the Bootstrap container class, and this div contains HTML5 header and main semantic elements. The header element uses the jumbotron class for its basic formatting. As you'll see later in this chapter, though, the custom style sheet overrides the formatting of this class to add a background image. The main element contains a form element that defines the format for the rest of the page. This form element contains two Bootstrap rows that contain the HTML elements and server controls that make up the page.

The first row is divided into two columns. The first column contains a form group with a label element, the drop-down list that the label identifies, and the SQL data source that the drop-down list is bound to. Here, the AutoPostBack property for the drop-down list is set to True so the page will post back to the server when the user selects a product. In addition, the DataSourceID, DataTextField, and DataValueField properties specify how the drop-down list is bound to the SQL data source.

The first form group is followed by four more form groups, each of which contains a Label server control that displays information about the selected product. Label controls are used here because their content will be changed by the C# code. In contrast, the content of the label element won't change.

Before you go on, you should remember from chapter 3 that the form-group class defines a row on a form. Because of that, the form groups shown here actually define rows within the first column of the outer row (the div element with the row class). Then, one or more columns are defined within the inner rows (the div elements with the form-group class).

The aspx file for the Order page (Order.aspx)

```aspx
<%@ Page Language="C#" AutoEventWireup="true" CodeFile="Order.aspx.cs"
    Inherits="Ch04Cart.Order" %>

<!DOCTYPE html>
<html xmlns="http://www.w3.org/1999/xhtml">
<head runat="server">
    <title>Chapter 4: Shopping Cart</title>
    <meta name="viewport" content="width=device-width, initial-scale=1" />
    <link href="Content/bootstrap.min.css" rel="stylesheet" />
    <link href="Content/site.css" rel="stylesheet" />
    <script src="Scripts/jquery-1.9.1.min.js"></script>
    <script src="Scripts/bootstrap.min.js"></script>
</head>
<body>
<div class="container">
    <header class="jumbotron"><%-- image set in site.css --%></header>
    <main><form id="form1" runat="server" class="form-horizontal">
        <div class="row"><%-- row 1 --%>
            <div class="col-sm-8"><%-- product drop down and info column --%>
                <div class="form-group">
                    <label class="col-sm-5">Please select a product:</label>
                    <div class="col-sm-6">
                        <asp:DropDownList ID="ddlProducts" runat="server"
                            AutoPostBack="True" DataSourceID="SqlDataSource1"
                            DataTextField="Name" DataValueField="ProductID"
                            CssClass="form-control"></asp:DropDownList>
                        <asp:SqlDataSource ID="SqlDataSource1" runat="server"
                            ConnectionString=
                                '<%$ ConnectionStrings:HalloweenConnection %>'
                            SelectCommand="SELECT [ProductID], [Name],
                            [ShortDescription], [LongDescription],
                            [ImageFile], [UnitPrice] FROM [Products]
                            ORDER BY [Name]"></asp:SqlDataSource>
                    </div>
                </div>
                <div class="form-group">
                    <div class="col-sm-12">
                        <h4><asp:Label ID="lblName" runat="server"></asp:Label>
                        </h4></div></div>
                <div class="form-group">
                    <div class="col-sm-12">
                        <asp:Label ID="lblShortDescription" runat="server">
                    </asp:Label></div></div>
                <div class="form-group">
                    <div class="col-sm-12">
                        <asp:Label ID="lblLongDescription" runat="server">
                    </asp:Label></div></div>
                <div class="form-group">
                    <div class="col-sm-12">
                        <asp:Label ID="lblUnitPrice" runat="server">
                    </asp:Label></div></div>
            </div>
            <div class="col-sm-4"><%-- product image column --%>
                <asp:Image ID="imgProduct" runat="server" /></div>
        </div><%-- end of row 1 --%>
```

Figure 4-17   The aspx code for the Order page (part 1 of 2)

The second column in the first row is much simpler and contains a single Image server control. This control displays the image that's associated with the selected product.

The second row contains a div element that spans all twelves columns of the row. Then, that element contains two form groups. The first form group contains a label, a text box control, and two validation controls that will test that the text box contains a value and that it ranges from 1 to 500.

The second form group contains two button controls. Here, the OnClick property for the Add to Cart button names the event handler that will be executed when the button is clicked. In contrast, the Go to Cart button uses the PostBackUrl property to indicate that the Cart.aspx page should be requested when that button is clicked. Since its CausesValidation property is set to False, the validation controls for the txtQuantity text box won't be executed when the Go to Cart button is clicked.

The aspx file for the Order page (continued)

```
<div class="row"><%-- row 2 --%>
    <div class="col-sm-12">
        <div class="form-group">
            <label class="col-sm-1">Quantity:</label>
            <div class="col-sm-3">
                <asp:TextBox ID="txtQuantity" runat="server"
                    CssClass="form-control"></asp:TextBox></div>
            <div class="col-sm-8">
                <asp:RequiredFieldValidator ID="RequiredFieldValidator1"
                    runat="server" ControlToValidate="txtQuantity"
                    CssClass="text-danger" Display="Dynamic"
                    ErrorMessage="Quantity is a required field.">
                </asp:RequiredFieldValidator>
                <asp:RangeValidator ID="RangeValidator1" runat="server"
                    ControlToValidate="txtQuantity"
                    CssClass="text-danger" Display="Dynamic"
                    ErrorMessage="Quantity must range from 1 to 500."
                    MaximumValue="500" MinimumValue="1" Type="Integer">
                </asp:RangeValidator></div>
        </div>
        <div class="form-group">
            <div class="col-sm-12">
                <asp:Button ID="btnAdd" runat="server" Text="Add to Cart"
                    OnClick="btnAdd_Click" CssClass="btn" />
                <asp:Button ID="btnCart" runat="server" Text="Go to Cart"
                    PostBackUrl="~/Cart.aspx" CausesValidation="False"
                    CssClass="btn" /></div>
        </div>
    </div>
</div><%-- end of row 2 --%>
</form></main>
</div>
</body>
</html>
```

Description

- The Order page and the Cart page that you'll see in figure 4-19 use Bootstrap for most of their formatting as described in chapter 3.

- The drop-down list is bound to a SqlDataSource control that retrieves product data from the Halloween database. The AutoPostBack property for this list is set to True so the page will post back to the server when a different product is selected and the product for that data can be retrieved and displayed.

- The Go to Cart button uses the PostBackUrl property so the Cart page is displayed when the button is clicked.

Figure 4-17   The aspx code for the Order page (part 2 of 2)

The C# code for the Order page

Figure 4-18 presents the code for the Order page's code-behind file, Order. aspx.cs. This code starts with a using directive for the System.Data namespace, which is part of the .NET Framework. This statement lets you use the classes that work with SQL data without having to fully qualify them.

The remaining code for the form is stored within a namespace that has the same name as the project, in this case, Ch04Cart. Then, the class for the page is coded within this namespace.

The code for this page starts by declaring a class-level variable that will hold a Product object that represents the item that the user has selected from the drop-down list. This variable is assigned a Product object by the second statement in the Page_Load method, which gets the Product object by calling the GetSelectedProduct method.

The Page_Load method starts by calling the DataBind method of the drop-down list if the page is being loaded for the first time (IsPostBack isn't True). This method binds the drop-down list to the SQL data source, which causes the data source to retrieve the data specified in its SelectCommand property.

Then, the Page_Load method calls the GetSelectedProduct method, which is coded in this file. This method gets the data for the selected product from the SQL data source and returns a Product object. That object is stored in the selectedProduct variable, which is available to all of the methods in this class.

Finally, the Page_Load method formats the labels and the image control to display the data for the selected product. At that point, the Order page is sent back to the user's browser.

For many applications, you don't need to call the DataBind method in the Page_Load method when you use data binding. Instead, you let ASP.NET automatically bind any data-bound controls. Unfortunately, this automatic data binding doesn't occur until after the Page_Load method has been executed. In this case, because the GetSelectedProduct method won't work unless the drop-down list has already been bound, the application calls the DataBind method to force the data binding to occur earlier than it normally would.

If the user clicks the Add to Cart button, the btnAdd_Click method is executed. After checking that the page is valid, this method calls the GetCart method of the CartItemList class to get the cart that's stored in session state. Remember that if a cart doesn't already exist in session state, this method creates a new CartItemList object and stores it in session state. Also remember that GetCart is a static method, so you call it from the class rather than an object created from the class.

Next, this method determines whether the cart already contains an item for the selected product. To do that, it uses the indexer of the CartItemList object to get the CartItem object with the product ID of the product. If an item isn't found with this product ID, the AddItem method of the CartItemList object is called to add an item with the selected product and quantity to the list. In contrast, if an item is found with the product ID, the AddQuantity method of the CartItem object is called to add the quantity to the item. Finally, this method uses Response.Redirect to go to the Cart.aspx page.

The code-behind file for the Order page (Order.aspx.cs)

```csharp
//default using directives
using System.Data;

namespace Ch04Cart
{
    public partial class Order : System.Web.UI.Page
    {
        private Product selectedProduct;

        protected void Page_Load(object sender, EventArgs e) {
            //bind drop-down list on first load
            if (!IsPostBack) ddlProducts.DataBind();

            //get and show product on every load
            selectedProduct = this.GetSelectedProduct();
            lblName.Text = selectedProduct.Name;
            lblShortDescription.Text = selectedProduct.ShortDescription;
            lblLongDescription.Text = selectedProduct.LongDescription;
            lblUnitPrice.Text = selectedProduct.UnitPrice.ToString("c") + " each";
            imgProduct.ImageUrl = "Images/Products/" + selectedProduct.ImageFile;
        }
        private Product GetSelectedProduct() {
            //get row from SqlDataSource based on value in drop-down list
            DataView productsTable = (DataView)
                SqlDataSource1.Select(DataSourceSelectArguments.Empty);
            productsTable.RowFilter = string.Format("ProductID = '{0}'",
                ddlProducts.SelectedValue);
            DataRowView row = productsTable[0];

            //create a new product object and load with data from row
            Product p = new Product();
            p.ProductID = row["ProductID"].ToString();
            p.Name = row["Name"].ToString();
            p.ShortDescription = row["ShortDescription"].ToString();
            p.LongDescription = row["LongDescription"].ToString();
            p.UnitPrice = (decimal)row["UnitPrice"];
            p.ImageFile = row["ImageFile"].ToString();
            return p;
        }
        protected void btnAdd_Click(object sender, EventArgs e) {
            if (IsValid) {
                //get cart from session state and selected item from cart
                CartItemList cart = CartItemList.GetCart();
                CartItem cartItem = cart[selectedProduct.ProductID];

                //if item isn't in cart, add it; otherwise, increase its quantity
                if (cartItem == null) {
                    cart.AddItem(selectedProduct,
                                Convert.ToInt32(txtQuantity.Text));
                }
                else {
                    cartItem.AddQuantity(Convert.ToInt32(txtQuantity.Text));
                }
                Response.Redirect("~/Cart.aspx");
            }
        }
    }
}
```

Figure 4-18   The C# code for the Order page

The aspx code for the Cart page

Figure 4-19 shows the aspx code in the container div for the second page of the Shopping Cart application, Cart.aspx, also shown in figure 4-1. Here, the shopping cart is displayed in a ListBox control, and the Bootstrap columns for this page causes the Remove and Empty buttons to flow to the right of the list box.

These two buttons, as well as the CheckOut button, use an OnClick property to name the event handler that's executed when the button is clicked. In contrast, the Continue button uses the PostBackUrl property to return to the Order.aspx page. All four buttons are styled using the Bootstrap button classes.

The lblMessage label is used to display messages to the user. Notice here that the EnableViewState property of this label is set to False. That way, the value of this label isn't maintained between HTTP requests. So if an error message is displayed in this label, it won't be displayed the next time the page is displayed.

The container div of the aspx file for the Cart page (Cart.aspx)

```
<div class="container">
  <header class="jumbotron"><%-- image set in site.css --%></header>
  <main><form id="form1" runat="server" class="form-horizontal">
    <div class="row"><%-- row 1 --%>
        <div class="col-sm-12"><h1>Your shopping cart</h1></div>
        <div class="col-sm-6"><%-- cart display column --%>
            <div class="form-group">
                <div class="col-sm-12"><asp:ListBox ID="lstCart"
                    runat="server" CssClass="form-control"></asp:ListBox></div>
            </div>
        </div>
        <div class="col-sm-6"><%-- cart edit buttons column --%>
            <div class="form-group">
                <div class="col-sm-12"><asp:Button ID="btnRemove"
                    runat="server" Text="Remove Item"
                    OnClick="btnRemove_Click" CssClass="btn" /></div>
                <div class="col-sm-12"><asp:Button ID="btnEmpty"
                    runat="server" Text="Empty Cart" OnClick="btnEmpty_Click"
                    CssClass="btn" /></div>
            </div>
        </div>
    </div><%-- end of row 1 --%>
    <div class="row"><%-- row 2 --%>
        <div class="col-sm-12">
            <div class="form-group"><%-- message label --%>
                <asp:Label ID="lblMessage" runat="server"
                    EnableViewState="False"
                    CssClass="text-info col-sm-12"></asp:Label>
            </div>
            <div class="form-group"><%-- buttons --%>
                <div class="col-sm-12">
                    <asp:Button ID="btnContinue" runat="server"
                        PostBackUrl="~/Order.aspx" Text="Continue Shopping"
                        CssClass="btn" />
                    <asp:Button ID="btnCheckOut" runat="server"
                        Text="Check Out" OnClick="btnCheckOut_Click"
                        CssClass="btn" />
                </div>
            </div>
        </div>
    </div><%-- end of row 2 --%>
  </form></main>
</div>
```

Description

- The Cart.aspx page uses a list box to display the shopping cart.

- The lblMessage server control has its EnableViewState property set to False so messages set by the C# code will clear when the page posts back.

- The btnContinue button uses cross-page posting to post back to the Order.aspx page. The other buttons post back to the Cart page, where the event handler specified by the OnClick property of the button is executed.

Figure 4-19   The aspx code for the Cart page

The C# code for the Cart page

Figure 4-20 presents the code-behind file for the Cart page. Like the Order page, this code starts with a series of using directives that Visual Studio added when the page was created. Also like the Order page, the remaining code is stored within the Ch04Cart namespace.

The code for the Cart class starts by declaring a class-level variable that will hold the CartItemList object for the shopping cart. Then, each time the page is loaded, the Page_Load method calls the GetCart method of the CartItemList class to retrieve the shopping cart from session state and store it in this variable.

If the page is being loaded for the first time, the Page_Load method also calls the DisplayCart method. This method starts by clearing the list box that will display the shopping cart items. Then, it uses a for loop to add an item to the list box for each item in the shopping cart list. Notice that this statement uses the Count property of the CartItemList object to get the number of CartItem objects in the cart, and the Display method of the CartItem objects to get the strings to display in the list box control.

If the user clicks the Remove Item button, the btnRemove_Click method is executed. This method begins by making sure that the cart contains at least one item and that an item in the shopping cart list box is selected. If so, the RemoveAt method of the CartItemList object is used to delete the selected item from the shopping cart. Then, the DisplayCart method is called to refresh the items in the list box. If not, the user is notified to select an item to remove.

If the user clicks the Empty Cart button, the btnEmpty_Click method is executed. This method calls the Clear method of the CartItemList object to clear the shopping cart. Then, it calls the Clear method of the Items collection of the list box to clear that list.

Please note, though, that instead of using the Clear method to clear the list box, this method could call the DisplayCart method. Similarly, the btnRemove_Click method could use the Remove method of the Items collection of the list box to remove the item at the selected index instead of calling the DisplayCart method. This just shows that there is usually more than one way that methods like these can be coded.

Also note that the Cart page doesn't contain a method for the Click event of the Continue Shopping button. That's because this button uses the PostBackUrl property to post directly to the Order.aspx page. As a result, the Cart page isn't executed if the user clicks the Continue Shopping button.

The code-behind file for the Cart page (Cart.aspx.cs)

```csharp
// default using directives

namespace Ch04Cart
{
    public partial class Cart : System.Web.UI.Page
    {
        private CartItemList cart;

        protected void Page_Load(object sender, EventArgs e)
        {
            // retrieve cart object from session state on every postback
            cart = CartItemList.GetCart();
            // on initial page load, add cart items to list control
            if (!IsPostBack) this.DisplayCart();
        }
        protected void btnRemove_Click(object sender, EventArgs e)
        {
            // if cart contains items and user has selected an item...
            if (cart.Count > 0) {
                if (lstCart.SelectedIndex > -1) {
                    // remove selected item from cart and re-display cart
                    cart.RemoveAt(lstCart.SelectedIndex);
                    this.DisplayCart();
                }
                else { // if no item is selected, notify user
                    lblMessage.Text = "Please select the item to remove.";
                }
            }
        }
        private void DisplayCart()
        {
            // remove all current items from list control
            lstCart.Items.Clear();

            // loop through cart and add each item's display value to the list
            for (int i = 0; i < cart.Count; i++) {
                lstCart.Items.Add(cart[i].Display());
            }
        }
        protected void btnEmpty_Click(object sender, EventArgs e)
        {
            // if cart has items, clear both cart and list control
            if (cart.Count > 0) {
                cart.Clear();
                lstCart.Items.Clear();
            }
        }
        protected void btnCheckOut_Click(object sender, EventArgs e)
        {
            lblMessage.Text = "Sorry, that function hasn't been "
                            + "implemented yet.";
        }
    }
}
```

Figure 4-20   The C# code for the Cart page

The custom CSS for the Shopping Cart application

The Shopping Cart application uses Bootstrap CSS classes for most of its layout and styling. However, it also uses a custom style sheet that overrides some of the Bootstrap styles and adds two new rule sets. You can see this style sheet in figure 4-21.

The first four rule sets in this style sheet override styles in the Bootstrap style sheet. The first rule set changes the container class by adding a solid grey border around it and adding space between the border and the top of the browser. If you look at the browser window in figure 4-1, you can see how these styles affect the appearance of the page.

The second rule set changes the jumbotron class by making the banner image the background. Then, it makes the image size responsive to changes in the viewport size by setting the background-size property to 100%. Finally, it adds space above the jumbotron. Again, you can look back at figure 4-1 to see how these styles affect the appearance of the jumbotron.

The third rule set changes the btn class by setting the margin-bottom property to 1em. This adds space below each button that is assigned to this class. That makes the buttons lay out better when the viewport narrows and the buttons stack on top of each other.

The fourth rule set overrides the Bootstrap style for label elements so they are a normal font weight. This is necessary if you don't want a label to be bold, since that's the Bootstrap default for label elements.

The last two rules sets in this style sheet are for two of the server controls on the form. These rules sets select the controls by id. The first one makes the text for the label that displays the unit price bold. The second one sets the minimum height of the list box that displays the cart items to 8em.

The CSS file for the Shopping Cart application

```
/*** Bootstrap overrides ***/
.container {
    border:1px solid #cecece;
    margin-top: 1em;
}

.jumbotron {
    background: url("/Images/banner.jpg");
    background-size: 100% 100%;
    margin-top: 1em;
}

.btn {
    margin-bottom: 1em;
}

label {
    font-weight: normal;
}

/*** server controls ***/
#lblUnitPrice {
    font-weight: bold;
}

#lstCart {
    min-height: 8em;
}
```

Description

- This CSS style sheet adjusts the Bootstrap container, jumbotron, and btn classes and overrides the default Bootstrap style for the label element.

- It also adds some custom styles for individual label and list box server controls.

Figure 4-21   The custom CSS for the Shopping Cart application

Perspective

The purpose of this chapter has been to get you started with the development of multi-page web applications. Now, if this chapter has worked, you should be able to develop multi-page applications of your own. Yes, there's a lot more to learn, but you should be off to a good start.

Frankly, though, much of the C# code in the Shopping Cart application is difficult, even in a simple application like this one. So if your experience with C# is limited, you may have trouble understanding some of the code. You may also have trouble writing the same type of code for your new applications.

If that's the case, we recommend that you get our latest C# book. It will quickly get you up to speed with the C# language. It will show you how to use dozens of the .NET classes, like the List<T> class, and some of the newer C# features like string interpolation, lambda expressions, and expression bodied properties and methods. It focuses on how to develop object-oriented Windows applications, and is a terrific on-the-job reference. And it is the perfect companion to this book, which assumes that you already know C#.

Terms

class library
HTTP redirect message
cross-page posting
custom property
absolute URL
relative URL
data source
bind a data source
session state
session state object
session ID
cookie
Data Transfer Object (DTO)

Summary

- In an ASP.NET web application, the Models folder is used for non-page classes, the App_Data folder is used for database files, and the Bin folder is used for compiled assemblies such as *class libraries*.

- By default, the starting page for a web application is the Default.aspx page, but you can change that to whichever page you want.

- In the code-behind file for a web form, you can use the Transfer method to go to another page without going back to the browser. Or, you can use the Redirect method to send an *HTTP redirect message* to the browser that causes the browser to request the new page.

- With *cross-page posting*, the PostBackUrl property of a button specifies the page that's requested when the user clicks the button. Then, you can use the PreviousPage property along with the FindControl method or *custom properties* to get the data from the previous page.

- To identify the page that control should be transferred to, you can use an *absolute* or a *relative URL*.

- In an ASP.NET web application, a *data source* can be used to get the data from specific rows and columns of a database like a SQL Server database. Then, you can *bind* the data source to a control like a drop-down list. You can also use C# to get data from a data source.

- ASP.NET uses *session state* to create a *session state object* for each user of an application. This object can be used to store data that's used across the pages of an application.

- To make session state work, ASP.NET creates a *session ID* that's sent to the browser as a *cookie*. Then, the browser returns this ID to the server with each request so the server can associate the user with the right session state object.

Exercise 4-1   Build the Shopping Cart application

This exercise guides you through the process of building a Shopping Cart application like the one that's presented in this chapter. To save time, though, you'll start from a web application that has the folders and files for the images, database, non-page classes, and style sheets needed by the application.

Open the web application and review its folders and files

1. Open the web application named Ex04Cart in the C:\aspnet46_cs directory. Then, run the application to see that an error message is displayed in the browser, which means the starting page hasn't been set. Stop the application and set the starting page to the Order form.

2. Run the application again. When the Order page is displayed, click on the Go to Cart button to go to the Cart page. Note that both forms have all of the controls that are required, but only the Go to Cart button works.

3. Stop the application, return to Visual Studio, and review the folders and files. Note that the Models folder contains the three class files that this application uses, the App_Data folder contains a SQL Server database (Halloween.mdf), and the Content folder contains the Bootstrap style sheets and a custom style sheet named site.css. Note also that the aspx files for the web forms include all of the controls including the validation controls, but their code-behind files contain only starts for the Page_Load method.

4. Open the Web.config file and note that unobtrusive validation has been turned off for the entire web application with the Web.config setting shown in figure 2-13 of chapter 2.

Build out the Order page

5. Open the Order form in Source view.

6. Add a SqlDataSource control right after the code for the drop-down list, and configure the data source to get product data from the Halloween database as shown in figures 4-8 and 4-9. Use HalloweenConnection as the name of the connection string for the database, and click on the Test Query button in the last step to see the data that's returned by the data source.

7. Switch to Design view and display the smart tag menu for the drop-down list. Then, set Enable AutoPostBack to True, and bind the drop-down list to the data source as described in figure 4-10. If necessary, click the Refresh Schema link so you can see the field names in the drop-down lists of the dialog box.

8. Run the application to see how the drop-down list works. Now, you should be able to select a product from the list. Although the page will post back when you do that, nothing else will happen. Stop the application and return to Visual Studio.

Add the C# code for the Order form

As you enter the C# code for the Order form, be sure to take full advantage of the IntelliSense and snippets that Visual Studio provides.

9. In Design view, double-click outside the body of the Order form to switch to the code-behind file in the Code Editor. You'll be taken to the start of the event handler for the Load event. Before coding the Load event handler, add a using directive for the System.Data namespace, as shown in figure 4-18.

10. Add a class-level declaration for a Product object before the Load event handler, as shown in figure 4-18. This is the object that's defined by the Product class in the Models folder.

11. Enter the GetSelectedProduct method that's shown in figure 4-18. This should be coded right after the code for the Load event handler. The GetSelectedProduct method gets the data for the product that's selected in the drop-down list. Then, it instantiates a new Product object. Last, it puts the database data for the product in the properties of the Product object, and it returns that Product object.

12. Enter the code for the Load event handler that binds the SQL data source to the drop-down list the first time the page is requested. After that, add the code that displays the data and image for the selected product in the Order form each time the page is requested. To do that, use the GetSelectedProduct method that you just entered.

13. Run the application to test the code. Now, when you select a product from the list, the appropriate data for the product should be displayed on the page.

14. In Design view, double-click on the Add to Cart button to open the Code Editor and start an event handler for the Click event of that button. Then, add code to the event handler so it adds the selected product to the session object. To do that, you can use the GetCart and AddItem methods of the CartItemList class, the indexer of the CartItemList class, and the AddQuantity method of the CartItem class, as shown in figure 4-18.

Build out the Cart page and add its C# code

15. Open the aspx file for the Cart page in Design view, and set the PostBackUrl property of the Continue Shopping button so it displays the Order page. Now, test that change to make sure this button works correctly.

16. Select the Cart page in the Solution Explorer, and then click the View Code button at the top of the Solution Explorer window to display the code-behind file in the Code Editor. Then, before the Load event handler, declare a class-level CartItemList variable that can be accessed by all the methods for this form.

17. Code the DisplayCart method that's shown in figure 4-20. Here, lstCart refers to the list box that's on the form.

18. Code the Load event handler. Within this event handler, you can use the GetCart method of the CartItemList class to get the cart from session state, and you can use the DisplayCart method to display the cart items in the list box, as shown in figure 4-20.

19. Run the application to test this code. Now, when you select a product on the Order page, enter a quantity, and click the Add to Cart button, the application should add the item to the cart and display it in the Cart page.

20. Add the event handlers for the Click events of the Remove, Empty, and Check Out buttons. To start the event handler for each button, switch to Design view and double-click on the button. Then, add the code for the event handlers as shown in figure 4-20.

Test everything and experiment

21. At this point, the entire application should work correctly. If it doesn't, find the problem and fix it.

22. If you want to experiment with any aspect of this application, do that now. For instance, add the total price (quantity times unit price) for each item in the cart so each line in the cart looks like this:

    ```
    Austin Powers (2 @ $79.99 each = $159.98)
    ```

23. When you're through experimenting, close the solution.

5

How to test and debug ASP.NET applications

If you've done much programming, you know that testing and debugging are often the most difficult and time-consuming phase of program development. Fortunately, Visual Studio includes an integrated debugger that can help you locate and correct even the most obscure bugs. And ASP.NET includes a trace feature that displays useful information as your ASP.NET pages execute.

In this chapter, you'll learn how to use both of these debugging tools. You'll also learn how to use Browser Link to test an application in two or more browsers at the same time. You'll learn how to use the browser's developer tools to analyze the HTML and CSS for a page And you'll learn how to use Visual Studio's Diagnostic Tools to analyze a web application's performance.

How to test an ASP.NET web application

When you *test* a web application, you try to make it fail. In other words, the goal of testing is to find all of the errors. When you *debug* an application, you find the cause of all of the errors that you've found and fix them.

To test an ASP.NET application, you typically start by running it from Visual Studio in the default browser. Then, you test the application with other web browsers to make sure it works right in all of them, even if they're all using the same application at the same time.

How to test a web application

Unless you've changed it, Windows uses Internet Explorer as its default browser. Figure 5-1 presents six different ways you can run a web application with the default browser. Three of these techniques start the debugger so you can use its features to debug any problems that might arise. The other three don't start the debugger.

All of the techniques in this figure except the View in Browser command start the application and display the application's designated start page. However, the View in Browser command displays the selected page. For example, if you right-click the Cart page and choose View in Browser, the Cart page will be displayed. This command is useful if you want to test a page without having to navigate to it from the designated start page.

Once you've thoroughly tested an application with your default browser, you'll want to test it for *browser incompatibilities*. To do that, you need to run your application in all of the common browsers to make sure it looks and works the same in all of them. One way to do that is to run the application in each browser separately. Another way is to run the application in two or more browsers at the same time. Both of these techniques are presented in this figure. Note that if you run an application in two or more browsers at the same time, the debugger won't be available from those browsers. However, you can still run the application with debugging in a separate browser if you want to debug it while the other browsers are still open.

When you're working with database applications, you'll also need to test for *concurrency errors*. Those errors can occur when two different users try to make changes to the same row in a database table at the same time. Generally you'll need to run the application in two or more browsers at the same time to test for these types of errors. You'll learn more about concurrency issues in section 3 of this book.

The browser menu in the Standard toolbar

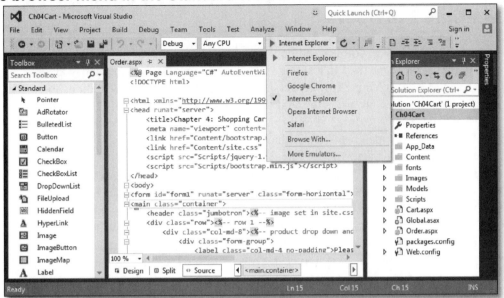

How to run an application in the default browser with debugging

- Click the browser name in the Standard toolbar, press F5, or choose the Debug→Start Debugging command.

How to run an application without debugging

- Press Ctrl+F5, choose Debug→Start Without Debugging, or right-click a page in the Solution Explorer and choose View in Browser.

How to stop an application that's run with debugging

- Press Shift+F5, click the Stop Debugging button in the Debug toolbar, or choose Debug→Stop Debugging.

How to run an application in a different browser

- If you want to change the default browser, click on the down arrow to the right of the browser name in the Standard toolbar, as shown above. Then, run the application.
- If you want to run an application in a different browser without changing the default, click on Browse With in the drop-down list or Browse With in the shortcut menu for a form. Then, in the Browse With dialog box, select the browser you want to use and click the Browse button to run the application without debugging.

How to run an application in two or more browsers at the same time

- In the Browse With dialog box described above, hold down the Ctrl key, select the browsers you want to use, and then click the Browse button.
- When you run an application in two or more browsers at the same time, the debugger isn't available from those browsers. To use the debugger, you have to run the application in a separate browser with debugging as described above.

Figure 5-1   How to test a web application

How to use Browser Link to test a web application in multiple browsers

In the last figure, you learned how to open your page in two or more browsers at the same time to test your web application. Once you identify an issue and make a change to your web application, though, it can be tedious to refresh all the open browsers to see if the change fixed the problem. Fortunately, Visual Studio has a feature called *Browser Link* that makes this process easier by refreshing all the open browsers with one click.

Figure 5-2 shows how to use the Browser Link feature. Here, the Shopping Cart application is being run in both Chrome and Internet Explorer at the same time. You can see that these two browsers are connected to Browser Link by pointing to the Refresh button to the right of the browser name as shown here.

When you make changes to the HTML for a web page, you can refresh all of the linked browsers by simply clicking the Refresh button or using its keyboard shortcut. Then, you can switch to each browser to see the changes. Note that you don't have to save the changes when you use one of these techniques. Instead, Visual Studio saves the changes for you.

When you make changes to the CSS for a web page, you can see the changes in the browsers without even clicking the Refresh button. This is made possible by the CSS Auto-Sync feature. This can save you a lot of time when you're trying to make small adjustments to the look of a web page.

The Browser Link and the CSS Auto-Sync features are enabled by default in Visual Studio 2015. If you want to turn off either of these features, though, you can use the Browser Link drop-down menu shown in this figure. You can also use this menu to open the Browser Link dashboard. This dashboard displays all connected browsers and includes a link that takes you to more information about Browser Link. Also, if Browser Link isn't working, this dashboard will tell you what prerequisites are needed.

Browser Link works by using an ASP.NET library called SignalR. SignalR creates a communication channel between ASP.NET and the browsers you select. Browser Link also registers an HTTP module with ASP.NET that dynamically inserts, or injects, script elements into pages sent from the server. Because of that, no browser plugin is required. Note that no code is actually added to the HTML files when you use Browser Link, so these script elements won't be included when the web application is deployed. If you want to learn more about how SignalR works and how you can use it in your ASP.NET web applications, you can go to http://asp.net/signalr.

The Cart application running in Chrome and IE at the same time

The Refresh button and Browser Link menu in the Standard toolbar

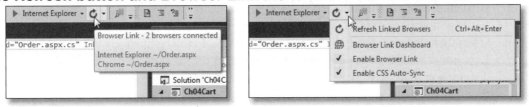

How to view all linked browsers

- Hover your mouse over the Refresh button in the Standard toolbar to see a list of the browsers that are connected to your web application.

Two ways to refresh all linked browsers

- Click on the Refresh button, or press Ctrl+Alt+Enter.

Description

- You can use *Browser Link* to refresh all connected browsers after you make a change.
- From the Browser Link drop-down menu, you can open the Browser Link dashboard, enable or disable the Browser Link functionality, and enable or disable CSS Auto-Sync.
- For HTML changes, you need to refresh the connected browsers as described above.
- For CSS changes, if Enable CSS Auto-Sync is checked, any changes you make are pushed to the linked browsers as soon as you make them, without a refresh.

Figure 5-2   How to use Browser Link to test a web application in multiple browsers

How to use the browser's developer tools

When you test your application and find that the pages aren't formatted correctly in all browsers, you need to change the HTML or CSS so the formatting is correct. In some cases, though, it's hard to figure out what HTML or CSS needs to be changed. To help you with that, the major browsers provide *developer tools* that let you view the HTML that's rendered by the web server and the CSS styles that are applied to the HTML. Figure 5-3 presents the basic skills for working with the developer tools in the five major browsers.

To start, you can open or close the developer tools in Chrome, Firefox, and IE by pressing F12. Because of that, these tools are sometimes called *F12 tools*. If you're using Opera or Safari, though, you have to use other techniques as described in this figure to open and close the developer tools.

The screen in this figure shows the developer tools in Internet Explorer. To display the HTML and CSS for a page, you use the DOM Explorer tab as shown here. The left pane of this tab displays the HTML in a hierarchical structure. Then, you can expand and collapse elements using the arrowheads to the left of the elements. In this case, the div element that's assigned to the Bootstrap container class has been expanded so you can see that it contains a header element and a main element. In addition, the main element has been expanded so you can see that it contains a form element.

If you want to see the styles that have been applied to any element, you just select that element. Then, the styles are displayed in the right pane of the DOM Explorer tab. In this figure, for example, you can see some of the styles for the div element that's assigned to the container class. Also notice the *bread crumbs* trail that's displayed at the bottom of the left pane when you select an element. This trail shows where the selected element is located in the HTML hierarchy.

In addition to listing the styles for each rule set, the right pane shows what style sheet contains the rule set. In this example, you can see three rule sets for the container class: the first one is in the site.css style sheet, and the other two are in the bootstrap.min.css style sheet. Notice that one of the rules sets in the bootstrap.min.css style sheet is coded within a media query. This media query indicates that the styles in the rule set should be applied only if the width of the viewport is 768 pixels or more.

Although it's not shown here, you should know that if any style is overridden, it will appear with a line through it. That can be helpful when you're trying to figure out why your styles aren't working the way you expect.

One of the best uses for the developer tools is to determine the cause of formatting and style issues. Another is to see the HTML that's generated by ASP.NET for viewstate and server controls, or to see the JavaScript that's generated for the validation controls or Browser Link. In fact, you can see the beginning of the first Browser Link script tag in the screen capture in this figure.

Although this figure shows the developer tools for Internet Explorer, the developer tools for the other browsers are much the same. The best way to learn how to use these tools is to experiment with them. You can also learn about all of the functionality provided by these tools by searching for a training video online.

Internet Explorer with the DOM Explorer of the developers tools open

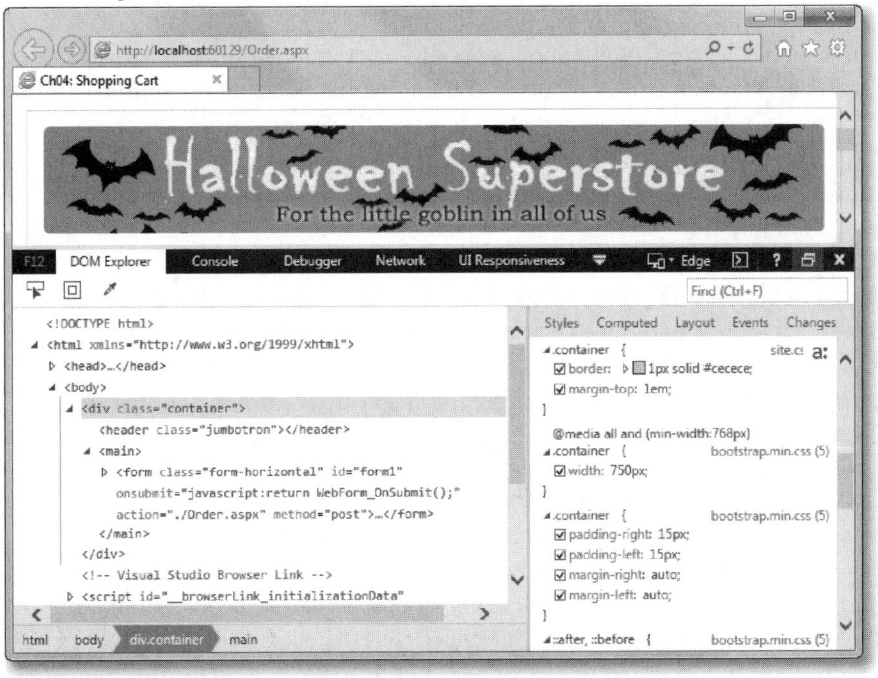

How to open and close the developer tools in Chrome, Firefox, and IE

- Press F12 to open. Or, right-click an element in the page and select Inspect Element.
- Press F12 to close. Or, click on the X in the upper right corner of the tools panel.

How to open and close the developer tools in Opera and Safari

- Right-click an element in the page and select Inspect Element to open.
- Click on the X in the upper right corner of the tools panel to close.
- In Safari, you first need to enable the developer tools. For information on how to do that, you can go to http://debugbrowser.com/#safari.

How to view the rendered HTML and CSS styles

- Open the appropriate panel by clicking on its tab. In IE, the tab is called DOM Explorer. In Firefox, it's called Inspector. In Chrome, Safari, and Opera, it's called Elements.
- Expand the nodes to navigate to the element you want. Then, click on that element.
- The HTML for a page is shown in the left pane, and the CSS styles that have been applied to the selected element are shown in the right pane.

Description

- The *developer tools* of the major browsers provide some excellent debugging features, like viewing the HTML rendered by the web server and viewing the styles applied to those HTML elements.
- These tools are often called *F12 tools* because of how they're opened in some browsers.

Figure 5-3   How to use the browser's developer tools

How to use the Exception Assistant

As you test an ASP.NET application, you may encounter runtime errors that prevent an application from executing. When that happens, an *exception* is thrown. Often, you can write code that anticipates these exceptions, catches them, and processes them appropriately. If an exception isn't caught, however, the application enters break mode and the Exception Assistant displays a dialog box like the one in figure 5-4.

As you can see, the Exception Assistant dialog box indicates the type of exception that occurred and points to the statement that caused the error. In many cases, this information is enough to determine what caused the error and what should be done to correct it. For example, the Exception Assistant dialog box in this figure indicates that the input string isn't in a correct format, and that the problem was encountered in this line of code for the Order page:

```
cart.AddItem(selectedProduct,
             Convert.ToInt32(txtQuantity.Text));
```

Based on that information, you can assume that the Text property of the txtQuantity control contains a value that can't be converted to an integer, since the AddItem method of the cart object accepts an integer as its second parameter. This could happen if the application didn't check that the user entered an integer value into this control. (To allow this error to occur, the range validator for the Quantity text box on the Order page was disabled.)

Many of the exceptions you'll encounter will be system exceptions like the one shown here. These exceptions apply to general system operations such as arithmetic operations and the execution of methods. If your applications use databases, you can also encounter ADO.NET and data provider exceptions. If, for example, the connection string for a database is invalid, a data provider exception will occur. And if you try to add a row to a data table with a key that already exists, an ADO.NET error will occur. More about this in section 3.

In some cases, you won't be able to determine the cause of an error just by analyzing the information in the Exception Assistant dialog box. Then, to get more information about the possible cause of an exception, you can use the list of troubleshooting tips in the dialog box. The items in this list are links that display additional information in a Help window. You can also use the other links in this dialog box to search for more help online, to display the content of the exception object, and to copy the details of the exception to the clipboard. If you still can't determine the cause of an error, you can use the Visual Studio debugger to help you locate the problem.

The Exception Assistant dialog box

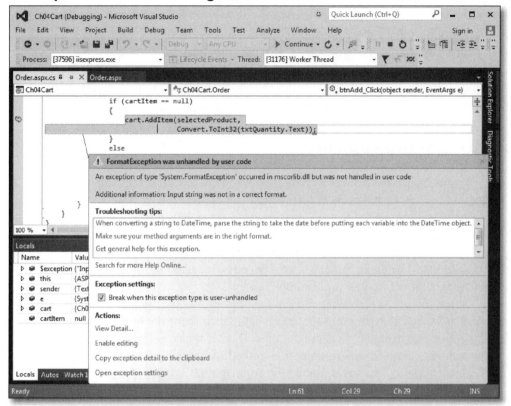

Description

- If you run an application with debugging and an *exception* occurs, the application enters break mode and the Exception Assistant displays a dialog box like the one above.

- The Exception Assistant provides the name and description of the exception, and it points to the statement in the program that caused the error. It also includes a list of troubleshooting tips that you can click on to display more information.

- The information provided by the Exception Assistant is often all you need to determine the cause of an error. If not, you can close this window and then use the debugging techniques presented in this chapter to determine the cause.

- If you continue program execution after an exception occurs, ASP.NET terminates the application and sends a Server Error page to the browser. This page is also displayed if you run an application without debugging. It provides the name of the application, a description of the exception, and the line in the program that caused the error.

Figure 5-4   How to use the Exception Assistant

How to use the debugger

The topics that follow introduce you to the basic techniques for using the Visual Studio *debugger* to debug an ASP.NET application. Note that these techniques are almost identical to the techniques you use to debug a Windows application. If you've debugged Windows applications, then, you shouldn't have any trouble debugging web applications.

How to use breakpoints

Figure 5-5 shows how to use *breakpoints* in an ASP.NET application. Note that you can set a breakpoint before you run an application or as an application is executing. Remember, though, that an application ends after it generates a page. So if you switch from the browser to Visual Studio to set a breakpoint, the breakpoint won't be taken until the next time the page is executed. If you want a breakpoint to be taken the first time a page is executed, then, you'll need to set the breakpoint before you run the application.

After you set a breakpoint and run the application, the application enters *break mode* before it executes the statement that contains the breakpoint. In this illustration, for example, the application will enter break mode before it executes the statement that caused the exception in the last figure to occur. Then, you can use the debugging features to debug the application.

In some cases, you may want to set more than one breakpoint. You can do that either before you begin the execution of the application or while the application is in break mode. Then, when you run the application, it will stop at the first breakpoint. And when you continue execution, the application will execute up to the next breakpoint.

Once you set a breakpoint, it remains active until you remove it. In fact, it remains active even after you close the project. If you want to remove a breakpoint, you can use one of the techniques presented in this figure.

You can also work with breakpoints from the Breakpoints window. To disable a breakpoint, for example, you can remove the check mark in front of the breakpoint. Then, the breakpoint isn't taken until you enable it again. You can also move to a breakpoint in the Code Editor window by selecting the breakpoint in the Breakpoints window and then clicking on the Go To Source Code button at the top of this window, or by right-clicking on the breakpoint in the Breakpoints window and choosing Go To Source Code from the shortcut menu.

If you experiment with the Breakpoints window, you'll see that it also provides other features like labeling groups of breakpoints, filtering breakpoints, and setting break conditions and hit counts. Most of the time, though, you won't need these more advanced features.

The Order page with a breakpoint

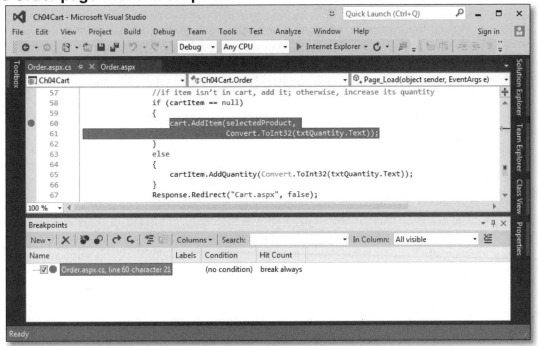

How to set and clear breakpoints

- To set a breakpoint, click in the margin indicator bar to the left of the statement at which you want the break to occur. The statement will be highlighted and a breakpoint indicator (a large red dot) will appear in the margin. You can set a breakpoint before you run an application or while you're debugging the application.

- To remove a breakpoint, click the breakpoint indicator. To remove all breakpoints at once, use the Debug→Delete All Breakpoints command.

- To disable all breakpoints, use the Debug→Disable All Breakpoints command. You can later enable the breakpoints by using the Debug→Enable All Breakpoints command.

- To display the Breakpoints window, use the Debug→Windows→Breakpoints command. This window is most useful for enabling and disabling existing breakpoints, but you can also use it to go to, add, modify, move, delete, label, or filter breakpoints.

Description

- When ASP.NET encounters a *breakpoint*, it enters *break mode* before it executes the statement on which the breakpoint is set.

- You can only set a breakpoint on a line that contains an executable statement.

- If you point to a breakpoint in the margin indicator bar, two icons appear. The first one lets you display the Breakpoint Settings window, which you can use to set conditional breakpoints as well as tracepoints (see figure 5-6). The second one lets you disable or enable a breakpoint.

Figure 5-5   How to use breakpoints

How to use tracepoints

Visual Studio also provides a feature called *tracepoints*. A tracepoint is a special type of breakpoint that performs an action when it's encountered. Figure 5-6 shows how tracepoints work.

To set a tracepoint, you use the Breakpoint Settings window to indicate what you want to do when the tracepoint is "hit." In most cases, you'll log a message to the Output Window and continue execution. The message you log can include variable values and other expressions as well as special keywords.

For example, the message shown here will include the value of the SelectedValue property of the ddlProducts control. You can see the output from this tracepoint in the Output window in this figure. Here, the first tracepoint message was displayed the first time the page was requested. The second message was displayed when a product was selected from the drop-down list.

Notice that the Output window is also used to display Visual Studio messages like the first three shown in this figure. Because of that, this window is displayed automatically when you run an application. If you close it and want to reopen it without running the application again, you can use the View→Output command.

By default, program execution continues after the tracepoint action is performed. If that's not what you want, you can remove the check mark from the Continue Execution option. Then, the program will enter break mode when the tracepoint action is complete.

After you set a tracepoint on a statement, the statement will be highlighted and a breakpoint indicator will appear in the margin. If program execution will continue after the tracepoint action is performed, the indicator will appear as a large diamond. But if the program will enter break mode, the standard breakpoint indicator is used.

Tracepoints are useful in situations where a standard breakpoint would be cumbersome, like in the execution of a loop. For example, suppose you have a loop that does 100 iterations, and an exception occurs in the middle somewhere. Imagine how tedious it would be to manually continue execution until you get to the error. In contrast, a tracepoint will give you a report of the loop's execution with just one click of the Start Debugging button.

The Order page with a tracepoint in the Breakpoint Settings window

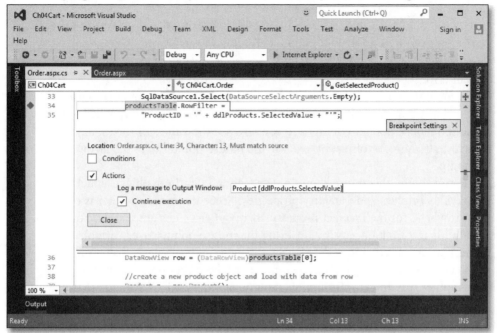

Output from the tracepoint in the Output window

Description

- A *tracepoint* is a special type of breakpoint that lets you perform an action. When ASP.NET encounters a tracepoint, it performs the action. Then, it continues execution if the Continue Execution option is checked or enters break mode if it isn't.

- You typically use tracepoints to print messages to the Output window. A message can include text, values, and special keywords. To include the value of a variable or other expression, place the variable or expression inside curly braces.

- To set a tracepoint, right-click on a statement and choose Breakpoint→Insert Tracepoint. Then, complete the Breakpoint Settings section and click Close. You can also convert an existing breakpoint to a tracepoint by pointing to its indicator and then clicking the Settings icon.

- If program execution will continue after the tracepoint action is performed, the tracepoint will be marked with a large red diamond, as shown above. Otherwise, it will be marked like any other breakpoint.

Figure 5-6   How to use tracepoints

How to work in break mode

Figure 5-7 shows the Order page in break mode. In this mode, the next statement to be executed is highlighted. Then, you can use the debugging information that's available to try to determine the cause of an exception or a logical error.

A great way to get information about what your code is doing is to use *data tips*. A data tip displays the current value of a variable or property when you hover the mouse pointer over it. You can also see the values of the members of an array, structure, or object by placing the mouse pointer over the arrowhead in a data tip.

For example, this figure shows a data tip for a CartItem object, which displays its Product and Quantity properties. Since the mouse pointer is over the arrowhead for the Product property, its member values are visible. You can see all this information, just by hovering the mouse pointer over variables and properties. When you move the mouse, the data tip disappears. However, you can keep it open by clicking on the pin icon to the right of a data tip.

Another way to get information about what your code is doing is to use *performance tips*, or PerfTips. A PerfTip displays to the right of the last statement to be executed, and it shows you how many milliseconds elapsed during the previous step. If you click on a PerfTip, it will take you to the Diagnostic Tools window that you'll learn about later in this chapter.

You can also see the values of variables and properties in the debugging windows in the bottom of the Visual Studio window. For example, the Locals window is visible in this figure. You'll learn more about the Locals window and some of the other debugging windows in a minute.

Once you're in break mode, you can use a variety of commands to control the execution of the application. The commands that are available from the Debug menu or the Debug toolbar are summarized in the table in this figure. You can also use shortcut keys to start these commands.

To execute the statements of an application one at a time, you use the Step Into command. Each time you use this command, the application executes the next statement, then returns to break mode so you can check the values of properties and variables and perform other debugging functions. The Step Over command is similar to the Step Into command, but it executes the statements in called methods without interruption (they are "stepped over").

The Step Out command executes the remaining statements in a method without interruption. When the method finishes, the application enters break mode before the next statement in the calling method is executed.

If your application gets caught in a processing loop so it keeps executing indefinitely without generating a page, you can force it into break mode by choosing the Debug→Break All command. This command lets you enter break mode any time during the execution of an application.

The Shopping Cart application in break mode

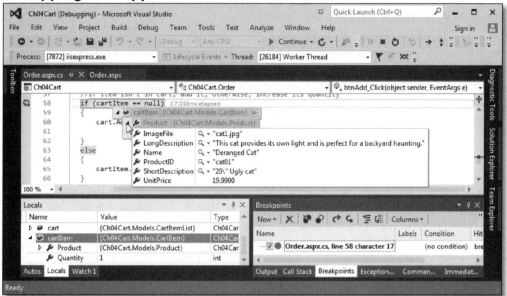

Commands in the Debug menu and toolbar

Command	Keyboard	Function
Start/Continue	F5	Start or continue execution of the application.
Break All	Ctrl+Alt+Break	Stop execution and enter break mode.
Stop Debugging	Shift+F5	Stop debugging and end execution of the application.
Restart	Ctrl+Shift+F5	Restart the entire application.
Step Into	F11	Execute one statement at a time.
Step Over	F10	Execute one statement at a time except for called methods.
Step Out	Shift+F11	Execute the remaining lines in the current method.

Description

- When you enter break mode, the debugger highlights the next statement to be executed. Then, you can use the debugging windows and the buttons in the Debug menu and toolbar to control the execution of the program and determine the cause of an exception.

- To display the value of a variable or property in a *data tip,* position the mouse pointer over the variable or property in the Code Editor window. You can also use the pin icon to the right of a data tip to pin the data tip so it remains displayed.

- To display the members of an array, structure, or object in a data tip, position the mouse pointer over it to display its data tip, and then point to the arrow to the left of the data tip.

- You can use the Step Into, Step Over, and Step Out commands to execute one or more statements and return to break mode.

- To stop an application that's caught in a loop, switch to the Visual Studio window and use the Debug→Break All command.

Figure 5-7   How to work in break mode

How to use the debugging windows to monitor variables

If you need to see the values of several application variables or properties, you can do that using the Autos, Locals, or Watch windows. By default, these windows are displayed in the lower left corner of the IDE when an application enters break mode. If they're not displayed, you can display them by selecting the appropriate command from the Debug→Windows menu.

The contents of the Locals and Watch windows are illustrated in figure 5-8. The Locals window displays information about the variables within the scope of the current method. If the code in a form is currently executing, this window also includes information about the form and all of the controls on the form. The Autos window is similar to the Locals window, but it only displays information about the variables used in the current statement and the previous statement.

Unlike the Autos and Locals windows, the Watch windows let you choose the values that are displayed. For example, the Watch window in this figure displays the SelectedValue property of the ddlProducts control. You can also add properties of the page or of business classes to a Watch window, as well as the values of expressions. In fact, an expression doesn't have to exist in the application for you to add it to a Watch window.

To add an item to a Watch window, you can type it directly into the Name column. Alternatively, if the item appears in the Code Editor window, you can highlight it in that window and then drag it to a Watch window. You can also highlight the item in the Code Editor or a data tip and then right-click on it and select the Add Watch command to add it to the Watch window that's currently displayed. You can display up to four Watch windows.

The Immediate window is useful for displaying the values of variables or properties that don't appear in the Code Editor window. To display a value, you type a question mark followed by the name of the variable or property. For instance, the first query in the Immediate window in this figure displays a CartItem's properties. In the second query, you can see that IntelliSense is available to help you enter expressions into this window.

The commands that you enter into the Immediate window remain there until you exit from Visual Studio or explicitly delete them using the Clear All command in the shortcut menu for the window. That way, you can edit and reuse the same commands from one execution of an application to another without having to reenter them.

To execute a command that you've already entered in the Immediate window, scroll through the commands in the window to find the one you want. As you scroll, the commands are displayed at the bottom of the window. Then, you can select one and press Enter to execute it.

The Locals window and a Watch window

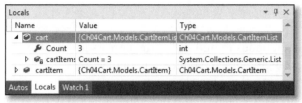

The Immediate window

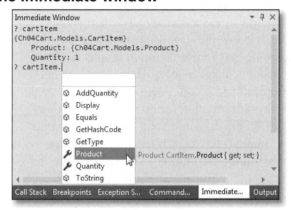

Description

- The Locals window displays information about the variables within the scope of the current method.

- The Watch windows let you view the values of variables and expressions that you specify, called *watch expressions*. You can display up to four Watch windows by using the Debug→Windows→Watch command.

- To add a watch expression, type a variable name or expression into the Name column, or highlight a variable or expression in the Code Editor window and drag it to the Watch window. You can also right-click on a variable, highlighted expression, or data tip in the Code Editor window and choose Add Watch.

- To delete a row from a Watch window, right-click the row and choose Delete Watch. To delete all the rows in a Watch window, right-click the window and choose Select All to select the rows, then right-click and choose Delete Watch.

- You can use the Immediate window to display specific values from a program during execution. To display a value in the Immediate window, enter a question mark followed by the expression whose value you want to display. Then, press the Enter key.

- To remove all commands and output from the Immediate window, right-click the window and choose the Clear All command from the shortcut menu. To execute an existing command, scroll to find it, select it, and press Enter.

- To display any of these windows, click on its tab if it's visible or select the appropriate command from the Debug→Windows menu.

Figure 5-8   How to use the debugging windows to monitor variables

How to use the Diagnostic Tools window to monitor performance

Up until now, you've learned techniques to find and correct errors in your C# code. In some cases, though, the problem with an application may be its performance. For instance, your page may load too slowly or it may appear to freeze when you click a button. Although Visual Studio has long had tools that let you troubleshoot these kinds of problems, these tools are now combined into a single Diagnostic Tools window. Figure 5-9 presents this window.

By default, the Diagnostic Tools window opens automatically when you run an application with debugging. This window presents information in two ways. First, the upper half of the window displays information in graphs along a timeline. Then, the lower half of the window displays detailed information in tabs. These graphs and tabs are synchronized and interact with each other.

The Diagnostic Tools window displays information for break events, memory usage, and CPU usage. Break events are the break, output, and IntelliTrace events that occur during a debugging session. (IntelliTrace records the execution of an application and is available only with the Enterprise edition.) The Events timeline shows when each of these events occurs, and the Events tab shows additional information about each event. A common use for this information is to see how many milliseconds elapsed between breakpoints.

The Process Memory timeline shows how much memory an application is using as it executes. To compare memory usage at different locations within the processing of an application, you can use the Memory Usage tab. This tab lets you take a snapshot of the current memory usage. Then, you can take additional snapshots later and compare them to previous snapshots to see how they differ.

The CPU Utilization timeline indicates the percentage of the CPU an application is using. The CPU Usage tab has instructions on how to run the CPU Usage Tool without debugging. This tool isn't available for ASP.NET applications, though.

How to debug client-side code

In addition to server-side C# code, most modern web applications contain client-side code like JavaScript. Fortunately, you can use breakpoints, data tips, and the debugging windows that you've learned about in this chapter with client-side code too. In figure 5-9, for instance, you can see the bootstrap.js file in the debugger with a breakpoint, a data tip, and several debugging windows.

Notice in this figure that when Visual Studio is in break mode, it displays a Script Documents section at the top of the Solution Explorer. This section lists all of the JavaScript files associated with the aspx file, including those generated by Visual Studio. That way, you can view and debug these files.

If you're going to use these debugging features with client-side code, we recommend that you make Internet Explorer your default browser. That's because these features don't work as well with other browsers.

The Diagnostic Tools window with a close up of the Events tab

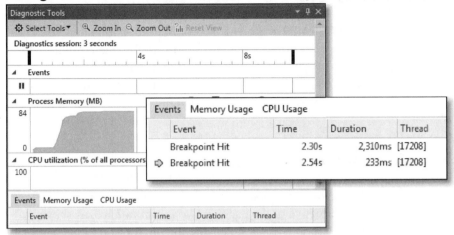

The bootstrap.js file in break mode

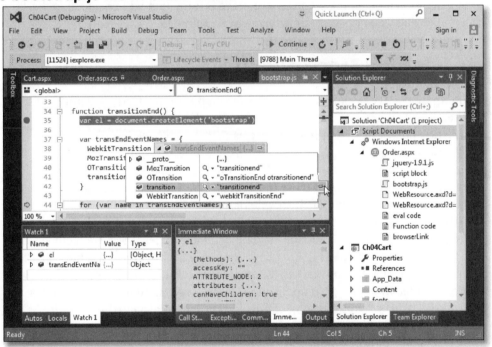

Description

- You can use the Diagnostic Tools window to find performance issues with your web application. A common use of this window is to see how much time has elapsed between breakpoints.

- You can use breakpoints, data tips, and the debugging windows with client-side JavaScript code just like you do with server side C# code. This works best in IE.

- The Script Documents section of the Solution Explorer displays all the JavaScript files associated with an aspx file, including those generated by Visual Studio.

Figure 5-9   How to use the Diagnostic Tools window and debug client-side code

How to use the trace feature

The *trace feature* is an ASP.NET feature that displays information that you can't get by using the debugger. The trace feature is most useful when trouble shooting a web application that you can't debug in Visual Studio, such as a production web application on a remote server. When you're working from Visual Studio, though, you shouldn't need the trace feature because the debugger works so well.

How to enable the trace feature

To use the trace feature, you must first enable tracing. To do that, you add a Trace attribute to the Page directive of the page that you want to trace, as shown in the first code example in figure 5-10. Or, to enable tracing for every page in the web application, you add an element to the Web.config file, as shown in the second code example in this figure. Then, trace information will be added to the end of each page's output each time the page is requested.

How to interpret trace output

In figure 5-10, you can see the start of the output for the Cart page after the user added an item to the shopping cart. After the request details, the trace information provides a list of trace messages that are generated as the application executes. Here, ASP.NET automatically adds Begin and End messages when major page events such as PreInit, Init, and InitComplete occur. If you scroll down to see all of these trace messages, you can see the variety of events that are raised during the life cycle of a page.

After the trace messages, you'll find information about the controls used by the page, the items in the session state object, the cookies that were included with the HTTP request, the HTTP request headers, and the server variables. In this figure, for example, you can see the session state and cookies data for the Cart page of the Shopping Cart application. In this case, an item named Cart has been added to the session state object. In addition, a cookie named ASP.NET_SessionId is used to keep track of the user's session ID so the user's session state object can be retrieved.

The beginning of the trace output for the Cart page

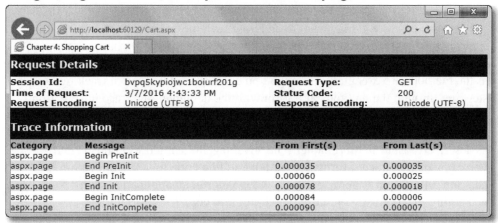

The session and cookies information for the Cart page

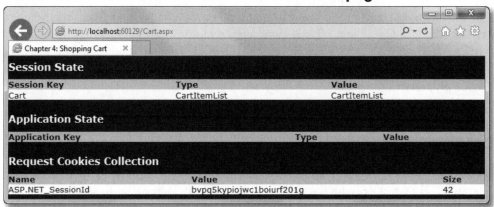

A Page directive that enables tracing for the Cart page

```
<%@ Page Language="C#" AutoEventWireup="true" CodeFile="Cart.aspx.cs"
Inherits="Cart" Trace="true" %>
```

A Web.config setting that enables tracing for the entire web application

```
<system.web>
    <trace enabled="true" pageOutput="true" />
</system.web>
```

Description

* The ASP.NET *trace feature* traces the execution of a page and displays trace information in tables at the bottom of that page.

* To activate the trace feature for a page, you add a Trace attribute set to True to its Page directive. To activate the trace feature for the web application, you add a trace element to the Web.config file as shown above.

Figure 5-10   How to enable the trace feature and interpret trace output

How to create custom trace messages

In some cases, you may want to add your own messages to the trace information that's generated by the trace feature. This can help you track the sequence in which the methods of a form are executed or the changes in the data as the methods are executed. Although you can also do this type of tracking by stepping through the methods of a form with the debugger, the trace information gives you a static listing of your messages.

Note, however, that you can also create this type of listing using tracepoints as described earlier in this chapter. The advantage to using tracepoints is that you can generate trace information without adding code to your application. In addition, this output is generated only when you run an application with debugging. In contrast, you have to add program code for custom trace messages, and the trace output is generated whenever the trace feature is enabled. If you don't have access to the debugger, though, trace messages are a good troubleshooting option.

To add messages to the trace information, you use the Write or Warn method of the TraceContext object. This is summarized in figure 5-11. The only difference between these two methods is that messages created with the Warn method appear in red. Notice that to refer to the TraceContext object, you use the Trace property of the page.

When you code a Write or Warn method, you can include both a category and a message or just a message. If you include a category, it will show in the category column in the trace output. If you include just a message, the category column is left blank, as shown in this figure. In most cases, you'll include a category because it makes it easy to see the sequence in which the methods were executed. However, leaving the category blank can make it easier to see your custom messages in a long list of trace output.

If you want to determine whether tracing is enabled before executing a Write or Warn method, you can use the IsEnabled property of the TraceContext object as shown in the example in this figure. Normally, though, you won't check the IsEnabled property because trace statements are executed only if tracing is enabled.

Common members of the TraceContext class

Property	Description
IsEnabled	True if tracing is enabled for the page.

Method	Description
Write(message)	Writes a message to the trace output.
Write(category, message)	Writes a message to the trace output with the specified category.
Warn(message)	Writes a message in red type to the trace output.
Warn(category, message)	Writes a message in red type to the trace output with the specified category.

Code that writes a custom trace message

```
if (Trace.IsEnabled)
{
    Trace.Write("Binding products drop-down list.");
}
```

A portion of a trace that includes a custom message

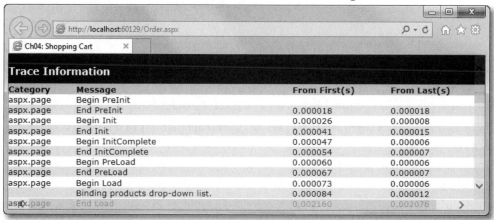

Description

- You can use the TraceContext object to write your own messages to the trace output. The TraceContext object is available through the Trace property of a page.

- Use the Write method to write a basic text message. Use the Warn method to write a message in red type.

- Trace messages are written only if tracing is enabled for the page. To determine whether tracing is enabled, you use the IsEnabled property of the TraceContext object.

- Traces messages in red and trace messages without a category can be easier to find in a long list of trace information.

Figure 5-11   How to create custom trace messages

Perspective

As you can now appreciate, Visual Studio provides a powerful set of tools for debugging ASP.NET applications. For simple applications, you can usually get the debugging done just by using breakpoints, data tips, and the Autos or Locals window. You may also need to step through critical portions of code from time to time.

For complex applications, though, you may discover the need for some of the other features that are presented in this chapter. With tools like these, a difficult debugging job becomes manageable.

Terms

testing	breakpoint
debugging	break mode
browser incompatibilities	tracepoint
concurrency error	data tip
Browser Link	performance tip
developer tools	watch expression
exception	trace feature
debugger	

Summary

- When you *test* an application, you try to find all of its errors. When you *debug* an application, you find the causes of the errors and fix them.

- To test for *browser incompatibilities*, you run a web application in all of the common browsers.

- To test a database application for *concurrency errors*, you run the application in more than one browser at the same time and then change the same rows in the database.

- You can use the browser's *developer tools* to find problems in your HTML and CSS, and Visual Studio's *Browser Link* to view changes in all open browsers.

- Visual Studio's *debugger* lets you set a *breakpoint*, step through the statements in an application when it is in *break mode*, and view the changes in the data after each statement is executed. This works on both server-side and client-side code.

- *Tracepoints* are like breakpoints but they also let you perform actions like printing messages in the Output window.

- *Data tips* provide an easy way to view the data when an application is in break mode. But you can also use the Locals, Watch, and Immediate windows for this.

- You can use the Diagnostic Tools window to monitor performance issues.

- The *trace feature* is useful when you have to test an application and Visual Studio isn't available. This happens when the web application has already been deployed on a remote server.

Exercise 5-1   Use the Visual Studio debugger

In this exercise, you'll use the debugger to step through the Shopping Cart application that you studied in chapter 4. However, you'll work with another version of it so you can experiment without changing the original version.

Use breakpoints, step through statements, and view data tips

1. Open the Ex05Cart web application in the aspnet46_cs directory. Then, set the starting page to the Order page.

2. Display the code for the Order page, and set a breakpoint on the statement in the Load event handler that calls the GetSelectedProduct method.

3. Run the application in the default browser. When the application enters break mode, point to the IsPostBack property to see that its value in the data tip is false. Then, point to the data tip and click the pin icon so the data tip remains open.

4. Use the Debug→Step Into command to execute the next statement. Notice that this statement is in the GetSelectedProduct method. Click the Step Into button in the Debug toolbar two more times to see that only one statement is executed each time.

5. Use the Debug→Step Out command to skip over the remaining statements in the GetSelectedProduct method. This should return you to the Page_Load method.

6. Click the Continue button in the Debug toolbar. This should execute the remaining statements in the Page_Load method and display the Order page.

7. Select another product from the combo box. This should cause the application to enter break mode again and stop on the statement that calls the GetSelectedProduct method. Notice that the data tip for the IsPostBack property is still displayed, but now its value is True.

8. Press the F10 key to execute the Step Over command. This should step over all statements in the GetSelectedProduct method and enter break mode before the next statement in the Page_Load method is executed.

9. Point to the selectedProduct variable to see its data tip, and then point to the arrowhead to its left to see the values of its members. Click outside the data tip to make it disappear.

10. Next, point to the Text property of the label variables that follow to display their data tips, and pin those data tips so they stay open. If necessary, drag the pinned data tips so you can see them better. Then, step through the statements that assign the product properties to the Text property of the labels and note how these values change.

Use the Locals and Autos window, a Watch window, and the Immediate window

11. Click on the Locals window tab and note the values that are displayed. Click the arrowhead to the left of the form object (this) to expand it and review the information that's available. When you're done, click the arrowhead again to collapse the information for this object.

12. Remove the breakpoint from the Page_Load method. Then, set another breakpoint on the statement in the GetSelectedProduct method that sets the value of the selected product's name, continue execution of the application, and select another product. When the application enters break mode again, click on the Autos window tab and note the variables that are displayed. Press F10 twice and see how the variables displayed in the Autos window change.

13. Display a Watch window. Add the Name column of the DataViewRow object to this window by selecting it and then dragging it from the Code Editor window. In the Watch window, it should look something like this:

    ```
    row["Name"].ToString()
    ```

    Then, enter an expression into the Watch window that displays the Count property of the DataView object. It should look something like this:

    ```
    productsTable.Count
    ```

14. Enter the same expression into the Immediate window, preceded by a question mark. Press the Enter key to see the value that's displayed. It should be 1.

15. Click the Stop Debugging button in the Debug toolbar to end the application. Note that the debugging windows close but the breakpoint remains in the Code Editor even after you have stopped debugging.

Exercise 5-2   Use the trace feature

In this exercise, you'll use the trace feature of ASP.NET to display trace output on the Order page of the Shopping Cart application that you created in the exercises for chapter 4.

1. If it's not already open, open the Ex05Cart web application. Then, use the Debug→Delete All Breakpoints command to delete any previous breakpoints.

2. Display the Order page in the Web Forms Designer in Source view. Then, enable tracing for the page by adding a Trace attribute to the Page directive as shown in figure 5-10.

3. Run the application and scroll down to see the trace output displayed below the controls on the Order page. View the trace information. In particular, review the session state information.

4. Add a product to the cart and go to the Cart page. Notice that the trace output isn't displayed on that page. Click on Continue Shopping to go back to the Order page. View the session state information again and notice there is now a Cart object in the session state data. When you're done, close the application.

Use custom trace messages

5. Add two custom trace messages to the GetSelectedProduct method as shown in figure 5-11. Put the first message at the top of this method. To do that, use the Trace.Warn method with the method name as the category and have the message indicate that the method is starting. Put the second message at the bottom of the GetSelectedProduct method, right before the return statement. Use the Trace.Write method, but don't include a category, and have the message indicate that a new Product object has been created.

6. Run the application to see what messages are displayed.

Section 2

ASP.NET essentials

The six chapters in this section expand upon the essentials that you learned in section 1. To start, chapter 6 shows you how to work with the server controls that can be used for developing web pages. Then, chapter 7 shows you how to work with the validation controls, and chapter 8 presents the several ways that you can manage the state of an application or form.

The next three chapters present features of ASP.NET that make it easier to develop professional web applications. Chapter 9 shows you how to use master pages to create pages with common elements. Chapter 10 shows you how to incorporate Bootstrap CSS and components in your pages, including components that make it easy for users to navigate through your site. And chapter 11 shows you how to use ASP.NET routing to provide friendly URLs that improve search engine optimization.

To a large extent, each of the chapters in this section is an independent unit. As a result, you don't have to read these chapters in sequence. If, for example, you want to know more about state management after you finish section 1, you can go directly to chapter 8. Eventually, though, you're going to want to read all six chapters. So unless you have a compelling reason to skip around, you may as well read the chapters in sequence.

6

How to use the standard server controls

In section 1, you learned the basic skills for working with some of the common server controls: labels, text boxes, buttons, and drop-down lists. Now, you'll learn more about working with those controls as well as how to use the rest of the standard server controls.

An introduction
to the standard server controls

The standard server controls are the ones in the Standard group of the Toolbox. These are the ones that get data from and present data in a web form.

The server controls you'll use the most

The two tables in figure 6-1 summarize the standard *server controls* that you'll use the most. If you've developed Windows applications or HTML pages, you should already be familiar with the operation of most of these controls. For instance, labels, text boxes, check boxes, radio buttons, drop-down lists, and buttons work the same way in Web Forms that they work in Windows applications and HTML pages.

In fact, the ASP.NET server controls are rendered as HTML elements. This is summarized by the second column in the tables in this figure, which present the HTML elements that ASP.NET generates for each type of control. For instance, a Label control is rendered as a span element, and a TextBox control is rendered as an input element. Similarly, some controls get rendered as two or more HTML elements. For instance, an ImageMap control gets rendered as an img element plus a related map element, and a DropDownList control gets rendered as a select element plus one option element for each item in the list.

What isn't shown in this table is that the type attribute of an HTML input element determines how the element looks and works. For instance, a typical text box is rendered as an input element with its type attribute set to "text", a check box is rendered as an input element with its type attribute set to "checkbox", and a file upload control is rendered as an input element with its type attribute set to "file".

For the most part, you don't need to know what HTML elements the server controls are rendered to. But if you use CSS to format those controls, you do need to know what elements are generated so you can code the selectors for the rule sets correctly. If necessary, you can view the source code when a page is rendered in a browser, but this table gives you a general idea of what you can expect.

This figure also answers the question: When should you use HTML elements instead of server controls, and vice versa? In brief, you should use HTML elements whenever the contents aren't going to change. If, for example, a label that identifies a text box isn't going to change, you should use the HTML label element instead of the Label control. In contrast, if the label is going to display text that is changed by the code-behind file based on user actions, the Label control is the right choice.

The other time to use server controls is when you don't know how to code the HTML that you need. Then, you can use the Properties window to set the properties for the corresponding server control and get the result that you want without using HTML. This makes sense when you just want to prototype an application and don't want to take the time to learn how to code the HTML. In the long run, though, you should learn how to use HTML instead of server controls whenever the data in the elements isn't going to change.

Common server controls

Name	HTML	Prefix	Description
Label	span	lbl	A label that displays descriptive information.
TextBox	input	txt	A text box that lets the user enter or modify a text value.
CheckBox	input/label	chk	A check box that can be turned on or off.
RadioButton	input/label	rdo	A radio button that can be turned on or off, but only one button in a group can be on.
Button	input	btn	A button that submits a page for processing.
LinkButton	<a>	lbtn	A link button that submits a page for processing.
ImageButton	input	ibtn	An image button that submits a page for processing.
Image	img	img	A control that displays an image.
ImageMap	img/map	imap	A control that displays an image with one or more clickable areas that submit the page for processing.
HyperLink	<a>	hlnk	A link that goes to another page or position on a page.
FileUpload	input	upl	A file upload control that consists of a text box and a Browse button that lets the user upload one or more files.

List server controls

Name	HTML	Prefix	Description
DropDownList	select/option	ddl	A drop-down list that lets the user choose one item.
ListBox	select/option	lst	A list box that lets the user choose one or more items.
CheckBoxList	input/label	cbl	A list of check boxes that can be turned on or off.
RadioButtonList	input/label	rbl	A list of radio buttons, but only one can be turned on or off.
BulletedList	ul or ol/li	blst	A bulleted list or numbered list.

When to use HTML elements instead of server controls

- When the contents of the controls aren't going to change, you should use HTML elements instead of server controls because server controls have some overhead.

When to use server controls instead of HTML

- When the contents of the controls are going to change, you should use server controls so it's easy to change the controls by using C# in the code-behind file.
- If you don't know how to code the HTML for the elements you want to use, server controls can help you get around that. Just add the controls to a form, use the Properties window to set their properties, and let ASP.NET generate the HTML.

Description

- In the tables above, the HTML column shows the HTML elements that are rendered for each *server control*. The Prefix column shows prefixes that are commonly used in the IDs for these controls.

Figure 6-1   The standard server controls that you'll use the most

How to use C# to work with the data in server controls

Like other objects, server controls have events that are fired when certain actions are performed on them. The table at the top of figure 6-2 summarizes some of these events for the common controls. When you click on a button control, for example, the Click event is fired. And when you change the text in a text box, the TextChanged event is fired.

If your application needs to respond to an event, you code a method called an *event handler*. When you generate an event handler from Visual Studio, as explained in chapter 2, an event attribute that names the event handler is added to the aspx code for the control. Then, you enter the C# code for the event handler in the code-behind file. This is illustrated by the first example in this figure. Here, the OnClick attribute of a button named btnCancel indicates that an event handler named btnCancel_Click will be executed when the Click event of the control is raised.

Often, though, you'll use the Load event handler to load data into the server controls of a form. This is illustrated by the second example in this figure. Here, data from a database is used to change the Text properties of two Label controls and the ImageUrl property of an Image control. This example is taken from the Cart application that you studied in chapter 4, and it shows how easy it is to change the data in server controls.

The third example in this figure presents a method that gets the data from server controls and stores it in a Customer object that is then saved in the Session object. Here, the Text property is used to get the data from two text boxes, and the SelectedValue property is used to get the data from a DropDownList control and a RadioButtonList control. You'll learn more about working with the list controls as you go through this chapter.

You can also use one event handler to handle events from two or more controls. To do that, you name the same event handler in the event attribute of each control. For instance, you can use the same event handler for the Click event of two different buttons. You'll see an example of an event handler like this later in this chapter.

Common control events

Event	Attribute	Controls
`Click`	`OnClick`	Button, image button, link button, image map
`Command`	`OnCommand`	Button, image button, link button
`TextChanged`	`OnTextChanged`	Text box
`CheckedChanged`	`OnCheckedChanged`	Check box, radio button
`SelectedIndexChanged`	`OnSelectedIndexChanged`	Drop-down list, list box, radio button list, check box list

A Click event hander

The aspx for a button control

```
<asp:Button id="btnCancel" runat="server" Text="Cancel Order"
    OnClick="btnCancel_Click" />
```

The event handler for the Click event of the control

```
protected void btnCancel_Click(object sender, EventArgs e)
{
    Session.Remove("Cart");
    Response.Redirect("Order.aspx");
}
```

A Load event handler that changes the data in server controls

```
protected void Page_Load(object sender, EventArgs e) {
    if (!IsPostBack) ddlProducts.DataBind();
    selectedProduct = this.GetSelectedProduct();
    lblName.Text = selectedProduct.Name;
    lblShortDescription.Text = selectedProduct.ShortDescription;
    imgProduct.ImageUrl = "Images/Products/" + selectedProduct.ImageFile;
}
```

A method that gets data from controls and puts them into a Customer object

```
private void GetCustomerData()
{
    if (customer == null)
        customer = new Customer();
    customer.EmailAddress = txtEmail.Text;
    customer.FirstName = txtFirstName.Text;
    customer.State = ddlState.SelectedValue;
    customer.ContactVia = rblContact.SelectedValue;
    Session["Customer"] = customer;
}
```

Description

- You can code *event handlers* that are called when a button is clicked, a value in a text box is changed, a check box or radio button is checked or unchecked, or the selection in a list is changed. Often, though, you'll process the data in the Load event handler for the page.

Figure 6-2   How to use C# to work with the data in server controls

How to set the focus, default button, tab order, and access keys for a form

Before you learn how to use specific server controls, figure 6-3 shows you how to do some housekeeping for the controls on a form. First, it shows how to set the control that receives the *focus* when the form is rendered in the browser. To do that, you use the DefaultFocus property of the form. In the aspx example in this figure, this property is set to the txtName control, which is the first text box on the form, so the user can start entering data in that text box.

Second, this figure shows how to set the *default button* for a form. That's the button that's activated by default when you press the Enter key. To identify that button, you set the DefaultButton property of the form. In the aspx example in this figure, this property is set to the btnSubmit button. Because of that, the form is posted back to the server when the Enter key is pressed, and the event handler for the Click event of that button is executed.

Third, this figure shows how to set the *tab order* for the controls on a form. That's the order in which the focus is moved from one control to another when the user presses the Tab key. By default, this is the sequence of the controls in the HTML, not including labels, and most browsers include links in the tab order. That means that if you set the focus to the first control on the form, the tab order is likely to work the way you want it to. Otherwise, you can use the TabIndex property to set the tab order for specific controls, but you usually won't need to do that.

Last, this figure shows how to set the *access keys* for the controls on a form. These let the user select controls by using keyboard shortcuts. If, for example, you designate N as the access key for an input field that accepts a customer's name, the user can move the focus directly to this field by pressing Alt+N in Internet Explorer, Chrome, Safari or Opera, or Alt+Shift+N in Firefox. (Press the Option key rather than the Alt key on a Mac.)

To create an access key, you add the AccessKey property to the control you want to create the keyboard shortcut for. Note, however, that the access keys that you define can conflict with the access keys that are defined for a browser. For example, most browsers use Alt+D to highlight the URL in the address bar. Because of that, you'll want to be sure to test them with all the modern browsers.

When you use access keys with text boxes that are identified by label elements or Label controls, you can assign the access key to the label and then underline the appropriate letter of the label. In this case, you should also code the for attribute for a label element or the AssociatedControlID property for a Label control to specify the control that should receive the focus when the user presses the access key.

You can also specify an access key for a button control as illustrated by the aspx code in this figure. However, you can't underline the access key in a Button control. That's because buttons are rendered by an input element that has "submit" as its type attribute, and that type of element doesn't provide a way to format the text that's displayed by the button.

The form properties for setting the focus and default button

Property	Description
`DefaultFocus`	Sets the focus to the control that's identified.
`DefaultButton`	Sets the default button to the button that's identified.

The control properties for setting the tab order and access keys

Property	HTML	Description
`AssociatedControlID`	`for`	Associates a label with a control.
`TabIndex`	`tabindex`	Sets the tab order for a control with a value of 0 or more. To take a control out of the tab order, use a negative value, like -1.
`AccessKey`	`accesskey`	Sets a keyboard key that can be pressed in with a control key to move the focus to the control.

The aspx code for a form

```
<form id="form1" runat="server" DefaultFocus="txtName"
    DefaultButton="btnSubmit">
    <label for="txtName"><u>N</u>ame:</label>
    <asp:TextBox ID="txtName" runat="server" AccessKey="N"></asp:TextBox>
    <asp:Label runat="server" AssociatedControlID="txtEmail"
        AccessKey="M">E<u>m</u>ail:</asp:Label>
    <asp:TextBox ID="txtEmail" runat="server" TabIndex="-1"></asp:TextBox>
    <asp:Button ID="btnSubmit" runat="server" AccessKey="S" Text="Submit" />
</form>
```

Description

- To set the control that receives the *focus* when a form is first displayed, you can use the DefaultFocus property of the form. You can also use the focus method of C# or JavaScript to set the focus on a control.

- To set the *default button* that causes a form to be submitted when the user presses the Enter key, you can use the DefaultButton property of the form.

- The *tab order* for a form is the sequence in which the controls receive the focus when the Tab key is pressed. By default, the tab order is the order of the controls in the HTML, not including labels, and most browsers include links in the default tab order.

- *Access keys* are shortcut keys that the user can press to move the focus to specific controls on a form. If you assign an access key to a label, the focus is moved to the control that's associated with the label since labels can't receive the focus.

- To show the user what the access key for a text box is, you can underline the letter for the key in the label that identifies the text box.

- To use an access key, you press a control key plus the access key. For IE, Chrome, Safari, and Opera, use the Alt key (Option key on a Mac). For Firefox, use Alt+Shift. Also, be aware that you can't use some letters. For example, most browsers use Alt+D to highlight the URL in the address bar. So, you'll need to test your access keys in the major browsers.

Figure 6-3   How to set the focus, default button, tab order, and access keys for a form

How to use the common server controls

The topics that follow show you how to use some of the common server controls. For the most part, it's just a matter of dragging a control onto a form and using the Properties window to set the Appearance and Behavior properties that make the control work the way you want it to. You can also work with these properties directly in the aspx code if you prefer.

How to use labels and text boxes

Figure 6-4 presents the properties that you need for working with *labels* and *text boxes*. For both of these controls, the Text property specifies the text that's stored in the control.

For a label, the AssociatedControlID property specifies the control that the label identifies. Although you don't need to set this property for all controls, you do need to set it when you provide an access key for a label, as shown in the last figure. Also, setting this property improves your website's user accessibility by allowing an assistive device for a visually-impaired user to say what control the label is for. Note that this property is converted to a for attribute in the HTML for the label.

For a text box, the TextMode property determines whether the box can accept and display one or more lines of text (SingleLine or MultiLine). Then, for a multiline text box, you can use the Rows property to specify the number of lines that are shown in the text box and the Wrap property to specify whether the lines are automatically wrapped when they exceed the width of the box.

For both single and multiline text boxes, you can use the MaxLength property to specify the maximum number of characters that the user can enter into the box. You can also use the Columns property to specify the width of the box in characters. Although you can also use CSS to set the appearance of a text box, including its width, please note that ASP.NET generates an HTML textarea element for a multiline text box, not an input element.

For a SingleLine control (the default), the TextMode property can be used to specify the HTML type attribute for the input element that's generated for the control. If, for example, you set the TextMode property to Password, the characters that the user enters are masked so they can't be read.

Beyond that, the TextMode property can be used to specify values like those listed in this figure that are converted to the HTML5 type attributes. For instance, the TextMode property can be set to "Email" if the text box is supposed to get an email address, and it can be set to "Phone" if the text box is supposed to get a telephone number. For semantic reasons, it's good to set these HTML5 attributes because they indicate what type of data each control is for.

At present, though, support for the HTML5 type attributes varies from one browser to another. At this writing, for example, Firefox, Chrome, Internet Explorer, and Opera support the Email type by providing automatic data validation for the entry in the text box, but Safari treats an Email text box just like any other text box. Similarly, Chrome and Opera fully support the Date

Common label properties

Property	HTML	Description
AssociatedControlID	for	Associates a label with a control. Sometimes, this property is required, like when working with check boxes and radio buttons.
Text		The text content of the label.

Common text box properties

Property	Description
TextMode	The type of text box. SingleLine (the default) creates a standard text box, MultiLine creates a text box that has more than one line of text, and Password causes the characters that are entered to be masked. This property can also be used to generate the HTML5 type attribute for the input element that is rendered for a text box.
Text	The text content of the text box.
MaxLength	The maximum number of characters that can be entered into the text box.
Wrap	Determines whether or not text wraps automatically when it reaches the end of a line in a multiline text box. The default is True.
ReadOnly	Determines whether the user can change the text in the text box. The default is False, which means that the text can be changed.
Columns	The width of the text box in characters. The actual width is based on the font that's used for the entry.
Rows	The height of a multiline text box in lines. The default value is 0, which sets the height to a single line.

Common TextMode values for the HTML5 type attributes for input elements

Email	Url	Phone	Number	Range
Date	Time	Search	Color	

The aspx for a label and a multiline text box

```
<label for="txtMessage">Please enter any special instructions</label>
<asp:TextBox ID="txtMessage" runat="server" Rows="5" TextMode="MultiLine">
</asp:TextBox>
```

The aspx for a text box that gets an email address

```
<asp:TextBox ID="txtEmail" runat="server" TextMode="Email"></asp:TextBox>
```

Description

- The HTML5 TextMode values get rendered as type attributes for input elements. For semantic reasons, it's good to use these attributes because they indicate what type of data each control is for.

- At present, the HTML5 type values are supported at varied levels by desktop and laptop browsers, but mobile devices provide better support. For instance, most mobile devices adjust the keyboard for the email, url, and tel types to make data entry easier.

Figure 6-4   How to use labels and text boxes

type by offering a calendar widget when the text box receives the focus, Safari supports the Date type by displaying up an down arrows that you can use to change the date, but the other browsers treat a Date text box just like any other text box.

In contrast, the browsers for mobile devices do a better job of supporting the HTML5 type attributes. For instance, the iPhone and iPad support the Email and Phone types by displaying a keyboard that is optimized for email or phone entries. For that reason, we recommend that you use the TextMode property to set the HTML5 type attributes for TextBox controls. Doing this can't hurt anything because the HTML5 type attributes are ignored if they aren't supported.

How to use check boxes and radio buttons

Figure 6-5 shows how to use the controls for *check boxes* or *radio buttons*. The main difference between these two types of controls is that only one radio button in a group can be selected, but check boxes are independent so more than one can be checked.

To create a group of radio buttons, you specify the same name for the GroupName property of each button in the group. If you want to create two or more groups of radio buttons on a single form, you use a different group name for each group. Note, however, that if you don't specify a group name for a radio button, that button won't be a part of any group. Instead, it will be processed independently of any other radio buttons on the form.

To specify whether a radio button or check box should be checked when a form is rendered in a browser, you use the Checked property. But since only one radio button in a group can be selected, you should only set the Checked property to True for one button. If you set this property to True for more than one button in a group, the last one will be selected.

If you want to use C# to get the value of a check box (whether it's checked or unchecked) whenever the user changes it, you start by adding an event property for the CheckedChanged event to the control. Then, you can code an event handler for this event like the one for the chkNewProducts check box shown in this figure. The one statement in this handler assigns the value of the Checked property of the check box to the NewProductInfo property of a customer object. That value will either be true or false, depending on whether or not the box is checked.

If you want to use C# to get the value of a radio button whenever the user selects it, you add an event property for the CheckedChanged event to the control just like you do for a check box. Then, you code an event handler for this event like the one for the rdoTwitter radio button shown in this figure. Since this event only occurs when the user selects the button, the one statement in this handler assigns a value of "Twitter" to the ContactBy property of a customer object.

The second radio button example shows how you can use if statements to find out which radio button in a group has been selected. Here, the first if statement tests whether the button with an id of "rdoTwitter" is selected. In this statement, the condition is just the checked property of the control, which tests whether that property is true. If it is, the code sets the ContactBy property of

Common check box and radio button properties

Property	Description
Text	The text that's displayed next to the check box or radio button.
Checked	Indicates whether the check box or radio button is selected. The default is False.
GroupName	The name of the group that the radio button belongs to (not used for check boxes).

Three check boxes and two radio buttons in a browser

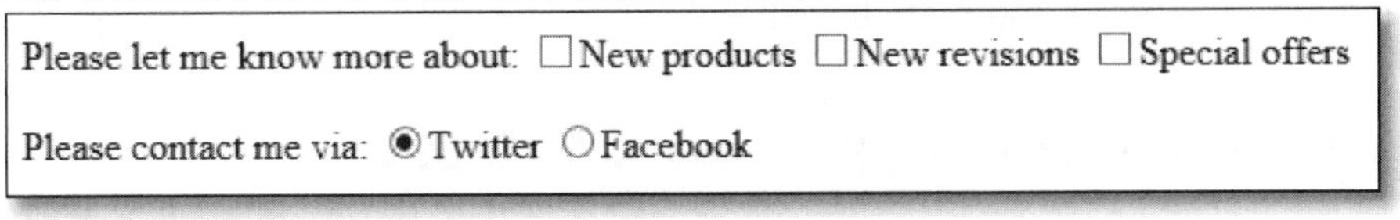

Please let me know more about: ☐ New products ☐ New revisions ☐ Special offers

Please contact me via: ◉ Twitter ◯ Facebook

The aspx code for the three check boxes

```
<asp:CheckBox ID="chkNewProducts" runat="server" Text="New products" />
<asp:CheckBox ID="chkRevisions" runat="server" Text="New revisions" />
<asp:CheckBox ID="chkSpecial" runat="server" Text="Special offers" />
```

C# code that gets the value of the first check box whenever it changes

```
protected void chkNewProducts_CheckedChanged(object sender, EventArgs e)
{
    customer.NewProductInfo = chkNewProducts.Checked;
}
```

The aspx code for the two radio buttons

```
<asp:RadioButton ID="rdoTwitter" runat="server"
    Checked="True" GroupName="ContactBy" Text="Twitter" />
<asp:RadioButton ID="rdoFacebook" runat="server"
    GroupName="ContactBy" Text="Facebook" />
```

C# code that gets the value of a radio button when it is turned on

```
protected void rdoTwitter_CheckedChanged(object sender, EventArgs e)
{
    customer.ContactVia = "Twitter";
}
```

Two if statements that set a value for the checked radio button

```
if (rdoTwitter.Checked) customer.ContactVia = "Twitter";
if (rdoFacebook.Checked) customer.ContactVia = "Facebook";
```

Description

- A *check box* displays a single option that the user can either check or uncheck.

- *Radio buttons* present a group of options from which the user can select just one.

- For a check box, the CheckedChanged event is raised whenever its checked property is changed. For a radio button, this event is raised only when its checked property is changed to checked.

- To determine whether a check box or radio button is selected, test its checked property.

Figure 6-5   How to use check boxes and radio buttons

a customer object to "Twitter". Then, the second statement tests whether the second button is checked, and it sets the ContactBy property to "Facebook" if it is. Since only one of these buttons can be checked, only one of the conditions in these if statements can be true.

If you use CSS to format check boxes and radio buttons, remember that each one is rendered as an input element followed by a label element that contains the text. Since this is the reverse of how labels and input elements are normally sequenced, this can make your CSS selectors more complicated. As you'll see later in this chapter, however, check box lists and radio button lists can simplify the CSS. And in chapter 10, you'll see how using Bootstrap can simplify the formatting of check boxes and radio buttons.

How to use image and hyperlink controls

Figure 6-6 shows how to use an *image control*. You've seen this control used to display a product image in the Shopping Cart application of chapter 4. To do that, you just set the ImageURL control to the URL of the image that you want displayed.

For user accessibility, though, it's also good to set the AlternateText property of an image control. That way, an assistive device for a visually-impaired user can read a description of the control.

If you need to set the width or height of an image, you can set the Width or Height property. Otherwise, the image will be displayed at its full size, unless the width or height is specified by CSS. In general, though, the images that you use should be the size that you want, so you shouldn't have to set their widths or heights. To convert the images to the right size, you can use an image editor.

This figure also shows how to use a *hyperlink control*. This control navigates to the web page specified in the NavigateUrl property when the user clicks the control. To display text for a hyperlink control, you set the Text property or code the text as content between the start and end tags. Either way, the text is underlined by default, although you can use CSS to change that.

The other alternative is to display an image for a hyperlink. To do that, you set the ImageUrl property to the URL of the image you want to display. Then, the control navigates to the web page that's specified when the user clicks on the image.

Remember, though, that you shouldn't use these controls unless the images or links are going to be changed by C# code based on the actions of the user. Otherwise, you should use an HTML img element to display an image and an <a> element for a link.

Common image properties

Property	Description
ImageUrl	The absolute or relative URL of the image.
AlternateText	The text that's used in place of the image if the browser can't display the image.
Width	The width of the image.
Height	The height of the image.

The aspx for an image control

```
<asp:Image ID="imgProduct" runat="server" />
```

C# code that sets the URL and alternate text of an image control

```
imgProduct.ImageUrl = "Images/Products/" + selectedProduct.ImageFile;
imgProduct.AlternateText = selectedProduct.AlternateText;
```

Common hyperlink properties

Property	Description
NavigateUrl	The absolute or relative URL of the page that's displayed when the control is clicked.
Text	The text that's displayed for the control.
ImageUrl	The absolute or relative URL of the image that's displayed for the control.

A hyperlink in a browser

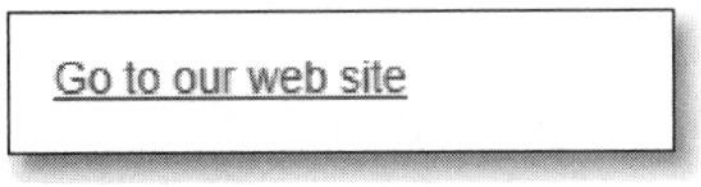

Go to our web site

The aspx for the hyperlink control

```
<asp:HyperLink ID="HyperLink1" runat="server"
    NavigateUrl="http://www.murach.com">Go to our website
</asp:HyperLink>
```

Description

- An *image control* displays a graphic image, typically in GIF (Graphic Interchange Format), JPEG (Joint Photographic Experts Group), or PNG (Portable Network Graphics) format.

- If you don't specify the Height or Width properties of an image control, the image will be displayed at full size or at the size specified by CSS. Most of the time it's best to use CSS rather than the Height and Width properties of the image.

- When a *hyperlink control* is clicked, it navigates to another web page or another location on the same page. The properties let you display either text or an image for the link.

Figure 6-6   How to use image and hyperlink controls

How to use the file upload control

Figure 6-7 shows how to use a *file upload control*. This control lets a user upload one or more files to a website. As this figure shows, this control is rendered as a text box that lets the user enter the path of each file to be uploaded, plus a Browse button that displays a dialog box that lets the user locate and select a file so the path is automatically put into the text box.

To upload the selected file or files, you must also provide a separate control that does a postback, like the Upload button in this figure. When the user clicks this button, the page is posted and the paths for the files that have been selected are sent to the server along with the HTTP request.

The first example in this figure shows the aspx code that declares a file upload control and an Upload button. Note here that the file upload control doesn't include a property that specifies where the file should be saved on the server. That's because the file upload control doesn't automatically save the uploaded file. Instead, you must write code that calls the SaveAs method of this control. The second example in this figure shows how to write this code.

Before you call the SaveAs method, you should test the HasFile property to make sure the user has selected a file. If the user has selected a valid file and it was successfully uploaded to the server, the HasFile property will be True. Then, you can use the FileName property to get the name of the selected file, and you can combine the file name with the path where you want the file saved. In this figure, the file is stored in the C:\Uploads directory.

You should know that if the directory you save the file to doesn't exist, ASP.NET throws a DirectoryNotFoundException, which is in the IO namespace. Because of that, You should use a try-catch statement with the code that calls the SaveAs method, as shown in the figure.

To illustrate the use of the PostedFile.ContentLength property, the event handler in this figure uses this property to get the size of the uploaded file. Then, it displays this size in the message for a successful upload.

If you use the AllowMultiple property with the file upload control, the user can select more than one file for uploading. This ASP.NET property gets rendered as the HTML5 multiple attribute. The only major browsers that don't support this attribute are Internet Explorer versions before version 10. But since IE8 and IE9 are still used by a small but significant portion of the market, you may want to put off using the AllowMultiple property until more IE users switch to version 10 or above. For more information about using it and for examples that use it, you can search the Internet.

A property of the file upload control

Property	Description
AllowMultiple	If True, the user can upload more than one file.

Properties and methods of the FileUpload class

Property	Description
HasFile	If True, the user has selected a file to upload.
FileName	The name of the file to be uploaded.
PostedFile	The HttpPostedFile object that represents the file that was posted. You can use this object's ContentLength property to determine the size of the posted file.

Method	Description
SaveAs(string)	Saves the posted file to the specified path. Throws an error if the path doesn't exist.

A label, file upload control, and button control in a browser

The aspx code for the controls

```
<asp:FileUpload ID="FileUpload1" runat="server" />
<asp:Button ID="btnUpload" runat="server" Text="Upload"
    OnClick="btnUpload_Click" />
```

The Click event handler for the button control

```
protected void btnUpload_Click(object sender, EventArgs e)
{
    if (FileUpload1.HasFile) {
        string path = "C:\\Uploads\\" + FileUpload1.FileName;
        try {
            FileUpload1.SaveAs(path);
            lblMessage.Text = $"File uploaded to {path}.<br>" +
                $"File size is {FileUpload1.PostedFile.ContentLength}.";
        }
        catch(System.IO.DirectoryNotFoundException ex) {
            lblMessage.Text = ex.Message;
        }
    }
}
```

Description

- The *file upload control* displays a text box and a Browse button that lets the user browse the file system to locate a file to be uploaded. You must provide a control to post the page.

- In the code-behind file, you must call the SaveAs method of the upload control to save the file.

Figure 6-7   How to use the file upload control

How to use the button controls

Most web forms have at least one button control that the user can click to submit the form to the server for processing. That button is commonly called a *submit button*. In the topics that follow, you'll learn how to use all three of the ASP.NET button controls: buttons, link buttons, and image buttons.

How to use buttons, link buttons, and image buttons

Figure 6-8 presents the three types of button controls. These controls differ only in how they appear to the user. This is illustrated by the three buttons shown in this figure. As you can see, a *button* displays text within a rectangular area. A *link button* displays text that looks like a hyperlink. And an *image button* displays an image.

This figure also presents the aspx for the three buttons that are illustrated. For the button and link button, the Text property provides the text that's displayed for the control. For the image button, the ImageUrl property provides the URL address of the image that's displayed on the button. To make an image button accessible to the visually impaired, you should also code its AlternateText property.

When a user clicks one of the button controls, ASP.NET raises two events: Click and Command. Then, you can provide event handlers for one or both of these events. The Click event is raised before the Command event. In this figure, you can see an event handler for the Click event of the Add to Cart button.

Note that the event handler for the Click event receives two arguments. The sender argument represents the control that was clicked. Because this argument has a type of object, you need to cast it to a button control if you want to access the properties and methods of the control. You might want to do that, for example, if you code a method that handles the processing for more than one button. Then, you can use the ID property of the control to determine which button was clicked.

The second argument that's passed to the event handler of a Click event is the e argument, which contains information about the event. You aren't likely to use this second argument for buttons and link buttons, because it doesn't contain much information. For an image button, on the other hand, you can use this argument to determine where the user clicked on the image. To do that, you can use the X and Y properties of the e argument, which return the X and Y coordinates for where on the image the user clicked.

Of course, the Click and Command event handlers are executed only if the page posts back to itself. In contrast, if a value is specified for the PostBackUrl property, the page at the specified URL is executed and displayed. This is the cross-page posting feature you learned about in chapter 4.

Common properties for Button, LinkButton, and ImageButton controls

Property	Description
Text	(Button and LinkButton only) The text displayed by the button. For a LinkButton control, the text can also be coded as content between the start and end tags.
ImageUrl	(ImageButton only) The image displayed for the button.
AlternateText	(ImageButton only) The text displayed if the browser can't display the image.
CausesValidation	If True (the default), page validation occurs when the button is clicked.
CommandName	An object that's passed to the Command event when a user clicks the button.
CommandArgument	A string value that's passed to the Command event when a user clicks the button.
PostBackUrl	The URL of the page that is requested when the user clicks the button.

Button, LinkButton, and ImageButton controls

The aspx for the three buttons

```
<asp:Button ID="btnAdd" runat="server" Text="Add to cart"
    OnClick="btnAdd_Click" /> 
<asp:LinkButton ID="lbtnCheckOut" runat="server"
    PostBackUrl="~/Checkout.aspx">Check Out</asp:LinkButton> 
<asp:ImageButton ID="ibtnCart" runat="server" AlternateText="Cart"
    ImageUrl="~/Images/cart.gif" PostBackUrl="~/Cart.aspx" />
```

An event handler for the Click event of a button control

```
protected void btnAdd_Click(object sender, EventArgs e)
{
    this.AddInvoice();
    Response.Redirect("~/Confirmation.aspx");
}
```

Description

- The *button*, *link button*, and *image button* controls are *submit buttons*.

- If the PostBackUrl property isn't coded for one of these buttons, the page is posted back to the server when the button is clicked, and the Click and Command events are raised. You can code event handlers for either or both of these events.

- If the PostBackUrl property is coded for one of these buttons, the page specified in the PostBackUrl property is loaded and executed.

- Two arguments are passed to the Click event handler: sender and e. Sender is the control that the user clicked, and e contains information about the events. For an image button, e has X and Y properties for the X and Y coordinates where the image was clicked.

Figure 6-8   How to use buttons, link buttons, and image buttons

How to use the Command event

Figure 6-9 shows how you can use the Command event to process a group of button controls with a single event handler. Like the Click event, this event receives both a sender argument and an e argument. In this case, though, the e argument represents a CommandEventArgs object.

Two properties of the CommandEventArgs class are shown in this figure. You can use these properties to get the values in the CommandName and CommandArgument properties of a control. When you create a button control, you can set the CommandName and CommandArgument properties to any string value. Then, you can test them in the Command event handler to determine how the application should respond when the user clicks the button.

The example in this figure illustrates how this works. The first part of the example shows the aspx code for four button controls. Note here that a different CommandName value is assigned to each button. Note too that the same event handler is named in the OnCommand attributes. That way, the same event handler will handle the Command event of all four controls. Although you can also assign CommandArgument values to each control, that isn't needed for this example.

The second part of this example shows an event handler that processes the Command event of all four controls. To do that, it uses a switch statement that tests the value of the CommandName property of the e argument, and calls a different method for each value. Since this value indicates which button was clicked, the effect is to call the right method for the button that was clicked.

By the way, you can use Visual Studio to generate the start of an event handler for the Command event. To do that, you go to Design view in the aspx page and then click on a button you want an event handler for. Then, you click on the Events button at the top of the Properties window (the one with the lightning bolt icon). This brings up a window with different sections that list all the events available for that button. In the Action section, double-click on the Command event. This creates an event handler for that event in the code-behind file, adds an OnCommand attribute to the button, and takes you to the code-behind file. In fact, you can use this technique to create event handlers for any server control.

Properties of the CommandEventArgs class

Property	Description
CommandName	The value in the CommandName property for the control that generated the Command event.
CommandArgument	The value in the CommandArgument property for the control that generated the Command event.

Four buttons in a browser

The aspx for the four buttons with CommandName properties

```
<asp:Button ID="btnFirst" runat="server" Text="<<"
    CommandName="First" OnCommand="NavigationButtons_Command" />
<asp:Button ID="btnPrevious" runat="server" Text="<"
    CommandName="Previous" OnCommand="NavigationButtons_Command" />
<asp:Button ID="btnNext" runat="server" Text=">"
    CommandName="Next" OnCommand="NavigationButtons_Command" />
<asp:Button ID="btnLast" runat="server" Text=">>"
    CommandName="Last" OnCommand="NavigationButtons_Command" />
```

An event handler for the Command events of the buttons

```
protected void NavigationButtons_Command(object sender, CommandEventArgs e)
{
    switch (e.CommandName) {
        case "First":
            GoToFirstRow();
            break;
        case "Previous":
            GoToPreviousRow();
            break;
        case "Next":
            GoToNextRow();
            break;
        case "Last":
            GoToLastRow();
            break;
    }
}
```

Description

- The Command event is raised whenever a user clicks a button control. It can be used instead of the Click event when you want to use one event handler for a group of buttons.

- The e argument that's passed to a Command event handler is a CommandEventArgs object. It contains the values of the CommandName and CommandArgument properties of the control that was clicked.

Figure 6-9   How to use the Command event

How to use the list controls

If you look back to figure 6-1, you can see that ASP.NET provides five different list controls. The topics that follow will show you how to use them.

How to create drop-down lists and list boxes

Figure 6-10 presents the properties for creating *drop-down lists* and *list boxes* as well as the items that they contain. To illustrate, the aspx code in this figure creates a list box with four list items that lets the user select more than one item. Also, the first item in the list is selected when the list is rendered in a browser.

Note here that the Value property for a list item only has to be coded when the value is different from the content for the list item. That's true for the third item in the list because it's content is "Text Message" and its value is "Text". In contrast, the values for the other three controls are the same as their content so the Value properties aren't required.

After you add any list control to a form, you can use the Collection Editor to add the items for the control. In fact, the items in the aspx code were generated from the items in the Collection Editor in this figure. The easiest way to start the Collection Editor for a list control is to click on the control's smart tag and select Edit Items.

When you first display the ListItem Collection Editor, the list is empty. Then, you can click the Add button below the Members list to add an item to the list. When you do, the item appears in the Members list and its properties appear in the Properties list. The first property lets you disable a list item so it doesn't appear in the list. The other three properties correspond to those in the second table in this figure. When you set the Text property for an item, the Value property defaults to the same value, but you can change that if that isn't what you want.

You can also set the items in a list control dynamically, either with code or with a data source control. In fact, you've already seen a couple examples of this. For example, the Future Value application of chapter 2 uses code to add items to a monthly investment amount drop-down list. And the product drop-down list on the Order page of the Shopping Cart application of chapter 4 is bound to a SqlDataSource control that gets the items for its list from a database.

Common properties of list box controls

Property	Description
Rows	Specifies the number of items that are displayed in a list box at one time. If all of the items can't be displayed, a scroll bar is added to the list box.
SelectionMode	Indicates whether a list box allows one (Single) or more (Multiple) selections.

Common properties of list items

Property	Description
Text	The text that's displayed for the list item.
Value	A string value associated with the list item.
Selected	Indicates whether the item is selected.

The aspx for a list box

```
<asp:ListBox ID="lstContactVia" runat="server" SelectionMode="Multiple">
    <asp:ListItem Selected="True">Twitter</asp:ListItem>
    <asp:ListItem>Facebook</asp:ListItem>
    <asp:ListItem Value="Text">Text Message</asp:ListItem>
    <asp:ListItem>Email</asp:ListItem>
</asp:ListBox>
```

The Collection Editor for creating and editing lists

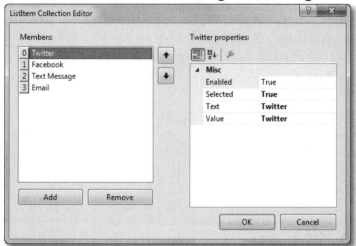

Description

- A *drop-down list* lets the user select one item in a list. A *list box* lets the user select one or more items in the list.

- To use the Collection Editor to add or edit the items in any list control, select Edit Items from the smart tag menu for the control. Or, select the control and then click the ellipsis button that appears when you select the Items property in the Properties window.

Figure 6-10   How to create drop-down lists and list boxes

How to use the properties for working with list controls

Figure 6-11 presents some common properties for working with list controls. As you just saw, these controls contain ListItem objects that define the items in the list. Then, you can use the properties in the first table in this figure to get the selected ListItem object, the index of the selected object, or the value of the selected object.

This is illustrated by the examples in this figure. All three are for drop-down lists, but they work the same for any type of list control. Here, the first example gets the value of the selected item in the list. And the second example gets the text for the selected item in the list.

The third example gets the value of the selected item right after it is changed because it is coded in the event handler for a list control's SelectedIndexChanged event. This event occurs any time the item that's selected changes between posts to the server. If you want the page to post immediately when the user selects an item, you should set the AutoPostBack property of the control to True.

By default, the SelectedIndex property of a drop-down list is set to zero, which means that the first item is selected. In contrast, the SelectedIndex property of a list box is set to -1 by default, which means that none of the items in the list are selected. Then, you can check if the user has selected an item in a list box by using code like this:

```
if (lstContactVia.SelectedIndex > -1) { ... }
```

You can also select an item by setting the SelectedIndex property to the appropriate index value. You can clear the selection from a list box by setting this property to -1. And you can select an item by setting the SelectedValue property to the appropriate value.

Common properties of list controls

Property	Description
SelectedItem	The ListItem object for the selected item, or the ListItem object for the item with the lowest index if more than one item is selected in a list box.
SelectedIndex	The index of the selected item, or the index of the first selected item if more than one item is selected in a list box. If no item is selected in a list box, the value of this property is -1.
SelectedValue	The value of the selected item, or the value of the first selected item if more than one item is selected in a list box. If no item is selected in a list box, the value of this property is an empty string ("").

A common event of all list controls

Event	Description
SelectedIndexChanged	This event is raised when the user selects a different item in a list.

The aspx code for a drop-down list

```
<asp:DropDownList ID="ddlDay" runat="server">
    <asp:ListItem Value="1">Sunday</asp:ListItem>
    <asp:ListItem Value="2">Monday</asp:ListItem>
    <asp:ListItem Value="3">Tuesday</asp:ListItem>
    <asp:ListItem Value="4">Wednesday</asp:ListItem>
    <asp:ListItem Value="5">Thursday</asp:ListItem>
    <asp:ListItem Value="6">Friday</asp:ListItem>
    <asp:ListItem Value="7">Saturday</asp:ListItem>
</asp:DropDownList>
```

C# code that gets the value of the selected item in the drop-down list

```
int dayNumber = Convert.ToInt32(ddlDay.SelectedValue);
```

C# code that gets the text for the selected item in the drop-down list

```
string dayName = ddlDay.SelectedItem.Text;
```

C# code that uses the SelectedIndexChanged event of the drop-down list

```
protected void ddlDay_SelectedIndexChanged(object sender, EventArgs e)
{
    int dayNumber = Convert.ToInt32(ddlDay.SelectedValue);
}
```

Description

- The properties of a list control let you get the selected ListItem object, the index of the selected object, or the value of the selected object.
- You can set a list control's AutoPostBack property to True if you want the page to post back as soon as the user selects an item.

Figure 6-11   How to use the properties for working with list controls

How to use the members for list item collections

Figure 6-12 presents some common members for working with a collection of list item objects. To get the item at a specific index, for example, you can use the indexer. And to get a count of the number of items in the collection, you can use the Count property.

The method in this summary that you're most likely to use is the Add method. It adds an item to the end of a collection. The examples in this figure show two different ways you can use this method.

The first example shows the for loop that was used in the Future Value application of chapter 2 to load the values from 50 to 500 into a drop-down list. Here, the Add method is used to add an item with the specified string value. When you code the Add method this way, the value you specify is assigned to both the Text and Value properties of the item.

However, if you want to assign different values to the Text and Value properties of an item, you use the technique in the second example. Here, a new list item object is created with two string values. The first string is stored in the Text property, and the second string is stored in the Value property. Then, the Add method is used to add the new item to the list item collection of the drop-down list.

Notice in both of these examples that the Items property is used to refer to the collection of list item objects for the control. You can also use the SelectedIndex property of a control to refer to an item at a specific index. For example, you could use a statement like this to remove the selected item from a drop-down list:

```
ddlDay.Items.RemoveAt(ddlDay.SelectedIndex);
```

Common property of a list control

Property	Description
Items	The collection of ListItem objects that represents the items in the control. This property returns a ListItemCollection object.

Common members of a ListItemCollection object

Property	Description
Count	The number of items in the collection.
Indexer	**Description**
[integer]	A ListItem object that represents the item at the specified index.
Method	**Description**
Add(string)	Adds a new item to the end of the collection, and assigns the string value to both the Text and Value properties of the item.
Add(ListItem)	Adds the specified list item to the end of the collection.
Insert(integer, string)	Inserts an item at the specified index location in the collection, and assigns the specified string value to the Text property of the item.
Insert(integer, ListItem)	Inserts the specified list item at the specified index in the collection.
Remove(string)	Removes the item whose Value property equals the specified string.
Remove(ListItem)	Removes the specified list item from the collection.
RemoveAt(integer)	Removes the item at the specified index from the collection.
Clear()	Removes all the items from the collection.

C# code that loads items into a drop-down list using strings

```
for (int i = 50; i <= 500; i += 50)
{
    ddlMonthlyInvestment.Items.Add(i.ToString());
}
```

C# code that loads items into a drop-down list using ListItem objects

```
ddlDay.Items.Add(new ListItem("Sunday", "1"));
ddlDay.Items.Add(new ListItem("Monday", "2"));
ddlDay.Items.Add(new ListItem("Tuesday", "3"));
```

Description

- The ListItemCollection object is a collection of ListItem objects. Each ListItem object represents one item in the list.
- Items in a ListItemCollection object are numbered from 0.
- When you load items into a list box using strings, both the Text and Value properties of the list item are set to the string value you specify.
- To set the Text and Value properties of a list item to different values, you must create a list item object and then add that item to the collection.

Figure 6-12   How to use the members for list item collections

How to use check box lists and radio button lists

Earlier in this chapter, you learned how to use radio buttons and check boxes. But ASP.NET also provides *check box lists* and *radio button lists* that you can use to create lists of check boxes and radio buttons. As figure 6-13 shows, these controls work like the other list controls.

In the aspx code for the check box list and radio button list in this figure, you can see the ListItem objects. You can use the Collection Editor to add these objects after you add a check box list or radio button list to a form. Like check boxes and radio buttons, more than one item can be checked in a check box list, but only one item can be selected in a radio button list. You can also use the SelectedValue property to get or set the value of the selected item in a radio button list, but note in the second example that this code is simpler for a radio button list than it is when you're using radio buttons in a group.

Like a list box, you can select more than one item in a check box list. Because of that, you'll usually determine whether an item in the list is selected by using the Selected property of the item. This is illustrated in the first example in this figure. Here, the Items property of a check box list is used to get the item at index 0. Then, the Selected property of that item is used to determine if the item is selected. Notice here that you can't refer to individual check boxes by name when you use a check box list.

To set the layout of the items in a radio button or check box list, you use the properties shown in this figure. The RepeatLayout property determines how ASP.NET aligns the buttons or check boxes in a list. By default, ASP.NET uses a table and generates the input and label elements for the boxes or buttons within the rows and columns of the table.

Similarly, the RepeatDirection property determines whether the controls are listed horizontally or vertically. And the RepeatColumns property specifies the number of columns in the radio button or check box list. If you experiment with these properties, you should get the boxes and buttons aligned the way you want them. And this can be much easier than using CSS to align check boxes and radio buttons that aren't in lists.

How to use bulleted lists

The BulletedList control lets you create a *bulleted* or *numbered list*. It works like the other list controls, but it has different properties. For instance, the BulletStyle property determines whether the list will be bulleted or numbered, and the BulletImageUrl, FirstBulletNumber, and DisplayMode properties provide other formatting details. If you experiment with these properties, you should be able to get the results that you want. Unless you're going to work with the items in the list in code, though, you should use HTML ul or ol tags instead of this server control.

Properties for formatting radio button and check box lists

Property	Description
`RepeatLayout`	Specifies whether ASP.NET should use a table (Table), an unordered list (UnorderedList), an ordered list (OrderedList), or normal HTML flow (Flow) to format the list when it renders the control. The default is Table.
`RepeatDirection`	Specifies the direction in which the controls should be repeated. The available values are Horizontal and Vertical. The default is Vertical.
`RepeatColumns`	Specifies the number of columns for the controls. The default is 0.

A check box list and a radio button list in a browser

Please let me know about:

☑ New products ☐ Special offers ☐ New editions

Please contact me via:

◉ Twitter

○ Facebook

The aspx code for the check box list

```
Please let me know about:
<asp:CheckBoxList ID="cblAbout" runat="server" RepeatDirection="Horizontal">
    <asp:ListItem Value="New" Selected="True">New products</asp:ListItem>
    <asp:ListItem Value="Special">Special offers</asp:ListItem>
    <asp:ListItem Value="Revisions">New editions</asp:ListItem>
</asp:CheckBoxList>
```

A statement that checks if the first item in a check box list is selected

```
if (cblAbout.Items[0].Selected) { /* do something */ }
```

The aspx code for the radio button list

```
Please contact me via:
<asp:RadioButtonList ID="rblContactVia" runat="server">
    <asp:ListItem Selected="True">Twitter</asp:ListItem>
    <asp:ListItem>Facebook</asp:ListItem>
</asp:RadioButtonList>
```

A statement that gets the value of the selected item in a radio button list

```
customer.ContactVia = rblContactVia.SelectedValue;
```

Description

- A *radio button list* presents a list of mutually exclusive options.

- A *check box list* presents a list of independent options.

- These controls contain a collection of ListItem objects that you refer to through the Items property of the control. They also have SelectedItem, SelectedIndex, and SelectedValue properties.

Figure 6-13   How to use check box lists and radio button lists

A CheckOut page that uses server controls

Now, to show you how the server controls can be used in a web page, this chapter ends by presenting a CheckOut page of the Shopping Cart application.

The user interface

Figure 6-14 shows the user interface for the CheckOut page of the application. It starts with text boxes and a drop-down list that are identified by HTML label elements. Then, after the last text box, this form uses a check box list and a radio button list. Those are followed by two Button controls and a LinkButton control.

Most of the styling and layout for this page is done with Bootstrap. However, some of the layout for the check box and radio button lists is done by the tables that ASP.NET has generated for these controls. Specifically, the input and label elements that are generated for the check boxes and radio buttons are stored in the cells of tables.

In this figure, you can see some messages that are displayed because the user didn't enter a value or select a value from a list. In fact, all of the text boxes and the drop-down list on this page have required field validators. They aren't shown in the aspx code in the next figure, though, because the focus of this chapter is the server controls. In the next chapter, though, you'll learn about validation controls in detail.

A CheckOut page that uses standard server controls

Description

- HTML label elements are used to identify all of the server controls on this page. The last two controls before the buttons are a check box list and a radio button list.

- The layout and styling of the page is done using the Bootstrap classes you learned about in chapter 3.

- All of the text boxes and the drop-down list have required field validators, but they aren't shown in the aspx code in the next figure.

Figure 6-14   A CheckOut page that uses standard server controls

The aspx code

Figure 6-15 presents the aspx code for the form element of the CheckOut page. Here, you can see the use of some of the label elements and server controls. For brevity, though, the code for the other labels and text boxes has been omitted. In addition, the code for the required field validators isn't shown.

On page 1 of this listing, you can see how the properties for the form element are set. Because the DefaultFocus property is set to the first text box on the form, the user will be able to use the Tab key to move from the first text box to those that follow. Because the DefaultButton property is set to the Check Out button, the user will be able to press the Enter key to submit the form to the server.

Then, notice that the TextMode properties of the email text boxes in the Contact Information section are set to Email. They determine the HTML5 type attributes of the input elements that are rendered for the text boxes. Similarly, the TextMode property of the phone number text box is set to Phone, although that control isn't included in this aspx code. Both of these properties indicate what type of data is expected, and the browsers for some mobile devices will display keyboards that are appropriate for those entries.

Of special note is the way the state drop-down list in the Billing Address section uses a SQL data source to add list items for each state to the list. The text that's displayed for each item is the state name, and the value for each item is the state code. The ListItem object that is coded within the drop-down list sets the Text and Value fields for the first item in the list to empty strings. Then, if the user doesn't select an item from the list, a required field validator will be activated so the form won't be submitted to the server.

Finally, notice how the MaxLength property of the text box for the zip code is set to 5. That way, no more than five characters can be entered into that text box.

The aspx code for the form on the CheckOut page   **Page 1**

```
<form id="form1" runat="server" class="form-horizontal"
    DefaultFocus="txtEmail1" DefaultButton="btnCheckOut">

    <h1>Check Out Page</h1>

    <h3>Contact Information</h3>
    <div class="form-group">
        <label class="control-label col-sm-3">Email Address:</label>
        <div class="col-sm-5">
            <asp:TextBox ID="txtEmail1" runat="server" CssClass="form-control"
                TextMode="Email"></asp:TextBox>
        </div>
        <div class="col-sm-4"><%-- required field validator --%></div>
    </div>
    <div class="form-group">
        <label class="control-label col-sm-3">Email Re-entry:</label>
        <div class="col-sm-5">
            <asp:TextBox ID="txtEmail2" runat="server" CssClass="form-control"
                TextMode="Email"></asp:TextBox>
        </div>
        <div class="col-sm-4"><%-- required field validator --%></div>
    </div>
    <%-- divs, labels, and text boxes for first name, last name, and phone --%>

    <h3>Billing Address</h3>
    <%-- divs, labels, and text boxes for address and city --%>
    <div class="form-group">
        <label class="control-label col-sm-3">State:</label>
        <div class="col-sm-5">
            <asp:DropDownList ID="ddlState" runat="server"
                AppendDataBoundItems="True" DataSourceID="SqlDataSource1"
                DataTextField="StateName" DataValueField="StateCode"
                CssClass="form-control">
                <asp:ListItem Text="" Value="" Selected="True"></asp:ListItem>
            </asp:DropDownList>
            <asp:SqlDataSource ID="SqlDataSource1" runat="server"
                ConnectionString="<%$ ConnectionStrings:HalloweenConnection %>"
                SelectCommand="SELECT [StateCode], [StateName] FROM [States]
                ORDER BY [StateCode]">
            </asp:SqlDataSource>
        </div>
        <div class="col-sm-4"><%-- required field validator --%></div>
    </div>
    <div class="form-group">
        <label class="control-label col-sm-3">Zip code:</label>
        <div class="col-sm-5">
            <asp:TextBox ID="txtZip" runat="server" CssClass="form-control"
                MaxLength="5"></asp:TextBox>
        </div>
        <div class="col-sm-4"><%-- required field validator --%></div>
    </div>
```

Figure 6-15   The aspx code for the CheckOut page (part 1 of 2)

The Optional Data section on page 2 of figure 6-15 contains a CheckBoxList control and a RadioButtonList control. The RepeatColumns property of the check box list is set to 2, and you can see how that is rendered in figure 6-14. Similarly, the RepeatDirection property of the radio button list is set to Horizontal, and you can see how that is rendered in the previous figure, too.

Following this section are two Button controls and a LinkButton control. The Check Out button and the Cancel button both have an OnClick attribute that indicates what method in the code-behind file is executed when the pages posts back. In contrast, the Continue Shopping link button has a PostBackUrl property instead of an OnClick attribute. Because of that, the page posts to the URL in that property, rather than to itself, when this button is clicked.

Finally, the Cancel and Continue Shopping buttons have their CausesValidation properties set to False. This means the validation that's specified by the validation controls on the page won't be done when these buttons are clicked. In contrast, the CausesValidation property isn't set for the Check Out button. Since the default value of this property is True, this means that the validation is done when the Check Out button is clicked.

The aspx code for the form on the CheckOut page   Page 2

```
<h3>Optional Data</h3>
<div class="form-group">
    <div class="col-sm-12">
        <label>Please let me know about:</label>
        <asp:CheckBoxList ID="cblAboutList" runat="server"
            RepeatColumns="2">
            <asp:ListItem Value="New" Selected="True">New products
            </asp:ListItem>
            <asp:ListItem Value="Special">Special offers</asp:ListItem>
            <asp:ListItem Value="Revisions">New editions</asp:ListItem>
            <asp:ListItem Value="Local">Local events</asp:ListItem>
        </asp:CheckBoxList>
    </div>
</div>
<div class="form-group">
    <div class="col-sm-12">
        <label>Please contact me via:</label>
        <asp:RadioButtonList id="rblContactVia" runat="server"
            RepeatDirection="Horizontal">
            <asp:listitem selected="true">Twitter</asp:listitem>
            <asp:listitem>Facebook</asp:listitem>
            <asp:listitem value="text">Text message</asp:listitem>
            <asp:listitem>Email</asp:listitem>
        </asp:RadioButtonList>
    </div>
</div>

<div class="form-group">
    <div class="col-sm-12">
        <asp:Button ID="btnCheckOut" runat="server" Text="Check Out"
          CssClass="btn" OnClick="btnCheckOut_Click" />
        <asp:Button ID="btnCancel" runat="server" Text="Cancel Order"
          CssClass="btn" CausesValidation="False"
          OnClick="btnCancel_Click" />
        <asp:LinkButton ID="lbtnContinueShopping" runat="server"
          CssClass="btn" PostBackUrl="~/Order.aspx"
          CausesValidation="False">Continue Shopping</asp:LinkButton>
    </div>
</div>

</form>
```

Figure 6-15   The aspx code for the CheckOut page (part 2 of 2)

The code-behind file for the CheckOut page

Figure 6-16 presents the code-behind file for the CheckOut page. The first thing to notice about this code is that it contains a private Customer object. This will store customer information retrieved from Session state or from the page, and it is used by most of the methods in the file.

As you've seen before, the Page_Load event handler first tests to see whether the page is a postback. If it isn't, that means it's being requested for the first time. In that case, this method gets the Customer object from the Session object if there is one, and it calls the LoadCustomerData method to load the data from the Customer object into the controls of the CheckOut page. Once the data is loaded in to the page's controls, it will be preserved between postbacks in ViewState. That's why you only have to retrieve the customer information from the Session object the first time the page loads.

In the LoadCustomerData method, you can see how the data from the customer object is loaded into the controls. But note that this is only done if the customer object isn't null. If the object isn't null, it means that the user entered the data for the CheckOut page, continued shopping, and then returned to the CheckOut page.

If the user clicks the Check Out button, the btnCheckOut_Click event handler is executed. It first checks to see if the data in the controls is valid. If it is, this method calls the GetCustomerData method to get the data from the controls on the form and save the data in the properties of the customer object. After that, it uses the Response.Redirect method to go to the Confirmation page.

In the GetCustomerData method, you can see how the statements get the data from the controls and save them in the properties of the customer object. When all of the data has been stored in the customer object, the object is added to the Session object.

On the other hand, if the user clicks the Cancel Order button, the btnCancel_Click event handler is executed. This method removes the Cart and Customer objects from the Session object, and redirects to the Order page.

The code-behind file for capturing the data

```
public partial class CheckOut : System.Web.UI.Page
{
    private Customer customer;
    protected void Page_Load(object sender, EventArgs e)
    {
        if (!IsPostBack)
        {
            customer = (Customer)Session["Customer"];
            LoadCustomerData();
        }
    }

    protected void btnCheckOut_Click(object sender, EventArgs e)
    {
        if (IsValid)
        {
            GetCustomerData();
            Response.Redirect("~/Confirmation.aspx");
        }
    }
    protected void btnCancel_Click(object sender, EventArgs e)
    {
        Session.Remove("Cart");
        Session.Remove("Customer");
        Response.Redirect("~/Order.aspx");
    }
    private void LoadCustomerData()
    {
        if (customer != null)
        {
            txtFirstName.Text = customer.FirstName;
            // load data into other text boxes from customer object
            ddlState.SelectedValue = customer.State;
            rblContactVia.SelectedValue = customer.ContactVia;
            cblAboutList.Items[0].Selected = customer.NewProductsInfo;
            cblAboutList.Items[1].Selected = customer.SpecialPromosInfo;
            cblAboutList.Items[2].Selected = customer.NewRevisionsInfo;
            cblAboutList.Items[3].Selected = customer.LocalEventsInfo;
        }
    }
    private void GetCustomerData()
    {
        if (customer == null) customer = new Customer();

        customer.FirstName = txtFirstName.Text;
        // get data from the other text boxes and load into customer object
        customer.State = ddlState.SelectedValue;
        customer.ContactVia = rblContactVia.SelectedValue;
        customer.NewProductsInfo = cblAboutList.Items[0].Selected;
        customer.SpecialPromosInfo = cblAboutList.Items[1].Selected;
        customer.NewRevisionsInfo = cblAboutList.Items[2].Selected;
        customer.LocalEventsInfo = cblAboutList.Items[3].Selected;
        Session["Customer"] = customer;
    }
}
```

Figure 6-16   The code-behind file for the CheckOut page

An introduction to the other standard server controls

Now that you've learned how to use the common server controls, you may be wondering what the other controls do and whether you need to learn how to use them. So here's a quick introduction to them.

When and how to use the other standard server controls

The table at the top of figure 6-17 summarizes some of the other standard server controls that you may be interested in. In particular, the Wizard and MultiView controls let you set up several steps or views that get user entries in a single web form. For instance, you can set up all of the steps of a CheckOut procedure with one Wizard control, as shown in the next figure. One benefit of doing that is you can get the data from all of the steps or views in a single code-behind file.

You can get the same result by using an HTML div element for each step and then using jQuery to move from one step to the next. With that approach, all of the data is collected by a single web form just as it is with a Wizard control.

Similarly, the ASP.NET Calendar control is a useful control. But the jQuery UI DatePicker widget works even better.

The message here is that if you're a professional ASP.NET developer, you should also know how to use jQuery, how to use the jQuery UI (User Interface) *widgets*, and what jQuery *plugins* are available. Then, you can decide how best to achieve the results you want. For example, controls like the Wizard and MultiView controls can work well for quickly prototyping an application. Then, when the prototype is working the way you want, you can redo it using jQuery.

To learn more about these and other server controls, you can search the Internet. For example, if you want to find out how to create a table that you can change as an application executes, you can learn about the Table control. This control provides a type of container that consists of columns and cells. If you need to create a generic container, you can use the Panel control instead. You can add static text like the text that's generated by the Literal control to this control, as well as other controls.

Other standard server controls that you may want to use

Name	Description
Calendar	Displays a calendar that lets the user select a date.
Wizard	Lets you build the steps of a procedure in a single web form.
MultiView	Acts as a container for View controls, and lets you provide two or more views in a single web form.
View	Acts as a container for other controls and HTML.
Table	Lets you work with an HTML table, rows, and cells using server-side code.
Panel	Acts as a container for other controls and HTML that can be displayed or hidden as a group.
Literal	Sends HTML or other text directly to the browser.

jQuery UI widgets that you should be aware of

Control	Description
DatePicker	A calendar that can be toggled from a text box or dislayed inline.
Accordion	Collapsible content panels that can be displayed by clicking on a header.
Tabs	A set of tabs that reveals one tab's contents at a time when its tab is clicked.
Dialog	A modal dialog box that is resizable and draggable.

Some common types of jQuery plugins that you should be aware of

Control	Description
Lightbox	Can be used to open a larger version of a thumbnail image, and then lets the user use the next and previous buttons to step through the set of images.
Carousel	Displays one or more images and lets the user use the next and previous buttons to step through the set of images.
Slideshow	Automatically presents one image at a time from a set of images.

Description

- The ASP.NET Calendar control displays a calendar that lets the user select a date, but the jQuery UI control works even better.
- The Wizard and MultiView controls let you provide several different steps or views in a single form, but you can get the same result by using HTML div tags that are manipulated by jQuery.
- If you're an ASP.NET developer, you should know how to use jQuery, the jQuery UI *widgets*, and jQuery *plugins*. Then, you can decide whether you want to use an ASP.NET control or jQuery to get the results that you want.
- The Table and Panel controls let you work with HTML table and div tags in code.
- The Literal control lets you add a string literal to the HTML sent to the browser.
- To learn more about using any of the ASP.NET server controls, you can search the Internet for information and examples, which are plentiful.

Figure 6-17   When and how to use the other standard server controls

How to use the Wizard control

To give you a better idea of how the Wizard control works and how you can use it, figure 6-18 presents an example of this control in use. Here, you can see three steps of a checkout procedure. Remember that all of the data collected in these steps is in a single web form, so you can capture all of the data in a single code-behind file.

After you add a Wizard control to a form, you can use the Wizard Collection Editor to add the steps that you want to the Wizard. These are added as WizardStep controls, as shown in the aspx code in this figure. When you're through with the Collection Editor, ASP.NET adds the sidebar links and buttons to the steps that let the user move from one step to another.

At that point, you can add the HTML and controls for each step. You can also use the templates and styles that ASP.NET provides for the controls that are generated by the Wizard. This shows how useful the Wizard Control can be for prototyping. Then, you can decide whether the result is the way you want it, or whether you want to convert it to another approach.

Three steps of a Wizard control

The starting aspx for a Wizard control

```
<asp:Wizard ID="Wizard1" runat="server" ActiveStepIndex="0">
    <WizardSteps>
        <asp:WizardStep runat="server" Title="Step 1:Contact Info">
            <h2>Contact information</h2>
            ...
        </asp:WizardStep>
        <asp:WizardStep runat="server" Title="Step 2:Shipping Method">
            <h2>Shipping method</h2>
            ...
        </asp:WizardStep>
        <asp:WizardStep runat="server" Title="Step 3:Credit Card Info">
            <h2>Credit card information</h2>
            ...
        </asp:WizardStep>
    </WizardSteps>
</asp:Wizard>
```

Description

- To add or remove the steps for a Wizard, you can use the WizardStep Collection Editor. Then, after you set up the steps, you can add the controls and HTML for each of the steps.

- The sidebar that provides the links for the steps and the Next, Previous, and Finish buttons are generated by ASP.NET. If you don't want the sidebar to be displayed, you can set the DisplaySideBar property of the Wizard control to False.

- Because all of the steps are on one web page, you can get the data from the controls for all of the steps in a single code-behind file.

Figure 6-18   How to use the Wizard control

Perspective

Now that you've finished this chapter, you should be able to use the common server controls whenever you need them in your applications. If necessary, you can refer to the figures in this chapter to see what properties you need to set for the common controls. But otherwise, you can add a control to a form, select it in the Designer, and use the Properties windows to figure out what properties you need to set.

Remember, though, that you should use HTML elements instead of server controls whenever the data in the elements isn't going to change while the application runs. You may also want to use JavaScript and jQuery, jQuery UI, or jQuery plugins instead of server controls like the Wizard and MultiView controls. That's why every ASP.NET developer should also know how to use HTML, CSS, JavaScript, and jQuery, and that's why you should have *Murach's HTML5 and CSS3, Murach's JavaScript,* and *Murach's jQuery* in your professional library.

Terms

server control	file upload control
event handler	submit button
focus	button
default button	link button
tab order	image button
access key	drop-down list
label	list box
text box	check box list
check box	radio button list
radio button	bulleted list
image control	numbered list
hyperlink	

Summary

- The *server controls* in the Standard group of the Visual Studio Toolbox are the ones that you use to get data entries from users and to display data for users. These controls are rendered into HTML elements when a form is displayed in a browser.

- You can code event handlers for the Click and Command events of *buttons*, the TextChanged event of a *text box*, the CheckChanged event of *check boxes* and *radio buttons*, and the SelectedIndexChanged event of list controls like *drop-down lists* and *list boxes*.

- To make it easier for users to work with the controls of a form, you can set the starting *focus* and the *default button* for each form. You should also make sure the *tab order* provides for easy movement through the controls of the form, and you may also want to provide *access keys* for some of the controls.

- In general, you should use HTML elements instead of server controls when the data in the controls isn't going to change. However, you may also want to use server controls when you don't know how to code the HTML elements, even though the data in the controls isn't going to change.

- One of the benefits of using server controls is that they provide properties that make it easy to change their data with C# code. The Properties window in the Designer also makes it easy to set the properties of the controls.

- With ASP.NET, a list control is treated as a ListItemCollection object that contains ListItem objects. The ListItem Collection Editor makes it easy to create the list items for a list control, and the members of the collection object provide the property, indexer, and methods that let you use C# for working with the items.

- You can also add items to the ListItemCollection of a list control dynamically. You can do this in code or with a data source control.

- Although ASP.NET provides advanced server controls like the Calendar, Wizard, and MultiView controls, you should be aware that you can get the same or better results by using jQuery, jQuery UI *widgets*, and jQuery *plugins*. Then, you need to decide which approach to use for your website.

Exercise 6-1   Modify the Check Out page

In this exercise, you'll modify the Check Out page of the Shopping Cart application that's presented in this chapter.

Open, review, and run the Shopping Cart application

1. Open the Ex06Cart web application that's in the aspnet46_cs directory, and review the Order and Cart pages to see that they're like the ones in chapter 4.

2. Test the application to see how it works. Without entering any data on the Check Out page, click the Check Out button to see that all of the text boxes and the drop-down list have required field validators.

3. Enter valid data for all of the fields and click on the Continue Shopping button. Return to the Check Out page by clicking on the Cart button in the Order page and then on the Check Out button in the Cart page. Note that the data you entered in step 2 hasn't been saved.

4. Enter valid data again and then go to the Confirmation page by clicking on the Check Out button. Note that this page lists the entries that you made on the Check Out page. Then, close the browser and switch to Visual Studio.

5. Review the code in the Customer.cs file in the Models folder to see the properties of the Customer object. Then, review the code-behind file for the Check Out page to see how the user entries are stored in the Customer object and how the Customer object is stored in the Session object when the Check Out button is clicked.

6. Review the code-behind file for the Confirmation page to see how the Customer object is retrieved from the Session object and the properties in the Customer object are displayed on the web page.

Use the Command event to handle the click events of two buttons

7. Add a new Button control between the Check Out and Cancel Order buttons. Set its ID property to btnSaveContinue, its Text property to "Save and Continue Shopping", its CssClass property to btn, and its CommandName property to "Continue".

8. Set the CommandName property for the Check Out button to "Confirm". Then, use the Properties window to create an event handler for the Command event of that button that's named SaveData.

9. Set the Command event for the Save and Continue Shopping button so it also executes the SaveData event handler when it's clicked.

10. Copy the code from the btnCheckOut_Click event handler and paste it into the new SaveData event handler. Then, change the code so it uses the CommandName property of the e argument to determine which button was clicked and then redirects to the appropriate page.

11. Delete the OnClick attribute for the Check Out button so the event handler for the Click event isn't executed when the button is clicked.

12. Run the application, add an item to the cart, and then click the Check Out button. When the Check Out page is displayed, complete the form and then click the Save and Continue Shopping button. Return to the Check Out page to see that the information you entered has now been saved.

13. Click on the Check Out button to see that it still works like it did before. Close the application when you're done.

7

How to use the validation controls

In chapter 2, you learned the basic skills for using two of the validation controls: the required field validator and the range validator. Now, you'll learn more about using those controls as well as how to use the other validation controls. As you'll see, you can use the validation controls to perform most of the data validation required by web forms.

Introduction to the validation controls

ASP.NET provides six *validation controls* that you can use to validate the data on a web form. You'll learn the basic skills for using these controls in the topics that follow.

How ASP.NET processes the validation controls

Figure 7-1 summarizes the *validation controls* that are available with ASP.NET. As you learned in chapter 2, the first five controls are called *validators*. These are the controls that you use to check that the user has entered valid data into the input controls on a web form. In contrast, you use the validation summary control to display a summary of all the errors on a page.

To refresh your memory about how the validation controls work, this figure summarizes the key points. To start, you should realize that the validation tests are typically done on the client before the page is posted to the server. That way, a round trip to the server isn't required if any invalid data is detected.

In most cases, client-side validation is done when the focus leaves an input control that has validators associated with it. That can happen when the user presses the Tab key to move to the next control or clicks another control to move the focus to that control.

However, the required field validator works a bit differently. When you use this validator, the validation isn't done until the user clicks a button whose CausesValidation property is set to True. The exception is if the user enters a value into an input control and then tries to clear the value. In that case, an error will be detected when the focus leaves the control.

To perform client-side validation, a browser must support JavaScript and JavaScript must be enabled. Because that's the norm, validation is usually done on the client. In case JavaScript isn't enabled in the browser, though, validation is always done on the server when a page is submitted. ASP.NET does this validation after it initializes the page.

When ASP.NET performs the validation tests on the server, it sets the IsValid property of each validator to True or False. In addition, it sets the IsValid property of the page to True or False based on whether the IsValid property of all the input data is true. Thus, you should test the IsValid property for the page to make sure it's true before processing any of the data that's been submitted. In the example in this figure, you can see how this property is tested in the event handler for the Click event for an Add button.

If you want to bypass client-side validation and just perform the validation on the server, you can set the EnableClientScript property of the validation controls to False. Then, the JavaScript for client-side validation isn't generated, and the validation is only done on the server.

The validation controls provided by ASP.NET

Name	Description
RequiredFieldValidator	Checks that an entry has been made.
CompareValidator	Checks an entry against a constant value or the value of another control. Can also be used to check for a specific data type.
RangeValidator	Checks that an entry is within a specified range.
RegularExpressionValidator	Checks that an entry matches a pattern that's defined by a regular expression.
CustomValidator	Checks an entry on the server using C# validation code. Can also check the entry in client-side code, although this is optional.
ValidationSummary	Displays a summary of error messages from the other validation controls.

Typical code for processing a page that contains validation controls

```
protected void btnAdd_Click(object sender, EventArgs e)
{
    if (Page.IsValid)
    {
        // code for processing the valid data
    }
}
```

Description

- If a browser has JavaScript enabled, the *validation controls* do their validation on the client. That way, the validation is done and error messages are displayed without the page being posted to the server.

- Validation is always done on the server too, right after the page is initialized, so the validation is done whether or not the browser supports JavaScript.

- Validation is always done when you click a button whose CausesValidation property is set to True. To create a button that doesn't cause validation, you can set this property to False.

- Validation is also done on the client when the focus leaves an input control. The exception is a required field validator, which does its validation only when you click a button whose CausesValidation property is set to True or when you enter a value into a control and then clear and leave the control.

- If a validation control finds invalid data, the IsValid property of that control is set to False and the IsValid property of the page is set to False. You can test these properties in your C# code.

- If you want to perform validation only on the server, you can set the EnableClientScript properties of the validation controls to False. Then, the JavaScript for validation on the client isn't generated.

Figure 7-1   How ASP.NET processes the validation controls

How to set the properties of the validators

Figure 7-2 summarizes the common properties for the validators. These are the ones you can use with any validator. The most important property is the ControlToValidate property, which associates the validator with an input control on the page.

The Display property determines how the error message for a validator is displayed. In most cases, Dynamic works the best because space is only generated for the message when it is displayed. In some cases, though, the other options can be useful.

You use the ErrorMessage and Text properties to specify messages that are displayed when the validator detects an error. You can set one or both of these properties depending on whether you use a validation summary control. If you want the same message in both the validator and the validation summary control, just set the ErrorMessage property. But if you want different messages, set the ErrorMessage property to the message you want in the validation summary control and the Text property to the message you want in the validator.

You use the CssClass property to specify the CSS class that should be applied to the message that's displayed by the validation control. For example, you might want to use the Bootstrap text-danger class for your validators, which makes a control's error message display in red. You'll learn more about classes like this in chapter 10.

If the Enabled property of a validator is set to True, the validation test for the validator is performed. But if you want to skip the validation that's done by a validator, you can set this property to False. In contrast, the EnableClientScript property determines whether the client-side JavaScript for the validation is generated. If this property is set to False, the validation is only done on the server.

Besides the properties in the table in this figure, you will use other properties for specific controls. You will find most of these in the Behavior category of the Properties window when the validator is selected in the Designer. For instance, you can use the drop-down list for the Operator property when you're setting the properties for a compare validator. You'll learn more about these properties as you read about specific validators.

Common validator properties

Property	Description
ControlToValidate	The ID of the control to be validated.
Display	Determines how the error message is to be displayed. Static is the default and allocates space for the message in the page layout. Dynamic allocates space only when an error occurs. None displays errors only in a validation summary control.
Text	The message that's displayed in the validator.
ErrorMessage	The message that's displayed in the validation summary control when the validation fails. This message is also displayed in the validator if the Text property hasn't been set.
CssClass	The CSS class that's applied to the validator's message.
Enabled	Indicates whether the validation control is enabled.
EnableClientScript	Indicates whether the validation will be done on the client.
SetFocusOnError	Indicates whether the focus will be moved to the control if it's invalid.
ValidationGroup	Indicates which group the validation control is part of.

The Behavior category in the Properties window for a Compare validator

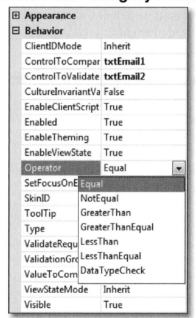

Description

- The Appearance category in the Properties window provides the Display, ErrorMessage, Text, and CssClass properties.
- The Behavior category provides the properties that you need to get the control to behave the way you want it to.

Figure 7-2   How to set the properties of the validators

How to provide for unobtrusive validation

In chapter 2, you were introduced to *unobtrusive validation*. When it's used, the validation on the client uses jQuery, which is a JavaScript library. The benefit of using jQuery is that it reduces the amount of JavaScript that has to be generated and takes advantage of jQuery features like cross-browser compatibility.

Even though unobtrusive validation is on by default when you start a new web application, it has been turned off in all of the applications that you've studied so far. But now, figure 7-3 shows the easiest way to implement unobtrusive validation. That is, by installing the NuGet package for it.

After you install the NuGet package using the procedure in this figure, you'll see that a Scripts folder has been added to the Project. This folder contains minified and un-minified versions of the JavaScript file for jQuery. It also contains a map file that maps the minified version to the un-minified version to aid in debugging the minified file.

It's important to note that if you've already installed the Bootstrap NuGet package, you already have a Scripts folder in your application. In that case, the unobtrusive validation NuGet package might update the jQuery files in the Scripts folder to a different version than what Bootstrap installed. If that happens, you'll need to change the script tags in the head element of your pages to make sure you're referring to the correct version of jQuery.

The NuGet package for unobtrusive validation also adds an assembly named AspNet.ScriptManager.jQuery to your application. You can see this file in the References folder for the project. This assembly will automatically register the jQuery library with the ASP.NET ScriptManager. That's how the unobtrusive validation feature knows where to find the jQuery files it needs.

Now that you know the easiest way to implement unobtrusive validation, we recommend that you do that for all of your production applications. For most of the applications in this book, however, unobtrusive validation is turned off to keep things simple.

The NuGet Package Manager page

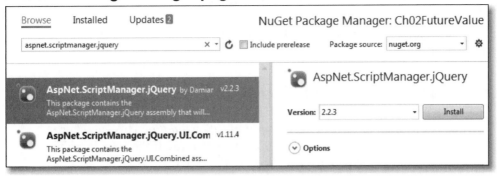

How to install the NuGet package for jQuery validation

- Right-click on the project and select Manage NuGet Packages.
- Click on Browse, then type "aspnet.scriptmanager.jquery" in the search box.
- In the left pane, click on the AspNet.ScriptManager.jQuery package. Then, in the right pane, click on the Install button.

Description

- *Unobtrusive validation* is on by default when you start a new web application from the Empty template.
- The easiest way to provide unobtrusive validation is to install the NuGet package for it. This creates a Scripts folder if you don't already have one, downloads the JavaScript files for jQuery to that folder, and downloads an assembly that registers jQuery with the ScriptManager and manages the validation.
- If you already have the Bootstrap NuGet package installed, the NuGet package for unobtrusive validation might replace the jQuery files that were downloaded by Bootstrap with a different version. If that happens, you'll need to update the script tags in the head element of each page so they refer to the correct version of jQuery.

Note

- As this book goes to the printer, a newer version of the NuGet package that includes jQuery 3.0.0 has become available. Unfortunately, this version of jQuery may conflict with some versions of the Bootstrap NuGet package. If you run into this problem, you can select an earlier version of the NuGet package for jQuery validation from the Version drop-down list. Note that in the future, it's likely that a newer version of Bootstrap will be released that works with the newer version of jQuery.

Figure 7-3   How to provide for unobtrusive validation

How to use the validators

In the topics that follow, you'll learn how to use the validators as you develop applications.

How to use the required field validator

Figure 7-4 shows how to use the *required field validator*. This validator checks that the user entered a value into an input control. If the user doesn't enter a value, the validator's error message is displayed.

The three examples in this figure illustrate how you can use the required field validator. In the first example, this validator is used to check for a required entry in a text box. To do that, its ControlToValidate property is set to the ID property of the text box. Then, if the user doesn't enter anything into the text box, the text in the ErrorMessage property is displayed.

The second and third examples show how you can use the InitialValue property of the required field validator to check that the user changed the initial value of a control. For this to work right, this property must be set to the initial value of the field that's being validated.

In the second example, this technique is used with a text box. Here, the initial value of the text box indicates the format for a date entry. If the user doesn't change this value, the validation test will fail. This doesn't work as well as you might want it to, though, because the users have to delete the initial value in the field before they can enter the new value, which isn't as easy as entering a value into an empty text box.

The third example uses the InitialValue property with a list box. Here, the InitialValue property is set to None, which is the value of the first item in the list. That way, if the user doesn't select another item, the validation test will fail. You can also use this technique with a drop-down list or a radio button list.

Notice in all three of these examples that the default ID property for each validator has been changed to a meaningful value. Although you won't typically do this unless a control is referred to in code, this can help make it easier to see at a glance what a validator does. So you might want to consider assigning a meaningful id to your validators too.

A property of the required field validator

Property	Description
InitialValue	The initial value of the control that's validated. If this value isn't changed, the validation fails. The default is an empty string.

A validator that checks for a required entry

```
<asp:TextBox ID="txtName" runat="server"></asp:TextBox>
<asp:RequiredFieldValidator ID="rfvName" runat="server"
    ControlToValidate="txtName" CssClass="text-danger"
    ErrorMessage="You must enter a name." >
</asp:RequiredFieldValidator>
```

A validator that checks that an initial value is changed

```
<asp:TextBox ID="txtBirthDate" runat="server">mm/dd/yyyy</asp:TextBox>
<asp:RequiredFieldValidator ID="rfvBirthDate" runat="server"
    ControlToValidate="txtBirthDate" CssClass="text-danger"
    InitialValue="mm/dd/yyyy"
    ErrorMessage="You must enter a birthdate.">
</asp:RequiredFieldValidator>
```

A required field validator that forces an option to be chosen from a list box

```
<asp:ListBox ID="lstCardType" runat="server">
    <asp:ListItem Selected="True" Value="None">Select a credit card
    </asp:ListItem>
    <asp:ListItem Value="Visa">Visa</asp:ListItem>
    <asp:ListItem Value="MC">MasterCard</asp:ListItem>
    <asp:ListItem Value="AmEx">American Express</asp:ListItem>
</asp:ListBox>
<asp:RequiredFieldValidator ID="rfvCardType" runat="server"
    ControlToValidate="lstCardType" CssClass="text-danger"
    InitialValue="None"
    ErrorMessage="You must select a credit card type.">
</asp:RequiredFieldValidator>
```

Description

- The *required field validator* checks that the user entered data into an input control. It's typically used with text box controls, but it can also be used with list controls.

- If you set the InitialValue property of a required field validator, you should set the starting value for the field that's being validated to the same value. This technique can be used to show the format that should be used for an entry.

- Most of the validation controls that you'll see in the next few topics pass their validation tests if the user doesn't enter a value. As a result, you'll often need to provide a required field validator along with other validation controls.

Figure 7-4   How to use the required field validator

How to use the compare validator

Figure 7-5 shows how you use the *compare validator*. This validator lets you compare the value entered into an input control with a constant value or the value of another control. You can also use the compare validator to make sure that the value is a particular data type.

To define a compare validator, you use the four properties shown in this figure. To compare the input data with a constant value, you specify the value in the ValueToCompare property. Then, you set the Operator property to indicate the type of comparison you want to perform, and you set the Type property to the type of data you're comparing.

The first example illustrates how this works. Here, the value entered into a text box is tested to be sure that it's an integer that's greater than zero. Then, if the user enters a value that isn't an integer, or if the user enters an integer that isn't greater than zero, the error message will be displayed.

To test for just a data type, you set the Type property to the type of data you're testing for, and you set the Operator property to DataTypeCheck. This is illustrated by the second example. Here, the value entered into a text box is tested to be sure that it's an integer.

The third example shows how to compare the value of an input control with the value of another control. To do that, you set the Operator and Type properties just as you do when you compare an input value with a constant. Instead of setting the ValueToCompare property, however, you set the ControlToCompare property to the ID of the control whose value you want to compare. This example tests that a date that's entered into one text box is after the date entered into another text box.

When you work with compare validators, you should know that if the user doesn't enter a value into a control, the control will pass the test of its compare validator. Because of that, you must use a required field validator along with the compare validator if you want to be sure that the user enters a value into a control.

You should also realize that if you compare the value of a control against the value of another control, the validation test will pass if the user doesn't enter a value into the other control or the value of the other control can't be converted to the correct type. To avoid that problem, you'll want to be sure that the other control is also validated properly.

Properties of the compare validator

Property	Description
ValueToCompare	The value that the control specified in the ControlToValidate property should be compared to.
Operator	The type of comparison to perform (Equal, NotEqual, GreaterThan, GreaterThanEqual, LessThan, LessThanEqual, or DataTypeCheck).
Type	The data type for the comparison (String, Integer, Double, Date, or Currency).
ControlToCompare	The ID of the control that the value of the control specified in the ControlToValidate property should be compared to.

A compare validator that checks for a value greater than zero

```
<asp:TextBox ID="txtQuantity" runat="server"></asp:TextBox>
<asp:CompareValidator ID="cvQuantity" runat="server"
    ControlToValidate="txtQuantity" CssClass="text-danger"
    Type="Integer"
    Operator="GreaterThan"
    ValueToCompare="0"
    ErrorMessage="Quantity must be greater than zero.">
</asp:CompareValidator>
```

A compare validator that checks for an integer value

```
<asp:TextBox id="txtYears" runat="server"></asp:TextBox>
<asp:CompareValidator ID="cvYears" runat="server"
    ControlToValidate="txtYears" CssClass="text-danger"
    Operator="DataTypeCheck"
    Type="Integer"
    ErrorMessage="Years must be an integer.">
</asp:CompareValidator>
```

A compare validator that compares the values of two text boxes

```
<asp:TextBox ID="txtStartDate" runat="server"></asp:TextBox>
<asp:TextBox ID="txtEndDate" runat="server"></asp:TextBox>
<asp:CompareValidator ID="cvDates" runat="server"
    ControlToValidate="txtEndDate" CssClass="text-danger"
    Operator="GreaterThan"
    Type="Date"
    ControlToCompare="txtStartDate"
    ErrorMessage="End Date must be after Start Date.">
</asp:CompareValidator>
```

Description

- The *compare validator* compares the value entered into a control with a constant value or with the value entered into another control.

- You can also use the compare validator to check that the user entered a specific data type.

- If the user doesn't enter a value in the input control, the compare validator passes its validation test.

Figure 7-5   How to use the compare validator

How to use the range validator

The *range validator*, shown in figure 7-6, validates user input by making sure that it falls within a given range of values. To specify the valid range, you set the MinimumValue and MaximumValue properties. You must also set the Type property to the type of data you're checking. For instance, the first example in this figure checks that the user enters an integer between 1 and 14 into a text box.

The second example in this figure shows how you can set the range for a range validator at runtime. Here, you can see that the MinimumValue and MaximumValue properties aren't set when the range validator is declared. Instead, they're set when the page is loaded for the first time. In this case, the MinimumValue property is set to the current date, and the MaximumValue property is set to 30 days after the current date.

Like the compare validator, you should realize that the range validator will pass its validation test if the user doesn't enter anything into the associated control. Because of that, you'll need to use a required field validator along with the range validator if the user must enter a value.

Properties of the range validator

Property	Description
MinimumValue	The minimum value allowed for the control.
MaximumValue	The maximum value allowed for the control.
Type	The data type for the comparison (String, Integer, Double, Date, or Currency).

A range validator that checks for a numeric range

```
<asp:TextBox ID="txtDays" runat="server"></asp:TextBox>
<asp:RangeValidator ID="rvDays" runat="server"
    ControlToValidate="txtDays" CssClass="text-danger"
    Type="Integer"
    MinimumValue="1"
    MaximumValue="14"
    ErrorMessage="Days must be between 1 and 14.">
</asp:RangeValidator>
```

How to set a range at runtime

A range validator that checks a date range that's set at runtime

```
<asp:TextBox ID="txtArrival" runat="server"></asp:TextBox>
<asp:RangeValidator ID="rvArrival" runat="server"
    ControlToValidate="txtArrival" CssClass="text-danger"
    Type="Date"
    ErrorMessage="You must arrive within 30 days.">
</asp:RangeValidator>
```

Code that sets the minimum and maximum values when the page is loaded

```
protected void Page_Load(object sender, EventArgs e)
{
    if (!IsPostBack)
    {
        DateTime today = DateTime.Today;
        rvArrival.MinimumValue = today.ToShortDateString();
        rvArrival.MaximumValue = today.AddDays(30).ToShortDateString();
    }
}
```

Description

- The *range validator* checks that the user enters a value that falls within the range specified by the MinimumValue and MaximumValue properties. These properties can be set when the range validator is created or when the page is loaded.

- If the user enters a value that can't be converted to the correct data type, the validation fails.

- If the user doesn't enter a value in the input control, the range validator passes its validation test.

Figure 7-6   How to use the range validator

How to use the regular expression validator

A *regular expression* is a string made up of special pattern-matching symbols. You'll learn more about these symbols and how they work in the next figure.

You can use regular expressions with the *regular expression validator* to make sure that a user's entry matches a specific pattern, like one for a zip code, phone number, or email address. Figure 7-7 shows how to use the regular expression validator.

As you can see, the ValidationExpression property specifies the regular expression the input data must match. For instance, the code for the first regular expression validator in this figure specifies that the input data must contain five decimal digits (\d{5}). And the regular expression for the second validator specifies that the input data must be in the format of a U.S. phone number.

If you access the Regular Expression Editor that's shown in this figure, you can select one of the expressions provided by Visual Studio. These expressions define common patterns for phone numbers and postal codes in the United States and some other countries, as well as social security numbers, email addresses, and URLs.

You can also create a custom expression that's based on a standard expression by selecting an expression in the Regular Expression Editor so its pattern appears in the text box at the bottom of the dialog box. Then, you can modify the expression and click on the OK button to insert it into the aspx code for the validator.

A property of the regular expression validator

Property	Description
`ValidationExpression`	A string that specifies a regular expression. The regular expression defines a pattern that the input data must match to be valid.

The Regular Expression Editor dialog box

A regular expression validator that validates five-digit numbers

```
<asp:TextBox ID="txtZipCode" runat="server"></asp:TextBox>
<asp:RegularExpressionValidator ID="revZipCode" runat="server"
    ControlToValidate="txtZipCode" CssClass="text-danger"
    ValidationExpression="\d{5}"
    ErrorMessage="Must be a five-digit U.S. zip code.">
</asp:RegularExpressionValidator>
```

A regular expression validator that validates U.S. phone numbers

```
<asp:TextBox ID="txtPhone" runat="server"></asp:TextBox>
<asp:RegularExpressionValidator ID="revPhone" runat="server"
    ControlToValidate="txtPhone" CssClass="text-danger"
    ValidationExpression="((\(\d{3}\) ?)|(\d{3}-))?\d{3}-\d{4}"
    ErrorMessage="Must be a valid U.S. phone number.">
</asp:RegularExpressionValidator>
```

Description

- The *regular expression validator* matches the user's entry with the pattern specified by the *regular expression* in the ValidationExpression property. If the entry doesn't match the pattern, the validation fails. If the user doesn't enter a value, the validation test passes.

- ASP.NET provides some common regular expressions that you can access from the Regular Expression Editor. To display its dialog box, select the validation control in the Designer, select the ValidationExpression property in the Properties window, and click its ellipsis button.

- You can also use the Regular Expression Editor to create a custom expression that's based on a standard expression. To do that, select the standard expression and then edit it in the Validation Expression text box.

Figure 7-7   How to use the regular expression validator

How to create regular expressions

Figure 7-8 presents the basic elements of regular expressions. Although the .NET Framework provides many other elements that you can use in regular expressions, you can create expressions of considerable complexity using just the ones shown here. In fact, all of the standard expressions provided by ASP.NET use only these elements.

To start, you can specify any ordinary character, such as a letter or a decimal digit. If a character must be an A, for example, you just include that character in the expression. To include a character other than an ordinary character, you must precede it with a backslash. For example, \(specifies that the character must be a left parenthesis, \] specifies that the character must be a right bracket, and \\ specifies that the character must be a backslash. A backslash that's used in this way is called an *escape character*.

You can also specify a *character class*, which consists of a set of characters. For example, \d indicates that the character must be a decimal digit, \w indicates that the character must be a *word character*, and \s indicates that the character must be a *whitespace character*. The uppercase versions of these elements—\D, \W, and \S—match any character that is not a decimal digit, word character, or whitespace character.

To create a list of possible characters, you enclose them in brackets. For example, [abc] specifies that the character must be the letter a, b, or c, and [a-z] specifies that the character must be a lowercase letter. One common construct is [a-zA-Z], which specifies that the character must be a lowercase or uppercase letter.

You can also use *quantifiers* to indicate how many of the preceding element the input data must contain. To specify an exact number, you just code it in braces. For example, \d{5} specifies that the input data must be a five-digit number. You can also specify a minimum number and a maximum number of characters. For example, \w{6,20} specifies that the input data must contain from six to twenty word characters. You can also omit the maximum number to require just a minimum number of characters. For example, \w{6,} specifies that the input data must contain at least 6 word characters. You can also use the *, ?, and + quantifiers to specify zero or more, zero or one, or one or more characters.

If the input data can match one or more patterns, you can use the vertical bar to separate elements. For example, \w+|\s{1} means that the input data must contain one or more word characters or a single whitespace character.

To create groups of elements, you use parentheses. Then, you can apply quantifiers to the entire group or you can separate groups with a vertical bar. For example, (AB)|(SB) specifies that the input characters must be either AB or SB. And (\d{3}-)? specifies that the input characters must contain zero or one occurrence of a three-digit number followed by a hyphen.

This of course is just an introduction to regular expressions. For more information, try searching the Internet. The information is plentiful, and you can probably find an example of an expression that does just what you're looking for.

Common regular expression elements

Element	Description
Ordinary character	Matches any character other than ., $, ^, [, {, (, |,), *, +, ?, or \.
\	Matches the character that follows.
\d	Matches any decimal digit (0-9).
\D	Matches any character other than a decimal digit.
\w	Matches any word character (a-z, A-Z, and 0-9).
\W	Matches any character other than a word character.
\s	Matches any white space character (space, tab, new line, etc.).
\S	Matches any character other than a whitespace character.
[abcd]	Matches any character included between the brackets.
[^abcd]	Matches any character that is not included between the brackets.
[a-z]	Matches any characters in the indicated range.
{n}	Matches exactly *n* occurrences of the preceding element or group.
{n,}	Matches at least *n* occurrences of the preceding element or group.
{n,m}	Matches at least *n* but no more than *m* occurrences of the preceding element.
*	Matches zero or more occurrences of the preceding element.
?	Matches zero or one occurrence of the preceding element.
+	Matches one or more occurrences of the preceding element.
		Matches any of the elements separated by the vertical bar.
( )	Groups the elements that appear between the parentheses.

Examples of regular expressions

Expression	Example	Description
\d{3}	289	A three digit number.
\w{8,20}	Frankenstein	At least eight but no more than twenty word characters.
\d{2}-\d{4}	10-3944	A two-digit number followed by a hyphen and a four-digit number.
\w{1,8}.\w{1,3}	freddy.jpg	Up to eight letters or numbers, followed by a period and up to three letters or numbers.
(AB)|(SB)-\d{1,5}	SB-3276	The letters AB or SB, followed by a hyphen and a one- to five-digit number.
\d{5}(-\d{4})?	93711-2765	A five-digit number, optionally followed by a hyphen and a four-digit number.
\w*\d\w*	arm01	A text entry that contains at least one numeral.
[xyz]\d{3}	x023	The letter x, y, or z, followed by a three-digit number.

Description

- For more information and for specific types of expressions, you can search the Internet.

Figure 7-8   How to create regular expressions

How to use a custom validator

If none of the other validators provide the data validation that your program requires, you can use a *custom validator*. Then, you can code your own validation routine that's executed when the page is submitted to the server.

Figure 7-9 shows how you use a custom validator. In this example, a custom validator is used to check that a value entered by the user is a prime number. To do that, the code includes an event handler for the ServerValidate event of the custom validator. This event occurs whenever validation is performed on the server, which means it's done when the form is submitted

When the ServerValidate event occurs, the event handler receives an argument named args that you can use to validate the data the user entered. The Value property of this argument contains the user's entry. Then, the event handler can perform the tests that are necessary to determine if this value is valid. If it is valid, the event handler assigns a True value to the IsValid property of the args argument so the validator passes its test. If it isn't valid, the event handler assigns a False value to the IsValid property of this argument so the validator doesn't pass its test. This causes the error message specified by the validator to be displayed in the browser.

In this figure, for example, the event handler calls a private method named IsPrimeNumber that returns a Boolean value. Although this method isn't shown here, all you need to know is that it does some calculations to determine if the number it receives is a prime number. If it is, this method returns a value of True. Otherwise, it returns a value of False. In either case, the returned value is assigned to the IsValid property of the args argument.

In addition to writing validation code that's executed on the server, you can include optional client-side validation code for a custom validator. That way, a round trip to the server isn't required for the validation to be done.

To use client-side validation, you start by coding a JavaScript function that tests if a value is valid. This is illustrated in the third example in this figure. Then, you identify that function on the ClientValidationFunction property of the validator.

Notice here that the JavaScript function must accept two arguments just like the C# event handler. Then, you can use the Value property of the second argument to get the value the user entered, and you can use the IsValid property to indicate whether the value passes the test. Also notice that this function and the function it calls are coded within a script element. This element can be coded in the head element along with the other script elements. Alternatively, you can store the JavaScript in a separate file. Then, this file must be identified by a script tag in the aspx file just like the other JavaScript files.

Properties of the ServerValidateEventArgs class

Property	Description
Value	The text string to be validated.
IsValid	A Boolean property that you set to True if the value passes the validation test or to False if it fails.

The aspx code for a text box and a custom validator

```
<asp:TextBox ID="txtPrime" runat="server"></asp:TextBox>
<asp:CustomValidator ID="cuvPrime" runat="server" CssClass="text-danger"
    ControlToValidate="txtPrime" ValidateEmptyText="true"
    ErrorMessage="Number must be a prime number."
    OnServerValidate="cuvPrime_ServerValidate"
    ClientValidationFunction="cuvPrime_ClientValidate">
</asp:CustomValidator>
```

C# code for the custom validation

```
protected void cuvPrime_ServerValidate(object source,
    ServerValidateEventArgs args)
{
    args.IsValid = IsPrimeNumber(args.Value);
}
private bool IsPrimeNumber(string value) { ... }
```

JavaScript code for the optional client-side validation

```
<script>
    function cuvPrime_ClientValidate(source, args) {
        args.IsValid = isPrimeNumber(args.Value);
    }
    function isPrimeNumber(value) { ... }
</script>
```

Description

- You can use a *custom validator* to validate input data using the tests you specify.

- You code the validation tests for a custom validator within an event handler for the ServerValidate event of the validator. This event is raised whenever validation is performed on the server.

- To start the event handler for the ServerValidate event, you can double-click on the custom validator control in the Designer. Then, you can use the properties of the args argument that's passed to this event handler to test the input data (args.Value) and indicate whether the data passed the validation test (args.IsValid).

- If you set the IsValid property of the args argument to False, the error message you specified for the custom validator is displayed in the browser.

- You can also add optional client-side validation by coding a custom JavaScript function and identifying it on the ClientValidationFunction property. This function also tests the data in the args.Value argument and sets the result in the args.IsValid argument.

- The custom validator provides a ValidateEmptyText property that you can set to True if you want the validation test to run even if the user doesn't enter a value.

Figure 7-9   How to use a custom validator

Validation techniques

Now that you're familiar with the validators, you're ready to learn how to use the validation summary control and validation groups.

How to use the validation summary control

The *validation summary control* lets you summarize all the errors on a page. The summary can be a simple message like "There were errors on the page," or a more elaborate message that includes information about each error. The summary can be displayed directly on the page or in a separate message box.

Figure 7-10 shows how to use the validation summary control. The only tricky part of using this control is knowing how to code the Text and ErrorMessage properties of a validator. To display the same message in both the validator and the validation summary control, for example, you set the ErrorMessage property to that message.

To display different messages, you set the ErrorMessage property to the message you want in the summary control and the Text property to the message you want in the validator. This is illustrated in the example in this figure. Here, the message for each field in the validation control specifies the name of the field, and the message in the validator describes the error. Note that in this case, the message in the validator is coded as content of the control rather than in the Text property.

If you don't want to display individual error messages in the summary control, just set the HeaderText property of the control to the generic message you want to display. Then, leave the ErrorMessage property of each validator blank. Otherwise, you can set the HeaderText property to a value like the one in this figure, or you can leave it at its default value so no heading is displayed. Last, if you want to display an error message in the validation summary control but not in a validator, you can set the Display property of the validator to None.

By default, the error messages displayed by a validation summary control are formatted as a bulleted list as shown in this figure. However, you can display the errors in a list or paragraph by setting the DisplayMode property. You can also display the error messages in a message box rather than on the web page by setting the ShowMessageBox property to True and the ShowSummary property to False.

If you use the default bulleted list for a summary control, the error messages will be in li elements within a ul element. Because of that, you can use CSS to format those elements. That's how the summary control in this figure works.

If you choose a different display mode, though, it can be difficult to find out what HTML elements are generated for the summary control. That's because these elements are generated by JavaScript or jQuery when errors are detected on the client, which means that you can't find out what the elements are by viewing the source code for a page. In this case, you may want to use some of the appearance properties of the control for formatting, such as the BorderColor, BorderStyle, and BorderWidth properties.

Properties of the validation summary control

Property	Description
DisplayMode	Specifies how the error messages from the validators are displayed. The options are BulletList (the default), List, and SingleParagraph.
HeaderText	The text that's displayed before the list of error messages.
ShowSummary	A Boolean value that determines whether the validation summary is displayed on the web page. The default is True.
ShowMessageBox	A Boolean value that determines whether the validation summary is displayed in a message box. The default is False.

The aspx code for a validation summary control and two validators

```
<asp:ValidationSummary ID="ValidationSummary1" runat="server"
    CssClass="summary text-danger"
    HeaderText="Please correct these entries:" />
<h3>Contact information</h3>
<label for="txtEmail1">Email address: </label>
<asp:TextBox ID="txtEmail1" runat="server"></asp:TextBox>
    <asp:RequiredFieldValidator ID="rfvEmail1" runat="server"
        ControlToValidate="txtEmail1" CssClass="text-danger"
        Display="Dynamic" ErrorMessage="Email address">Email is required
    </asp:RequiredFieldValidator><br />
<label for="txtEmail2">Email Re-entry: </label>
<asp:TextBox ID="txtEmail2" runat="server"></asp:TextBox>
    <asp:CompareValidator ID="cvEmail2" runat="server"
        ControlToValidate="txtEmail2" CssClass="text-danger"
        ControlToCompare="txtEmail1" Display="Dynamic"
        ErrorMessage="Email re-entry">Must match first email
    </asp:CompareValidator>
```

How the error messages appear on the web page

```
Please correct these entries:
    • Email address
    • Email re-entry
```

Contact Information

Email address: [   ] Email is required

Email re-entry: [grace@yahoo.com] Must match first email

Description

- The *validation summary control* displays a summary of the error messages that are generated by the page's validators. These messages can be displayed on the form or in a message box.

- The error messages in a summary control come from the ErrorMessage properties of the page's validators. If you want to display a different message in a validator, set the Text property of the validator or code the text as the content of the control.

- If you want to display a message in the validation summary but not in the validator, you can set the validators Display property to None.

Figure 7-10   How to use the validation summary control

How to use validation groups

The *validation group* feature of ASP.NET lets you group validation controls and specify which group should be validated when a page is posted. Figure 7-11 presents a simple example that shows how to use these groups.

To illustrate, the web page in this figure provides for choosing a city on the West Coast or the East Coast. If the user selects a city from the West Coast drop-down list and clicks the Submit button below that control, only the validator for that drop-down list should be executed. Similarly, if the user selects a city from the East Coast drop-down list and clicks the Submit button below that control, only the validator for that drop-down list should be executed. To implement this type of validation, you can use a different validation group for each drop-down list and button.

The first example in this figure shows the West Coast drop-down list and a validator that's assigned to a validation group named West. Then, the second example shows a button that submits the page. Here, the button specifies West as its validation group. Because of that, only the West Coast drop-down list will be validated when the user posts the form. For this to work, the CausesValidation property of the button must be set to True, but that's the default for a button.

The third example shows how you can invoke the West validator or the East validator that's used to validate the second drop-down list in your C# code depending on which Submit button is clicked. To accomplish that, each button includes a CommandName property. Then, the C# code checks the value of that property when the OnCommand event occurs to see which button was clicked, and the Validate method of the Page class is executed with the name of the validation group as its argument. That causes the Validate method of each validator in the group to be executed. In this case, that's a single validator, but additional validators for one or more controls can be assigned to the same group.

If you use validation groups, you should know that any validation controls that don't have a ValidationGroup property are considered part of the *default group*. The validators in this group are executed only when the page is posted with a button or other control that causes validation but doesn't specify a validation group, or when the Page.Validate method is called without specifying a validation group. Because that can make validation groups difficult to work with, they have limited application.

Part of a web form that accepts a city from the east or west coast

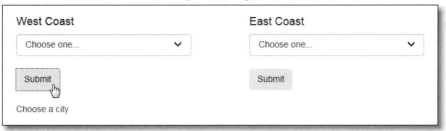

A drop-down list with a validator that specifies a validation group

The aspx code

```
<asp:DropDownList ID="ddlWestCities" runat="server" CssClass="form-con-
trol">
    <asp:ListItem>Choose one...</asp:ListItem>
    <asp:ListItem Value="Seattle">Seattle, WA</asp:ListItem>
    <asp:ListItem Value="Portland">Portland, OR</asp:ListItem>
    <asp:ListItem Value="San Francisco">San Francisco, CA</asp:ListItem>
    <asp:ListItem Value="Los Angeles">Los Angeles, CA</asp:ListItem>
</asp:DropDownList>
<asp:RequiredFieldValidator ID="rfvWestCity" runat="server"
    ErrorMessage="Choose a city" ControlToValidate="ddlWestCities"
    InitialValue="Choose one..." ValidationGroup="West"
    CssClass="text-danger"></asp:RequiredFieldValidator>
```

A button that starts the validation of the group

```
<asp:Button ID="btnSubmitWest" runat="server" Text="Submit"
    ValidationGroup="West" CommandName="West" CssClass="btn"
    OnCommand="SubmitButtons_Command" />
```

C# code that conditionally validates the group

```
protected void SubmitButtons_Command(object sender, CommandEventArgs e)
{
    if (e.CommandName == "West")
        Page.Validate("West");
    else
        Page.Validate("East");
}
```

Description

- A *validation group* is a group of validators that are run when a page is posted.
- To group validators, set the ValidationGroup property for each validator. To run the validators for the group, set this property for a control that causes validation.
- You can also use C# code to do the validation for a group by using the Page.Validate method with the name of the validation group as the argument.
- Any validators that don't specify the ValidationGroup property are part of the *default group*. This group is executed when started by a button or control that doesn't specify a validation group or when the Page.Validate method is used without an argument.

Figure 7-11   How to use validation groups

A CheckOut page that uses validation controls

Now, to show you how the validation controls work in a complete application, this chapter ends by presenting a CheckOut page that uses most of the validation controls.

The user interface

Figure 7-12 presents the user interface for the CheckOut page. At the top of this page, you can see a validation summary control that lists the fields that need to be corrected. Then, to the right of those fields, you can see the error messages that describe what's wrong.

In the shipping-address portion of the page, you can see the check box that determines whether the shipping address is the same as the billing address. If the user checks this box, the page is posted to the server, the four shipping-address fields and their validators are disabled, and the page is returned to the browser. If the user unchecks this box, this process is reversed. Either way, when the user clicks the Check Out button, the appropriate validators are executed. In this figure, the shipping fields and their validators aren't enabled so only the other validators are executed when the user clicks the Check Out button.

The Check Out page with validation

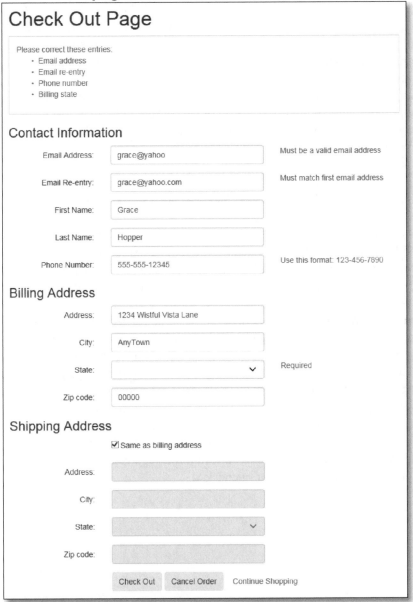

Description

- This web form has a validation summary control at the top of the form that doesn't show unless the validators detect errors, along with several validation controls.

- When the user clicks on the check box that indicates whether the shipping address is the same as the billing address, the page is posted to the server and the text boxes and validators for the shipping fields are either enabled or disabled.

Figure 7-12   The CheckOut page for the Shopping Cart application

The aspx code

Figure 7-13 presents some of the aspx code for the CheckOut page. Here, the validation summary control is at the top of the form so its content is displayed prominently on the page. This is followed by the labels, controls, and validators for the user entries.

As you can see, the validators for all of the fields have one message in the ErrorMessage property and another in the text content for the field. As a result, the first message is displayed in the validation summary control, and the second message is displayed in the validator.

If you look down the page to the first required field validator for the shipping-address portion of the page, you can see another way to provide the message that's displayed in the validator. Here, the Text property for the validator is used to store the message.

The first block of code in this figure also illustrates the use of a regular expression validator and a compare validator. In the regular expression validator for the first email address entry, the regular expression is one that is provided by the Regular Expression Editor. So even though it's long and complicated, you can trust it to do its job.

In the compare validator, the email address entry in the related text box is compared with the address in the preceding text box. Because the Operator property isn't specified, an equal comparison is assumed. As a result, the error messages are displayed if the entries in the first two text boxes aren't equal.

In the aspx code for the shipping-address portion of the page, you can see the code for the check box that determines whether the shipping address is different from the billing address. To make this form work right, the AutoPostBack property of the check box is set to True. Also, by default, its CausesValidation property is set to False. As a result, the page is posted back to the server when this button is checked or unchecked.

The start of the aspx code for the CheckOut page

```
<asp:ValidationSummary ID="ValidationSummary1" runat="server"
    CssClass="text-danger summary"
    HeaderText="Please correct these entries:" />
<h3>Contact Information</h3>
<div class="form-group">
    <label class="control-label col-sm-3">Email Address:</label>
    <div class="col-sm-5">
        <asp:TextBox ID="txtEmail1" runat="server" CssClass="form-control"
            TextMode="Email"></asp:TextBox></div>
    <div class="col-sm-4">
        <asp:RequiredFieldValidator ID="rfvEmail1" runat="server"
            ErrorMessage="Email address" CssClass="text-danger"
            Display="Dynamic" ControlToValidate="txtEmail1">Required
        </asp:RequiredFieldValidator>
        <asp:RegularExpressionValidator ID="revEmail1" runat="server"
            ErrorMessage="Email address" CssClass="text-danger"
            Display="Dynamic"
            ValidationExpression="\w+([-+.']\w+)*@\w+([-.]\w+)*\.\w+([-.]\w+)*"
            ControlToValidate="txtEmail1">Must be a valid email address
        </asp:RegularExpressionValidator></div></div>
<div class="form-group">
    <label class="control-label col-sm-3">Email Re-entry:</label>
    <div class="col-sm-5">
        <asp:TextBox ID="txtEmail2" runat="server" CssClass="form-control"
            TextMode="Email"></asp:TextBox></div>
    <div class="col-sm-4">
        <asp:RequiredFieldValidator ID="rfvEmail2" runat="server"
            ErrorMessage="Email re-entry" CssClass="text-danger"
            Display="Dynamic" ControlToValidate="txtEmail2">Required
        </asp:RequiredFieldValidator>
        <asp:CompareValidator ID="cvEmail2" runat="server"
            ErrorMessage="Email re-entry" CssClass="text-danger"
            Display="Dynamic" ControlToValidate="txtEmail2"
            ControlToCompare="txtEmail1">Must match first email address
        </asp:CompareValidator></div></div>
```

The start of the aspx code for the shipping-address portion of the page

```
<div class="form-group">
    <div class="col-sm-offset-3 col-sm-9">
        <asp:CheckBox ID="chkSameAsBilling" runat="server"
            AutoPostBack="True"
            OnCheckedChanged="chkSameAsBilling_CheckedChanged" />
        <label>Same as billing address</label></div></div>
<div class="form-group">
    <label class="control-label col-sm-3">Address:</label>
    <div class="col-sm-5">
        <asp:TextBox ID="txtShipAddress" runat="server"
            CssClass="form-control"></asp:TextBox></div>
    <div class="col-sm-4">
        <asp:RequiredFieldValidator ID="rfvShipAddress" runat="server"
            ErrorMessage="Shipping address" Text="Required"
            CssClass="text-danger" Display="Dynamic"
            ControlToValidate="txtShipAddress">
        </asp:RequiredFieldValidator></div></div>
```

Figure 7-13   Some of the aspx code for the CheckOut page

The C# code

Figure 7-14 shows some of the C# code in the code-behind file for the page. This is like the code you reviewed in the previous chapter, with two exceptions.

First, the GetCustomerData method not only gets the data for the contact information and the billing address, but also the data for the shipping address. As you can see, though, the information it gets for the shipping data depends on whether the Same as Billing Address checkbox is checked. If it is, the GetCustomerData method uses the billing address information it just added to the customer object to fill the shipping address properties. Otherwise, the GetCustomerData method retrieves the shipping information from the shipping data controls on the page.

Second, the last event handler in this figure is executed when the CheckedChanged event of the check box occurs. This event occurs when the user checks or unchecks the box. To cause a postback when the check box is changed, its AutoPostBack property has been set to True. Also, the CausesValidation property of a check box is set to False by default, so checking the box won't cause validation.

Within this event handler, you can see a series of statements that set the value of the Enabled property for the shipping-address fields and the required field validators for those fields. To do that, the Not operator (!) is used to toggle the values so they become true if they're false and false if they're true.

You could take this code one step further and set the values in the shipping fields to empty strings when the box is checked. That would remove any data that might be in those fields.

You could also use JavaScript and jQuery to handle the CheckedChanged event on the client instead of on the server. Then, a round trip wouldn't be required each time the user changes the check box, and you wouldn't need the CheckedChanged event handler in the code-behind file. Since this is a better way to handle the check box changes, this is one more reason for learning how to use JavaScript and jQuery.

Some of the C# code in the code-behind file for the CheckOut page

```csharp
private Customer customer;
protected void Page_Load(object sender, EventArgs e)
{
    if (!IsPostBack) {
        customer = (Customer)Session["Customer"];
        LoadCustomerData();
    }
}
protected void btnCheckOut_Click(object sender, EventArgs e)
{
    if (IsValid) {
        GetCustomerData();
        Response.Redirect("~/Confirmation.aspx");
    }
}
private void LoadCustomerData()
{
    if (customer != null) {
        ...
        txtShipAddress.Text = customer.ShippingAddress;
        txtShipCity.Text = customer.ShippingCity;
        ddlShipState.SelectedValue = customer.ShippingState;
        txtShipZip.Text = customer.ShippingZip;
    }
}
private void GetCustomerData()
{
    if (customer == null) customer = new Customer();
    ...
    if (chkSameAsBilling.Checked) {
        customer.ShippingAddress = customer.Address;
        customer.ShippingCity = customer.City;
        customer.ShippingState = customer.State;
        customer.ShippingZip = customer.Zip;
    }
    else {
        customer.ShippingAddress = txtShipAddress.Text;
        customer.ShippingCity = txtShipCity.Text;
        customer.ShippingState = ddlShipState.SelectedValue;
        customer.ShippingZip = txtShipZip.Text;
    }
    Session["Customer"] = customer;
}
protected void chkSameAsBilling_CheckedChanged(object sender, EventArgs e)
{
    rfvShipAddress.Enabled = !rfvShipAddress.Enabled;
    rfvShipCity.Enabled = !rfvShipCity.Enabled;
    rfvShipState.Enabled = !rfvShipState.Enabled;
    rfvShipZip.Enabled = !rfvShipZip.Enabled;

    txtShipAddress.Enabled = !txtShipAddress.Enabled;
    txtShipCity.Enabled = !txtShipCity.Enabled;
    ddlShipState.Enabled = !ddlShipState.Enabled;
    txtShipZip.Enabled = !txtShipZip.Enabled;
}
```

Figure 7-14   Some of the C# code for the CheckOut page

Perspective

Now that you've completed this chapter, you should be able to create web forms that provide most or all of the data validation that your applications require. Keep in mind, though, that after you add validators to a form, you need to test them thoroughly to be sure that they detect all invalid entries. Although that can be time-consuming, it's an essential part of developing professional web applications.

Terms

validation control	regular expression validator
validator	regular expression
unobtrusive validation	custom validator
required field validator	validation summary control
compare validator	validation group
range validator	default group

Summary

- ASP.NET provides six *validation controls*, including five *validators* and one validation summary control.

- If a browser has JavaScript enabled, as most browsers do, the validation that's specified by the validators is done on the client. But, it's always done on the server too. In the code-behind file for a page, the IsValid property of the page can be tested to see whether the data in all of the controls is valid.

- When *unobtrusive validation* is on, jQuery is used for the validation that's done on the client. Since jQuery is a JavaScript library, this means that ASP.NET generates less JavaScript code for the page. To implement unobtrusive validation, you can install the NuGet package for it.

- The *required field validator* lets you check to see if an entry has been made. The *compare validator* lets you compare an entry to another entry or a constant. And the *range validator* lets you check whether an entry falls within a specified range.

- The *regular expression validator* lets you check an entry to see whether it conforms to a pattern that's defined by a *regular expression*. Visual Studio's Regular Expression Editor lets you select regular expressions for common entries like email addresses and phone numbers.

- A *custom validator* lets you provide your own validation code in the code-behind file for the page. You can also add optional client-side validation code.

- A *validation summary control* lets you display error messages for the entries in a separate portion of the page as well as in the validators.

- *Validation groups* let you validate one group of controls at a time.

Exercise 7-1   Modify the CheckOut page

In this exercise, you'll modify the CheckOut page that's presented in this chapter.

Open, review, and run the CheckOut page

1. Open the Ex07Cart web application that's in the aspnet46_cs directory, and review the CheckOut page and its code-behind file. Refer back to these files as you test the application to see how the aspx and C# code works.

2. Test the application to see how it works. Without entering any data on the CheckOut page, click the Check Out button to see how the error messages are displayed in the validation summary control as well as in the validators.

3. Click on the check box to check it and note that the validation messages disappear. Next, click on the Check Out button again, and note that no error messages are displayed for the shipping fields. Then, click in one of the shipping text boxes and note that it is disabled.

4. Click on the check box again to uncheck it, and click on the Check Out button again. Then, note that error messages are displayed for all of the fields.

5. Test the validators for each field by entering both valid and invalid entries and clicking on the Check Out button. In the first text box, for example, enter an invalid email address to see how the regular expression validator works. And in the second text box, enter a value that's different from the one in the first text box.

6. Eventually, enter valid data for all fields, and click the Check Out button. Then, in the Confirmation page, note the data that has been retrieved from the customer object.

Implement unobtrusive validation for the web application

7. Open the Web.config file and note that unobtrusive validation has been turned off for the web application. Now, delete the elements that turn it off, and test the application again. Note that the application won't run because it needs a ScriptResourceMapping for jQuery.

8. Install the NuGet package for unobtrusive validation as shown in figure 7-3, making sure to select a version before 3.0.0. Note the new assembly in the References section of the Solution Explorer, and check to see if the jQuery files in the Scripts folder have new version numbers. If so, update the script tags in the head element of the applications pages as needed. Then, test the application again. This time, the validation should work.

Add validators to the web form

9. Add an initial value of 999-999-9999 to the phone number field to show the format for the phone number entry. Next, add an InitialValue property to the required field validator for this text box that has the same initial value. Then, test this change to see how it works.

10. Add a regular expression validator for the billing zip code field so it will accept an entry in either of these formats: 99999 or 99999-9999. The validator message should be: "Use this format: 99999 or 99999-9999", and the ErrorMessage and CssClass properties should be the same as they are for the required field validator. Then, test to make sure that both formats are accepted as valid and that the right messages are displayed in the validation summary control and the validator.

11. Add a "Date of birth" field after the Phone number field. Don't add a required field validator for this field because it will be optional, but add a regular expression validator for the field that tests to make sure the data is in this format: mm/dd/yyyy. Also, set the initial value for the text field to "mm/dd/yyyy", and be sure to provide appropriate messages for both the validation summary control and the validator. For the regular expression, you can use this code:

```
[01]?\d\/[0-3]\d\/\d{4}
```

Modify the Customer class and two code-behind files

12. Open the Customer.cs file in the Models folder, and add a birthdate property to the Customer class. To keep this simple, the property should be a string (not a DateTime value).

13. Open the code-behind file for the CheckOut page, and modify the code so the birthdate entry is added to the customer object when the Check Out button is clicked and retrieved from the customer object if the page is displayed again.

14. Open the code-behind file for the Confirmation page, and modify the code so the birthdate entry is displayed when a valid form has been posted back to the CheckOut page and the Confirmation page is displayed.

15. When you're through testing and experimenting, close the application.

8

How to work with state, cookies, and URL encoding

In chapters 2 and 4, you were introduced to the way that view state and session state are used. Now you'll learn more about using these states, and you'll also learn how and when to use application state and caching. Beyond that, you'll learn how to use cookies and URL encoding to pass data between the server and the client. Because HTTP is a stateless protocol, these are essential skills for every web developer.

How to use view state

For the most part, *view state* is automatic. Because of that, you don't have to set any properties or write any code to use it. Nevertheless, you should understand how view state works and how to use it to your advantage. In some cases, you may even want to add your own data to view state.

How to work with view state

As the summary in figure 8-1 says, view state works by saving data in the HTML stream that's sent to the browser when a page is requested. This data is saved as a hidden input field named _VIEWSTATE. Because the field is hidden, it isn't displayed in the browser. And because the field is an input field, it's automatically sent back to the server when the user posts the page.

View state is used to retain the values of the form and control properties that you set in code. In the Future Value application of chapter 2, for example, the values in the drop-down list were set by code. As a result, those values don't need to be reset by code each time the page is posted back to the server. Instead, they're automatically reset by view state.

The EnableViewState property of a page and its controls determines if view state is enabled, which it is by default. Although this is usually what you want, you may occasionally want to disable view state. One reason for doing that is to get a control to work the way you want it to. Another reason is to improve performance when view state gets so large that it degrades performance. In practice, though, you probably won't turn off view state until you discover that it's creating either a programming or performance problem.

If, for example, you change the value of a control property in code, but you want the initial value of that property restored each time the page is loaded, you can turn off view state to get the page to work right. Or, if a page is never posted back to itself, you can turn off view state to improve performance. To disable view state for a control, page, or entire application, you can use the techniques in this figure.

To disable view state for all but a few controls on a page, you can use the technique under the fourth heading in this figure, but this is tricky. First, you need to set the EnableViewState property of the page and controls that you want to use view state for to True. That's because you can't enable view state for any controls if view state is turned off for the page. Then, you set the ViewStateMode property of the Page directive to disabled so view state is disabled for all controls. Last, you set the ViewStateMode property for each of the controls that you want view state enabled for to True.

To determine the size of view state, you can enable the ASP.NET trace feature as described in chapter 5. Then, you can scroll to the Control Tree section of the trace output to see which controls are using view state and how many bytes they're using. That way, you can tell whether it's worth the effort to turn view state off.

View state concepts

- *View state* is an ASP.NET feature that provides for retaining the values of page and control properties that change from one execution of a page to another.

- Before ASP.NET sends a page back to the client, it determines what changes the program has made to the properties of the page and its controls. These changes are encoded in a string that's assigned to the value of a hidden input field named _VIEWSTATE.

- When the page is posted back to the server, the _VIEWSTATE field is sent back to the server along with the HTTP request. Then, ASP.NET retrieves the property values from the _VIEWSTATE field and uses them to restore the page and control properties.

- ASP.NET also uses view state to save the values of the page properties it uses, such as IsPostBack.

- View state is *not* used to restore data entered by a user into a text box or any other input control unless the control responds to change events.

- If view state is enabled for a data-bound control, the control will not be bound again when the page is reposted. Instead, the control's values will be restored from view state.

Two cases when you may want to disable view state

- When restoring the control properties for a page affects the way you want the form to work, you may want to disable view state for one or more controls.

- When the size of the view state field gets so large that it affects performance, you may want to disable view state for one or more controls or for an entire page.

How to disable view state

- To disable view state for a control, set the control's EnableViewState property to False.

- To disable view state for an entire page, set the EnableViewState property of the Page directive to False. That disables view state for all the controls on the page.

- To disable view state for the entire application, set the EnableViewState attribute of the pages element in the system.web element of the Web.config file to False.

How to enable view state for selected controls

- Set the EnableViewState property of the page and the controls whose view state you want to enable to True.

- Set the ViewStateMode property of the Page directive to Disabled.

- Set the ViewStateMode property of the selected controls to Enabled.

How to determine the size of view state for a page

- Enable the page's trace feature by setting the Trace attribute of the Page directive to True as described in chapter 5. Then, scroll down to the Control Tree section of the trace output to see the number of bytes of view state used by the page and its controls.

Figure 8-1   How to work with view state

How to use view state for your own data

Although view state is designed to automatically save page and control property values across round trips to the browser, you can also add your own data to view state. To do that, you store the data in a *view state object* that's created from the StateBag class as shown in figure 8-2.

Like the session state object, the view state object contains a collection of key/value pairs that represent the items saved in view state. To access this object, you use the ViewState property of the page. Then, you can use the methods listed in this figure to work with the view state object.

To illustrate, the first two examples in this figure show how you can add or update a view state item named TimeStamp. The third example shows how to retrieve that item. And the last example shows how to remove it. Notice in the third example that because a view state item is stored as an object type, the code must cast the object to the DateTime data type.

Keep in mind that you usually use session state, not view state, to save data across round trips. Occasionally, though, it does make sense to use view state for passing small amounts of data, especially when you want to associate the data with a specific page. In chapter 21, you'll see an example of that.

Common members of the StateBag class

Indexer	Description
`[name]`	The value of the view state item with the specified name. If you set the value of an item that doesn't exist, that item is created.

Property	Description
`Count`	The number of items in the view state collection.
`Keys`	A collection of keys for all of the items in the view state collection.
`Values`	A collection of values for all of the items in the view state collection.

Method	Description
`Add(name, value)`	Adds an item to the view state collection. If the item already exists, its value is updated.
`Clear()`	Removes all items from the view state collection.
`Remove(name)`	Removes the item with the specified name from the view state collection.

A statement that adds or updates a view state item

```
ViewState.Add("TimeStamp", DateTime.Now);
```

Another way to add or update a view state item

```
ViewState["TimeStamp"] = DateTime.Now;
```

A statement that retrieves the value of a view state item

```
DateTime timeStamp = (DateTime) ViewState["TimeStamp"];
```

A statement that removes an item from view state

```
ViewState.Remove("TimeStamp");
```

Description

- View state is implemented with a *view state object* that's defined by the StateBag class. This class defines a collection of view state items.
- Although the form and control properties are automatically saved in view state, you can also save other data in view state.
- To access the view state object for a page, you use the ViewState property of the page.
- Usually you'll use session state, not view state, to save data across round trips to the server.

Figure 8-2   How to use view state for your own data

How to use session state

In chapter 4, you learned some basic skills for using session state to save data across round trips. The topics that follow review and expand on that information.

How to work with session state

As you have learned, ASP.NET uses *session state* to track the state of each user of an application. To do that, it creates a *session state object* that contains a unique *session ID* for each user's session. This ID is passed back to the browser as part of a response and returned to the server with the next request. ASP.NET can then use the session ID to get the session state object that's associated with the request.

To manage a user session, you can store data in the session state object as shown in figure 8-3. Since you've already seen how session state is used in the Shopping Cart application, you shouldn't have any trouble understanding these examples. The first one adds or updates a session state item named Email. The second one retrieves the value of the Email item and stores it in a string variable. And the third one removes the Email item from session state.

All three of these examples assume that session state is being accessed from the code-behind file of a web page. In that case, you refer to the session state object by using the Session property of the page. To access session state from outside of a web page, however, you use the Session property of the HttpContext object for the current request, as illustrated in the fourth example.

Note that the HttpContext class used in this example is stored in the System.Web namespace. Because of that, you'll typically include a using directive for this namespace. Otherwise, you'll need to qualify any references to the HttpContext class with System.Web.

Common members of the HttpSessionState class

Indexer	Description
`[name]`	The value of the session state item with the specified name. If you set the value of an item that doesn't exist, that item is created.

Property	Description
`SessionID`	The unique ID of the session.
`Count`	The number of items in the session state collection.

Method	Description
`Add(name, value)`	Adds an item to the session state collection. If the item already exists, its value is updated.
`Clear()`	Removes all items from the session state collection.
`Remove(name)`	Removes the item with the specified name from the session state collection.

A statement that adds or updates a session state item

```
Session["Email"] = email;
```

A statement that retrieves the value of a session state item

```
string email = Session["Email"].ToString();
```

A statement that removes an item from session state

```
Session.Remove("Email");
```

A statement that retrieves a session state item from a non-page class

```
string email = HttpContext.Current.Session["Email"].ToString();
```

Description

- ASP.NET uses *session state* to track the state of each user of an application. To do that, it creates a *session state object* that contains a *session ID*. This ID is passed to the browser and then back to the server with the next request so the server can identify the session state object associated with that request.

- Because session state sends only the session ID to the browser, it doesn't slow response time. Session state can slow performance on the server side, though, because session state objects are maintained in server memory by default. In a moment, you'll learn about other options for maintaining session state on the server.

- To work with the data in session state, you use the HttpSessionState class, which defines a collection of session state items.

- To access the session state object from the code-behind file for a web form, use the Session property of the page.

- To access the session state object from a class other than a code-behind file, use the Current property of the HttpContext class to get the HttpContext object for the current request. Then, use the Session property to get the session state object.

- The HttpContext class is stored in the System.Web namespace.

Figure 8-3   How to work with session state

When to save and retrieve session state items

Most ASP.NET developers use session state in a consistent way. First, an application retrieves data from session state and stores it in variables. Then, the application uses these variables when it processes the user events. Finally, the application saves the updated variables back to session state so they can be retrieved the next time the page is posted back to the server.

If an item in session state is used within a single method in an application, you can retrieve, process, and save that item within that method. However, it's more common for an application to use a session state item in two or more methods. Because of that, it makes sense to retrieve the item when the application first starts and save it just before it ends. To do that, you can use the Load and PreRender events of the page, as shown in figure 8-4.

The first two examples in this figure are taken from the Shopping Cart application of chapter 4, so you shouldn't have any trouble understanding them. The first example uses the GetCart method of the CartItemList class to get a CartItemList object from the session state object, and it stores it in a variable named cart. The second example updates the cart by removing an item from it if an item in the cart is selected.

The third example shows how to use an event handler for the PreRender event to update an item named "Count" with the value of a variable named sessionCount. Note, however, that this event handler is only needed because sessionCount is a value-based variable, which means that the value is actually stored in the variable.

In contrast, if you update a reference-type variable such as a string or other object variable, the session state item is updated automatically when you update the object. That's because the variable contains a pointer to the object, not the data itself. Then, since the session state item also contains a pointer to that object, you don't have to update the session state item explicitly. That's the way the CartItemList object in the session state object is handled in the first two examples in this figure.

The page events that can be used to get and save session state data

Event	Handler name	Description
Load	Page_Load	This event occurs when a page is requested from the server, after all controls have been initialized and view state has been restored. You can use the handler for this event to test whether the session state object already exists, to get data from it if it does, and to create one if it doesn't.
PreRender	Page_PreRender	This event occurs after all the control events for the page have been processed but before the HTML that will be sent back to the browser is generated. You can use it to update value-type variables in the object, but you don't need to do that for reference-type variables.

A Load event handler that gets the session state object named cart

```
private CartItemList cart;
protected void Page_Load(object sender, EventArgs e)
{
    cart = CartItemList.GetCart();
    if (!IsPostBack) DisplayCart();
}
```

A Click event handler that updates the cart object

```
protected void btnRemove_Click(object sender, EventArgs e)
{
    if (cart.Count > 0)
    {
        if (lstCart.SelectedIndex > -1)
        {
            cart.RemoveAt(lstCart.SelectedIndex);
            DisplayCart();
        }
        else
        {
            lblMessage.Text = "Please select the item you want to remove.";
        }
    }
}
```

A PreRender event handler that updates a value in the cart object

```
protected void Page_PreRender(object sender, EventArgs e)
{
    cart["Count"] = sessionCount;
}
```

Description

- You only need to update a session state item explicitly if it's stored in a value-type variable, like an integer. If it's stored in a reference-type variable, like a custom object, the session state item is updated when the variable is updated. That's because the variable is a pointer to the object that's updated.

Figure 8-4   When to save and retrieve session state items

Options for storing session state data and tracking session IDs

By default, ASP.NET stores session state data in server memory and tracks user sessions using cookies. However, as figure 8-5 shows, ASP.NET actually provides four options for storing session state data and two options for tracking session IDs. It's good, then, to be familiar with all these options in case you ever need them.

The default for storing session state data is *in-process mode*. With this mode, session state data is stored in server memory within the same process that your ASP.NET application runs. This is the most efficient way to store session state data, but it only works for applications that are hosted on a single web server.

If your application has so many users that a single web server can't carry the load, you can deploy the application on two or more servers. When you do that, you need to store session state data in a location that can be accessed by all of the servers. To do that, you can use either the *State Server mode* or the *SQL Server mode* that are described in the first table in this figure.

The last option for storing session state data is *custom mode*. With this mode, you create your own *session state store provider* that saves and retrieves session state data. You might use this option, for example, if you want to save session state data in an Oracle database instead of Microsoft SQL Server.

Fortunately, the programming requirements for all four session state modes are identical. So you can change an application from one mode to another without changing any of the application's code, with one caveat. If you haven't made your custom objects *serializable* when working in in-process mode, you'll need to do so when you move to state server or SQL server mode.

By default, ASP.NET maintains session state by sending the session ID for a user session to the browser as a *cookie*. Then, the cookie is returned to the server with the next request so the server can associate the browser with the session. This is called *cookie-based session tracking*, and this is the most reliable and secure way to track sessions.

If a browser doesn't support cookies, however, session state won't work unless you switch to *cookieless session tracking*. Cookieless session tracking works by adding the session ID to the URL that's used to request the ASP.NET page. Unfortunately, because the URL is visible to the user and isn't encrypted, the use of cookieless session tracking creates a security risk.

Ideally, then, you should use cookie-based session tracking when cookies are supported and cookieless session tracking when they're not. As you can see in the third table and the code example, ASP.NET lets you do that by modifying the system.web element in the Web.config file. In this example, the mode attribute indicates that in-process mode should be used. The cookieless attribute indicates that cookies should be used if they're supported, and URLs should be used if they're not. And the timeout attribute increases the time that the session will be maintained without activity to 30 minutes.

If you use a mode other than in-process mode, you're probably going to be in a large shop. In that case, you should be able to get help from the server manager when it's time to set the attributes in the Web.config file.

Four modes for storing session state data

Mode	Description
In-process	Stores the data in IIS server memory in the same process as the application. This is the default, but it's only suitable when a single server is used for the application.
State Server	Stores the data in server memory under the control of the *ASP.NET state service*. This service can be accessed by other IIS servers, so it can be used when an application is hosted on a web farm.
SQL Server	Stores the data in a SQL Server database. This mode is used for applications that require more than one IIS server. This mode is slower than In-process mode and State Server mode, but it's the most reliable.
Custom	Lets you write your own *session state store provider* class for session state data.

Two options for tracking session IDs

Option	Description
Cookie-based	Uses cookies.
Cookieless	The session ID is encoded as part of the URL.

Attributes of the session state element in the Web.config file

Attribute	Values
`Mode`	Off, InProc (the default), StateServer, SQLServer, or Custom.
`Cookieless`	UseCookies (the default). AutoDetect uses cookies if they're supported and a query string if they're not. UseUri uses a query string.
`Timeout`	The minutes that a session should be maintained without any user activity. The default is 20.
`StateConnectionString`	The server name or IP address and port number (always 42424) of the server that runs the ASP.NET state service.
`SqlConnectionString`	A connection string for the instance of SQL Server that contains the database that's used to store the session state data.
`AllowCustomSqlDatabase`	A Boolean value that determines if the SqlConnectionString can specify the name of the database used to store state information.

A sessionState element in the Web.config file that uses in-process mode

```
<system.web>
    <sessionState mode="InProc" cookieless="AutoDetect" timeout="30" />
</system.web>
```

Description

- The programming requirements for all four session state modes are the same, but the State Server and SQL Server modes require objects in session state to be *serializable*. To make an item serializable, add a Serializable attribute to its class declaration.

Figure 8-5   Options for storing session state data and tracking session IDs

How to use application state and caching

In contrast to session state, which stores data for a single user session, application state and caching let you store data that's shared by all users of an application. In the topics that follow, you'll learn how to use application state and caching.

How application state and caching work

Figure 8-6 presents the concepts you need for working with *application state* and *caching*. To start, an *application* is made up of all the pages, code, and other files that are located under a single directory in an IIS web server.

The first time a user requests a page that resides in an application's directory, ASP.NET initializes the application. During that process, ASP.NET creates an *application object* from the HttpApplication class, an *application state object* from the HttpApplicationState class, and a *cache object* from the Cache class. You can use the application state object or the cache object to store data in server memory that can be accessed by any page that's part of the application.

These objects exist until the application ends, which normally doesn't happen until IIS shuts down. However, the application is also restarted each time you rebuild the application or edit the application's Web.config file.

So which application-level storage should you use? Generally, you'll want to use the cache object, because it's more flexible. This is because you can set expiration dates for items stored in the cache, and because the server is allowed to *scavenge* the cache when memory is running low. Because of this, you can store just about anything you want in the cache without worrying about negatively affecting the server, as long as you remember that the items may not be there when you come back for them. So, always check for null values in your code before trying to use something you've retrieved from cache.

Caching is typically used to store application-specific data that changes infrequently. For example, you might use the cache to store discount terms and tax rates for an ordering system, or a list of the 50 states. Although you could retrieve this type of information from a database each time it's needed, it can be retrieved more quickly from cache. As a result, using cached data can improve your application's performance.

In contrast, items stored in application state stay in memory until they are specifically removed or until the application ends. This can have a negative effect on a server's performance if a lot of data is stored. For this reason, it's best to use application state for small items of data, such as keeping track of the users that are logged on to an application that provides a chat room or a forum.

Application concepts

- An ASP.NET *application* is the collection of pages, code, and other files within a single directory on a web server. In most cases, an ASP.NET application corresponds to a single Visual Studio web project.

- An application begins when the first user requests a page that's a part of the application. Then, ASP.NET initializes the application before it processes the request for the page.

- As part of its initialization, ASP.NET creates an *application object* from the HttpApplication class, an *application state object* from the HttpApplicationState class, and a *cache object* from the Cache class. These objects exist for the duration of the application, and items stored in application state or cache are available to all users of the application.

- Once an application has started, it doesn't normally end until the web server is shut down. However, if you rebuild the application or edit the Web.config file, the application will be restarted the next time a user requests a page that's part of the application.

Cache concepts

- Items stored in the cache object don't necessarily stay in server memory until the application ends. They can be set with an expiration date, and they can be *scavenged* by the server to recover memory when memory is low.

- Because of the way caching works, you can store larger amounts of data in the cache. However, you'll always need to check whether the data is still there before using it.

- The cache object is typically used to store data that changes infrequently, such as a list of states or countries. Storing data like this in cache improves performance by reducing the number of times you need to retrieve it from the database or other data store.

- Caching in ASP.NET can be done declaratively with output caching, and cache items can be removed automatically via dependencies, but that's beyond the scope of this book. Caching can also be used by data source server controls.

Application state concepts

- Items stored in the application state object stay in server memory until they are specifically removed, or until the application ends. Because this can stress the server, application state should be used sparingly.

- Application state is most appropriate for storing small items of data that change as an application executes, such as how many users have requested the application.

- To make sure the application object is not accessed by more than one user at a time, it should be locked while updating and unlocked when the update is completed.

Figure 8-6   How application state and caching work

How to work with application state and cache data

Figure 8-7 presents the details for working with application state and cache data. The first table in this figure shows the members that are common to both classes, while the second and third tables show some methods specific to the Cache and HttpApplicationState classes.

As you can see from the examples below the tables, the techniques you use to add items to and retrieve items from application state and cache are similar to the techniques you use to work with items in session state. The main difference is that you use the Application or Cache property of the page to access the objects from a code-behind file, and you use the Application or Cache property of the HttpContext object for the current request to access the objects from a class other than a code-behind file.

However, if you want to set an expiration for an item you're adding to the cache, you'll need to use the Insert method of the Cache object. The Insert method is an overloaded method, but the one you'll most commonly use to set an expiration is shown in the second table in this figure. There are five parameters for this method.

The first and second parameters are the name and value of the object to be stored, just like with the Add method. The third parameter is a CacheDependency object. While not illustrated here, cache dependencies allow you to automatically remove an item from the cache when something it is associated with changes. For example, if your cached item is associated with an item in a database, the cached item can be removed when the item in the database changes. Most of the time, though, you'll enter a value of null for this parameter.

The fourth and fifth parameters determine the expiration time for the cached item. The fourth parameter sets an absolute expiration, such as 20 minutes from now, while the fifth parameter sets a sliding expiration, such as 20 minutes from the last time the item was accessed. If you try to set a value for both of these parameters, you'll get an error. Rather, you must set only one, and then use the System.Web.Caching.Cache enumeration to set a value of NoAbsoluteExpiration or NoSlidingExpiration for the other, as shown in the last example in this figure.

Common members of the HttpApplicationState and Cache classes

Indexer	Description
[name]	The value of the item with the specified name. If you set the value of an item that doesn't exist, that item is created.

Property	Description
Count	The number of items in the collection.

Method	Description
Add(name, value)	Adds an item to the collection.
Remove(name)	Removes the item with the specified name from the collection.

The Insert method of the Cache class

Method	Description
Insert(name, value, dependency, absolute, sliding)	Adds an item to the cache collection with a CacheDependency object (which can be null) and either an absolute expiration (like 20 minutes from now) or a sliding expiration (like 20 minutes from last usage). Use the System.Web.Caching.Cache enumeration for the expiration.

Common methods of the HttpApplicationState class

Method	Description
Clear()	Removes all items from the application state collection.
Lock()	Locks the application state collection so only the current user can access it.
Unlock()	Unlocks the application state collection so other users can access it.

Two statements that add items to application state and cache

```
Application.Add("ClickCount", 0);
Cache.Add("states", states);
```

Two statements that retrieve an item from application state and cache

```
int applicationCount = Convert.ToInt32(Application["ClickCount"]);
List<string> states = (List<string>)Cache["states"];
```

Two statements that retrieve an item from a non-page class

```
int applicationCount =
    Convert.ToInt32(HttpContext.Current.Application["ClickCount"]);
List<string> states = (List<string>)HttpContext.Current.Cache["states"];
```

A statement that adds an item to cache with an absolute expiration time

```
Cache.Insert("states", states, null, DateTime.Now.AddMinutes(20),
    System.Web.Caching.Cache.NoSlidingExpiration);
```

Figure 8-7   How to work with application state and cache data

How to work with application events

Besides providing storage, the application object also raises several events that you can use to run code at various points in the life of an application, such as when it starts, when it ends, or when an error occurs. One of the uses of these events is to initialize the values of application state items, as shown in figure 8-8. To work with these events, you first add a Global.asax file to the project using one of the techniques described in this figure.

When you first add this file, it will contain declarations for one or more event handlers depending on which technique you use to add it. Then, you can add code to any of these event handlers, and you can add additional event handlers. This figure summarizes the four events you're most likely to use.

The example in this figure shows how you can initialize and update a session state item named HitCount that keeps track of the number of times a new session is started for an application. In this example, the Application_Start event handler retrieves the current hit count number from a database and adds an application state item named HitCount to the application state object. Similarly, the Application_End event handler saves the HitCount item to the database so it will be accurate when it's retrieved the next time the application starts. Although the HalloweenDB class that includes the methods that are used to retrieve and update the count isn't shown here, all you need to know is that the GetHitCount method retrieves the current hit count from the database as an integer value, and the UpdateHitCount method saves the integer value to the database.

The updating of the HitCount item takes place in the Session_Start event handler, which is raised whenever a new user session begins. Note that the code that updates the HitCount item uses the Lock and Unlock methods of the Application object.

When you're working with application state data, you'll want to lock the application state collection when you modify any of its data. To minimize the length of time the application state object is locked, you should do as little processing as possible between the Lock and Unlock methods.

If you don't lock the application state collection while the count is updated, two or more users could access the count at the same time. To illustrate why that's a problem, let's assume that three users access the count item at the same time when its value is 11. Then, when each of those users increment the count it becomes 12, and that's the value that each user stores in the application state collection. In this case, though, the correct count should be 14.

Four common application events

Event	Description
`Application_Start`	This event is raised when the first page of an application is requested by any user. It is often used to initialize the values of application state items.
`Application_End`	This event is raised when an application is about to terminate. It can be used to write the values of application state items to a database or file.
`Session_Start`	This event is raised when a user session begins. It can be used to initialize session state items, update application state items, or authorize user access.
`Session_End`	This event is raised when a user session is about to terminate. It can be used to free resources held by the user or to log the user off the application. It is raised only when in-process mode is used.

A Global.asax file that creates an object in application state

```
public class Global : System.Web.HttpApplication
{
    protected void Application_Start(object sender, EventArgs e)
    {
        // Code that runs on application startup
        Application.Add("HitCount", HalloweenDB.GetHitCount());
    }
    protected void Application_End(object sender, EventArgs e)
    {
        //  Code that runs on application shutdown
        HalloweenDB.UpdateHitCount(Application["HitCount"]);
    }
    protected void Session_Start(object sender, EventArgs e)
    {
        // Code that runs when a new session is started
        Application.Lock();
            int hitCount = Convert.ToInt32(Application["HitCount"]) + 1;
            Application["HitCount"] = hitCount;
        Application.UnLock();
    }
}
```

Two ways to add a Global.asax file to your application

- Right-click the project in the Solution Explorer and select Add→New Item. Then, select Global Application Class in the Web→General section and click Add. The file will contain handlers for the events listed above, as well as for Application_BeginRequest, Application_AuthenticateRequest, and Application_Error.

- Create a project using the Empty template with folders and core references for Web Forms. The file will contain only an event handler for the Application_Start event.

Description

- The Global.asax file provides event handlers for application events, including when the application starts, when the application ends, and when a user's individual session starts and ends.

Figure 8-8   How to work with application events

How to use cookies and URL encoding

Earlier in this chapter, you learned that view state data is stored in a hidden field on a page that's sent to and from the browser. That's one way to maintain data between round trips. Two others are using cookies and URL encoding.

How to create cookies

A *cookie* is a name/value pair that is stored on the client's computer. For instance, the name of the first cookie in figure 8-9 is ASP.NET_SessionId, and its value is

`jsswpu5530hcyx2w3jfa5u55`

This is a typical session ID for a cookie that's generated by ASP.NET to keep track of a session. The other cookie examples are typical of cookies that you create yourself.

To create a cookie, you instantiate an object from the HttpCookie class. Then, you include it in the HTTP response that the server sends back to the browser, and the user's browser stores the cookie either in its own memory or in a text file on the client machine's disk.

A cookie that's stored in the browser's memory is called a *session cookie* because it exists only for that session. When the browser session ends, the contents of any session cookies are lost. Session cookies are what ASP.NET uses to track session ID's. In contrast, *persistent cookies* are written to disk, so they are maintained after the browser session ends. Whether session or persistent, though, once a cookie is sent to a browser, it's automatically returned to the server with each HTTP request.

Besides using cookies for session IDs, you can use cookies to save information that identifies each user so the users don't have to enter that information each time they visit your website. You can also use cookies to store information that lets you personalize the web pages that are displayed for a user.

When you use cookies to store this type of information, you should keep in mind that some users may have disabled cookies on their browsers. In that case, you won't be able to save cookies on the user's computer. Unfortunately, ASP.NET doesn't provide a way for you to determine whether a user has disabled cookies. As a result, if you use cookies in an application, you may need to notify the user that cookies must be enabled to use that application.

This figure also presents some properties of the HttpCookie class. Then, the first example shows how to create a session cookie. Here, both the cookie's name and value are specified in the constructor. Because the Expires property isn't set, it's given a default value of 12:00 a.m. on January 1, 0001. Because this date has already passed, the cookie is deleted when the session ends.

If you don't set the value of a cookie when you create it, you can use the Value property to set it later on. In addition, you can use the Expires property to set the expiration date for a persistent cookie. This is illustrated by the second example in this figure.

Examples of cookies

```
ASP.NET_SessionId=jsswpu5530hcyx2w3jfa5u55
Email=grace@yahoo.com
user_ID=4993
```

Two ways to create a cookie

```
New HttpCookie(name)
New HttpCookie(name, value)
```

Common properties of the HttpCookie class

Property	Description
Expires	A DateTime value that indicates when the cookie should expire.
Name	The cookie's name.
Secure	A Boolean value that indicates whether the cookie should be sent only when a secure connection is used. See chapter 19 for information on secure connections.
Value	The string value assigned to the cookie.

Code that creates a session cookie

```
HttpCookie nameCookie = new HttpCookie("UserName", userName);
```

Code that creates a persistent cookie

```
HttpCookie nameCookie = new HttpCookie("UserName");
nameCookie.Value = userName;
nameCookie.Expires = DateTime.Now.AddYears(1);
```

Description

- A *cookie* is a name/value pair that's stored in the user's browser or on the user's disk.

- A web application sends a cookie to a browser via an HTTP response. Then, each time the browser sends an HTTP request to the server, it attaches any cookies that are associated with that server.

- By default, ASP.NET uses a cookie to store the session ID for a session, but you can also create and send your own cookies to a user's browser.

- A *session cookie* is kept in the browser's memory and exists only for the duration of the browser session. A *persistent cookie* is kept on the user's disk and is retained until the cookie's expiration date.

- To create a cookie, you specify its name or its name and value. To create a persistent cookie, you must also set the Expires property to the time you want the cookie to expire.

Figure 8-9   How to create cookies

How to work with cookies

After you create a cookie, you work with it using the members of the HttpCookieCollection class shown in figure 8-10. This class defines a collection of HttpCookie objects. To refer to a cookie in a cookies collection, for example, you use the indexer of the collection. And to add a cookie to the collection, you use the Add method of the collection.

The key to working with cookies is realizing that you must deal with two instances of the HttpCookieCollection class. The first one contains the collection of cookies that have been sent to the server from the client. You access this collection using the Cookies property of the HttpRequest object. The second one contains the collection of cookies that will be sent back to the browser. You access this collection using the Cookies property of the HttpResponse object.

To send a new cookie to the client, you create the cookie and then add it to the collection of cookies in the HttpResponse object. This is illustrated in the first example in this figure. Here, a cookie named UserName is created and added to the HttpResponse object.

The second example shows you how to retrieve the value of a cookie that's sent from the browser. Here, the Request property of the page is used to refer to the HttpRequest object. Then, the indexer of the Cookies collection of the request object is used to get the cookie, and the Value property of the cookie is used to get the cookie's value.

The last example in this figure shows how to delete a persistent cookie. You might think that you'd use the Remove method of the HttpCookieCollection class to do that. However, all the remove method does is remove the cookie from the collection on the server. It won't affect a cookie saved to disk on the user's computer. Rather, if you want to remove a persistent cookie from a user's computer before the expiration date is up, you need to follow this example.

First, you create a cookie with the same name as the cookie you want to delete, and you set its Expires property to a time in the past. In this example, the date is set to one second before the current time. Then, you add the cookie to the HttpResponse object so it's sent back to the browser. When the browser receives the cookie, it replaces the existing cookie with the new cookie. When the client's system detects that the cookie has expired, it deletes it.

Common members of the HttpCookieCollection class

Indexer	Description
[name]	The cookie with the specified name.
Property	**Description**
Count	The number of cookies in the collection.
Method	**Description**
Add(cookie)	Adds a cookie to the collection.
Clear()	Removes all cookies from the collection.
Remove(name)	Removes the cookie with the specified name from the collection.

A method that creates a new cookie and adds it to the HttpResponse object

```
private void AddCookie()
{
    HttpCookie nameCookie = new HttpCookie("UserName", txtUserName.Text);
    nameCookie.Expires = DateTime.Now.AddYears(1);
    Response.Cookies.Add(nameCookie);
}
```

A method that retrieves the value of a cookie from the HttpRequest object

```
protected void Page_Load(object sender, EventArgs e)
{
    if (!IsPostBack)
        if (!(Request.Cookies["UserName"] == null))
            lblUserName.Text = "Welcome back, "
                            + Request.Cookies["UserName"].Value + ".";
}
```

A method that deletes a persistent cookie

```
private void DeleteCookie()
{
    HttpCookie nameCookie = new HttpCookie("UserName");
    nameCookie.Expires = DateTime.Now.AddSeconds(-1);
    Response.Cookies.Add(nameCookie);
}
```

Description

- Cookies are managed in collections defined by the HttpCookieCollection class.
- To access the cookies collection for a request or response, use the Cookies property of the HttpRequest or HttpResponse object. To refer to these objects, use the Request and Response properties of the page.
- To delete a persistent cookie, create a cookie with the same name as the cookie you want to delete and set its Expires property to a time that has already passed. Then, when the client's system detects that the cookie has expired, it deletes it.

Figure 8-10   How to work with cookies

How to enable or disable cookies

If an application relies on the use of cookies, you'll want to be sure that cookies are enabled in your browser as you test the application. Conversely, to test an application that's intended to work even if cookies have been disabled, you'll need to disable cookies in your browser. To do that, you can use the techniques presented in figure 8-11.

If you're using Internet Explorer, you use a slider control to determine what cookies are allowed. The default setting is Medium, which enables both session and persistent cookies. To disable both types of cookies, you can select a privacy setting that blocks all cookies. Alternatively, you can use the dialog box that's displayed when you click the Advanced button to override the default settings so your browser accepts session cookies but disables persistent cookies.

This figure also describes how to enable or disable cookies if you're using Google Chrome or Mozilla Firefox. Although these techniques differ from browser to browser and they may change in later browser versions, you should be able to figure out what you need to do for any browser that you use.

An Internet Explorer dialog box with disabled cookies

How to enable or disable cookies for Internet Explorer

1. Click the Tools icon to the right of the address bar, then select Internet Options.

2. Select the Privacy tab, then use the slider control in the Settings group to set the security level to accept or block cookies.

3. To enable or disable persistent cookies and session cookies separately, click the Advanced button and select from the advanced privacy settings.

How to enable or disable cookies for Google Chrome

1. Click the menu icon to the right of the address bar, and then select Settings.

2. Scroll to the bottom of the page and click on the Show Advanced Settings link.

3. Click the Content Settings button in the Privacy group, then select the Block Sites From Setting Any Data button.

How to enable or disable cookies for Mozilla Firefox

1. Click the menu icon to the right of the address bar, and then select Options.

2. Click the Privacy icon. Then, select the Use Custom Settings for History option from the Firefox Will drop-down list.

3. Check or uncheck the Accept Cookies From Sites option, and select an item from the Keep Until drop-down list.

Figure 8-11   How to enable or disable cookies

How to use URL encoding

URL encoding provides another way to maintain state by storing information in a page on the client. This information is stored in a *query string* that's added to the end of the URL, as shown in figure 8-12. Since using query strings is a common technique, you've probably seen them used on search sites like Google and shopping sites like Ebay and Amazon.

At the top of this figure, you can see two URLs that include query strings. The first one includes a single attribute named cat (for category), and the second one includes two attributes named cat and prod. As you can see, you add a query string by coding a question mark after the URL. Then, you code the name of the first attribute, an equals sign, and the value you want to assign to the attribute. To include another attribute, you code an ampersand (&), followed by the name and value of the attribute.

In most cases, you'll use query strings within hyperlinks or anchor (<a>) elements to pass information from one page of an application to another. The second example in this figure shows how to use query strings with hyperlinks. Here, the NavigateUrl property of the hyperlink indicates that it will link to a page named Product.aspx. In addition, the URL includes a query string that contains category and product attributes. The Product page can then use the values of these attributes to display information for the specified product.

You use query strings with anchor elements in the much the same way. This is illustrated in the third example in this figure. Here, the href attribute specifies the URL with the query string.

To retrieve the values included in a query string, you use the QueryString property of the Request object as illustrated in the fourth example. The two statements in this example retrieve the two values passed by the query string in the second and third examples.

The fifth example shows that you can also use query strings in the URLs that you code for Redirect, RedirectPermanent, or Transfer methods. Here, the URL contains a query string with a single attribute that contains a category ID. You should also realize that you can code query strings in the PostBackUrl property of a button control, although you're not likely to do that.

The last example shows a newer way to store information in a URL. This type of URL is often called an *SEO-friendly URL,* or just a *friendly URL,* because they help with search engine optimization. You'll learn more about how to work with friendly URLs in chapter 11.

Two URLs with query strings

```
~/Order.aspx?cat=costumes
~/Order.aspx?cat=props&prod=rat01
```

A hyperlink with a URL that includes a query string

```
<asp:HyperLink ID="HyperLink1" runat="server"
    NavigateUrl="~/Product.aspx?cat=fx&amp;prod=fog01">Fog machine
</asp:HyperLink>
```

An anchor element with a URL that includes a query string

```
<a href="product.aspx?cat=fx&prod=fog01">Fog machine</a>
```

Statements that retrieve the values of the query string attributes

```
string categoryID = Request.QueryString["cat"];
string productID = Request.QueryString["prod"];
```

Code that uses a URL with a query string in a Redirect method

```
Response.Redirect("~/Order.aspx?cat=" + categoryID);
```

An SEO-friendly URL

```
~/Order.aspx/props/rat01
```

Description

- When you use *URL encoding*, a *query string* with attributes that consist of name/value pairs is added to the end of a URL. Query strings are frequently used in hyperlinks and anchor <a> elements to pass information from one page of an application to another or to display different information on the same page.

- Query strings can also be used in the URLs that are specified for Response. Redirect, Response.RedirectPermanent, or Server.Transfer calls, and they can be used in the PostBackUrl property of a button control.

- When you use a hyperlink, an anchor element, or a Redirect or Transfer method that specifies a URL for the current page, the page is processed as if it's being requested for the first time.

- To code a query string, follow the URL with a question mark, the name of the attribute, an equals sign, and a value. To code two or more attributes, separate them with ampersands (&) and don't include any spaces in the query string.

- To retrieve the value of a query string attribute, use the QueryString property of the HttpRequest object and specify the attribute name. To refer to the HttpRequest object, use the Request property of the page.

- Different browsers impose different limits on the number of characters in the query string of a URL. Most browsers provide for a URL with at least 2000 characters, however.

- A recent development with URL encoding is *SEO-friendly URLs*, or *friendly URLs*, that improve search engine optimization. You'll learn about friendly URLs in chapter 11.

Figure 8-12   How to use URL encoding

An application that uses cookies, application state, and caching

To show you how cookies, application state, and caching can be used in an application, this chapter ends by showing two pages of the Shopping Cart application with a couple of added features.

The Order and CheckOut pages

Figure 8-13 shows the Order and CheckOut pages for the Shopping Cart application that you studied in section 1. But now, the Order page includes a Welcome message with the user's first name. This name is stored in a cookie when the user completes the CheckOut page that's shown in this figure. After that, the name is retrieved from the cookie whenever the Order page is requested.

In addition, the footer of the Order page now contains two lines of data. The first one shows a timestamp that's stored in the cache object for the application. As you'll see in a minute, this timestamp remains in the cache for only 10 minutes. The second line shows the number of times that this page has been accessed during the life of this application. This value is kept in the application state object.

This figure also shows the aspx code for the new items on the Order page. Here, you can see that all of the items are displayed in label controls. Although this chapter doesn't show the aspx code for the CheckOut page, the IDs for its four controls are txtFirstName, txtLastName, btnContinue, and btnCancel.

An Order page that uses a cookie and application state

The CheckOut page

The aspx code for the welcome message and the footer on the Order page

```
<main>
    ...
    <div class="col-sm-12"><asp:Label ID="lblWelcome" runat="server"
        CssClass="text-capitalize text-info"></asp:Label></div>
    ...
</main>
<footer class="text-center">
    Cache Timestamp: <asp:Label ID="lblCacheTimestamp" runat="server">
    </asp:Label>
    <br />
    Number of Page Hits: <asp:Label ID="lblPageHits" runat="server">
    </asp:Label>
</footer>
```

Figure 8-13   An application that uses cookies, application state, and caching

The critical C# code for the Order and CheckOut pages

Figure 8-14 presents the critical C# code in the code-behind files for the Order and CheckOut forms. Look first at the code for the CheckOut page. There, the Click event handler for the Continue button starts by setting a DateTime object named "expiry" to 5 minutes after the current time. Then, the next two statements call the SetCookie method to add FirstName and LastName cookies to the HTTP response for this application. Note, however, that both of these cookies will last for only five minutes. The last statement in this event handler redirects to the Order page.

Now, look at the code for the Load event handler for the Order page. After the SQL data source is bound to the drop-down list, the item named "HitCount" is retrieved from the application state object and stored in an integer variable named hitCount. Then, this variable is increased by one, and the HitCount item in application state is set to the value of this variable. Last, the value of the hitCount variable is converted to a string and stored in the second label in the footer of the page.

The next block of code in the Load event handler for the Order page gets the FirstName cookie from the request object. If it isn't null, the value of this cookie is concatenated in the string for the Welcome message, and the message is put into the label at the start of the main element. That displays the message below the header on the Order page.

The third block of code uses caching to get the value of the Timestamp item from the cache object. If the item is null, it sets the object named "cacheTimestamp" to the current date and time. Then, it uses the Insert method of the Cache object to add that item to the cache with a time before expiration of 10 minutes. Note that a using directive for the System.Web.Caching namespace is included at the beginning of this file, so it isn't necessary to qualify the Cache enumeration that's used by the last parameter of this method. Last, this block of code puts the value of the item into the second label control in the footer of the page.

The critical code in the code-behind file for the Order page

```
...
using System.Web.Caching;

protected void Page_Load(object sender, EventArgs e)
{
    // bind drop-down list and update page hit count on first load
    if (!IsPostBack)
    {
        ddlProducts.DataBind();
        Application.Lock();
            int hitCount = Convert.ToInt32(Application["HitCount"]);
            hitCount++;
            Application["HitCount"] = hitCount;
        Application.UnLock();
        lblPageHits.Text = hitCount.ToString();
    }
    // get and show product data on every load
    ...

    // get firstname from cookie and set welcome message if it exists
    HttpCookie firstName = Request.Cookies["FirstName"];
    if (firstName != null)
        lblWelcome.Text = "<h4>welcome back, " + firstName.Value + "!</h4>";

    // get timestamp from cache, then display it
    // or set timestamp in cache to now plus 10, then display
    object cacheTimestamp = Cache.Get("Timestamp");
    if (cacheTimestamp == null)
    {
        cacheTimestamp = DateTime.Now;
        Cache.Insert("Timestamp", cacheTimestamp, null,
            DateTime.Now.AddMinutes(10), Cache.NoSlidingExpiration);
    }
    lblCacheTimestamp.Text = cacheTimestamp.ToString();
}
```

The critical code in the code-behind file for the Check Out page

```
protected void btnContinue_Click(object sender, EventArgs e)
{
    if (IsValid)
    {
        DateTime expiry = DateTime.Now.AddMinutes(5);
        SetCookie("FirstName", txtFirstName.Text, expiry);
        SetCookie("LastName", txtLastName.Text, expiry);
    }
    Response.Redirect("~/Order.aspx");
}

private void SetCookie(string name, string value, DateTime expiry)
{
    HttpCookie cookie = new HttpCookie(name, value);
    cookie.Expires = expiry;
    Response.Cookies.Add(cookie);
}
```

Figure 8-14   The critical C# code for the Order and CheckOut pages

Perspective

If this chapter has succeeded, you should now be able to use view state, session state, application state, caching, cookies, and URL encoding whenever they're appropriate for your applications. As you work with these techniques, you'll often find that you need two or more of them in a single application. Most web applications, for example, use both view state and session state. And many applications also use caching, cookies, and URL encoding.

Terms

view state	application state
view state object	application state object
session state	caching
session state object	cache object
session ID	scavenging the cache
in-process mode	cookie
session state store provider	session cookie
cookie-based session tracking	persistent cookie
cookieless session tracking	URL encoding
serializable	query string
application	SEO-friendly URL
application object	friendly URL

Summary

- *View state* is implemented by a *view state object* that retains the values of page and control properties that change from one execution of a page to another. These values are encoded in a string that's assigned to a hidden input field that's passed to and from the browser.

- Two reasons for disabling view state for a page or control are (1) because view state restores data that you don't want restored, and (2) because view state storage is so large that it affects the performance of the page.

- ASP.NET uses *session state* to track each user's session. To do that, it creates a *session state object* that contains a *session ID*, and it passes this ID to and from the browser. The server uses this ID to get the session state object for the user.

- To work with the items in a view state object or a session state object, you can use the indexer, properties, and methods of their classes: the StateBag class for view state and the HttpSessionState class for session state.

- To get data from a session state object, you often use the Load event handler for a page. To get or update the data in the object, you can use any event handler. And to update value-based data, you can use the PreRender event handler, although you don't need to do that for reference-based data.

- Although *cookies* are normally used to pass the session ID for a session state object to and from the browser, you can also set up *cookieless session tracking*. Then, the session ID is coded in the URL for the page. A third option uses a cookie if cookies are supported by a browser or the URL if they aren't.

- When an *application* starts, ASP.NET creates an *application object*, an *application state object*, and a *cache object*. These objects exist as long as the application is running on IIS, and items stored in the application state object and cache object are available to all users of the application.

- The application state object is best used for small items of data, but the cache object can be used for larger items since they don't have to stay in server memory until the application ends. Instead, cache items can have expiration dates, and they can be *scavenged* by the server if memory is needed.

- You can create a Global.asax file for an application that lets you create event handlers for application and session events like the start or end of an application or session.

- A *cookie* is a name/value pair that's stored in the user's browser or on the user's disk. A web application can send a cookie to a browser in an HTTP response. Then, the browser returns the cookie in its HTTP request.

- A *session cookie* exists only for the duration of a browser session. A *persistent cookie* is kept on the user's disk and is retained until the cookie expires.

- *URL encoding* lets you pass data from one page of an application to another by attaching name/value pairs in a *query string* at the end of the URL.

Exercise 8-1   Modify the Shopping Cart application

In this exercise, you'll modify and enhance the Shopping Cart application that's in figures 8-13 and 8-14. Although the way this application works isn't entirely realistic, this exercise will give you a chance to use cookies, session state, and caching.

Open, review, and run the Shopping Cart application

1. Open the Ex08Cart web application that's in the aspnet46_cs directory, and review the code-behind files for the Order and CheckOut pages to see that they're like the ones in figure 8-14.

2. Test the application to see how it works. To go to the CheckOut page, go first to the Cart page, then click its Check Out button. On the CheckOut page, enter a first name and last name and click on the Continue button. Note that this displays the Order page with a Welcome message displayed.

3. Go back to the CheckOut page, and note that the first name and last name fields are empty. Then, enter a different first name and last name and click on the Continue button to see that the Welcome message has been changed. Now, stop the application and return to Visual Studio.

4. Enable the trace feature for the Order page as described at the bottom of figure 8-1. Next, run the application and scroll down to see the number of bytes used for view state. Then, turn the trace feature off.

Use cookies or session state to restore the data in the CheckOut page

5. Modify the code-behind file for the CheckOut page so the first and last name fields are restored when the user returns to this page by getting the data from the cookies that are created. Then, test this change. Remember, though, that the cookies have just a five minute life, so you may have to enter the first and last name fields again when you test this change.

6. Test this change again. This time, make sure that the Welcome message is correct if you change the entry in the first name field after it has been restored from the cookie. In other words, if you change the field from Mary to Anne, the Welcome message should reflect that.

7. Comment out the code for using cookies to restore the entries on the CheckOut page. Then, write new code that uses session state to store the first and last name entries after the user enters them, and to restore those entries when the user returns to this page. This should also let the user change the values in the restored entries and have the changes be reflected in the Welcome message. Now, test this change.

Use caching to keep track of the hit count

8. In the code-behind file for the Order page, comment out the code that uses application state to keep track of the hit count. Then, write new code that uses caching to do that with a 5-minute life for the item, and test that change.

9. When you're through testing and experimenting, close the application.

9

How to work with master pages

As you develop the pages of a web application, you'll find that many pages require some of the same elements like headers, navigation bars, and footers. For example, both the Order and Cart pages of the Shopping Cart application have the same header. The easiest way to create pages with common elements like that is to use master pages, and that's what you'll learn how to do in this chapter. In fact, we recommend that you use master pages for every web application you develop.

How to create master pages

A *master page* is a page that provides the common elements for the other pages of a website. For instance, master pages make it easy to include headers, navigation menus, and footers that are used by the other pages. In the topics that follow, you'll learn how to create master pages in your ASP.NET applications.

An introduction to master pages

Figure 9-1 shows the basics of how master pages work. As you can see, the page that's actually sent to the browser is created by combining elements from a master page and a *content page*. The content page provides the content that's unique to each page in the application, while the master page provides the elements that are common to all pages.

In this example, the master page (Site.master) provides a header at the top of each page, a navigation menu at the side of each page, and a default footer at the bottom of each page. However, you can't see the footer in this example because its content has been overridden by the content page. You'll see how that works later in this chapter.

The master page also includes *content placeholders* that indicate where the content from each content page should be displayed. In this example, the content page is the Order.aspx page, and its content is displayed in the main placeholder for the master page.

Notice that the name of the content page is Order.aspx, the same as the Order page that you saw in chapter 4. In other words, when you use master pages, the individual pages of your web application become the content pages.

The Shopping Cart application with a master page
Master page (Site.master) and Content page (Order.aspx)

Rendered page

Description

- A *master page* provides a framework for presenting the content of the pages of a web application. As a result, master pages make it easy to create pages with a consistent look.

- The pages that provide the content that's displayed in a master page are called *content pages*. The content of each content page is displayed in one or more of the master page's *content placeholders*.

Figure 9-1   An application that uses a master page

How to create a master page

Figure 9-2 shows how to add a master page to a project using the Add→Web Forms Master Page command in the shortcut menu for a project. Note, however, that this command isn't available if this is the first time you've added a master page using Visual Studio 2015. In that case, you'll need to add the master page by displaying the Add New Item dialog box and then selecting the Web Forms Master Page template. After that, you should be able to use the shortcut menu to add a master page.

This figure also shows the starting aspx code for a master page. This code includes two ContentPlaceHolder controls: one in the head element and one in the form element. The one in the head element can contain any element that would normally be coded within the head element, such as links to external style sheets or JavaScript files. The one in the form element marks the location where the content from the content page will be displayed.

To develop the content of the master page, you add elements outside of the ContentPlaceHolder controls. Like any page, you can add HTML elements and server controls, and you can structure the page with HTML5 semantic elements. For instance, in the second code example in this figure, you can see that a header element that contains an image has been added within the form element. In addition, an aside element with a nav element that contains two HyperLink controls has been added to the form. Next, the div element was changed to a main element, an h1 element was added within that element, and the name of the content placeholder control that is now within the main element was changed to mainPlaceholder. Finally, a footer element was added at the bottom of the form.

Although a master page starts with only two content placeholders, you can add other placeholders if you want. That's the case for the placeholder in the footer element in this example. To create another content placeholder, you simply drag the ContentPlaceHolder control from the Standard group of the Toolbox onto the master page and give it a unique ID. You can also delete either of the content placeholders that are added to the master page by default, but you won't typically do that.

Because an application can have more than one master page, you can use one master page for one set of pages within an application and another master page for another set of pages. That way, you can give each set of pages a distinctive page layout. For example, you can use one master page for all of the shopping pages of a web application, and another master page for the checkout pages. Then, each content page specifies which master page to use.

If you look at the starting code for a master page, you can see that it starts with a Master directive with attributes that are similar to those in the Page directive for a content page. Although it isn't included in the starting Master directive, another important attribute is the ClientIDMode attribute. You'll learn about this attribute next.

The starting code for a master page named Site.Master

```
<%@ Master Language="C#" AutoEventWireup="true" CodeBehind="Site.master.cs"
    Inherits="Ch09Cart.Site" %>

<!DOCTYPE html>
<html xmlns="http://www.w3.org/1999/xhtml">
<head runat="server">
    <title></title>
    <asp:ContentPlaceHolder id="head" runat="server">
    </asp:ContentPlaceHolder>
</head>
<body>
    <form id="form1" runat="server">
    <div>
        <asp:ContentPlaceHolder id="ContentPlaceHolder1" runat="server">
        </asp:ContentPlaceHolder>
    </div>
    </form>
</body>
</html>
```

The form element of the Site.Master page after content is added

```
<form id="form1" runat="server">
    <header><img src="Images/banner.jpg" /></header>
    <aside>
        <nav>
            <asp:HyperLink runat="server" NavigateUrl="~/Home.aspx">
                Home</asp:HyperLink>
            <asp:HyperLink runat="server" NavigateUrl="~/Cart.aspx">
                Cart</asp:HyperLink>
        </nav>
    </aside>
    <main>
        <h1>Welcome to my website!</h1>
        <asp:ContentPlaceHolder ID="mainPlaceholder" runat="server">
        </asp:ContentPlaceHolder>
    </main>
    <footer>
        <asp:ContentPlaceHolder ID="footerPlaceHolder" runat="server">
        </asp:ContentPlaceHolder>
    </footer>
</form>
```

How to add a master page to a project

- Right-click on the project in the Solution Explorer, then select Add→Web Forms Master Page, enter a name for the page in the resulting dialog box, and click OK.

Description

- A new master page starts with two content placeholder controls, but you can add more.

- Elements you add to the master page *outside* of a content placeholder will automatically appear on every content page that uses the master page.

Figure 9-2   How to create a master page

How to work with the ClientIDMode attribute

Figure 9-3 shows two versions of the Cart page after it has been updated to use a master page. Because the Cart page uses Bootstrap classes for most of its formatting, the two versions are nearly identical. If you look closely, however, you'll see that the height of the list box is different in the two versions. In addition, the font color and weight of the label at the bottom of the page are different. That's because the CSS rule sets that specify the minimum height for the list box and the font for the label are being applied to the second version but not the first.

To understand why this is happening, you need to know how ASP.NET creates a *client id*. That's the id attribute that ASP.NET assigns to an HTML element when it renders HTML to the browser. As you have seen, ASP.NET typically uses the ID attribute of a server control as the client id. For example, a list box with an ID of "lstCart" will be rendered as a select element with an id of "lstCart".

However, if a server control is placed inside a parent control, such as a ContentPlaceHolder control, ASP.NET uses a combination of the parent control's ID and the server control's ID to create the client id. You can see how this can be a problem if your CSS expects the id to be "lstCart" but ASP.NET generates an id of "mainPlaceHolder_lstCart". And that's what's going on in this figure.

The good news is that you can control how a client id is created by using the ClientIDMode attribute of a page or a control. The table in this figure shows the available values for this attribute, and the code examples show the client ids that are created for a control with an id of "lstCart" when using each of the modes.

The default value of the ClientIDMode for a page is Predictable. Then, since the default value for all controls is Inherit, their mode will also be Predictable. This mode is called Predictable because you can predict the client id that ASP.NET is going to produce based on the IDs of the parent control and the server control. For instance, a control with an ID of lstCart in a placeholder with an ID of mainPlaceHolder will end up with a client id of mainPlaceHolder_lstCart.

If you are starting a web application from scratch, you'll probably want to leave these settings alone and use the generated client ids when you write CSS and JavaScript code for your pages. But if you're converting existing pages so they use a master page and you've already written the CSS for them, you may want to change the page's ClientIDMode attribute to Static. Or, if you're converting an older application with CSS that's expecting the ASP.NET-generated client ids, you may want to change the ClientIDMode to AutoID. If you don't want to change the ClientIDMode for the entire page, you can change it for individual content placeholders on the master page or for individual controls that you add to the content pages.

A page with the ClientIDMode attribute set to Predictable and Static

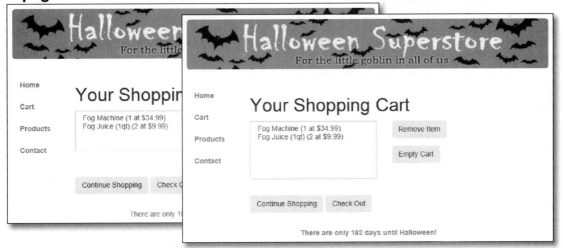

Values of the ClientIDMode attribute

Value	Description
Predictable	The client id is the name of the parent container added to the name of the server control. This is a page's default value. (For a data-bound parent control that generates multiple rows, the value of the control's ClientIDRowSuffix property is added to the end of the child control's id. If this property is blank, a sequential number is added.)
Static	The client id is the same as the server control ID. This can cause id conflicts, such as when there are several instances of the same user control on a page.
AutoID	The client id is based on the conventions of ASP.NET versions prior to 4.0.
Inherit	The control inherits the parent's ClientIDMode. This is the default value for a control.

The HTML generated for a list box with an ID of lstCart
inside a content placeholder with an ID of mainPlaceHolder

When ClientIDMode is Predictable

```
<select name="ctl00$mainPlaceHolder$lstCart"
        id="mainPlaceHolder_lstCart">...</select>
```

When ClientIDMode is Static

```
<select name="ctl00$mainPlaceHolder$lstCart"
        id="lstCart">...</select>
```

When ClientIDMode is AutoID

```
<select name="ctl00$mainPlaceHolder$lstCart"
        id="ctl00_mainPlaceHolder_lstCart">...</select>
```

Description

- A *client id* is the value of the HTML id attribute that will be generated for a control.
- The ClientIDMode attribute of a page or a control determines how client ids will be generated. This affects the ID selectors you use in the CSS or JavaScript for a page.

Figure 9-3   How to use the ClientIDMode attribute

How to create and develop content pages

Once you create a master page, you can create and develop the content pages for the master page. The topics that follow show how.

How to create a content page

Figure 9-4 shows two ways to create a content page. Note that when you use the first technique, a page with a generic name like WebForm1 is created. Because of that, you may want to use the second technique instead. If you use this technique, though, you should know that the Add→Web Form with Master Page command won't be available from the shortcut menu for a project if you haven't previously added a content page from the Add New Item dialog box.

The code example in this figure shows the code that's generated when you create a new content page named Order. Although the Page directive includes the same information as a regular ASP.NET page, it also includes a MasterPageFile attribute that specifies the master page that you selected.

Unlike normal ASP.NET pages, though, content pages don't include a DOCTYPE directive or any structural HTML elements such as html, head, body, or form elements. That's because those elements are provided by the master page. Instead, the content page includes one ASP.NET Content control for each content placeholder in the master page. In this case, because the master page contains three placeholders, the content page contains three Content controls.

As you can see, the ContentPlaceHolderID properties of these elements identify which placeholders they're associated with. Then, you place the content for the page between the start and end tags of the Content elements. Note that the default ID values for the Content controls are Content1, Content2, and Content3. Most of the time, though, you'll want to change these defaults to more meaningful names.

This figure also includes a procedure for converting a regular page to a content page. You'll need to follow this procedure if you start a web application without using master pages, and later decide to use them. Unfortunately, though, Visual Studio doesn't provide a way to automatically do this. As a result, you'll have to manually edit each of the pages to add the MasterPageFile attribute to the Page directive, remove the DOCTYPE directive and structural HTML elements (html, head, body, and form), and add one or more Content controls.

Because this conversion procedure is error prone, it pays to use master pages for all but the simplest of applications, even if each master page contains only the content placeholders. Then, when you're ready to provide a consistent look to the pages within the application, you can enhance the master pages.

For the record, you can also use two other methods for specifying which master page is used for a content page. First, you can add a masterPageFile attribute to the pages element in the Web.config file that specifies the master page that will apply to all content pages that don't specify a master file. Second, you can specify the master page at runtime by setting the MasterPageFile

The starting code for a new content page that uses Site.Master

```
<%@ Page Title="" Language="C#" MasterPageFile="~/Site.Master"
    AutoEventWireup="true" CodeBehind="Order.aspx.cs"
    Inherits="Ch09Cart.Order" %>

<asp:Content ID="Content1" ContentPlaceHolderID="headPlaceholder"
    runat="server"></asp:Content>

<asp:Content ID="Content2" ContentPlaceHolderID="mainPlaceholder"
    runat="server"></asp:Content>

<asp:Content ID="Content3" ContentPlaceHolderID="footerPlaceHolder"
    runat="server"></asp:Content>
```

Two ways to add a content page to a project

- Right-click on the master page in the Solution Explorer, then choose Add Content Page. The new content page will be named WebForm*number*.aspx by default.
- Right-click on the project in the Solution Explorer and select Add→Web Form with Master Page. Then, enter a name for the content page in the resulting dialog box and click OK. In the Select a Master Page dialog box that appears, select the master page you want to use and click OK.

How to convert a regular ASP.NET page to a content page

- Add a MasterPageFile attribute to the Page directive and set its value to the URL of the master page. You can also add an optional Title attribute to the Page directive.
- Add one or more Content controls outside the html element. For each Content control, set its ContentPlaceHolderID property to the correct content placeholder of the master page. Then, move the original contents of the page inside the Content controls.
- If the head element contains other elements the page needs, like link or script elements, add a Content control and set its ContentPlaceHolderID property to the content placeholder that's in the master page's head element. Then, move the needed elements inside this control.
- Delete everything that's outside the Content controls except the Page directive.

Description

- The aspx for a content page contains a Page directive and one or more Content controls.
- The Page directive includes a MasterPageFile attribute that specifies the name of the master page, and a Title attribute that works like the title element of the head element.
- The Content controls correspond to the placeholders of the master page. Then, you enter the content for the page within these Content controls.

Figure 9-4   How to create a content page

attribute of the page in the Page_PreInit method. Note, however, that the Web Forms Designer doesn't support either of these techniques, so you won't be able to view or edit the content pages in Design view.

How to add content to a page

Figure 9-5 shows how a content page appears in Design view when you use Bootstrap to format the page. As you can see, the master page elements are displayed along with the contents of the Content controls for the content placeholder in the body of the master page. However, the display isn't formatted the way it will look in a browser. Because of that, you'll need to display the page in a browser to be sure it looks the way you want it to.

Note that if you're not using Bootstrap or a similar framework to format a page, Design view will give you a more accurate representation of what the page will look like with the master page content. Regardless of that, you should know that you can't edit any of the master page elements from this view.

To add content to a content page, you use the same techniques that you use for adding content to any other page. You can enter text, HTML elements, and server controls directly into Source view, or you can drag elements or controls from the Toolbox to the content area in either Source or Design view. Just be sure that the elements are going into the Content control. In this figure, for example, you can see the aspx code for the Content control in the main element of the Cart page after three controls have been added to it.

If you work with a master page that has more than one content placeholder in the body element, there will be a separate Content control in the content page for each placeholder. For instance, a master page might have one placeholder in its header element, one in its main element, and another in its footer element. Then, when you add content to a content page, you need to make sure you're adding the right content to the right Content control.

The beginning of the Cart page in Design view

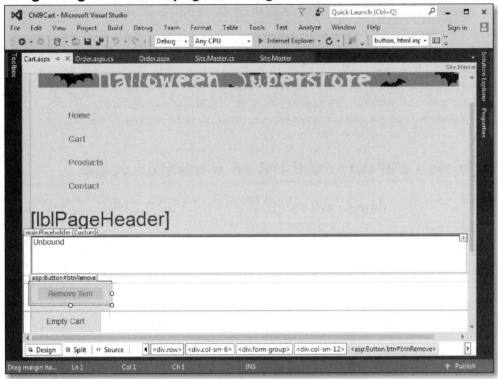

The aspx code for the controls in the Content control

```
<asp:Content ID="mainContent" ContentPlaceHolderID="mainPlaceholder"
    runat="server">
    <asp:ListBox ID="lstCart" runat="server"></asp:ListBox>
    <asp:Button ID="btnRemove" runat="server"
        Text="Remove Item" OnClick="btnRemove_Click" CssClass="btn" />
    <asp:Button ID="btnEmpty" runat="server"
        Text="Empty Cart" OnClick="btnEmpty_Click" CssClass="btn" />
    ...
</asp:Content>
```

Description

- To add content to a content page, you add text, HTML elements, or server controls in Source view or Design view, just as you would for any other page. Just be sure that what you add is within the right Content control.

- When you display a content page in Design view, the elements from the master page are displayed, but you can't edit them.

- If you're using Bootstrap to format your web page as shown above, the display in Design view probably won't look right. In that case, you can preview the page in a browser.

- If you're not using Bootstrap or another framework to format your web page, you should be able to see a more accurate representation of how the content page appears within the master page in Design view.

Figure 9-5   How to add content to a page

How to customize content pages

In many applications, you'll want a basic look and feel for the application as a whole, but you'll want to be able to customize individual pages or groups of pages. One way to do that is with *nested master pages*, which are master pages that are also content pages for other master pages. The problem with nested master pages is that they can quickly become confusing and hard to maintain. For this reason, this topic will present two other ways to customize individual pages.

How to add default content to a master page

Default content is a good way to handle scenarios where most of the pages of an application will be the same, but a few pages will need to make some changes to the master page content. For example, you may want to remove the navigation menu from the checkout pages. Or, you may want to put a login button in the header of some but not all of the pages in an application.

Figure 9-6 shows how to add two types of default content to a master page. First, if you add a title element to the head element in the master page, that title will be displayed in the browser's title bar or tab for all pages, unless it's overridden.

Second, if you add content in a placeholder on a master page, that content will be displayed in all pages, unless it's overridden. In the example in this figure, the default content in the placeholder is a Label control that will be used to display the number of days until Halloween.

How to display and override the default content on a content page

Figure 9-6 also shows how to display and override two types of default content on the master page. First, you can override the title by coding the Title attribute of the Page directive for a content page. If you don't override it, the value of the title element in the master page will be displayed.

Second, you can display the default content in a placeholder by deleting the Content control that's associated with it from the content page. In contrast, if you want to override the default content, you can add the content you want displayed to the associated Content control. Or, you can leave the Content control empty if you don't want any content displayed.

An easy way to work with the Content control for a placeholder is to use the placeholder's smart tag menu from the content page. In this figure, for example, you can see the menu that's displayed when a Content control is associated with a placeholder. In this case, you can select the Default to Master's Content command to delete the Content control so the default content on the master page will be displayed. Once the Content control is deleted, the command on this menu changes to Create Custom Content. You can use this command to add another Content control for the placeholder if necessary.

The smart tag menu for a placeholder on a content page

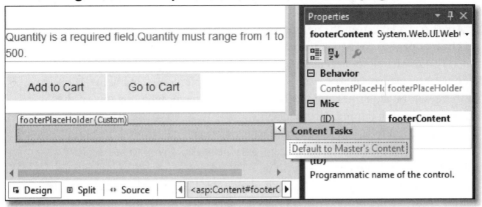

How to set a default title in a master page and override it in a content page

To set the default title in a master page, enter the content for the title element
```
<title>Ch09: Shopping Cart</title>
```

To override it in a content page, use the Title attribute of the Page directive
```
<%@ Page Title="Your Shopping Cart" Language="C#" ... %>
```

How to set default content in a master page
```
<asp:ContentPlaceHolder id="footerPlaceHolder" runat="server">
    <asp:Label ID="lblDaysUntilHalloween" runat="server"></asp:Label>
</asp:ContentPlaceHolder>
```

How to display a placeholder's default content in a content page

- Delete the Content control associated with the placeholder that has the default content. You can do that manually or by choosing Default to Master's Content from the placeholder's smart tag menu.

How to override a placeholder's default content in a content page

- Add content to the Content control for the related placeholder that's added when you create the content page. If you've deleted a Content control, you can add a new one by choosing Create Custom Content from the placeholder's smart tag menu.

Description

- To provide *default content* that can be overridden by a content page, add content to a placeholder in a master page. This content is overridden by the Content control that's generated for the placeholder when a new content page is created, but you can display the default content by deleting this Content control.

Figure 9-6   How to add default content to a master page and how to override it

How to expose a public property in a master page

Another way to provide content on a master page that can be overridden by a content page is to use *public properties*. For instance, you can use a public property for an h1 element that will be displayed at the top of every page. Then, the content pages can override the value in this h1 element. This helps to insure that there will be an h1 heading at the top of every page, which is one of the principles of search engine optimization.

To *expose* a public property in a master page, you can use the technique in figure 9-7. The example in this figure only provides a way to set the text of the h1 element, but you can also provide a get accessor for getting the value of an exposed property. In this example, the content pages only need to set the heading's text, so the property on the master page is a write-only property.

When you use public properties, you can expose properties of the master page itself, such as its width. You can expose entire server controls, such as a message label. And you can expose individual properties of a server control, such as the Text property of a message label. In general, you should expose only what you're going to work with. So, if all you need to do is change a label's text, you should expose only the Text property, not the entire label control.

How to access a public property from a content page

The easiest way to access a master page's public properties from a content page is by adding a MasterType directive to the content page as shown in figure 9-7. Then, you use the TypeName or VirtualPath attribute to specify the type of object that's returned by the content page's Master property. In this example, the master page is Site.master, so its type is Site. As a result, you either add Site in the TypeName attribute, or you add the path to the master page in the VirtualPath attribute. Either option will work, but Visual Studio provides IntelliSense for the VirtualPath attribute.

After you add the MasterType directive, you can work with the content page's Master property to access any public property on the master page, as shown in this figure. Here, the HeaderText property is being updated to the heading that will be displayed at the top of the page, "Your Shopping Cart".

You should also know that you can work with the content page's Master property even if you don't add a MasterType directive. In that case, though, the Master property will return an object of type Master, and you'll need to cast it to the specific type you want to work with, like this:

```
MasterPage mp = (Site)Master;
```

To avoid this awkward bit of casting, you'll usually want to use the MasterType directive.

Attributes of the MasterType directive

Attribute	Description
TypeName	Specifies the type name for the master page. For instance, for a master page named Site.Master, the TypeName is Site.
VirtualPath	Specifies the path to the master page file that generates the type. When you use this attribute, IntelliSense helps you pick the master page.

How to expose a public property in a master page

The aspx code for the element in the master page

```
<main class="col-sm-9">
    <h1><asp:Label ID="lblPageHeader" runat="server"></asp:Label></h1>
    <asp:ContentPlaceHolder ID="mainPlaceholder" runat="server">
    </asp:ContentPlaceHolder>
</main>
```

The C# in the code-behind file that exposes the property

```
public string HeaderText
{
    set { lblPageHeader.Text = value;  }
}
```

How to access a master page's public property from a content page

The MasterType directive for a content page

```
<%@ MasterType VirtualPath="~/Site.Master" %>
```

The C# code in the code-behind file that accesses the public property

```
Master.HeaderText = "Your Shopping Cart";
```

Description

- You can create *public properties* in a master page that expose elements of the master page to the content pages. A public property can have both get and set accessors, just a get accessor, and or just a set accessor.

- You can use public properties to *expose* properties of the master page itself, such as the width; server controls on the master page, such as a text box; or individual properties of a server control, such as the Text property of a label.

- To access a master page's public properties, a content page must have a MasterType directive with either a TypeName or VirtualPath attribute. The MasterType directive goes below the Page directive.

Figure 9-7   How to expose and access properties in a master page

The Shopping Cart application

To give you a better idea of how master pages work, this chapter ends by presenting two pages of the shopping cart application that use the same master page.

Two pages of the Shopping Cart application

Figure 9-8 presents the Order page and Cart page of the Shopping Cart application. Here, the header, the sidebar with four links, and the footer are part of the master page. The title of "Ch09: Shopping Cart" is also part of the master page, but the Cart page has added a value of "Your Shopping Cart" to the Title attribute of its Page directive. Because of that, this value overrides the default title for the Cart page.

This master page has two more types of default content. First, it provides a default but empty h1 element at the top of the content for each page. Because the master page exposes the Text property for this element, it can be changed by the content pages. In this example, the Cart page has done that, but the Order page hasn't.

Second, the master page provides content for its footer. This is a label that shows the number of days left until Halloween. Note that this label is displayed in the Cart page, but overridden in the Order page.

The Order page

The Cart page

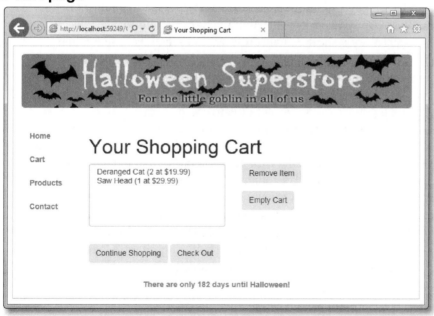

Figure 9-8   Two Shopping Cart pages that use a master page

The aspx code for the master page

Figure 9-9 presents the aspx code for the master page of the Shopping Cart application. To start, you should notice that the content for the title element in the document head is "Ch09: Shopping Cart". As a result, this title will be displayed in the browser's title bar or tab for all pages, unless it's overridden.

The head element contains the link and script tags needed by all the pages in the application, although they're not shown here to save space. In addition, the document head contains the content placeholder that's added by default. This placeholder can be used by the content pages to add other elements to the document head.

Next, notice that the page uses HTML5 semantic elements to structure its content. The header element uses the Bootstrap Jumbotron class to display the image at the top of the page. The aside element creates the sidebar on the left side of the page, and the bulleted list within the aside element creates the navigation menu in the sidebar. Note that because the DisplayMode property of this list is set to "Hyperlink", the value of each list item will be displayed as a hyperlink. The main element contains an h1 element with a label, along with a content placeholder for the main element. And the footer element contains the content placeholder for the footer, along with the default content for the placeholder.

In addition to these HTML5 elements, the master page uses Bootstrap classes to format the page, along with an external style sheet to augment or override the Bootstrap styles or provide additional formatting for the page. Because the external style sheet contains references to the IDs of individual controls, the master page's ClientIDMode attribute is set to Static in the Master directive. That way, the IDs will be rendered the way the style sheet expects. However, you could also set the ClientIDMode of the content placeholders instead of setting the mode in the Master directive.

Unlike other pages you've seen in this book that use Bootstrap, the form element for this page is coded directly inside the container div rather than inside the main element. That's because the BulletedList control that the page uses to provide a navigation menu is a server control, and server controls don't work unless they're coded within a form element. Although you could use regular <a> tags here instead of the BulletedList control, it's often better to use server controls for the navigation on a master page. That way, you can use the tilde operator to resolve the file path for each URL. This is important in a master page, since the content pages can be in different directories.

The aspx code for the master page

```aspx
<%@ Master Language="C#" AutoEventWireup="true" CodeBehind="Site.master.cs"
    Inherits="Ch09Cart.Site" ClientIDMode="Static" %>
<!DOCTYPE html>
<html xmlns="http://www.w3.org/1999/xhtml">
<head runat="server">
    <title>Ch09: Shopping Cart</title>
    <%-- link and script tags go here --%>
    <asp:ContentPlaceHolder ID="headPlaceholder" runat="server">
    </asp:ContentPlaceHolder>
</head>
<body>
<div class="container">
    <form id="form1" runat="server" class="form-horizontal">
        <header class="jumbotron"><%-- image set in site.css --%></header>

        <div class="row">
            <aside class="col-sm-2"><nav>
                <asp:BulletedList ID="blNav" DisplayMode="HyperLink"
                    runat="server" CssClass="nav nav-pills nav-stacked">
                    <asp:ListItem Value="~/Order.aspx">Home</asp:ListItem>
                    <asp:ListItem Value="~/Cart.aspx">Cart</asp:ListItem>
                    <asp:ListItem Value="~/Products.aspx">Products</asp:ListItem>
                    <asp:ListItem Value="~/ContactUs.aspx">Contact</asp:ListItem>
                </asp:BulletedList>
            </nav></aside>

            <main class="col-sm-9">
                <h1><asp:Label ID="lblPageHeader" runat="server"></asp:Label></h1>
                <asp:ContentPlaceHolder ID="mainPlaceholder" runat="server">
                </asp:ContentPlaceHolder>
            </main>
        </div><%-- end of row --%>

        <footer class="text-center text-info">
            <asp:ContentPlaceHolder ID="footerPlaceHolder" runat="server">
                <asp:Label ID="lblDaysUntilHalloween" runat="server"></asp:Label>
            </asp:ContentPlaceHolder>
        </footer>

    </form>
</div><%-- end of container --%>
</body>
</html>
```

Description

- This master page uses a BulletedList server control for navigation so it can use the tilde operator in the Value property of each list item. Because of that, these controls are coded within the form element. That's usually easier than using <a> elements for the links.

- The text of the Label control in the main element is exposed as a public write-only property so its value can be set by a content page.

- The Label control in the footer element is the footer's default content, but this content can be overridden by a content page.

Figure 9-9   The aspx code for the master page

The code-behind file for the master page

Master pages have events just like regular ASP.NET pages. So it's important to realize that most of these events are raised *after* the corresponding events for the content page are raised. For example, the Page Load event for the master page will be processed after the Page Load event for the content page.

Likewise, any control events for the master page are processed after any control events for the content page. Note, however, that the Load events for both the content page and the master page are processed before any of the control events are processed.

Content pages also have a Page Load Completed event that is raised after the Page Load events for the content and master page have fired. This can be a good place to put content page code that needs to run after some code in the master page's Page Load event has run.

With that in mind, figure 9-10 presents the code-behind file for the master page of the Shopping Cart application. This file includes a Page_Load method that's executed when the master page loads. As you can see, this method calls a method named DaysUntilHalloween that calculates and returns the number of days remaining until October 31. Then, an appropriate message is assigned to the Text property of the lblDaysUntilHalloween label. Remember, though, that this text is default content that can be overridden by a content page. Because of this, the code must first check to make sure the label is there before trying to set its content.

This code-behind file also includes a write-only public property that allows content pages to change the text in the master page's h1 element. If the content page doesn't add any text to this property, the page won't have a page heading. That's because the aspx page hasn't specified any content for this h1 heading.

The code-behind file for the master page

```
public partial class Site : System.Web.UI.MasterPage
{
    public string HeaderText {
        set { lblPageHeader.Text = value;  }
    }

    protected void Page_Load(object sender, EventArgs e)
    {
        if (lblDaysUntilHalloween != null) {
            int daysUntil = DaysUntilHalloween();
            switch (daysUntil) {
                case 0:
                    lblDaysUntilHalloween.Text = "Happy Halloween!";
                    break;
                case 1:
                    lblDaysUntilHalloween.Text = "Tomorrow is Halloween!";
                    break;
                default:
                    lblDaysUntilHalloween.Text =
                        $"There are only {daysUntil} days until Halloween!";
                    break;
            }
        }
    }

    private int DaysUntilHalloween()
    {
        DateTime today = DateTime.Today;
        DateTime halloween = new DateTime(today.Year, 10, 31);
        if (today > halloween) halloween = halloween.AddYears(1);
        TimeSpan span = halloween - today;
        return span.Days;
    }
}
```

Description

- Most events for the content page are raised before the corresponding events for the master page. Similarly, events for a content page's controls are raised before events for the master page's controls.

- Content pages also have a Page Load Completed event that is raised after the Page Load events for the content and master page have fired.

- This master page exposes a public property that lets the content pages set the text of the label inside the h1 element.

- The Load event of this master page is used to display the number of days until Halloween in the label in the footer. However, because the label is default content that can be overridden, the code first checks to make sure the label is there.

Figure 9-10   The code-behind file for the master page

The aspx code for the Order page

When you create a content page, ASP.NET generates one Content control for each placeholder in the master page. By default, then, each content page for the Shopping Cart application contains three Content controls: one for the placeholder in the head element, one for the placeholder in the main element, and one for the placeholder in the footer element. Notice in figure 9-11, though, that the Content control for the placeholder in the head element has been deleted. That's because no additional link or script tags need to be added for this page, so deleting this control simplifies this page.

The first Content control contains the main content for the page. This is the same content that would normally be included in the form element of a page. Since you've already seen this content, only its Bootstrap div tags are shown here so you can see how the content is structured.

The second Content control overrides the default content for the footer. Note that this control doesn't contain any content. Because of that, the default content is replaced with nothing. Keep in mind, though, that you can replace default content with anything you want.

The Order page also leaves the Title attribute in the Page directive empty, which is how it is by default when the content page is created. Because it's empty, the Order page will display the master page's title in the browser.

Finally, notice that this page doesn't include a MasterType directive. Because the code-behind file for this page doesn't use the public property that's exposed by the master page, it doesn't need to include this directive.

The Page directive and Content controls for the Order content page

```
<%@ Page Title="" MasterPageFile="~/Site.Master" AutoEventWireup="true"
    Language="C#" CodeBehind="Order.aspx.cs" Inherits="Ch09Cart.Order" %>

<asp:Content ID="mainContent" ContentPlaceHolderID="mainPlaceholder"
    runat="server">
    <div class="row"><%-- row 1 --%>
        <div class="col-sm-8">
            <%-- product drop-down list and info column --%>
        </div>
        <div class="col-sm-4">
            <%-- product image column --%>
        </div>
    </div><%-- end of row 1 --%>

    <div class="row"><%-- row 2 --%>
        <div class="col-sm-12"><%-- quantity text box --%></div>
        <div class="col-sm-12"><%-- Add and Go to Cart buttons --%></div>
    </div><%-- end of row 2 --%>
</asp:Content>

<asp:Content ID="footerContent" ContentPlaceHolderID="footerPlaceHolder"
    runat="server"></asp:Content>
```

Description

- The Order page contains a Content control named mainContent, which is associated with the master page placeholder named mainPlaceholder. All of the HTML and server controls for the Order page are in this Content control.

- The Order page also contains a Content control named footerContent, which is associated with the master page placeholder named footerPlaceHolder. This overrides the default content in the master page footer. Because no content is included for the footer, though, the label will be blank.

- The Order page doesn't need any specific CSS or JavaScript files, so it doesn't have a Content control for the placeholder in the master page's head element.

- The Order page leaves the Title attribute of the Page directive blank, so the Order page uses the title value of the master page.

- Because the code-behind file for the Order page doesn't use the master page's public property, it doesn't need a MasterType directive.

Figure 9-11   The aspx code for the Order page

The aspx code for the Cart page

Figure 9-12 presents the aspx code for the Cart page of the Shopping Cart application. Like the Order page, this page doesn't need to add anything to the head element of the master page, so the Content control for the placeholder in the head element has been deleted. The Content control for the placeholder in the footer has also been deleted. That means that this page doesn't override the default content for the footer in the master page.

Notice too that this page adds content to the Title attribute of the Page directive. This means that the content of the Title attribute, rather than the master page's title content, will be displayed in the browser for this page. Also, because the code-behind file for this page uses the public HeaderText property that's exposed by the master page, this page includes a MasterType directive. This directive uses the VirtualPath attribute to specify the path to the master page.

The Load event handler in the code-behind file for the Cart page

Figure 9-12 also presents the Page_Load method of the code-behind file for the Cart page. Here, the Cart page adds a value to the public HeaderText property of the master page. This means that the Cart page will have a page heading of "Your Shopping Cart".

The directives and Content control for the Cart content page

```
<%@ Page Title="Your Shopping Cart" Language="C#"
    MasterPageFile="~/Site.Master" AutoEventWireup="true"
    CodeBehind="Cart.aspx.cs" Inherits="Ch09Cart.Cart" %>
<%@ MasterType VirtualPath="~/Site.Master" %>

<asp:Content ID="mainContent" ContentPlaceHolderID="mainPlaceholder"
    runat="server">
    <div class="row"><%-- row 1 --%>
        <div class="col-sm-6">
            <%-- cart display column --%>
        </div>
        <div class="col-sm-6">
            <%-- cart edit buttons column --%>
        </div>
    </div>

    <div class="row"><%-- row 2 --%>
        <div class="col-sm-12">
            <%-- message label and buttons --%>
        </div>
    </div>
</asp:Content>
```

The load event for the Cart content page

```
protected void Page_Load(object sender, EventArgs e)
{
    Master.HeaderText = "Your Shopping Cart";

    cart = CartItemList.GetCart();
    if (!IsPostBack)
        DisplayCart();
}
```

Description

- The Cart.aspx page adds a value to the Title attribute of the Page directive. As a result, that value, rather than the master page's title value, will display in the browser.

- The Cart page has a MasterType directive with a VirtualPath attribute that's set to the URL of the master page. That way, the code-behind file for this page can access the master page's public properties.

- Like the Order page, the Cart page doesn't need any specific CSS or JavaScript files, so the Content control for the placeholder in the master page's head element has been deleted.

- The Content control that's associated with the placeholder in the master page's footer has also been deleted so the default content in the master page will be displayed.

- The code-behind file for the Cart page sets the value of the master page's HeaderText property in its Load event so that value will be displayed at the top of the page.

Figure 9-12   The aspx code and Load event handler for the Cart page

Perspective

Because master pages are so valuable, we recommend that you use them for all but the simplest applications, even if you start out with nothing in your master pages but placeholders. Then, when you're ready to provide a professional look to your pages, you can enhance the master pages, which will also enhance all of your content pages.

The alternative is to convert regular content pages so they use the master pages that you develop later on. But that's a time-consuming and error-prone procedure. How much better it is to think ahead.

Terms

master page	client id
content page	public property
content placeholder	expose a property
default content	

Summary

- *Master pages* let you provide a consistent look and feel to all of the pages in a web application. A master page provides the elements that are the same for all of the pages. The *content pages* provide the elements that vary from page to page.

- Master pages work by providing *content placeholders* that receive the contents of the pages of the web application. Master pages can also provide *default content* within these placeholders that can be overridden by the content pages when necessary.

- The ClientIDMode attribute of a master page or a control determines how the *client ids* for the controls are generated by ASP.NET. The setting for this attribute is important when the IDs are used by the selectors in the CSS for a page.

- You can code *public properties* in the code-behind file for a master page that *expose* properties in the master page to the content pages. Then, the content pages can access and work with those public properties.

Exercise 9-1   Work with master pages

In this exercise, you'll modify the Shopping Cart application that's presented in this chapter. That will give you a better feel for how master pages work and show you how easy it is to work with them.

Open, run, and review the Shopping Cart application

1. Open the Ex09Cart web application that's in the aspnet46_cs directory. Then, test the application to see how it works and note that the last two links in the navigation list don't work.

2. Review the aspx, code-behind, and CSS files for both the master and content pages to see how everything works. Notice that the code-behind class for the master page includes a second public property named FormClass that can be used to change the class property for the form. You'll use this property in a minute.

Modify the Order page

3. Change the Order page so it displays the default content for the footer by using the technique in figure 9-6.

4. In the aspx file for the Order page, add content to the Title attribute in the Page directive so "Your Shopping Page" will be displayed in the browser's title bar or tab.

5. In the code-behind file for the Order page, use the exposed property in the master page to set the h1 heading for the Order page to "Your Shopping Page", as shown in figure 9-7. Now, test this page to make sure everything is working.

Modify the Cart page

6. In the aspx file for the Order page, override the default content in the footer and replace it with "Your Shopping Cart" by using the technique in figure 9-6.

7. In the code-behind file for the Cart page, comment out the code that uses the exposed property in the master page to set the h1 heading. Now, test this page to make sure everything is working.

Create a Checkout page

8. Create a new content page named CheckOut.aspx that uses the Site.Master master page. Note that it has three Content controls.

9. Delete the first Content control since no additional link or script tags are needed for this page.

10. In the Content control for the main placeholder, add an h1 element that displays "Check Out Page" (don't use the exposed property in the master page to set this heading). Also, change the content for the title element for the page to "Check Out Page". Now, display this page to be sure it's formatted properly.

Create a second master page

11. Create a second master page named CheckOut.Master. The content for this page should be the same as the Site.Master content, but without the aside and nav elements and without the h1 element in the main element. Also, the placeholder should be deleted from the footer and the Label control should display "Check Out Page". The easiest way to create this content is to copy it from the Site.Master page and then delete the content that isn't needed.

12. Switch the Checkout page to the new master page. Then, delete the Content control for the placeholder for the footer since it's been deleted from the master. Now, display this page in your browser to see how it looks.

Use another public property

13. Change the class that's used by the form in the Site.Master page to form-vertical. Then, display the Order and CheckOut pages to see that the formatting doesn't look as good as it did with horizontal formatting.

14. Add a statement to the Page_Load event handler for the Order page that sets the public FormClass property that's declared by the master page to form-horizontal each time the page is loaded. Do the same for the Cart page. Then, test these pages again to see that they look the way they did before.

15. When you're through experimenting, close the application.

10

How to work with Bootstrap in ASP.NET

In chapter 3, you learned the basics of how to use Bootstrap for responsive web design. Now, in this chapter, you'll learn even more about Bootstrap with a focus on how to make it work with ASP.NET. As you'll see, that can require some adjustments because ASP.NET doesn't always render the HTML that Bootstrap needs.

You should know, though, that there's more to learn about Bootstrap than what's presented here. That includes more classes and components, as well as best practices for making Bootstrap accessible. That's why each section in this chapter starts with a URL to the appropriate documentation.

How to use the Bootstrap CSS classes

In chapter 3, you learned about the Bootstrap grid system and how to use the form-control class to style the input, textarea, and select controls in a form. You also learned the basics of styling buttons and images.

In the topics that follow, you'll learn even more about styling buttons and images, as well as how to style check boxes, radio buttons, list controls, and tables. You'll also learn more about working with the CSS classes for text, and you'll learn about the CSS classes that provide context.

How to work with the CSS classes for buttons

The table in figure 10-1 shows some of the Bootstrap CSS classes for working with buttons. To start, you always use the btn class for a button. In addition, you can use the other two classes to style a button and specify its size.

The first example in this figure shows five buttons that are each created using a different element or server control. Because all of these elements and controls use the btn and btn-default classes, they all look the same when displayed on a page. Note, though, that the <a> element and the HyperLink and LinkButton controls are only displayed as buttons because the btn-default class is applied. If this class or another contextual class wasn't applied, they would appear as links. However, the btn class will still apply spacing and other formatting to the links.

The second example in this figure illustrates the four different button sizes. To specify a size, you use one of the btn-*size* classes. Note that there isn't a class for creating a medium-sized button. That's because this is the default size if a size class isn't applied.

The Bootstrap documentation gives two recommendations for working with buttons. First, it recommends that you use HTML button elements for cross-browser consistency. Even so, you're usually okay using Button and LinkButton controls, which render as <input> and <a> tags. But if you find that you need to use a button element, you can do that and still work with the button on the server. To do that, you just code the runat="server" attribute on the element. You'll learn the details of how that works later in this chapter.

Second, the Bootstrap documentation recommends that you add a role="button" attribute when you style <a> elements to appear as buttons. That way, a screen reader will recognize the element as a button. You should keep this in mind when working with HyperLink and LinkButton controls, since they render to <a> elements.

The URL for the Bootstrap CSS classes documentation

`http://getbootstrap.com/css/`

Common CSS classes for working with buttons

Class	Description
btn	Provides the default formatting and styling for a button element.
btn-*context*	Provides more styling, such as borders and colors, and makes links look like buttons. Example: btn-default. See figure 10-6 for more information about contextual classes.
btn-*size*	Makes the button a specified size. Example: btn-lg.

Anchor and button HTML elements and server controls styled as buttons

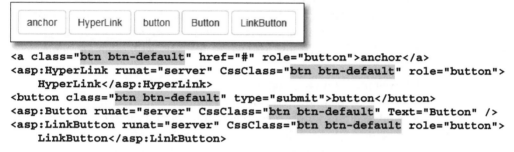

```
<a class="btn btn-default" href="#" role="button">anchor</a>
<asp:HyperLink runat="server" CssClass="btn btn-default" role="button">
    HyperLink</asp:HyperLink>
<button class="btn btn-default" type="submit">button</button>
<asp:Button runat="server" CssClass="btn btn-default" Text="Button" />
<asp:LinkButton runat="server" CssClass="btn btn-default" role="button">
    LinkButton</asp:LinkButton>
```

Button server controls styled at various sizes

```
<asp:Button runat="server" CssClass="btn btn-lg" Text="Large" />
<asp:Button runat="server" CssClass="btn" Text="Default" />
<asp:Button runat="server" CssClass="btn btn-sm" Text="Small" />
<asp:Button runat="server" CssClass="btn btn-xs" Text="Extra Small" />
```

Description

- The Bootstrap button classes let you control the appearance and size of a button. You can use these classes with <a> and button elements as well as with HyperLink, Button, and LinkButton controls.

- For anchor elements and HyperLink and LinkButton controls, the btn class provides spacing and padding, but it doesn't style the link to look like a button.

- To style a link like a button, you can use a btn-*context* class. When you do that, you should include the role="button" attribute for accessibility.

Figure 10-1   How to work with the CSS classes for buttons

How to work with the CSS classes
for check boxes and radio buttons

The table in figure 10-2 shows some of the Bootstrap CSS classes for working with check boxes and radio buttons. You can use these classes with individual check box and radio button controls as well as with check box list and radio button list controls.

The first example in this figure shows how to use two of these classes with two CheckBox controls. Here, the checkbox class is applied to the div elements that contain both check boxes. In addition, the disabled class is applied to the second div element, and the Enabled property of the check box within this div is set to False. Although the Enabled property alone will cause the check box to be disabled, the "not allowed" cursor will only be displayed when the mouse hovers over the check box. By applying the disabled class to the div element, this cursor will also be displayed when the mouse hovers over the label that's associated with the check box. The disabled class also works this way with other elements, such as buttons.

The second example shows a group of three radio buttons. Here, the radio-inline class is assigned to the label that contains each radio button so the buttons are displayed on a single line. In addition, the last radio button is disabled using the same technique that was used in the first example.

The third example shows how to use the checkbox class with a CheckBoxList control. Although check box lists and radio button lists can be easier to create than individual check box and list box controls, they are more difficult to format when using Bootstrap. That's because you have less control over the HTML that's sent to the browser when you use these controls. Because the RepeatLayout property of the check box list shown here is set to "UnorderedList", for example, a ul element with an li element is generated for each check box. Because these aren't the elements that Bootstrap expects for a list of check boxes, though, they're not formatted like other check boxes. If you compare the check boxes in the third example with the check boxes in the first example, you'll see that both the vertical and horizontal spacing are different. Because of that, you may need to adjust the CSS for your application so it styles these controls the way you want.

Another issue when using list controls is that if you set the RepeatDirection property to Horizontal, no adjustment will be made on smaller screens. In other words, your page won't be responsive if you use this setting. If you use this setting, then, you should consider setting the RepeatColumns property to 2 so the list will look right on smaller screens. Or, you should consider using individual check boxes or radio buttons instead.

One final issue with check box and radio button list controls is that you can't use the disabled class with them. Because of that, the "not allowed" cursor is displayed only when the mouse hovers over a check box or radio button in a list control, not the label that's associated with it. Also, a pointer is displayed when the mouse hovers over a check box or radio button in a list control instead of the hand cursor that's displayed when the mouse hovers over an individual check box or radio button that has a Bootstrap class applied to it.

Common CSS classes for working with check boxes and radio buttons

Class	Description
`checkbox`	Provides default styling and padding for a check box element.
`checkbox-inline`	Makes a series of check box elements appear on the same line.
`radio`	Provides default styling and padding for a radio button element.
`radio-inline`	Makes a series of radio button elements appear on the same line.
`disabled`	Provides a "not allowed" cursor for the associated label.

CheckBox controls with default styling and a "not allowed" cursor

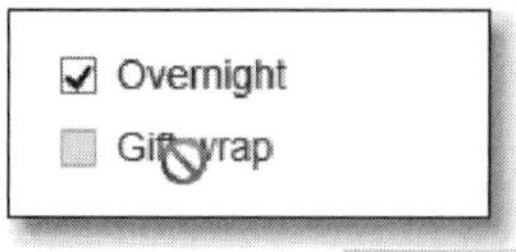

```
<div class="checkbox">
    <label><asp:CheckBox ID="chkOvernight runat="server" Checked="True" />
        Overnight</label>
</div>
<div class="checkbox disabled">
    <label><asp:CheckBox ID="chkWrap" runat="server" Enabled="False" />
        Gift wrap</label>
</div>
```

RadioButton controls styled to display inline

```
<label class="radio-inline">
    <asp:RadioButton ID="rdoGround" runat="server" GroupName="Shipping" />
        Ground</label>
<label class="radio-inline">
    <asp:RadioButton ID="rdo2Day" runat="server" GroupName="Shipping" />
        2nd Day</label>
<label class="radio-inline disabled">
    <asp:RadioButton ID="rdoOvernight" runat="server" GroupName="Shipping"
        Enabled="False" />Overnight</label>
```

A CheckBoxList control with default styling

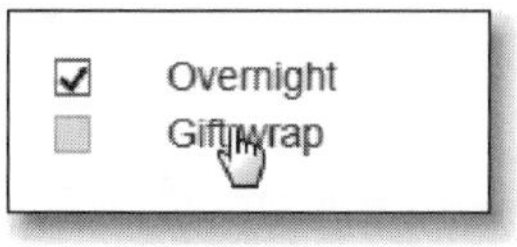

```
<asp:CheckBoxList ID="cblOptions" runat="server" CssClass="checkbox"
    RepeatLayout="UnorderedList">
    <asp:ListItem Selected="True">Overnight</asp:ListItem>
    <asp:ListItem Enabled="False">Gift wrap</asp:ListItem>
</asp:CheckBoxList>
```

Description

- The Bootstrap classes for check boxes and radio buttons let you control the appearance of these items as well as the items in a check box or radio button list.

- It can be harder to style CheckBoxList and RadioButtonList controls with Bootstrap.

Figure 10-2   How to work with the CSS classes for check boxes and radio buttons

How to work with the CSS classes for images

The first table in figure 10-3 shows some of the Bootstrap CSS classes for working with images. Then, the example below that table shows three img elements with different classes applied to them. Note that even though each img element uses the same image, the appearance of the image is different depending on which class is applied. Also note that you can use the classes shown here with Image controls as well as with img elements.

How to work with the CSS classes for lists

The second table in figure 10-3 shows some of the Bootstrap CSS classes for working with lists. You can use these classes for both HTML ul and ol elements, as well as for the BulletedList control since it renders to a ul or ol element. The first example below this table shows the result of applying the list-unstyled class to an unordered list. This class removes the default styling for the list and the left margin from its list items. Because of that, it appears as a simple, left-aligned list of items with no bullets or numbers.

The second example for working with ordered and unordered lists uses a BulletedList control. Here, the list-inline class has been applied to the control. Because a bulleted list is rendered as an unordered list with no bullets by default, the list items are displayed on a single line with no bullets.

Common CSS classes for working with images

Class	Description
`img-rounded`	Gives an image rounded corners.
`img-circle`	Makes an image appear circular.
`img-thumbnail`	Puts a small border around an image.
`img-responsive`	Makes an image scale relative to the element that contains it.

Img elements styled with various shapes

```
<img src="Images/MurachLogo.jpg" class="img-rounded" />
<img src="Images/MurachLogo.jpg" class="img-circle" />
<img src="Images/MurachLogo.jpg" class="img-thumbnail" />
```

Common CSS classes for working with ordered and unordered lists

Class	Description
`list-unstyled`	Removes the default styling from the list and the left margin from the items in a list.
`list-inline`	Makes the items in a list display in a horizontal line.

An unordered list element with default styling removed

```
C#
Visual Basic
```

```
<ul class="list-unstyled">
    <li>C#</li>
    <li>Visual Basic</li>
</ul>
```

A BulletedList control styled to display inline

```
HTML  JavaScript  jQuery  ASP.NET
```

```
<asp:BulletedList runat="server" CssClass="list-inline">
    <asp:ListItem>HTML</asp:ListItem>
    <asp:ListItem>JavaScript</asp:ListItem>
    <asp:ListItem>jQuery</asp:ListItem>
    <asp:ListItem>ASP.NET</asp:ListItem>
</asp:BulletedList>
```

Description

- The Bootstrap image classes let you control the appearance and size of an image.
- The Bootstrap list classes make it easy to change how the items in an ordered list, unordered list, and bulleted list are displayed.

Figure 10-3   How to work with the CSS classes for images and lists

How to work with the CSS classes for HTML tables

The table in figure 10-4 shows some of the Bootstrap CSS classes for working with HTML tables. Then, the first example shows an HTML table that uses the default Bootstrap styling. Note that for the Bootstrap table classes to work correctly, an HTML table must have thead and tbody elements as shown here.

The second example shows another table with additional styling applied. Here, the table-striped class is used to apply alternating colors to the rows of the table. (Although it's hard to tell here, the first and third rows in the body of the table have a light gray background.) The table-bordered class is used to add a border around the table and between cells. And the table-condensed class is used to make the table more compact.

By the way, if you use the table-striped class, you should know that it won't work in Internet Explorer 8. In addition, this class may not be listed in the completion list that's provided by IntelliSense like the other table classes are.

It's important to note that the table-responsive class works differently than the other CSS classes for working with tables. Instead of applying this class directly to an HTML table, you apply it to a div element that contains an HTML table that has one or more of the Bootstrap table classes applied to it. Then, if the viewport narrows so the data in each cell of the table can't be displayed on a single line, horizontal scrolling is added to the table.

You can also use the CSS classes shown here with the Table server control. Note, however, that the thead and tbody elements aren't rendered for a Table control by default. To fix that, you can set the TableSection property of the TableHeaderRow element to "TableHeader". This adds both thead and tbody elements to the rendered HTML.

Common CSS classes for working with HTML tables

Class	Description
table	Provides default styling for an HTML table element.
table-bordered	Adds a border around the table and between cells.
table-striped	Adds alternating colors to the table rows.
table-hover	Makes the color of a row change when you hover over it.
table-condensed	Reduces the amount of cell padding to make the table more compact.
table-responsive	Adds horizontal scrolling to the table when the viewport narrows so the data in the columns doesn't roll over. Applied to a div element that contains a table element that uses the Bootstrap table class.

A table with default styling

Department	Phone Number
General	555-555-5555
Customer Service	555-555-5556
Billing and Accounts	555-555-5557

```
<table class="table">
    <thead>
        <tr><th>Department</th><th>Phone Number</th></tr>
    </thead>
    <tbody>
        <tr><td>General</td><td>555-555-5555</td></tr>
        <tr><td>Customer Service</td><td>555-555-5556</td></tr>
        <tr><td>Billing and Accounts</td><td>555-555-5557</td></tr>
    </tbody>
</table>
```

A condensed table with a border and alternating stripes

Department	Phone Number	Extension
General	555-555-5555	1
Customer Service	555-555-5555	2
Billing and Accounts	555-555-5557	3

```
<table class="table table-striped table-bordered table-condensed">...
```

Description

- You must include the thead and tbody elements in your table for the Bootstrap table classes to work properly.
- To use these elements with the Table server control, you set the value of the TableSection property of the TableHeaderRow element to "TableHeader".

Figure 10-4   How to work with the CSS classes for HTML tables

How to work with the CSS classes for text

The table in figure 10-5 shows some of the Bootstrap CSS classes for working with text. The classes shown here consist of the alignment classes and the transformation classes.

The alignment classes control where the text of an element displays on the page relative to the element that contains it. For instance, the <p> elements in the example below the table are coded within a div tag that spans six Bootstrap columns. As you can see, the first <p> element is aligned at the right side of the div, the second <p> element is centered in the div, and the third <p> element is aligned at the left side of the div.

The transformation classes control how the text of an element is capitalized. For instance, the text in the first span element in this example displays in all uppercase letters, even though the text in the HTML is in lowercase letters. Similarly, the text in the second span element displays with the first letter of each word capitalized, and the text in the third span element displays in all lowercase letters.

Common CSS classes for text

Class	Description
`text-left`	Aligns text to the left within the parent element.
`text-right`	Aligns text to the right within the parent element.
`text-center`	Aligns text in the center of the parent element.
`text-lowercase`	Makes all text in the element lower case.
`text-uppercase`	Makes all text in the element upper case.
`text-capitalize`	Capitalizes the first letter of every word in the element.

Some examples of the text CSS classes

```
                                        This text is RIGHT-ALIGNED.
                    This Text Is Centered.
This text is left-aligned.
```

```html
<p class="text-right">
    This text is <span class="text-uppercase">right-aligned</span>.
</p>
<p class="text-center">
    <span class="text-capitalize">This text is centered.</span>
</p>
<p class="text-left">
    This text is <span class="text-lowercase">LEFT-ALIGNED</span>.
</p>
```

Description

- The Bootstrap classes for text control the alignment and capitalization for the text.
- The alignment classes, text-left, text-right, and text-center, control where the text of an element is displayed on the page relative to the element that contains it.
- The transformation classes, text-lowercase, text-uppercase, and text-capitalize, control the capitalization for the text of an element.

Figure 10-5   How to work with the CSS classes for text

How to work with the CSS classes that provide context

Figure 10-6 presents the contextual classes that are available with Bootstrap. These classes apply a color to an element depending on its context.

The first table in this figure shows the four main CSS classes for providing context. These classes are available to most elements. In addition, their colors are usually the same regardless of what Bootstrap theme you use. You'll learn more about Bootstrap themes later in this chapter.

The second table in this figure shows four more contextual classes. Unlike the classes in the first table, these tend to have more limited uses. For example, the primary class is used mostly with buttons and text, and the default class is used mostly with buttons. Also, the colors for these classes are often different depending on the Bootstrap theme you use.

The examples in this figure show how to use some of these contextual classes. The first example shows how six buttons appear with six different classes applied. Note that each class is prefixed with *btn-* to indicate that the class is being applied to a button. You can use Visual Studio's IntelliSense feature to find out what prefixes you can use with the contextual classes.

The second example shows how two of these classes are applied to the text in two span elements. Here, the text-success class indicates that the color for the success class should be applied to the text within the span element. In contrast, the bg-primary class indicates that the background of the text should be changed to the color specified by the primary class.

The last example illustrates that you can sometimes use the contextual classes without a prefix. Here, the info class is assigned to a td element of a table. Because of that, the cell is displayed with the background color for that class.

The four main contextual classes available to most elements

Class	Description	Default color
success	Indicates a successful or positive outcome or action	Green
info	Indicates neutral information	Light blue
warning	Indicates something that might need attention	Yellow
danger	Indicates a dangerous or negative outcome or action	Red

Four more contextual classes

Class	Used by	Description	Default Color
primary	buttons, text	Emphasizes an element or information	Dark blue
muted	text	Deemphasizes information	Gray
default	buttons	Default styling of a button	White background
active	multiple elements	Applies the hover color to the element	

Some examples of the contextual classes

```
<asp:Button runat="server" CssClass="btn btn-default" Text="Default" />
<asp:Button runat="server" CssClass="btn btn-primary" Text="Primary" />
<asp:Button runat="server" CssClass="btn btn-success" Text="Success" />
<asp:Button runat="server" CssClass="btn btn-info" Text="Info" />
<asp:Button runat="server" CssClass="btn btn-warning" Text="Warning" />
<asp:Button runat="server" CssClass="btn btn-danger" Text="Danger" />
```

```
<span class="text-success">This sentence is SUCCESS.</span>
<span class="bg-primary">This background is PRIMARY.</span>
```

```
<tr><td class="info">Info</td><td>Remote Access</td>...</tr>
```

Description

- The contextual classes are typically combined with a prefix that indicates the element or component being styled. In the examples above, for instance, btn- indicates that a button is being styled, text- indicates that text is being styled, and bg- indicates that the background is being styled.

- The contextual classes can also be used without a prefix with some elements such as a table cell.

- You can use IntelliSense in Visual Studio to see all of the prefixes and contextual classes that are available.

Figure 10-6   How to work with the CSS classes that provide context

How to use the Bootstrap components

Up until now, you've seen how to apply Bootstrap CSS classes to standard HTML elements and server controls. However, Bootstrap also provides its own *components*. These components use predefined HTML elements and CSS classes to create user interface elements like button groups, navigation bars, and thumbnail images. You saw one of these components, the jumbotron component, in chapter 3. Now, you'll learn how to work with other Bootstrap components.

How to work with glyphicons

A *glyph* is a character or symbol, and you can use glyphs to decorate or add meaning to elements. For example, you can add a glyph to a button or link to indicate its purpose. Bootstrap includes over 250 glyphs from the Halflings set at glyphicons.com. They are located in the fonts folder that's added to your application when you install the NuGet package for Bootstrap. Because these glyphs have been made available free of charge to Bootstrap users, you are asked to include a link to the glyphicons.com website whenever you use these glyphs.

To use a *glyphicon* component, you include the base glyphicon class along with the class for the individual glyph you want to use. You can see how this works in the first two examples in figure 10-7.

It's important to note that you can't code the glyphicon classes directly on other components, including server controls. In the first example in this figure, for instance, you might think that you could code the glyphicon and glyphicon-align-*position* classes on the CssClass property of each LinkButton control. But instead, you must code these classes on elements such as span elements that are coded as content of the LinkButton controls. Note that the span elements themselves can't include any content.

If you use glyphicons, you should be aware that they don't have any padding by default. If you're going to use a glyphicon with text, then, as shown in the second example, you'll need to add space between the glyph and the text. You can do that using CSS, or you can add a non-breaking space to the HTML.

If you review the Bootstrap documentation for glyphicons, you'll see that it contains information about how to make them accessible. This is particularly important if you're using them to add meaning, as in the first example in this figure. In that case, you'll want to be sure to include content that reflects that meaning and that can be read by screen readers. On the other hand, if a glyphicon is used just for decoration, it should be hidden by setting the aria-hidden attribute to True so it don't confuse screen readers.

How to work with badges

A *badge* component lets you highlight text within an element. This is illustrated in the last example in figure 10-7. Here, the LinkButton control contains a badge with the number 2. Note that the content of the badge is coded in the span element that contains the badge class. Also note that the appearance

The URL for the Bootstrap components documentation

http://getbootstrap.com/components/

The URL for the Glyphicons website

http://glyphicons.com/

LinkButton controls with glyphicons

```
<asp:LinkButton runat="server" CssClass="btn btn-default">
    <span class="glyphicon glyphicon-align-left"></span></asp:LinkButton>
<asp:LinkButton runat="server" CssClass="btn btn-default">
    <span class="glyphicon glyphicon-align-center"></span></asp:LinkButton>
<asp:LinkButton runat="server" CssClass="btn btn-default">
    <span class="glyphicon glyphicon-align-right"></span></asp:LinkButton>
<asp:LinkButton runat="server" CssClass="btn btn-default">
    <span class="glyphicon glyphicon-align-justify"></span></
asp:LinkButton>
```

Hyperlink controls with glyphicons

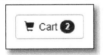

```
<ul class="list-inline">
    <li><asp:HyperLink NavigateUrl="~/Order.aspx" runat="server">
            <span class="glyphicon glyphicon-home"></span>Home
        </asp:HyperLink></li>
    <li><asp:HyperLink NavigateUrl="~/Cart.aspx" runat="server">
            <span class="glyphicon glyphicon-shopping-cart"></span>Cart
        </asp:HyperLink></li>
    <li><asp:HyperLink NavigateUrl="~/Products.aspx" runat="server">
            <span class="glyphicon glyphicon-tasks"></span>Products
        </asp:HyperLink></li>
</ul>
```

A LinkButton control with a badge

```
<asp:LinkButton runat="server" CssClass="btn btn-default">
    <span class="glyphicon glyphicon-shopping-cart"></span>Cart
    <span class="badge">2</span></asp:LinkButton>
```

Description

- A *glyph* is a character or symbol that you use to decorate or add meaning to an element.

- A *badge* provides for highlighting text within an element.

- The classes for *glyphicons* and badges can't be coded directly on a control or component. Instead, they can be coded in span elements that are contained by the control or component.

Figure 10-7   How to work with glyphicons and badges

of this badge will change depending on its context. For instance, it's grey with white text in a normal link, but white with blue text in a link with a btn-primary class. It also collapses so it's hidden if it doesn't contain any text.

How to work with button groups

The table in figure 10-8 shows some of the Bootstrap CSS classes that create *button groups*, and the three examples show some of the ways to use these classes. In the first example, four Button controls are grouped together within a div element that has the btn-group class applied to it. As you can see, this class provides the formatting that makes the buttons in the group look like a menu bar.

If you use a button group to create a menu bar, you'll typically justify the buttons as shown in the second example. This causes all the buttons to be the same size and for the group to span the width of the parent element. Note that for this to work with button elements or controls that render to button elements, you must code each button as a button group as shown here. Then, you must code those groups within another element that applies the btn-group-justified class. In contrast, if you use <a> elements or LinkButton controls for the button group, you don't need to use button groups for each button.

Regardless of whether you use buttons or links, you should know that Internet Explorer 8 doesn't add borders to a justified button group. Because of that, you should always code each button or link within its own button group when you create a justified button group.

In the third example, two div elements each with two buttons are coded as button groups. Then, these two div elements are coded within another div element that has the btn-toolbar class applied to it. As you can see, this class combines the two button groups but leaves space between them so you can see which buttons are related to each other.

In addition to using button groups as shown in this figure, you can use them as part of a button dropdown component. You'll learn how to use this component next.

Common CSS classes for creating button groups

Class	Description
`btn-group`	Groups two or more buttons on a single line with no padding between them.
`btn-toolbar`	Combines button groups with appropriate padding between groups.
`btn-group-`*size*	Applies sizing to all buttons in a group. Example: btn-group-lg.
`btn-group-vertical`	Stacks buttons in a group vertically rather than horizontally.
`btn-group-justified`	Makes buttons equal size and span the width of the parent element.

A basic button group

```
<div class="btn-group">
  <asp:Button runat="server" CssClass="btn btn-default" Text="Home" />
  <asp:Button runat="server" CssClass="btn btn-default" Text="Cart" />
  <asp:Button runat="server" CssClass="btn btn-default" Text="Products" />
  <asp:Button runat="server" CssClass="btn btn-default" Text="Contact Us" />
</div>
```

A group of justified buttons

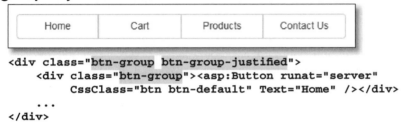

```
<div class="btn-group btn-group-justified">
    <div class="btn-group"><asp:Button runat="server"
        CssClass="btn btn-default" Text="Home" /></div>
    ...
</div>
```

A toolbar with two button groups

```
<div class="btn-toolbar">
  <div class="btn-group">
    <asp:Button runat="server" CssClass="btn btn-default" Text="Home" />
    <asp:Button runat="server" CssClass="btn btn-default" Text="Cart" />
  </div>
  <div class="btn-group">
    <asp:Button runat="server" CssClass="btn btn-default" Text="About" />
    <asp:Button runat="server" CssClass="btn btn-default" Text="Contact Us" />
  </div>
</div>
```

Description

- You can use the classes shown above to group associated buttons together.
- You can also use button groups to create button dropdowns as shown in figure 10-9.

Figure 10-8   How to work with button groups

How to work with button dropdowns

Figure 10-9 shows how to create a *button dropdown*. A button dropdown displays a menu when it's clicked and lets the user select an item from that menu. Then, the page that's associated with the selected item is displayed. To create a button dropdown, you use the CSS classes and the HTML5 data attribute shown in this figure.

The first example in this figure presents a basic button dropdown. Notice that this dropdown is coded within a div element that uses the btn-group class that you learned about in the last figure. Then, it contains a LinkButton control and a ul element. Note that you could also use a HyperLink control instead of the LinkButton control, since they both render to an <a> element.

Within the LinkButton control is a span element that uses the caret class. This class causes a caret to be displayed to the right of the text on the button. That makes it obvious that this is a button dropdown and not a standard button. Then, the dropdown-toggle class is applied to the button to style the button as a dropdown. Finally, the data-toggle data attribute of the button is set to "dropdown" so the button behaves like a button dropdown.

The ul element that follows the LinkButton control defines the items in the menu. The dropdown-menu class is applied to this element so it's styled as a dropdown. Then, each li element within the list contains an <a> element that specifies the URL of the page to be displayed when the item is clicked.

An important thing to know about the basic button dropdown is that clicking on it only toggles the dropdown menu so it's either displayed or hidden. It won't cause a postback to the server, even if you use a link button. If you need a button dropdown to cause a postback, you can create a *split button dropdown* like the one shown in the second example.

In this example, the button dropdown includes two server controls. The first one is a standard Button control like the ones you've seen throughout this book. Because it doesn't include a PostbackUrl property, it will cause a postback to the server when it's clicked. The second one is a LinkButton control that's similar to the one in the first example. The only difference is that it just displays a caret. When this button is clicked, the menu is displayed so the user can select an item, or it's hidden if it's already displayed.

Just like the glyphicon components you learned about earlier, the caret doesn't have any padding by default. When you code a basic button dropdown, then, you need to add space between the text and the caret. One way to do that is to add a non-breaking space as shown in the first example. You can also use CSS to add space. Keep in mind, though, that if you use both basic and split button dropdowns, you'll want to be sure that the extra space is added only to the carets in the basic button dropdowns.

Although the two examples shown here each contain a single button dropdown, you should know that you can also code button dropdowns within a group of buttons like the ones you saw in the previous figure. To do that, you just nest the div element for the button dropdown within the div element for a button group.

CSS classes and an HTML5 data attribute for creating button dropdowns

Class	Description
dropdown-toggle	Applies styling to a button that will function as a dropdown.
dropdown-menu	Applies styling to an unordered list that contains the items in the dropdown.
divider	Applies styling to a list item that acts as a divider between other items.
dropup	Makes the list items drop up rather than down.
caret	Displays a caret.

Attribute	Description
data-toggle	If set to "dropdown", makes a button dropdown.

A button dropdown

```
<div class="btn-group">
    <asp:LinkButton runat="server"
        CssClass="btn btn-default dropdown-toggle" data-toggle="dropdown">
        Products <span class="caret"></span></asp:LinkButton>
    <ul class="dropdown-menu">
        <li><a href="Masks.aspx">Masks</a></li>
        <li><a href="Costumes.aspx">Costumes</a></li>
    </ul>
</div>
```

A split button dropdown

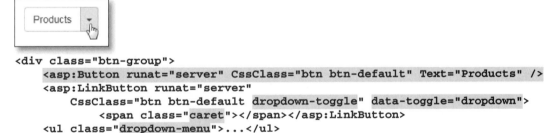

```
<div class="btn-group">
    <asp:Button runat="server" CssClass="btn btn-default" Text="Products" />
    <asp:LinkButton runat="server"
        CssClass="btn btn-default dropdown-toggle" data-toggle="dropdown">
            <span class="caret"></span></asp:LinkButton>
    <ul class="dropdown-menu">...</ul>
</div>
```

Description

- You can use the classes and attribute shown above to create a *button dropdown*, which is a button that displays a menu of links when clicked.

- To create a button dropdown, you must code the button in a button group, along with a list that includes the items to be displayed in the menu.

- To include a caret on a dropdown button, you must use a LinkButton or HyperLink control.

Figure 10-9   How to work with button dropdowns

How to work with list groups

The table in figure 10-10 shows some of the Bootstrap CSS classes that you can use to create *list groups*. As its name implies, a list group is simply a group of items displayed in a list.

In the first example in this figure, you can see how the items in an unordered list are styled as a list group. Here, the list-group class is applied to the ul element, and the list-group-item class is applied to each li element in the list. You'll typically use a list like this if you just want to display information.

If you want to display links or buttons in a list, you should code them within a div element that uses the list-group class. This is illustrated in the second example in this figure. Here, the list consists of a series of <a> elements, and the list-group-item class is applied to each of these elements. In addition, a badge is included on each item.

Unfortunately, the list group component doesn't provide for applying alternating colors to the items in the list by default. If you want to do that, though, you can add a CSS rule set that looks like this:

```
.list-group li:nth-child(odd) {
    background-color: lightgrey;
}
```

This CSS will work in most modern browsers, but it won't work in Internet Explorer 8.

Note that list groups don't display properly with ASP.NET Button controls. If you want to use server controls, then, you should use LinkButton controls since they render to <a> elements. Or, you can use HTML button elements and make them run at the server, which you'll learn how to do later in this chapter.

Common CSS classes for creating list groups

Class	Description
`list-group`	Groups two or more items in a list or div element.
`list-group-item`	Styles the individual items in a list group.
`list-group-item-`*context*	Applies a context class to a list group item. Example: list-group-item-danger.
`active, disabled`	Highlights or grays out the list group item.

A basic list group

```
<ul class="list-group">
    <li class="list-group-item">Costumes</li>
    <li class="list-group-item">Masks</li>
    <li class="list-group-item">Props</li>
    <li class="list-group-item">Special Effects</li>
</ul>
```

A list group of links with badges

```
<div class="list-group">
    <a href="Costumes.aspx" class="list-group-item">
        <span class="badge">6</span>Costumes</a>
    ...
    <a href="Effects.aspx" class="list-group-item">
        <span class="badge">6</span>Special Effects</a>
</div>
```

Description

- The CSS classes for *list groups* let you display items, like links, buttons, and list items, in a list. You can also nest a list group within another list group.

- You can use the LinkButton control or the HTML button element to create a list group, but you shouldn't use Button controls because they're not styled properly.

- If you use LinkButton controls or HTML button elements, you should also use the btn class so the buttons are styled properly.

Figure 10-10   How to work with list groups

How to work with alerts

The first table in figure 10-11 shows some of the Bootstrap CSS classes that you can use to create *alerts*, along with an HTML5 data attribute that you can use with alerts. In its simplest form, an alert can consist of an element such as a div that contains text and has the alert class applied to it. In most cases, though, an alert will be more complex like the one shown in this figure. In addition to text, this alert contains a close button and a link. It's also given a context.

You should notice four things about this alert. First, the base alert class is applied to the div element that contains the alert. An alert-*context* class that provides the appropriate color for the alert is also applied to this div, as well as the alert-dismissible class that provides for closing the alert.

Second, the close class is applied to the HTML button within the div element. This class provides for closing the alert. Also, the data-dismiss data attribute of this button tells Bootstrap to dismiss the alert when the button is clicked. Note that even though this button is coded first in the HTML, it displays in the far right corner of the alert.

Third, the text of the close button uses the × character entity instead of the letter "X". This is the HTML5 character entity for the multiplication sign, and it's often recommended that you use it for close buttons because it lays out better. However, screen readers for the visually impaired will read this character entity as the word "multiplication". Because of that, you should include an aria attribute such as

```
aria-label="Close Success dialog box"
```

when you use this character entity.

Finally, the alert-link class is applied to the link in the alert so the link matches the styling of the alert itself. In this case, since the alert uses the success context class, the alert-link class styles the link to match that class.

When you work with alerts in Visual Studio, you might notice that IntelliSense displays two similar classes: alert-dismissible and alert-dismissable. Although either class will work, the Bootstrap documentation uses the alert-dismissible class as shown here.

How to work with breadcrumbs

Figure 10-11 also shows how to create *breadcrumbs*. As you can see in the example in this figure, breadcrumbs provide navigation links that are relative to the user's current location in a website. Here, the breadcrumbs are coded as an ordered list. Notice that the active class has been applied to the last item in the list. This class indicates the current page, and it displays the text of the item in a different color than the other items. Also notice that the last item doesn't contain a link.

In addition to creating breadcrumbs using HTML and Bootstrap classes, you can create them dynamically using server-side code. You'll learn how to do that later in this chapter.

Common CSS classes and an HTML5 data attribute for creating alerts

Class	Description
`alert`	Wraps text and HTML in a contextual message area.
`alert-`*context*	Applies a context class to an alert. Example: alert-warning.
`alert-dismissible`	Makes an alert dismissible. The div for the alert should include a button that uses the close class and the data-dismiss attribute.
`alert-link`	Styles links to match the styling of the alert that contains the link.
`close`	Provides for closing an alert.

Attribute	Description
`data-dismiss`	Tells Bootstrap to dismiss the alert.

A dismissible alert with a link

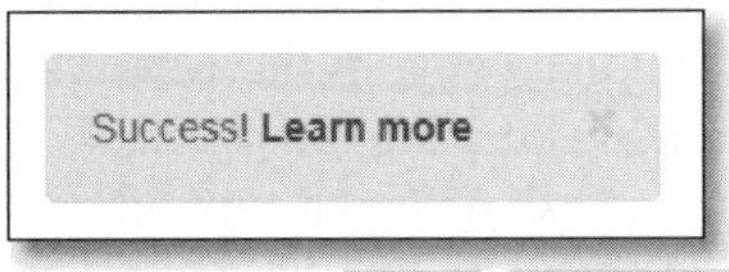

Success! **Learn more**

```
<div class="alert alert-success alert-dismissible">
    <button class="close" data-dismiss="alert">&times;</button>
    Success! <a href="#" class="alert-link">Learn more</a>
</div>
```

Common CSS classes for creating breadcrumbs

Class	Description
`breadcrumb`	Makes an ordered list element display inline with separators between items.
`active`	Indicates the current page.

A breadcrumb with four segments

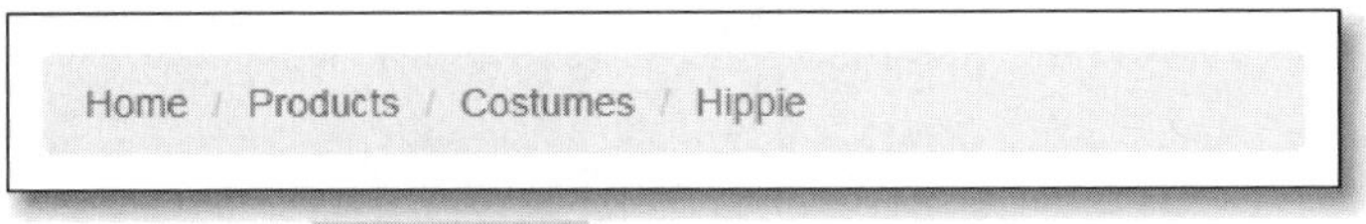

Home / Products / Costumes / Hippie

```
<ol class="breadcrumb">
    <li><a href="Default.aspx">Home</a></li>
    <li><a href="Products.aspx">Products</a></li>
    <li><a href="Costumes.aspx">Costumes</a></li>
    <li class="active">Hippie</li>
</ol>
```

Description

- *Alerts* let you provide contextual feedback in your application. To do that, you use the alert class along with a contextual class like alert-success or alert-info.

- If you make an alert dismissible, the user can close it by clicking on the "x" that's displayed. This feature uses JavaScript along with the Bootstrap classes.

- *Breadcrumbs* display navigation links that are relative to the user's current location.

Figure 10-11 How to work with alerts and breadcrumbs

How to work with thumbnails

In some cases, you'll want to display images at a small size so you can fit more on a page. When a group of small images is displayed, the images are typically referred to as *thumbnails*. Although this name implies that an image is about the size of a thumbnail, it can be used to refer to any small image.

Figure 10-12 shows how to use two Bootstrap CSS classes to create thumbnails. In the first example, the thumbnail class is applied to three <a> elements that contain images. (Only the code for the first thumbnail is shown here.) Notice that the <a> element for the first thumbnail is coded within a div element that provides the width of the div in columns. When you do that, the image will span the width of the div up to its actual size. This will also cause the images to lay out properly in smaller viewports.

The second example shows how to add a caption to a thumbnail component. To do that, you apply the thumbnail class to a div element that contains the <a> element with the image and another div element that contains the caption. Then, you apply the caption class to the inner div element. In this example, the caption consists of a heading and a paragraph with two button elements.

Just as you can with breadcrumbs, you can create thumbnails dynamically using server-side code. You'll learn how to do that later.

Common CSS classes for creating thumbnails

Class	Description
thumbnail	Provides the default styling and padding for a thumbnail image.
caption	Provides the default styling and padding for the HTML and text that accompanies a thumbnail.

Three basic thumbnails

```
<div class="col-md-4">
    <a href="#" class="thumbnail"><img src="/Images/Products/cat1.jpg" /></a>
</div>
...
```

Three thumbnails with captions

```
<div class="col-md-4">
    <div class="thumbnail">
        <a href="#"><img src="/Images/Products/cat1.jpg" alt="cat" /></a>
        <div class="caption text-center">
            <h6>Deranged Cat</h6>
            <p><button class="btn btn-primary">Buy</button>
                <button class="btn btn-default">Save</button></p>
        </div>
    </div>
</div>
...
```

Description

- A *thumbnail* is a small version of an image that can be used to make downloading the image faster and to save space on a web page that contains multiple images.

Figure 10-12   How to work with thumbnails

How to work with navs

The table in figure 10-13 shows some of the Bootstrap CSS classes that you can use to create *nav* components. Nav components provide another way to create a simple menu bar. As you'll see in the next figure, though, you're more likely to use them as part of a navbar component.

The first example in this figure shows how to create a basic nav with tabs, the second example shows how to create a nav with justified tabs, and the third example shows how to create a nav with pills. If you compare these examples, you'll see that the only difference between a tab and a pill is in the appearance of the active item.

Notice in all three of these examples that the list of nav items are coded within an HTML5 nav element. This provides accessibility for the items. If for some reason you need to put a nav component within an element other than a nav element, you should include the role="navigation" attribute on that element.

To create a nav component in ASP.NET, you can use an HTML ul element as shown in the first two examples or a BulletedList control as shown in the third example. If you use a BulletedList control, you should set its DisplayMode property to HyperLink so the list items are displayed as links. You can also set this property to LinkButton to display the items as links. If you do that, though, the page will post back to the server when you click a link, which usually isn't what you want.

If you include the Value property for a list item in a BulletedList control, you should know that the value of that property will be used as the value of the href attribute of the link that's rendered to the browser. Otherwise, the text content of the list item will be used as the value of the href attribute. In the example in this figure, each of the list items contains a Value property that specifies the name of the page to be displayed when the link is clicked.

You should also know that the list items for a BulletedList control don't have a CssClass property that you can use to apply Bootstrap classes. However, you can still apply these classes by coding a standard class property. For example, the active class is applied to the first list item in this example so its background is blue. If you use the class property like this, you should know that Visual Studio will warn you that it isn't valid. Even so, the class will still be rendered to the browser.

You can also add button dropdowns to the nav items in a nav component. To add a button dropdown, you just nest it within a list item. Then, you apply the dropdown class to that list item.

Common CSS classes for creating navs

Class	Description
nav	Groups two or more nav items.
nav-tabs	Styles the nav items in a single line with the active item displayed as a tab.
nav-pills	Styles the nav items in a single line with the active item displayed as a pill.
nav-stacked	Causes nav items to be stacked vertically.
nav-justified	Makes nav items equal in size and span the width of the parent element.
active	Styles the active nav item differently than the other nav items.

An unordered list styled as tabs

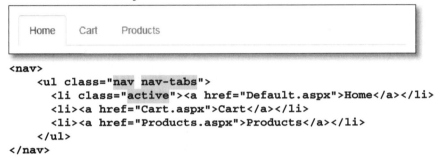

```
<nav>
    <ul class="nav nav-tabs">
      <li class="active"><a href="Default.aspx">Home</a></li>
      <li><a href="Cart.aspx">Cart</a></li>
      <li><a href="Products.aspx">Products</a></li>
    </ul>
</nav>
```

An unordered list styled as justified tabs

```
<nav><ul class="nav nav-tabs nav-justified">...</ul></nav>
```

A BulletedList server control styled as pills

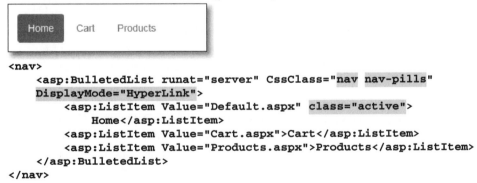

```
<nav>
    <asp:BulletedList runat="server" CssClass="nav nav-pills"
    DisplayMode="HyperLink">
        <asp:ListItem Value="Default.aspx" class="active">
            Home</asp:ListItem>
        <asp:ListItem Value="Cart.aspx">Cart</asp:ListItem>
        <asp:ListItem Value="Products.aspx">Products</asp:ListItem>
    </asp:BulletedList>
</nav>
```

Description

- You can use the CSS classes for *navs* to create tabs and pills. The difference between a tab and a pill is in the appearance of the active item.
- Nav components should be placed within an HTML5 nav element for accessibility.

Figure 10-13   How to work with navs

How to work with default navbars

The Bootstrap *navbar* component creates a responsive menu bar that collapses to a dropdown menu on narrower viewports. This is a popular feature used by many websites. In fact, once you learn about navbars, you'll probably start to notice them on the websites you visit.

The table in figure 10-14 shows some of the Bootstrap CSS classes and HTML5 data attributes that you can use to create a default navbar. Note that to save space, the "navbar" portion of some of the class names has been omitted. For example, the classes in the fourth entry of the table are actually navbar-header, navbar-nav, and navbar-brand. Also note that you don't need to understand exactly what each class and attribute does to create a navbar. So, this topic will only point out the most important things to know.

The example in this figure shows how a default navbar looks at two different viewport widths. At desktop width, the brand and all the links in the menu bar are displayed across the top of the page. In contrast, only the brand and a button that displays a dropdown menu when clicked are displayed at mobile width.

The HTML shows how to create a navbar like this. As you can see, the navbar is coded within a nav element for accessibility, and that element is coded as the first element within the container div for the page. Both the navbar and navbar-default classes are applied to the nav element.

Within the nav element is a div element that has the container-fluid class applied. This groups the navbar items together and applies the appropriate spacing to those items.

Within this second div element are two additional div elements. The first one defines the head of the navbar. It contains the button that's displayed on mobile viewports and a link with brand information that's displayed on all viewports. The brand is typically text or an image that displays the home page when clicked. It's displayed at the left side of the navbar by default and the button is displayed at the right side of the navbar by default.

Notice that the button element uses two of the classes and both of the data attributes presented here. These classes and attributes provide for collapsing the navbar and displaying and hiding the menu on smaller viewports. Also notice the sr-only and icon-bar classes that are applied to the span elements within the button element. The sr-only class provides text that can be read by screen readers. The icon-bar class causes the lines to be displayed on the button.

The second div element represents the body of the navbar, which contains the links for the menu. It uses the collapse and navbar-collapse classes so the navbar works properly in smaller viewports. It also includes an id attribute whose value is identified by the data-target attribute of the button element in the header.

The links for the navbar shown here are coded within two ul elements. The nav class that you learned about in the last figure as well as the navbar-nav class are applied to both of these elements. In addition, the navbar-right class is applied to the second ul element so the links it contains are aligned at the right side of the navbar. Because no alignment is specified for the first set of links, they're aligned at the left.

Common CSS classes and HTML5 data attributes for creating navbars

Class	Description
navbar	Creates a responsive menu bar that collapses in smaller viewports.
navbar-default	Styles the individual nav items in a horizontal bar with borders.
navbar-*alignment*	Aligns the nav items to the right or the left. Example: navbar-right.
-header, -nav, -brand	Identify and style the head, body, and brand information of the navbar.
-toggle, -collapse, collapsed, collapse	Identify and style the parts of the navbar that collapse and toggle.

Attribute	Description
data-toggle	If set to "collapse", makes a navbar collapsible.
data-target	Identifies the HTML element that will be changed.

A default navbar at desktop width and collapsed at mobile width

```
<div class="container">
  <nav class="navbar navbar-default">
    <div class="container-fluid">
      <div class="navbar-header">
        <button type="button" class="navbar-toggle collapsed"
                data-toggle="collapse" data-target="#mainMenu">
          <span class="sr-only">Toggle navigation</span>
          <span class="icon-bar"></span>
          <span class="icon-bar"></span>
          <span class="icon-bar"></span>
        </button>
        <a class="navbar-brand" href="Default.aspx">Halloween Store</a>
      </div>
      <div class="collapse navbar-collapse" id="mainMenu">
        <ul class="nav navbar-nav">
          <li class="active"><a href="Default.aspx">Home</a></li>
          <li><a href="Products.aspx">Products</a></li>
          <li><a href="Cart.aspx">Cart</a></li></ul>
        <ul class="nav navbar-nav navbar-right">
          <li><a href="ContactUs.aspx">Contact Us</a></li>
          <li><a href="AboutUs.aspx">About Us</a></li></ul>
      </div>
    </div>
  </nav>
  ...
</div>
```

Figure 10-14   How to work with default navbars

How to work with static, fixed, and inverse navbars

In addition to the default navbars that you learned about in the last topic, you can create static, fixed, and inverse navbars as shown in figure 10-15. A static navbar is one that's displayed at the top of the page and that scrolls out of sight when you scroll down the page. In contrast, a fixed navbar can be displayed at the top or bottom of the page and it's always visible, even when you scroll. Unlike default navbars, which span the width of the element that contains them, static and fixed navbars span the width of the viewport.

Both static and fixed navbars can be styled as default navbars as shown in the previous figure, or as inverse navbars. An inverse navbar is simply a navbar that has a dark background color and a light foreground color rather than a light background color and a dark foreground color.

The table in this figure shows some of the Bootstrap CSS classes that you can use to create all three of these types of navbars. Then, the examples that follow show a static navbar, a navbar that's fixed at the bottom of the screen, and an inverse navbar that's fixed at the bottom of the screen.

The most important thing to notice about the static navbar is that its nav element is coded as a sibling of the page's container div element, and it comes before that div element. In contrast, the nav element for a default navbar and a fixed navbar is coded as a child of the container div.

The most important thing to know when fixing a navbar to the top or bottom of the screen is that you typically need to adjust the padding of the page's body element. If you don't, the navbar can overlay the content at the top or bottom of the page. In this figure, for example, 70 pixels of padding have been added below the body. 50 pixels were added to accommodate the height of the navbar, and an additional 20 pixels were added to provide space between the page's content and the navbar.

Note that the rest of the HTML for a static, fixed, or inverse navbar is the same as shown in the last figure for a default navbar. When you create a static or fixed navbar, though, you might want to use the container class instead of the container-fluid class for the div element within the nav element. That's because the container class provides additional left and right padding, which leaves room for the scrollbar at the right side of the screen. You can see how that works in the second example in this figure.

Although the examples in this figure and the last figure should get you off to a good start, you should know that there's a lot more you can do with navbars than what's presented here. For example, you can add brand images, buttons, search forms, and more. For more information, please see the Bootstrap documentation.

More CSS classes for creating navbars

Class	Description
navbar-static-top	Makes the navbar the full width of the viewport; scrolls off the screen when the user scrolls down.
navbar-fixed-top	Makes the navbar stay at the top of the screen even when the user scrolls. Will overlay other content unless you add padding to the top of the body.
navbar-fixed-bottom	Makes the navbar stay at the bottom of the screen even when the user scrolls. Will overlay other content unless you add padding to the bottom of the body.
navbar-inverse	Modifies the look of the navbar by inverting its default colors.

A static navbar that's displayed at the top of the screen

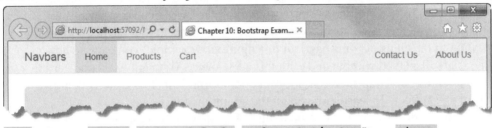

```
<nav class="navbar navbar-default navbar-static-top">...</nav>
<div class="container">...</div>
```

A navbar that's fixed at the bottom of the screen

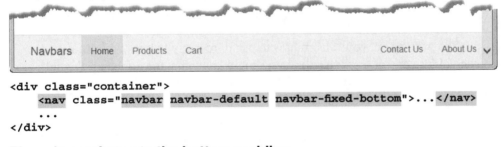

```
<div class="container">
    <nav class="navbar navbar-default navbar-fixed-bottom">...</nav>
    ...
</div>
```

The rule set that sets the bottom padding
```
body { padding-bottom: 70px; }
```

An inverse navbar that's fixed at the bottom of the screen

```
<nav class="navbar navbar-inverse navbar-fixed-bottom">...</nav>
```

Figure 10-15   How to work with static, fixed, and inverse navbars

How to work with Bootstrap themes

As you know, you can override the styles that Bootstrap provides with your own custom styles. In many cases, that's all you'll need to do to make your web pages look the way you want them to. But you can also override the Bootstrap styles with a number of different *themes*, which provide alternate styles for the elements on a web page. That's what you'll learn to do in the two topics that follow.

How to work with the bootstrap-theme style sheet

When you download the Bootstrap NuGet package as described in chapter 3, four CSS files are added to the Content folder. These files are shown in the table in figure 10-16. Up until now, you've only used the main bootstrap style sheet. However, you can also use the bootstrap-theme style sheet to apply additional styling to the elements on a page. In this figure, for example, you can see how alerts are displayed without and with this style sheet. Although it may be hard to tell here, the bootstrap-theme style sheet applies gradients to the alerts that give them a 3D effect. To learn more about the styling that this style sheet applies, you can refer to the documentation at the URL shown at the top of this figure.

It's important to note that the bootstrap-theme style sheet doesn't take the place of the main style sheet. Instead, it augments the main style sheet. Because of that, you must code its link tag after the link tag for the main style sheet. Then, if you want to override either of the Bootstrap style sheets, you code a link tag to your own custom style sheets after those style sheets. You can see how this works in the example in this figure.

In the next figure, you'll learn how to use third-party themes with Bootstrap. When you use one of these themes, you should know that the bootstrap-theme style sheet can interfere with them. Because of that, you shouldn't use this style sheet when you use a third-party theme.

The URL for the bootstrap-theme style sheet documentation

`http://getbootstrap.com/examples/theme/`

The CSS files that are downloaded with the Bootstrap NuGet package

File	Description
`bootstrap.css`	The main Bootstrap style sheet.
`bootstrap.min.css`	The minified version of the main Bootstrap style sheet.
`bootstrap-theme.css`	An optional Bootstrap style sheet with augmented styles such as 3D effects for buttons and alerts.
`bootstrap-theme.min.css`	The minified version of the Bootstrap theme style sheet.

How to add the bootstrap-theme style sheet to a web page

```
<link href="Content/bootstrap.min.css" rel="stylesheet" />
<link href="Content/bootstrap-theme.min.css" rel="stylesheet" />
<link href="Content/site.css" rel="stylesheet" />
```

Styling applied to alerts with the main and bootstrap-theme style sheets

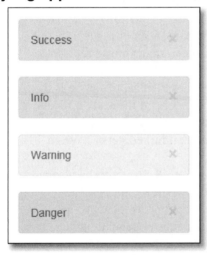

Description

- The bootstrap-theme style sheet downloads automatically with the Bootstrap NuGet package.

- The bootstrap-theme style sheet adds styling such as gradients that give a 3D effect to alerts and buttons. Often, the default styling of the main Bootstrap style sheet will be all you need for your project.

- If you use the bootstrap-theme style sheet, be sure to code its link tag after the tag for the main Bootstrap style sheet and before the tags for your own style sheets.

- If you use custom themes as described in the next figure, you shouldn't use the bootstrap-theme style sheet.

Figure 10-16   How to work with the bootstrap-theme style sheet

How to change your Bootstrap theme

In addition to the bootstrap-theme style sheet that comes with the NuGet package for Bootstrap, several websites provide other themes that you can use with Bootstrap. Some of these themes are available for free, but you must pay for others. One of the most popular sites for free themes is Bootswatch, whose URL is shown at the top of figure 10-17.

To use the Bootswatch website, you just scroll down the page until you see the theme you want to use. In this figure, for example, you can see two of the available themes and some of the basic styling they apply. If you want to see some of the additional styling that a theme applies, you can click on the Preview button for that theme. Then, the page that's displayed shows the styling that the theme applies to many of the common elements and components.

To use a theme, you start by clicking on the Download button. When you do, the source code for the bootstrap.min.css file is displayed for that theme. Then, you can right-click on the page and select Save As to save this file to your web application. If you want to download the non-minified file instead, you can click the arrowhead to the right of the Download button and then choose the bootstrap.css file.

Unlike the bootstrap-theme style sheet that you learned about in the previous figure, the style sheets that are available from the Bootswatch website replace the main Bootstrap style sheet rather than augmenting it. Because of that, the minified and non-minified files for these style sheets have the same names as the files for the main Bootstrap style sheet. When you save one of these style sheets, then, you'll probably want to give it a different name so it doesn't override the main style sheet. For example, you might name the minified version of the Superhero theme bootstrap-superhero.min.css.

If you're using a master page, you can then switch back and forth between the main Bootstrap style sheet and the Bootswatch style sheet simply by changing the file name in the link tag for that page. That makes it easy to try different Bootswatch themes too. If you're not using a master page, though, you may want to rename the main Bootstrap style sheet and then rename the Bootswatch style sheet you want to use to bootstrap.min.css. That way, you won't need to change the link tag in every page that uses Bootstrap.

The URL of the Bootswatch website

`http://bootswatch.com/`

The Bootswatch website with two themes displayed

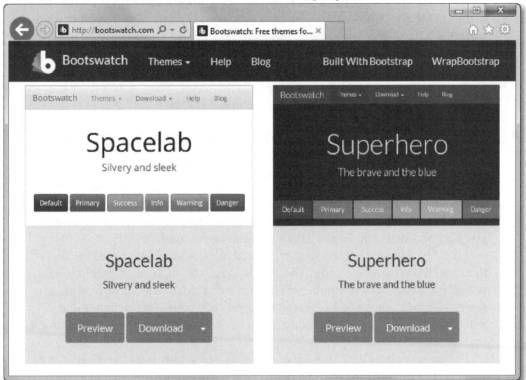

Description

- You can download Bootstrap themes in addition to the one that's downloaded with the NuGet package for Bootstrap.

- One of the most popular websites for Bootstrap themes is the Bootswatch website shown above.

- To download a theme from Bootswatch, go to the URL above and scroll down to the theme you want to use. Then, click the arrowhead to the right of the Download button and select the bootstrap.css or bootstrap.min.css file to display its source code. Finally, right-click on the page, select Save As, and enter the name and location for the file in the dialog box that's displayed.

- The style sheets that are available from Bootswatch replace the main Bootstrap style sheet rather than augmenting it. Because of that, you'll typically change the name of the downloaded file so it reflects the name of the theme.

- You can also see how many of the elements and components will look with a theme by clicking the Preview button.

- To use a Bootswatch style sheet, you can just replace the link tag for the main Bootstrap style sheet with a link tag for the Bootswatch style sheet.

Figure 10-17   How to change your Bootstrap theme

How to control the rendered HTML

Throughout this chapter, you've learned how to use Bootstrap with ASP.NET controls. That includes how to make adjustments when a control isn't rendered to the HTML that Bootstrap needs. In some cases, though, it can be difficult to make the adjustments you need to render the correct HTML. Then, you may want to generate the HTML dynamically in server-side code.

In the topics that follow, you'll learn two ways to do that. First, you'll learn how you can work with HTML elements on the server. Then, you'll learn how to use two ASP.NET controls to render the required HTML.

How to work with HTML elements on the server

In some cases, it can be easier to control the rendered HTML by coding that HTML directly in the aspx code rather than using server controls. The problem with using HTML is that you can't work with it in server-side code by default. But you can easily fix that by adding the runat="server" attribute to the elements you want to work with. Figure 10-18 shows two examples of this.

The first example is for a span element that's used to display a badge. In this case, the value of the badge should change as the application executes so it displays a count of the number of items in a cart. Since that must be done in server-side code, the span element in the aspx code contains a runat attribute with the value "server". It also contains an id attribute that can be used to refer to the element.

You can see how the id attribute is used in the code-behind file. Here, the InnerText property of the span element refers to the contents of that element. Then, the number of items in the shopping cart is assigned to that property, so that value is displayed in the badge.

You should know that you could also use an ASP.NET Label control to render the same HTML as the span element shown here. To do that, you would simply set its CssClass property to "badge". In more complicated situations, though, it's better to use HTML.

To illustrate, consider the second example in this figure. This example starts by showing part of a navbar component on a master page. In this case, the navbar should change as the application executes so the active class is applied to the navbar item that represents the current page. To do that, the runat="server" attribute is coded on both the li and ul elements for the navbar. In addition, an id attribute is coded on the ul element so it can be referred to from the server-side code. Note that this navbar is coded within a form element so it can be processed on the server.

You can see how this works in the code for the Load event handler of the master page shown here. This code uses a foreach statement to loop through the controls in the ul element, checking if each item is an instance of HtmlGenericControl. If it is, that means it's an li element. In that case, the control is cast to an HtmlGenericControl and stored in a variable named li. Then, the control within that li element is cast to a HyperLink object and stored in a variable named a.

How to set the value that's displayed in a badge

In the aspx file

```
<span id="spanCount" runat="server" class="badge"></span>
```

In the code-behind file

```
spanCount.InnerText = CartItemList.GetCart().Count.ToString();
```

How to mark the current page in a navbar on a master page as active

In the aspx file for the master page

```
<div class="collapse navbar-collapse" id="mainMenu">
    <ul id="navList" runat="server" class="nav navbar-nav">
        <li runat="server">
            <asp:HyperLink NavigateUrl="~/Order.aspx" runat="server">
                Home</asp:HyperLink></li>
        <li runat="server">
            <asp:HyperLink NavigateUrl="~/Cart.aspx" runat="server">
                Cart</asp:HyperLink></li>
        <li runat="server">
            <asp:HyperLink NavigateUrl="~/ContactUs.aspx" runat="server">
                Contact Us</asp:HyperLink></li>
    </ul>
</div>
```

In the Load event handler of the code-behind file for the master page

```
if (!IsPostBack) // on initial load
{
    foreach (Control ctl in navList.Controls)
    {
        if (ctl is HtmlGenericControl)
        {
            // get the current li element and its child <a> element
            var li = (HtmlGenericControl)ctl;
            var a = (HyperLink)li.Controls[1];

            // if the current navigation link is the active page...
            if (Page.AppRelativeVirtualPath.Contains(a.NavigateUrl))
            {
                // set Bootstrap active class
                li.Attributes.Add("class", "active");
                return; // end loop after marking current page active
            }
        }
    }
}
```

Description

- If a server control doesn't work with Bootstrap, you can use an HTML element instead.

- To work with an HTML element on the server, include the runat="server" attribute.

- A using directive for the System.Web.UI.HtmlControls namespace has been added to the code-behind file for the master page shown above to make it easier to refer to the HTML controls.

Figure 10-18   How to work with HTML elements on the server

Next, the page's AppRelativeVirtualPath property is checked to see if the HyperLink's URL matches the URL of the current page. If it does, a class attribute with the value "active" is added to the li element. Finally, the return statement ends the loop.

How to use the Literal control to render HTML

Another way to render the HTML you need is to use the ASP.NET Literal control. When you use this control, its content is rendered to the browser just as it is. Because of that, you can add the HTML you want to render directly to this control.

This is illustrated in the first example in figure 10-19. Here, an ol element that's coded in the master page will be used to display the breadcrumbs for each content page. To accomplish that, a Literal control is coded within the ol element. This control will be used as a container for the li elements that make up the breadcrumbs.

The code for the master page contains two public methods that will be used by the content pages to create the appropriate li elements for the page. The AddBreadcrumbLink method accepts a URL and text and then appends an li element that contains an anchor tag with that URL and text to the Literal control's Text property. In contrast, the AddCurrentPage method appends just an li element with the text that's passed to it. Note that the active class is applied to this element to indicate that it's for the current page.

Each content page calls these methods to generate the li elements for the breadcrumbs. To create a breadcrumb for a page other than the current page, it calls the AddBreadcrumbLink method. To create a breadcrumb for the current page, it calls the AddCurrentPage method. You can see the result here.

How to use the Repeater control to render HTML

Although you can use a Literal control for just about any situation, a Repeater control works better if you need to generate a series of components. In the second example in figure 10-19, for instance, a Repeater control is used to generate the HTML for a series of thumbnails that use data from a database. Although the Repeater control is an older data control, it's easy to work with so many programmers still use it for simple tasks. In section 3 of this book, you'll learn how to use other controls like this for working with data.

The DataSourceID property of the Repeater control identifies the source of data it will display. In this case, the source is a SqlDataSource control that retrieves data from the Products table of the Halloween database. Then, the ItemTemplate element within the Repeater control defines how each item in the data source is displayed. In this case, the template contains a thumbnail with a caption that displays the product name, unit price, and long description. You'll learn more about how templates like this work in chapter 13. For now, you just need to know that the ItemTemplate element in this Repeater control will render the HTML for a thumbnail for every product that's returned by the SQL statement in the SqlDataSource control.

How to use a Literal control to display breadcrumbs

In the aspx file for the master page

```
<ol class="breadcrumb">
    <asp:Literal ID="litBreadcrumb" runat="server"></asp:Literal>
</ol>
```

In the code-behind file for the master page

```
public void AddBreadcrumbLink(string url, string text) {
    litBreadcrumb.Text += $"<li><a href='{url}'>{text}</a></li>";
}
public void AddCurrentPage(string text) {
    litBreadcrumb.Text += $"<li class='active'>{text}</li>";
};
```

In the code-behind file for a content page

```
Master.AddBreadcrumbLink("/Order.aspx", "Home");
Master.AddBreadcrumbLink("/Products.aspx", "Products");
Master.AddCurrentPage("Costumes");
```

How the breadcrumb looks in the browser

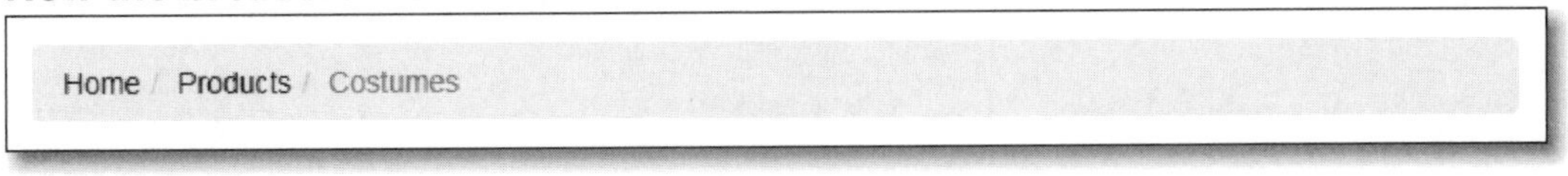

Home / Products / Costumes

How to use a Repeater control to display a series of thumbnails

```
<div class="row">
    <asp:Repeater ID="Repeater1" runat="server"
        DataSourceID="SqlDataSource1">
        <ItemTemplate>
            <div class="col-sm-6 col-md-3">
                <div class="thumbnail">
                    <img src='/Images/Products/<%# Eval("ImageFile") %>'
                        alt='<%# Eval("Name") %>' />
                    <div class="caption">
                        <h3><%# Eval("Name") %></h3>
                        <p><b>Price: <%# Eval("UnitPrice", "{0:c}") %></b>
                        <br><br><%# Eval("LongDescription") %></p>
                    </div>
                </div>
            </div>
        </ItemTemplate>
    </asp:Repeater>
</div>
<asp:SqlDataSource runat="server" ID="SqlDataSource1"
    ConnectionString='<%$ ConnectionStrings:HalloweenConnection %>'
    SelectCommand="SELECT [ProductID], [Name], [LongDescription],
    [UnitPrice], [ImageFile] FROM [Products] ORDER BY [Name]">
</asp:SqlDataSource>
```

Description

- You can use Literal and Repeater controls to build the HTML that Bootstrap needs.

Figure 10-19   How to use the Literal and Repeater controls to render HTML

Perspective

In this chapter, you learned more about how to use the classes and components of Bootstrap to style your web applications. In particular, you learned how to make Bootstrap work with ASP.NET. You learned to do this by applying classes to server controls, by working with HTML elements on the server, and by generating HTML dynamically. You also learned how to use themes to change the styles that Bootstrap applies by default.

It's important to know, though, that there's much more to Bootstrap than what's presented here. For example, Bootstrap lets you float elements to the left or right, create blocks, make elements visible or invisible based on the viewport size, format text by making it larger, smaller, bold, italic, and more. In addition, Bootstrap provides many more components than those presented here, such as progress bars, panels, and carousels. And, of course, there are all sorts of ways to make Bootstrap accessible for users with disabilities. For more about all the things you can do with Bootstrap, please see the documentation at the URLs presented in this chapter.

Terms

component	button dropdown	thumbnail
glyph	split button dropdown	nav
glyphicon	list group	navbar
badge	alert	theme
button group	breadcrumb	

Summary

- Bootstrap CSS classes let you style HTML elements such as buttons, check boxes, images, and tables. They also provide alignment and transformation classes for working with text, and classes that provide context for most elements.

- Bootstrap *components* let you create user interface elements such as *button groups*, *navbars*, and *thumbnails*. The Bootstrap *glyphicon* component uses the Halflings set from glyphicon.com to create *glyphs*.

- Bootstrap comes with an optional bootstrap-theme.css style sheet that augments the main Bootstrap style sheet by adding styling such as 3-D effects for buttons and alerts.

- You can also replace the main Bootstrap style sheet with a third-party *theme*. A popular website for Bootstrap themes is Bootswatch.com.

- You can generate HTML dynamically in server-side code by coding HTML elements, a Literal control, or a Repeater control in your aspx code.

- To work with an HTML element in server-side code, you must include the runat="server" attribute on that element. If you use a Literal control, you can use server-side code to add the HTML you need as the content of that control. And if you use a Repeater control, you can generate a series of components that display data from a data source such as a database.

Exercise 10-1   Review Bootstrap CSS and components

In this exercise, you'll review a Shopping Cart application that uses Bootstrap to give you a better feel for how Bootstrap works.

1. Open the Ex10Cart_1 web application that's in the aspnet46_cs directory.

2. Run the application to see how it works. Note that each button on the navbar has a glyphicon, the Products button is a dropdown, and the Cart button has a badge that shows how many items are in the cart.

3. Navigate to different pages of the application to see how the breadcrumb links change. Be sure to navigate to pages for the various product categories.

4. Narrow the browser to see how the navbar behaves at different widths. When you're done, close the browser.

5. Review the code for the application to see how it works. In particular, review the aspx and code-behind file for the master page to see the code for displaying the breadcrumbs and marking the current page in the navbar. When you're done, close the solution.

Exercise 10-2   Use Bootstrap in an application

In this exercise, you'll modify another version of the Shopping Cart application by adding Bootstrap CSS classes and a Repeater control.

Open, run, and review the application

1. Open the Ex10Cart_2 web application that's in the aspnet46_cs directory and run it. Note that this version has nav tabs instead of a navbar, that the Products page doesn't display any product data, and that the formatting of the Contact Us and About Us pages could be improved.

2. Narrow the browser and see that the nav component behaves differently than the navbar component that you saw in exercise 10-1.

Update the Bootstrap CSS classes

3. Add Bootstrap classes to the footer element for the master page that center its text and capitalize the first letter of each word in its text.

4. Change the Bootstrap contextual class for the Add to Cart button on the Order page from default to primary. Do the same for the Continue Shopping button on the Cart page.

5. Add Bootstrap classes to the table on the Contact Us page to give it a border and alternating row colors. If the table-striped class isn't included in the IntelliSense completion list, enter it by hand.

6. Add Bootstrap classes to make the ul element on the About Us page a list group component. Then, if you're feeling adventurous, add a rule set to the site.css file to give the list group an alternating background color of lightgrey.

7. Save all your changes. Then, go back to the browser, do a refresh, and review the changes you've just made.

Add thumbnail components for the products in the database

8. Display the aspx file for the Products page. Note that it has an empty Repeater control and a SqlDataSource control that selects Product information from the database. Also note that the value of the DataSourceID property of the Repeater control has been set to the value of the ID of this SqlDataSource control.

9. Add an ItemTemplate element to the Repeater control. Then, use figure 10-19 as a guide to create a thumbnail component for each product that's returned by the SqlDataSource. For simplicity, you can include just an h4 element that contains the product name in the caption. Be sure to use the Eval method to bind the ImageFile and name fields as shown in this figure, and center the name for each product.

10. When you're done, run the application and navigate to the Products page to see how it looks. Narrow the browser to see how the page adjusts at different widths.

11. When you're done, stop the application and then close the solution.

11

How to work with friendly URLs and routing

ASP.NET offers routing features that let you provide friendly URLs for your pages. When ASP.NET first added routing, you had to work with it manually in code. Now, though, the FriendlyUrls feature provides a more automated way to add friendly URLs to your applications. In this chapter, you'll learn how to work with friendly URLs using both techniques. You'll also learn how to use both of these techniques together in the same application.

An introduction to friendly URLs

Before you learn about the two different ways to work with friendly URLs, you should know what they are and what benefits they provide. Figure 11-1 presents this information.

What is a friendly URL?

As you learned in chapter 1, a URL consists of several parts, including protocol, domain, path, and file name. Also, as you learned in chapter 8, one way to pass data between the pages of a website is to use URL encoding with *query strings* that are coded at the end of the URLs. This is illustrated by the first code example in this figure, whose query string contains a ProductID value of cat01.

In contrast, when you use *friendly URLs*, the data that's passed between pages becomes part of the URL itself. You can see this in the second code example in this figure. Here, the cat01 parameter is simply the last segment of the URL.

Two benefits of friendly URLs

One of the main benefits of friendly URLs is improved *search engine optimization*, or *SEO*. That's why friendly URLs are sometimes called *SEO-friendly URLs*. They improve SEO because all friendly URL pages get archived by the search engines. In contrast, most search engines don't archive the query string in a traditional URL.

In this figure, for example, the traditional URL with a query string is this:

```
http://halloweenstore.com/Order.aspx?ProductID=cat01
```

However, most search engines will only archive this portion of it:

```
http://halloweenstore.com/Order.aspx
```

In contrast, the entire friendly URL in this figure will be archived.

Friendly URLs also benefit users because they're easier to read and remember. For instance, you can probably imagine a customer typing the second URL in this figure into the address bar of a browser. But it's not so easy to imagine a customer typing in the first one.

Friendly URLs in a Shopping Cart application

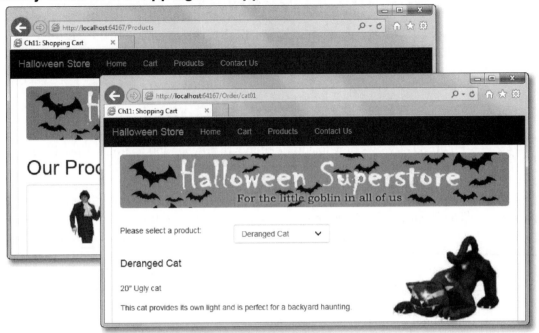

A URL with a query string parameter

```
http://halloweenstore.com/Order.aspx?ProductID=cat01
```

A friendly URL with the same parameter

```
http://halloweenstore.com/Order/cat01
```

Two benefits of friendly URLs

- They improve search engine optimization because URLs with parameters are archived.
- They are easier for users to read and remember.

Friendly URLs in the Shopping Cart application and their actual file paths

Friendly URL	Actual file path
/ContactUs	/ContactUs.aspx
/Cart	/Cart.aspx
/Products	/Products.aspx
/Order/cat01	/Order.aspx
/Order/hippie01	/Order.aspx

Two ways to provide friendly URLs in ASP.NET Web Forms

- Install and configure the FriendlyUrls feature.
- Manually map routes in code with ASP.NET routing.

Figure 11-1   An introduction to friendly URLs

How to use the FriendlyUrls feature

FriendlyURLs is a feature that automatically converts traditional URLs to friendly URLs. In the topics that follow, you'll learn how to install and set up FriendlyUrls, how to work with it in your applications, and how to change some of its default functionality.

How to install and set up FriendlyUrls

Figure 11-2 shows how to add FriendlyUrls to your application by installing its NuGet package. This package adds a folder named App_Start to your application with a file named RouteConfig.cs. It also adds two additional files named Site.Mobile.Master and ViewSwitcher.ascx that you'll learn about later.

The RouteConfig.cs file contains a static class named RouteConfig as shown in the first example in this figure. It also includes two using directives that are required by the code for the RegisterRoutes method within this class. For example, the first statement in this method creates a new object from the FriendlyUrlSettings class, which is stored in the Microsoft.AspNet.FriendlyUrls namespace. This object contains settings that are used by the FriendlyUrls feature, and it's stored in a variable named settings.

The second statement sets the AutoRedirectMode property of the FriendlyUrlSettings object to RedirectMode.Permanent. That way, when a user accesses a traditional URL and the FriendlyUrls feature redirects them to a friendly URL, the application also sends a 301 Permanent Redirect header to the user's browser. Then, the next time the user tries to access the traditional URL, the browser will automatically take them to the friendly URL. 301 Permanent Redirects also help search engines update their indexes to the friendly URL.

If your URLs change, though, using 301 Permanent Redirects can cause problems. This is particularly true during development, when you might change an application's navigation structure. If you do that, you'll need to clear the cache of every browser you use to test the application.

For this reason, it's better to change the AutoRedirectMode setting to RedirectMode.Temporary during development so your application issues a 302 Temporary Redirect header. Then, when you're ready to deploy your web application to production, you can change the setting back to Permanent.

The third statement in the RegisterRoutes method calls the EnableFriendlyUrls method of the RouteCollection parameter, passing the FriendlyUrlSettings object as an argument. This enables the FriendlyUrls feature for the web application using the settings you specified. Later in this chapter, you'll learn about another argument that you can pass to this method to customize the behavior of FriendlyUrls.

Although the code in the RouteConfig class is generated for you, you need to add code to the Global.asax file to make FriendlyUrls work. This code, shown in the second example in this figure, calls the RegisterRoutes method when the application starts and passes it the static Routes property of the RouteTable class. This property contains the collection of *routes* for the application, which are the URL patterns used in the friendly URLs.

The NuGet Package Manager page

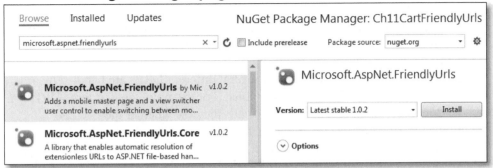

How to install the NuGet package for FriendlyUrls

- Right-click on the project and select Manage NuGet Packages.
- Click on Browse and type "microsoft.aspnet.friendlyurls" in the search box.
- In the left pane, click on the Microsoft.AspNet.FriendlyUrls package. Then, in the right pane, click on the Install button. For this package, you'll be asked to accept the license terms from Microsoft.

The RouteConfig class that's added to the App_Start folder

```
using System.Web.Routing;
using Microsoft.AspNet.FriendlyUrls;

public static class RouteConfig
{
    public static void RegisterRoutes(RouteCollection routes)
    {
        var settings = new FriendlyUrlSettings();
        settings.AutoRedirectMode = RedirectMode.Permanent;
        routes.EnableFriendlyUrls(settings);
    }
}
```

The code you must add to the Global.asax file to make FriendlyUrls work

```
using System.Web.Routing;

protected void Application_Start(object sender, EventArgs e)
{
    RouteConfig.RegisterRoutes(RouteTable.Routes);
}
```

Description

- The NuGet package for FriendlyUrls installs an App_Start folder with a RouteConfig.cs file. This file contains a static RouteConfig class with a static RegisterRoutes method.
- You must also add code to the Global.asax file that calls the RegisterRoutes method when the application starts and passes the static Routes property of the RouteTable class, which contains the collection of routes for the application.
- A *route* is the URL pattern used in a friendly URL.

Figure 11-2   How to install and set up FriendlyUrls

How to work with FriendlyUrls

Once you install and set up FriendlyUrls, you don't need to do anything else to make it work. Instead, it will automatically convert a traditional URL like /Order.aspx to a friendly one like /Order.

The table in figure 11-3 shows how several different URLs are handled by a web application that has FriendlyUrls enabled. For example, the first three URLs will be directed to the Order.aspx page. That's the case whether the URL is traditional, like the first one, or friendly, like the second and third ones.

The third URL in the table contains a parameter of cat01. To determine which parts of a URL are parameters, FriendlyUrls analyzes each segment of the URL. Then, if it doesn't find a corresponding folder or aspx file for the segment, it adds that segment to a list of strings.

To retrieve this list of strings, you use the GetFriendlyUrlSegments method as shown in the second example in this figure. This is an extension method of the Request object, and it requires the using directive shown in the first example. Note that to access this method from outside a web page, you use the Request property of the HttpContext object for the current request.

Once you have the list of friendly URL parameters, you can use the Count property to see how many strings it contains. Then, you can retrieve the parameter you want by its index.

The third code example shows how to create a friendly URL in code using the Href method of the FriendlyUrl object. On this method, you code each segment of the URL and each parameter as a separate argument. Although you can also create a friendly URL using string concatenation, it's easier to use the Href method, especially when you create a URL that has many parameters.

How to work with file paths

When you use FriendlyUrls (or the ASP.NET routing that you'll learn about later), it can sometimes have unexpected effects on the file paths that ASP.NET renders for static resources. These are things like images, CSS files, and JavaScript files. Figure 11-3 shows three ways to deal with the file paths for static resources so they won't cause problems.

All three techniques make the file paths relative to the root directory of the site rather than to the current file. First, you can start the file path with a forward slash ("/"). Second, for a server control, you can use the tilde operator in the file path, which causes the URL to be based on the root directory of the site.

Third, for an HTML element, you can make the path relative to the root directory by using the ResolveUrl method of the page along with the tilde operator. This resolves any conflicts that might occur when the page is rendered.

Although it's not shown here, you can also use another technique to get around this problem with images. Rather than using img elements in your HTML, you can use CSS to treat the images as background images for other HTML elements.

The default functionality of the FriendlyUrls feature

URL typed in browser	Handled by	URL displayed in browser
`/Order.aspx`	Order.aspx page	`/Order`
`/Order`	Order.aspx page	`/Order`
`/Order/cat01`	Order.aspx page	`/Order/cat01`
`/Products.aspx`	Products.aspx page	`/Products`
`/Products`	Products.aspx page	`/Products`

A using directive for the FriendlyUrls namespace

```
using Microsoft.AspNet.FriendlyUrls;
```

How to retrieve a FriendlyUrls parameter

In a code-behind file

```
// URL being processed: /Order/cat01
var segments = Request.GetFriendlyUrlSegments();
int count = segments.Count;      // 1
string productID = segments[0];  // cat01
```

In a non-page class

```
var segments = HttpContext.Current.Request.GetFriendlyUrlSegments();
```

A statement that creates a friendly URL

```
var url = FriendlyUrl.Href("~/Order", productID);  // ~/Order/cat01
```

Three ways to code a file path that's relative to the root directory

Start the path with a forward slash

```
<link href="/Styles/Order.css" rel="stylesheet" />
```

Use the tilde operator with server controls

```
<asp:Image ID="Image1" runat="server" ImageUrl="~/Images/banner.jpg" />
```

Use the tilde operator and the ResolveURL method with HTML elements

```
<img src='<%=ResolveUrl("~/Images/banner.jpg")%>' alt="Halloween Store" />
```

Description

- The FriendlyUrls functionality automatically converts a traditional URL like /Order.aspx to a friendly URL like /Order. You don't have to map any routes or do anything other than set it up as described in the last figure.

- The FriendlyUrls feature analyzes the segments of a friendly URL to determine which ones are parameters, and it stores the parameters in a list of strings. You can retrieve this list of strings using the GetFriendlyUrlSegments method of the Request object.

- You can use the Href method of the FriendlyUrl object to create a friendly URL in code so you can redirect to that URL.

- When using FriendlyUrls, you should code paths to static resources like image, CSS, and JavaScript files so they're relative to the root directory.

Figure 11-3   How to work with FriendlyUrls and file paths

How to change the default behavior of FriendlyUrls

Although the FriendlyUrls feature automatically converts traditional URLs to friendly URLs, there may be times when you want to change some of its default behavior. Figure 11-4 shows how to do that.

To start, you should know that FriendlyUrls uses a *resolver object* to determine how it handles URLs. This object is defined by the WebFormsFriendlyUrlResolver class. To change the behavior of this object, you create a custom resolver object that inherits the WebFormsFriendlyUrlResolver class and overrides one or more of its methods. Then, you pass the custom resolver object as the second parameter of the EnableFriendlyUrls method that you learned about in figure 11-2.

The table in figure 11-4 shows the methods that are most commonly overridden. The first one is the TrySetMobileMasterPage method, which attempts to change the value of the page's MasterPageFile property to a mobile specific master page for mobile devices. This mobile master page is the one named Site.Mobile.Master that's installed with the NuGet package for FriendlyUrls. It contains a user control named ViewSwitcher.ascx, which is also installed with the NuGet package. When FriendlyUrls determines that the browser is a mobile browser, it calls the TrySetMobileMasterPage method so the application will use the mobile master page. Then, the user can use the ViewSwitcher control on this page to switch back to the desktop master page if they choose to.

This default behavior lets you create a different user experience for mobile devices. Then, you just need to set up the mobile master page and the content pages the way you want them. In some cases, though, you won't want to use a different master page and content pages for mobile devices. If you use Bootstrap, for example, it automatically takes care of adjusting the pages for mobile devices. In that case, you'll want to override the TrySetMobileMasterPage method. The examples in this figure show you how to do that.

The first example shows the using directive you'll need to work with the WebFormsFriendlyUrlResolver class. The second example creates a new class called MyUrlResolver that inherits the WebFormsFriendlyUrlResolver class. Then, it overrides the TrySetMobileMasterPage method. This method simply returns a false value to keep your application from switching to the mobile master page. The third example shows how to pass a new instance of the custom MyUrlResolver class as the second argument of the EnableFriendlyUrls method.

You'll see how to override the other two methods shown in this figure later in this chapter. The ConvertToFriendlyUrl method is the one that actually converts a traditional URL to a friendly one, and you can override it to provide URLs that differ from the defaults. The PreprocessRequest method is called after the handler that will process a friendly URL has been determined, but before it's called. You can override this method to make sure that all requests for a page are handled the way you want.

Some of the methods of the WebFormsFriendlyUrlResolver class

Method	Description
`TrySetMobileMasterPage`	Tries to set the MasterPageFile property for the page to a mobile specific master page. Returns a Boolean value.
`ConvertToFriendlyUrl`	Converts a URL with a file extension to a friendly URL.
`PreprocessRequest`	Called after the handler that should process the friendly URL has been determined, but before that handler is called.

A using directive for working with the WebFormsFriendlyUrlResolver class

```
using Microsoft.AspNet.FriendlyUrls.Resolvers;
```

Code that keeps the application from changing to the mobile master page

```
public class MyUrlResolver : WebFormsFriendlyUrlResolver
{
    protected override bool TrySetMobileMasterPage(HttpContextBase ctx,
    System.Web.UI.Page page, string mobileSuffix)
    {
        return false;
    }
}
```

A RegisterRoutes method that uses the custom resolver

```
public static void RegisterRoutes(RouteCollection routes)
{
    var settings = new FriendlyUrlSettings();
    settings.AutoRedirectMode = RedirectMode.Permanent;
    routes.EnableFriendlyUrls(settings, new MyUrlResolver());
}
```

Description

- The FriendlyUrls feature uses a *resolver object* called WebFormsFriendlyUrlResolver to determine how it will handle URLs.

- You can change the default behavior of the resolver object by creating a new class that inherits the WebFormsFriendlyUrlResolver class and overrides one or more of its methods. Then, you can pass an instance of the custom class as the second parameter of the EnableFriendlyUrls method in the RegisterRoutes method.

- One reason to use a custom resolver is to override the resolver's default behavior of switching to a mobile master page for mobile devices. This mobile master page downloads with the NuGet package for FriendlyUrls, but you may not want to use it if you're using Bootstrap.

Figure 11-4   How to change the default behavior of FriendlyUrls

The aspx code for FriendlyUrls in the Shopping Cart application

When you use the FriendlyUrls feature, you should use friendly URLs anytime the aspx code for a page refers to another page. In figure 11-5, for example, you can see the aspx code in the Shopping Cart application that contains friendly URLs. Here, the NavigateUrl property for each link in the navbar on the master page contains a friendly URL. In addition, the PostBackUrl property for the Go to Cart button on the Order page and the Continue Shopping button on the Cart page contain friendly URLs.

The Repeater control on the Products page also uses a friendly URL. Here, the img element for each product is coded within an <a> element that links to the Order page. As you can see, the href attribute for this link is coded as a friendly URL that includes a product ID so that product is displayed when the link is clicked.

The last example in this figure is for the Products drop-down list on the Order page. As you can see, an event property has been added for the SelectedIndexChanged event. This event fires when the user selects a product from the drop-down list. You'll see the code for the event handler that handles this event in the next figure.

Some of the aspx code for the navbar on the master page

```
<div class="collapse navbar-collapse" id="mainMenu">
    <ul class="nav navbar-nav">
        <li><asp:HyperLink NavigateUrl="~/Order" runat="server">
                Home</asp:HyperLink></li>
        <li><asp:HyperLink NavigateUrl="~/Cart" runat="server">
                Cart</asp:HyperLink></li>
        <li><asp:HyperLink NavigateUrl="~/Products" runat="server">
                Products</asp:HyperLink></li>
        <li><asp:HyperLink NavigateUrl="~/ContactUs" runat="server">
                Contact Us</asp:HyperLink></li>
    </ul>
</div>
```

The aspx code for the Go to Cart button on the Order page

```
<asp:Button ID="btnCart" runat="server" Text="Go to Cart"
    PostBackUrl="~/Cart" CausesValidation="False" CssClass="btn" />
```

The aspx code for the Continue Shopping button on the Cart page

```
<asp:Button ID="btnContinue" runat="server"
    PostBackUrl="~/Order" Text="Continue Shopping" CssClass="btn" />
```

The aspx code for the Repeater control on the Products page

```
<asp:Repeater ID="Repeater1" runat="server" DataSourceID="SqlDataSource1">
    <ItemTemplate>
        <div class="col-sm-6 col-md-3">
            <div class="thumbnail">
                <a href='/Order/<%# Eval("ProductID") %>'>
                    <img src='/Images/Products/<%# Eval("ImageFile") %>'
                        alt='<%# Eval("Name") %>' /></a>
                <div class="caption">
                    <h3><%# Eval("Name") %></h3>
                    <p><b>Price: <%# Eval("UnitPrice", "{0:c}") %></b>
                    <br><br><%# Eval("LongDescription") %></p>
                </div>
            </div>
        </div>
    </ItemTemplate>
</asp:Repeater>
```

The aspx code for the drop-down list on the Order page

```
<asp:DropDownList ID="ddlProducts" runat="server" AutoPostBack="True"
    DataSourceID="SqlDataSource1" DataTextField="Name"
    DataValueField="ProductID" CssClass="form-control"
    OnSelectedIndexChanged="ddlProducts_SelectedIndexChanged">
</asp:DropDownList>
```

Description

- A friendly URL should be used anytime a URL for a page is referred to in aspx code.

- In addition to the code shown above, all of the link and script tags in the header of all the pages are coded so their file paths are relative to the root directory.

Figure 11-5   The aspx code that implements FriendlyUrls

The C# code for FriendlyUrls
in the Shopping Cart application

Figure 11-6 presents the C# code for this version of the Shopping Cart application that uses FriendlyUrls. To start, when the page is loaded and it's not being posted back, the product ID is retrieved from the URL using code like you saw earlier in this chapter. Then, if a parameter is found, its value is passed to a method named ShowSelectedProduct, which displays the product on the page. If a parameter isn't found, a method named Reload is called.

The Reload method creates a friendly URL for the Order page that includes the ID of the product that is currently selected in the drop-down list on the page. In this case, because the page isn't being posted back, that's the product ID for the first product in the list. Then, the Redirect method of the Response object is used to redirect to the Order page so the first product is displayed.

The Reload method is also called when the user selects another product from the Products drop-down list. To accomplish that, an event handler is coded for the SelectedIndexChanged event of the drop-down list. Note that because the page is posted back when this event fires, the code in the Page_Load event handler isn't executed. Instead, just the Reload method is executed. Then, this method gets the ID of the product the user selected, creates a friendly URL for the Order page that includes that ID, and redirects to this URL.

The last method shown in this figure is for the event handler that's executed when the user clicks the Add to Cart button on the Order page. The last statement in this event handler calls the Redirect method of the Response method to redirect to the Cart page using a friendly URL.

You should know that the code presented here implements the Post-Redirect-Get (PRG) pattern, which you'll learn about in chapter 21. This pattern makes sure that the URL parameter in the browser's address bar matches the product being displayed on the page.

The C# code for the Order page that redirects to a friendly URL

```csharp
protected void Page_Load(object sender, EventArgs e)
{
    if (!IsPostBack)
    {
        ddlProducts.DataBind();

        string id = "";
        var segments = Request.GetFriendlyUrlSegments();
        if (segments.Count > 0) id = segments[0];

        if (id == "") Reload();
        else ShowSelectedProduct(id);
    }
}

protected void ddlProducts_SelectedIndexChanged(object sender, EventArgs e)
{
    Reload();
}

private void Reload()
{
    var id = ddlProducts.SelectedValue;
    var url = FriendlyUrl.Href("~/Order", id);
    Response.Redirect(url);
}

protected void btnAdd_Click(object sender, EventArgs e)
{
    if (Page.IsValid)
    {
        .
        .
        Response.Redirect("~/Cart");
    }
}
```

Description

- If the Order page isn't being posted back, the parameter for the product ID is retrieved from the URL if it exists and the ShowSelectedProduct method is called to display the product on the page. If the parameter doesn't exist, the Reload method is called.

- The Reload method uses the Href method of the FriendlyUrl object to create a friendly URL that includes the ID of the product that's currently selected in the drop-down list. Then, it redirects to that URL.

- The Reload method is also called if the user selects a different product from the drop-down list. To accomplish that, the SelectedIndexChanged event handler is wired to that control.

- When the user clicks the Add to Cart button on the Order page, a friendly URL is used in the Redirect method of the Response object to redirect to the Cart page.

- This application also uses a custom resolver that overrides the TrySetMobileMasterPage method so the mobile master page isn't used on mobile devices.

Figure 11-6   The C# code that implements FriendlyUrls

How to use ASP.NET routing

ASP.NET routing also lets you add friendly URLs to your application. Unlike the FriendlyUrls feature, though, it isn't automatic. Instead, you must manually code the URL routes you want the application to use. This makes ASP.NET routing more difficult to use than the FriendlyUrls feature, but it also gives you more control over the navigation structure of your site.

How to use friendly URLs with ASP.NET routing

When you use traditional URLs or the FriendlyURLs feature, the navigation structure of a website mirrors the physical structure. If, for example, you want the Order page to be in a Shop menu, you have to create a Shop directory and place the Order.aspx file in it. In contrast, when you use ASP.NET routing, you can organize the physical files for a website without worrying about the navigation structure of the website.

The two pages and the table in figure 11-7 show how this works. In the two pages, you can see that the URLs in the address bar and the Shop button dropdown in the navbar make it appear that the Products, Order, and Cart pages are in a Shop directory. If you look at the table, though, you'll see that the friendly URLs for these file paths point to Cart.aspx, Products.aspx, and Order. aspx files that are in the root directory. To accomplish that, you have to map the routes for the application as shown next.

Friendly URLs in a Shopping Cart application that uses ASP.NET routing

Friendly URLs in the Shopping Cart application and their actual file paths

Friendly URL	Actual file path
/ContactUs	/ContactUs.aspx
/Shop/Cart	/Cart.aspx
/Shop/Products	/Products.aspx
/Shop/Order/cat01	/Order.aspx
/Shop/Order/hippie01	/Order.aspx

Description

- When you use ASP.NET routing, you can map routes for URLs that don't depend on the directory structure of the site. For example, the Friendly URLs shown in the table above make it appear that the Cart, Products, and Order pages are in a Shop directory when they're actually in the root directory.

- To make the appearance of the site correspond with the structure indicated by the Friendly URLs, a Shop button dropdown has been added to the navbar for this version of the application. This dropdown includes links to the Products, Order, and Cart pages.

Figure 11-7   How to use friendly URLs with ASP.NET routing

How to create a custom route collection

To use ASP.NET routing, you must first map your application's routes. As you learned earlier in this chapter, a *route* is a URL pattern that identifies a page. A route can be either static or dynamic. The difference is that a *static route* will always be the same, like Shop/Cart, but a *dynamic route* will contain at least one placeholder that represents a URL parameter, like Shop/Order/cat01.

To use ASP.NET routing, you start by declaring a RegisterRoutes method like the one that's used with FriendlyUrls. You can add this method to the Global.asax file, or you can add it to a RouteConfig class that you create. If you add it to a RouteConfig class, you should add an App_Start folder to your project and then store the RouteConfig class in that folder. Then, you can add code to the Application_Start event handler in the Global.asax file that calls the RegisterRoutes method just like you do when you use FriendlyUrls.

Once you declare the RegisterRoutes method, you can add the code to map your routes within that method as shown in the example in figure 11-8. To map a route, you use the MapPageRoute method of the RouteCollection parameter that's passed to the RegisterRoutes method. The common parameters for the MapPageRoute method are summarized in the table in this figure. The first three parameters are required for any route, but all five can be used for dynamic routes.

The first three routes in this figure show how static routes are coded. Here, the MapPageRoute method is passed the name of the route, the friendly URL for the route, and the URL for the physical file that the route maps to. In the second static route, for example, Shop/Cart is the friendly URL, and it maps to the Cart.aspx file in the root directory of the application.

In contrast, the last statement in this method creates a dynamic route. Here, the friendly URL includes a parameter named productID that's coded within braces, and it maps to the Order.aspx file in the root directory. Then, the fifth parameter provides a default value of an empty string for this parameter. To do that, it creates a new RouteValueDictionary object with productID as its key and an empty string as its value. As a result, an empty string is the default value for the parameter when the route is called and a value isn't passed to it. Note that if you don't provide a default value for the parameter and the user enters the URL with no parameter, a "404 File Not Found" error will occur if the page doesn't provide for URLs with no parameters. Because of that, it's a best practice to provide default values for parameters.

You should also notice here that a value of false is coded for the fourth parameter. Because of that, ASP.NET doesn't check whether the user has the authority to access the page.

In addition to the routes that you code within the RegisterRoutes method, you should start this method by executing the Ignore method of the Routes property. This tells the routing framework to ignore any of the .axd resource files that are used by ASP.NET. That way, ASP.NET routing won't interfere with other ASP.NET functions. This line of code appears by default in ASP.NET MVC projects, and it must come before any mapping code.

Common parameters of the MapPageRoute method

Parameter	Description
`routeName`	The name of the route.
`routeURL`	The friendly URL for the route. For dynamic routes, the pattern should contain placeholders within braces for the parameters.
`physicalFile`	The physical file that the route maps to.
`checkPhysicalUrlAccess`	A Boolean value that indicates whether ASP.NET should validate that the user has the authority to access the physical URL. (The route URL is always checked.) The default value is True.
`defaults`	A RouteValueDictionary object that contains default values for the route parameters.

A RegisterRoutes method with custom routes

```
public static class RouteConfig
{
    public static void RegisterRoutes(RouteCollection routes)
    {
        // ignore WebResource.axd file
        routes.Ignore("{resource}.axd/{*pathInfo}");

        // map static routes
        routes.MapPageRoute("ContactUs", "ContactUs", "~/ContactUs.aspx");
        routes.MapPageRoute("ShopCart", "Shop/Cart", "~/Cart.aspx");
        routes.MapPageRoute("ShopProducts", "Shop/Products",
            "~/Products.aspx");

        // map a dynamic route with a default value for the parameter
        routes.MapPageRoute("ShopOrder", "Shop/Order/{productID}",
            "~/Order.aspx", false,
            new RouteValueDictionary { { "productID", "" } });
    }
}
```

Description

- When you use ASP.NET routing, you can add the RegisterRoutes method to the Global.asax file, or you can code it in a RouteConfig class that you create.

- Within the RegisterRoutes method, you map a route for every friendly URL you want to create. To add a route to the collection of routes for an application, you use the MapPageRoute method of the RouteCollection object that's passed to the RegisterRoutes method when the application starts.

- A route can be either static or dynamic. A *static route* is always the same. A *dynamic route* contains one or more placeholders that represent parameters.

- Just as you do when you use FriendlyUrls, you need to add code to the Application_Start event handler to register the routes that you create.

- The Ignore method of the Routes property tells the routing framework to ignore any of the .axd resource files used by ASP.NET so routing doesn't interfere with other ASP.NET functions.

Figure 11-8   How to create a custom route collection

How to work with route parameters

Figure 11-9 shows how you can retrieve parameters from a URL when you use ASP.NET routing. To do that, you use the Values collection of a page's RouteData property, as shown in the first example. As you can see, you can use the parameter name as the indexer for the Values collection. This must be the same as the name of the placeholder that was used on the dynamic route.

Notice that before you retrieve a parameter value, you must use the ContainsKey method of the Values collection to be sure that the URL includes the parameter. Otherwise, you'll get an error when the application tries to retrieve a parameter that doesn't exist.

You can also retrieve URL parameters from outside of a web page. To do that, you use the current request's RequestContext property to get the RouteData property. Then, you use the Values collection of that property, as shown in the second example in this figure.

Unlike FriendlyUrls, which stores URL parameters in a list of strings, the Values collection of the RouteData property stores items as objects. This means that when you retrieve them, you must cast them to their specific data types. Once you retrieve and cast a parameter from the Values collection, you can work with it in code like any other variable.

Besides retrieving route parameters in code, you can use them with data source controls. For instance, the third example in this figure shows a SqlDataSource control that uses a route parameter as a select parameter. You'll learn more about select parameters in chapter 13. For now, you just need to know that it provides the value for a parameter in the SQL statement for a data source. In this example, for instance, the SELECT statement includes a parameter named ProductID that determines the product that's retrieved.

Within the SelectParameters element for the data source, a RouteParameter element is used to get the value of the parameter from the page's route data. Here, the RouteKey property is the name given to the placeholder in the code that maps the route. The Name property is the name of the field in the SELECT statement. And the Type property is the data type of the value. All three of these properties are required, and you can also set an optional DefaultValue property. Note that, as of this writing, you can only use this technique with ASP.NET routing.

How to retrieve a route parameter

In a code-behind file

```
if (RouteData.Values.ContainsKey("productID"))
{
    string id = RouteData.Values["productID"].ToString();
}
```

In a non-page class

```
if (HttpContext.Current.Request.RequestContext.RouteData.Values.ContainsKey(
    "productID"))
{
    string id = HttpContext.Current.Request.RequestContext.
        RouteData.Values["productID"].ToString();
}
```

How to use a route parameter as the parameter for a SQL data source

```
<asp:SqlDataSource ID="SqlDataSource1" runat="server"
    ConnectionString='<%$ ConnectionStrings:HalloweenDatabase %>'
    SelectCommand="SELECT [ProductID], [Name], [LongDescription],
        [CategoryID], [UnitPrice], [ImageFile] FROM [Products] WHERE
        ([ProductID] = @ProductID)">
    <SelectParameters>
        <asp:RouteParameter RouteKey="productID" Name="ProductID"
            DefaultValue="pow01" Type="String">
        </asp:RouteParameter>
    </SelectParameters>
</asp:SqlDataSource>
```

Description

- If a page is running in response to a request made through ASP.NET routing, the page's RouteData property provides access to the parameter values that are in the URL.

- Before retrieving the value of a parameter, you should check that a parameter with the key you want exists in the collection of keys.

- To use a route parameter as the select parameter for a SQL data source, you code a RouteParameter element within the SelectParameters element of the data source as shown above.

Figure 11-9   How to work with route parameters

The aspx code for ASP.NET routing in the Shopping Cart application

Figure 11-10 shows some of the aspx code for this version of the Shopping Cart application. Here, you can see the code for the Shop button dropdown in the navbar on the master page. Notice that the NavigateUrl property for each of the items in the dropdown include "Shop" as part of the path for the friendly URL.

This figure also shows the aspx code for the Go to Cart button on the Order page and the Continue Shopping button on the Cart page. These controls are like the ones for the FriendlyUrls version of this application, but the friendly URLs used in their PostBackUrl properties include "Shop" in the path.

Finally, this figure shows some of the code for the Repeater control on the Products page. The code for this control is also like the code for the FriendlyUrls version, but it too includes "Shop" in the path for the href attribute of the <a> element.

Some of the aspx code for the navbar on the master page

```
<div class="collapse navbar-collapse" id="mainMenu">
    <ul class="nav navbar-nav">
        <li class="dropdown">
            <a href="#" class="dropdown-toggle" data-toggle="dropdown"
                role="button" aria-haspopup="true" aria-expanded="false">
                Shop<span class="caret"></span></a>
            <ul class="dropdown-menu">
                <li><asp:HyperLink NavigateUrl="~/Shop/Products"
                        runat="server">View Products</asp:HyperLink></li>
                <li><asp:HyperLink NavigateUrl="~/Shop/Order"
                        runat="server">Place Order</asp:HyperLink></li>
                <li role="separator" class="divider"></li>
                <li><asp:HyperLink NavigateUrl="~/Shop/Cart"
                        runat="server">Cart</asp:HyperLink></li>
            </ul>
        </li>
        <li><asp:HyperLink NavigateUrl="~/ContactUs" runat="server">
                Contact Us</asp:HyperLink></li>
    </ul>
</div>
```

The aspx code for the Go to Cart button on the Order page

```
<asp:Button ID="btnCart" runat="server" Text="Go to Cart"
    PostBackUrl="~/Shop/Cart" CausesValidation="False" CssClass="btn" />
```

The aspx code for the Continue Shopping button on the Cart page

```
<asp:Button ID="btnContinue" runat="server"
    PostBackUrl="~/Shop/Order" Text="Continue Shopping" CssClass="btn" />
```

Some of the aspx code for the Repeater control on the Products page

```
<asp:Repeater ID="Repeater1" runat="server" DataSourceID="SqlDataSource1">
    <ItemTemplate>
        <div class="col-sm-6 col-md-3">
            <div class="thumbnail">
                <a href='/Shop/Order/<%# Eval("ProductID") %>'>...</a>
        ...
    </ItemTemplate>
</asp:Repeater>
```

Description

- The navbar on the master page, the Go to Cart button on the Order page, and the Continue Shopping button on the Cart page all use friendly URLs.

- The Repeater control on the Products page is identical to the one used by the FriendlyUrls version of this application shown in figure 11-5, except that the link to the Order page uses a friendly URL that includes "Shop" in its path.

Figure 11-10   The aspx code that implements ASP.NET routing

The C# code for ASP.NET routing
in the Shopping Cart application

Figure 11-11 shows some of the C# code for the Order page that uses ASP.NET routing. Because the basic processing for this version is the same as for the FriendlyUrls version, I'll just point out the differences here.

To start, instead of retrieving the parameter from a URL segment, the Page_Load event handler uses code like the code you saw in figure 11-9 to check if the Values collection of the page's RouteData object contains a productID parameter. If it does, that parameter is retrieved and stored in the id variable.

If the productID parameter isn't found or its value is an empty string (the default value), the Reload method is called. This method starts by getting the ID of the product that's selected in the drop-down list, just like the the FriendlyUrls version of the application. Instead of creating the friendly URL using the Href method, though, it creates the URL by concatenating the file path, which includes "Shop", with the product ID. Then, it redirects to that URL.

The only other difference is in the event handler that's executed when the user clicks the Add to Cart button on the Order page. Instead of using the Href method to create the friendly URL, that URL is just coded on the Redirect method. Like the URL in the Reload method, the path for this URL includes "Shop".

Some of the C# code for the Order page

```
protected void Page_Load(object sender, EventArgs e)
{
    if (!IsPostBack)
    {
        ddlProducts.DataBind();

        string id = "";
        if (RouteData.Values.ContainsKey("productID"))
        {
            id = RouteData.Values["productID"].ToString();
        }
        if (id == "") Reload();
        else ShowSelectedProduct(id);
    }
}

protected void ddlProducts_SelectedIndexChanged(object sender, EventArgs e)
{
    Reload();
}

private void Reload()
{
    var id = ddlProducts.SelectedValue;
    Response.Redirect("~/Shop/Order/" + id);
}
.
.
.
protected void btnAdd_Click(object sender, EventArgs e)
{
    if (Page.IsValid)
    {
        .
        .
        .
        Response.Redirect("~/Shop/Cart");
    }
}
```

Description

- If the Order page isn't being posted back and a route parameter for the product ID is found, the parameter is retrieved from the page's route data and the product is displayed on the page. Otherwise, the Reload method is called. The Reload method is also called if the user selects a different product from the drop-down list.

- The Reload method creates a friendly URL using the ID of the product that's selected in the drop-down list. Then, it redirects to that URL.

- When the user clicks the Add to Cart button on the Order page, a custom route is used in the Redirect method of the Response object to redirect to the Cart page.

Figure 11-11   The C# code that implements ASP.NET routing

How to combine ASP.NET routing with FriendlyUrls

In some cases, you'll use ASP.NET routing along with FriendlyUrls. For example, suppose you want to use a Shop menu like the one you saw in the ASP.NET routing version of the Shopping Cart application, but you don't want to have to manually map non-custom routes like the one you saw for the ContactUs page in figure 11-8. Then, you can use FriendlyUrls for the routes that match the physical structure of the website, and you can use ASP.NET routing for those that don't. In the topics that follow, you'll learn some additional techniques for working with route collections and URL parameters when you combine FriendlyUrls with ASP.NET routing.

How to create route collections

When you use ASP.NET routing with FriendlyUrls, you can just map the custom routes for ASP.NET routing in the RegisterRoutes method of the RouteConfig class that's created when you install FriendlyUrls. This is illustrated in the first example in figure 11-12. Here, you can see that the RegisterRoutes method contains both the code for using FriendlyUrls and the custom routes for using ASP.NET routing. Notice that the code for FriendlyUrls comes first, which is a requirement if you use both ASP.NET routing and FriendlyUrls.

When you map custom routes, URLs that correspond to those routes will be handled by ASP.NET routing. In contrast, URLs that don't correspond to those routes will be handled by the FriendlyUrls feature. Because a custom route isn't included for the ContactUs page, for example, a request for that page will be handled by FriendlyUrls. In addition, any requests for the Cart, Products, and Order pages with URLs that match the directory structure will be handled by FriendlyUrls. You'll learn more about that and how you can change how this works in just a minute.

How to retrieve URL parameters

The second example in figure 11-12 shows how to retrieve a URL parameter when you use both ASP.NET routing and FriendlyUrls. To do that, you combine the two techniques you learned about earlier in this chapter. To start, you check if the Values collection of the RouteData object contains the parameter you want to retrieve. If it does, that means that ASP.NET routing is being used, and you can retrieve the parameter value from the Values collection. Otherwise, it means that FriendlyUrls is being used, and you can retrieve the URL segment that contains the parameter.

A RegisterRoutes method for FriendlyUrls and ASP.NET routing

```
public static void RegisterRoutes(RouteCollection routes)
{
    // set up basic FriendlyUrls functionality
    var settings = new FriendlyUrlSettings();
    settings.AutoRedirectMode = RedirectMode.Temporary;
    routes.EnableFriendlyUrls(settings, new MyUrlResolver());

    // map custom static routes
    routes.MapPageRoute("ShopCart", "Shop/Cart", "~/Cart.aspx");
    routes.MapPageRoute("ShopProducts", "Shop/Products", "~/Products.aspx");

    // map a custom dynamic route with a default value for the parameter
    routes.MapPageRoute("ShopOrder", "Shop/Order/{productID}",
        "~/Order.aspx", false,
        new RouteValueDictionary { { "productID", "" } });
}
```

Code in a code-behind file that retrieves a URL parameter

```
string id = "";
if (RouteData.Values.ContainsKey("productID")) {
    // handled by ASP.NET routing - get the named parameter
    id = RouteData.Values["productID"].ToString();
}
else {
    // handled by FriendlyUrls - get the URL segment
    var segments = Request.GetFriendlyUrlSegments();
    if (segments.Count > 0) id = segments[0];
}
```

Description

- When you combine ASP.NET routing with FriendlyUrls, you need to make sure that you call the EnableFriendlyUrls method in the RegisterRoutes method before you map any routes for ASP.NET routing.

- The routes that you map for ASP.NET routing are the ones that are different from the FriendlyUrls default mapping.

- To retrieve a URL parameter, you start by checking if the page contains a parameter with the given ID. If it does, you know that the parameter is from an ASP.NET route. In that case, you get the parameter from the Values collection of the page's RouteData property.

- If the page doesn't contain a parameter with the given ID, you use the GetFriendlyUrlSegments method of the Request object to get the segments of the URL and then retrieve the parameter from that collection.

Figure 11-12   How to create route collections and retrieve URL parameters

How to get ASP.NET routing to handle some or all URLs

When a page is requested for an application, the URL for the request determines whether ASP.NET routing or FriendlyUrls is used. To illustrate, the table in figure 11-13 shows three different URLs that can be used to navigate to the Order.aspx page. If you assume that the application that contains this page includes the custom routes shown in figure 11-12, the first URL will be handled by ASP.NET routing and the second and third URLs will be handled by FriendlyUrls.

Although this will work correctly no matter what URL is used to access the page, the URL that's displayed in the browser will vary. This can be confusing for users, and it can affect how search engines index your site. Because of that, you may want to create a custom resolver class that causes most or all URLs for a page to be handled by ASP.NET routing.

The first code example in this figure shows how to create a custom resolver that converts traditional URLs to friendly URLs. To do that, it overrides the ConvertToFriendlyUrl method of the WebFormsFriendlyUrlResolver class. The code for this method checks the path parameter to see if the URL is for the Order page. If it is, it adds /Shop to the start of the path, removes .aspx from the path, and then returns the new URL. Otherwise, it returns the value from the base class method. With this custom resolver, the third URL in the table is now handled by ASP.NET routing, but the second URL is still handled by FriendlyUrls.

The second code example shows a custom resolver that causes all URLs to be handled by ASP.NET routing. It does this by overriding the PreprocessRequest method as well as the ConvertToFriendlyUrl method. The PreprocessRequest method uses the HTTP context object to get the URL, and then checks if the URL is for the Order page. If it is, it adds ~/Shop to the start of the path and then redirects to the page using ASP.NET routing. Otherwise, it calls the base class method.

You should be aware that this technique requires some additional overhead, since the redirection causes an extra round trip to the server. Because of that, you should only override the PreprocessRequest method if there's a compelling reason to do so. One such reason is when you're using a route parameter with a data source, as described in figure 11-9. In that case, the page won't work properly if it's handled by FriendlyUrls, so you'll need to make sure it's always handled by ASP.NET routing.

Three URLs that map to Order.aspx but are handled differently

URL	Handled by	URL in the browser
`/Shop/Order/cat01`	ASP.NET routing	`/Shop/Order/cat01`
`/Order/cat01`	FriendlyUrls	`/Order/cat01`
`/Order.aspx`	FriendlyUrls	`/Order`

A custom resolver that causes ASP.NET routing to handle the third URL

```
public class MyUrlResolver : WebFormsFriendlyUrlResolver
{
    // called when url is traditional (e.g. /Order.aspx)
    public override string ConvertToFriendlyUrl(string path)
    {
        if (path.Contains("Order"))
            return "~/Shop" + path.Replace(".aspx", "");
        return base.ConvertToFriendlyUrl(path);
    }
}
```

A custom resolver that causes ASP.NET routing to handle all URLs

```
public class MyUrlResolver : WebFormsFriendlyUrlResolver
{
    // called when url is traditional (e.g. /Order.aspx)
    public override string ConvertToFriendlyUrl(string path)
    {
        // same as above
    }

    // called when url is friendly (e.g. /Order or /Order/cat01
    public override void PreprocessRequest(HttpContextBase ctx,
    IHttpHandler hdlr)
    {
        string path = ctx.Request.CurrentExecutionFilePath;
        if (path.Contains("Order"))
            ctx.Response.Redirect("~/Shop" + path);
        base.PreprocessRequest(ctx, hdlr);
    }
}
```

Description

- You can make ASP.NET routing handle most of the URLs for a page by overriding the ConvertToFriendlyUrl method of the WebFormsFriendlyUrlResolver class or all of the URLs by overriding the ConvertToFriendlyUrl and PreprocessRequest methods.

- The code within the ConvertToFriendlyUrl method can convert a traditional URL that meets specific criteria to a friendly URL by removing the file extension, adjusting the URL as needed, and returning it. If a URL doesn't meet the criteria, the method should just call the base ConvertToFriendlyUrl method and return its value.

- The code within the PreprocessRequest method can change the path for a friendly URL that meets specific criteria by getting the URL from the Response object, changing it as needed, and then redirecting to the new URL. If a URL doesn't meet the criteria, the method should just call the base PreprocessRequest method.

Figure 11-13   How to get ASP.NET routing to handle some or all URLs

The C# code for the Shopping Cart application that combines FriendlyUrls and ASP.NET routing

Because the aspx code for this version of the Shopping Cart application is identical to the code for the ASP.NET routing version, it's not shown again here. However, some of the C# code has changed. That code is shown in figure 11-14.

The Page_Load event handler for the Order page starts by getting the product ID parameter that's passed with the request for the page using the technique you saw in figure 11-12. If a parameter isn't found, the Reload method is called. This method is identical to the one for the FriendlyUrls version of this page, except that the URL that's created includes "Shop" as part of its path.

Like the Reload method, the event handler that's executed when the user clicks the Add to Cart button uses the Href method to create a friendly URL that includes "Shop" as part of its path. Then, it redirects to that URL.

This application also uses a custom resolver that overrides the ConvertToFriendlyUrl method. This is similar to the method you saw in figure 11-13, but it converts traditional URLs for the Order, Products, and Cart pages to friendly URLs that include "Shop" in their paths.

Some of the C# code for the Order page

```
protected void Page_Load(object sender, EventArgs e)
{
    if (!IsPostBack)
    {
        ddlProducts.DataBind();

        string id = "";
        if (RouteData.Values.ContainsKey("productID"))
        {
            id = RouteData.Values["productID"].ToString();
        }
        else
        {
            var segments = Request.GetFriendlyUrlSegments();
            if (segments.Count > 0) id = segments[0];
        }

        if (id == "") Reload();
        else ShowSelectedProduct(id);
    }
}

protected void ddlProducts_SelectedIndexChanged(object sender, EventArgs e)
{
    Reload();
}

private void Reload()
{
    var id = ddlProducts.SelectedValue;
    var url = FriendlyUrl.Href("~/Shop", "Order", id);
    Response.Redirect(url);
}
.
.
protected void btnAdd_Click(object sender, EventArgs e)
{
    if (Page.IsValid)
    {
        .
        .
        var url = FriendlyUrl.Href("~/Shop", "Cart");
        Response.Redirect(url);
    }
}
```

The code for the overridden ConvertToFriendlyUrl method in the custom resolver

```
public override string ConvertToFriendlyUrl(string path)
{
    if (path.Contains("Order") || path.Contains("Products") ||
    path.Contains("Cart"))
        return "~/Shop" + path.Replace(".aspx", "");
    return base.ConvertToFriendlyUrl(path);
}
```

Figure 11-14   The C# code that implements FriendlyUrls and ASP.NET routing

Perspective

The FriendlyUrls feature and ASP.NET routing can be used individually or together to add friendly URLs to your web applications. These features make an application easier for users to navigate and easier for you to code and maintain. They also give you the flexibility to choose a routing solution that's fully automated, fully customized to your navigation structure, or somewhere in between.

Terms

query string	route
friendly URL	resolver object
SEO (search engine optimization)	ASP.NET routing
SEO-friendly URL	static route
FriendlyUrls	dynamic route

Summary

- *Friendly URLs* don't have a file extension and can include parameters as part of the URL. They improve *search engine optimization (SEO)* and make URLs easier to read.

- *FriendlyUrls* is an ASP.NET feature that automatically converts traditional URLs to friendly ones. To do that, it generates the routes for an application for you. A *route* is the URL pattern that's used in a friendly URL.

- You can also use a custom *resolver object* to change the default behavior of FriendlyUrls.

- When you use FriendlyUrls, you retrieve parameters using the GetFriendlyUrlSegments method of the pages Request object.

- *ASP.NET routing* lets you manually map friendly URLs for your site. That lets developers create navigation structures that don't depend on the directory structure.

- To work with ASP.NET routing, you must define your site's routes at application startup. A route can be *static* or *dynamic*.

- You map your site's routes to its physical files by using the MapPageRoute method of the static Routes property of the RouteTable class.

- When you use ASP.NET routing, you retrieve parameters using the Values collection of the page's RouteData object.

- You can also use ASP.NET routing in conjunction with FriendlyUrls.

- When using FriendlyUrls or ASP.NET routing, you should make sure that file paths of static resources are relative to the root directory.

Exercise 11-1   Use friendly URLS with the Shopping Cart application

In this exercise, you'll modify another version of the Shopping Cart application so it works with FriendlyUrls, you'll map some custom routes using ASP.NET routing, and you'll create a custom resolver object.

Open, run, and review the Shopping Cart application

1. Open the Ex11Cart web application that's in the aspnet46_cs directory. Then, start the application and click on the links in the navbar. Note that the URLs that display in the browser's address bar include the .aspx file extension.

2. Click on the Home link to display a page that describes how the finished application works. Point to any of these links to see that they use friendly URLs. Then, click on a link to see that you get a "404 File Not Found" error.

Add FriendlyUrls to the application

3. Add the FriendlyUrls NuGet package to the application. When the package is finished installing, review the information in the readme.txt file that's displayed. Then, update the Global.asax file using this information.

4. Open the RouteConfig.cs file in the new App_Start folder and review it. Then, change the AutoRedirectMode property from Permanent to Temporary. *If you skip this step, some of the following exercise steps won't work right.*

5. Run the application and click on the links in the navbar. Notice that the URLs in the browser's address bar are now friendly, even though you didn't change the URLs in the HyperLink controls for the navbar.

6. End the application. Then, open the master page and change the HyperLink controls for the navbar so they use friendly URLs. Also use friendly URLs in the PostBackUrl properties of the Go to Cart button on the Order page, the Continue Shopping button on the Cart page, and the Redirect method that's executed when the user clicks the Add to Cart button on the Order page.

Fix the Order page so it uses the parameter in the URL

7. Run the application, go to the Home page, and click the friendly URL in the first column that has the cat01 parameter. Notice that the Order page loads but doesn't display the product with this code. Also notice that the URL parameter that's displayed in the browser's address bar doesn't change when you select other products from the drop-down list.

8. Display the code-behind file for the Order page, and uncomment the using directive at the top of the page and the private Reload method.

9. In the Load event handler, comment out the call to the ShowSelectedProduct function. Then, use figure 11-6 as a guide to add code that gets the parameter if it exists and then calls the ShowSelectedProduct method. If the parameter doesn't exist, the code should call the Reload method. Be sure this code runs only when the page is not being posted back.

10. Add an event handler for the SelectedIndexChanged event of the drop-down list. This event handler should call the Reload method.

11. Run the application, go back to the Home page, and click on the same link you did in step 7. This time, the Order page should display the product with the cat01 code. Select other products from the drop-down list, and notice that the URL in the browser's address bar includes the parameter.

Map some routes with ASP.NET routing

12. Run the application, go to the Home page, and click on one of the links that includes "Shop" in its path. Just as before, these links return a "404 File Not Found" error.

13. Add custom routes to the RegisterRoutes method in the RouteConfig.cs file so the friendly URLs for the Products, Order, and Cart pages include "Shop" in their paths, and the route for the Order page includes a parameter for the product ID. Use figure 11-12 as a guide if necessary.

14. Change the code in the Load event handler for the Order page so it uses the Values collection of the page's RouteData object if a "productID" parameter exists in that collection, or the GetFriendlyUrlSegments method if it doesn't exist. Again, you can use figure 11-12 as a guide if necessary.

15. Change the code in the Reload method so the friendly URL it creates includes "Shop" in its path. Also include "Shop" in the URL in the Redirect method that's called when the user clicks the Add to Cart button.

16. Update the NavigateUrl properties of the HyperLink controls on the master page for the Products, Order, and Cart pages so they include "Shop". Do the same for the PostBackUrl properties of the Go to Cart button on the Order page and the Continue Shopping button on the Cart page.

17. Run the application, go back to the Home page, and click on the links that include "Shop" to see that they all work. Also, click on the links in the Shop menu of the navbar and note the URL in the browser's address bar.

Create a custom resolver object

18. Run the application, go to the Home page, and then click on the links in the second column that use traditional URLs for the Cart and Products pages. Notice that these URLs are still handled by FriendlyUrls, which you can tell because the URLs in the browser's address bar don't include "Shop".

19. Use figure 11-4 as a guide to add a new class to the RouteConfig.cs file named MyUrlResolver that inherits the WebFormsFriendlyUrlResolver class. Be sure to include the using directive shown in that figure.

20. Override the ConvertToFriendlyUrl method as shown in figure 11-14. Then, change the last statement in the RegisterRoutes method so it uses an object created from the new class as shown in figure 11-4.

21. Run the application, go back to the Home page, and click on the same links as in step 18. Notice that they all use ASP.NET routing now.

ASP.NET database programming

Since most ASP.NET applications store their data in databases, this section is devoted to the essentials of database programming. To start, chapter 12 introduces you to the concepts and terms you need to know for developing database applications.

Then, chapter 13 shows you how to use SQL data sources and the DataList control to get data from a database. Chapter 14 shows you how to use the GridView control to create more complex applications. Chapter 15 shows you how to use the DetailsView and FormView controls. And chapter 16 shows you how to use the ListView and DataPager controls. By using SQL data sources and the data controls, you'll be able to develop powerful applications with a minimum of code.

Next, chapter 17 shows you how to use object data sources to develop 3-layer database applications. If you already know how to use ADO.NET directly, you should be able to use object data sources when you complete this chapter. Otherwise, you will at least understand the concepts and recognize the need for learning ADO.NET.

Finally, chapter 18 shows you how to use model binding with the Entity Framework. This works because the Entity Framework includes a model with objects that are mapped to a database. Then, you can use model binding to bind these objects directly to a control like a GridView control without using a data source control.

12

An introduction to database programming

This chapter introduces you to the basic concepts and terms that apply to database applications. In particular, it explains what a relational database is and describes how you work with it using SQL. It also introduces the basic ADO.NET components that are used to access and update the data in relational databases.

An introduction to relational databases

In 1970, Dr. E. F. Codd developed a model for what was then a new and revolutionary type of database called a *relational database.* This type of database eliminated some of the problems that were associated with standard files and other database designs. By using the relational model, you can reduce data redundancy, which saves disk storage and leads to efficient data retrieval. You can also view and manipulate data in a way that is both intuitive and efficient. Today, relational databases are the de facto standard for database applications.

How a table is organized

The model for a relational database states that data is stored in one or more *tables.* It also states that each table can be viewed as a two-dimensional matrix consisting of *rows* and *columns.* This is illustrated by the relational table in figure 12-1. Each row in this table contains information about a single product.

In practice, the rows and columns of a relational database table are sometimes referred to by the more traditional terms, *records* and *fields.* In fact, some software packages use one set of terms, some use the other, and some use a combination. In this book, we've used the terms *rows* and *columns* for consistency.

If a table contains one or more columns that uniquely identify each row in the table, you can define these columns as the *primary key* of the table. For instance, the primary key of the Products table in this figure is the ProductID column. Here, the primary key consists of a single column. However, a primary key can also consist of two or more columns, in which case it's called a *composite primary key.*

In addition to primary keys, some database management systems let you define additional keys that uniquely identify each row in a table. If, for example, the Name column in the Products table contains a unique name for each product, it can be defined as a *non-primary key.* In SQL Server, this is called a *unique key,* and it's implemented by defining a *unique key constraint* (also known simply as a *unique constraint*). The only difference between a unique key and a primary key is that a unique key can contain a null value and a primary key can't.

Indexes provide an efficient way to access the rows in a table based on the values in one or more columns. Because applications typically access the rows in a table by referring to their key values, an index is automatically created for each key you define. However, you can define indexes for other columns as well. If, for example, you frequently need to sort the rows in the Products table by the CategoryID column, you can set up an index for that column. Like a key, an index can include one or more columns.

The Products table in a Halloween database

Primary key		Columns					
ProductID	Name	ShortDescripti...	LongDescription	CategoryID	ImageFile	UnitPrice	OnHand
arm01	Freddie Arm	Life-size Freddy...	This arm will gi...	props	arm1.jpg	20.9500	200
bats01	Flying Bats	Bats flying in fr...	Bats flying in fr...	props	cool1.jpg	69.9900	25
bl01	Black Light	Black light with...	Create that cree...	fx	blacklight1.jpg	19.9900	200
cat01	Deranged Cat	20" Ugly cat	This cat provid...	props	cat1.jpg	19.9900	45
fog01	Fog Machine	600W Fog mac...	The perfect fog...	fx	fog1.jpg	34.9900	100
fogj01	Fog Juice (1qt)	1 qt Bottle of fo...	Fill up your fog ...	fx	fogjuice1.jpg	9.9900	500
frankc01	Frankenstein	Frankenstein co...	Have all your fri...	costumes	frank1.jpg	39.9900	100
fred01	Freddie	Freddie Krueger...	The ultimate in ...	masks	freddy1.jpg	29.9900	50
head01	Michael Head	Mini Michael M...	For classic horr...	props	head1.jpg	29.9900	100
head02	Saw Head	Jigsaw head sca...	Perfect for getti...	props	head2.jpg	29.9900	100
hippie01	Hippie	Women's hippi...	Share the peace...	costumes	hippie1.jpg	79.9900	40
jar01	JarJar	Jar Jar Binks	Meesa happy t...	costumes	jarjar1.jpg	59.9900	25
martian01	Martian	Martian costume	Now includes a...	costumes	martian1.jpg	69.9900	100
mum01	Mummy	Mummy mask	All wrapped up ...	masks	mummy1.jpg	39.9900	30
pow01	Austin Powers	Austin Powers ...	Be the most sh...	costumes	powers1.jpg	79.9900	25
rat01	Ugly Rat	16" Rat	This guy is sure...	props	rat1.jpg	14.9900	75
rat02	Uglier Rat	20" Rat	Yuch! This one ...	props	rat2.jpg	19.9900	50
skel01	Life-size Skeleton	Life-size plastic ...	This blown plas...	props	skel1.jpg	14.9500	10
skullfog01	Skull Fogger	2,800 cubic foo...	This fogger put...	fx	skullfog1.jpg	39.9500	50
str01	Mini-strobe	Black mini stro...	Perfect for crea...	fx	strobe1.jpg	13.9900	200
super01	Superman	Superman cost...	Look, up in the ...	costumes	superman1.jpg	39.9900	100
tlm01	T&L Machine	Thunder & Lig...	Flash! Boom! Cr...	fx	tlm1.jpg	99.9900	10
vader01	Darth Vader Ma...	The legendary ...	OB1 has taught...	masks	vader1.jpg	19.9900	100

Rows

Concepts

- A *relational database* uses *tables* to store and manipulate data. Each table consists of one or more *records*, or *rows*, that contain the data for a single entry. Each row contains one or more *fields*, or *columns*, with each column representing a single item of data.

- Most tables contain a *primary key* that uniquely identifies each row in the table. The primary key often consists of a single column, but it can also consist of two or more columns. If a primary key uses two or more columns, it's called a *composite primary key*.

- In addition to primary keys, some database management systems let you define one or more *non-primary keys*. In SQL Server, these keys are called *unique keys*, and they're implemented using *unique key constraints*. Like a primary key, a non-primary key uniquely identifies each row in the table.

- A table can also be defined with one or more *indexes*. An index provides an efficient way to access data from a table based on the values in specific columns. An index is automatically created for a table's primary and non-primary keys.

Figure 12-1   How a table is organized

How the tables in a database are related

The tables in a relational database can be related to other tables by values in specific columns. The two tables shown in figure 12-2 illustrate this concept. Here, each row in the Categories table is related to one or more rows in the Products table. This is called a *one-to-many relationship*.

Typically, relationships exist between the primary key in one table and the *foreign key* in another table. The foreign key is simply one or more columns in a table that refer to a primary key in another table. In SQL Server, relationships can also exist between a unique key in one table and a foreign key in another table.

Although one-to-many relationships are the most common, two tables can also have a one-to-one or many-to-many relationship. If a table has a *one-to-one relationship* with another table, the data in the two tables could be stored in a single table. Because of that, one-to-one relationships are used infrequently.

In contrast, a *many-to-many relationship* is usually implemented by using an intermediate table, called a *linking table*, that has a one-to-many relationship with the two tables in the many-to-many relationship. In other words, a many-to-many relationship can usually be broken down into two one-to-many relationships.

The relationship between the Categories and Products tables

CategoryID	ShortName	LongName
costumes	Costumes	Costumes
fx	FX	Special Effects
masks	Masks	Masks
props	Props	Props
NULL	NULL	NULL

Primary key

Foreign key

ProductID	Name	ShortDescripti...	LongDescription	CategoryID	ImageFile	UnitPrice	OnHand
arm01	Freddie Arm	Life-size Freddy...	This arm will gi...	props	arm1.jpg	20.9500	200
bats01	Flying Bats	Bats flying in fr...	Bats flying in fr...	props	cool1.jpg	69.9900	25
bl01	Black Light	Black light with...	Create that cree...	fx	blacklight1.jpg	19.9900	200
cat01	Deranged Cat	20" Ugly cat	This cat provid...	props	cat1.jpg	19.9900	45
fog01	Fog Machine	600W Fog mac...	The perfect fog...	fx	fog1.jpg	34.9900	100
fogj01	Fog Juice (1qt)	1 qt Bottle of fo...	Fill up your fog ...	fx	fogjuice1.jpg	9.9900	500
frankc01	Frankenstein	Frankenstein co...	Have all your fri...	costumes	frank1.jpg	39.9900	100
fred01	Freddie	Freddie Krueger...	The ultimate in ...	masks	freddy1.jpg	29.9900	50
head01	Michael Head	Mini Michael M...	For classic horr...	props	head1.jpg	29.9900	100
head02	Saw Head	Jigsaw head sca...	Perfect for getti...	props	head2.jpg	29.9900	100
hippie01	Hippie	Women's hippi...	Share the peace...	costumes	hippie1.jpg	79.9900	40
jar01	JarJar	Jar Jar Binks	Meesa happy t...	costumes	jarjar1.jpg	59.9900	25
martian01	Martian	Martian costume	Now includes a...	costumes	martian1.jpg	69.9900	100
mum01	Mummy	Mummy mask	All wrapped up ...	masks	mummy1.jpg	39.9900	30
pow01	Austin Powers	Austin Powers ...	Be the most sh...	costumes	powers1.jpg	79.9900	25
rat01	Ugly Rat	16" Rat	This guy is sure...	props	rat1.jpg	14.9900	75
rat02	Uglier Rat	20" Rat	Yuch! This one ...	props	rat2.jpg	19.9900	50
skel01	Life-size Skeleton	Life-size plastic ...	This blown plas...	props	skel1.jpg	14.9500	10
skullfog01	Skull Fogger	2,800 cubic foo...	This fogger put...	fx	skullfog1.jpg	39.9500	50
str01	Mini-strobe	Black mini stro...	Perfect for crea...	fx	strobe1.jpg	13.9900	200
super01	Superman	Superman cost...	Look, up in the ...	costumes	superman1.jpg	39.9900	100
tlm01	T&L Machine	Thunder & Lig...	Flash! Boom! Cr...	fx	tlm1.jpg	99.9900	10
vader01	Darth Vader Ma...	The legendary ...	OB1 has taught...	masks	vader1.jpg	19.9900	100

Concepts

- The tables in a relational database are related to each other through their key columns. For example, the CategoryID column is used to relate the Categories and Products tables above. The CategoryID column in the Products table is called a *foreign key* because it identifies a related row in the Categories table.

- Usually, a foreign key corresponds to the primary key in the related table. In SQL Server, however, a foreign key can also correspond to a unique key in the related table.

- When two tables are related via a foreign key, the table with the foreign key is referred to as the *foreign key table* and the table with the primary key is referred to as the *primary key table*.

- The relationships between the tables in a database correspond to the relationships between the entities they represent. The most common type of relationship is a *one-to-many* relationship as illustrated by the Categories and Products tables. A table can also have a *one-to-one relationship* or a *many-to-many relationship* with another table.

Figure 12-2   How the tables in a database are related

How the columns in a table are defined

When you define a column in a table, you assign properties to it as indicated by the design of the Products table in figure 12-3. The two most important properties for a column are Name, which provides an identifying name for the column, and Data Type, which specifies the type of information that can be stored in the column. With SQL Server, you can choose from *system data types* like the ones in this figure, and you can define your own data types that are based on the system data types. As you define each column in a table, you generally try to assign the data type that will minimize the use of disk storage because that will improve the performance of the queries later.

In addition to a data type, you must indicate whether the column can store a *null value*. A null represents a value that's unknown, unavailable, or not applicable. The Products table, for example, allows nulls in its ImageFile column.

You can also assign a *default value* to each column. Then, that value is assigned to the column if another value isn't provided. If a column doesn't allow nulls and doesn't have a default value, you must supply a value for the column when you add a new row to the table. Otherwise, an error will occur.

Each table can also contain a numeric column whose value is generated automatically by the DBMS. In SQL Server, a column like this is called an *identity column*, and you establish it using the Identity, Identity Seed, and Identity Increment properties. Identity columns are often used as the primary key for a table.

A *check constraint* defines the acceptable values for a column. For example, you can define a check constraint for the Products table in this figure to make sure that the UnitPrice column is greater than zero. A check constraint like this can be defined at the column level because it refers only to the column it constrains. If the check constraint for a column needs to refer to other columns in the table, however, it can be defined at the table level.

After you define the constraints for a database, they're managed by the DBMS. If, for example, a user tries to add a row with data that violates a constraint, the DBMS sends an appropriate error code back to the application without adding the row to the database. The application can then respond to the error code.

Another alternative is to validate the data that is going to be added to a database before the program tries to add it. That way, the constraints shouldn't be needed and the program should run more efficiently. In many cases, both data validation and constraints are used. That way, the programs run more efficiently if the data validation routines work, but the constraints are there in case the data validation routines don't work or aren't coded.

The Server Explorer design view window for the Products table

	Name	Data Type	Allow Nulls	Default
🔑	ProductID	varchar(10)	☐	
	Name	varchar(50)	☐	
	ShortDescription	varchar(200)	☐	
	LongDescription	varchar(2000)	☐	
	CategoryID	varchar(10)	☐	
	ImageFile	varchar(30)	☑	
	UnitPrice	money	☐	
	OnHand	int	☐	
			☐	

▲ **Keys** (1)
    PK_Products (Primary Key, Clustered: ProductID)
Check Constraints (0)
Indexes (0)
▲ **Foreign Keys** (1)
    FK_Products_Categories   (CategoryID)
Triggers (0)

Common SQL Server data types

Type	Description
bit	A value of 1 or 0 that represents a True or False value.
char, varchar, nchar, nvarchar	Any combination of letters, symbols, and numbers.
date, time, datetime, smalldatetime	Alphanumeric data that represents a date, a time, or both a date and time. Various formats are acceptable.
decimal, numeric	Numeric data that is accurate to the least significant digit. The data can contain an integer and a fractional portion.
float, real	Floating-point values that contain an approximation of a decimal value.
bigint, int, smallint, tinyint	Numeric data that contains only an integer portion.
money, smallmoney	Monetary values that are accurate to four decimal places.

Description

- The *data type* that's assigned to a column determines the type of information that can be stored in the column. Depending on the data type, the column definition can also include its length, precision, and scale.

- Each column definition also indicates whether or not the column can contain *null values*. A null value indicates that the value of the column is not known.

- A column can be defined with a *default value*. Then, that value is used for the column if another value isn't provided when a row is added to the table.

- A column can also be defined as an *identity column*. An identity column is a numeric column whose value is generated automatically when a row is added to the table.

- To restrict the values that a column can hold, you define *check constraints*. Check constraints can be defined at either the column level or the table level.

Note

- When you select a column in design view, its properties are displayed in the Properties window. Then you can use this window to change any of the properties of the column, including those that aren't displayed in design view.

Figure 12-3   How the columns in a table are defined

The design of the Halloween database

Now that you've seen how the basic elements of a relational database work, figure 12-4 shows the design of the Halloween database that's used in the programming examples throughout this book. Although this database may seem complicated, its design is actually much simpler than most databases you'll encounter when you work on actual database applications.

The purpose of the Halloween database is to track orders placed at an online Halloween products store. To do that, the database must track not only invoices, but also products and customers.

The central table for this database is the Invoices table, which contains one row for each order placed by the company's customers. The primary key for this table is the InvoiceNumber column, which is an identity column. As a result, invoice numbers are generated automatically by SQL Server whenever new invoices are created.

The LineItems table contains the line item details for each invoice. The primary key for this table is a combination of the InvoiceNumber and ProductID columns. The InvoiceNumber column relates each line item to an invoice, and the ProductID column relates each line item to a product. As a result, each invoice can have only one line item for a given product.

The Products and Categories tables work together to store information about the products offered by the Halloween store. The Category table has just three columns: CategoryID, ShortName, and LongName. The CategoryID column is a code with up to 10 characters that uniquely identifies each category. The ShortName and LongName columns provide two different descriptions of the category that an application can use, depending on how much room is available to display the category information.

The Products table contains one row for each product. Its primary key is the ProductID column. The Name, ShortDescription, and LongDescription columns provide descriptive information about the product. The ImageFile column provides the name of a separate image file that depicts the product, if one exists. This column specifies just the name of each image file, not the complete path. In the applications in this book, the image files are stored in a directory named Images beneath the application's main directory, so the application knows where to find them. If an image isn't available for a product, this column contains a null value.

The Customers table contains a row for each customer who has purchased from the Halloween Store. The primary key for this table is the customer's email address. The other columns in this table contain the customer's name, address, and phone number. The State column relates each customer to a state in the States table. The primary key for the States table is the 2-character StateCode column.

The tables that make up the Halloween database

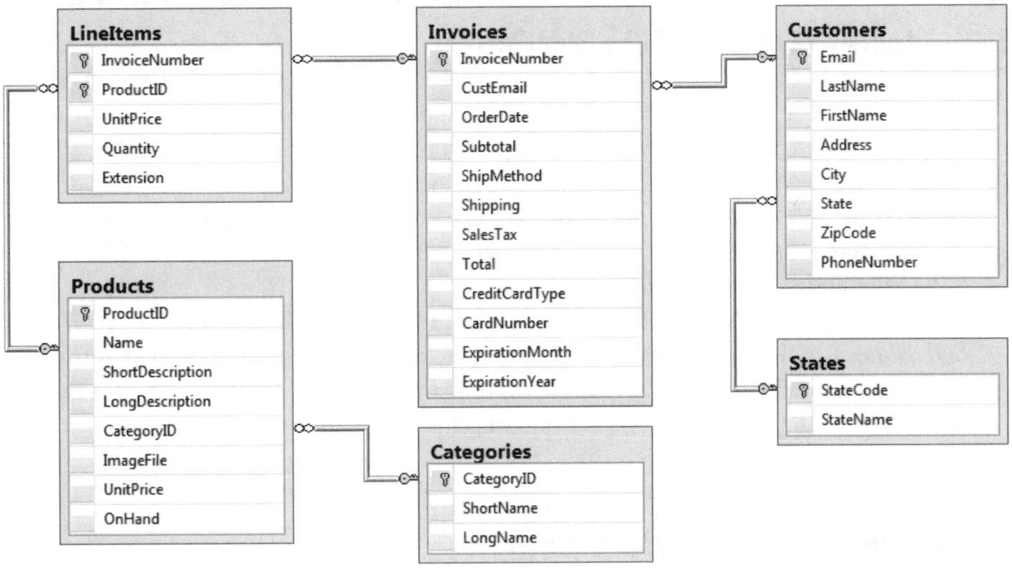

Description

- The Categories table contains a row for each product category. Its primary key is CategoryID, a variable-length code with up to 10 characters that identifies each category.

- The Products table contains a row for each product. Its primary key is ProductID, a variable-length code with up to 10 characters that identifies each product. CategoryID is a foreign key that relates each product to a row in the Categories table.

- The States table contains a row for each state. Its primary key is StateCode, a 2-character code that identifies each state.

- The Customers table contains a row for each customer. Its primary key is Email, which identifies each customer by his or her email address. State is a foreign key that relates each customer to a row in the States table.

- The Invoices table contains a row for each invoice. Its primary key is InvoiceNumber, an identity column that's generated automatically when a new invoice is created. CustEmail is a foreign key that relates each invoice to a row in the Customers table.

- The LineItems table contains one row for each line item of each invoice. Its primary key is a combination of InvoiceNumber and ProductID. InvoiceNumber is a foreign key that relates each line item to an invoice, and ProductID is a foreign key that relates each line item to a product.

- The relationships between the tables in this diagram appear as links, where the endpoints indicate the type of relationship. A key indicates the "one" side of a relationship, and the infinity symbol (∞) indicates the "many" side.

Figure 12-4   The design of the Halloween database

How to use SQL to work with the data in a relational database

To access or update the data in a relational database, you use a standard language called *SQL (Structured Query Language)*. In practice, SQL is either pronounced as the letters S-Q-L or as sequel, and the writing in this section assumes the sequel pronunciation. In the topics that follow, you'll learn about the four *SQL statements* that retrieve and update data: the SELECT, INSERT, UPDATE, and DELETE statements.

Although SQL is a standard language, each DBMS is likely to have its own *SQL dialect*, which includes extensions to the standard language. So when you use SQL, you need to make sure that you're using the dialect that's supported by your DBMS. In this chapter and throughout this book, all of the SQL examples are for Microsoft SQL Server's dialect, which is called *Transact-SQL*.

How to query a single table

Figure 12-5 shows how to use a SELECT statement to query a single table in a database. In the syntax summary at the top of this figure, you can see that the SELECT clause names the columns to be retrieved and the FROM clause names the table that contains the columns. You can also code a WHERE clause that gives criteria for the rows to be selected. And you can code an ORDER BY clause that names one or more columns that the results should be sorted by and indicates whether each column should be sorted in ascending or descending sequence (ascending is the default).

If you study the SELECT statement below the syntax summary, you can see how this works. Here, the SELECT statement retrieves three columns from the Products table. It selects a row only if the CategoryID column for the row has a value of "props." And it sorts the returned rows by UnitPrice, so the least expensive products are listed first.

This figure also shows the *result table*, or *result set*, that's returned by the SELECT statement. A result set is a logical table that's created temporarily within the database. When an application requests data from a database, it receives a result set.

Although it's not shown here, you should realize that a result set can include columns that are calculated from other columns in the table. For example, you could create a column for the total value of each product in the Products table by multiplying the OnHand column in that table by the UnitPrice column. This type of column is called a *calculated column*, and it exists only in the results of the query.

Simplified syntax of the SELECT statement

```
SELECT column-1 [, column-2]...
FROM table-1
[WHERE selection-criteria]
[ORDER BY column-1 [ASC|DESC] [, column-2 [ASC|DESC]]...]
```

A SELECT statement that retrieves and sorts selected columns and rows from the Products table

```
SELECT ProductID, Name, UnitPrice
FROM Products
WHERE CategoryID = 'props'
ORDER BY UnitPrice
```

The result set defined by the SELECT statement

	ProductID	Name	UnitPrice
1	skel01	Life-size Skeleton	14.95
2	rat01	Ugly Rat	14.99
3	rat02	Uglier Rat	19.99
4	cat01	Deranged Cat	19.99
5	arm01	Freddie Arm	20.95
6	head01	Michael Head	29.99
7	head02	Saw Head	29.99
8	bats01	Flying Bats	69.99

Concepts

- To access and update the data in a relational database, you use *Structured Query Language*, or *SQL* (pronounced as sequel or the letters S-Q-L).

- The SELECT statement is a *SQL statement* that gets data from a database and returns it in a *result table*, or *result set*. A result set is a logical set of rows that consists of all of the columns and rows requested by the SELECT statement.

- A result set can include *calculated columns* that are calculated from other columns in the table.

- To select all of the columns in a table, you can code an asterisk (*) in place of the column names. For example, this statement will select all of the columns from the Products table:
  ```
  SELECT * FROM Products
  ```
  However, this technique is typically not used in production applications because it can retrieve more data than is needed or introduce errors if the table changes.

Figure 12-5   How to query a single table

How to join related data from two or more tables

Figure 12-6 presents the syntax of the SELECT statement for retrieving related data from two tables. This type of operation is called a *join* because the data from the two tables is joined together into a single result set. For example, the SELECT statement in this figure joins data from the Categories and Products tables into a single result set.

An *inner join* is one of the most common types of joins. When you use an inner join, rows from the two tables in the join are included in the result set only if their related columns match. These matching columns are specified in the FROM clause of the SELECT statement. In the SELECT statement in this figure, for example, rows from the Categories and Products tables are included only if the value of the CategoryID column in the Categories table matches the value of the CategoryID column in one or more rows in the Products table. If there aren't any products for a particular category, that category won't be included in the result set.

Notice that the SELECT clause in this statement doesn't indicate which table contains each column. That's because each of the columns exists in only one of the tables. If a column existed in both tables, however, you would need to indicate which table you wanted to retrieve the column from. If you wanted to retrieve the CategoryID column from the Categories table, for example, you would need to code that column like this:

```
Categories.CategoryID
```

Although this figure shows how to join data from two tables, you should know that you can extend this syntax to join data from additional tables. If, for example, you want to include data from the LineItems table in the results shown in this figure, you can code the FROM clause of the SELECT statement like this:

```
FROM Categories
    INNER JOIN Products
        ON Categories.CategoryID = Products.CategoryID
    INNER JOIN LineItems
        ON Products.ProductID = LineItems.ProductID
```

Then, in the column list of the SELECT clause, you can include any of the columns in the LineItems table.

The syntax of the SELECT statement for joining related data from two tables

```
SELECT column-list
FROM table-1
    [INNER] JOIN table-2
    ON table-1.column-1 {=|<|>|<=|>=|<>} table-2.column-2
[WHERE selection-criteria]
[ORDER BY column-list]
```

A SELECT statement that joins data from the Products and Categories tables

```
SELECT ShortName, ProductID, Name, UnitPrice
FROM Categories INNER JOIN Products
    ON Categories.CategoryID = Products.CategoryID
ORDER BY Categories.CategoryID
```

The result set defined by the SELECT statement

	ShortName	ProductID	Name	UnitPrice
1	Costumes	frankc01	Frankenstein	39.99
2	Costumes	hippie01	Hippie	79.99
3	Costumes	jar01	JarJar	59.99
4	Costumes	martian01	Martian	69.99
5	Costumes	pow01	Austin Powers	79.99
6	Costumes	super01	Superman	39.99
7	FX	tlm01	T&L Machine	99.99
8	FX	fog01	Fog Machine	34.99
9	FX	fogj01	Fog Juice (1qt)	9.99
10	FX	skullfog01	Skull Fogger	39.95
11	FX	str01	Mini-strobe	13.99
12	FX	bl01	Black Light	19.99
13	Masks	fred01	Freddie	29.99
14	Masks	mum01	Mummy	39.99
15	Masks	vader01	Darth Vader ...	19.99
16	Props	rat01	Ugly Rat	14.99
17	Props	rat02	Uglier Rat	19.99
18	Props	skel01	Life-size Skel...	14.95
19	Props	head01	Michael Head	29.99
20	Props	head02	Saw Head	29.99
21	Props	cat01	Deranged Cat	19.99
22	Props	arm01	Freddie Arm	20.95
23	Props	bats01	Flying Bats	69.99

Concepts

- A *join* lets you combine data from two or more tables into a single result set.
- One common type of join is an *inner join*. This type of join returns rows from both tables only if their related columns match.

Figure 12-6   How to join related data from two or more tables

How to add, update, and delete data in a table

Figure 12-7 presents the basic syntax of the SQL INSERT, UPDATE, and DELETE statements. You use these statements to add new rows to a table, to update the data in existing rows, and to delete existing rows.

To add a single row to a table, you use an INSERT statement with the syntax shown in this figure. With this syntax, you specify the name of the table you want to add the row to, the names of the columns you're supplying data for, and the values for those columns. In the example, the INSERT statement adds a row to the Categories table and supplies a value for each of the three columns in that table. If a table allows nulls or provides default values for some columns, though, the INSERT statement doesn't have to provide values for those columns. In addition, an INSERT statement never provides a value for an identity column because that value is generated by the DBMS.

To change the values of one or more columns in one or more rows, you use the UPDATE statement. On this statement, you specify the name of the table you want to update, expressions that indicate the columns you want to change and how you want to change them, and a condition that identifies the rows you want to change. In the example, the UPDATE statement changes the ShortName value for just the one row in the Categories table that has a CategoryID value of "food."

To delete one or more rows from a table, you use the DELETE statement. On this statement, you specify the table you want to delete rows from and a condition that indicates the rows you want to delete. In the example, the DELETE statement deletes just the one row in the Categories table whose CategoryID column is "food."

Note that you can code both the UPDATE and DELETE statements without a WHERE clause. If you do that, however, every row in the table will be updated or deleted, which can be catastrophic. Because of that, you should be sure to include a WHERE clause whenever necessary.

How to add a single row

The syntax of the INSERT statement for adding a single row
```
INSERT [INTO] table-name [(column-list)]
    VALUES (value-list)
```

A statement that adds a single row to a table
```
INSERT INTO Categories (CategoryID, ShortName, LongName)
    VALUES ('food', 'Spooky Food', 'The very best in Halloween cuisine')
```

How to update rows

The syntax of the UPDATE statement
```
UPDATE table-name
    SET expression-1 [, expression-2]...
    [WHERE selection-criteria]
```

A statement that changes the value of the ShortName column for a selected row
```
UPDATE Categories
    SET ShortName = 'Halloween cuisine'
    WHERE CategoryID = 'food'
```

How to delete rows

The syntax of the DELETE statement
```
DELETE [FROM] table-name
    [WHERE selection-criteria]
```

A statement that deletes a specified category
```
DELETE FROM Categories
    WHERE CategoryID = 'food'
```

Description
- You use the INSERT, UPDATE, and DELETE statements to maintain the data in a database table.
- The INSERT statement can be used to add one or more rows to a table. Although the syntax shown above is for adding just one row, there is another syntax for adding more than one row.
- The UPDATE and DELETE statements can be used for updating or deleting one or more rows in a table using the syntax shown above.

Warning
- If you code an UPDATE statement without a WHERE clause, all of the rows in the table will be updated. Similarly, if you code a DELETE statement without a WHERE clause, all of the rows in the table will be deleted.

Figure 12-7   How to add, update, and delete data in a table

How to work with other database objects

In addition to the tables you've already learned about, relational databases can contain other database objects like views and stored procedures. In the topics that follow, you'll be introduced to these objects.

How to work with views

A *view* is a predefined query that's stored in a database. To create a view, you use the CREATE VIEW statement as shown in figure 12-8. This statement causes the SELECT statement you specify to be stored with the database. In this case, the CREATE VIEW statement creates a view named CustomersMin that retrieves four columns from the Customers table.

To access a view, you issue a SELECT statement that refers to the view. This causes a *virtual table*—a temporary table that's created on the server—to be created from the SELECT statement in the view. Then, the SELECT statement that referred to the view is executed on this virtual table to create the result set.

Although views can be quite useful, they require some additional overhead. That's because every time an application refers to a view, the virtual table has to be created from scratch. If that's a problem, an alternative is to use stored procedures.

A CREATE VIEW statement for a view named CustomersMin

```
CREATE VIEW CustomersMin AS
    SELECT LastName, FirstName, State, Email
    FROM Customers
```

A SELECT statement that uses the CustomersMin view

```
SELECT * FROM CustomersMin
WHERE State = 'CA'
ORDER BY LastName, FirstName
```

The virtual table that's created from the view

	LastName	FirstName	State	Email
1	Molunguri	A	AL	A8@webemaxmjKd.com
2	Antosca	Andrew	MI	AAntosca@netYduo.com
3	Antony	Abdul	NC	Abdul70@matminvV.edu
4	Johnson	Ajith	CA	Ajith@xgMaster.edu
5	Rose	Alan	FL	Alan@NsiYYGE.net
6	Browning	Albert	GA	Albert@masterxmlrad.com
7	Litterson	Anthony	PA	ALitterson@mastermaster.c
8	Lee	Andra	NY	Andra91@webtechdotca.edu
9	Latheef	Andrea c.	FL	Andrea c.@sWGrUDweb.com

The result set that's created from the virtual table

	LastName	FirstName	State	Email
1	Amalie	Dennis	CA	DAmalie@ShwildOHrad.com
2	Arutla	Jerry I.	CA	Jerry I.@progwildbioY.com
3	Blake	John	CA	John@netEw.edu
4	Bommana	Ilya	CA	IIBommana@radassoc.net
5	Brown	Srikanth	CA	Srikanth@XyRbduocare.gov
6	Carroll	Sam	CA	Sam91@OSZqIKrNxmlE.gov
7	Condron	Michael	CA	Michael@zmasterftRW.com
8	Curless	Darald	CA	Darald@DDiHYzrmaste.net
9	Diop	John	CA	JoDiop@netcaremaste.edu

Description

- A *view* consists of a SELECT statement that's stored with the database. Because views are stored as part of the database, they can be managed independently of the applications that use them.

- When you refer to a view, a *virtual table* is created on the server that represents the view. Then, the result set is extracted from this virtual table. For this reason, a view is also called a *viewed table*.

- Views can be used to restrict the data that a user is allowed to access or to present data in a form that's easy for the user to understand. In some databases, users may be allowed to access data only through views.

Figure 12-8   How to work with views

How to work with stored procedures

A *stored procedure* is a set of one or more SQL statements that are stored together in a database. To create a stored procedure, you use the CREATE PROCEDURE statement as shown in figure 12-9. Here, the stored procedure contains a single SELECT statement. To use the stored procedure, you send a request for it to be executed.

When the server receives the request, it executes the stored procedure. If the stored procedure contains a SELECT statement like the one in this figure, the result set is sent back to the calling program. If the stored procedure contains INSERT, UPDATE, or DELETE statements, the appropriate processing is performed.

Notice that the stored procedure in this figure accepts an *input parameter* named @State from the calling program. The value of this parameter is then substituted for the parameter in the WHERE clause so only customers in the specified state are included in the result set.

When it's done with its processing, a stored procedure can also pass *output parameters* back to the calling program. In addition, stored procedures can include *control-of-flow language* that determines the processing that's done based on specific conditions.

A CREATE PROCEDURE statement
for a procedure named spCustomersByState

```
CREATE PROCEDURE uspCustomersByState @State char AS
    SELECT LastName, FirstName, State, Email
    FROM Customers
    WHERE State = @State
    ORDER BY LastName, FirstName
```

The result set that's created when the stored procedure is executed with the @State variable set to 'CA'

	LastName	FirstName	State	Email
1	Armalie	Dennis	CA	DArmalie@ShwildOHrad.com
2	Arutla	Jerry I.	CA	Jerry I.@progwildbioY.com
3	Blake	John	CA	John@netEw.edu
4	Bommana	Ilya	CA	IlBommana@radassoc.net
5	Brown	Srikanth	CA	Srikanth@XyRbduocare.gov
6	Carroll	Sam	CA	Sam91@OSZqlKrNxmlE.gov
7	Condron	Michael	CA	Michael@zmasterftRW.com
8	Curless	Darald	CA	Darald@DDiHYzrmaste.net
9	Diop	John	CA	JoDiop@netcaremaste.edu

Concepts

- A *stored procedure* consists of one or more SQL statements that have been compiled and stored with the database. A stored procedure can be started by application code on the client.

- Stored procedures can improve database performance because the SQL statements in each procedure are only compiled and optimized the first time they're executed. In contrast, SQL statements that are sent from a client to the server have to be compiled and optimized every time they're executed.

- In addition to SELECT statements, a stored procedure can contain other SQL statements such as INSERT, UPDATE, and DELETE statements. It can also contain *control-of-flow language*, which lets you perform conditional processing within the stored procedure.

- Like views, stored procedures can be used to restrict the data that a user is allowed to access.

Figure 12-9   How to work with stored procedures

An introduction to ADO.NET

ADO.NET (*ActiveX Data Objects*) is the primary data access API for the .NET Framework. It provides the classes that are used when you develop database applications. The topics that follow introduce you to the important ADO.NET concepts.

How the basic ADO.NET components work

Figure 12-10 presents the primary ADO.NET objects that are used when you develop database applications. To start, the data that's retrieved from a database is stored in a *dataset* that contains one or more *data tables*. Then, the data in the data tables can be displayed in one or more controls on the page. When the data in a control is updated, the change is reflected in the data table and is passed on to the database.

To manage the flow of data between a dataset and a database, ADO.NET uses a *data adapter*. The data adapter uses *commands* that define the SQL statements to be issued. If a command contains a SELECT statement, for example, the command connects to the database using a *connection* and passes the SELECT statement to the database. After the SELECT statement is executed, the result set it produces is sent back to the data adapter, which stores the results in the data table.

To update the data in a database, the data adapter can use a command that contains an INSERT, UPDATE, or DELETE statement for a data table. Then, the command uses the connection to connect to the database and perform the requested operation.

When you use a SQL data source to work with the data in a database as shown in chapter 4, the data is stored in a dataset by default. Then, the data source provides the information ADO.NET needs to connect to the database, and it specifies the SQL statements ADO.NET uses to retrieve and update the data. You'll learn more about that in the chapters that follow.

The ADO.NET classes for the data adapters, commands, and connections that work directly with a database are provided by the *.NET data providers*. The .NET Framework currently includes data providers for SQL Server, OLE DB, and ODBC. You can use a SQL data source to work with any of these data providers. (Although the .Net Framework also includes a data provider for Oracle, it has been deprecated and you shouldn't use it).

Although it's not apparent in this figure, the data in a dataset is independent of the database that the data was retrieved from. In fact, when you use a SQL data source, the connection to the database is automatically closed after each operation. Because of that, the application must work with the copy of the data that's stored in the dataset. The architecture that's used to implement this type of data processing is referred to as a *disconnected data architecture*.

Although a disconnected data architecture is more complicated than a connected architecture, it improves system performance by using fewer system resources for maintaining connections. It also works well with ASP.NET web applications, which are inherently disconnected.

Basic ADO.NET objects

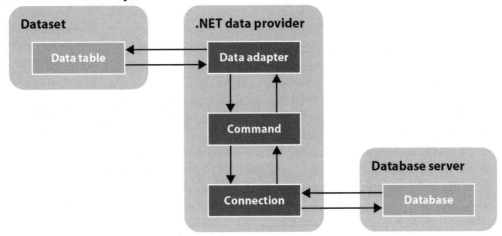

Description

- ADO.NET uses two types of objects to access the data in a database: *datasets*, which can contain one or more *data tables*, and *.NET data provider* objects, which include data adapters, commands, and connections.

- A dataset stores data from the database so it can be accessed by the application. The .NET data provider objects retrieve data from and update data in the database.

- To retrieve data from a database and store it in a data table, a *data adapter* object issues a SELECT statement that's stored in a *command* object. Next, the command object uses a *connection* object to connect to the database and retrieve the data. Then, the data is passed back to the data adapter, which stores the data in a table within the dataset.

- To update the data in a database based on the data in a data table, the data adapter object issues an INSERT, UPDATE, or DELETE statement that's stored in a command object. Then, the command object uses a connection to connect to the database and update the data.

- When you use a SQL data source, it specifies the information for connecting to the database and for retrieving and updating data.

- The data provider remains connected to the database only long enough to retrieve or update the specified data. Then, it disconnects from the database and the application works with the data via the dataset object. This is referred to as a *disconnected data architecture*.

- All of the ADO.NET objects are implemented by classes in the System.Data namespace of the .NET Framework. However, the specific classes used to implement the connection, command, and data adapter objects depend on the .NET data provider you use.

Figure 12-10   How the basic ADO.NET components work

Concurrency and the disconnected data architecture

Although the disconnected data architecture has advantages, it also has some disadvantages. One of those is the conflict that can occur when two or more users retrieve and then try to update data in the same row of a table. This is called a *concurrency* problem. This is possible because once a program retrieves data from a database, the connection to that database is dropped. As a result, the database management system can't manage the update process.

To illustrate, consider the situation shown in figure 12-11. Here, two users are using the Products table at the same time. These users could be using the same page of a website or different pages that have accessed the Products table. Now, suppose that user 1 modifies the unit price in the row for a product and updates the Products table in the database. Suppose too that user 2 modifies the description in the row for the same product, and then tries to update the Products table in the database. What will happen? That will depend on the *concurrency control* that's used by the programs.

When you use ADO.NET, you have two choices for concurrency control. First, you can use *optimistic concurrency*, which checks whether a row has been changed since it was retrieved. If it has, the update or deletion will be refused and a *concurrency exception* will be thrown. Then, the program should handle the error. For example, it could display an error message that tells the user that the row could not be updated and then retrieve the updated row so the user can make the change again.

Second, you can use the *"last in wins"* technique, which works the way its name implies. Since no checking is done with this technique, the row that's updated by the last user overwrites any changes made to the row by a previous user. For the example above, the row updated by user 2 will overwrite changes made by user 1, which means that the description will be right but the unit price will be wrong. Since errors like this corrupt the data in a database, optimistic concurrency is used by most programs.

If you know that concurrency will be a problem, you can use a couple of programming techniques to limit concurrency exceptions. If a program uses a dataset, one technique is to update the database frequently so other users can retrieve the current data. The program should also refresh its dataset frequently so it contains the recent changes made by other users.

Another way to avoid concurrency exceptions is to retrieve and work with just one row at a time. That way, it's less likely that two users will update the same row at the same time. In contrast, if two users retrieve the same table, they will of course retrieve the same rows. Then, if they both update the same row in the table, even though it may not be at the same time, a concurrency exception will occur when they try to update the database.

Two users who are working with copies of the same data

What happens when two users try to update the same row

- When two or more users retrieve the data in the same row of a database table at the same time, it is called *concurrency*. Because ADO.NET uses a disconnected data architecture, the database management system can't prevent this from happening.

- If two users try to update the same row in a database table at the same time, the second user's changes could overwrite the changes made by the first user. Whether or not that happens depends on the *concurrency control* that the programs use.

- With *optimistic concurrency*, the program checks to see whether the database row that's going to be updated or deleted has been changed since it was retrieved. If it has, a *concurrency exception* occurs and the update or deletion is refused. Then, the program should handle the exception.

- If optimistic concurrency isn't in effect, the program doesn't check to see whether a row has been changed before an update or deletion takes place. Instead, the operation proceeds without throwing an exception. This is referred to as "*last in wins*" because the last update overwrites any previous update. And this can lead to errors in the database.

How to avoid concurrency errors

- For many applications, concurrency errors rarely occur. As a result, optimistic concurrency is adequate because the users will rarely have to resubmit an update or deletion that is refused.

- If concurrency is likely to be a problem, a program that uses a dataset can be designed so it updates the database and refreshes the dataset frequently. That way, concurrency errors are less likely to occur.

- Another way to avoid concurrency errors is to design a program so it retrieves and updates just one row at a time. That way, there's less chance that two users will retrieve and update the same row at the same time.

Figure 12-11   Concurrency and the disconnected data architecture

How to work with data
without using a data adapter

By default, when you use a SQL data source to work with the data in a database, a data adapter is used to retrieve that data and store it in a dataset as described earlier in this chapter. You should know, however, that you can also work with the data in a database without using a data adapter. Figure 12-12 shows you how.

As you can see, you still use command and connection objects to access the database. Instead of using a data adapter to execute the commands, though, you execute the commands directly. When you do that, you also have to provide code to handle the result of the command. If you issue a command that contains an INSERT, UPDATE, or DELETE statement, for example, the result is an integer that indicates the number of rows that were affected by the operation. You can use that information to determine if the operation was successful.

If you execute a command that contains a SELECT statement, the result is a result set that contains the rows you requested. To read through the rows in the result set, you use a *data reader* object. Although a data reader provides an efficient way of reading the rows in a result set, you can't use it to modify those rows. In addition, it only lets you read rows in a forward direction. Once you read the next row, the previous row is unavailable. Because of that, you typically use a data reader to retrieve and work with a single database row at a time or to retrieve rows that won't change.

As you'll see in the next chapter, you can use this technique with a SQL data source instead of using a dataset. That can improve the efficiency of an application. You can also use this technique with object data sources as described in chapter 17. As you'll see in that chapter, though, you have to write all of the data access code yourself when you use object data sources.

ADO.NET components for accessing a database directly

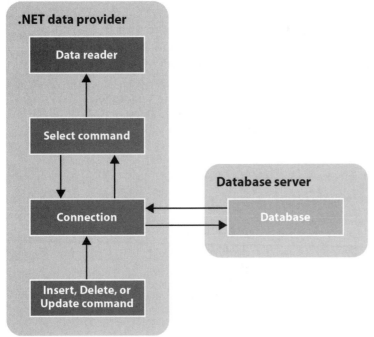

Description

- Instead of using a data adapter to execute commands to retrieve, insert, update, and delete data from a database, you can execute those commands directly.

- To retrieve data from a database, you execute a command object that contains a SELECT statement. Then, the command object uses a connection to connect to the database and retrieve the data. You can then read the results one row at a time using a *data reader* object.

- To insert, update, or delete data in a database, you execute a command object that contains an INSERT, UPDATE, or DELETE statement. Then, the command object uses a connection to connect to the database and update the data. You can then check the value that's returned to determine if the operation was successful.

- If you use this technique in an application that maintains the data in a database, you typically work with a single row at a time. Because of that, the chance of a concurrency error is reduced.

- To use this technique with ASP.NET applications, you can use object data sources. See chapter 17 for details.

Figure 12-12   How to work with data without using a data adapter

Perspective

This chapter has introduced you to the basic concepts of relational databases and the basic SQL statements. With that as background, you're ready to learn how to develop ASP.NET database applications with SQL data sources, ASP.NET data controls, and object data sources.

Before you continue, though, you should know that there's a lot more to SQL and SQL Server than what has been presented in this chapter. For a complete treatment of SQL Server, please refer to the latest edition of our SQL Server book.

Terms

relational database	SQL dialect
table	Transact-SQL
record	result table
row	result set
field	calculated column
column	join
primary key	inner join
composite primary key	view
non-primary key	virtual table
unique key	stored procedure
unique key constraint	input parameter
unique constraint	output parameter
index	control-of-flow language
foreign key	ADO.NET
foreign key table	ActiveX Data Objects .NET
primary key table	dataset
one-to-many relationship	data table
one-to-one relationship	.NET data provider
many-to-many relationship	data adapter
linking table	command
data type	connection
system data type	disconnected data architecture
null value	concurrency
default value	concurrency control
identity column	optimistic concurrency
check constraint	concurrency exception
SQL (Structured Query Language)	last in wins
SQL statement	data reader

Summary

- A *relational database* consists of *tables* that store data in *rows* and *columns*. A *primary key* is used to identify each row in a table.

- The tables in a relational database are related by *foreign keys* in one table that have the same values as primary keys in another table. Usually, these tables have a *one-to-many* relationship.

- Each column in a database table is defined with a *data type* that determines what can be stored in that column. In addition, the column definition specifies whether the column allows *null values* or has a *default value*.

- To work with the data in a database, you use *SQL (Structured Query Language)*. To access and update the data in a database, you use these *SQL statements*: SELECT, INSERT, UPDATE, and DELETE.

- The SELECT statement returns data from one or more tables in a *result set*. To return data from two or more tables, you *join* the tables based on the data in related fields. An *inner join* returns a result set that includes data only if the related fields match.

- A *view* consists of a SELECT statement that's stored with the database.

- A *stored procedure* consists of one or more SQL statements that have been compiled and stored with the database.

- Stored procedures and views can be used to restrict the data that a user is allowed to access. Stored procedures can also improve database performance because they're only compiled and optimized the first time they're executed.

- *ADO.NET (ActiveX Data Objects)* is the primary data access API for the .NET Framework. It provides the classes that are used by the *data provider* when you develop database applications with SQL data sources. The members in these classes can also be used directly by the programmer.

- ADO.NET uses a *disconnected data architecture*, which means that the database is disconnected from the web server as soon as each database operation is completed. This has some advantages, but it can also lead to *concurrency* problems. These occur when two or more users try to update the same row in a database table at the same time.

13

How to use
SQL data sources

In this chapter, you'll learn more about using the SqlDataSource control, which lets you access data from a relational database with little or no programming. Along the way, you'll also learn how to use the DataList control, which lets you create a list of the data that's retrieved by a data source.

How to create a SQL data source

In chapter 4, you learned the basics of using the SqlDataSource control to get data from a SQL Server database. Now, in the topics that follow, you'll learn more about how to use this control, which can be referred to as a *SQL data source*.

Just as in chapter 4, all of the applications in this chapter and in the rest of this section use the Microsoft *SQL Server 2014 Express LocalDB* database engine that comes with Visual Studio 2015. Because LocalDB is based on SQL Server 2014, the applications you develop with LocalDB are compatible with applications you develop with SQL Server 2014. The only difference is the connection string you use to connect to the database.

How the SqlDataSource control works

Figure 13-1 illustrates how the SqlDataSource control works and presents its basic properties. In the example in this figure, the data source is bound to a drop-down list that displays all the categories in the Categories table. You can see the SELECT statement that retrieves this data in the SelectCommand property of the SqlDataSource control.

The ConnectionString property of the data source provides the information that's needed to connect to the database that contains the Categories table. In this case, the property refers to a connection string that's stored in the application's Web.config file. You'll learn more about that later in this chapter.

A SqlDataSource that's bound to a drop-down list

The aspx code for the SqlDataSource control

```
<asp:SqlDataSource ID="SqlDataSource1" runat="server"
    ConnectionString="<%$ ConnectionStrings:HalloweenConnection %>"
    SelectCommand="SELECT [CategoryID], [LongName] FROM [Categories]
        ORDER BY [LongName]">
</asp:SqlDataSource>
```

Basic SqlDataSource control properties

Property	Description
ID	The ID for the SqlDataSource control.
Runat	Must specify "server."
ConnectionString	The connection string. In most cases, you should use a <%$ expression to specify the name of a connection string saved in the Web.config file (see figure 13-4).
ProviderName	The name of the .NET data provider used to access the database. The default is System.Data.SqlClient.
SelectCommand	The SQL SELECT statement executed by the data source to retrieve data.

Description

- A SqlDataSource control (or *SQL data source*) provides the information an application needs to connect to a database and retrieve the data needed by the application. It can also be used to insert, update, and delete data.

- A SQL data source can be bound to another control, such as a drop-down list or a DataList control. Then, the data that's retrieved by the data source is displayed in that control.

Figure 13-1   How the SqlDataSource control works

How to choose a data source type

In chapter 4, you learned how to create a SqlDataSource control by dragging the control from the Toolbox to a form and then using the Configure Data Source command in its smart tag menu to start the Configure Data Source wizard. When you use this technique, the data source type is automatically set to Database.

You can also create a SQL data source using the Choose Data Source command in the smart tag menu of a bindable control. The exact technique for doing that varies depending on the control you're binding.

To create a SQL data source for a drop-down list, for example, you select the Choose Data Source command to start the Data Source Configuration Wizard. Then, you can choose New Data Source from the drop-down list in the first dialog box that's displayed and click OK. The technique for creating a SQL data source from a DataList control is similar. The only difference is that the Choose Data Source command in the control's smart tag menu includes a drop-down list that lets you select New Data Source.

Regardless of the bindable control you use, the Data Source Configuration Wizard dialog box shown in figure 13-2 is displayed. From this dialog box, you can select the Database icon and click OK. That drops the data source control onto the form next to the bindable control and brings you to the Configure Data Source dialog box.

How to choose a data connection

The Configure Data Source dialog box, also shown in figure 13-2, lets you choose the data connection you want to use to connect to the database. From this dialog box, you can select a database file that's included in the App_Data folder of the project, or you can select an existing connection (one you've already created for this project or for another project). You can also click the New Connection button to display the Add Connection dialog box that's shown in the next figure.

To be sure you use the right connection, you can click the button with the plus sign on it to display the connection string. In this example, you can see that the connection string will attach the Halloween.mdf file at the specified location to the LocalDB engine. Here, DataDirectory refers to the project's App_Data folder.

Note that when you run an application that uses LocalDB, the database engine is started if it isn't already running, and the database is attached. In addition, the first time you try to connect to the LocalDB engine, an instance of the engine has to be created before it's started. Because of that, the connection may fail with a timeout message. If that happens, you should wait a few seconds while the creation finishes and then run the application again.

The dialog boxes for choosing a data source type and connection

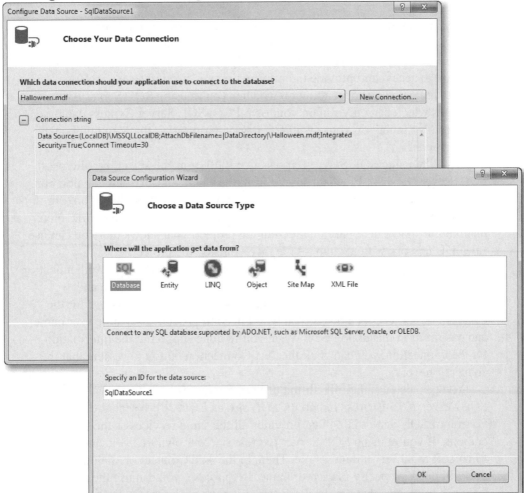

How to choose a data source type

- When you drag a SqlDataSource control onto the form, the data source type is automatically set to Database and the first page of the Configure Data Source wizard shown above is displayed.

- To use the Data Source Configuration Wizard to choose a data source type, use the Choose Data Source command in the smart tag menu of a bindable control, select the Database icon in the dialog box that's displayed, and click OK.

How to choose a connection

- If your project contains a database file or you've previously created a connection for the database you want to use, you can select the file or connection from the drop-down list. To see the connection string for that connection, click the + button below the list.

- To create a new connection, click the New Connection button.

Figure 13-2   How to choose a data source type and connection

How to create a connection

If you click the New Connection button from the Configure Data Source dialog box shown in figure 13-2, the Add Connection dialog box shown in figure 13-3 is displayed. This dialog box helps you identify the database that you want to access and provide the information you need to access it. How you do that, though, varies depending on whether you're using SQL Server Express LocalDB, which can only run on your own PC; a SQL Server Express database server that's running on your own PC; or a database server that's running on a remote server.

If you're using SQL Server Express LocalDB, you can select the Microsoft SQL Server Database File data source from the Change Data Source dialog box. Then, you just identify the database file in the Add Connection dialog box. In this figure, for example, the connection is for the Halloween database file. Note that the file shown here isn't included in the project. That shows that you can use LocalDB to work with a database file that's outside the project.

For the logon information, you should select the Use Windows Authentication option. Then, SQL Server Express LocalDB will use the login name and password that you use to log in to Windows as the name and password for the database server too. As a result, you won't need to provide a separate user name and password in this dialog box. When you're done supplying the information for the connection, you can click the Test Connection button to be sure that the connection works.

You can also use the full edition of SQL Server 2014 Express instead of SQL Server 2014 Express LocalDB. *SQL Server Express* is a scaled-back version of SQL Server 2014 that provides all the same services as the full editions. If you're using SQL Server Express on your own PC, you can use the Microsoft SQL Server data source. Then, in the Add Connection dialog box, you will need to specify the server name. In this case, you can use the localhost keyword to specify that the database server is running on the same PC as the application. This keyword should be followed by a backslash and the name of the database server: SqlExpress. Alternatively, you can select the server name from the drop-down list, which will include your computer name like this: ANNE-PC\SQLEXPRESS. If you will be porting your applications from one computer to another, though, it's best to use localhost.

After you enter the name of the server, you can enter or select the name of the database you want to connect to. You can also enter the required logon information. Just as you do when you use SQL Server Express LocalDB, though, you typically use Windows authentication with SQL Server Express.

If you need to connect to a SQL Server database that's running on a database server that's available through a network, you can use the Microsoft SQL Server data source just like you do for SQL Server Express. This works for SQL Server 2005, 2008, 2012, and 2014 databases. Then, you need to get the connection information from the network or database administrator. This information will include the name of the database server, logon information, and the name of the database. Once you establish a connection to the database, you can use that connection for all of the other applications that use that database.

The dialog boxes for defining a connection

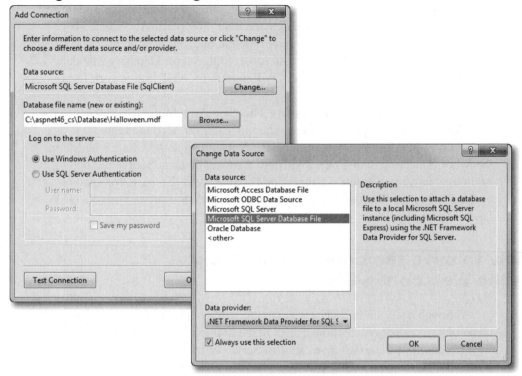

Description

- The first time you create a connection, the Change Data Source dialog box is displayed so you can select the data source and data provider you want to use. If you check the Always Use This Selection option, your selections will be used each time you create a connection. To change these options, click the Change button in the Add Connection dialog box.

- To create a connection for a database file that uses SQL Server Express LocalDB, use the Microsoft SQL Server Database File data source. Then, specify the name and path for the file and enter the information that's required to log on to the server in the Add Connection dialog box.

- To create a connection for a database on a local or remote SQL Server database server, use the Microsoft SQL Server data source. Then, specify the name of the server that contains the database, enter the information that's required to log on to the server, and specify the name of the database you want to connect to in the Add Connection dialog box.

- To be sure that the connection is configured properly, you can click the Test Connection button in the Add Connection dialog box.

Figure 13-3   How to create a connection

The first time you create a connection, Visual Studio automatically displays the Change Data Source dialog box so you can select the data source and data provider you want to use. In most cases, the data provider that's selected by default when you select a data source will be the one you want to use. If you select the Microsoft SQL Server or Microsoft SQL Server Database File data source, for example, the data provider will default to .NET Framework Data Provider for SQL Server.

You can also check the Always Use This Selection option if you want to use the selected data provider by default. Then, if you ever need to create a connection for a different type of database, you can click the Change button in the Add Connection dialog box to display the Change Data Source dialog box again. If you want to create a connection for an Access database, for example, you can select the Microsoft Access Database File data source to use the OLE DB data provider.

How to save the connection string in the Web.config file

Although you can hard-code connection strings into your programs, it's much better to store connection strings in the application's Web.config file. That way, if you move the database to another server or make some other change that affects the connection string, you won't have to change every instance of the connection string and then recompile the application. Instead, you can simply change the connection string in the Web.config file.

As figure 13-4 shows, ASP.NET can store connection strings in the Web. config file automatically if you check the Yes box in the next step of the Configure Data Source wizard. That way, you don't have to manually edit the Web.config file or write code to retrieve the connection string. When you select this check box, the connection string will automatically be saved with the name that you supply.

This figure also shows the entries made in the Web.config file when a connection string is saved. Here, the Web.config file has a connectionStrings element that contains an add element for each connection string. In the example, the connection string is named HalloweenConnectionString, and the connection string refers to a LocalDB database named Halloween that's stored in the project's App_Data folder.

Last, this figure shows how the aspx code that's generated for a data source can refer to the connection string by name. Here, the shaded portion of the example shows the value of the ConnectionString property. As you can see, it begins with the word ConnectionStrings followed by a colon and the name of the connection string you want to use. Note that this code is automatically generated by the Configure Data Source wizard, so you don't have to write it yourself.

The dialog box for saving the connection string in the Web.config file

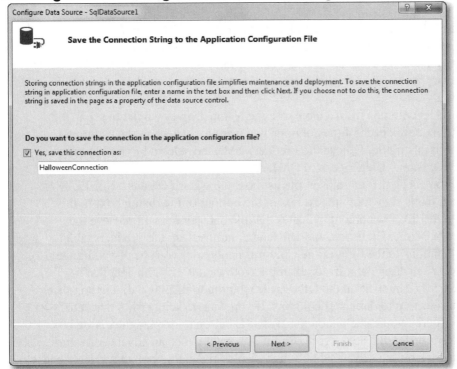

The ConnectionStrings section of the Web.config file

```
<connectionStrings>
    <add name="HalloweenConnection"
        connectionString="Data Source=(LocalDB)\MSSQLLocalDB;
        AttachDbFilename=|DataDirectory|\Halloween.mdf;
        Integrated Security=True" providerName="System.Data.SqlClient" />
</connectionStrings>
```

Aspx code that refers to a connection string in the Web.config file

```
<asp:SqlDataSource ID="SqlDataSource1" runat="server"
    ConnectionString="<%$ ConnectionStrings:HalloweenConnection %>"
    SelectCommand="SELECT [CategoryID], [LongName] FROM [Categories]
        ORDER BY [LongName]">
</asp:SqlDataSource>
```

Description

- ASP.NET applications can store connection strings in the Web.config file.

- If you save the connection string in the Web.config file, the ConnectionString property of the data source control will include a special code that retrieves the connection string from the Web.config file.

- If you don't save the connection string in the Web.config file, the ConnectionString property will specify the actual connection string.

- It's best to always save the connection string in the Web.config file. Then, if the location of the database changes, you can change the connection string in the Web. config file rather than in each data source that uses the connection.

Figure 13-4   How to save the connection string in the Web.config file

How to configure the SELECT statement

Figure 13-5 shows how to configure the SELECT statement for a data source as you proceed through the steps of the wizard. The easiest way to do that is to choose the columns for the query from a single table or view. You can also specify a custom SQL statement or stored procedure as shown later in this chapter.

To select columns from a table, use the Name drop-down list to select the table. Then, check each of the columns you want to retrieve in the Columns list box. In this figure, I chose the Products table and selected four columns: ProductID, Name, UnitPrice, and OnHand.

As you check the columns in the list box, the wizard creates a SELECT statement that's shown in the text box at the bottom of the dialog box. In this case, the SELECT statement indicates that the data source will retrieve the ProductID, Name, UnitPrice, and OnHand columns from the Products table.

The buttons to the right of the Columns list box let you specify additional options for selecting data. If, for example, you want to sort the data that's retrieved, you can click on the ORDER BY button to display a dialog box that lets you select up to three sort columns. If you want to select rows that satisfy certain criteria, you can click on the WHERE button to display the dialog box that's described in the next figure. And if you want to use an advanced feature, you can click on the Advanced button to display the dialog box that's described in figure 13-18.

When you finish specifying the data you want the data source to retrieve, click Next. This takes you to a dialog box that includes a Test Query button. If you click this button, the wizard immediately retrieves the data that you specified. You can then look over this data to make sure the query retrieves the data you expected. If it doesn't, you can click the Back button and adjust the query as needed.

The dialog box for defining the SELECT statement

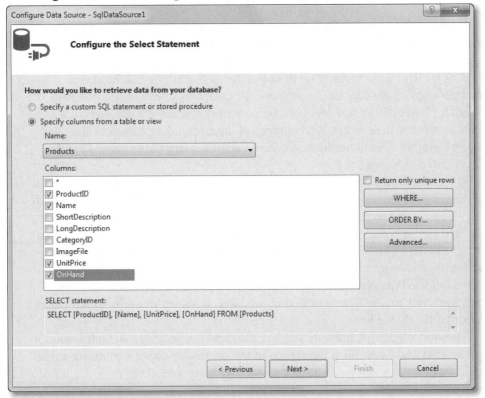

Description

- To configure the SELECT statement, you choose whether you want to use a custom SQL statement or specify the columns from a table or view in the database.

- If you choose to select the columns from a table or view, you can choose the table or view and columns you want retrieved. You can click the ORDER BY button to specify how the records should be sorted. And you can click the WHERE button to specify the selection criteria as shown in figure 13-6.

- If you choose to use custom SQL statements, the next dialog box lets you enter the SQL statements as shown in figure 13-8 or click the Query Builder button to build the query as shown in figure 13-9.

Figure 13-5   How to configure the SELECT statement

How to create a WHERE clause

If you click on the WHERE button shown in the first dialog box in figure 13-5, the Add WHERE Clause dialog box in figure 13-6 is displayed. It lets you create a WHERE clause and parameters for the SELECT statement.

A WHERE clause is made up of one or more conditions that limit the rows retrieved by the SELECT statement. To create these conditions, the Add WHERE Clause dialog box lets you compare the values in the columns of a database table with several different types of data, including a literal value, the value of another control on the page, the value of a query string passed via the page's URL, or a cookie.

For example, the SELECT statement shown in figure 13-5 will use a WHERE clause that compares the CategoryID column in the Products table with the category selected from a drop-down list named ddlCategory. To create this WHERE clause, you select CategoryID in the Column drop-down list, the equals operator in the Operator drop-down list, and Control in the Source drop-down list. Next, you select ddlCategory in the Control ID drop-down list. When you do, the SelectedValue property of the control is automatically selected. Then, when you click on the Add button, this condition is shown in the WHERE clause section of the dialog box.

The Add WHERE Clause dialog box also lets you specify a default value for a parameter. This is useful if the source of the parameter doesn't contain a value. You'll learn more about the different sources for a parameter next.

The Add WHERE Clause dialog box

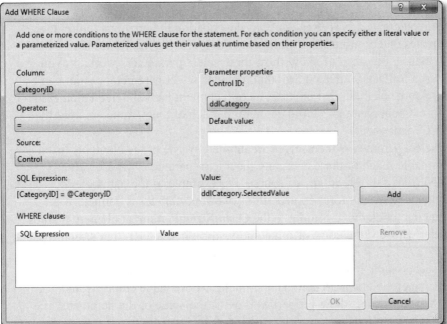

The WHERE clause section after a condition has been added

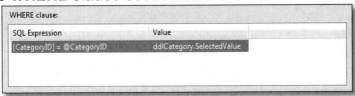

Description

- The Add WHERE Clause dialog box lets you specify a WHERE clause for the SELECT statement.

- The WHERE clause consists of one or more conditions that you construct by using the controls in this dialog box. To create a condition, you select the column you want to compare, the operator you want to use for the comparison, and the source of the data to use for the comparison. Then, you must click Add to add the condition to the list of WHERE clause conditions.

- The source of the data for the comparison can be a literal value, the value of another control on the form, a cookie, an HTML form field, a profile property, a query string in the URL for the page, a value stored in session state, or a route.

- You can also specify a default value for a parameter. Then, that value is used if the source doesn't contain a value.

Remember

- After you construct a condition, be sure to click the Add button to add the condition to the generated WHERE clause.

Figure 13-6   How to create a WHERE clause

How select parameters work

When you create a WHERE clause as described in the previous figure, the wizard creates one or more *select parameters* that provide the values used by the WHERE clause. Figure 13-7 shows how these select parameters work. As you can see, each SqlDataSource control that includes select parameters is defined by a SqlDataSource element that includes a child element named SelectParameters. Then, this element contains a child element for each of the parameters used by the SELECT statement.

The select parameters themselves are defined by one of the elements listed in the first table. Each of these elements specifies a parameter whose value is obtained from a different type of source. For example, if the parameter's value is obtained from a form control, this *control parameter* is defined by a ControlParameter element. Similarly, the QueryStringParameter element defines a parameter whose value comes from a query string in the URL that's used for the page.

The second table in this figure lists the properties used by the ControlParameter element to define a parameter whose value comes from a form control. As you can see, these properties provide the name of the parameter, the SQL data type used for the parameter, the ID of the form control that provides the value, the name of the property used to obtain the value, and, optionally, a default value for the parameter.

The code example in this figure shows the aspx code generated for a SqlDataSource control with a SELECT statement that includes the WHERE clause shown in the previous figure. Here, the SELECT statement uses one parameter named CategoryID. This parameter is defined by a ControlParameter element whose Name property is set to CategoryID. The SQL data type for this parameter is String, and the parameter's value is obtained from the SelectedValue property of the form control whose ID is ddlCategory.

Please note that the code in this example is generated by the Web Forms Designer when you configure the data source using the Configure Data Source wizard. As a result, you don't have to write this code yourself.

Elements used to define select parameters

Element	Description
SelectParameters	Contains a child element for each parameter used by the data source's SELECT statement.
Parameter	Defines a parameter with a constant value.
ControlParameter	Defines a parameter that gets its value from a control on the page.
QueryStringParameter	Defines a parameter that gets its value from a query string in the URL used to request the page.
FormParameter	Defines a parameter that gets its value from an HTML form field.
SessionParameter	Defines a parameter that gets its value from an item in session state.
ProfileParameter	Defines a parameter that gets its value from a profile property.
CookieParameter	Defines a parameter that gets its value from a cookie.
RouteParameter	Defines a parameter that gets its value from a route.

Properties of the ControlParameter element

Property	Description
Name	The parameter name.
Type	The SQL data type of the parameter.
ControlID	The ID of the web form control that supplies the value for the parameter.
PropertyName	The name of the property from the web form control that supplies the value for the parameter.
DefaultValue	The value that's used if a value isn't provided by the specified property of the web form control.

The aspx code for a SqlDataSource control that includes a select parameter

```
<asp:SqlDataSource ID="SqlDataSource2" runat="server"
    ConnectionString="<%$ ConnectionStrings:HalloweenConnection %>"
    SelectCommand="SELECT [ProductID], [Name], [UnitPrice], [OnHand]
        FROM [Products] WHERE ([CategoryID] = @CategoryID)
        ORDER BY [ProductID]">
    <SelectParameters>
        <asp:ControlParameter Name="CategoryID" Type="String"
            ControlID="ddlCategory" PropertyName="SelectedValue" />
    </SelectParameters>
</asp:SqlDataSource>
```

Description

- The SelectParameters element defines the *select parameters* that are used by the SELECT statement of a data source. The aspx code that defines these parameters is generated automatically when you use the Add WHERE Clause dialog box to create parameters.

- A *control parameter* is a parameter whose value is obtained from another control on a web form, such as the value selected by a drop-down list. Control parameters are defined by the ControlParameter element.

- Once you understand how to use control parameters, you shouldn't have any trouble learning how to use the other types of parameters on your own.

Figure 13-7   How select parameters work

How to use custom statements and stored procedures

Earlier in this chapter, you learned how to configure the SELECT statement for a SQL data source by selecting columns from a table. If you need to code a SELECT statement that's more complex than what you can create using this technique, you can define your own custom statements. To do that, you can enter the statements directly, or you can use the Query Builder. You can also use stored procedures that have been defined within the database.

How to enter custom statements

If you select the first option from the dialog box shown in figure 13-5 and then click the Next button, the dialog box shown in figure 13-8 is displayed. As you can see, this dialog box includes tabs that let you enter SELECT, UPDATE, INSERT, and DELETE statements for the data source. In this case, the SELECT statement is the same as the one that was generated by the wizard as shown earlier in this chapter. Because of that, you might think that you wouldn't need to enter a custom SELECT statement. Keep in mind, though, that when you create a SELECT statement by selecting columns from a table, you have no control over the UPDATE, INSERT, and DELETE statements that are generated. So if you want to use statements other than those that are generated automatically, you can do that by entering custom statements.

How to select stored procedures

If the stored procedures you want to use to select, insert, update, and delete data have already been defined in the database, you can easily use them in a SQL data source. To do that, you select the Stored Procedure option from the appropriate tab of the dialog box shown in figure 13-8. Then, you select the stored procedure you want to use for the operation from the drop-down list that becomes available.

The dialog box for entering a custom SELECT statement

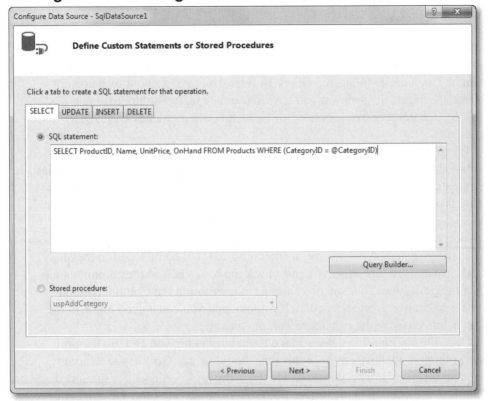

Description

- To use custom statements with a SQL data source, select the SQL Statement option and then enter the statement into the text box. You can enter SELECT, UPDATE, INSERT, and DELETE statements by selecting the appropriate tab.

- You can also use the Query Builder to generate custom statements, as shown in the next figure.

- To use stored procedures with a SQL data source, select the Stored Procedure option and then select the stored procedure you want to use from the drop-down list that's displayed.

- When you use custom statements, Visual Studio doesn't generate UPDATE, INSERT, and DELETE statements from the SELECT statement you enter. Because of that, you have to enter each of these statements yourself or use the Query Builder to generate them.

Figure 13-8   How to enter custom statements or select stored procedures

How to create a SELECT statement with the Query Builder

The *Query Builder* makes it easy to generate SQL statements without even knowing the proper syntax for them. Even if you do know the proper syntax, it can be much easier to use the Query Builder than to enter your own custom statements. Figure 13-9 shows you how to use the Query Builder to create a SELECT statement. You can use similar techniques to create other SQL statements.

When the Query Builder window opens, the Add Table dialog box is displayed. This dialog box, which isn't shown in this figure, lists all of the tables and views in the database that the data source is connected to. You can use this dialog box to add one or more tables to the *diagram pane* of the Query Builder window so you can use them in your query. In this figure, for example, the Products table has been added to the diagram pane.

In the *grid pane*, you can see the columns that will be included in the query. To add columns to this pane, you just check the boxes before the column names in the diagram pane. You can also enter an expression in the Column column of the grid pane to create a calculated column, and you can enter a name in the Alias column to give the calculated column a name.

Once the columns have been added to the grid pane, you can use the Sort Type column to identify any columns that should be used to sort the returned rows and the Sort Order column to give the order of precedence for the sort if more than one column is identified. The Query Builder uses these specifications to build the ORDER BY clause for the SELECT statement.

You can use the Filter column to establish the criteria to be used to select the rows that will be retrieved by the query. For the query in this figure, a parameter named @CategoryID is specified for the CategoryID column. As a result, only the products whose CategoryID column matches the value of the @CategoryID parameter will be retrieved.

Notice in this figure that the Output column for the CategoryID column in the grid pane isn't selected. That means that this column won't be included in the query output. However, it's included in the grid pane so it can be used to specify the filter criteria.

The Query Builder dialog box

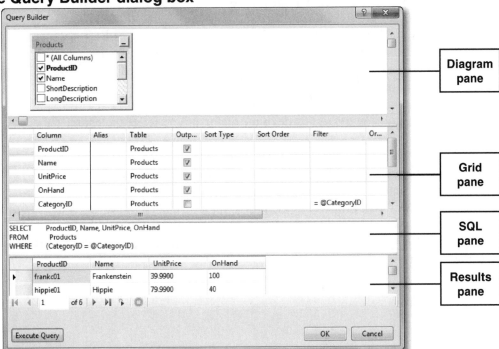

Description

- The *Query Builder* is displayed if you choose to enter a custom SQL statement, and then click the Query Builder button in the dialog box that follows.

- The Query Builder lets you build a SELECT statement by choosing columns from one or more tables and views and specifying the sort order and filter criteria for each column.

- When you first start the Query Builder, a dialog box is displayed that lets you select the database tables you want to include in the query. Each table you select is displayed in the *diagram pane* at the top of the Query Builder window.

- If you add two related tables to the diagram pane, the Query Builder automatically joins the two tables by including a Join phrase in the From clause.

- To include a column from a table, use the check box that appears next to the column in the diagram pane. This adds the column to the *grid pane*. Then, you can specify any sorting or filtering requirements for the column.

- You can use a parameter in an expression in the Filter column to create a parameterized query. If you use one or more parameters in the query, the Data Source Configuration Wizard lets you specify the source of each parameter value, as described in figure 13-10.

- As you select columns and specify sort and selection criteria, the Query Builder builds the SELECT statement and displays it in the *SQL pane*.

- To display the results of the query in the *results pane*, click the Execute Query button. If the query includes parameters, you will be asked to enter the value of each parameter.

Figure 13-9   How to create a SELECT statement with the Query Builder

How to define the parameters

If you specify one or more parameters when you create a SELECT statement with the Query Builder, the next dialog box lets you define those parameters as shown in figure 13-10. Here, the list box on the left side of the dialog box lists each of the parameters you created in the Query Builder. To define the source for one of these parameters, you select the parameter in this list box. Then, you can use the controls on the right side of the dialog box to select the parameter's source.

In this example, the source of the CategoryID parameter is set to the SelectedValue property of the control named ddlCategory. When I selected the ddlCategory control, the SelectedValue property was selected by default. If you want to use a different property as the source for a parameter, however, you can click the Show Advanced Properties link to display a list of the parameter properties. Then, you can set the PropertyName property to the control property you want to use.

The dialog box for defining parameters

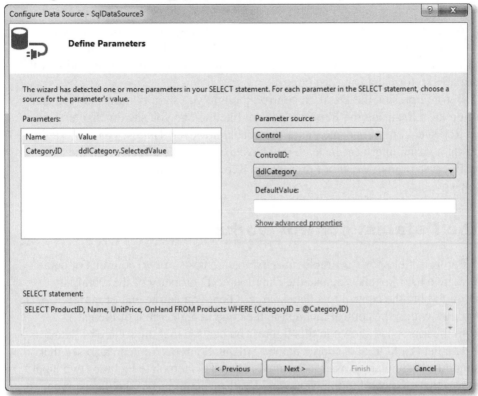

Parameter sources

Source	Description
Control	The parameter's value comes from a control on the page.
QueryString	The parameter's value comes from a query string in the URL used to request the page.
Form	The parameter's value comes from an HTML form field.
Session	The parameter's value comes from an item in session state.
Profile	The parameter's value comes from a profile property.
Cookie	The parameter's value comes from a cookie.
Route	The parameter's value comes from a route.

Description

- If you specify one or more parameters when you create a custom SELECT statement, the next dialog box lets you define those parameters.
- To define a parameter, you specify the source of the value for each parameter. You can also specify a default value for the parameter.

Figure 13-10   How to define the parameters

How to use the DataList control

A DataList control displays items from a repeating data source such as a data table. In the topics that follow, you'll learn how the DataList control works, you'll learn how to create the templates that define a DataList control, and you'll learn how to format a DataList control.

Before I present the DataList control, though, you should know that you can also create a list using the Repeater control like the one you saw in chapter 11. The Repeater control has one major drawback, however. That is, you can't define it using a visual interface. Instead, you have to enter code directly into the aspx file. Because of that, we won't present the Repeater control in this section of the book.

How the DataList control works

Figure 13-11 shows a simple *data list* that consists of two columns of data. To create a list like this, you use the DataSourceID property of the DataList control to bind the control to a data source. Then, you define one or more *templates* within the control that define the content and format of the list.

In the aspx code shown in this figure, you can see that the source of data for the data list is a SQL data source named SqlDataSource2. You can also see that a single Item template is used to create this list. This template includes two label controls that are bound to the Name and UnitPrice columns of the data source. You'll learn about the expressions you use to accomplish this binding later in this chapter. Also, in chapter 18 you'll learn how to make this kind of binding easier with model binding.

A simple list displayed by a DataList control

```
Austin Powers $79.99
Frankenstein $39.99
Hippie $79.99
JarJar $59.99
Martian $69.99
Superman $39.99
```

The aspx code for the DataList control

```
<asp:DataList ID="DataList1" runat="server" DataSourceID="SqlDataSource2">
    <ItemTemplate>
        <asp:Label ID="lblName" runat="server"
            Text='<%# Eval("Name") %>' />
        <asp:Label ID="lblUnitPrice" runat="server"
            Text='<%# Eval("UnitPrice", "{0:C}") %>' />
    </ItemTemplate>
</asp:DataList>
```

Basic properties of the DataList control

Property	Description
ID	The ID for the DataList control.
Runat	Must specify "server."
DataSourceID	The ID of the data source to bind the data list to.

Description

- A *data list* displays a list of items from the data source that it's bound to. To bind a data list to a data source, use the Choose Data Source command in the control's smart tag menu.

- To define the information to be displayed in a data list, you create one or more *templates*. Visual Studio provides a designer interface you can use to create the templates as shown in the next figure.

- To display the data from a column in the data source in a data list, you add a control to a template and then bind that control. See figure 13-15 for more information.

- You can use a DataList control for edit operations as well as display operations. However, you're more likely to use the GridView, DetailsView, FormView, and ListView controls for edit operations.

Figure 13-11   How the DataList control works

How to define the templates for a data list

Figure 13-12 shows you how to define the templates for a data list. The table in this figure lists the templates you're most likely to use. Although you can also create templates that let the user select and edit items in the list, you're not likely to use a DataList control for these functions. Instead, you'll use the GridView, DetailsView, FormView, or ListView controls that are described in the next three chapters.

The only template that's required for a data list is the Item template, which defines how each item in the data source is displayed. Depending on the requirements of your application, though, you may need to use one or more of the other templates as well. For example, you'll typically use a Header template to create headings that are displayed in the first row of the data list.

To define the templates for a data list, you work in *template-editing mode*. At the top of this figure, for example, you can see the Item template for a list that includes four columns. This template is displayed by default when you enter template-editing mode. To display a different template, you can use the Display drop-down list in the smart tag menu for the control. You can also display a group of related templates by selecting the group name from this list. For example, you can display both the Header and Footer templates by selecting the Header and Footer Templates item.

If a data list consists of two or more columns, you can place the text and controls in each template within a table. That way, you can set the width of each column in the data list by setting the widths of the columns in the table. In addition, if you add two or more templates to a data list, you can align the columns in the templates by setting the widths of the corresponding table columns to the same values. In this illustration, for example, I set the widths of the corresponding columns in the Item template and the Header template to the same values.

Note that if you're using Bootstrap, you don't have to place the contents of each template in a table to set the column widths. Instead, you can assign a Bootstrap CSS column class to the text or control in each column. You'll see how that works later in this chapter.

Before I go on, you should realize that you use templates to define the content of a data list and not its appearance. For example, you use the AlternatingItem template to display different content for every other row in a data list, not to shade or highlight every other row. To format a data list, you use styles as shown in the next figure.

The Item template in template-editing mode

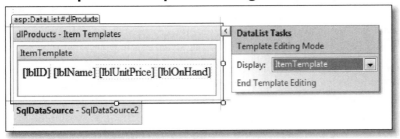

A Header template

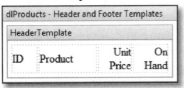

Common template elements for a data list

Element	Description
HeaderTemplate	Displayed before the first item in the data source.
FooterTemplate	Displayed after the last item in the data source.
ItemTemplate	Displayed for each item in the data source.
AlternatingItemTemplate	Displayed for alternating items in the data source.
SeparatorTemplate	Displayed between items.

Description

- The templates you define for a data list specify what content to display and what controls to use to display it. At the least, you must create an Item template that defines the items from the data source that you want to display.

- To create a template, choose Edit Templates from the smart tag menu for the control to display the control in *template-editing mode*. Then, select the template or group of templates you want to edit from the smart tag menu.

- To add text to a template, click in the template and begin typing. To add a control to a template, drag the control from the Toolbox onto the template, then use the Properties window or the control's smart tag menu to set its properties. When you're finished, choose End Template Editing from the smart tag menu.

- To line up the text and controls in two or more templates, place them in tables within the templates and set the column widths to the same values. Or, if you're using Bootstrap, assign a column class to the text or control in each column.

- When you set the data source for a DataList control, Visual Studio creates a default Item template. This template includes a text box for each column in the data source preceded by text that identifies the column.

Figure 13-12   How to define the templates for a data list

How to format a data list

To format a data list, you can use one of the techniques presented in figure 13-13. If you're using Bootstrap, the best way to format a data list is to use the Bootstrap CSS classes for working with tables. For example, you can use the table and table-striped classes to create a table whose rows have alternating colors. This works because a data list is rendered to a table.

To refresh your memory on some of the Bootstrap classes that are available for working with tables, you can refer back to figure 10-4 in chapter 10. Then, later in this chapter, you'll see how Bootstrap table classes are used with a data list when you review the aspx code for the Product List application.

You can also use the other techniques presented in this figure to format a data list. You can use these techniques instead of Bootstrap classes or in addition to Bootstrap classes. The easiest way to format a data list is to use the Auto Format dialog box. This dialog box lets you select one of 17 predefined schemes that use different combinations of colors and borders for the items in the data list.

Another way to format a data list is to use the Format page of the Properties dialog box shown in this figure. This dialog box lets you set the colors, fonts, alignment, and other formatting options for the data list and each of its templates. Note that you can use this dialog box to customize an Auto Format scheme or to design your own scheme.

The Auto Format and Properties dialog boxes provide convenient ways to format a data list. However, you can also apply formatting directly from the Properties window. To do that, you use the properties in the Appearance and Style sections of this window, which are available when you display the properties by category. The properties in the Appearance section apply to the data list as a whole, and the properties in the Style section apply to the templates that make up the data list. To set the properties for the Item template, for example, you can expand the ItemStyle group, and to set the properties for the Header template, you can expand the HeaderStyle group.

This figure also presents the five style elements you're most likely to use with a data list. When you format the templates in a data list by applying a scheme, by using the Properties dialog box, or by using the Properties window, the appropriate style elements are generated for you. Of course, you can also format a data list by entering style elements directly into the aspx code. That's not usually necessary, however.

The Format page of the Properties dialog box

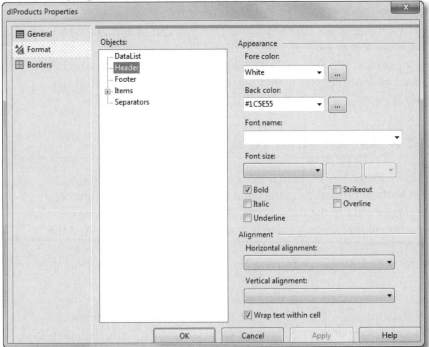

Common style elements for a data list

Element	Description
HeaderStyle	The style used for the header.
FooterStyle	The style used for the footer.
ItemStyle	The style used for each item in the data source.
AlternatingItemStyle	The style used for alternating items in the data source.
SeparatorStyle	The style for the separator.

The asp tag for a Header style

```
<HeaderStyle BackColor="#1C5E55" ForeColor="White" />
```

Description

- Because a data list is rendered as a table, you can use the Bootstrap CSS classes for working with tables to format a data list.

- You can also format a data list by applying a predefined scheme, by using the Properties dialog box, by using the Properties window, or by editing the aspx code.

- To apply a scheme, choose Auto Format from the control's smart tag menu and then select the scheme you want to apply.

- To use the Properties dialog box, choose Property Builder from the control's smart tag menu and then set the properties for the data list and its templates.

- To use the Properties window to format a template, expand the style property for that template and then set its properties.

Figure 13-13   How to format a data list

How to use data binding

Once you've configured a data source control, you can bind it to a web form control to automatically display the data retrieved by the data source on the page. In the following topics, you'll learn how to bind a list control to a data source and how to bind controls defined within the templates of another control like a DataList control.

How to bind a list control to a data source

Figure 13-14 shows how to bind a list control to a data source. To do that, you use the three properties in the table in this figure. The DataSourceID property provides the ID of the data source. The DataTextField property provides the name of the data source field that's displayed in the list. And the DataValueField property provides the name of the data source field that is returned by the SelectedValue property when the user selects an item from the list.

You can set these properties manually by using the Properties window or by editing the aspx code. Or, you can use the Data Source Configuration Wizard shown at the top of this figure to set these properties. To do that, display the smart tag menu for the list and select Choose Data Source. Then, use the wizard's controls to set the data source, display field, and value field.

The code example in this figure shows a drop-down list that's bound to a data source named SqlDataSource1. The field named LongName provides the values that are displayed in the drop-down list, and the field named CategoryID supplies the value that's returned by the SelectedValue property when the user selects an item from the list.

The Data Source Configuration Wizard for binding a drop-down list

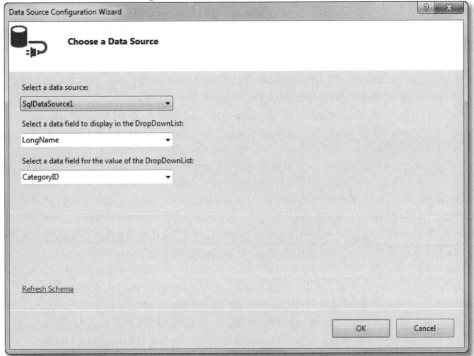

List control properties for data binding

Property	Description
DataSourceID	The ID of the data source to bind the list to.
DataTextField	The name of the data source field that should be displayed in the list.
DataValueField	The name of the data source field whose value should be returned by the SelectedValue property of the list.

The aspx code for a drop-down list that's bound to a SQL data source

```
<asp:DropDownList ID="ddlCategory" runat="server"
    AutoPostBack="True" DataSourceID="SqlDataSource1"
    DataTextField="LongName" DataValueField="CategoryID">
</asp:DropDownList>
```

Description

- You can bind any of the controls that inherit the ListControl class to a data source. That includes the list box control, the drop-down list control, the check box list control, and the radio button list control.
- You can use the Data Source Configuration Wizard to select the data source for a list control, the data field to display in the list, and the data value to return for the selected item.
- You can also use the DataTextFormatString property of a list control to specify a format string you want to apply to the text that's displayed in the control.

Figure 13-14   How to bind a list control to a data source

How to bind the controls in a template

Figure 13-15 shows how you can bind the controls in a template to columns of a data source. This technique can be used with any control that uses templates and specifies a data source. That includes the data controls that you'll learn about in the next three chapters. In the application in the next two figures, you'll see how these binding techniques are used for a DataList control.

To bind a control to a column of the data source, you use the DataBindings dialog box. From this dialog box, you can select the Field Binding option and then select the field you want to bind to from the first drop-down list. If you want to format the bound data, you can also select a format from the second drop-down list.

By default, you bind the Text property of a control so the bound data is displayed in the control. However, you may occasionally want to bind to another property. For example, you might want to bind the Enabled or Visible property of a control to a Boolean field. To do that, you simply select the property you want to bind from the Bindable Properties list.

As you make selections in the DataBindings dialog box, Visual Studio generates an Eval method that contains the data binding expression that's used to bind the control. You can see the syntax of the Eval method in this figure along with two examples. If you compare these examples with the binding options in the DataBindings dialog box, you shouldn't have any trouble understanding how this method works.

Although the drop-down lists in the DataBindings dialog box make it easy to create a data binding expression, you can also create your own custom binding expressions. To do that, you just select the Custom Binding option and then enter the binding expression in the Code Expression text box. You might want to do that, for example, if you need to apply a custom format to the data. Or, you might want to code a custom expression that uses the Bind method instead of the Eval method.

Unlike the Eval method, which only provides for displaying bound data, the Bind method provides for both displaying and updating data. This method implements a feature called *two-way binding*. You'll see an application that uses two-way binding in the next chapter.

The DataBindings dialog box for binding a control

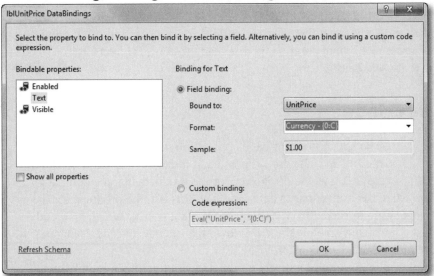

The syntax of the Eval and Bind methods

```
<%# {Eval|Bind}(NameString [, FormatString]) %>
```

Code examples

```
<%# Eval("Name") %>
<%# Eval("UnitPrice", "{0:C}") %>
<%# Bind("UnitPrice", "{0:C}") %>
```

Description

- To bind a control in a template, select the Edit DataBindings command from the smart tag menu for the control to display the DataBindings dialog box. Then, select the property you want to bind to (usually Text), select the Field Binding option, and select the field you want to bind to from the Bound To drop-down list.

- If you want to apply a format to the bound data, select a format from the Format drop-down list.

- As you specify the binding for a control, Visual Studio generates a data binding expression that uses the Eval method. You can see this method in the Code Expression box at the bottom of the DataBindings dialog box.

- You can also create a custom binding expression by selecting the Custom Binding option and then entering the expression in the Code Expression text box.

- The Eval method provides only for displaying data from a data source in a control. In contrast, the Bind method provides for *two-way binding*, which means that it can be used to display as well as update data from a data source.

Note

- If the Field Binding option isn't enabled, you can click the Refresh Schema link to enable it.

Figure 13-15   How to bind the controls in a template

A Product List application

Now that you understand the basic techniques for creating and working with SQL data sources and bound controls, you're ready to see a Product List application that uses them.

The user interface

Figure 13-16 shows a simple one-page application that demonstrates the use of two SQL data sources. The drop-down list at the top of the page is bound to a SQL data source that gets the categories for the products that the company offers. Then, when the user selects a category from this list, the products for the selected category are retrieved from a second SQL data source, which is bound to a DataList control that's below the drop-down list. As a result, the products are displayed in the DataList control.

Since this application relies entirely on the data binding that's established in the Web Forms Designer, the code-behind file for this application contains no C# code. Although this is a simple application, even complicated applications that insert, update, and delete database data can often be written with little or no code.

That's not to say that most ASP.NET database applications are code-free. In the next three chapters, for example, you'll see applications that require database handling code. In particular, these applications require code to detect database errors and concurrency violations and display appropriate error messages. Also, as you'll learn in chapter 17, you can use object data sources to build 3-layer applications that require extensive amounts of database handling code.

The Product List application displayed in a web browser

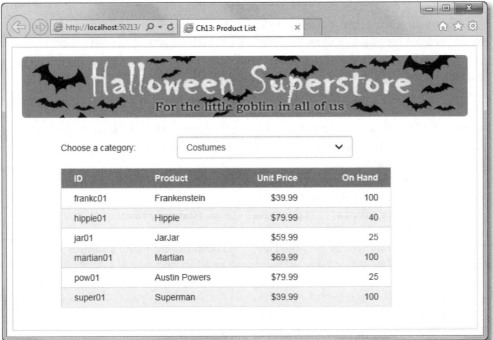

Description

- The Product List application uses two SqlDataSource controls to get category and product data from a SQL Server database and display it in two bound controls.

- The drop-down list near the top of the form displays the product categories. This control is bound to the first data source control.

- The DataList control, which is bound to the second data source control, displays the data for the products that are in the category that's selected in the drop-down list.

- This application requires no C# code in the code-behind file.

Figure 13-16   The Product List application

The aspx file

Figure 13-17 presents the aspx code for the Product List application. To make it easier for you to follow this code, I've shaded parts of the data source controls and the controls they're bound to. Because this application relies entirely on the data binding declared in this aspx file, it doesn't require any C# code.

The first control is the drop-down list that's bound to the first SqlDataSource control, SqlDataSource1. Here, the AutoPostBack property for the drop-down list is set to True so the page is automatically posted back to the server when the user selects a category.

The second control is the first SqlDataSource control, which uses this SELECT statement to get the required data:

```
SELECT [CategoryID], [LongName] FROM [Categories]
    ORDER BY [LongName]
```

As a result, this data source gets the CategoryID and LongName columns for each row in the Categories table and sorts the result based on the LongName column. Then, these columns are used by the drop-down list that's bound to this data source.

The third control is a DataList control that's bound to the second SqlDataSource control, SqlDataSource2. Because this application uses Bootstrap, it can use the Bootstrap CSS classes for tables to format the DataList control. (Remember that a DataList control is rendered as a table.) In this case, the CssClass property uses the table class to provide the default styling for the table, it uses the table-bordered class to add a border around the table and between cells, it uses the table-striped class to add alternating colors to the table rows, and it uses the table-condensed class to make the table more compact.

The Header template for this control includes four span elements that contain the headings for the table. Each span element includes a class attribute that specifies the width of the column using a Bootstrap column class. Then, the Item template defines the labels that display the data in the rows that are retrieved by the data source. As you can see, the Text properties of these labels are bound to a column in the data source. Also notice that the labels in the Item template use the same Bootstrap column classes as the span elements in the Header template. Because of that, the columns in the two templates are aligned. In addition, the last two columns in each template use the Bootstrap text-right class so the numeric data and the corresponding headings are right aligned.

The last element for the DataList control defines the style for the header. Like the HeaderStyle element you saw in figure 13-13, this element formats the header with a white font on a dark green background. In this case, though, the styles are stored in a class in the style sheet.

The Default.aspx file   **Page 1**

```
<body>
<div class="container">
    <header class="jumbotron"><%-- image set in site.css --%></header>
    <main>
    <form id="form1" runat="server" class="form-horizontal">
        <div class="form-group">
            <label id="lblCategory" for="ddlCategory"
                class="col-xs-4 col-sm-offset-1 col-sm-3 control-label">
                Choose a category:</label>
            <div class="col-xs-8 col-sm-5">
                <asp:DropDownList ID="ddlCategory" runat="server"
                    AutoPostBack="true" DataSourceID="SqlDataSource1"
                    DataTextField="LongName" DataValueField="CategoryID"
                    CssClass="form-control">
                </asp:DropDownList>
                <asp:SqlDataSource ID="SqlDataSource1" runat="server"
                    ConnectionString='<%$ ConnectionStrings:HalloweenConnection %>'
                    SelectCommand="SELECT [CategoryID], [LongName]
                        FROM [Categories] ORDER BY [LongName]">
                </asp:SqlDataSource>
            </div>
        </div>

        <div class="form-group">
            <div class="col-xs-12 col-sm-offset-1 col-sm-9">
                <asp:DataList ID="dlProducts" runat="server"
                    DataKeyField="ProductID" DataSourceID="SqlDataSource2"
                    CssClass="table table-bordered table-striped
                        table-condensed">
                    <HeaderTemplate>
                        <span class="col-xs-3">ID</span>
                        <span class="col-xs-3">Product</span>
                        <span class="col-xs-3 text-right">Unit Price</span>
                        <span class="col-xs-3 text-right">On Hand</span>
                    </HeaderTemplate>
                    <ItemTemplate>
                        <asp:Label ID="lblID" runat="server"
                            Text='<%# Eval("ProductID") %>'
                            CssClass="col-xs-3" />
                        <asp:Label ID="lblName" runat="server"
                            Text='<%# Eval("Name") %>' CssClass="col-xs-3" />
                        <asp:Label ID="lblUnitPrice" runat="server"
                            Text='<%# Eval("UnitPrice", "{0:C}") %>'
                            CssClass="col-xs-3 text-right" />
                        <asp:Label ID="lblOnHand" runat="server"
                            Text='<%# Eval("OnHand") %>'
                            CssClass="col-xs-3 text-right" />
                    </ItemTemplate>
                    <HeaderStyle CssClass="bg-halloween" />
                </asp:DataList>
```

Figure 13-17   The aspx file for the Product List application (part 1 of 2)

On page 2 of this listing, you can see the fourth control, which is the SqlDataSource that's used by the DataList control. It uses this SELECT statement:

```
SELECT [ProductID], [Name], [UnitPrice], [OnHand]
    FROM [Products]
    WHERE ([CategoryID] = @CategoryID)
    ORDER BY [ProductID]
```

Here, the WHERE clause specifies that only those rows whose CategoryID column equals the value of the CategoryID parameter should be retrieved. To make this work, the ControlParameter element specifies that the value of the CategoryID parameter is obtained from the SelectedValue property of the ddlCategory control.

The Default.aspx file   Page 2

```
<asp:SqlDataSource ID="SqlDataSource2" runat="server"
ConnectionString="<%$ ConnectionStrings:HalloweenConnection %>"
SelectCommand="SELECT [ProductID], [Name], [UnitPrice],
    [OnHand] FROM [Products]
    WHERE ([CategoryID] = @CategoryID)
    ORDER BY [ProductID]">
    <SelectParameters>
        <asp:ControlParameter ControlID="ddlCategory"
            Name="CategoryID" PropertyName="SelectedValue"
            Type="String" />
    </SelectParameters>
</asp:SqlDataSource>
    </div>
    </div>
    </form>
    </main>
</div>
</body>
```

Figure 13-17   The aspx file for the Product List application (part 2 of 2)

How to use the advanced features of a SQL data source

The SqlDataSource control provides several advanced features that you may want to use in your applications. These features are explained in the topics that follow.

How to create a data source that can update the database

Much like ADO.NET data adapters, a SQL data source can include INSERT, UPDATE, and DELETE statements that let you automatically update the underlying database based on changes made by the user to bound data controls. To automatically generate these statements, you can check the first box in the dialog box shown in figure 13-18, which is displayed when you click on the Advanced button in the dialog box shown in figure 13-5. You can also check the box for optimistic concurrency, which enhances the generated statements so they check whether updated or deleted rows have changed since the data source retrieved the original data.

Note that for this to work, the primary key column of the table you're updating must be included in the SELECT statement. That's because this column is used to identify a row that's being updated or deleted. So if the Generate option in the Advanced SQL Generation Options dialog box isn't enabled, it's probably because you haven't selected the primary key column.

The code in this figure shows the aspx elements that are generated when you request INSERT, UPDATE, and DELETE statements without using optimistic concurrency. Here, the InsertCommand, UpdateCommand, and DeleteCommand properties provide the statements, and the InsertParameters, UpdateParameters, and DeleteParameters child elements define the parameters used by these statements. Because optimistic concurrency isn't used, these statements will update the database whether or not the data has changed since it was originally retrieved, which could lead to corrupt data.

If you check the Use Optimistic Concurrency check box, though, the update and delete commands will include WHERE clauses that compare the value of each column with the value originally retrieved. Because these values are passed as parameters, the generated aspx code will include additional elements that define these parameters. The SqlDataSource control will also include two additional properties. The first one indicates that optimistic concurrency should be used, and the second one indicates the format that should be used for the names of the parameters that will hold the original column values. Then, if the value of any column has changed since it was originally retrieved, the update or delete operation will be refused, and your application needs to provide code that handles that situation. You'll see how that works in chapter 14.

The Advanced SQL Generation Options dialog box

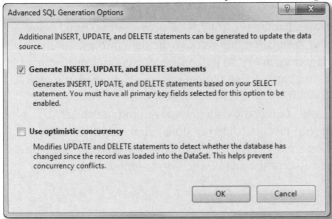

The aspx code for a SqlDataSource control that uses action queries

```
<asp:SqlDataSource ID="SqlDataSource1" runat="server"
    ConnectionString="<%$ ConnectionStrings:HalloweenConnection %>"
    SelectCommand="SELECT [CategoryID], [ShortName], [LongName]
                    FROM [Categories]"
    InsertCommand="INSERT INTO [Categories] ([CategoryID], [ShortName],
                    [LongName]) VALUES (@CategoryID, @ShortName, @LongName)"
    UpdateCommand="UPDATE [Categories] SET [ShortName] = @ShortName,
                    [LongName] = @LongName WHERE [CategoryID] = @CategoryID"
    DeleteCommand="DELETE FROM [Categories]
                    WHERE [CategoryID] = @CategoryID">
    <DeleteParameters>
        <asp:Parameter Name="CategoryID" Type="String" />
    </DeleteParameters>
    <UpdateParameters>
        <asp:Parameter Name="ShortName" Type="String" />
        <asp:Parameter Name="LongName" Type="String" />
        <asp:Parameter Name="CategoryID" Type="String" />
    </UpdateParameters>
    <InsertParameters>
        <asp:Parameter Name="CategoryID" Type="String" />
        <asp:Parameter Name="ShortName" Type="String" />
        <asp:Parameter Name="LongName" Type="String" />
    </InsertParameters>
</asp:SqlDataSource>
```

Description

- To automatically generate INSERT, UPDATE, and DELETE statements for a data source, check the first box in the dialog box that you get by clicking on the Advanced button in the first dialog box in figure 13-5. To generate enhanced versions of the UPDATE and DELETE statements that use optimistic concurrency, check the second box too.

- The InsertCommand, UpdateCommand, and DeleteCommand properties in the aspx code define the INSERT, UPDATE, and DELETE statements used by a data source. If these statements require parameters, the InsertParameters, UpdateParameters, and DeleteParameters elements specify those parameters.

Figure 13-18   How to create a SQL data source that can update the database

How to change the data source mode

As you may remember from chapter 12, ADO.NET provides two basic ways to retrieve data from a database. You can either retrieve the data into a dataset, which retains a copy of the data in memory so it can be accessed multiple times and updated if necessary. Or, you can retrieve the data using a data reader, which lets you retrieve the data in forward-only, read-only fashion.

When you create a SQL data source, the data is retrieved into a dataset by default. If the data will be read just once and not updated, though, you can usually improve the application's performance by retrieving the data using a data reader. To do that, just set the value of the DataSourceMode property shown in figure 13-19 to DataReader.

How to use caching

ASP.NET's caching feature lets you save the data retrieved by a data source in cache memory on the server. That way, the next time the data needs to be retrieved, the cached data is used instead of getting it from the database again. Since this reduces database access, it often improves an application's overall performance.

To cache the data that's retrieved by a SQL data source, you use the properties of the data source that are presented in figure 13-19. To enable caching, you simply set the EnableCaching property to True. Then, you can use the CacheDuration property to specify how long data should be kept in the cache. If, for example, the cached data rarely changes, you can set a long cache duration value such as 30 minutes or more. If the data changes more frequently, you can set a shorter cache duration value.

But what if the data in the database changes before the duration expires? In that case, the user will view data that is out of date. Sometimes, that's okay so you don't have to worry about it. Otherwise, you can minimize the chance of this happening by setting a shorter duration time.

The DataSourceMode property

Property	Description
DataSourceMode	DataSet or DataReader. The default is DataSet, but you can specify DataReader if the data source is read-only.

A SqlDataSource control that uses a data reader

```
<asp:SqlDataSource ID="SqlDataSource1" runat="server"
    ConnectionString="<%$ ConnectionStrings:HalloweenConnection %>"
    DataSourceMode="DataReader"
    SelectCommand="SELECT [CategoryID], [LongName]
        FROM [Categories]
        ORDER BY [LongName]"
</asp:SqlDataSource>
```

SqlDataSource properties for caching

Property	Description
EnableCaching	A Boolean value that indicates whether caching is enabled for the data source. The default is False.
CacheDuration	The length of time in seconds that the cached data should be saved in cache storage.
CacheExpirationPolicy	If this property is set to Absolute, the cache duration timer is started the first time the data is retrieved and is not reset to zero until after the time has expired. If this property is set to Sliding, the cache duration timer is reset to zero each time the data is retrieved. The default is Absolute.
CacheKeyDependency	A string that provides a key value associated with the cached data. If you provide a key for the cached data, you can use the key value to programmatically expire the cached data at any time.

A SqlDataSource control that uses caching

```
<asp:SqlDataSource ID="SqlDataSource1" runat="server"
    ConnectionString="<%$ ConnectionStrings:HalloweenConnection %>"
    EnableCaching="True" CacheDuration="60"
    SelectCommand="SELECT [CategoryID], [LongName]
        FROM [Categories]
        ORDER BY [LongName]"
</asp:SqlDataSource>
```

Description

- The DataSourceMode property lets you specify that data should be retrieved using a data reader rather than being stored in a dataset. For read-only data, a data reader is usually more efficient.

- The data source caching properties let you specify that data should be stored in cache storage for a specified period of time. For data that changes infrequently, caching can improve performance.

Figure 13-19   How to change the data source mode and use caching

Perspective

In this chapter, you've learned how to use the SqlDataSource control with a DataList control. As you will see, however, the real power of a SQL data source lies in how it can be used with data controls like the GridView, DetailsView, FormView, and ListView controls. Those are the controls that you'll learn how to use in the next three chapters.

When you use SQL data sources as shown in this chapter, the code that's used to manage the user interface is mixed with the code that's used to work with the application's database. One easy way to separate these concerns is to use stored procedures instead of SQL statements with the SqlDataSource control. That way, the SQL statements that access and update the database are in the database itself, separated from the presentation code.

Another way to separate the concerns is to use ObjectDataSource controls instead of SqlDataSource controls, as shown in chapter 17. Then, you create and use data access classes to work with the data, so the code isn't in the aspx file. You can also use the Entity Framework and model binding as shown in chapter 18. Then, you can bind the objects of the Entity Framework, which are mapped to a database, directly to a control like a GridView control without using a data source control.

Terms

SQL data source	control parameter	results pane
SQL Server Express	Query Builder	data list
LocalDB	diagram pane	template
SQL Server Express	grid pane	template-editing mode
select parameter	SQL pane	two-way binding

Summary

- A *SQL data source* provides the information an application needs to connect to a database and retrieve the data needed by the application. A SQL data source can also be used to insert, update, and delete data.

- When you connect a SQL data source to a database, you can select a *SQL Server Express LocalDB* file on your own computer or you can create a connection to a SQL Server database on a database server. Either way, it's best to store the connection string in the web.config file for the application.

- The Configure Data Source wizard helps you generate the SELECT statement for a SQL data source including the *select* and *control parameters* used in the WHERE clause. This wizard also lets you enter custom SQL statements with parameters, select stored procedures, and use the *Query Builder* to generate SQL statements.

- The DataList control (or *data list*) displays a list of items from the data source that it's bound to. To define the information that's displayed in the list, you can create one or more *templates* for the list. To format the data in the list, you can use the Properties window, the Properties dialog box, or Bootstrap classes.

- You can *bind* a SQL data source to any list control like a drop-down list or list box. You can also bind a SQL data source to the controls that are within a template of a data control like a data list.

- The Configure Data Source wizard lets you automatically generate the INSERT, UPDATE, and DELETE statements for a SQL data source based on the SELECT statement for the data source, with or without optimistic concurrency.

- You can make a SQL data source more efficient by setting its properties so you use a data reader to retrieve data instead of retrieving the data into a dataset. If the data rarely changes, you can also improve performance by setting the properties of a data source so the retrieved data is stored in a *cache*.

Exercise 13-1   Create a DataList application

In this exercise, you'll create an application that lists line items by invoice. To do that, you'll use two SqlDataSource controls and two bound controls. When you're done, the application should look like this:

Create a drop-down list and the data source it's bound to

1. Open the Ex13InvoiceLineItems application in the aspnet46_cs directory. This application contains the starting page and the database, image, and style sheet used by the page.

2. Add a drop-down list to the page within the div that follows the label in the first form group. Then, select the Choose Data Source command from the smart tag menu for the list, and then select New Data Source from the first drop-down list in the Data Source Configuration Wizard.

3. Configure the data source as shown in figures 13-2 through 13-6, using the Halloween.mdf file in the App_Data folder for the data connection. The data source should include the InvoiceNumber column from the Invoices table for all invoices whose Total column is greater than 300. To create the WHERE clause for the SELECT statement, select None from the Source drop-down list.

4. When the Data Source Configuration Wizard is displayed again, accept the defaults so the InvoiceNumber column is displayed in the drop-down list and stored as the value of the drop-down list.

5. Change the name of the drop-down list to ddlInvoice and set its AutoPostBack property to True. Then, in the aspx code, review the SELECT statement and the select parameter that were generated for the SqlDataSource control.

Create another data source and bind it to a data list

6. Add another SqlDataSource control to the page within the div element of the second form group. Configure this data source so it uses the connection string that's in the Web.config file, so it selects the ProductID, UnitPrice, Quantity, and Extension columns from the LineItems table, and so it selects only the line items for the invoice that's selected from the drop-down list.

7. Add a DataList control to the form before the SqlDataSource control you just created, set its data source to that SqlDataSource control, assign the Bootstrap form-control class to the data list, and change its name to dlLineItems. Then, run the application to see how the data is displayed.

Modify the templates for the data list

8. Display the smart tag menu for the DataList control, and select the Edit Templates command to display the Item template. Then, delete the literal text for each column, but leave the labels.

9. Select the label for the UnitPrice column, display its smart tag menu, and select Edit DataBindings. Then, use the DataBindings dialog box to apply the Currency format to that column. Do the same for the Extension column. When you're done, exit from template-editing mode.

10. Remove the br elements that follow the Label controls in the datalist, and assign the col-xs-3 Bootstrap class to each label. In addition, assign the text-right class to the UnitPrice, Quantity, and Extension labels.

11. Add a Header template with four span elements that contain the text for the column headings shown above. Assign the same Bootstrap CSS classes to these elements that you assigned to the corresponding labels in the Item template. Then, run the application to see how the data list is displayed.

Format the data list

12. Assign these Bootstrap table classes to the DataList control: table, table-bordered, table-striped, and table-condensed. In addition, add a HeaderStyle element that assigns the bg-halloween class that's defined in the site.css file.

13. Run the application one more time to see how it's formatted. Select a different invoice from the drop-down list to make sure this works. Then, close the browser.

14

How to use the GridView control

In this chapter, you'll learn how to use the GridView control. This control lets you display the data from a data source in the rows and columns of a table. It includes many advanced features, such as automatic paging and sorting. It lets you update and delete data with minimal C# code. And its appearance is fully customizable.

How to customize the GridView control

The GridView control is one of the most powerful user interface controls available in ASP.NET 4.6. It provides many options that let you customize its appearance and behavior. In the following topics, you'll learn how to define fields, customize the contents and appearance of those fields, enable sorting, and provide for custom paging.

How the GridView control works

As figure 14-1 shows, the GridView control displays data provided by a data source in a row and column format. In fact, the GridView control renders its data as an HTML table with one Tr element for each row in the data source, and one Td element for each column in the data source.

The GridView control at the top of this figure displays the data from the Categories table of the Halloween database. Here, the first three columns of the control display the data from the three columns of the table.

The other two columns of this control display buttons that the user can click to edit or delete a row. In this example, the user has clicked the Edit button for the masks row, which placed that row into edit mode. In this mode, text boxes are displayed in place of the labels for the short and long name columns, the Edit button is replaced by Update and Cancel buttons, and the Delete button is removed.

The table in this figure lists some of the basic properties of the GridView control, and the aspx code in this figure is the code that creates the GridView control above it. By default, this control contains one column for each of the columns in the data source. These columns are defined by BoundField elements, which are coded within a Columns element. The GridView control in this figure, for example, contains a Columns element with three BoundField elements. Notice that all three BoundField elements contain an ItemStyle element that defines the width of the column. The Columns element also contains two CommandField elements that define the button columns.

Most of the aspx code for a GridView control is created automatically by Visual Studio when you drag the control from the Toolbox onto the form and when you use the configuration wizard to configure the data source. However, you typically modify this code to customize the appearance and behavior of this control.

A GridView control that provides for updating a table

CategoryID	ShortName	LongName				
costumes	Costumes	Costumes		Edit		Delete
fx	FX	Special Effects		Edit		Delete
masks	Masks	Masks		Update	Cancel	
props	Props	Props		Edit		Delete

The aspx code for the GridView control shown above

```
<asp:GridView ID="GridView1" runat="server" AutoGenerateColumns="False"
            DataSourceID="SqlDataSource1" DataKeyNames="CategoryID">
    <Columns>
        <asp:BoundField DataField="CategoryID" HeaderText="ID"
                        ReadOnly="True" SortExpression="CategoryID">
            <ItemStyle Width="100px" />
        </asp:BoundField>
        <asp:BoundField DataField="ShortName" HeaderText="Short Name"
                        SortExpression="ShortName">
            <ItemStyle Width="150px" />
        </asp:BoundField>
        <asp:BoundField DataField="LongName" HeaderText="Long Name"
                        SortExpression="LongName">
            <ItemStyle Width="200px" />
        </asp:BoundField>
        <asp:CommandField ButtonType="Button" ShowEditButton="True"
                          CausesValidation="False" />
        <asp:CommandField ButtonType="Button" ShowDeleteButton="True"
                          CausesValidation="False" />
    </Columns>
</asp:GridView>
```

Basic properties of the GridView control

Property	Description
DataSourceID	The ID of the data source to bind to.
DataKeyNames	The names of the primary key columns separated by commas.
AutoGenerateColumns	Specifies whether the control's columns should be automatically generated.
SelectedIndex	Specifies the row to be initially selected.

Description

- The GridView control displays data from a data source in a row and column format. The data is rendered as an HTML table.

- To create a GridView control, drag the GridView icon from the Data group of the Toolbox.

- To bind a GridView control to a data source, use the smart tag menu's Choose Data Source command.

Figure 14-1   How the GridView control works

How to define the fields in a GridView control

By default, a GridView control displays one column for each column in the data source. If that's not what you want, you can choose Edit Columns from the control's smart tag menu to display the Fields dialog box shown in figure 14-2. Then, you can use this dialog box to delete fields you don't want to display, change the order of the fields, add additional fields like command buttons, and adjust the properties of the fields.

The Available Fields list box lists all of the available sources for GridView fields, while the Selected Fields list box shows the fields that have already been added to the GridView control. To add an additional field to the GridView control, select the field you want to add in the Available Fields list box and click Add. To change the properties for a field, select the field in the Selected Fields list, and use the Properties list.

The table in this figure lists some of the properties you're most likely to want to change. For example, the HeaderText property determines the text that's displayed for the field's header row, the ItemStyle.Width property sets the width for the field, and the DataFormatString property specifies how you want a field formatted.

Instead of defining each bound field you want to include in a GridView control, you can have the control generate the fields for you automatically. To do that, you select the Auto-generate Fields option in the Fields dialog box. Then, a field will be automatically generated for each column in the data source. Because of that, you'll want to remove any bound fields that were added to the Selected Fields list by default. If you don't, these fields will appear in the GridView control twice.

Note that if you choose to have the bound fields generated automatically, the aspx code for those fields isn't generated until runtime. That means that you can't change the appearance or behavior of these fields at design time. Because of that, you're not likely to use auto-generated fields.

The Fields dialog box

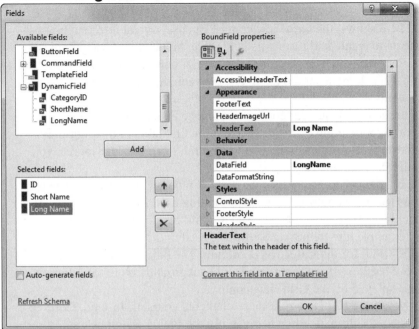

Commonly used field properties

Property	Description
`DataField`	For a bound field, the name of the column in the underlying data source that the field should be bound to.
`DataFormatString`	A format string used to format the data. For example, use {0:c} to format a decimal value as currency.
`ItemStyle.Width`	The width of the field.
`ReadOnly`	True if the field is used for display only.
`NullDisplayText`	The text that's displayed if the data field is null.
`ConvertEmptyStringToNull`	If True (the default), empty strings are treated as nulls when data is updated in the database. Set this property to False if the underlying database field doesn't allow nulls.
`HeaderText`	The text that's displayed in the header row for the field.
`ShowHeader`	True if the header should be displayed for this field.

Description

- By default, the GridView control displays one column for each column in the data source.

- To define the fields that you want to display in the GridView control, display the Fields dialog box by selecting the Edit Columns command from the control's smart tag menu.

- Another way to add a field to a GridView control is to use the Add New Column command in the smart tag menu. You'll see how to use this technique to add command buttons to a DetailsView control in the next chapter.

Figure 14-2   How to define the fields in a GridView control

Elements used to create and format fields

As figure 14-3 shows, the GridView control can use several different types of child elements to create and format its fields. The first element listed here is the Columns element, which defines the collection of columns that are displayed by the control. This element should be placed between the start and end tags for the GridView control.

Between the start and end tags for the Columns element, you can place any combination of the remaining elements listed in the first table in this figure. For example, to create a column that's bound to a column from the data source, you use the BoundField element.

The second table in this figure lists the various types of style elements you can use with a GridView control to set the formatting used for different parts of the control. Some of these elements are used as child elements of the column elements. For example, the ItemStyle element is used in the code example in this figure to set the width for the CategoryID column. The other style elements in this example are used to set the foreground and background colors for different types of rows displayed by the GridView control.

Note that you don't have to create these elements yourself. Instead, these elements are created automatically when you use the Fields dialog box as described in the previous figure, when you use the Properties window to specify the styles for an element, or when you apply a scheme to the GridView control using the Auto Format command.

Also note that, like a DataList control, a GridView control is rendered as an HTML table. Because of that, you can also use Bootstrap classes instead of some of the Style elements shown here. You'll learn more about that next.

Column field elements

Element	Description
Columns	The columns that are displayed by a GridView control.
asp:BoundField	A field bound to a data source column.
asp:ButtonField	A field that displays a button.
asp:CheckBoxField	A field that displays a check box.
asp:CommandField	A field that contains Select, Edit, Delete, Update, or Cancel buttons.
asp:HyperlinkField	A field that displays a hyperlink.
asp:ImageField	A field that displays an image.
asp:TemplateField	Lets you create a column with custom content.

Style elements

Element	Description
RowStyle	The style used for data rows.
AlternatingRowStyle	The style used for alternating data rows.
SelectedRowStyle	The style used when the row is selected.
EditRowStyle	The style used when the row is being edited.
EmptyDataRowStyle	The style used when the data source is empty.
ItemStyle	The style used for an individual field.
HeaderStyle	The style used for the header row.
FooterStyle	The style used for the footer row.
PagerStyle	The style used for the pager row.

The aspx code for a control that uses field and style elements

```
<asp:GridView ID="GridView1" runat="server" AutoGenerateColumns="False"
              DataKeyNames="CategoryID" DataSourceID="SqlDataSource1">
  <Columns>
    <asp:BoundField DataField="CategoryID" HeaderText="ID" ReadOnly="true">
      <ItemStyle Width="100px" />
    </asp:BoundField>
    .
    .
  </Columns>
  <HeaderStyle BackColor="LightGray" ForeColor="White" Font-Bold="True" />
  <RowStyle BackColor="White" ForeColor="Black" />
  <SelectedRowStyle BackColor="Gray" ForeColor="White" Font-Bold="True" />
  <FooterStyle BackColor="LightGray" ForeColor="Blue" />
  <PagerStyle BackColor="LightGray" ForeColor="Blue"
              HorizontalAlign="Center" />
</asp:GridView>
```

Description

- The GridView control uses several child elements to define the column fields in a row and the styles used to format the data.

Figure 14-3   Elements used to create and format fields

How to use Bootstrap CSS classes to format a GridView control

Like the DataList control you learned about in the last chapter, ASP.NET renders a GridView control to the browser as an HTML table. Because of that, you can style a GridView control with the Bootstrap CSS classes for HTML tables. For example, figure 14-4 shows a GridView control that uses the base Bootstrap table, table-bordered, table-striped, and table-condensed classes.

You can also use Bootstrap classes with the Style elements you learned about in the last figure. You can do that by setting the CssClass property of the Style element to the Bootstrap class you want to apply. In this figure, for example, the CssClass property of the ItemStyle element is used to apply Bootstrap column classes that specify the widths of the individual columns. Note that if you don't specify the column widths, the widths will grow and shrink depending on the size of the content. To maintain consistent widths, then, you'll want to use the column classes.

As you learned in chapter 10, an HTML table must have thead and tbody elements for the Bootstrap classes to work properly. However, ASP.NET doesn't include these elements by default when it renders a GridView control to the browser. Fortunately, you can get ASP.NET to render these elements by adding an event handler for the GridView control's PreRender event as shown in this figure. If the GridView control can be empty, you start by checking that the header row isn't null. If it isn't, you set the TableSection property of the GridView control's HeaderRow property to the TableHeader value of the TableRowSection enumeration. Note that most of the applications in this book that use a GridView control assume that the control isn't empty, so they don't include the if statement shown here.

A GridView control that uses Bootstrap CSS classes for styling

ID	Short Name	Long Name
costumes	Costumes	Costumes
fx	FX	Special Effects
masks	Masks	Masks
props	Props	Props

The aspx code for the control

```
<div class="col-xs-12 table-responsive">
    <h1>Category List</h1>
    <asp:GridView ID="grdCategories" runat="server"
        AutoGenerateColumns="False" DataSourceID="SqlDataSource1"
        CssClass="table table-bordered table-striped table-condensed"
        OnPreRender="grdCategories_PreRender">
        <Columns>
            <asp:BoundField DataField="CategoryID" HeaderText="ID">
                <ItemStyle CssClass="col-xs-2" />
            </asp:BoundField>
            <asp:BoundField DataField="ShortName" HeaderText="Short Name">
                <ItemStyle CssClass="col-xs-4" />
            </asp:BoundField>
            <asp:BoundField DataField="LongName" HeaderText="Long Name">
                <ItemStyle CssClass="col-xs-6" />
            </asp:BoundField>
        </Columns>
    </asp:GridView>
    <asp:SqlDataSource ID="SqlDataSource1"...></asp:SqlDataSource>
</div>
```

The PreRender event handler in the code-behind file

```
protected void grdCategories_PreRender(object sender, EventArgs e)
{
    if (grdCategories.HeaderRow != null)
        grdCategories.HeaderRow.TableSection = TableRowSection.TableHeader;
}
```

Description

- Since ASP.NET renders a GridView control as an HTML table, you can use the Bootstrap CSS classes for HTML tables to style GridView controls.

- You can also use Bootstrap CSS classes with the Style elements shown in figure 14-3. To do that, you set the CssClass property of the Style element to the class you want to apply.

- For the Bootstrap table classes to be applied properly, an HTML table must have thead and tbody elements. Because ASP.NET doesn't render these elements for a GridView control by default, you must add code to the control's PreRender event handler that sets the value of the TableSection property of the control's HeaderRow property to TableHeader.

Figure 14-4   How to use Bootstrap CSS classes to format a GridView control

How to enable sorting

The GridView control has a built-in ability to let the user sort the rows based on any or all of the columns displayed by the control. As figure 14-5 shows, all you have to do to enable sorting is set the AllowSorting property to True and provide a SortExpression property for each column you want to allow sorting for. When sorting is enabled for a column, the user can sort the data by clicking the column header. The first time it's clicked, the data will be sorted in ascending order. The second time it's clicked, the data will be sorted in descending order. And so on.

Note that a SortExpression property is automatically generated for each BoundField column that's included by default or that you create with the Fields dialog box. As a result, instead of adding SortExpression properties for the columns you want to allow sorting for, you must remove the SortExpression properties for the columns you don't want to allow sorting for. You can use the Fields dialog box to do that by clearing the SortExpression properties. Or, you can use the HTML Editor to delete the SortExpression properties.

The code example in this figure allows sorting for three of the five fields displayed by the GridView control. For the first two fields, the SortExpression property simply duplicates the name of the data source column the field is bound to. If, for example, the user clicks the header of the ProductID column, the data is sorted on the ProductID field.

In some cases, though, you may want the sort expression to be based on two or more columns. To do that, you just use commas to separate the sort field names. In this example, the sort expression for the CategoryID column is "CategoryID, Name". That way, any rows with the same category ID will be sorted by the Name column. Note that the first time the CategoryID column header is clicked, the rows will be sorted by the Name column in ascending order within the CategoryID column in ascending order. If the CategoryID column header is clicked again, the category IDs will remain in ascending order, but the names will be sorted in descending order.

It's important to note that the GridView control doesn't actually do the sorting. Instead, it relies on the underlying data source to sort the data. As a result, sorting will only work if the data source provides for sorting. For a SqlDataSource, this means that you need to use the default DataSet mode.

A GridView control with sorting enabled

ID	Name	Category	Unit Price	On Hand
pow01	Austin Powers	costumes	$79.99	25
frankc01	Frankenstein	costumes	$39.99	100
hippie01	Hippie	costumes	$79.99	40
jar01	JarJar	costumes	$59.99	25
martian01	Martian	costumes	$69.99	100
super01	Superman	costumes	$39.99	100
bl01	Black Light	fx	$19.99	200
fogj01	Fog Juice (1qt)	fx	$9.99	500
fog01	Fog Machine	fx	$34.99	100
str01	Mini-strobe	fx	$13.99	200
skullfog01	Skull Fogger	fx	$39.95	50
tlm01	T&L Machine	fx	$99.99	10

The aspx code for the control shown above

```
<asp:GridView ID="GridView1" runat="server" AutoGenerateColumns="False"
    DataKeyNames="CategoryID" DataSourceID="SqlDataSource1"
    UseAccessibleHeader="true" AllowSorting="True"
    CssClass="table table-bordered table-striped table-condensed"
    OnPreRender="GridView1_PreRender">
    <Columns>
        <asp:BoundField DataField="ProductID" HeaderText="ID"
            ReadOnly="True" SortExpression="ProductID">
            <ItemStyle CssClass="col-xs-1" /></asp:BoundField>
        <asp:BoundField DataField="Name" HeaderText="Name"
            SortExpression="Name">
            <ItemStyle CssClass="col-xs-4" /></asp:BoundField>
        <asp:BoundField DataField="CategoryID" HeaderText="Category"
            SortExpression="CategoryID, Name">
            <ItemStyle CssClass="col-xs-2" /></asp:BoundField>
        <asp:BoundField DataField="UnitPrice" HeaderText="Unit Price"
            DataFormatString="{0:c}">
            <ItemStyle CssClass="col-xs-2 text-right" />
            <HeaderStyle CssClass="text-right" /></asp:BoundField>
        <asp:BoundField DataField="OnHand" HeaderText="On Hand">
            <ItemStyle CssClass="col-xs-2 text-right" />
            <HeaderStyle CssClass="text-right" />
        </asp:BoundField>
    </Columns>
</asp:GridView>
```

Description

- To enable sorting, set the AllowSorting property to True. Then, add a SortExpression property to each column you want to allow sorting for.

- For sorting to work, the DataSourceMode property of the data source must be set to DataSet mode, which it is by default.

Figure 14-5   How to enable sorting

How to enable paging

Paging refers to the ability of the GridView control to display bound data one page at a time, along with paging controls that let the user select which page of data to display next. As figure 14-6 shows, the GridView control lets you enable paging simply by setting the AllowPaging property to True.

When you enable paging, an additional row is displayed at the bottom of the GridView control to display the paging controls. If you want, you can provide a PagerStyle element to control how this row is formatted. In the example in this figure, the pagerStyle class is assigned to the PagerStyle element. This class adds space to the left of each page number. In addition, the HorizontalAlign property of the PagerStyle element centers the pager controls. Although you might think that you could center the controls using a CSS class, this can be difficult to do because of the complex HTML that ASP.NET renders for a pager row. So in most cases, you'll need to format a pager row using properties of the PagerStyle element like the one shown here.

Unlike sorting, the GridView control doesn't delegate the paging function to the underlying data source. Like sorting, however, paging works only for data sources that are in DataSet mode.

Before going on, you should know that Bootstrap also includes a component that provides for pagination. Although you can use this component with the GridView control, the procedure for getting this to work can be involved. For more information, you can search online for "Bootstrap pagination with GridView".

A GridView control with paging enabled

ID	Name	Category	Unit Price	On Hand
arm01	Freddie Arm	props	$20.95	200
bats01	Flying Bats	props	$69.99	25
bl01	Black Light	fx	$19.99	200
cat01	Deranged Cat	props	$19.99	45
fog01	Fog Machine	fx	$34.99	100
fogj01	Fog Juice (1qt)	fx	$9.99	500
frankc01	Frankenstein	costumes	$39.99	100
fred01	Freddie	masks	$29.99	50
head01	Michael Head	props	$29.99	100
head02	Saw Head	props	$29.99	100

1 2 3

The aspx code for the control shown above

```
<asp:GridView ID="GridView1" runat="server" AllowPaging="true"
    AutoGenerateColumns="False" DataKeyNames="CategoryID"
    DataSourceID="SqlDataSource1" UseAccessibleHeader="true"
    CssClass="table table-bordered table-striped table-condensed"
    OnPreRender="GridView1_PreRender">
    <Columns>
        <asp:BoundField DataField="ProductID" HeaderText="ID"
            ReadOnly="True">
            <ItemStyle CssClass="col-xs-1" /></asp:BoundField>
        <asp:BoundField DataField="Name" HeaderText="Name">
            <ItemStyle CssClass="col-xs-4" /></asp:BoundField>
        <asp:BoundField DataField="CategoryID" HeaderText="Category">
            <ItemStyle CssClass="col-xs-2" /></asp:BoundField>
        <asp:BoundField DataField="UnitPrice" HeaderText="Unit Price"
            DataFormatString="{0:c}">
            <ItemStyle CssClass="col-xs-2 text-right" />
            <HeaderStyle CssClass="text-right" />
        </asp:BoundField>
        <asp:BoundField DataField="OnHand" HeaderText="On Hand">
            <ItemStyle CssClass="col-xs-2 text-right" />
            <HeaderStyle CssClass="text-right" />
        </asp:BoundField>
    </Columns>
    <PagerStyle CssClass="pagerStyle" HorizontalAlign="Center" />
</asp:GridView>
```

Description

- To enable *paging*, set the AllowPaging property to True. Then, add a PagerStyle element to define the appearance of the pager controls. You can also add a PagerSettings element as described in the next figure to customize the way paging works.

- For paging to work, the DataSourceMode property of the data source must be set to DataSet mode, which it is by default.

Figure 14-6   How to enable paging

How to customize paging

Figure 14-7 shows how you can customize the way paging works with a GridView control. To start, the two properties in the first table let you enable paging and specify the number of data rows that will be displayed on each page. The default setting for the second property is 10.

You can also customize the appearance of the pager area by including a PagerSettings element between the start and end tags of a GridView control. Then, you can use the properties in the second table for the customization. The most important of these properties is Mode, which determines what buttons are displayed in the pager area. If, for example, you set the mode to NextPrevious, only Next and Previous buttons will be displayed.

If you specify Numeric or NumericFirstLast for the Mode property, individual page numbers are displayed in the pager area so the user can go directly to any of the listed pages. You can then use the PageButtonCount property to specify how many of these page numbers should be displayed in the pager area. Note that if you specify NumericFirstLast, the first and last buttons are displayed only if the total number of pages exceeds the value you specify for the PageButtonCount property and the first or last page isn't displayed.

The remaining properties in this table let you control the text or image that's displayed for the various buttons. By default, the values for the First, Previous, Next, and Last buttons use less-than and greater-than signs, but the example shows how you can change the text for these buttons.

When you use paging, you should know that, by default, all of the rows from the data source are retrieved each time a different page is displayed. If the data source contains a large number of rows, this can be inefficient. Because of that, ASP.NET 4.5 added two properties to the GridView control that you can use to read just the rows you need for each page.

The first property, AllowCustomPaging, lets you enable custom paging. Then, when the user clicks a pager control to display another page of data, the application can respond to the PageIndexChanging event. Among other things, the event handler for this event must set the second new property, VirtualItemCount, to the total number of rows in the data source. For more information on how to code this event handler, please see online help.

Properties of the GridView control that affect paging

Property	Description
`AllowPaging`	Set to True to enable paging.
`PageSize`	Specifies the number of rows to display on each page. The default is 10.

Properties of the PagerSettings element

Property	Description
`Mode`	Controls what buttons are displayed in the pager area. You can specify NextPrevious, NextPreviousFirstLast, Numeric, or NumericFirstLast.
`FirstPageText`	The text to display for the first page button. The default is <<, which displays as <<.
`FirstPageImageUrl`	The URL of an image file used to display the first page button.
`PreviousPageText`	The text to display for the previous page button. The default is <, which displays as <.
`PreviousPageImageUrl`	The URL of an image file used to display the previous page button.
`NextPageText`	The text to display for the next page button. The default is >, which displays as >.
`NextPageImageUrl`	The URL of an image file used to display the next page button.
`LastPageText`	The text to display for the last page button. The default is >>, which displays as >>.
`LastPageImageUrl`	The URL of an image file used to display the last page button.
`PageButtonCount`	The number of page buttons to display if the Mode is set to Numeric or NumericFirstLast.
`Position`	The location of the pager area. You can specify Top, Bottom, or TopAndBottom.
`Visible`	Set to False to hide the pager controls.

Example

A PagerSettings element

```
<PagerSettings Mode="NextPreviousFirstLast"
          NextPageText="Next" PreviousPageText="Prev"
          FirstPageText="First" LastPageText="Last" />
```

The resulting pager area

```
First  Prev  Next  Last
```

Description

- You can use the PageSize property of the GridView element to specify the number of rows to display on each page.
- You can also add a PagerSettings element to control the appearance of the pager area.
- By default, each time a different page is displayed, all the rows in the data source are read. To avoid that, you can use the AllowCustomPaging and VirtualItemCount properties. For more information, see online help.

Figure 14-7 How to customize paging

A list application
that uses a GridView control

Now that you've learned the basics of working with a GridView control, the following topics present the design and code for an application that uses a GridView control to list the rows of a data source. As you'll see, this application provides for sorting and paging and requires just the C# code you saw in figure 14-4 for the PreRender event of the control.

The Product List application

Figure 14-8 presents the Product List application. Here, the data from the Products table of the Halloween database is displayed in a GridView control. The data is displayed 8 rows at a time, and numeric page buttons are displayed at the bottom of the GridView control so the user can navigate from page to page. In addition, the user can sort the data by clicking the column headings for the ID, Name, and Category columns.

The Product List application

Description

- The Product List application uses a GridView control to display a list of all the products in the Products table. The GridView control is bound to a SqlDataSource control that works in DataSet mode.

- Sorting is enabled for the first three columns. That way, the user can sort the product data by ID, Name, or Category.

- Paging is enabled with 8 products displayed on each page.

- Currency formatting is applied to the Unit Price column.

Figure 14-8   The Product List application

The aspx file

Figure 14-9 shows the body of the aspx code for this application, which is stored in the Default.aspx file. Because you've already been introduced to all of the code in the aspx file, you should be able to follow it without much trouble. So I'll just point out a few highlights.

First, the GridView control is formatted mostly by using Bootstrap CSS classes. You can see these classes in the CssClass property of this control. Note that because the table-striped class is included, it isn't necessary to include RowStyle and AlternatingRowStyle elements.

The Columns element for the GridView control contains five BoundField child elements that define the fields displayed by the grid. All five columns are retrieved from the SQL data source. The first three of these BoundField elements include the SortExpression property to allow sorting. The fourth BoundField element includes the DataFormatString property to apply currency formatting. The ItemStyle elements for the first three BoundField elements set the widths of the fields, and the ItemStyle elements for the last two fields set the widths of the fields and right-align the fields. The last two BoundField elements also include a HeaderStyle element that right-aligns the headers for the fields.

A PagerSettings element is used to specify the types of pager controls to display. Then, a PagerStyle element assigns the pagerStyle class to the pager area, which applies some basic styles like a boldface font. It also sets the background color for the pager area and centers the pager buttons in the pager area.

Finally, the SqlDataSource control uses this Select statement to retrieve data from the Halloween database:

```
SELECT [ProductID], [Name], [CategoryID],
    [UnitPrice], [OnHand] FROM [Products]
```

Because the DataSourceMode property isn't set, the default of DataSet mode is used, which means that sorting and paging can be enabled.

The code-behind file

The code-behind file for this application includes an event handler for the PreRender event of the GridView control, also shown in figure 14-9. This event handler contains a single statement that causes thead and tbody elements to be included in the table that's rendered for the GridView. To refresh your memory on how this works, you can refer back to figure 14-4.

The body of the Default.aspx file

```
<body>
<div class="container">
    <header class="jumbotron"><%-- image set in site.css --%></header>
    <main class="row">
    <form id="form1" runat="server">
        <div class="col-xs-12 table-responsive">
            <asp:GridView ID="grdProducts" runat="server"
                AutoGenerateColumns="False" DataKeyNames="ProductID"
                DataSourceID="SqlDataSource1" AllowPaging="True"
                PageSize="8" AllowSorting="True"
                CssClass="table table-bordered table-striped table-condensed"
                OnPreRender="grdProducts_PreRender">
                <Columns>
                    <asp:BoundField DataField="ProductID" HeaderText="ID"
                        ReadOnly="True" SortExpression="ProductID">
                        <ItemStyle CssClass="col-xs-1" />
                    </asp:BoundField>
                    <asp:BoundField DataField="Name" HeaderText="Name"
                        SortExpression="Name">
                        <ItemStyle CssClass="col-xs-4" />
                    </asp:BoundField>
                    <asp:BoundField DataField="CategoryID"
                        HeaderText="Category"
                        SortExpression="CategoryID, Name">
                        <ItemStyle CssClass="col-xs-2" />
                    </asp:BoundField>
                    <asp:BoundField DataField="UnitPrice"
                        HeaderText="Unit Price" DataFormatString="{0:c}">
                        <ItemStyle CssClass="col-xs-2 text-right" />
                        <HeaderStyle CssClass="text-right" />
                    </asp:BoundField>
                    <asp:BoundField DataField="OnHand" HeaderText="On Hand">
                        <ItemStyle CssClass="col-xs-2 text-right" />
                        <HeaderStyle CssClass="text-right" />
                    </asp:BoundField>
                </Columns>
                <HeaderStyle CssClass="bg-halloween" />
                <PagerSettings Mode="NumericFirstLast" />
                <PagerStyle CssClass="pagerStyle" BackColor="#8C8C8C"
                    HorizontalAlign="Center" />
            </asp:GridView>
            <asp:SqlDataSource ID="SqlDataSource1" runat="server"
            ConnectionString="<%$ ConnectionStrings:HalloweenConnection %>"
                SelectCommand="SELECT [ProductID], [Name], [CategoryID],
                    [UnitPrice], [OnHand] FROM [Products]">
            </asp:SqlDataSource>
        </div>
    </form>
    </main>
</div>
</body>
```

The event handler for the Prerender event of the GridView control

```
protected void grdProducts_PreRender(object sender, EventArgs e)
{
    grdProducts.HeaderRow.TableSection = TableRowSection.TableHeader;
}
```

Figure 14-9   The aspx and code-behind files for the Product List application

How to update GridView data

Another impressive feature of the GridView control is its ability to update data in the underlying data source with little additional code. Before you can set that up, though, you must configure the data source with Update, Delete, and Insert statements as described in the last chapter. Once you've done that, you can set up a GridView control so it calls the Update and Delete statements, which you'll learn how to do next. Then, you'll learn how to insert a row into a GridView control.

How to work with command fields

A *command field* is a GridView column that contains one or more command buttons. Figure 14-10 shows five of the command buttons that you can include in each row of a GridView control. Please note, however, that the Update and Cancel buttons are displayed only when a user clicks the Edit button to edit a row. You can't display these buttons in separate command fields.

When the user clicks a Delete button, the GridView control calls the data source control's Delete method, which deletes the selected row from the underlying database. Then, the GridView control redisplays the data without the deleted row.

When the user clicks the Edit button, the GridView control places the selected row in *edit mode*. In this mode, the labels used to display the editable bound fields are replaced by text boxes so the user can enter changes. Also, the row is formatted using the style attributes provided by the EditRowStyle element. Finally, the Edit button itself is replaced by Update and Cancel buttons. Then, if the user clicks the Update button, the GridView control calls the data source control's Update method, which updates the underlying database. But if the user clicks Cancel, any changes made by the user are discarded and the original values are redisplayed.

The Select button lets the user select a row. Then, the selected row is displayed with the settings in the SelectedRowStyle element. Also, the SelectedIndex and SelectedRow properties are updated to reflect the selected row. The Select button is most often used in combination with a FormView or DetailsView control to create pages that show the details for an item selected from the GridView control. You'll learn how this works in chapter 15.

The two tables in this figure show the properties of a CommandField element. For instance, you can set the ShowEditButton property to True to display an Edit button in a command field. And you can use the EditText property to set the text that's displayed on that button.

Although a single command field can display more than one button, it's common to create separate command fields for Select, Edit, and Delete buttons. It's also common to set the CausesValidation property of the Select and Delete buttons to False since the operations these buttons perform don't require any data validation. On the other hand, you'll usually leave the CausesValidation property of the Edit button set to True so validation is performed when the user clicks the Update button. Later in this chapter, you'll learn how to use validation controls with the Edit button by creating template fields.

The Fields dialog box for working with a command field

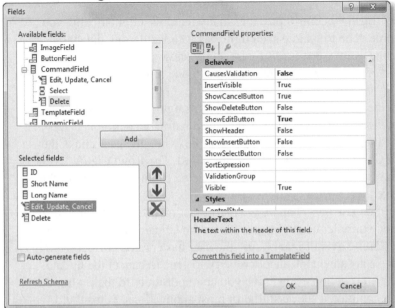

Properties of the CommandField element

Property	Description
ButtonType	Specifies the type of button displayed in the command field. Valid options are Button, Link, or Image.
CausesValidation	Specifies whether validation should be performed if the user clicks the button.
ValidationGroup	Specifies the name of the group to be validated if CausesValidation is True.

Properties that show buttons and set the text or images they display

Button	Show	Text	Image
Cancel	ShowCancelButton	CancelText	CancelImage
Delete	ShowDeleteButton	DeleteText	DeleteImage
Edit	ShowEditButton	EditText	EditImage
Select	ShowSelectButton	SelectText	SelectImage
Update	n/a	UpdateText	UpdateImage

Code that defines two command fields

```
<asp:CommandField ButtonType="Button" ShowEditButton="True" />
<asp:CommandField ButtonType="Button" ShowDeleteButton="True"
    CausesValidation="False" />
```

Description

- A *command field* adds buttons that let the user edit, delete, or select data.
- The CommandField element also provides for an Insert button, but the GridView control doesn't directly support insert operations.

Figure 14-10   How to work with command fields

How to use events raised by the GridView control

Although the GridView control provides many features automatically, you still must write some code to handle such things as data validation, database exceptions, and concurrency errors. As figure 14-11 shows, most of this code will be in the form of event handlers that respond to one or more of the events raised by the GridView control.

If you look at the list of events in the table in this figure, you'll see that several of them come in pairs, with one event raised before an action is taken and the other after the action completes. For example, when the user clicks the Delete button in a GridView row, two events are raised. The RowDeleting event is raised before the row is deleted, and the RowDeleted event is raised after the row has been deleted.

The most common reason to handle the before-action events is to provide data validation. For example, when the user clicks the Update button, you can handle the RowUpdating event to make sure the user has entered correct data. If not, you can set the e argument's Cancel property to True to cancel the update.

In contrast, the after-action events give you an opportunity to make sure the database operation completed successfully. In most applications, you should test for two conditions. First, you should check for any database exceptions by checking the Exception property of the e argument. If this property refers to a valid object, an exception has occurred and you can notify the user with an appropriate error message.

Second, if optimistic concurrency is used, you should check to see if a concurrency violation has occurred. To do that, you can check the AffectedRows property of the e argument. If this property is zero, which means no rows have been changed, a concurrency error has probably occurred, and you can notify the user with an appropriate error message.

When you use optimistic concurrency, remember that the Where clause in an Update or Delete statement tries to find a row that has the same values as when the row was originally retrieved. If that row can't be found, which means that another user has updated one of the columns or deleted the row, the update or delete operation never takes place so no rows are affected.

When you try to update a row, one of the most common exceptions is caused by an attempt to store a null value in a database column that doesn't allow null values. This occurs when the user doesn't enter a value in one of the columns that's being updated. In this case, you can display an appropriate error message and set the e argument's ExceptionHandled property to True to suppress further processing of the exception. You can also set the KeepInEditMode property to True to leave the GridView control in edit mode. This is illustrated by the event handler that's coded in this figure.

Another event you may use is the RowDataBound event, which occurs when a row is bound to the GridView control. This event is commonly used to format a cell in a row based on the cell's value. If the value of the cell is less than zero, for example, you might assign a different background color to it. To do that, you can use the Row property of the e argument that's passed to the event handler to get the current row. Then, you can use the Cell property with an index to get a cell in the row. Finally, you can set the properties of the cell as appropriate.

Events raised by the GridView control

Event	Raised when ...
RowCancelingEdit	The Cancel button of a row in edit mode is clicked.
RowDataBound	Data binding completes for a row.
RowDeleted	A row has been deleted.
RowDeleting	A row is about to be deleted.
RowEditing	A row is about to be edited.
RowUpdated	A row has been updated.
RowUpdating	A row is about to be updated.
SelectedIndexChanged	A row has been selected.
SelectedIndexChanging	A row is about to be selected.

An event handler for the RowUpdated event

```
protected void GridView1_RowUpdated(object sender,
    GridViewUpdatedEventArgs e)
{
    if (e.Exception != null)
    {
        lblError.Text = "A database error has occurred. " +
            "Message: " + e.Exception.Message;
        e.ExceptionHandled = true;
        e.KeepInEditMode = true;
    }
    else if (e.AffectedRows == 0)
    {
        lblError.Text = "Another user may have updated that category. " +
            "Please try again.";
    }
}
```

Description

- The GridView control raises various events that can be handled when data is updated.

- The RowUpdating and RowDeleting events are often used for data validation. You can cancel the update or delete operation by setting the e argument's Cancel property to True.

- You can handle the RowUpdated and RowDeleted events to ensure that the row was successfully updated or deleted.

- To determine if a SQL exception has occurred, check the Exception property of the e argument. If an exception has occurred, the most likely cause is a null value for a column that doesn't accept nulls. To suppress the exception, you can set the ExceptionHandled property to True. And to keep the control in edit mode, you can set the KeepInEditMode property to True.

- To determine how many rows were updated or deleted, check the AffectedRows property of the e argument. If this property is zero and an exception has *not* been thrown, the most likely cause is a concurrency error.

Figure 14-11   How to use events raised by the GridView control

How to insert a row in a GridView control

You may have noticed that although the GridView control lets you update and delete rows, it has no provision for inserting new rows. When you use the GridView control in concert with a FormView or DetailsView control, though, you can provide for insert operations with a minimum of code. You'll learn how to do that in chapter 15. Another alternative is to create a page that lets you insert data into a GridView control by using the technique described in figure 14-12.

To provide for insertions, you must first create a set of input controls such as text boxes into which the user can enter data for the row to be inserted. Next, you must provide a button that the user can click to start the insertion. Then, in the Click event handler for this button, you can set the insert parameter values to the values entered by the user and call the data source's Insert method to add the new row.

This is illustrated by the code in this figure. Here, if the insertion is successful, the contents of the text boxes are cleared. But if an exception is thrown, an error message is displayed. This message indicates that an exception has occurred and uses the Message property of the Exception object to display the message that's stored in the Exception object.

Notice in this example that the Click event handler starts by checking the IsValid property to be sure that the validation that's done by the validation controls for the input controls is successful. Also notice that a parameter is generated for each column in the Categories table. If a table contains an identity column, though, a parameter won't be generated for that column. That makes sense because the value of this column is set by the database when the row is inserted.

Method and properties of the SqlDataSource class for inserting rows

Method	Description
`Insert()`	Executes the Insert command defined for the data source.

Property	Description
`InsertCommand`	The Insert command to be executed.
`InsertParameters["name"]`	The parameter with the specified name.

Property of the Parameter class for inserting rows

Property	Description
`DefaultValue`	The default value of a parameter. This value is used if no other value is assigned to the parameter.

Code that uses a SqlDataSource control to insert a row

```
protected void btnAdd_Click(object sender, EventArgs e)
{
    if (IsValid)
    {
        var parameters = SqlDataSource1.InsertParameters;
        parameters["CategoryID"].DefaultValue = txtID.Text;
        parameters["ShortName"].DefaultValue = txtShortName.Text;
        parameters["LongName"].DefaultValue = txtLongName.Text;
        try {
            SqlDataSource1.Insert();
            txtID.Text = "";
            txtShortName.Text = "";
            txtLongName.Text = "";
        }
        catch (Exception ex) {
            lblError.Text = "A database error has occurred. " +
                "Message: " + ex.Message;
        }
    }
}
```

Description

- The GridView control doesn't support insert operations, but you can use the GridView's data source to insert rows into the database. When you do, the new row will automatically be shown in the GridView control.

- To provide for inserts, the page should include controls such as text boxes for the user to enter data and a button that the user can click to insert the data.

- To use a SqlDataSource control to insert a database row, first set the DefaultValue property of each insert parameter to the value you want to insert. Then, call the Insert method.

- The Insert method may throw a SqlException if a SQL error occurs. The most likely cause of the exception is a primary key constraint violation.

Figure 14-12   How to insert a row in a GridView control

A maintenance application that uses a GridView control

To give you a better idea of how you can use a GridView control to update, delete, and insert data, the following topics present an application that maintains the Categories table in the Halloween database.

The Category Maintenance application

Figure 14-13 introduces you to the Category Maintenance application. It lets the user update, delete, and insert rows in the Categories table of the Halloween database. Here, a GridView control is used to display the rows in the Categories table along with Edit and Delete buttons. In this figure, the user has clicked the Edit button for the third data row, placing that row in edit mode.

Below the GridView control, three text boxes let the user enter data for a new category. Then, if the user clicks the Add New Category button, the data entered in these text boxes is used to add a category row to the database. Although it isn't apparent from this figure, required field validators are used for each text box. Also, there's a label control below the GridView control that's used to display error messages when an update, delete, or insert operation fails.

The Category Maintenance application

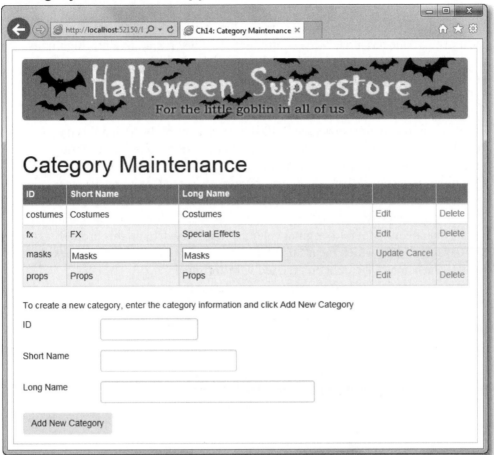

Description

- The Category Maintenance application uses a GridView control to let the user update or delete rows in the Categories table.

- To edit a category, the user clicks the Edit button. This places the GridView control into edit mode. The user can then change the Short Name or Long Name and click Update. Or, the user can click Cancel to leave edit mode.

- To delete a category, the user clicks the Delete button.

- The user can add a category to the table by entering data into the text boxes below the GridView control and clicking the Add New Category button.

- If the user attempts to update or add a row with a column that is blank, an error message is displayed.

Figure 14-13   The Category Maintenance application

The aspx file

Figure 14-14 shows the aspx listing for the body of this application. Since most of this code has already been introduced, I'll just point out a few highlights.

Part 1 of this figure shows the aspx code for the GridView control. It specifies that the data source is SqlDataSource1 and the primary key for the data is CategoryID. The five columns defined in the Columns element display the three columns from the data source, an Edit button, and a Delete button.

Part 2 of this figure shows the SqlDataSource control. Note that this data source includes the ConflictDetection and OldValuesParameterFormatString properties. The ConflictDetection property indicates how update and delete operations are handled. By default, this property is set to CompareAllValues, which means that optimistic concurrency checking will be done. The OldValuesParameterFormatString property indicates the format of the parameter names that are used to hold original column values. By default, this property is set to original_{0}, which means that the name of each original parameter will include the name of the column prefixed with "original_".

As a result of these two property values, these statements are used to retrieve, delete, update, and insert category rows:

```
SELECT [CategoryID], [ShortName], [LongName]
    FROM [Categories]

DELETE FROM [Categories]
    WHERE [CategoryID] = @original_CategoryID
      AND [ShortName] = @original_ShortName
      AND [LongName] = @original_LongName

UPDATE [Categories]
    SET [ShortName] = @ShortName,
        [LongName] = @LongName
    WHERE [CategoryID] = @original_CategoryID
      AND [ShortName] = @original_ShortName
      AND [LongName] = @original_LongName

INSERT INTO [Categories]
    ([CategoryID], [ShortName], [LongName])
    VALUES (@CategoryID, @ShortName, @LongName)
```

Here, the Where clauses implement optimistic concurrency by looking for rows that have the values originally retrieved. Then, the DeleteParameters, UpdateParameters, and InsertParameters elements define the parameters used by these statements.

Finally, part 3 of this figure shows the input controls used to enter the data for a new category. As you can see, each text box is validated by a required field validator that makes sure the user has entered data for the field. This validation is performed when the user clicks the Add New Category button. In addition, the MaxLength property is coded for each text box so the user can't enter more characters than are allowed by the associated column in the data source.

The body of the Default.aspx file   **Page 1**

```
<body>
<div class="container">
    <header class="jumbotron"><%-- image set in site.css --%></header>
    <main class="row">
    <form id="form1" runat="server" class="form-horizontal">
        <div class="col-xs-12 table-responsive">
            <h1>Category Maintenance</h1>
            <asp:GridView ID="grdCategories" runat="server"
                AutoGenerateColumns="False" DataKeyNames="CategoryID"
                DataSourceID="SqlDataSource1"
                CssClass="table table-bordered table-condensed table-hover"
                OnPreRender="grdCategories_PreRender"
                OnRowDeleted="grdCategories_RowDeleted"
                OnRowUpdated="grdCategories_RowUpdated">
                <Columns>
                    <asp:BoundField DataField="CategoryID" HeaderText="ID"
                        ReadOnly="True">
                        <ItemStyle CssClass="col-xs-1" />
                    </asp:BoundField>
                    <asp:BoundField DataField="ShortName"
                        HeaderText="Short Name"
                        SortExpression="ShortName">
                        <ItemStyle CssClass="col-xs-3" />
                    </asp:BoundField>
                    <asp:BoundField DataField="LongName"
                        HeaderText="Long Name"
                        SortExpression="LongName">
                        <ItemStyle CssClass="col-xs-5" />
                    </asp:BoundField>
                    <asp:CommandField CausesValidation="False"
                        ShowEditButton="True">
                        <ItemStyle CssClass="col-xs-1 text-danger" />
                    </asp:CommandField>
                    <asp:CommandField CausesValidation="False"
                        ShowDeleteButton="True">
                        <ItemStyle CssClass="col-xs-1" />
                    </asp:CommandField>
                </Columns>
                <HeaderStyle CssClass="bg-halloween" />
                <AlternatingRowStyle CssClass="altRow" />
                <EditRowStyle CssClass="warning" />
            </asp:GridView>
```

Notes

- The GridView control is bound to the SqlDataSource1 data source.
- The Columns element includes child elements that define five columns. Three are for the bound fields; the other two are for the command buttons.

Figure 14-14   The aspx file for the Category Maintenance application (part 1 of 3)

The body of the Default.aspx file   Page 2

```
<asp:SqlDataSource ID="SqlDataSource1" runat="server"
    ConnectionString="<%$ ConnectionStrings:HalloweenConnection %>"
    ConflictDetection="CompareAllValues"
    OldValuesParameterFormatString="original_{0}"
    SelectCommand="SELECT [CategoryID], [ShortName], [LongName]
        FROM [Categories]"
    DeleteCommand="DELETE FROM [Categories]
        WHERE [CategoryID] = @original_CategoryID
          AND [ShortName] = @original_ShortName
          AND [LongName] = @original_LongName"
    InsertCommand="INSERT INTO [Categories]
        ([CategoryID], [ShortName], [LongName])
        VALUES (@CategoryID, @ShortName, @LongName)"
    UpdateCommand="UPDATE [Categories]
        SET [ShortName] = @ShortName,
            [LongName] = @LongName
        WHERE [CategoryID] = @original_CategoryID
          AND [ShortName] = @original_ShortName
          AND [LongName] = @original_LongName">
    <DeleteParameters>
        <asp:Parameter Name="original_CategoryID" Type="String" />
        <asp:Parameter Name="original_ShortName" Type="String" />
        <asp:Parameter Name="original_LongName" Type="String" />
    </DeleteParameters>
    <InsertParameters>
        <asp:Parameter Name="CategoryID" Type="String" />
        <asp:Parameter Name="ShortName" Type="String" />
        <asp:Parameter Name="LongName" Type="String" />
    </InsertParameters>
    <UpdateParameters>
        <asp:Parameter Name="ShortName" Type="String" />
        <asp:Parameter Name="LongName" Type="String" />
        <asp:Parameter Name="original_CategoryID" Type="String" />
        <asp:Parameter Name="original_ShortName" Type="String" />
        <asp:Parameter Name="original_LongName" Type="String" />
    </UpdateParameters>
</asp:SqlDataSource>
```

Notes

- The SELECT statement retrieves all rows in the Categories table.
- The WHERE clauses in the DELETE and UPDATE statements provide for optimistic concurrency.

Figure 14-14   The aspx file for the Category Maintenance application (part 2 of 3)

The body of the Default.aspx file   **Page 3**

```
            <div class="col-xs-12">
                <p>To create a new category, enter the category information
                    and click Add New Category</p>
                <p><asp:Label ID="lblError" runat="server" EnableViewState="false"
                        CssClass="text-danger"></asp:Label></p>
                <div class="form-group">
                    <label for="txtID" class="col-sm-2">ID</label>
                    <div class="col-sm-3">
                        <asp:TextBox ID="txtID" runat="server" MaxLength="10"
                            CssClass="form-control"></asp:TextBox>
                    </div>
                    <div class="col-sm-offset-3 col-sm-4">
                        <asp:RequiredFieldValidator ID="rfvID" runat="server"
                            ControlToValidate="txtID" CssClass="text-danger"
                            ErrorMessage="ID is a required field">
                        </asp:RequiredFieldValidator>
                    </div>
                </div>
                <div class="form-group">
                    <label for="txtShortName" class="col-sm-2">Short Name</label>
                    <div class="col-sm-4">
                        <asp:TextBox ID="txtShortName" runat="server"
                            MaxLength="15" CssClass="form-control"></asp:TextBox>
                    </div>
                    <div class="col-sm-offset-2 col-sm-4">
                        <asp:RequiredFieldValidator ID="rfvShortName"
                            runat="server" ControlToValidate="txtShortName"
                            CssClass="text-danger"
                            ErrorMessage="Short Name is a required field">
                        </asp:RequiredFieldValidator>
                    </div>
                </div>
                <div class="form-group">
                    <label for="txtLongName" class="col-sm-2">Long Name</label>
                    <div class="col-sm-6">
                        <asp:TextBox ID="txtLongName" runat="server"
                            MaxLength="50" CssClass="form-control"></asp:TextBox>
                    </div>
                    <div class="col-sm-4">
                        // required field validator for long name
                    </div>
                </div>
                <asp:Button ID="btnAdd" runat="server" Text="Add New Category"
                    CssClass="btn" OnClick="btnAdd_Click" />
            </div>
        </form>
        </main>
    </div>
</body>
```

Notes

- The text boxes are used to enter data for a new row.
- The required field validators ensure that the user enters data for each column of a new row.

Figure 14-14   The aspx file for the Category Maintenance application (part 3 of 3)

The code-behind file

Although it would be nice if you could create a robust database application without writing any C# code, you must still write code to insert data into a GridView control and to catch and handle any database or concurrency errors that might occur. Figure 14-15 shows this code for the Category Maintenance application.

As you can see, this code-behind file consists of four event handlers and two helper methods. The first event handler, GridView1_PreRender, works just the the PreRender event handlers you've seen earlier in this chapter.

The second event handler, btnAdd_Click, starts by checking if the data is valid. If it is, it sets the values of the three insert parameters to the values entered by the user. Then, it calls the Insert method of the data source control. If an exception is thrown, The Database ErrorMessage method is called to display an appropriate error message.

The third event handler, grdCategories_RowUpdated, is called after a row has been updated. This method checks the Exception property of the e argument to determine if an exception has been thrown. If so, the Database ErrorMessage method is called to display an error message, the ExceptionHandled property is set to True to suppress the exception, and the KeepInEditMode property is set to True to leave the GridView control in edit mode. If an exception hasn't occurred, the e argument's AffectedRows property is checked. If it's zero, it means that a concurrency error has occurred and the ConcurrencyErrorMessage method is called to display an appropriate message.

The fourth event handler, grdCategories_RowDeleted, is called after a row has been deleted. Like the method that's called after a row is updated, this method checks if an exception has been thrown or if a concurrency error has occurred. The only difference is that this method doesn't set the KeepInEditMode property to True, since the control isn't in edit mode when the Delete button is clicked.

The Default.aspx.cs file

```
public partial class Default : System.Web.UI.Page
{
    protected void grdCategories_PreRender(object sender, EventArgs e)
    {
        grdCategories.HeaderRow.TableSection = TableRowSection.TableHeader;
    }
    protected void btnAdd_Click(object sender, EventArgs e)
    {
        if (IsValid) {
            var parameters = SqlDataSource1.InsertParameters;
            parameters["CategoryID"].DefaultValue = txtID.Text;
            parameters["ShortName"].DefaultValue = txtShortName.Text;
            parameters["LongName"].DefaultValue = txtLongName.Text;
            try {
                SqlDataSource1.Insert();
                txtID.Text = "";
                txtShortName.Text = "";
                txtLongName.Text = "";
            }
            catch (Exception ex) {
                lblError.Text = DatabaseErrorMessage(ex.Message);
            }
        }
    }
    protected void grdCategories_RowUpdated(object sender,
        GridViewUpdatedEventArgs e)
    {
        if (e.Exception != null) {
            lblError.Text = DatabaseErrorMessage(e.Exception.Message);
            e.ExceptionHandled = true;
            e.KeepInEditMode = true;
        }
        else if (e.AffectedRows == 0) {
            lblError.Text = ConcurrencyErrorMessage();
        }
    }
    protected void grdCategories_RowDeleted(object sender,
        GridViewDeletedEventArgs e)
    {
        if (e.Exception != null) {
            lblError.Text = DatabaseErrorMessage(e.Exception.Message);
            e.ExceptionHandled = true;
        }
        else if (e.AffectedRows == 0) {
            lblError.Text = ConcurrencyErrorMessage();
        }
    }
    private string DatabaseErrorMessage(string errorMsg)
    {
        return $"<b>A database error has occurred:</b> {errorMsg}";
    }
    private string ConcurrencyErrorMessage()
    {
        return "Another user may have updated that category. " +
            "Please try again";
    }
}
```

Figure 14-15   The code-behind file for the Category Maintenance application

How to work with template fields

Although using bound fields is a convenient way to include bound data in a GridView control, the most flexible way is to use template fields. A *template field* is simply a field that provides one or more templates that are used to render the column. You can include anything you want in these templates, including labels or text boxes, data binding expressions, and validation controls. In fact, including validation controls for editable GridView controls is one of the main reasons for using template fields.

How to create template fields

Figure 14-16 shows how to create template fields. The easiest way to do that is to first create a regular bound field and then convert it to a template field. This changes the BoundField element to a TemplateField element and, more importantly, generates ItemTemplate and EditItemTemplate elements that include labels and text boxes with appropriate binding expressions. In particular, each EditItemTemplate element includes a text box that uses the Bind method to implement two-way binding (please see figure 13-15 for more information about this method). Note, though, that the binding expression for the Item template shown here was also generated with the Bind method. That's because the data source uses optimistic concurrency. In that case, the Bind method must be used instead of the Eval method if the GridView control is used to delete rows from the database.

Once you've converted the bound field to a template, you can edit the template to add any additional elements you want to include, such as validation controls. In the code example in this figure, you can see that I added a RequiredFieldValidator control to the EditItem template for the ShortName column. That way, the user must enter data into the txtGridShortName text box. I also changed the names of the label and the text box that were generated for the Item and EditItem templates from their defaults (Label1 and TextBox1) to lblGridShortName and txtGridShortName.

You can also edit the templates from Design view. To do that, you use the same basic techniques that you use to work with the templates for a DataList control. The main difference is that each bound column in a GridView control has its own templates. In this figure, for example, you can see the EditItem template for the ShortName column.

Although a text box is included in the EditItem template for a column by default, you can also use other types of controls. For example, you can use a check box to work with a Boolean column, and you can use a Calendar control to work with a date column. You can also use a drop-down list that lets the user select a value from the list. To do that, you must create a separate data source that retrieves the data for the list. Then, you can bind the drop-down list to this data source by setting the DataTextField and DataValueField properties as shown in the last chapter, and you can bind the drop-down list to a column in the GridView's data source by setting its SelectedValue property using the DataBindings dialog box you saw in the last chapter.

How to edit templates

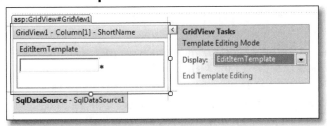

GridView template elements

Element	Description
ItemTemplate	The template used for an individual field.
AlternatingItemTemplate	The template used for alternate rows.
EditItemTemplate	The template used when the row is being edited.
HeaderTemplate	The template used for the header row.
FooterTemplate	The template used for the footer row.

A template field that includes a validation control

```
<asp:TemplateField HeaderText="Short Name">
    <ItemTemplate>
        <asp:Label ID="lblGridShortName" runat="server"
            Text='<%# Bind("ShortName") %>'></asp:Label>
    </ItemTemplate>
    <EditItemTemplate>
        <asp:TextBox ID="txtGridShortName" runat="server"
            Text='<%# Bind("ShortName") %>'></asp:TextBox>
        <asp:RequiredFieldValidator
            ID="rfvGridShortName" runat="server"
            ControlToValidate="txtGridShortName"
            ErrorMessage="Short Name is a required field."
            ValidationGroup="Edit">*</asp:RequiredFieldValidator>
    </EditItemTemplate>
</asp:TemplateField>
```

Description

- *Template fields* provide more control over the appearance of the columns in a GridView control than bound fields. A common reason for using template fields is to add validation controls.

- To create a template field, first use the Fields dialog box to create a bound field. Then, click the Convert This Field into a TemplateField link.

- To edit a template, choose Edit Templates from the smart tag menu for the GridView control. Then, select the template you want to edit in the smart tag menu and edit the template by adding text or other controls. You may also want to change the names of the labels and text boxes that were generated when you converted to a template field. When you're finished, choose End Template Editing from the smart tag menu.

Figure 14-16   How to create template fields

The template version
of the Category Maintenance application

Figure 14-17 shows a version of the Category Maintenance application that uses templates instead of bound fields in the GridView control. Then, each EditItem template includes a required field validator. In addition, the page uses a validation summary control to display any error messages that are generated by the required field validators.

The aspx code for the template version

Figure 14-18 shows the aspx code for the template version of the Category Maintenance application. Because this file is similar to the file shown in figure 14-14, this figure shows only the portions that are different. In particular, it shows the code for the GridView control and the ValidationSummary control. Because you've already been introduced to most of this code, I'll just point out a few highlights.

First, the GridView control uses template fields for the ShortName and LongName columns. These templates include required field validators to validate the text box input fields. Here, each validator is assigned to a validation group named Edit. Then, in the CommandField element for the Edit button, the CausesValidation property is set to True and the ValidationGroup property is set to Edit. As a result, when a row is displayed in edit mode, just the validators that belong to the Edit group will be invoked when the Update button is clicked.

Second, the ErrorMessage property of each of the Edit validators provides the error message that's displayed in the ValidationSummary control. For this control, you can see that the ValidationGroup is set to Edit so the right messages will be displayed. In addition, the Text property of each validator specifies that an asterisk will appear to the right of each field in the GridView control. If you look closely at the screen in the last figure, you can see that these asterisks are displayed in a dark color on a light row background.

Third, the text boxes in the EditItem templates for the Short Name and Long Name fields include the MaxLength property. That way, the user can't enter more characters than are allowed by the data source. This is another advantage of using templates with a GridView control.

Please note that even though a validation group is used for the validators in the GridView control, it isn't necessary to use another validation group for the validators outside the GridView control. Instead, when the user clicks the Add New Category button, the validation for the required field validators that aren't included in the Edit group will be done.

The Category Maintenance application with template fields

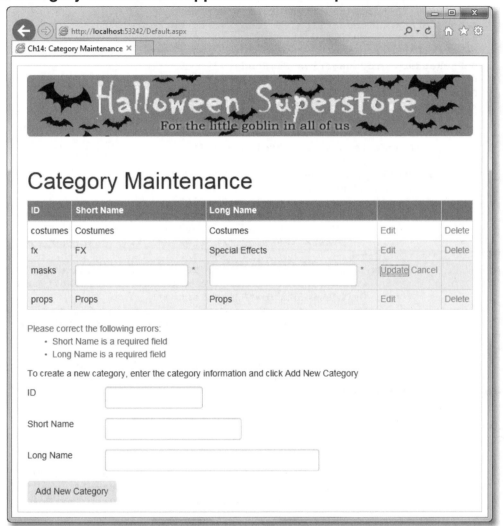

Description

- This version of the Category Maintenance application uses template fields in the GridView control, and the EditItem template for each editable field includes a required field validator.

- A ValidationSummary control is used to display the error messages generated by the required field validators.

- The text boxes in the EditItem templates for the Short Name and Long Name fields include the MaxLength property so the user can't enter more characters than are allowed by the data source.

Figure 14-17   The template version of the Category Maintenance application

The Default.aspx file

```
<asp:GridView ID="grdCategories" runat="server"
    AutoGenerateColumns="False" DataKeyNames="CategoryID"
    DataSourceID="SqlDataSource1"
    CssClass="table table-bordered table-condensed"
    OnPreRender="grdCategories_PreRender"
    OnRowDeleted="grdCategories_RowDeleted"
    OnRowUpdated="grdCategories_RowUpdated">
<Columns>
    <asp:BoundField DataField="CategoryID" HeaderText="ID"
        ReadOnly="True">
        <ItemStyle CssClass="col-xs-1" />
    </asp:BoundField>
    <asp:TemplateField HeaderText="Short Name">
        <EditItemTemplate>
            <div class="col-xs-11 col-edit">
                <asp:TextBox ID="txtGridShortName" runat="server"
                    MaxLength="15" CssClass="form-control"
                    Text='<%# Bind("ShortName") %>'></asp:TextBox>
            </div>
            <asp:RequiredFieldValidator ID="rfvGridShortName"
                runat="server" ControlToValidate="txtGridShortName"
                ValidationGroup="Edit" Text="*"
                ErrorMessage="Short Name is a required field"
                CssClass="text-danger"></asp:RequiredFieldValidator>
        </EditItemTemplate>
        <ItemTemplate>
            <asp:Label ID="lblGridShortName" runat="server"
                Text='<%# Bind("ShortName") %>'></asp:Label>
        </ItemTemplate>
        <ItemStyle CssClass="col-xs-4" />
    </asp:TemplateField>
    <asp:TemplateField HeaderText="Long Name">
        <EditItemTemplate>
            <div class="col-xs-11 col-edit">
                <asp:TextBox ID="txtGridLongName" runat="server"
                    MaxLength="50" CssClass="form-control"
                    Text='<%# Bind("LongName") %>'></asp:TextBox>
            </div>
            <asp:RequiredFieldValidator ID="rfvGridLongName"
                runat="server" ControlToValidate="txtGridLongName"
                ValidationGroup="Edit" Text="*"
                ErrorMessage="Long Name is a required field"
                CssClass="text-danger"></asp:RequiredFieldValidator>
        </EditItemTemplate>
        <ItemTemplate>
            <asp:Label ID="lblGridLongName" runat="server"
                Text='<%# Bind("LongName") %>'></asp:Label>
        </ItemTemplate>
        <ItemStyle CssClass="col-xs-5" />
    </asp:TemplateField>
```

Figure 14-18   The aspx code for the template version of the application (part 1 of 2)

The Default.aspx file   **Page 2**

```
        <asp:CommandField CausesValidation="True"
            ShowEditButton="True" ValidationGroup="Edit">
            <ItemStyle CssClass="col-xs-1" />
        </asp:CommandField>
        <asp:CommandField ShowDeleteButton="True">
            <ItemStyle CssClass="col-xs-1" />
        </asp:CommandField>
    </Columns>
    <HeaderStyle CssClass="bg-halloween" />
    <AlternatingRowStyle CssClass="altRow" />
    <EditRowStyle CssClass="warning" />
</asp:GridView>
.
.
.
<asp:ValidationSummary ID="ValidationSummary1" runat="server"
    HeaderText="Please correct the following errors:"
    ValidationGroup="Edit" CssClass="text-danger" />
.
.
```

Description

- The EditItem templates for the Short Name and Long Name fields include required field validators, which are assigned to a validation group named Edit. This group is also referenced in the code for the Edit button and the ValidationSummary control so only the validators in this group are included.

- The text boxes in the EditItem templates for the Short Name and Long Name fields include the MaxLength property so the user can't enter more characters than are allowed by the data source.

- The aspx code that's not shown in this figure is identical to the code in figure 14-14.

Figure 14-18   The aspx code for the template version of the application (part 2 of 2)

Perspective

The GridView control is ideal for any application that displays a list of items retrieved from a database, and nearly all applications have that need. It's also good for displaying search results and for maintaining tables that consist of just a few columns. If a table consists of many columns, though, you're more likely to use a GridView control to select the row to be updated or deleted and a DetailsView or FormView control to perform the update or delete operation. You'll learn how to do that in the next chapter.

Terms

paging	edit mode
command field	template field

Summary

- The GridView control displays data from a data source in a row and column format. Because the data is rendered as an HTML table, Bootstrap can be used to format the control. However, some special techniques are required.

- By default, the Gridview control displays one column for each column in the data source, but you can change those fields and add other types of fields to the control, like button, command, and hyperlink fields. Then, you can use style elements or Bootstrap CSS classes to format the fields.

- By default, the GridView control lets the users sort the rows based on the data in the columns. However, you do have to enable this feature and remove the sort expressions from those columns for which you don't want to allow sorting.

- To enable *paging* for a GridView control, you just need to set one property for the control. Then, you can customize the paging by adding a PagerSettings element to the aspx code for the control.

- *Command fields* are used to add buttons to a GridView control that let users edit, delete, or select data without requiring any C# code. To insert data, you have to use input controls such as text boxes and a button that users can click to start the insert operation. Then, the event handler for the Click event of that button adds the data to the data source that the GridView control is bound to.

- Although the GridView control provides many features automatically, you have to write C# code for handling such things as data validation, database exceptions, and concurrency errors. To do that, you can use the events that are raised by a GridView control, like the RowUpdating and RowUpdated events.

- A *template field* provides one or more templates for rendering a column. These fields can contain standard server controls, binding expressions, and validation controls. One common use of template fields is to provide the validation controls that validate the data in an editable GridView control.

Exercise 14-1   Create a Customer List application

In this exercise, you'll develop a page that displays customers in a GridView control that includes sorting and paging. When you're done, the page should look like this:

Create the GridView control and the SQL data source

1. Open the Ex14CustomerList application in the aspnet46_cs directory. This application contains the starting page and the database, image, and style sheet used by the page.

2. Add a GridView control within the div element for the form, and change its name to grdCustomers. Then, create a data source for the control that retrieves the LastName, FirstName, State, and City columns from the Customers table sorted by LastName.

3. Assign these Bootstrap table classes to the GridView control: table, table-bordered, table-striped, table-condensed.

4. Generate an event handler for the PrePrender event of the GridView, and add a statement to the event handler that will cause thead and tfoot elements to be included in the table that's rendered for the GridView.

5. Use the Fields dialog box to add an ItemStyle element to each bound field that sets the widths of the columns by using the CssClass property to assign the col-xs-3 style to first two fields and the col-xs-2 and col-xs-4 styles to the third and fourth fields respectively.

6. Run the application to see how it looks. Notice that all the customers are displayed on a single page.

Add paging to the GridView control

7. Display the smart tag menu for the GridView control and check the Enable Paging option.

8. Set the Mode property in the PagerSettings element for the GridView control to NextPreviousFirstLast. In addition, assign the pagerStyle class to the pager area in the PagerStyle element, set the background color of the pager area to #8C8C8C, and center the paging controls horizontally.

9. Run the application again, and use the paging controls to display different pages.

Add sorting to the GridView control

10. Display the smart tag menu for the GridView control and check the Enable Sorting option.

11. Remove the sort expressions from the FirstName and City fields, and set the sort expression for the State field so it sorts by city within state.

12. Run the application, and click the State heading. The rows should be sorted by city in ascending order within state in ascending order.

13. Click the State heading again. This time, the rows should be sorted by city in descending order within state in ascending order.

14. Continue experimenting if you want, and then close the browser.

15

How to use the DetailsView and FormView controls

In this chapter, you'll learn how to use the DetailsView and FormView controls. Although both of these controls are designed to work with the GridView control to display the details of the item selected in that control, they can also be used on their own or in combination with other types of list controls such as drop-down lists or list boxes.

How to use the DetailsView control

The following topics present the basics of working with the DetailsView control. However, much of what you'll learn in these topics applies to the FormView control as well.

An introduction to the DetailsView control

As figure 15-1 shows, the DetailsView control is designed to display the data for a single item of a data source. To use this control effectively, you must provide some way for the user to select which data item to display. The most common way to do that is to use the DetailsView control in combination with another control such as a GridView control or a drop-down list. At the top of this figure, you can see how the DetailsView control works with a drop-down list, and you'll see how it works with a GridView control later in this chapter.

Alternatively, you can enable paging for the DetailsView control. Then, a row of paging controls appears at the bottom of the DetailsView control, and the user can select a data item using those controls. You'll learn how this works in figure 15-3.

As the code example in this figure shows, you use the DataSourceID attribute to specify the data source that a DetailsView control should be bound to. Then, the Fields element contains a set of child elements that define the individual fields to be displayed by the DetailsView control. This is similar to the way the Columns element for a GridView control works.

Notice here that the width of the header section is specified only for the first bound field. Then, this same width is used for the other bound fields. In addition, the width of the item section isn't specified. Because of that, it takes up the remainder of the width of the control. In figure 15-3, you'll see that this works differently when you use Bootstrap classes.

A DetailsView control can be displayed in one of three modes. In ReadOnly mode, the data for the current data source row is displayed but can't be modified. In Edit mode, the user can modify the data for the current row. And in Insert mode, the user can enter data that will be inserted into the data source as a new row.

A DetailsView control that displays data for a selected product

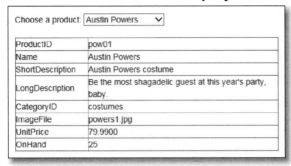

The aspx code for the DetailsView control shown above

```
<asp:DetailsView ID="DetailsView1" runat="server" AutoGenerateRows="False"
    DataKeyNames="ProductID" DataSourceID="SqlDataSource2" Width="450px">
    <Fields>
        <asp:BoundField DataField="ProductID" HeaderText="ProductID"
            ReadOnly="True">
            <HeaderStyle Width="125px" />
        </asp:BoundField>
        <asp:BoundField DataField="Name" HeaderText="Name" />
        <asp:BoundField DataField="ShortDescription"
            HeaderText="ShortDescription" />
        <asp:BoundField DataField="LongDescription"
            HeaderText="LongDescription" />
        <asp:BoundField DataField="CategoryID" HeaderText="CategoryID" />
        <asp:BoundField DataField="ImageFile" HeaderText="ImageFile" />
        <asp:BoundField DataField="UnitPrice" HeaderText="UnitPrice" />
        <asp:BoundField DataField="OnHand" HeaderText="OnHand" />
    </Fields>
</asp:DetailsView>
```

Three modes of the DetailsView control

Mode	Description
ReadOnly	Used to display an item from the data source.
Edit	Used to edit an item in the data source.
Insert	Used to insert a new item into the data source.

Description

- The DetailsView control displays data for a single row of a data source. It is typically used in combination with a drop-down list or GridView control that is used to select the item to be displayed.

- The DetailsView element includes a Fields element that contains a BoundField element for each field retrieved from the data source.

- You can edit the fields collection by choosing Edit Fields from the smart tag menu of a DetailsView control.

Figure 15-1   An introduction to the DetailsView control

Properties and child elements for the DetailsView control

The tables in figure 15-2 list the properties and child elements you can use to declare a DetailsView control. The first table lists the properties you're most likely to use for this control. You can use the DataKeyNames property to list the names of the primary key fields for the data source. And you can set the AutoGenerateRows property to True if you want the DetailsView control to automatically generate data fields. Then, you'll want to delete the Fields element that was added when you created the DetailsView control.

By the way, there are many other attributes you can use on the DetailsView element to specify the control's layout and formatting. For example, you can include attributes like Height, Width, BackColor, and ForeColor. To see all of the attributes that are available, you can use the HTML Editor's IntelliSense feature.

The second table in this figure lists the child elements that you can use between the start and end tags of the DetailsView element. Most of these elements provide styles and templates that control the formatting and content for the different parts of the DetailsView control. Like the DataList and GridView controls, the DetailsView control is rendered as a table. Because the generated code can be complicated, though, it's best to use the Style elements to format the control rather than using CSS to format the rendered table. The exception is if you're using Bootstrap. Then, you can use the Bootstrap table classes to provide the basic format for the rendered table. You can also use some of the other Bootstrap classes with the Style elements.

The Fields element can contain any of the child elements listed in the third table of this figure. These elements describe the individual fields that are displayed by the DetailsView control. Although this figure doesn't show it, these child elements can themselves include child elements to specify formatting. For example, you can include HeaderStyle and ItemStyle as child elements of a BoundField element to control the formatting for the header and item sections of a bound field. Here again, you can use the HTML Editor's IntelliSense feature to see what child elements are available and what attributes they support.

Note that when Visual Studio generates a BoundField element for a DetailsView control, it includes a SortExpression attribute just as it does for a GridView control. Because the DetailsView control doesn't support sorting, though, you can delete this attribute if you want to simplify the aspx code.

How to define the fields in a DetailsView control

Just like when you create a GridView control, one BoundField element is created for each column in the data source when you create a DetailsView control. Then, you can work with those fields or create additional fields using the Fields dialog box you saw in figure 14-2 of chapter 14. To display this dialog box, you choose the Edit Fields command from the control's smart tag menu. You can also use the HTML editor to create these fields manually. Or you can use the Add Field dialog box as described later in this chapter.

DetailsView control properties

Property	Description
DataSourceID	The ID of the data source to bind the DetailsView control to.
DataKeyNames	A list of field names that form the primary key for the data source.
AutoGenerateRows	If True, a row is automatically generated for each field in the data source. If False, you must define the rows in the Fields element.
DefaultMode	Sets the initial mode of the DetailsView control. Valid options are Edit, Insert, or ReadOnly.
AllowPaging	Set to True to allow paging.

DetailsView child elements

Element	Description
Fields	The fields that are displayed by a DetailsView control.
RowStyle	The style used for data rows in ReadOnly mode.
AlternatingRowStyle	The style used for alternate rows.
EditRowStyle	The style used for data rows in Edit mode.
InsertRowStyle	The style used for data rows in Insert mode.
CommandRowStyle	The style used for command rows.
EmptyDataRowStyle	The style used for data rows when the data source is empty.
EmptyDataTemplate	The template used when the data source is empty.
HeaderStyle	The style used for the header row.
HeaderTemplate	The template used for the header row.
FooterStyle	The style used for the footer row.
FooterTemplate	The template used for the footer row.
PagerSettings	The settings used to control the pager row.
PagerStyle	The style used for the pager row.
PagerTemplate	The template used for the pager row.

Fields child elements

Element	Description
asp:BoundField	A field bound to a data source column.
asp:ButtonField	A field that displays a button.
asp:CheckBoxField	A field that displays a check box.
asp:CommandField	A field that contains command buttons.
asp:HyperlinkField	A field that displays a hyperlink.
asp:ImageField	A field that displays an image.
asp:TemplateField	A column with custom content.

Figure 15-2   Attributes and child elements for the DetailsView control

How to enable paging

Like the GridView control, the DetailsView control supports paging. As figure 15-3 shows, a row of paging controls is displayed at the bottom of the DetailsView control when you set the AllowPaging attribute to True. Then, you can specify the paging mode by including a PagerSettings element, and you can include PagerStyle and PagerTemplate elements to specify the formatting and content of the pager controls.

Notice in the code example in this figure that Bootstrap table classes are used to format the table that ASP.NET renders for the DetailsView control. In addition, a Bootstrap column class is used to specify the width of the header section. Unfortunately, when you use a column class like this, you must code a HeaderStyle element for each bound field. You don't have to code an ItemStyle element, though, unless you don't want the item section to take up the remainder of the row width.

If the data source that's associated with a DetailsView control contains more than a few dozen items, paging isn't a practical way to provide for navigation. In most cases, then, a DetailsView control is associated with a list control that is used to select the item to be displayed. You'll learn how to create pages that work this way in the next figure.

A DetailsView control that allows paging

Product ID	bats01
Name	Flying Bats
Short Description	Bats flying in front of moon
Long Description	Bats flying in front of a full moon make for an eerie spectacle.
Category ID	props
Image File	cool1.jpg
Uni tPrice	69.9900
On Hand	25
<<<>>>	

The aspx code for the DetailsView control shown above

```
<asp:DetailsView ID="DetailsView1" runat="server" AutoGenerateRows="False"
    DataKeyNames="ProductID" DataSourceID="SqlDataSource1"
    AllowPaging="True" CssClass="table table-bordered table-condensed">
    <PagerSettings Mode="NextPreviousFirstLast" />
    <Fields>
        <asp:BoundField DataField="ProductID" HeaderText="Product ID"
            ReadOnly="True">
            <HeaderStyle CssClass="col-xs-3" />
        </asp:BoundField>
        <asp:BoundField DataField="Name" HeaderText="Name">
            <HeaderStyle CssClass="col-xs-3" />
        </asp:BoundField>
        <asp:BoundField DataField="ShortDescription"
            HeaderText="Short Description">
            <HeaderStyle CssClass="col-xs-3" />
        </asp:BoundField>
        .
        .
        <asp:BoundField DataField="UnitPrice" HeaderText="Unit Price">
            <HeaderStyle CssClass="col-xs-3" />
        </asp:BoundField>
        <asp:BoundField DataField="OnHand" HeaderText="On Hand">
            <HeaderStyle CssClass="col-xs-3" />
        </asp:BoundField>
    </Fields>
</asp:DetailsView>
```

Description

- The DetailsView control supports paging. Then, you can move from one item to the next by using the paging controls. This works much the same as it does for a GridView control, except that data from only one row is displayed at a time.

- For more information about paging, please refer to figure 14-6 in chapter 14.

Figure 15-3   How to enable paging

How to create a Master/Detail page

As figure 15-4 shows, a *Master/Detail page* is a page that displays a list of data items from a data source along with the details for one of the items selected from the list. The list of items can be displayed by any control that allows the user to select an item, including a drop-down list or a GridView control. Then, you can use a DetailsView control to display the details for the selected item. The page shown in figure 15-1 is an example of a Master/Detail page in which the master list is displayed as a drop-down list and a DetailsView control is used to display the details for the selected item.

A Master/Detail page typically uses two data sources. The first retrieves the items to be displayed by the control that contains the list of data items. For efficiency's sake, this data source should retrieve only the data columns necessary to display the list. For example, the data source for the drop-down list in figure 15-1 only needs to retrieve the ProductName and ProductID columns from the Products table in the Halloween database.

The second data source provides the data for the selected item. It usually uses a parameter to specify which row should be retrieved from the database. In the example in this figure, the data source uses a parameter that's bound to the drop-down list. That way, this data source automatically retrieves the data for the product that's selected by the drop-down list.

A Master/Detail page typically contains:

- A control that lets the user choose an item to display, such as a drop-down list or a GridView control.

- A data source that retrieves all of the items to be displayed in the list. The control that contains the list of data items should be bound to this data source.

- A DetailsView control that displays data for the item selected by the user.

- A data source that retrieves the data for the item selected by the user. The DetailsView control should be bound to this data source. To retrieve the selected item, this data source can use a parameter that's bound to the SelectedValue property of the control that contains the list of data items.

A SqlDataSource control with a parameter that's bound to a drop-down list

```
<asp:SqlDataSource ID="SqlDataSource2" runat="server"
    ConnectionString="<%$ ConnectionStrings:HalloweenConnection %>"
    SelectCommand="SELECT [ProductID], [Name], [ShortDescription],
        [LongDescription], [CategoryID], [ImageFile], [UnitPrice], [OnHand]
        FROM [Products]
        WHERE ([ProductID] = @ProductID)">
    <SelectParameters>
        <asp:ControlParameter ControlID="ddlProducts" Name="ProductID"
            PropertyName="SelectedValue" Type="String" />
    </SelectParameters>
</asp:SqlDataSource>
```

Description

- A *Master/Detail page* is a page that displays a list of items from a database along with the details of one item from the list. The DetailsView control is often used to display the details portion of a Master/Detail page.

- The list portion of a Master/Detail page can be displayed by any control that contains a list of data items, including a drop-down list or a GridView control.

- A Master/Detail page usually includes two data sources, one for the master list and the other for the DetailsView control.

Figure 15-4   How to create a Master/Detail page

How to update the data in a DetailsView control

Besides displaying data for a specific item from a data source, you can also use a DetailsView control to edit, insert, and delete items. You'll learn how to do that in the following topics.

An introduction to command buttons

Much like the GridView control, the DetailsView control uses command buttons to let the user edit and delete data. Thus, the DetailsView control provides Edit, Delete, Update, and Cancel buttons. In addition, the DetailsView control lets the user insert data, so it provides for two more buttons. The New button places the DetailsView control into Insert mode, and the Insert button accepts the data entered by the user and writes it to the data source. These command buttons are summarized in figure 15-5.

You can provide the command buttons for a DetailsView control in two ways. The easiest way is to use the AutoGenerate*xxx*Button properties, which are listed in the second table and illustrated in the code example. However, when you use these properties, you have no control over the appearance of the buttons. For that, you must use command fields as described in the next figure.

A DetailsView control with automatically generated command buttons

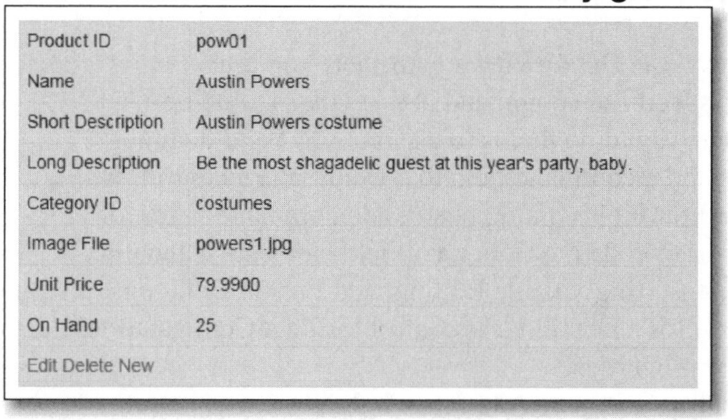

Product ID	pow01
Name	Austin Powers
Short Description	Austin Powers costume
Long Description	Be the most shagadelic guest at this year's party, baby.
Category ID	costumes
Image File	powers1.jpg
Unit Price	79.9900
On Hand	25
Edit Delete New	

Command buttons

Button	Description
Edit	Places the DetailsView control in Edit mode.
Delete	Deletes the current item and leaves the DetailsView control in ReadOnly mode.
New	Places the DetailsView control in Insert mode.
Update	Displayed only in Edit mode. Updates the data source, then returns to ReadOnly mode.
Insert	Displayed only in Insert mode. Inserts the data, then returns to ReadOnly mode.
Cancel	Displayed in Edit or Insert mode. Cancels the operation and returns to ReadOnly mode.

Properties that generate command buttons

Property	Description
`AutoGenerateDeleteButton`	Generates a Delete button.
`AutoGenerateEditButton`	Generates an Edit button.
`AutoGenerateInsertButton`	Generates a New button.

A DetailsView element that automatically generates command buttons

```
<asp:DetailsView ID="DetailsView1" runat="server"
    DataSourceID="SqlDataSource2" DataKeyNames="ProductID"
    AutoGenerateRows="False"
    AutoGenerateDeleteButton="True"
    AutoGenerateEditButton="True"
    AutoGenerateInsertButton="True">
</asp:DetailsView>
```

Description

- The DetailsView control supports six different command buttons.
- You can use the AutoGenerateDeleteButton, AutoGenerateEditButton, and AutoGenerateInsertButton properties to automatically generate command buttons.
- To customize command button appearance, use command fields instead of automatically generated buttons as described in the next figure.

Figure 15-5 An introduction to command buttons

How to add command buttons

Like the GridView control, the DetailsView control lets you use CommandField elements to specify the command buttons that should be displayed by the control. One way to do that is to use the Add Field dialog box shown in figure 15-6 to add a command field to a DetailsView control. Of course, you can also use the Edit Fields dialog box to add command fields, or you can use the HTML Editor to code the CommandField elements manually. You can also use the Enable Inserting, Enable Editing, and Enable Deleting options in the smart tag menu for a DetailsView control to add a CommandField element with the appropriate properties.

To create a command button using the Add Field dialog box, you select CommandField as the field type. When you do, four check boxes appear that let you select which command buttons you want to show in the command field. In addition, a drop-down list lets you choose whether the command buttons should be displayed as buttons or hyperlinks.

When you first display the Add Field dialog box for a command field, you'll notice that the Show Cancel Button check box is disabled. That's because this button can only be used in conjunction with the New/Insert and Edit/Update buttons. When you select one of these buttons, then, the Show Cancel Button check box is enabled and it's selected by default. That makes sense because you'll typically want to allow the user to cancel out of an insert or edit operation.

Note that the CommandField element includes attributes that let you specify the text or image to be displayed and whether the button causes validation. For more information about using these attributes, please refer back to chapter 14.

Before going on, you should realize that you can use the Add Field dialog box to create any of the elements shown in the third table in figure 15-2. To do that, you just select the type of field you want to create from the drop-down list at the top of the dialog box. Then, the appropriate options for that field type are displayed. If you experiment with this, you shouldn't have any trouble figuring out how it works.

The Add Field dialog box for adding a command field

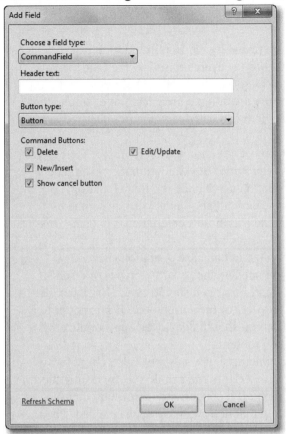

Code generated by the above dialog box

```
<asp:CommandField ButtonType="Button"
    ShowDeleteButton="True"
    ShowEditButton="True"
    ShowInsertButton="True" />
```

Description

- You can add command buttons to a DetailsView control to let the user update, insert, and delete data.

- The command buttons for a DetailsView control are similar to the command buttons for a GridView control. However, the DetailsView control doesn't provide a Select button, and it does provide New and Insert buttons. For more information about command buttons, please refer to figure 14-10 in chapter 14.

- To display the Add Field dialog box, choose Add New Field from the smart tag menu of the DetailsView control.

Figure 15-6   How to add command buttons

How to use events raised by the DetailsView control

Figure 15-7 lists the events that are raised by the DetailsView control. As you can see, these events are similar to the events raised by the GridView control. Most of these events come in pairs: one that's raised before an operation occurs, and another that's raised after the operation completes. For example, the ItemDeleting event is raised before an item is deleted, and the ItemDeleted event is raised after an item has been deleted.

As with the GridView control, the most common reason to handle the before events for the DetailsView control is to provide data validation. For example, when the user clicks the Update button, you can handle the ItemUpdating event to make sure the user has entered correct data. Then, you can set the e argument's Cancel property to True if the user hasn't entered correct data. This cancels the update.

The after-action events let you check that database operations have completed successfully. To do that, you need to check for two types of errors as illustrated in the example in this figure. First, you should check for database exceptions by testing the Exception property of the e argument. If it is not null, a database exception has occurred. Then, you should display an appropriate error message to let the user know about the problem.

If the data source uses optimistic concurrency, you should also check to make sure there hasn't been a concurrency error. You can do that by testing the AffectedRows property of the e argument. If a concurrency error has occurred, this property will be set to zero meaning that no rows have been changed. Then, you can display an appropriate error message.

If no errors occurred during the update operation, the ItemUpdated event shown in this figure ends by calling the DataBind method for the drop-down list control. This is necessary because view state is enabled for this control. As a result, this control will continue to display the old data unless you call its DataBind method to refresh its data. If view state were disabled for this control, the DataBind call wouldn't be necessary.

Events raised by the DetailsView control

Event	Description
`ItemCommand`	Raised when a button is clicked.
`ItemCreated`	Raised when an item is created.
`DataBound`	Raised when data binding completes for an item.
`ItemDeleted`	Raised when an item has been deleted.
`ItemDeleting`	Raised when an item is about to be deleted.
`ItemInserted`	Raised when an item has been inserted.
`ItemInserting`	Raised when an item is about to be inserted.
`ItemUpdated`	Raised when an item has been updated.
`ItemUpdating`	Raised when an item is about to be updated.
`PageIndexChanged`	Raised when the index of the displayed item has changed.
`PageIndexChanging`	Raised when the index of the displayed item is about to change.

An event handler for the ItemUpdated event

```
protected void DetailsView1_ItemUpdated(
    object sender, DetailsViewUpdatedEventArgs e)
{
    if (e.Exception != null)
    {
        lblError.Text = "A database error has occurred. " +
            "Message: " + e.Exception.Message;
        e.ExceptionHandled = true;
    }
    else if (e.AffectedRows == 0)
    {
        lblError.Text = "Another user may have updated that product. "
            + "Please try again.";
    }
    else
    {
        ddlProducts.DataBind();
    }
}
```

Description

- Like the GridView control, the DetailsView control raises events that you can use to test for database exceptions and concurrency errors.

- To determine if a SQL exception has occurred, test the Exception property of the e argument. If an exception has occurred, you can set the ExceptionHandled property to True to suppress the exception. You can also set the KeepInEditMode or KeepInInsertMode property to True to keep the control in Edit or Insert mode.

- If the AffectedRows property of the e argument is zero and an exception has not been thrown, a concurrency error has probably occurred.

- If the DetailsView control is used on a Master/Detail page, you should call the DataBind method of the master list control after a successful insert, update, or delete.

Figure 15-7   How to use events raised by the DetailsView control

How to create template fields

Like the GridView control, you can use template fields to control the appearance of the fields in a DetailsView control. You can do that to add validation controls or to use controls other than text boxes as described in the last chapter or to modify the text boxes that are displayed by default. Figure 15-8 illustrates how this works.

At the top of this figure, you can see two DetailsView controls displayed in Edit mode. The first control uses the default BoundField elements. Here, you can see that the text box for the long description isn't big enough to display all of the data in this column for the selected product, which makes it more difficult for the user to modify this field. In addition, to change the category, the user must enter the category ID. That makes it more likely that the user will enter a value that isn't valid.

The second DetailsView control illustrates how you can use templates to make it easier for the user to work with the data. Here, all of the text boxes have been resized so they're appropriate for the data they will display. In particular, the text box for the long description has been changed to a multi-line text box. In addition, the text box for the category ID has been replaced by a drop-down list that displays the category name. This control is bound to a separate data source that retrieves the category IDs and category names from the Categories table.

To create template fields for a DetailsView control, you use the same techniques you use to create template fields for a GridView control. That is, you convert bound fields to template fields, you switch to template-editing mode, and you select the template you want to edit. The table in this figure lists the five templates that are available for the template fields in a DetailsView control. In most cases, you'll define just the Item, EditItem, and InsertItem templates as shown in the code example in this figure.

The template field shown here is for the Name column of the Products table. Notice that the MaxLength attributes for the text boxes in this column are set so the user can't enter more characters than are allowed by the Name column. As you'll see in the aspx code for the Product Maintenance application that's presented next, this same technique is used to restrict the number of characters that can be entered for the ProductID, ShortDescription, LongDescription, and ImageFile columns.

A DetailsView control in Edit mode without and with templates

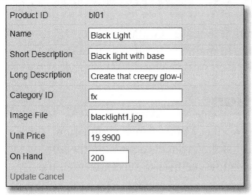
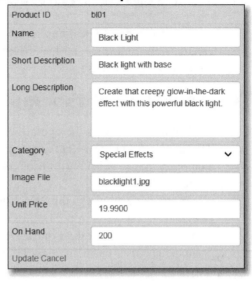

DetailsView template elements

Element	Description
ItemTemplate	The template used for an individual field.
AlternatingItemTemplate	The template used for alternating fields.
EditItemTemplate	The template used for a field in Edit mode.
InsertItemTemplate	The template used for a field in Insert mode.
HeaderTemplate	The template used for the header text for a field.

The aspx code for a custom template field

```
<asp:TemplateField HeaderText="Name:">
    <ItemTemplate>
        <asp:Label ID="lblName" runat="server" Text='<%# Bind("Name") %>'>
        </asp:Label>
    </ItemTemplate>
    <EditItemTemplate>
        <asp:TextBox ID="txtName" runat="server" Text='<%# Bind("Name") %>'
            CssClass="form-control" MaxLength="50">
        </asp:TextBox>
    </EditItemTemplate>
    <InsertItemTemplate>
        <asp:TextBox ID="txtName" runat="server" Text='<%# Bind("Name") %>'
            CssClass="form-control" MaxLength="50">
        </asp:TextBox>
    </InsertItemTemplate>
</asp:TemplateField>
```

Description

- You can use template fields to control the appearance of the fields in a DetailsView control using the same techniques you use to work with template fields in a GridView control. See figure 14-16 in chapter 14 for more information.

Figure 15-8   How to create template fields

The Product Maintenance application

The following topics present an application that uses GridView and DetailsView controls in a Master/Detail page to maintain the Products table in the Halloween database.

The operation of the application

Figure 15-9 shows the operation of the Product Maintenance application. This application uses a GridView control to list the product records on the left side of the page. This control uses paging to allow the user to scroll through the entire Products table.

When the user clicks the Select button for a product, the details for that product are displayed in the DetailsView control on the right side of the page. Then, the user can use the Edit or Delete button to edit or delete the selected product. The user can also click the New button to insert a new product.

The aspx file

Figure 15-10 shows the Default.aspx file for the Product Maintenance application. In part 1, you can see the GridView control that displays the products as well as the data source for this control. Notice that the SelectedIndex attribute of the GridView control is set to 0. That way, the information for the first product will be displayed in the DetailsView control when the page is first displayed.

The DetailsView control is shown in parts 2 and 3 of the listing. Here, the CssClass property assigns three Bootstrap table classes that control the overall appearance of the control. In addition, RowStyle and CommandRowStyle elements are included to control the colors used by the control. Since EditRowStyle and InsertRowStyle elements aren't included, these styles will default to the RowStyle.

To make it easier for the user to work with the data in the DetailsView control, all of the bound fields have been converted to template fields. Then, the EditItem and InsertItem templates for these fields were modified so the fields are displayed as shown in the second DetailsView control in figure 15-8. In addition, required field validators were added for each field except for the category ID and image file fields, and compare validators were added for the unit price and on hand fields. Finally, a command field that provides for Edit, Delete, and New buttons was added.

Before going on, you should notice the Bootstrap column classes that are used by the template fields. Here, each text box and drop-down list is coded within a div element that uses the col-xs-11 class. That way, these controls will take up eleven of the twelve columns that are available in the item section. Then, the col-edit and col-insert classes provide the spacing for these controls.

The first template field also includes a HeaderStyle element that uses a Bootstrap column class to specify the width of the header section. Unlike when

The Product Maintenance application

Description

- The Product Maintenance application uses a GridView control and a DetailsView control to let the user update the data in the Products table.

- To select a product, the user locates the product in the GridView control and clicks the Select button. This displays the details for the product in the DetailsView control. Then, the user can click the Edit button to change the product data or the Delete button to delete the product.

- To add a new product to the database, the user clicks the New button in the DetailsView control. Then, the user can enter the data for the new product and click the Insert button.

Figure 15-9   The Product Maintenance application

The Default.aspx file
Page 1

```
<%@ Page Language="C#" AutoEventWireup="true" CodeBehind="Default.aspx.cs"
Inherits="Ch15ProductMaintenance.Default" %>

<!DOCTYPE html>

<html xmlns="http://www.w3.org/1999/xhtml">
<head runat="server">
    <title>Ch15: Product Maintenance</title>
    <meta name="viewport" content="width=device-width, initial-scale=1" />
    <link href="Content/bootstrap.min.css" rel="stylesheet" />
    <link href="Content/site.css" rel="stylesheet" />
    <script src="Scripts/jquery-1.9.1.min.js"></script>
    <script src="Scripts/bootstrap.min.js"></script>
</head>
<body>
<div class="container">
  <header class="jumbotron"><%-- image set in site.css --%></header>
  <main class="row">
    <form id="form1" runat="server">
      <div class="col-sm-6 table-responsive">
        <asp:GridView ID="grdProducts" runat="server" SelectedIndex="0"
            AutoGenerateColumns="False" DataKeyNames="ProductID"
            DataSourceID="SqlDataSource1" AllowPaging="True"
            CssClass="table table-bordered table-striped table-condensed"
            OnPreRender="GridView1_PreRender">
            <Columns>
              <asp:BoundField DataField="ProductID" HeaderText="ID"
                  ReadOnly="True">
                  <ItemStyle CssClass="col-xs-2" />
              </asp:BoundField>
              <asp:BoundField DataField="Name" HeaderText="Name">
                  <ItemStyle CssClass="col-xs-6" />
              </asp:BoundField>
              <asp:BoundField DataField="CategoryID"
                  HeaderText="Category">
                  <ItemStyle CssClass="col-xs-3" />
              </asp:BoundField>
              <asp:CommandField ButtonType="Link"
                  ShowSelectButton="true">
                  <ItemStyle CssClass="col-xs-1" />
              </asp:CommandField>
            </Columns>
            <HeaderStyle CssClass="bg-halloween" />
            <PagerSettings Mode="NumericFirstLast" />
            <PagerStyle CssClass="pagerStyle"
                BackColor="#8c8c8c" HorizontalAlign="Center" />
            <SelectedRowStyle CssClass="warning" />
        </asp:GridView>
        <asp:SqlDataSource ID="SqlDataSource1" runat="server"
            ConnectionString="<%$ ConnectionStrings:HalloweenConnection %>"
            SelectCommand="SELECT [ProductID], [Name], [CategoryID],
                [UnitPrice], [OnHand] FROM [Products] ORDER BY [Name]">
        </asp:SqlDataSource>
      </div>
```

Figure 15-10   The aspx file for the Product Maintenance application (part 1 of 4)

The Default.aspx file   Page 2

```
<div class="col-sm-6">
  <asp:DetailsView ID="dvProduct" runat="server"
    DataSourceID="SqlDataSource2" DataKeyNames="ProductID"
    AutoGenerateRows="False"
    CssClass="table table-bordered table-condensed"
    OnItemDeleted="DetailsView1_ItemDeleted"
    OnItemDeleting="DetailsView1_ItemDeleting"
    OnItemInserted="DetailsView1_ItemInserted"
    OnItemUpdated="DetailsView1_ItemUpdated">
    <Fields>
      <asp:TemplateField HeaderText="Product ID">
        <ItemTemplate>
          <asp:Label runat="server" ID="lblProductID"
            Text='<%# Bind("ProductID") %>'></asp:Label>
        </ItemTemplate>
        <EditItemTemplate>
          <asp:Label runat="server" ID="lblProductID"
            Text='<%# Eval("ProductID") %>'></asp:Label>
        </EditItemTemplate>
        <InsertItemTemplate>
          <div class="col-xs-11 col-insert">
            <asp:TextBox runat="server" ID="txtProductID"
              Text='<%# Bind("ProductID") %>' MaxLength="10"
              CssClass="form-control"></asp:TextBox></div>
            <asp:RequiredFieldValidator ID="rfvProductID"
              runat="server" CssClass="text-danger"
              ControlToValidate="txtProductID"
              ErrorMessage="ProductID is a required field."
              Text="*"></asp:RequiredFieldValidator>
        </InsertItemTemplate>
        <HeaderStyle CssClass="col-xs-4" />
      </asp:TemplateField>
          .
          .
          .
      <asp:TemplateField HeaderText="Category">
        <ItemTemplate>
          <asp:Label runat="server" ID="lblCategory"
            Text='<%# Bind("CategoryID") %>'></asp:Label>
        </ItemTemplate>
        <EditItemTemplate>
          <div class="col-xs-11 col-edit">
            <asp:DropDownList runat="server" ID="ddlCategory"
              DataSourceID="SqlDataSource3"
              DataTextField="LongName" DataValueField="CategoryID"
              SelectedValue='<%# Bind("CategoryID") %>'
              CssClass="form-control"></asp:DropDownList></div>
        </EditItemTemplate>
        <InsertItemTemplate>
          <div class="col-xs-11 col-insert">
            <asp:DropDownList runat="server" ID="ddlCategory"
              DataSourceID="SqlDataSource3"
              DataTextField="LongName" DataValueField="CategoryID"
              SelectedValue='<%# Bind("CategoryID") %>'
              CssClass="form-control"></asp:DropDownList></div>
        </InsertItemTemplate>
      </asp:TemplateField>
          .
          .
          .
```

Figure 15-10   The aspx file for the Product Maintenance application (part 2 of 4)

The Default.aspx file

```
                    <asp:CommandField ButtonType="Link"
                        ShowDeleteButton="true"
                        ShowEditButton="true"
                        ShowInsertButton="true" />
                </Fields>
                <RowStyle BackColor="#e7e7e7" />
                <CommandRowStyle BackColor="#8c8c8c" ForeColor="white" />
            </asp:DetailsView>
            <asp:SqlDataSource ID="SqlDataSource2" runat="server"
                ConnectionString="<%$ ConnectionStrings:HalloweenConnection %>"
                ConflictDetection="CompareAllValues"
                OldValuesParameterFormatString="original_{0}"
                SelectCommand="SELECT [ProductID], [Name], [ShortDescription],
                        [LongDescription], [CategoryID], [ImageFile],
                        [UnitPrice], [OnHand]
                    FROM [Products]
                    WHERE ([ProductID] = @ProductID)"
                DeleteCommand="DELETE FROM [Products]
                    WHERE [ProductID] = @original_ProductID
                    AND [Name] = @original_Name
                    AND [ShortDescription] = @original_ShortDescription
                    AND [LongDescription] = @original_LongDescription
                    AND [CategoryID] = @original_CategoryID
                    AND (([ImageFile] = @original_ImageFile)
                     OR ([ImageFile] IS NULL AND @original_ImageFile IS NULL))
                    AND [UnitPrice] = @original_UnitPrice
                    AND [OnHand] = @original_OnHand"
                InsertCommand="INSERT INTO [Products] ([ProductID], [Name],
                        [ShortDescription], [LongDescription], [CategoryID],
                        [ImageFile], [UnitPrice], [OnHand])
                    VALUES (@ProductID, @Name, @ShortDescription,
                        @LongDescription, @CategoryID, @ImageFile,
                        @UnitPrice, @OnHand)"
                UpdateCommand="UPDATE [Products] SET [Name] = @Name,
                        [ShortDescription] = @ShortDescription,
                        [LongDescription] = @LongDescription,
                        [CategoryID] = @CategoryID,
                        [ImageFile] = @ImageFile,
                        [UnitPrice] = @UnitPrice,
                        [OnHand] = @OnHand
                    WHERE [ProductID] = @original_ProductID
                    AND [Name] = @original_Name
                    AND [ShortDescription] = @original_ShortDescription
                    AND [LongDescription] = @original_LongDescription
                    AND [CategoryID] = @original_CategoryID
                    AND (([ImageFile] = @original_ImageFile)
                     OR ([ImageFile] IS NULL AND @original_ImageFile IS NULL))
                    AND [UnitPrice] = @original_UnitPrice
                    AND [OnHand] = @original_OnHand">
                <SelectParameters>
                    <asp:ControlParameter ControlID="GridView1" Name="ProductID"
                        PropertyName="SelectedValue" Type="String" />
                </SelectParameters>
```

Figure 15-10   The aspx file for the Product Maintenance application (part 3 of 4)

The Default.aspx file

```
            <DeleteParameters>
              <asp:Parameter Name="original_ProductID" Type="String" />
              <asp:Parameter Name="original_Name" Type="String" />
              <asp:Parameter Name="original_ShortDescription" Type="String" />
              <asp:Parameter Name="original_LongDescription" Type="String" />
              <asp:Parameter Name="original_CategoryID" Type="String" />
              <asp:Parameter Name="original_ImageFile" Type="String" />
              <asp:Parameter Name="original_UnitPrice" Type="Decimal" />
              <asp:Parameter Name="original_OnHand" Type="Int32" />
            </DeleteParameters>
            <UpdateParameters>
              <asp:Parameter Name="Name" Type="String" />
              <asp:Parameter Name="ShortDescription" Type="String" />
              <asp:Parameter Name="LongDescription" Type="String" />
              <asp:Parameter Name="CategoryID" Type="String" />
              <asp:Parameter Name="ImageFile" Type="String" />
              <asp:Parameter Name="UnitPrice" Type="Decimal" />
              <asp:Parameter Name="OnHand" Type="Int32" />
              <asp:Parameter Name="original_ProductID" Type="String" />
              <asp:Parameter Name="original_Name" Type="String" />
              <asp:Parameter Name="original_ShortDescription" Type="String" />
              <asp:Parameter Name="original_LongDescription" Type="String" />
              <asp:Parameter Name="original_CategoryID" Type="String" />
              <asp:Parameter Name="original_ImageFile" Type="String" />
              <asp:Parameter Name="original_UnitPrice" Type="Decimal" />
              <asp:Parameter Name="original_OnHand" Type="Int32" />
            </UpdateParameters>
            <InsertParameters>
              <asp:Parameter Name="ProductID" Type="String" />
              <asp:Parameter Name="Name" Type="String" />
              <asp:Parameter Name="ShortDescription" Type="String" />
              <asp:Parameter Name="LongDescription" Type="String" />
              <asp:Parameter Name="CategoryID" Type="String" />
              <asp:Parameter Name="ImageFile" Type="String" />
              <asp:Parameter Name="UnitPrice" Type="Decimal" />
              <asp:Parameter Name="OnHand" Type="Int32" />
            </InsertParameters>
        </asp:SqlDataSource>
        <asp:SqlDataSource ID="SqlDataSource3" runat="server"
            ConnectionString='<%$ ConnectionStrings:HalloweenConnection %>'
            SelectCommand="SELECT [CategoryID], [LongName]
                FROM [Categories] ORDER BY [LongName]">
        </asp:SqlDataSource>
        <p>
          <asp:ValidationSummary ID="ValidationSummary1" runat="server"
              HeaderText="Please correct the following errors:"
              CssClass="text-danger" />
        </p>
        <p>
          <asp:Label ID="lblError" runat="server"
              EnableViewState="false" CssClass="text-danger"></asp:Label></p>
      </div>
    </form>
    </main>
  </div>
  </body>
  </html>
```

Figure 15-10   The aspx file for the Product Maintenance application (part 4 of 4)

you use bound fields, you only need to include the HeaderStyle element on one of the fields when you use template fields.

In parts 3 and 4 of figure 15-10, you can see the aspx code for the data source that the DetailsView control is bound to. This data source includes Delete and Update statements that use optimistic concurrency.

A data source is also included for the drop-down lists that are used to display the categories in the EditItem and InsertItem templates for the CategoryID field. You can see this data source in part 4 of this figure. If you look back at the definitions of the drop-down lists, you'll see how they're bound to this data source.

The code-behind file

Figure 15-11 shows the code-behind file for the Default page of the Product Maintenance application. Even though this application provides complete maintenance for the Products table, only five event handler methods are required. You learned about the first event handler in the last chapter. It adds thead and tbody elements to the table that's rendered for the GridView control so the Bootstrap table classes can be used with it.

The other event handlers respond to events raised by the DetailsView control. The first three handle database exceptions and concurrency errors for updates, deletions, and insertions. Note that the error-handling code for the insert method is simpler than the error-handling code for the update and delete methods. That's because optimistic concurrency doesn't apply to insert operations. As a result, there's no need to check the AffectedRows property to see if a concurrency error has occurred.

The last method, DetailsView1_ItemDeleting, handles a problem that can occur when you apply a format to a control that's bound to the data source. In this case, the currency format is applied to the unit price field in the Item template. Because this application uses optimistic concurrency, the original values of each field are passed to the Delete statement as parameters to make sure that another user hasn't changed the product row since it was retrieved. Unfortunately, the DetailsView control sets the value of the unit price parameter to its formatted value, which includes the currency symbol. If you allow this value to be passed on to the Delete statement, an exception will be thrown because the parameter value is in the wrong format.

Before the Delete statement is executed, then, the DetailsView1_ItemDeleting method is called. This method removes the currency symbol from the parameter value so the value will be passed to the Delete statement in the correct format.

The Default.aspx.cs file

```
public partial class Default : System.Web.UI.Page
{
    protected void GridView1_PreRender(object sender, EventArgs e)
    {
        GridView1.HeaderRow.TableSection = TableRowSection.TableHeader;
    }
    protected void DetailsView1_ItemUpdated(
        object sender, DetailsViewUpdatedEventArgs e)
    {
        if (e.Exception != null) {
            lblError.Text = DatabaseErrorMessage(e.Exception.Message);
            e.ExceptionHandled = true;
            e.KeepInEditMode = true;
        }
        else if (e.AffectedRows == 0)
            lblError.Text = ConcurrencyErrorMessage();
        else
            GridView1.DataBind();
    }
    protected void DetailsView1_ItemDeleted(
        object sender, DetailsViewDeletedEventArgs e)
    {
        if (e.Exception != null) {
            lblError.Text = DatabaseErrorMessage(e.Exception.Message);
            e.ExceptionHandled = true;
        }
        else if (e.AffectedRows == 0)
            lblError.Text = ConcurrencyErrorMessage();
        else
            GridView1.DataBind();
    }
    protected void DetailsView1_ItemInserted(
        object sender, DetailsViewInsertedEventArgs e)
    {
        if (e.Exception != null) {
            lblError.Text = DatabaseErrorMessage(e.Exception.Message);
            e.ExceptionHandled = true;
            e.KeepInInsertMode = true;
        }
        else
            GridView1.DataBind();
    }
    protected void DetailsView1_ItemDeleting(
        object sender, DetailsViewDeleteEventArgs e)
    {
        if (e.Values["UnitPrice"] != null)
            e.Values["UnitPrice"] =
                e.Values["UnitPrice"].ToString().Substring(1);
    }
    private string DatabaseErrorMessage(string errorMsg)
    {
        return $"<b>A database error has occurred:</b> {errorMsg}";
    }
    private string ConcurrencyErrorMessage()
    {
        return "Another user may have updated that category. Please try again";
    }
}
```

Figure 15-11   The code-behind file for the Product Maintenance application

How to use the FormView control

Besides the DetailsView control, ASP.NET also provides a FormView control. Like the DetailsView control, the FormView control is designed to display data for a single item from a data source. However, as you'll see in the following topics, the FormView control uses a different approach to displaying its data.

An introduction to the FormView control

Figure 15-12 presents an introduction to the FormView control. Although the FormView control is similar to the DetailsView control, it differs in several key ways. Most importantly, the FormView control isn't restricted by the HTML table layout of the DetailsView control, in which each field is rendered as a table row. Instead, the FormView control uses templates to render all of the fields as a single row by default. This gives you complete control over the layout of the fields within the row.

Because you have to use template fields with a FormView control, this control can be more difficult to work with than a DetailsView control that uses bound fields. As you learned earlier in this chapter, though, you can convert the bound fields used by a DetailsView control to template fields so you have more control over them. In that case, a FormView control is just as easy to work with.

When you create a FormView control and bind it to a data source, the Web Forms Designer will automatically create default templates for you, as shown in the first image in this figure. Then, you can edit the templates to achieve the layout you want. To do that, you choose Edit Templates from the smart tag menu. This places the control in template-editing mode, as shown in the second image in this figure. Here, the drop-down list shows the various templates you can use with a FormView control. For most applications, you'll use just the Item, EditItem, and InsertItem templates.

A FormView control after a data source has been assigned

A FormView control in template-editing mode

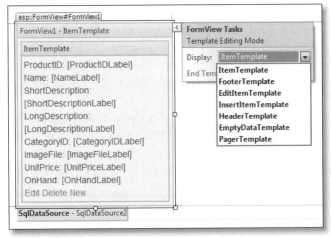

How the FormView control differs from the DetailsView control

- The DetailsView control can be easier to work with, but the FormView control provides more formatting and layout options.

- The DetailsView control can use BoundField elements or TemplateField elements with templates that use data binding expressions to define bound data fields. The FormView control can only use templates with data binding expressions to display bound data.

- The DetailsView control renders each field as a table row, but the FormView control renders all the fields in a template as a single table row.

Description

- A FormView control is similar to a DetailsView control, but its templates give you more control over how its data is displayed. To accomplish that, all the columns in the data source can be laid out within a single template.

- After you create a FormView control and assign a data source to it, you can edit the control's templates so the data is displayed the way you want.

Figure 15-12   An introduction to the FormView control

How to work with the Item template

When you use the Web Forms Designer to create a FormView control and bind it to a data source, the Web Forms Designer automatically generates basic templates for the FormView control. For instance, the code in figure 15-13 shows a typical Item template. This template is used to display the data from the data source in ReadOnly mode.

As you can see, the Item template consists of a literal header and a label control for each field in the data source. The Text attribute of each label control uses either the Bind or Eval method for data binding. The Eval method is used for columns that can't be modified. That's the case for the ProductID column in the Products table, since this is the key column.

To control the format and layout of the data that's displayed in ReadOnly mode, you can edit the Item template. To do that, it's common to use Bootstrap column classes as described in chapter 3. In particular, it's common to define two columns for the literal text and the labels so the labels are left-aligned. If you're not using Bootstrap, you can also use CSS to float the literal text to the left of the labels.

Note that if the data source includes Update, Delete, and Insert commands, the Item template will include command buttons that let the user edit, delete, or add new rows. Although these buttons are created as link buttons, you can easily change them to regular buttons or image buttons.

The Item template generated for a FormView control

```
<asp:FormView ID="FormView1" runat="server" DataKeyNames="ProductID"
    DataSourceID="SqlDataSource2">
    <ItemTemplate>
        ProductID:
        <asp:Label ID="ProductIDLabel" runat="server"
            Text='<%# Eval("ProductID") %>' /><br />
        Name:
        <asp:Label ID="NameLabel" runat="server"
            Text='<%# Bind("Name") %>' /><br />
        ShortDescription:
        <asp:Label ID="ShortDescriptionLabel" runat="server"
            Text='<%# Bind("ShortDescription") %>' /><br />
        LongDescription:
        <asp:Label ID="LongDescriptionLabel" runat="server"
            Text='<%# Bind("LongDescription") %>' /><br />
        CategoryID:
        <asp:Label ID="CategoryIDLabel" runat="server"
            Text='<%# Bind("CategoryID") %>' /><br />
        ImageFile:
        <asp:Label ID="ImageFileLabel" runat="server"
            Text='<%# Bind("ImageFile") %>' /><br />
        UnitPrice:
        <asp:Label ID="UnitPriceLabel" runat="server"
            Text='<%# Bind("UnitPrice") %>' /><br />
        OnHand:
        <asp:Label ID="OnHandLabel" runat="server"
            Text='<%# Bind("OnHand") %>' /><br />
    </ItemTemplate>
        .
        .
        .
</asp:FormView>
```

Description

- When you bind a FormView control to a data source, the Web Forms Designer generates an Item template that includes heading text and a bound label for each column in the data source.

- The Item template is rendered whenever the FormView control is displayed in ReadOnly mode.

- The Item template uses the Eval and Bind methods to create binding expressions for the columns in the data source (see figure 13-15 in chapter 13).

- If the data source includes Update, Delete, and Insert commands, the generated Item template will include Edit, Delete, and New buttons.

- The Web Forms Designer also generates an EditItem template and an InsertItem template, even if the data source doesn't include an Update or Insert command. For more information, see the next figure.

- You can modify a generated template so you can use Bootstrap column classes or standard CSS to control the format and layout of the data that's rendered for that template.

Figure 15-13   How to work with the Item template

How to work with the EditItem and InsertItem templates

As figure 15-14 shows, the Web Forms Designer also generates EditItem and InsertItem templates when you bind a FormView control to a data source. These templates are used to display the fields in Edit and Insert mode, and they're generated even if the data source doesn't have an Update or Insert command. As a result, you can delete these templates if your application doesn't allow for edits and inserts. Although this figure only shows an EditItem template, the InsertItem template is similar.

One drawback to using the FormView control is that once you edit the Item template so the data is arranged the way you want, you'll usually want to provide similar layout code in both the EditItem template and the InsertItem template. That way, the layout in all three modes will be similar. One way to do that is to copy the code in one template and paste it into another. Then, you can make the necessary adjustments, such as replacing the labels that were generated for the Item template with the text boxes that were generated for the EditItem or InsertItem template.

Depending on the complexity of the layout, it may take considerable work to get the templates looking the way you want them. In addition, if you later decide to change that layout, you'll have to make the change to all three templates. Unfortunately, there's no escaping this duplication of effort.

A generated EditItem template as displayed in a browser window

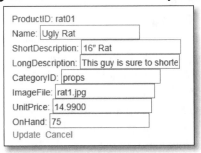

The aspx code for the EditItem template shown above

```
<EditItemTemplate>
    ProductID:
    <asp:Label ID="ProductIDLabel1" runat="server"
        Text='<%# Eval("ProductID") %>' />
    <br />
    Name:
    <asp:TextBox ID="NameTextBox" runat="server"
        Text='<%# Bind("Name") %>' />
    <br />
    ShortDescription:
    <asp:TextBox ID="ShortDescriptionTextBox" runat="server"
        Text='<%# Bind("ShortDescription") %>' />
    <br />
    .
    .                 The code generated for the LongDescription, CategoryID,
    .                 ImageFile, UnitPrice, and OnHand columns is similar to
    .                 the code generated for the ShortDescription column.
    .
    .
    <asp:LinkButton ID="UpdateButton" runat="server"
        CausesValidation="True" CommandName="Update" Text="Update" /> 
    <asp:LinkButton ID="UpdateCancelButton" runat="server"
        CausesValidation="False" CommandName="Cancel" Text="Cancel" />
</EditItemTemplate>
```

Description

- The EditItem template determines how the FormView control is rendered in Edit mode. It includes a text box for each editable bound column in the data source. The Text attribute for each text box uses a binding expression that binds the text box to its data source column.

- The EditItem template also includes Update and Cancel buttons.

- The InsertItem template is similar to the EditItem template. It determines how the FormView control is rendered in Insert mode.

Figure 15-14   How to work with the EditItem and InsertItem templates

A Shopping Cart application that uses a FormView control

To show the versatility of the FormView control, the following topics present a version of the Order page in the Shopping Cart application that was originally presented in chapter 9. That version of the application used simple label and image controls to display the information for the product selected by the user. Because data binding didn't work for those controls, C# code was required in the Page_Load event handler to set the values of the label and image controls. In contrast, this new version of the application takes advantage of the data binding ability of the FormView control, so no binding is required in the Page_Load event handler. Note that this application also uses some of the Bootstrap classes and components that you learned about in chapter 10.

The operation of the application

To refresh your memory, figure 15-15 shows the Order page displayed by the Shopping Cart application. As you can see, this page lets the user select a product from a drop-down list. When the user selects a product, the page displays the name, description, price, and an image of the selected product. Then, the user can order the product by entering a quantity and clicking the Add to Cart button.

This time, the product information is displayed within a FormView control, and Bootstrap classes are used to display the image to the right of the text. This demonstrates the layout flexibility of the FormView control. With a DetailsView control, it wouldn't be possible to display the image to the right of the text, because the DetailsView control displays each column of the data source in a separate table row.

The Order page of the Shopping Cart application

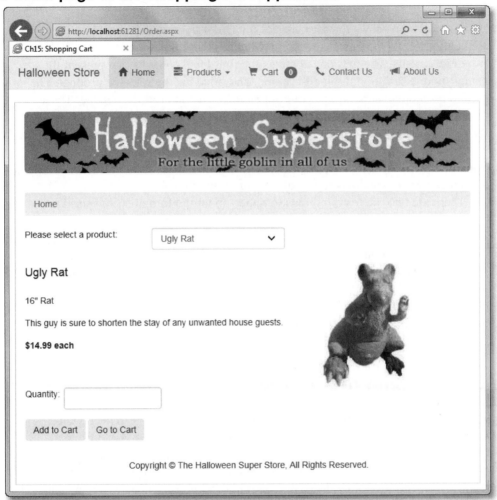

Description

- This is the Shopping Cart application that was originally presented in chapter 9, but this time it's implemented with a FormView control that displays the data for the selected product. It also uses some of the Bootstrap classes and components that you learned about in chapter 10.

- The Item template for the FormView control includes labels that are bound to the columns in the data source. It also includes an Image control whose ImageUrl property is bound to the ImageFile column in the data source.

- The alignment of the controls in the Item template of the FormView control is done using Bootstrap column classes.

Figure 15-15   The Shopping Cart application with a FormView control

The aspx file for the Order page

Figure 15-16 shows the aspx file for the Order page of the Shopping Cart application. Here, the FormView control includes an Item template that contains two div elements. The first one contains the four label controls that present the name, short description, long description, and price for the selected product. The second one contains the image control that displays the product's image. These div elements use Bootstrap column classes so the product image is displayed to the right of the labels.

Note that although the Web Forms Designer generated the EditItem and InsertItem templates, this application doesn't use them. As a result, those templates were deleted so they wouldn't clutter the listing.

There are two interesting things to notice about the format strings used in the binding expressions on this page. First, the format string used to bind the image control is this: "Images/Products/{0}". Since the ImageFile column in the Products table contains just the name of the image file for each product, not its complete path, this formatting expression prefixes the file name with the path Images/Products/ so the image file can be located.

Second, the format string used in the binding expression that displays the unit price is this: "{0:c} each". As a result, the price is displayed in currency format, followed by the word "each."

The code-behind file for the Order page

Figure 15-17 shows the code-behind file for the Order page. This code is similar to the code for the original version of this program that was presented back in chapter 9. However, there are two substantial differences. First, the only code in the Page_Load event handler is the code that sets the breadcrumb the first time the page is loaded. This event handler doesn't need to do any data binding because that's done automatically by the FormView control.

Second, the GetSelectedProduct method in this version is simpler than the one in the original version. That's because the data source for the DetailsView control retrieves a single row based on the item that's selected in the drop-down list. That means it's not necessary to filter the DataView object that's retrieved from the data source. Instead, the index value 0 is used to retrieve data from the first and only row of the data source.

The Order.aspx file   **Page 1**

```
<%@ Page Title="" Language="C#" MasterPageFile="~/Site.Master"
AutoEventWireup="true" CodeBehind="Order.aspx.cs" Inherits="Ch15Cart.Order" %>
<%@ MasterType VirtualPath="~/Site.Master" %>

<asp:Content ID="mainContent" ContentPlaceHolderID="mainPlaceholder"
    runat="server">

    <div class="row"><%-- row 1: drop-down list --%>
      <div class="form-group">
        <div class="col-sm-8">
          <label class="col-sm-5">Please select a product:</label>
          <div class="col-sm-6">
            <asp:DropDownList ID="ddlProducts" runat="server"
                AutoPostBack="True" DataSourceID="SqlDataSource1"
                DataTextField="Name" DataValueField="ProductID"
                CssClass="form-control">
            </asp:DropDownList>
            <asp:SqlDataSource ID="SqlDataSource1" runat="server"
                ConnectionString='<%$ ConnectionStrings:HalloweenConnection %>'
                SelectCommand="SELECT [ProductID], [Name], [ShortDescription],
                [LongDescription], [ImageFile], [UnitPrice]
                FROM [Products] ORDER BY [Name]">
            </asp:SqlDataSource>
          </div>
        </div>
      </div>
    </div><%-- end of row 1 --%>

    <div class="row"><%-- row 2: FormView control --%>
      <asp:FormView ID="FormView1" runat="server"
          DataSourceID="SqlDataSource2">
        <ItemTemplate>
          <div class="col-sm-8">
            <div class="form-group">
              <div class="col-sm-12">
                <h4><asp:Label Text='<%# Eval("Name") %>'
                    runat="server" /></h4></div></div>
            <div class="form-group">
              <div class="col-sm-12">
                <asp:Label Text='<%# Eval("ShortDescription") %>'
                    runat="server" /></div></div>
            <div class="form-group">
              <div class="col-sm-12">
                <asp:Label Text='<%# Eval("LongDescription") %>'
                    runat="server" /></div></div>
            <div class="form-group">
              <div class="col-sm-12">
                <asp:Label ID="lblUnitPrice" ClientIDMode="Static"
                    Text='<%# Eval("UnitPrice", "{0:c} each") %>'
                    runat="server" /></div></div>
          </div>
          <div class="col-sm-4">
            <asp:Image ID="imgProduct" runat="server"
                ImageUrl='<%# Eval("ImageFile", "Images/Products/{0}") %>' />
          </div>
        </ItemTemplate>
      </asp:FormView>
```

Figure 15-16   The aspx file for the Order page of the Shopping Cart application (part 1 of 2)

The Order.aspx file

```
<asp:SqlDataSource runat="server" ID="SqlDataSource2"
    ConnectionString='<%$ ConnectionStrings:HalloweenConnection %>'
    SelectCommand="SELECT [ProductID], [Name], [ShortDescription],
        [LongDescription], [ImageFile], [UnitPrice]
        FROM [Products]
    WHERE ([ProductID] = @ProductID)">
    <SelectParameters>
        <asp:ControlParameter ControlID="ddlProducts" Name="ProductID"
            PropertyName="SelectedValue" Type="String">
        </asp:ControlParameter>
    </SelectParameters>
</asp:SqlDataSource>
</div><%-- end of row 2 --%>

<div class="row"><%-- row 3: quantity, buttons --%>
    <div class="col-sm-12">
        <div class="form-group">
            <label class="col-sm-1">Quantity:</label>
            <div class="col-sm-3">
                <asp:TextBox ID="txtQuantity" runat="server"
                    CssClass="form-control"></asp:TextBox></div>
            <div class="col-sm-8">
                <asp:RequiredFieldValidator ID="RequiredFieldValidator1"
                    CssClass="text-danger" runat="server"
                    ControlToValidate="txtQuantity" Display="Dynamic"
                    ErrorMessage="Quantity is a required field.">
                </asp:RequiredFieldValidator>
                <asp:RangeValidator ID="RangeValidator1" runat="server"
                    CssClass="text-danger"
                    ControlToValidate="txtQuantity" Display="Dynamic"
                    ErrorMessage="Quantity must range from 1 to 500."
                    MaximumValue="500" MinimumValue="1" Type="Integer">
                </asp:RangeValidator></div>
        </div>
        <div class="form-group">
            <div class="col-sm-12">
                <asp:Button ID="btnAdd" runat="server" Text="Add to Cart"
                    onclick="btnAdd_Click" CssClass="btn btn-default" />
                <asp:Button ID="btnCart" runat="server" Text="Go to Cart"
                    PostBackUrl="~/Cart.aspx" CausesValidation="False"
                    CssClass="btn btn-default" />
            </div>
        </div>
    </div>
</div><%-- end of row 3 --%>

</asp:Content>
```

Figure 15-16   The aspx file for the Order page of the Shopping Cart application (part 2 of 2)

The Order.aspx.cs file

```
public partial class Order : System.Web.UI.Page
{
    protected void Page_Load(object sender, EventArgs e)
    {
        // set breadcrumb on first load;
        if (!IsPostBack)
        {
            Master.AddCurrentPage("Home");
        }
    }

    protected void btnAdd_Click(object sender, EventArgs e)
    {
        if (IsValid)
        {
            Product selectedProduct = GetSelectedProduct();
            CartItemList cart = CartItemList.GetCart();
            CartItem cartItem = cart[selectedProduct.ProductID];

            if (cartItem == null)
            {
                cart.AddItem(selectedProduct,
                            Convert.ToInt32(txtQuantity.Text));
            }
            else
            {
                cartItem.AddQuantity(Convert.ToInt32(txtQuantity.Text));
            }
            Response.Redirect("Cart.aspx", false);
        }
    }

    private Product GetSelectedProduct()
    {
        DataView productsTable = (DataView)
            SqlDataSource2.Select(DataSourceSelectArguments.Empty);
        DataRowView row = productsTable[0];

        Product p = new Product();
        p.ProductID = row["ProductID"].ToString();
        p.Name = row["Name"].ToString();
        p.ShortDescription = row["ShortDescription"].ToString();
        p.LongDescription = row["LongDescription"].ToString();
        p.UnitPrice = (decimal)row["UnitPrice"];
        p.ImageFile = row["ImageFile"].ToString();
        return p;
    }
}
```

Figure 15-17   The code-behind file for the Order page of the Shopping Cart application

Perspective

The DetailsView and FormView controls work well for any application that displays bound data one row at a time. The choice of which one to use depends mostly on how much control you want over the layout of the data. If you want to present a simple list of the fields in a row, the DetailsView control will automatically present data in that format. But if you need more control over the layout of the data, you'll want to use the FormView control.

Term

Master/Detail page

Summary

- The DetailsView control displays the data for a single row of a data source. Although this control supports paging, it is typically used in combination with a list or GridView control that lets the user select the item to be displayed.

- A *Master/Detail page* is a page that displays a list of items from a database along with the details for one item in the list. The DetailsView control is often used for the detail portion of the page.

- The DetailsView control provides for editing, updating, and inserting rows without requiring any C# code. To implement that, this control provides six different command buttons. But if you want to control the appearance of the buttons, you can use command fields instead of command buttons.

- To provide for data validation, database exceptions, and concurrency errors, you can write event handlers for the events of the DetailsView control.

- To control the appearance of the fields in a DetailsView control, you use template fields.

- The FormView control is similar to the DetailsView control, but the templates for the FormView control give you more control over how the data is displayed.

Exercise 15-1 Develop an application that uses a DetailsView control

In this exercise, you'll develop an application that lets the user select a customer from a GridView control and maintain that customer in a DetailsView control. To make that easier, you'll start from an application with a page that contains a GridView control that lists customers and validation summary and label controls that will be used to display error messages.

Review the starting code for the application

1. Open the Ex15CustMaintDetailsView application in the aspnet46_cs directory.

2. Review the aspx code for the SQL data source, and notice that it retrieves the Email, LastName, and FirstName columns from the Customers table.

3. Display the page in Design view, and notice that only the LastName and FirstName columns are displayed in the GridView control. That's because the Visible property of the Email column has been set to False. This column must be included in the data source, though, because it's the primary key of the Customers table, and it will be used to display the selected customer in a DetailsView control.

4. Run the application to see that you can page through the customers, but you can't select a customer.

Add a select function to the GridView control

5. Add a command field to the GridView control that will let the user select a customer. Add an ItemStyle element to this field that sets its width using the Bootstrap col-xs-1 class.

6. Run the application again and click the Select button for any customer. Notice how the formatting for the selected row changes. That's because a SelectedRowStyle element is included for the control.

Add a default DetailsView control

7. Add a DetailsView control at the beginning of the division that contains the validation summary control, set its name to dvCustomer, delete the generated Height and Width properties, and set its CssClass property so it uses these Bootstrap classes: table, table-bordered, and table-condensed.

8. Create a data source for the DetailsView control that retrieves each of the columns from the Customers table for the customer that's selected in the GridView control. Be sure to generate Insert, Update, and Delete statements and use optimistic concurrency.

9. Use the Add Field dialog box to add a command field that lets the user Edit, Delete, and Add rows. Then, use any Style elements you want to style the rows.

10. Run the application, display the last page of customers in the GridView control, and select customer "Barbara White". The data for that customer should be displayed in the DetailsView control.

11. Click the Edit button to see that the text boxes that let you edit the data for a customer are all the same size, and the text box for the address is too small to display the full address for this customer.

12. Click the Cancel button to exit from Edit mode, and close the browser window.

Create templates for the DetailsView control

13. Use the Fields dialog box to convert each of the bound fields in the DetailsView control to a template field.

14. Add another data source to the page below the data source for the DetailsView control. This data source should retrieve the StateCode and StateName columns from the States table and sort the results by the StateName column.

15. Replace the text box in the InsertItem template for the State field with a drop-down list name ddlCustomers, and bind the list to the data source you just created so the state name is displayed in the drop-down list and the state code is stored in the list. Then, use the DataBindings dialog box (see chapter 13) to bind the SelectedValue property of the drop-down list to the State field of the Customers table.

16. Enclose the text box or drop-down list within the InsertItem template for each field in a div element that assigns the col-xs-11 and col-align classes to the div. In addition, set the MaxLength property of each text box so the user can't enter more characters than are allowed by the database. (Email: 25 characters; LastName, FirstName, and PhoneNumber: 20 characters; Address: 40 characters; City: 30 characters; and ZipCode: 9 characters.)

17. Assign meaningful names to the text boxes in the InsertItem templates. Then, add a required field validator to each of these fields that displays an asterisk to the right of the text box and displays an error message in the validation summary control if a value isn't entered in the field.

18. Run the application and click the New button in the DetailsView control to make sure you have the controls in the InsertItem template formatted properly.

19. Copy the text boxes, validation controls, and drop-down list you created for the InsertItem templates to the EditItem templates of the same fields except for the Email field.

20. Run the application again and click the Edit button. The EditItem template should look just like the InsertItem template except the email field isn't editable.

Add code to check for database and concurrency errors

21. Add event handlers for the ItemUpdated, ItemDeleted, and ItemInserted events of the DetailsView control. The ItemUpdated and ItemDeleted methods should check for both database and concurrency errors, but the ItemInserted method should check only for database errors. Display an appropriate error message in the label at the bottom of the page if an error is detected. Otherwise, bind the GridView control so it reflects the current data.

22. Run the application and test it to make sure it works correctly.

16

How to use the ListView and DataPager controls

In this chapter, you'll learn how to use the ListView and DataPager controls. As you'll see, the ListView control works much like the GridView control you learned about in chapter 14. However, it provides features that make it more versatile than the GridView control. For example, you can use the ListView control to insert rows into a data source, and you can use it to display items from the data source in customized formats. You can also use the DataPager control in conjunction with the ListView control to implement paging.

How to use the ListView control

The ListView control is a highly customizable control that was introduced with ASP.NET 3.5. In the topics that follow, you'll learn the basic skills for defining the content and appearance of this control. In addition, you'll learn how to provide sorting, paging, and grouping for this control.

An introduction to the ListView control

Figure 16-1 presents a ListView control that provides for updating the data in the Categories table of the Halloween database. As you can see, this control presents the data in a row and column format just like the GridView control. In fact, if you compare this control to the GridView control shown in figure 14-1 of chapter 14, you'll see that these controls look quite similar. The main difference is that the ListView control includes an additional row for inserting a new row into the table.

The first table in this figure lists some of the basic properties of the ListView control. In most cases, these properties are set the way you want them by default. If you want to change the location of the row that provides for insert operations, though, you can do that by changing the value of the InsertItemPosition property.

To define the layout of a ListView control, you use the templates listed in the second table in this figure. At the least, a ListView control typically contains a Layout template and an Item template. You use the Layout template to define the overall layout of the control, and you use the Item template to define the layout that's used for each item in the data source. You'll see how these and many of the other templates can be used as you progress through this chapter.

A ListView control that provides for updating a table

		CategoryID	ShortName	LongName
Delete	Edit	costumes	Costumes	Costumes
Delete	Edit	fx	FX	Special Effects
Delete	Edit	masks	Masks	Masks
Delete	Edit	props	Props	Props
Insert	Clear			

Basic properties of the ListView control

Property	Description
DataSourceID	The ID of the data source to bind to.
DataKeyNames	The names of the primary key fields separated by commas.
InsertItemPosition	The location within the ListView control where the InsertItem template is rendered. You can specify FirstItem, LastItem, or None.

Template elements used by the ListView control

Element	Description
LayoutTemplate	Defines the basic layout of the control.
ItemTemplate	The template used for each item in the data source.
ItemSeparatorTemplate	The template used to separate items in the data source.
AlternatingItemTemplate	The template used for alternating items in the data source.
EditItemTemplate	The template used when a row is being edited.
InsertItemTemplate	The template used for inserting a row.
EmptyDataTemplate	The template used when the data source is empty.
SelectedItemTemplate	The template used when a row is selected.
GroupTemplate	The template used to define a group layout.
GroupSeparatorTemplate	The template used to separate groups of items.
EmptyItemTemplate	The template used for empty items in a group.

Description

- The ListView control displays data from a data source using templates. It can be used to edit and delete data as well as insert data.

- The template elements define the formatting that's used to display data. These templates are generated automatically when you configure a ListView control. See figure 16-2 for information on configuring this control.

- The Layout template defines the overall layout of the control. This template includes an element that's used as a placeholder for the data. Then, the other templates are substituted for this placeholder as appropriate.

Figure 16-1   An introduction to the ListView control

How to configure a ListView control

The easiest way to configure a ListView control is to use the Configure ListView dialog box shown in figure 16-2. Before you do that, though, you have to add the ListView control to the page and bind it to a data source. Then, you can use the Configure ListView command in the control's smart tag menu to display this dialog box.

When you use the Configure ListView dialog box to configure a ListView control, Visual Studio generates templates based on the options you choose. If you want to generate templates that use a standard row and column format, for example, you can select the Grid layout as shown here. Then, if you want to add formatting to the templates, you can select a style. In this figure, for example, you can see the Blues style.

If you use one of the predefined styles, you should know that it adds style attributes to the elements within the templates. Because this isn't a recommended way to use styles, you may want to move these styles to an external style sheet after they're generated. That can make it easier to work with these styles if you want to make changes.

The other options in this dialog box let you enable editing, inserting, deleting, and paging. Note that if the data source isn't defined with Update, Insert, and Delete commands, the Enable Editing, Enable Inserting, and Enable Deleting options won't be available. Even so, EditItem and InsertItem templates are generated for the ListView control. If your application won't provide for updating and inserting data, then, you may want to delete these templates.

The Item template that's generated for a ListView control depends on the columns in the data source that the control is bound to and whether you enable editing and deleting. If you enable editing and deleting, Edit and Delete buttons are added to this template. You'll learn more about how these buttons and the other buttons used by the ListView control work later in this chapter.

If you select the Enable Paging option, a DataPager control is also added to the ListView control. The exact format of this control depends on the option you choose from the drop-down list. You'll learn more about this later in this chapter too.

As you select options in the Configure ListView dialog box, a preview of the control is displayed in the Preview window. That way, you can be sure that the ListView control is generated the way you want. And that will save you time later if you need to customize the control.

The Configure ListView dialog box

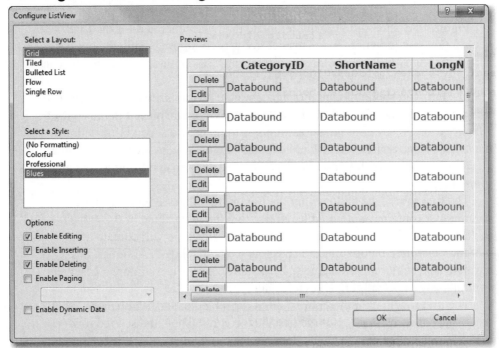

Description

- After you add a ListView control and bind it to a data source, you can configure it to generate many of the templates shown in figure 16-1. To do that, you use the Configure ListView dialog box.

- To display the Configure ListView dialog box, choose the Configure ListView command from the control's smart tag menu. Then, you can select a layout and style for the control, and you can enable editing, inserting, deleting, and paging.

- The EditItem and InsertItem templates are generated regardless of whether the data source provides for editing and inserting and whether editing and inserting are enabled for the ListView control.

- If you enable editing, an Edit button is added to the Item and AlternatingItem templates that lets the user switch to edit mode. If you enable deleting, a Delete button is added to the Item and AlternatingItem templates.

- If you enable inserting, the InsertItemPosition property is set to LastItem. This causes the InsertItem template to be displayed after the existing rows in the data source.

- If you enable paging, a DataPager control is added to the ListView control. See figures 16-6 and 16-7 for information on how to use this control.

Figure 16-2   How to configure a ListView control

How to work with the Layout template

Figure 16-3 shows the Layout template that was generated for the ListView control you saw in figure 16-1. This control was configured using the options shown in figure 16-2, except that no formatting was applied. That way, you can focus on the layout rather than the styles.

To start, you should notice that this template contains a table with two rows. The first row defines the layout of the data that will be displayed in the control. I'll have more to say about this row in just a minute. The second row defines the layout of the pager area. If I had enabled paging, this row would contain a DataPager control. In this case, however, paging isn't enabled, so the second row is empty.

The first row in the table within the Layout template contains a single column that contains another table. Notice that the id attribute of this table is set to itemPlaceholderContainer. This indicates that the table will contain a placeholder where items from the data source are displayed. Although this attribute isn't required, it's included by default when you configure a ListView control using the Configure ListView dialog box.

The first row in the inner table defines the table headers (th elements) that are displayed across the top of the ListView control. Then, the second row identifies where the data from the data source should be displayed. To do that, the ID attribute of this row is set to itemPlaceholder. To specify how the data is displayed, you use the other templates of the ListView control. In the next figure, for example, you'll see the code for a basic Item template.

Before going on, you should notice that each element within the Layout template has a runat attribute set to "server". Although this attribute isn't required, it's added by default when you configure the control. Note, however, that if this attribute is included on the itemPlaceholderContainer table, thead and tbody elements won't be rendered for the table. And that means that you won't be able to use the Bootstrap table classes to format the table. If you'll be using Bootstrap table classes, then, you'll want to remove this attribute.

If you use the Configure ListView dialog box as shown in the previous figure, the ListView control that's generated always contains a Layout template. If you're creating a simple layout, though, you should know that you can omit this template. For example, suppose you want to create a list of names and addresses formatted like this:

FirstName LastName
Address
City, State ZipCode

Since the Layout template for this list would contain only the item placeholder, it can be omitted.

You should also realize that you can't modify the Layout template for a ListView control from Design view. Instead, you'll need to work with it in Source view. As you'll learn later in this chapter, though, you may be able to work with the other templates from Design view depending on what layout you use.

The Layout template for the ListView control in figure 16-1

```
<LayoutTemplate>
    <table runat="server">
        <tr runat="server">
            <td runat="server">
                <table id="itemPlaceholderContainer" runat="server"
                       border="0" style="">
                    <tr runat="server" style="">
                        <th runat="server"></th>
                        <th runat="server">CategoryID</th>
                        <th runat="server">ShortName</th>
                        <th runat="server">LongName</th>
                    </tr>
                    <tr id="itemPlaceholder" runat="server">
                    </tr>
                </table>
            </td>
        </tr>
        <tr runat="server">
            <td runat="server" style="">
            </td>
        </tr>
    </table>
</LayoutTemplate>
```

Description

- The Layout template that's generated for a ListView control that uses a grid layout consists of a table with two rows and one column. The first row defines the layout of the data that's displayed in the control, and the second row defines the layout of the DataPager control if paging is enabled.

- The column in the first row of the table for the Layout template contains another table with two rows. The first row defines the headers that are displayed for the columns of the data source as well as a header for any buttons that are displayed by the control. The second row defines a placeholder where the data defined by the other templates will be displayed.

- By default, the ID of the control that's used as a placeholder is set to itemPlaceholder. If you want to use a different name, you can set the ItemPlaceholderID property of the ListView control to the name you want to use.

- You can modify the Layout template any way you like. The only requirement is that it must contain a placeholder element that runs on the server.

- Design view doesn't support displaying the Layout template. Because of that, you must work with this template in Source view.

Figure 16-3   How to work with the Layout template

How to work with the Item template

You use the Item template to define how the items from a data source are displayed within a ListView control. To illustrate, figure 16-4 shows the Item template that was generated for the ListView control in figure 16-1. The first thing you should notice here is that this template contains a single tr element. That's necessary because the element that defines the item placeholder in the Layout template is a tr element. Then, at runtime, the tr element in the Item template is substituted for the tr element in the Layout template.

By default, the Item template for a ListView control with a grid layout contains one column for each column in the data source. As you can see, the data from each column is displayed in a label that's bound to the data source using the Eval method. In addition, if editing or deleting is enabled for the ListView control, an additional column is included in the Item template. This column contains the Edit and Delete buttons that can be used to perform edit and delete operations.

In addition to the Item template, an AlternatingItem template is generated for you when you configure a ListView control. Unless you apply a style to the control, though, this template is identical to the Item template, so each row in the control has the same appearance. If you want every other row to have a different appearance, you can modify the Item and AlternatingItem templates as appropriate. For example, you might want to set the background color for the AlternatingItem template so it's different from the background color for the Item template. Note that in some cases, though, you can also do this using the Bootstrap table-striped class. You'll see an example of that when you do the exercise at the end of this chapter.

The Item template for the ListView control in figure 16-1

```
<ItemTemplate>
    <tr style="">
        <td>
            <asp:Button ID="DeleteButton" runat="server"
                CommandName="Delete" Text="Delete" />
            <asp:Button ID="EditButton" runat="server"
                CommandName="Edit" Text="Edit" />
        </td>
        <td>
            <asp:Label ID="CategoryIDLabel" runat="server"
                Text='<%# Eval("CategoryID") %>' />
        </td>
        <td>
            <asp:Label ID="ShortNameLabel" runat="server"
                Text='<%# Eval("ShortName") %>' />
        </td>
        <td>
            <asp:Label ID="LongNameLabel" runat="server"
                Text='<%# Eval("LongName") %>' />
        </td>
    </tr>
</ItemTemplate>
```

Description

- The Item template defines the layout of the data that's displayed in the ListView control. This template is substituted for the placeholder in the Layout template at runtime.

- The Item template that's generated for a ListView control with a grid layout consists of a single row with one column for each column in the data source. The data for each column is displayed in a label that's bound to the data source using the Eval method.

- If editing or deleting is enabled for the ListView control, an additional column that contains the buttons used to implement these operations is included in the Item template. See figure 16-11 for more information.

- You can modify the Item template any way you like to customize the layout that's used to display the data. To do that, you work in Source view since the Item template can't be displayed in Design view.

- The Item template is the only required template. If editing and inserting are enabled, however, you must also include EditItem and InsertItem templates. See figure 16-12 for more information on these templates.

Figure 16-4   How to work with the Item template

How to provide for sorting

Figure 16-5 shows how you provide sorting for a ListView control. To do that, you add a button to the Layout template for each column you want to sort by. The ListView control in this figure, for example, provides for sorting by using link buttons in the column headers for the first three columns.

To indicate that a button should be used for sorting, you set the CommandName property of the button to Sort. Then, you set the CommandArgument property of the button to the name of the column in the data source that you want to sort by. If the user clicks the Product ID button in the ListView control shown here, for example, the products will be sorted by the ProductID column. Similarly, if the user clicks the Name button, the products will be sorted by the Name column.

You can also sort by two or more columns in the data source. To do that, you separate the column names with commas. You can see how this works in the link button for the Category column in this figure. If you click this button, the products will be sorted by the Name column within the CategoryID column.

By the way, the sort order that's used for a ListView control is the same as the order that's used for a GridView control. That is, the first time you click a sort button, the column is sorted in ascending order. The second time you click the button, the column is sorted in descending order. If a sort button sorts by two or more columns, only the last column toggles between ascending and descending order. The other columns are always sorted in ascending order.

Also like the GridView control, the ListView control doesn't actually do the sorting. Instead, it relies on the underlying data source to sort the data. As a result, sorting will only work if the DataSourceMode property for the data source is set to DataSet.

A ListView control that provides for sorting

Product ID	Name	Category	Unit Price	On Hand
pow01	Austin Powers	costumes	$79.99	25
frankc01	Frankenstein	costumes	$39.99	100
hippie01	Hippie	costumes	$79.99	40
jar01	JarJar	costumes	$59.99	25
martian01	Martian	costumes	$69.99	100
super01	Superman	costumes	$39.99	100
bl01	Black Light	fx	$19.99	200
fogj01	Fog Juice (1qt)	fx	$9.99	500
fog01	Fog Machine	fx	$34.99	100
str01	Mini-strobe	fx	$13.99	200

The Layout template for the ListView control

```
<LayoutTemplate>
    <table class="col-xs-12 table-responsive">
        <tr><td><table id="itemPlaceholderContainer"
            class="table table-bordered table-condensed">
            <thead>
                <tr style="">
                    <th><asp:LinkButton ID="LinkButton1" runat="server"
                        CommandName="Sort" CommandArgument="ProductID">
                        Product ID</asp:LinkButton></th>
                    <th><asp:LinkButton ID="LinkButton2" runat="server"
                        CommandName="Sort" CommandArgument="Name">
                        Name</asp:LinkButton></th>
                    <th><asp:LinkButton ID="LinkButton3" runat="server"
                        CommandName="Sort"
                        CommandArgument="CategoryID, Name">
                        Category</asp:LinkButton></th>
                    <th class="text-right">Unit Price</th>
                    <th class="text-right">On Hand</th>
                </tr>
            </thead>
            <tbody>
                <tr runat="server" id="itemPlaceholder"></tr>
            </tbody>
        </table></td></tr>
    </table>
</LayoutTemplate>
```

Description

- To sort the data in a ListView control, you add a button to the Layout template, set the button's CommandName property to Sort, and set its CommandArgument property to the name of the column you want to sort by. To sort by two or more columns, separate the column names with commas.

- For sorting to work, the DataSourceMode property of the data source must be set to DataSet, which it is by default.

Figure 16-5   How to provide for sorting

How to provide for paging

To provide paging for a ListView control, you use the DataPager control. Figure 16-6 presents the basic skills for using this control. The easiest way to create this control is to select the Enable Paging option from the Configure ListView dialog box. When you do that, a drop-down list becomes available that lets you choose whether you want to add a *next/previous pager* or a *numeric pager*.

The ListView control at the top of this figure shows the default next/previous pager, and the first code example shows the aspx code for this pager. Notice that the DataPager control contains a Fields element. This element can contain one or more NextPreviousPagerField or NumericPagerField controls. In this case, the Fields element includes a single NextPreviousPagerField control. You'll learn more about the properties that you can code on this control in the next figure.

The second pager in this figure is a simple numeric pager. In the aspx code for this pager, you can see that the PageSize property is set to 4 so only four items will be displayed on each page. Then, the pager contains a NumericPagerField control with no properties. Because of that, the default settings for this control are used. That means that a maximum of five page buttons are displayed, along with an ellipsis button (…) if additional pages are available.

Note that you can also add a DataPager control by dragging it from the Toolbox. If you do that, though, you have to add the Fields element and the pager controls manually. Because of that, you'll rarely use this technique.

A ListView control that uses a next/previous pager

Product ID	Name	Category	Unit Price	On Hand
arm01	Freddie Arm	props	$20.95	200
bats01	Flying Bats	props	$69.99	25
bl01	Black Light	fx	$19.99	200
cat01	Deranged Cat	props	$19.99	45
fog01	Fog Machine	fx	$34.99	100
fogj01	Fog Juice (1qt)	fx	$9.99	500
frankc01	Frankenstein	costumes	$39.99	100
fred01	Freddie	masks	$29.99	50
head01	Michael Head	props	$29.99	100
head02	Saw Head	props	$29.99	100

First   Previous   Next   Last

The aspx code for the next/previous pager

```
<asp:DataPager ID="DataPager1" runat="server">
    <Fields>
        <asp:NextPreviousPagerField ButtonType="Button"
            ShowFirstPageButton="True" ShowLastPageButton="True" />
    </Fields>
</asp:DataPager>
```

A numeric pager

1 2 3 4 5 ...

The aspx code for the numeric pager

```
<asp:DataPager ID="DataPager1" runat="server" PageSize="4">
    <Fields>
        <asp:NumericPagerField />
    </Fields>
</asp:DataPager>
```

Description

- To provide paging for a ListView control, you use a DataPager control. To add a DataPager control to a ListView control, you can select the Enable Paging option in the Configure ListView dialog box and then select Next/Previous Pager or Numeric Pager from the drop-down list that's displayed.

- The DataPager control contains a Fields element that can contain two types of pager controls. The NextPreviousPagerField control can display first, previous, next, and last buttons. The NumericPagerField control can display page numbers as well as an ellipsis button if additional pages are available.

- You can customize the appearance of a DataPager control by adding two or more pager controls to it. See figure 16-7 for more information.

Figure 16-6   How to provide for paging

How to customize paging

Figure 16-7 shows how you can customize a DataPager control. To do that, you use the properties of the DataPager control and the NextPreviousPagerField and NumericPagerField controls shown in this figure. For example, to change the number of items that are displayed on each page, you set the PageSize property of the DataPager control.

Because the DataPager is a separate control, you don't have to place it inside the ListView control. Instead, you can place it anywhere you want on the page. If you do that, however, you need to set the PagedControlID property of the control. This property identifies the ListView control that it provides paging for.

By the way, the DataPager control can be used only with controls that implement the IPageableItemContainer interface. Currently, the ListView control is the only control that meets that criterion. In the future, however, you can expect other data-bound controls to implement this interface so their paging can be done from outside the controls.

The properties of the NextPreviousPagerField control shown in this figure determine the type of buttons that are used in the pager and which buttons are displayed. The default is to display Previous and Next buttons, but if you create the DataPager control from the Configure ListView dialog box, First and Last buttons are also displayed. Similarly, the properties of the NumericPagerField control determine the type of buttons that are used and the number of buttons that are displayed. The default is to display a maximum of five link buttons.

The code example in this figure shows a custom DataPager control that uses two next/previous pagers and one numeric pager. The resulting control is shown below this code. This should help you begin to see the flexibility that the DataPager control provides.

Before going on, you should notice the ButtonCssClass property that's included on both NexPreviousPagerField controls. This property is specific to this control and can be used to apply CSS styles. In this case, it's used to apply the Bootstrap btn and btn-default styles.

Properties of the DataPager control

Property	Description
PageSize	Specifies the number of items to be displayed on each page. The default is 10.
PagedControlID	The ID of the ListView control that the DataPager control provides paging for. Used only if the DataPager control is placed outside the ListView control.

Properties of the NextPreviousPagerField control

Property	Description
ButtonType	The type of buttons to be used. You can specify Button, Image, or Link.
ShowFirstPageButton	Determines whether the first page button is displayed. Default is False.
ShowPreviousPageButton	Determines whether the previous page button is displayed. Default is True.
ShowNextPageButton	Determines whether the next page button is displayed. Default is True.
ShowLastPageButton	Determines whether the last page button is displayed. Default is False.

Properties of the NumericPagerField control

Property	Description
ButtonCount	The maximum number of buttons to be displayed.
ButtonType	The type of buttons to be used. You can specify Button, Image, or Link.

The aspx code for a DataPager control that uses both types of pagers

```
<asp:DataPager ID="DataPager1" runat="server" PageSize="4">
    <Fields>
        <asp:NextPreviousPagerField ButtonType="Button"
            ButtonCssClass="btn btn-default" ShowFirstPageButton="True"
            ShowNextPageButton="False" ShowPreviousPageButton="False" />
        <asp:NumericPagerField ButtonCount="3" />
        <asp:NextPreviousPagerField ButtonType="Button"
            ButtonCssClass="btn btn-default" ShowLastPageButton="True"
            ShowNextPageButton="False" ShowPreviousPageButton="False" />
    </Fields>
</asp:DataPager>
```

The resulting DataPager control

Description

- You can use the PageSize property of the DataPager control to specify the number of items to display on each page.

- You can place a DataPager control outside of the ListView control. Then, you must set the PagedControlID property of the DataPager control to the ID of the ListView control you want to use it with.

- The NextPreviousPagerField and NumericPagerField controls also have properties that let you change the text or image for the buttons that are displayed.

Figure 16-7   How to customize paging

How to group ListView data

Another feature of the ListView control is its ability to group data so it's displayed in two or more columns. In figure 16-8, for example, you can see the beginning of a ListView control that groups product data into two columns.

The easiest way to create a control like this is to select the Tiled layout from the Configure ListView dialog box. When you do that, Layout and Group templates like the ones shown here are generated. In addition, the GroupItemCount property is included for the ListView control. This property determines the number of columns in the group, and it's set to 3 by default.

When you use Tiled layout, the Layout template includes a nested table just like it does for the Grid layout. In this case, though, the id attribute of the nested table is set to groupPlaceholderContainer to indicate that it will contain a placeholder where groups of data will be displayed. This placeholder is defined by the single row for the table, whose id attribute is set to groupPlaceholder. Then, the row that's defined by the Group template is substituted for this row at runtime.

The row in the Group template defines the placeholder for the items in the group. This row contains a single column with an id attribute that's set to itemPlaceholder. Just as it does when it's included in the Layout template, this id indicates where the data from the data source is displayed. Then, the other templates determine how the data is displayed. To do that, these templates must contain a single td element that's substituted for the td element in the Group template when the application is run.

The beginning of a ListView control with two columns

Name: Austin Powers ShortDescription: Austin Powers costume Category: Costumes UnitPrice: 79.9900 OnHand: 25	Name: Black Light ShortDescription: Black light with base Category: Special Effects UnitPrice: 19.9900 OnHand: 200
Name: Darth Vader Mask ShortDescription: The legendary Darth Vader Category: Masks UnitPrice: 19.9900 OnHand: 100	Name: Deranged Cat ShortDescription: 20" Ugly cat Category: Props UnitPrice: 19.9900 OnHand: 45

The Layout and Group templates for the control

```
<asp:ListView ID="ListView1" runat="server" DataSourceID="SqlDataSource1"
    GroupItemCount="2">
    <LayoutTemplate>
        <table runat="server">
            <tr runat="server">
                <td runat="server">
                    <table id="groupPlaceholderContainer" class="table">
                        <tr id="groupPlaceholder" runat="server"></tr>
                    </table>
                </td>
            </tr>
            .
            .
            .
        </table>
    </LayoutTemplate>
    <GroupTemplate>
        <tr id="itemPlaceholderContainer" runat="server">
            <td id="itemPlaceholder" runat="server">
            </td>
        </tr>
    </GroupTemplate>
    <ItemTemplate>
        .
        .
        .
    </ItemTemplate>
</asp:ListView>
```

Description

- You can use the Group template to display items in two or more columns. Then, the Group template replaces the element in the Layout template that has the ID "groupPlaceholder," and the Group template contains an element with the ID "itemPlaceholder" that's replaced by the Item template.

- To determine the number of columns in the group, you set the GroupItemCount property of the ListView control.

- The easiest way to create a Group template is to select the Tiled layout from the Configure ListView dialog box. Then, a group with three columns is created, and you can modify the aspx code to format the control any way you like.

Figure 16-8   How to group ListView data

A list application that uses a ListView control

Now that you've learned the basic skills for working with a ListView control, the following topics present the design and code for an application that uses this control to display a list of products. If you compare this application with the list application in chapter 14 that uses a GridView control, you'll begin to see the flexibility that the ListView control provides.

The Product List application

Figure 16-9 presents the Product List application. Here, you can see that the first column in the ListView control contains the product name for each row in the Products table of the Halloween database. Then, the second column contains the headings for the other product columns that are included in the list, and the third column contains the data from each of the product columns. This type of layout wouldn't be possible with the GridView control.

You should also notice the DataPager control that's used with the ListView control. This control specifies that only four products should be displayed on each page. It's implemented using a next/previous pager with custom values for the text that's displayed on the buttons.

The Product List application

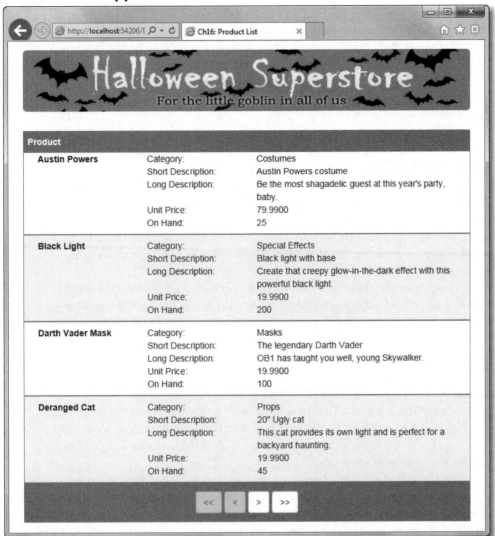

Description

- The ProductList application uses a ListView control to display a list of all the products in the Products table. The ListView control is bound to a SqlDataSource control that works in DataSet mode.

- The ListView control uses Item and AlternatingItem templates to display every other row with a different background color.

- A DataPager control is used within the ListView control to display four products on each page.

Figure 16-9   The Product List application

The aspx file

Figure 16-10 presents the aspx code for the Product List application. To generate the starting code for the ListView control used by this application, I selected the Flow layout from the Configure ListView dialog box. Unlike the code that's generated when you use the Grid layout, the code for Flow layout doesn't use tables. That makes it easy to apply styles using CSS.

The first page of this listing shows the Layout template for the ListView control. The two div elements in this template were generated by default. The first one is used as the container for the item placeholder. In this case, the item placeholder is coded within a span element.

The second div element contains the DataPager control that's used by the ListView control. By default, this element was generated with a style attribute, but that attribute was deleted and an id property was included instead. That way, the data pager can be formatted using CSS. Notice that the Bootstrap text-center class is also assigned to this div element to center the paging buttons in the control.

As you can see, the PageSize property for the DataPager control is set to 4. Then, a NextPreviousPagerField control is used to implement the pager. Here, the FirstPageText, PreviousPageText, NextPageText, and LastPageText properties of this control are set so the buttons display less-than and greater-than signs as shown in the previous figure.

The only other change that was made to this template is that a paragraph was added before the two div elements. This paragraph contains the literal text that's displayed at the top of the ListView control. Like the div element that contains the DataPager control, an id attribute was added to this paragraph so it could be formatted with CSS. In addition, a Bootstrap column class was assigned to the paragraph to specify its width.

The second page of this listing shows the Item template for the control. Considerable changes were made to the aspx code that was generated for this template to format the data so it looks as shown in the previous figure. In particular, div elements were added so the data could be formatted and aligned using Bootstrap row and column classes. If you review these elements and classes, you shouldn't have any trouble understanding how this works.

The third page of this listing shows the AlternatingItem template for the ListView control. This code is identical to the code for the Item template except that the outermost div element for this template is assigned to a custom class named altRow instead of to the class named itemRow. Then, CSS is used to assign a different background color for alternate rows.

The SqlDataSource control is also shown on the third page of this listing. Notice here that the data source retrieves data from both the Products and Categories tables. The Categories table is included so the LongName column can be displayed instead of the CategoryID column from the Products table.

The Default.aspx file   Page 1

```
<%@ Page Language="C#" AutoEventWireup="true" CodeBehind="Default.aspx.cs"
Inherits="Ch16ProductList.Default" %>

<!DOCTYPE html>

<html xmlns="http://www.w3.org/1999/xhtml">
<head runat="server">
    <title>Ch16: Product List</title>
    <meta name="viewport" content="width=device-width, initial-scale=1" />
    <link href="Content/bootstrap.min.css" rel="stylesheet" />
    <link href="Content/site.css" rel="stylesheet" />
    <script src="Scripts/jquery-1.9.1.min.js"></script>
    <script src="Scripts/bootstrap.min.js"></script>
</head>
<body>
  <div class="container">
    <header class="jumbotron"><%-- image set in site.css --%></header>
    <main>
      <form id="form1" runat="server">
        <asp:ListView ID="ListView1" runat="server"
            DataSourceID="SqlDataSource1" DataKeyNames="ProductID">
          <LayoutTemplate>
            <p id="product" class="col-xs-12">Product</p>
            <div runat="server" id="itemPlaceholderContainer">
              <span runat="server" id="itemPlaceholder" />
            </div>
            <div id="pager" class="text-center">
              <asp:DataPager runat="server" ID="DataPager1"
                  PageSize="4">
                  <Fields>
                    <asp:NextPreviousPagerField
                        ButtonType="Button"
                        ButtonCssClass="btn btn-default"
                        ShowFirstPageButton="True"
                        ShowLastPageButton="True"
                        FirstPageText="&lt;&lt;"
                        PreviousPageText="&lt;"
                        NextPageText="&gt;"
                        LastPageText="&gt;&gt;">
                    </asp:NextPreviousPagerField>
                  </Fields>
              </asp:DataPager>
            </div>
          </LayoutTemplate>
```

Figure 16-10   The aspx file for the Product List application (part 1 of 3)

The Default.aspx file

```
<ItemTemplate>
  <div class="row itemRow">
    <div class="col-sm-3 font-bold">
      <asp:Label Text='<%# Eval("Name") %>'
            runat="server" ID="NameLabel" />
    </div>
    <div class="col-sm-9">
      <div class="row">
        <div class="col-xs-5 col-sm-4">Category:</div>
        <div class="col-xs-7 col-sm-8">
          <asp:Label Text='<%# Eval("Category") %>'
                runat="server" ID="CategoryLabel" />
        </div>
      </div>
      <div class="row">
        <div class="col-xs-5 col-sm-4">
            Short Description:</div>
        <div class="col-xs-7 col-sm-8">
          <asp:Label runat="server"
              Text='<%# Eval("ShortDescription") %>'
              ID="ShortDescriptionLabel"/>
        </div>
      </div>
      <div class="row">
        <div class="col-xs-5 col-sm-4">Long Description:</div>
        <div class="col-xs-7 col-sm-8">
          <asp:Label Text='<%# Eval("LongDescription") %>'
                runat="server" ID="LongDescriptionLabel" />
        </div>
      </div>
      <div class="row">
        <div class="col-xs-5 col-sm-4">Unit Price:</div>
        <div class="col-xs-7 col-sm-8">
          <asp:Label Text='<%# Eval("UnitPrice") %>'
                runat="server" ID="UnitPriceLabel" />
        </div>
      </div>
      <div class="row">
        <div class="col-xs-5 col-sm-4">On Hand:</div>
        <div class="col-xs-7 col-sm-8">
          <asp:Label Text='<%# Eval("OnHand") %>' runat="server"
              ID="OnHandLabel" />
        </div>
      </div>
    </div>
  </div>
</ItemTemplate>
```

Figure 16-10   The aspx file for the Product List application (part 2 of 3)

The Default.aspx file   **Page 3**

```
            <AlternatingItemTemplate>
              <div class="row altRow">
                <div class="col-sm-3 font-bold">
                  <asp:Label Text='<%# Eval("Name") %>' runat="server"
                        ID="NameLabel" /></div>
                <div class="col-sm-9">
                  <div class="row">
                    <div class="col-xs-5 col-sm-4">Category:</div>
                    <div class="col-xs-7 col-sm-8">
                      <asp:Label Text='<%# Eval("Category") %>'
                            runat="server" ID="CategoryLabel" /></div>
                  </div>
                  <div class="row">
                    <div class="col-xs-5 col-sm-4">Short Description:</div>
                    <div class="col-xs-7 col-sm-8">
                      <asp:Label Text='<%# Eval("ShortDescription") %>'
                            runat="server" ID="ShortDescriptionLabel" /></div>
                  </div>
                  <div class="row">
                    <div class="col-xs-5 col-sm-4">Long Description:</div>
                    <div class="col-xs-7 col-sm-8">
                      <asp:Label Text='<%# Eval("LongDescription") %>'
                            runat="server" ID="LongDescriptionLabel" /></div>
                  </div>
                  <div class="row">
                    <div class="col-xs-5 col-sm-4">Unit Price:</div>
                    <div class="col-xs-7 col-sm-8">
                      <asp:Label Text='<%# Eval("UnitPrice") %>'
                            runat="server" ID="UnitPriceLabel" /></div>
                  </div>
                  <div class="row">
                    <div class="col-xs-5 col-sm-4">On Hand:</div>
                    <div class="col-xs-7 col-sm-8">
                      <asp:Label Text='<%# Eval("OnHand") %>' runat="server"
                            ID="OnHandLabel" /></div>
                  </div>
                </div>
              </div>
            </AlternatingItemTemplate>
          </asp:ListView>
          <asp:SqlDataSource ID="SqlDataSource1" runat="server"
              ConnectionString='<%$ ConnectionStrings:HalloweenConnection %>'
              SelectCommand="SELECT Products.ProductID, Products.Name,
                  Categories.LongName AS Category, Products.ShortDescription,
                  Products.LongDescription, Products.UnitPrice, Products.OnHand
                  FROM Products INNER JOIN Categories
                  ON Products.CategoryID = Categories.CategoryID
                  ORDER BY Products.Name">
          </asp:SqlDataSource>
        </form>
      </main>
    </div>
  </body>
</html>
```

Figure 16-10   The aspx file for the Product List application (part 3 of 3)

How to update ListView data

To update ListView data, you use the EditItem and InsertItem templates. I'll show you how to use these templates in just a minute. But first, I want to describe the various buttons you can use to work with data in a ListView control.

How to use buttons to perform update operations

You may recall that when you use a FormView control or a DetailsView control with templates to update data, the templates include buttons that let you insert, update, and delete data. You also use buttons to perform these operations using a ListView control. Although the buttons you need are generated automatically when you configure a ListView control, you will better understand how the ListView control works if you understand these buttons.

When the user clicks a button in a ListView control, the operation that's performed is determined by the value of the button's CommandName property. Figure 16-11 lists the predefined values for this property and describes their functions. For the most part, these values should be self-explanatory. For example, if the user clicks a button whose CommandName property is set to Edit, the row that contains that button is placed in Edit mode. In that mode, the row is displayed using the EditItem template. As you'll see in a minute, the EditItem template contains buttons whose CommandName properties are set to Update and Cancel. Then, if the user changes the data in that row and clicks the update button, the row in the database is updated. If the user clicks the cancel button instead, the original data is redisplayed using the Item template.

Notice that the ListView control can also contain a button whose CommandName property is set to Select. When this button is clicked, the selected row is displayed using the SelectedItem template. You can use a button like this to create a Master/Detail page like the one you saw in chapter 15 using a ListView control rather than a GridView control.

Buttons for working with the data in a ListView control

CommandName property	Description
Edit	Switches the ListView control to Edit mode and displays the data using the EditItem template.
Update	In Edit mode, saves the contents of the data-bound controls to the data source.
Cancel	Cancels the current operation. If a row is being edited, the original data is displayed using the Item template. If a row is being inserted, an empty InsertItem template is displayed.
Delete	Deletes the item from the data source.
Insert	Inserts the contents of the data-bound controls into the data source.
Select	Displays the contents of the data-bound controls using the SelectedItem template.

The aspx code for the Edit and Delete buttons in an Item template

```
<asp:Button ID="DeleteButton" runat="server"
    CommandName="Delete" Text="Delete" />
<asp:Button ID="EditButton" runat="server"
    CommandName="Edit" Text="Edit" />
```

Description

- To work with the data in a ListView control, you can use buttons whose CommandName properties are set to predefined values. Then, when the user clicks these buttons, they perform the functions shown above.

- Although you must set the CommandName property to one of the values shown above to perform the associated function, you can set the Text property to anything you like.

- You can also create buttons that perform custom functions by setting the CommandName property to a custom value. Then, you can use the ItemCommand event of the ListView control to determine which button was clicked and perform the appropriate action.

Figure 16-11   How to use buttons to perform update operations

How to work with the EditItem and InsertItem templates

To help you understand how the EditItem and InsertItem templates work, figure 16-12 presents these templates for the ListView control you saw back in figure 16-1. This control was used to maintain the data in the Categories table of the Halloween database.

If you review the code for the EditItem template, you'll see that it includes two buttons whose CommandName properties are set to Update and Cancel. Then, it includes a bound control for each of the three columns in the data source. The first column, CategoryID, is displayed in a label and is bound using the Eval method. That makes sense because this is the primary key for the table and shouldn't be changed. The other two columns, ShortName and LongName, are displayed in text boxes that are bound using the Bind method so they can be changed.

The InsertItem template is similar. Instead of update and cancel buttons, though, it includes insert and cancel buttons. Notice that although the CommandName property for the cancel button is set to Cancel just like it is for the cancel button in the EditItem template, the Text property is set to Clear instead of Cancel. That better describes what happens when this button is clicked. Also notice that all three columns in the data source are displayed in text boxes that are bound using the Bind method. That makes sense because all three values are required for a new category.

How to use events raised by the ListView control

The ListView control raises many of the same events as the DetailsView and FormView controls. For example, the ItemUpdating event is raised before an item is updated, and the ItemUpdated event is raised after an item has been updated. Similarly, the ItemInserting event is raised before an item is inserted, and the ItemInserted event is raised after an item has been inserted. And the ItemDeleting event is raised before an item is deleted, and the ItemDeleted event is raised after an item has been deleted.

You'll typically use the before events to provide data validation in the code-behind file, and you'll use the after events to provide error handling code if the operation wasn't successful. This works the same as in the maintenance applications of the last two chapters.

The EditItem template for the ListView control in figure 16-1

```
<EditItemTemplate>
    <tr style="">
        <td>
            <asp:Button ID="UpdateButton" runat="server"
                CommandName="Update" Text="Update" />
            <asp:Button ID="CancelButton" runat="server"
                CommandName="Cancel" Text="Cancel" /></td>
        <td>
            <asp:Label ID="CategoryIDLabel1" runat="server"
                Text='<%# Eval("CategoryID") %>' /></td>
        <td>
            <asp:TextBox ID="ShortNameTextBox" runat="server"
                Text='<%# Bind("ShortName") %>' /></td>
        <td>
            <asp:TextBox ID="LongNameTextBox" runat="server"
                Text='<%# Bind("LongName") %>' /></td>
    </tr>
</EditItemTemplate>
```

The InsertItem template for the ListView control in figure 16-1

```
<InsertItemTemplate>
    <tr style="">
        <td>
            <asp:Button ID="InsertButton" runat="server"
                CommandName="Insert" Text="Insert" />
            <asp:Button ID="CancelButton" runat="server"
                CommandName="Cancel" Text="Clear" /></td>
        <td>
            <asp:TextBox ID="CategoryIDTextBox" runat="server"
                Text='<%# Bind("CategoryID") %>' /></td>
        <td>
            <asp:TextBox ID="ShortNameTextBox" runat="server"
                Text='<%# Bind("ShortName") %>' /></td>
        <td>
            <asp:TextBox ID="LongNameTextBox" runat="server"
                Text='<%# Bind("LongName") %>' /></td>
    </tr>
</InsertItemTemplate>
```

Description

- The EditItem template determines how an item in the ListView control is rendered in edit mode. By default, it includes a label for each column in the data source that can't be modified and a text box for each column in the data source that can be modified. These controls are bound to the columns of the data source using the Eval and Bind methods.

- The InsertItem template is similar to the EditItem template. It determines the content that's rendered for a new item that's being inserted.

- The EditItem template also includes update and cancel buttons by default, and the InsertItem template includes insert and cancel buttons.

Figure 16-12   How to work with the EditItem and InsertItem templates

Perspective

In this chapter, you've seen how the templates of the ListView control provide for features that aren't available with the other data-bound controls. In particular, you saw how to use the Item and AlternatingItem templates in conjunction with the Layout template to display data. You saw how to use the Group template to display data in two or more columns. And you saw how to use the DataPager control to provide for paging.

You also saw how to use the EditItem and InsertItem templates along with the buttons that let you insert, update, and delete data. With this as background, you should now be able to use the ListView and DataPager controls in your own applications.

Terms

next/previous pager
numeric pager

Summary

- The ListView control works much like a GridView control but it provides features that make it more versatile, including automatic formatting, sorting, paging, grouping, editing, deleting, updating, and inserting.

- The ListView control displays the data from a data source using templates to format the data. These templates are generated automatically when you configure this control.

- To provide sorting for a ListView control, you add buttons at the top of the columns in the Layout template. Then, you set the CommandName property to Sort and the CommandArgument property to the name of the column you want to sort by.

- To provide paging for a ListView control, you use a DataPager control and configure it to work with the ListView control.

- To group the data for two or more items in a ListView control, you use the Group template.

- To edit, update, and insert data in a data source, you use buttons with their CommandName properties set to predefined values like Edit, Update, Delete, and Insert. The Edit and Insert buttons automatically work with the EditItem and InsertItem templates.

- When you use the ListView control, the code-behind file only needs to provide data validation and error handling for database operations.

Exercise 16-1   Create a Customer List application

In this exercise, you'll use a ListView control to create a simple customer list that provides for sorting and paging.

Create a basic ListView control with paging

1. Open the Ex16CustomerList application in the aspnet46_cs directory. This application contains the starting page and the database, image, and style sheet used by the page.

2. Add a ListView control to the form element of the page, and create a data source that retrieves the LastName, FirstName, State, City, and PhoneNumber columns from the Customers table, sorted by last name.

3. Display the Configure ListView dialog box, make sure Grid layout is selected, don't select a style, enable paging, and select the Numeric Pager item from the drop-down list that becomes available.

4. Switch to Source view, and delete the AlternatingItem, EditItem, InsertItem, and SelectedItem, templates since they aren't used by this application.

5. Run the application to see how the ListView control looks. Notice that some formatting has been applied to the DataPager control by styles in the site.css file. Now, experiment with the buttons in the DataPager control to see how they work.

Format the ListView and DataPager controls using Bootstrap

6. Modify the Layout template so Bootstrap styles can be applied to the rendered table. To do that, you'll need to delete the Runat attribute from the itemPlaceholderContainer table. You'll also need to code the first tr element within a thead element, and you'll need to code the second tr element within a tbody element.

7. Delete the Border and Style attributes from the itemPlaceholderContainer table, and replace them with a class attribute that assigns these Bootstrap classes: table, table-bordered, and table-striped. In addition, add a class attribute to the outer table of the Layout template that assigns the col-xs-12 and table-responsive classes.

8. Assign the text-center class to the td element that contains the DataPager control. In addition, assign the btn and btn-default classes to each NextPreviousPagerField control. To do that, you'll need to use the ButtonCssClass property.

9. Run the application again to see how the look of the ListView and DataPager controls have improved. Now, display different pages to see that the widths of the columns change depending on the data that's displayed.

10. Assign a width to each of the th elements by adding a col-xs class. The last name, city, and phone should be three columns wide, the first name should be two columns wide, and the state should be one column wide.

11. Run the application and display different pages to see that the widths of the columns now stay the same.

Add sorting to the ListView control

12. Replace the literal text for the LastName, State, and City columns with link buttons. Add a CommandName property to each link button with the value "Sort", add a CommandArgument property whose value is the name of the column to be sorted, and change the text that's display on the control as appropriate.

13. Run the application again, and notice that the headings for the columns that provide for sorting are displayed in white and the others are displayed in a light gray. Also notice that when you point to a heading that provides for sorting, it's displayed in black. This formatting is applied by styles in the site.css file. Now, make sure that the sorting works correctly.

17

How to use object data sources with ADO.NET

This chapter shows you how to use object data sources as an alternative to SQL data sources. The benefit of using object data sources is that they let you use a three-layer design in which the data access code is kept in data access classes. This lets you separate the presentation code from the data access code, but still lets you use the data binding features of ASP.NET.

To write the data access classes that are used with object data sources, you need to be able to use ADO.NET, which you'll be introduced to in this chapter. Once you understand the material presented in this chapter, you'll be in good shape to understand the Entity Framework and model binding material presented in the next one.

An introduction to object data sources

The following topics introduce you to object data sources, ADO.NET, and the 3-layer architecture that they let you implement.

How 3-layer applications work in ASP.NET

Today, a best practice for web development is to use a *3-layer architecture* that separates the presentation, business rules, and data access components of the application. The *presentation layer* includes the web pages that define the user interface. The *middle layer* includes the classes that manage the data access for those pages, and it may also include classes that implement *business rules* such as data validation requirements and discount policies. The *database layer* consists of the database itself.

In this chapter, you'll learn how to use *object data sources* to implement the 3-layer architecture. Figure 17-1 shows how this works. Here, you can see that the ObjectDataSource control serves as an interface between the data-bound controls in the presentation layer and the data access classes in the middle layer.

When you use an ObjectDataSource control, you must create a data access class to handle the data access for the control. This class provides at least one method that retrieves data from the database and returns it in a form that the ObjectDataSource control can handle. It can also provide methods to insert, update, and delete data. The data access class should be placed in the application's Model folder.

When you code a data access class, you can use any techniques you want to access the database. In this chapter, for example, you'll see data access classes that use ADO.NET. Then, in the next chapter, you'll see data access classes that use the Entity Framework. These classes can be used to work with data in a SQL Server database, in other types of databases such as Oracle or MySQL, or in other sources such as XML or plain text files.

If you have already developed data access classes for the database used by your application, you may be able to use those classes with an object data source. Often, though, it's better to develop the data access classes specifically for the ObjectDataSource controls that you're going to use. That way, you can design each class so it works as efficiently as possible.

Incidentally, Microsoft uses both the term *business object class* and the term *data object class* to refer to a class that provides data access for an object data source. Both this chapter and the next one, though, use the term *data access class* for this type of class. This is partly because the term makes it clear what the class does, and partly because some of the examples use static methods to provide the data access functions, which means an object is never instantiated from the class.

Also, you may be accustomed to using the term *3-tier architecture* for the *3-layer architecture* that's described in figure 17-1. Because some people use *3-tier* to refer to an architecture that puts the three layers on three different physical devices, though, this chapter uses the term *3-layer*. Although you could put each of the three layers on three separate devices, you don't have to.

The 3-layer architecture in ASP.NET

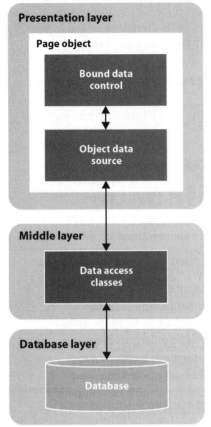

The three layers

- The **presentation layer** consists of the ASP.NET pages that manage the appearance of the application. This layer can include bound data controls and ObjectDataSource controls that bind the data controls to the data.

- The **middle layer** contains the *data access classes* that manage the data access for the application. This layer can also contain business objects that represent business entities such as customers, products, or employees and that implement business rules such as credit and discount policies.

- The **database layer** consists of the database that contains the data for the application. The SQL statements that do the database access can be saved in stored procedures within the database, but these SQL statements are often stored in the data access classes.

Description

- An *object data source* is implemented by the ObjectDataSource control, which lets you use data binding with the *3-layer architecture* for a database application.

- An object data source is similar to a SQL data source. However, instead of directly accessing a database, the object data source gets its data through a data access class that handles the details of database access.

Figure 17-1   How 3-layer applications work in ASP.NET

How to create and work with ADO.NET classes

To code the data access classes that you use with object data sources and the 3-layer architecture, you can use *ADO.NET* (*Active Data Objects*). Figure 17-2 presents the ADO.NET classes and members that are used by the applications in this chapter. Although there are other classes and members, these are the ones you'll use most often.

Before you can access the data in a database, you have to create a connection object that defines the connection to the database. On the constructor for this object, you can include a connection string that provides the information that's needed to connect to a database. That means it includes information such as the name of the database and the database server. It can also contain authentication information such as a user ID and password.

The two methods of this class that are shown in this figure let you open and close the connection. In general, you should leave a connection open only while data is being retrieved or updated. Later in this chapter you'll see some ways to close a connection without explicitly calling the Close method.

To execute a SQL statement against a SQL Server database, you create a SqlCommand object that contains the statement. Notice that the constructor for the object shown here accepts a string that contains the SQL statement to be executed, along with the SqlConnection object that will be used to connect to the database.

To execute a command object, you can use the two Execute methods shown in this figure. To execute a SELECT statement, for example, you use the ExecuteReader method. Then, the results are returned as a SqlDataReader object.

When you code the ExecuteReader method, you can include an argument that is a member of the CommandBehavior enumeration. One member that's used frequently is CloseConnection. This member causes the connection to be closed when the data reader is closed.

To execute an INSERT, UPDATE, or DELETE statement, you use the ExecuteNonQuery method. This method returns an integer value that indicates the number of rows that were affected by the command. If, for example, the command deletes a single row, the ExecuteNonQuery method returns 1.

If the SQL statement you're executing includes one or more parameters, you can use the Parameters property of the SqlCommand object to work with the parameters of this object. This property returns a SqlParameterCollection object. Then, you can use the AddWithValue method of the SqlParameterCollection class to add parameters to the collection.

To work with the data reader that's returned by the ExecuteReader method of a command object, you can use the members of the SqlDataReader class. To start, you can use the Read method to read the next row of data. Then, you can use the indexer shown here to access individual columns in the current row by name. Finally, when you're done using the data reader, you can use the Close method to close it.

How to create and work with a connection
A constructor for the SqlConnection class
```
new SqlConnection(connectionString)
```

Two methods of the SqlConnection class

Method	Description
Open()	Opens a connection to a database.
Close()	Closes a connection to a database.

How to create and work with a command
A constructor for the SqlCommand class
```
new SqlCommand(commandText, connection)
```

Some of the members of the SqlCommand class

Property	Description
Parameters	The SqlParameterCollection object with the parameters used by the command.

Method	Description
ExecuteReader([behavior])	Executes a query and returns the result as a SqlDataReader object. The behavior argument must be a member of the CommandBehavior enumeration.
ExecuteNonQuery()	Executes the command and returns the number of rows affected as an integer.

A method of the SqlParameterCollection class

Method	Description
AddWithValue(name, value)	Adds a named parameter and value to the collection.

How to create and work with a data reader
How to create a SqlDataReader object
```
sqlCommand.ExecuteReader([CommandBehavior.member])
```

Some of the members of the SqlDataReader class

Indexer	Description
[name]	Accesses the column with the specified name from the current row.

Method	Description
Read()	Reads the next row. Returns True if there are more rows. Otherwise, returns False.
Close()	Closes the data reader.

Description
- A SqlConnection object is required to establish a connection to a SQL Server database.
- A SqlCommand object is used to execute a SQL command against a SQL Server database. A SqlCommand object can contain one or more parameters.
- A SqlDataReader object provides read-only, forward-only access to the data in a database.

Figure 17-2   How to create and work with ADO.NET classes

How to use the ObjectDataSource control

Figure 17-3 presents the basics of working with the ObjectDataSource control. The image at the top of this figure shows how an ObjectDataSource control that's bound to a drop-down list appears in the Web Forms Designer. Then, the first code example shows the aspx code for the drop-down list and the object data source it's bound to. As with any other data source, you can add an object data source to a web page by dragging it from the Toolbox or by selecting the Choose Data Source command from a bindable control.

In the this example, you can see that the drop-down list is bound to the object data source using the DataSourceID property just as it is for a SQL data source. You can also see that the code for the ObjectDataSource control has just two properties besides the required ID and Runat properties. The TypeName property provides the name of the data access class, and the SelectMethod property provides the name of the method within that class that's used to retrieve the data. In this case, the data access class is ProductDB and the select method is GetAllCategories.

You'll use the other properties of the ObjectDataSource control shown here when you insert, update, and delete data. You'll learn more about these methods when you see the Category Maintenance application later in this chapter.

The second code example in this figure shows the GetAllCategories method of the ProductDB class. This method uses straightforward ADO.NET code to retrieve category rows from the Categories table and return a data reader that can be used to read the category rows. Notice, though, that the return type for this method is IEnumerable. Because the SqlDataReader class implements the IEnumerable interface, a data reader is a valid return object for this method. (You'll learn more about the return types that are acceptable for a select method in figure 17-9.)

This method is also preceded by an C# attribute that identifies it as a select method for a data access class. You'll learn about all the attributes you can use with data access classes in figure 17-11.

A drop-down list bound to an ObjectDataSource control

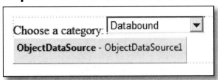

The code for the drop-down list and the ObjectDataSource control

```
<asp:DropDownList ID="ddlCategories" runat="server"
    AutoPostBack="True" DataSourceID="ObjectDataSource1"
    DataTextField="LongName" DataValueField="CategoryID">
</asp:DropDownList>
<asp:ObjectDataSource ID="ObjectDataSource1" runat="server"
    TypeName="ProductDB"
    SelectMethod="GetAllCategories">
</asp:ObjectDataSource>
```

The GetAllCategories method of the ProductDB class

```
[DataObjectMethod(DataObjectMethodType.Select)]
public static IEnumerable GetAllCategories()
{
    SqlConnection con = new SqlConnection(GetConnectionString());
    string sql = "SELECT CategoryID, LongName "
        + "FROM Categories ORDER BY LongName";
    SqlCommand cmd = new SqlCommand(sql, con);
    con.Open();
    SqlDataReader dr = cmd.ExecuteReader(CommandBehavior.CloseConnection);
    return dr;
}
```

Basic properties of the ObjectDataSource control

Property	Description
TypeName	The name of the data access class.
SelectMethod	The name of the method that retrieves the data.
UpdateMethod	The name of the method that updates the data.
DeleteMethod	The name of the method that deletes the data.
InsertMethod	The name of the method that inserts the data.
DataObjectTypeName	The name of a class that provides properties that are used to pass parameter values.
ConflictDetection	Specifies how concurrency conflicts will be detected. CompareAllValues uses optimistic concurrency checking. OverwriteValues, which is the default, does no concurrency checking.

Description

- The ObjectDataSource control specifies the name of the data access class and the methods used to select, update, delete, and insert data.

Figure 17-3   How to use the ObjectDataSource control

How to configure an ObjectDataSource control

Figure 17-4 shows how you can use the Configure Data Source dialog boxes to configure an ObjectDataSource control. As you can see, the first dialog box lets you choose the business object that will be associated with this object data source. The selection you make here will be specified in the TypeName property of the ObjectDataSource control. (Notice that Microsoft refers to the data access class as a *business object* in this wizard. In other contexts, though, Microsoft refers to the data access class as a *data object* or a *data component*.)

The drop-down list in the first dialog box lists all of the classes that are available in the Models folder. Note, though, that you might need to build the solution before this will work correctly. Then, if you check the "Show Only Data Components" box, only those classes that are marked as data components will be listed. In figure 17-11, you'll learn how to mark classes this way.

When you select a data access class and click Next, the second Configure Data Source dialog box is displayed. Here, you can select the method you want to use to retrieve data for the object data source. The one you select is specified in the SelectMethod property of the ObjectDataSource control. (In this step, the wizard uses a .NET feature called *reflection* to determine all of the available methods, and you'll learn more about reflection in a moment.)

If you choose a select method that requires parameters, the Define Parameters step lets you specify the source for each of the required parameters. Then, Visual Studio generates the elements that define the parameters required by the ObjectDataSource control. This works the same as it does for a SQL data source.

As you can see in this figure, the second Configure Data Source dialog box also provides tabs that let you specify the methods for update, insert, and delete operations. You'll see an application that uses these methods later in this chapter.

How to work with bound controls

Although you can bind a control such as a GridView control to an object data source, you can't always use the designer to select individual fields like you can when you use a SQL data source. That's because the fields are defined in the data access class and not directly in the data source. When you bind a drop-down list, for example, you may have to manually enter the names of the fields you want to display and use for the value of the control. Similarly, when you bind a GridView control, you may have to manually enter the name of each field you want to bind and, if the control provides for sorting, you may have to enter the name of the field for each sort expression. In addition, you may have to enter the appropriate field name or names for the DataKeyNames property of the control.

To avoid having to enter the names of these fields, you can code the select method so it returns a strongly-typed collection. You'll see an example like that later in this chapter. For now, just realize that because select methods that return a strongly-typed collection can make an object data source easier to work with, you should use them whenever that makes sense.

The dialog boxes for configuring a data source

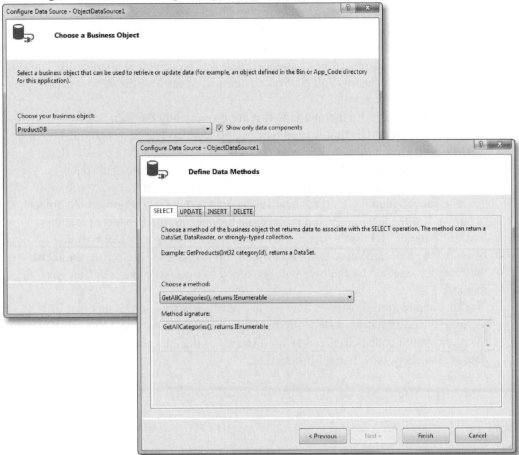

Description

- You can use the Configure Data Source dialog boxes to configure an ObjectDataSource control by choosing Configure Data Source from its smart tag menu.

- The Choose a Business Object step lets you select the data access class you want to use. If the class you want isn't listed, cancel the dialog box, select the Build→Build Solution command, and try again.

- The Define Data Methods step includes tabs that let you choose the methods you want to use for select, update, insert, and delete operations.

- If you choose a method that requires parameters, a Define Parameters step appears. This step lets you choose the source of each parameter required by the method. For example, you can specify that a drop-down list is used as the source for a parameter.

- If you create a new data source from a bound control, the Data Source Configuration Wizard asks you to choose a data source type. To create an object data source, select the Object option. Then, click the Next button to display the first dialog box shown above.

Figure 17-4   How to configure an ObjectDataSource control

A Product List application

To illustrate the basics of working with the ObjectDataSource control, figure 17-5 presents a Product List application. This application is identical in appearance to the Product List application that was presented in chapter 13. However, instead of using SqlDataSource controls to retrieve the data, it uses ObjectDataSource controls.

This figure also lists the methods that are provided by the data access class named ProductDB that is used by this application. The first method, GetAllCategories, returns an IEnumerable object (actually, a data reader) that contains the data for all of the categories in the Categories table. This data includes just the category ID and long name for each category.

The second method, GetProductsByCategory, returns an IEnumerable object (again, a data reader) that includes all of the products in the Products table that have the category ID that's supplied by a parameter. This parameter will be bound to the SelectedValue property of the drop-down list. As a result, the ID of the category selected by the user will be passed to the GetProductsByCategory method.

This application illustrates how the use of object data sources lets you separate the presentation code from the data access code. As you will see, all of the presentation code is in the aspx file. And all of the data access code is in the data access class that's named ProductDB.

The Product List application

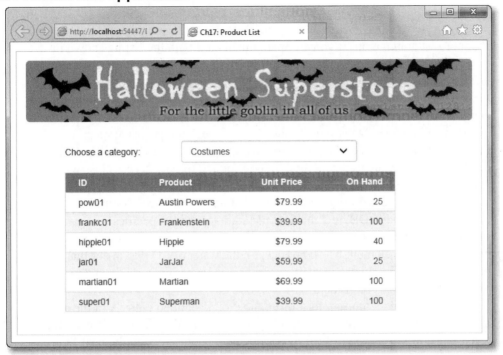

Methods of the ProductDB class

Method	Description
`GetAllCategories()`	Returns an IEnumerable object with the ID and long name of all the categories in the Categories table.
`GetProductsByCategory(categoryID)`	Returns an IEnumerable object with the ID, name, unit price, and on-hand quantity for all products in the Products table for the specified category.

Description

- The Category drop-down list is bound to an ObjectDataSource control that retrieves a list of categories from the Categories table.

- The DataList control is bound to a second ObjectDataSource control that uses a parameterized query to retrieve the products for a selected category. The CategoryID for the parameter is taken from the SelectedValue property of the drop-down list.

- Both ObjectDataSource controls use a data access class named ProductDB that contains the static methods that return a list of categories and the products for a specific category.

Figure 17-5   The Product List application

The aspx file

Figure 17-6 shows the main element of the Default.aspx page for the Product List application. If you compare this listing with the listing shown in figure 13-17, you'll discover that the only difference is that the SqlDataSource elements have been replaced by ObjectDataSource elements. In other words, the code for the drop-down list and DataList controls is identical whether the application uses a SQL data source or an object data source.

In the first ObjectDataSource control, the TypeName property specifies ProductDB, and the SelectMethod property specifies GetAllCategories. As a result, the GetAllCategories method in the ProductDB data access class will be called to retrieve the category data when the drop-down list is bound.

The TypeName property for the second ObjectDataSource control also specifies ProductDB, and the SelectMethod property specifies GetProductsByCategory. Then, a ControlParameter element within the SelectParameters element is used to declare the CategoryID parameter that's passed to the GetProductsByCategory method. This parameter is bound to the SelectedValue property of the drop-down list.

Because the data binding for this application is defined entirely in the aspx file, there is no code-behind file for this page. As a result, the only C# code for this application is in the ProductDB class, which is presented in the next figure.

The main element of the Default.aspx file

```
<main>
    <form id="form1" runat="server" class="form-horizontal">
        <div class="form-group">
            <label id="lblCategory" for="ddlCategory"
                class="col-xs-4 col-sm-offset-1 col-sm-3 control-label">
                Choose a category:</label>
            <div class="col-xs-8 col-sm-5">
                <asp:DropDownList ID="ddlCategory" runat="server"
                    CssClass="form-control" DataSourceID="ObjectDataSource1"
                    DataTextField="LongName" DataValueField="CategoryID"
                    AutoPostBack="true">
                </asp:DropDownList>
                <asp:ObjectDataSource runat="server" ID="ObjectDataSource1"
                    SelectMethod="GetAllCategories" TypeName="ProductDB">
                </asp:ObjectDataSource>
            </div>
        </div>

        <div class="form-group">
            <div class="col-xs-12 col-sm-offset-1 col-sm-9">
                <asp:DataList ID="dlProducts" runat="server"
                    DataKeyField="ProductID" DataSourceID="ObjectDataSource2"
                    UseAccessibleHeader="true"
                    CssClass="table table-bordered table-striped table-condensed">
                    <HeaderTemplate>
                        <span class="col-xs-3">ID</span>
                        <span class="col-xs-3">Product</span>
                        <span class="col-xs-3 text-right">Unit Price</span>
                        <span class="col-xs-3 text-right">On Hand</span>
                    </HeaderTemplate>
                    <ItemTemplate>
                        <asp:Label ID="lblID" runat="server"
                            Text='<%# Eval("ProductID") %>' CssClass="col-xs-3" />
                        <asp:Label ID="lblName" runat="server"
                            Text='<%# Eval("Name") %>' CssClass="col-xs-3" />
                        <asp:Label ID="lblUnitPrice" runat="server"
                            Text='<%# Eval("UnitPrice", "{0:C}") %>'
                            CssClass="col-xs-3 text-right" />
                        <asp:Label ID="lblOnHand" runat="server"
                            Text='<%# Eval("OnHand") %>'
                            CssClass="col-xs-3 text-right" />
                    </ItemTemplate>
                    <HeaderStyle CssClass="bg-halloween" />
                </asp:DataList>
                <asp:ObjectDataSource runat="server" ID="ObjectDataSource2"
                    SelectMethod="GetProductsByCategory" TypeName="ProductDB">
                    <SelectParameters>
                        <asp:ControlParameter ControlID="ddlCategory"
                            Name="CategoryID" PropertyName="SelectedValue"
                            Type="String"></asp:ControlParameter>
                    </SelectParameters>
                </asp:ObjectDataSource>
            </div>
        </div>
    </form>
</main>
```

Figure 17-6   The aspx file for the Product List application

The ProductDB class

Figure 17-7 presents the C# code for the ProductDB class. To create this class, you can right-click the Models folder and select Add→Class to display the Add New Item dialog box.

The ProductDB class has two public methods, GetAllCategories and GetProductsByCategory. It also has a private method, GetConnectionString. This method is used by both of the public methods to retrieve the connection string for the Halloween database.

As you can see, this class includes DataObject and DataObjectMethod attributes. These attributes are used to identify the class and methods as data objects, and you'll learn how to use them in figure 17-11. For now, just realize that they're used by the Configure Data Source wizard to determine which classes and methods to display when you configure an object data source.

The GetAllCategories method starts by creating a connection to the Halloween database. To get the connection, it calls the GetConnectionString method. Next, this method creates a string variable that contains the SELECT statement that will be used to retrieve data from the Halloween database:

```
SELECT CategoryID, LongName
FROM Categories
ORDER BY LongName
```

Then, a SqlCommand object is created using the string variable that contains the SELECT statement and the connection object as parameters. Finally, the connection is opened, the ExecuteReader method of the command object is called to create a data reader object that contains the requested data, and the data reader is returned to the object data source. Notice that the CloseConnection member of the CommandBehavior enumeration is passed to the ExecuteReader method. That way, the connection is closed when the data reader is closed.

The GetProductsByCategory method is slightly more complicated because it uses a parameter in its SELECT statement:

```
SELECT ProductID, Name, UnitPrice, OnHand
FROM Products
WHERE CategoryID = @CategoryID
ORDER BY ProductID
```

Here again, a SqlCommand object is created using this statement and the connection object. Then, a parameter named CategoryID is added to the command's Parameters collection. This parameter is assigned the value of the CategoryID parameter that's passed to the method. Finally, the connection is opened and the command is executed so it returns a data reader with the requested data.

The GetConnectionString method uses the ConfigurationManager class to retrieve the connection string named "HalloweenConnection" from the Web.config file. Unlike a SQL data source, however, an object data source doesn't save a connection string in the Web.config file when you configure it. Instead, you have to manually add the connection string to the Web.config file. To refresh your memory about the syntax of a connection string in this file, please refer to figure 13-4 in chapter 13.

The ProductDB class

```
...
using System.Collections;
using System.Configuration;
using System.Data;
using System.Data.SqlClient;
using System.ComponentModel;

[DataObject(true)]
public static class ProductDB
{
    [DataObjectMethod(DataObjectMethodType.Select)]
    public static IEnumerable GetAllCategories()
    {
        SqlConnection con = new SqlConnection(GetConnectionString());
        string sql = "SELECT CategoryID, LongName "
            + "FROM Categories ORDER BY LongName";
        SqlCommand cmd = new SqlCommand(sql, con);
        con.Open();
        SqlDataReader dr = cmd.ExecuteReader(CommandBehavior.CloseConnection);
        return dr;
    }

    [DataObjectMethod(DataObjectMethodType.Select)]
    public static IEnumerable GetProductsByCategory(string CategoryID)
    {
        SqlConnection con = new SqlConnection(GetConnectionString());
        string sql = "SELECT ProductID, Name, "
            + "UnitPrice, OnHand "
            + "FROM Products "
            + "WHERE CategoryID = @CategoryID "
            + "ORDER BY Name";
        SqlCommand cmd = new SqlCommand(sql, con);
        cmd.Parameters.AddWithValue("CategoryID", CategoryID);
        con.Open();
        SqlDataReader dr = cmd.ExecuteReader(CommandBehavior.CloseConnection);
        return dr;
    }

    private static string GetConnectionString()
    {
        return ConfigurationManager.ConnectionStrings
            ["HalloweenConnection"].ConnectionString;
    }
}
```

Note

- The DataObject and DataObjectMethod attributes are described in figure 17-11.

Figure 17-7   The ProductDB class for the Product List application

How to create a data access class

The most challenging aspect of using object data sources is developing the data access classes that they require. So the topics that follow explain how to design and implement these classes.

How to design a data access class

As figure 17-8 shows, the data access class used by an ObjectDataSource control can have four different types of methods that are used to select, insert, update, and delete data. You can use any method names that you want for these methods, and you can design the class so it has more than one of each of these types of methods. For example, the ProductDB class used in the previous figure has two select methods that are named GetAllCategories and GetProductsByCategory.

The data access methods can be static methods or instance methods. If you define them as instance methods, the ObjectDataSource control will create an instance of the data access class before it calls the method, and then destroy the object after the method has been executed. For this to work, the data access class must provide a parameterless constructor. In C#, though, a parameterless constructor is provided by default if the class has no constructors.

Because creating and destroying a data access object can affect performance, another option is to use static methods for the select, insert, update, and delete methods whenever possible. That way, the ObjectDataSource control won't have to create an instance of the data access class when it calls one of the data access methods.

Although you provide the names of the methods called by the ObjectDataSource control by using the SelectMethod, InsertMethod, UpdateMethod, and DeleteMethod properties, the ObjectDataSource control doesn't generate the parameters that will be passed to these methods until runtime. Because of that, the ObjectDataSource control must use a .NET feature called *reflection* to determine if a method it calls contains the correct parameters. It also uses reflection to determine the return type of a select method. As you'll see in the next figure, this lets you design a select method that can return the selected data in a variety of forms.

In case you haven't encountered reflection before, it's a .NET feature that provides information about compiled classes at runtime. For example, reflection can determine what methods are provided by a particular class. In addition, it can determine what parameters each method requires and the type returned by the method.

Types of methods in a data access class

Method type	Description
Select	Retrieves data from a database and returns it as an IEnumerable object.
Insert	Inserts data for one row into the underlying database. The values for the new row are passed via one or more parameters.
Update	Updates the data for one row in the underlying database. The values for the updated row, along with any values that are used to implement optimistic concurrency, are passed via one or more parameters.
Delete	Deletes a row from the underlying database. The key or keys for the row to be deleted, along with any values that are used to implement optimistic concurrency, are passed via one or more parameters.

How an object data source determines which method to call

- The name of the method used for select, insert, update, and delete operations is specified by the SelectMethod, InsertMethod, UpdateMethod, or DeleteMethod property.

- The ObjectDataSource control determines what parameters need to be passed to the data access class methods based on the data fields to be inserted, updated, or deleted and whether or not optimistic concurrency is used.

- The ObjectDataSource control uses reflection to determine the parameter signatures for the insert, update, and delete methods provided by the data access class.

- At runtime, if the class doesn't provide a method with the correct name and parameters, an exception is thrown.

Description

- A data access class can declare public methods that select, insert, update, and delete data. These methods can be instance methods or static methods.

- You can use any method names you want for the select, insert, update, and delete methods.

- If the select, insert, update, and delete methods are static methods, the methods are used without creating an instance of the data access class.

- If the select, insert, update, and delete methods are instance methods, an instance of the data access class is created and destroyed for each data access operation. In this case, the data access class must provide a parameterless constructor.

- You can use parameters to pass selection criteria or other data to the select, insert, update, and delete methods. For more information on the parameters used with insert, update, and delete methods, see figure 17-10.

- *Reflection* is a .NET feature that provides information about compiled classes and methods at runtime.

Figure 17-8   How to design a data access class

How to create a select method

Figure 17-9 shows how to design and code a select method that can be used with an ObjectDataSource control. The table at the top of this figure lists the four different types of values that a select method can return. The simplest is the IEnumerable interface, which can return a data reader or a data view since the DataReader and DataView classes implement the IEnumerable interface. You saw how to use a data reader in the Product List application.

The IEnumerable object can also be a strongly-typed collection that's created by using the generics feature of C#. This technique is illustrated in the example in this figure. Here, the select method starts by creating a List<> object that will store a list of Category objects. Then, a Category object is created for each row that's retrieved by the data reader. To do that, the values of the row are assigned to the properties of the object. Then, the Category object is added to the List<Category> object. Finally, the data reader is closed and the List<Category> object is returned to the object data source.

Notice in this example that the connection and command objects are created as part of using statements, and the statements that retrieve the data from the database are coded within the using blocks. Then, when the using blocks end, any resources associated with the objects are released. In addition, before the resources for the connection are released, the connection is closed. Because of that, it isn't necessary to explicitly close the connection. The use of using blocks is a best practice because it causes resources to be released as soon as they're no longer needed instead of waiting for them to be released by the .NET Framework's garbage collection feature.

The select method can also return a DataTable or DataSet object. Because a dataset can contain more than one table, the ObjectDataSource control simply uses the first table in the dataset. As a result, you must design the select method so the first table in the dataset contains the data you want to access.

The main advantage of returning a dataset is that the object data source can cache a dataset. Then, to enable caching, you can set the EnableCaching property to True for the ObjectDataSource control. In that case, the select method will be called only the first time the data is requested. For more information on caching, which works the same as it does for a SqlDataSource control, please refer back to chapter 13.

You can also pass parameters to the select method. In that case, the ObjectDataSource control must include a SelectParameters element. This element is added automatically if you use the Configure Data Source wizard to create the control. Then, you can create a ControlParameter element that binds a parameter to a control such as a drop-down list. You saw an example of this in figure 17-6.

Allowable return types for a select method

Return type	Description
IEnumerable	A collection such as an ArrayList, or a strongly-typed collection such as System. Collections.Generic.List. (Because the DataReader and DataView classes implement IEnumerable, the select method can also return a data reader or a data view.)
DataTable	If the select method returns a data table, the ObjectDataSource control automatically extracts a data view from the table and uses the view for data binding.
DataSet	If the select method returns a dataset, the ObjectDataSource control extracts a data view from the first data table in the dataset and uses the view for data binding.
Object	If the select method returns an object, the ObjectDataSource control wraps the object in an IEnumerable collection with just one item, then does the data binding as if the method returned an IEnumerable object.

A select method that returns a strongly-typed collection

```
public static List<Category> GetCategories()
{
    List<Category> categoryList = new List<Category>();
    string sql = "SELECT CategoryID, ShortName, LongName "
        + "FROM Categories ORDER BY LongName";
    using (SqlConnection con = new SqlConnection(GetConnectionString())) {
        using (SqlCommand cmd = new SqlCommand(sql, con)) {
            con.Open();
            SqlDataReader dr = cmd.ExecuteReader();
            Category category;
            while (dr.Read()) {
                category = new Category();
                category.CategoryID = dr["CategoryID"].ToString();
                category.ShortName = dr["ShortName"].ToString();
                category.LongName = dr["LongName"].ToString();
                categoryList.Add(category);
            }
            dr.Close();
        }
    }
    return categoryList;
}
```

Description

- The select method returns data retrieved from the underlying database. It can return the data in several forms, including a data reader, dataset, or strongly-typed collection.

- If the select method returns a dataset, the object data source can cache the data.

- The select method can return a strongly-typed collection using C#'s generics feature. To use this feature, the application must include a business class that defines the objects in the collection. See figure 17-10 for more information.

- If the select method accepts parameters, the parameters must be declared within the SelectParameters element of the ObjectDataSource control.

Figure 17-9   How to create a select method

How to create update, delete, and insert methods

Besides select methods, the data access class used by an object data source can provide methods that update, delete, and insert data in the underlying database. Before you can code these methods, you need to determine what parameters are required. Figure 17-10 summarizes how an object data source generates these parameters.

Any insert or delete method you create requires a single business object as its parameter. This business object must contain all the values required by the method, and you can give it any name you choose. If an update method doesn't provide for optimistic concurrency checking, it too requires a single business object as its parameter.

If an update method provides for optimistic concurrency checking, however, it requires two parameters as shown in the code at the top of this figure. One of the parameters must be a business object that provides the original values for the row to be updated, and the other parameter must be a business object that provides the new values for the row. Note that the name of the parameter for the business object that contains the new values can have any name you choose. However, the name of the parameter for the business object that contains the original values must be the same as the name of the parameter for the business object with the new values, preceded by the value of the OldValuesParameterFormatString property. In this example, the value of this property is original_, which is the default.

Two parameters are also required if the key column for a table is updatable. In that case, though, the object data source won't automatically generate two parameters. Because of that, you will need to set the ConflictDetection property of the object data source to CompareAllValues even if the update method doesn't provide for optimistic concurrency checking, and you will need to set the OldValuesParameterFormatString property accordingly. Then, you can use the property that contains the value for the key column of the object that contains the original values to identify the row to be updated.

The business objects that you pass to update, delete, and insert methods are defined by the class that's identified on the DataObjectTypeName property of the object data source. This class must meet the requirements listed in this figure. First, the class must provide a parameterless constructor. Since C# provides a parameterless constructor by default if a class isn't defined with any constructors, you can typically omit this constructor.

Second, the class must define a public property for each bound field that's passed from the bound control to the object data source. If the object data source is bound to a GridView or DetailsView control that uses BoundField elements, the names of these properties must be the same as the names specified for the DataField properties of those elements. In contrast, if the object data source is bound to a GridView or DetailsView control that uses TemplateField elements, or if the object data source is bound to a FormView or ListView control, the names of these properties must be the same as the names in the Eval and Bind methods of the bound controls.

A typical update method

```
public static int UpdateCategory(Category original_Category,
    Category category)
{
    string sql = "UPDATE Categories "
        + "SET ShortName = @ShortName, "
        + "LongName = @LongName "
        + "WHERE CategoryID = @original_CategoryID "
        + "AND ShortName = @original_ShortName "
        + "AND LongName = @original_LongName";
    using (SqlConnection con = new SqlConnection(GetConnectionString())) {
        using (SqlCommand cmd = new SqlCommand(sql, con)) {
            cmd.Parameters.AddWithValue("ShortName", category.ShortName);
            cmd.Parameters.AddWithValue("LongName", category.LongName);
            cmd.Parameters.AddWithValue("original_CategoryID",
                original_Category.CategoryID);
            cmd.Parameters.AddWithValue("original_ShortName",
                original_Category.ShortName);
            cmd.Parameters.AddWithValue("original_LongName",
                original_Category.LongName);
            con.Open();
            return cmd.ExecuteNonQuery();
        }
    }
}
```

How parameters are generated

- When the insert or delete method is called, one parameter of the business class type is generated and passed to the method. The parameter that's declared in the method can have any name you choose.

- One parameter of the business class type is also generated and passed to the update method when this method is called if optimistic concurrency isn't used. The parameter that's declared in the method can have any name you choose.

- If optimistic concurrency is specified, two parameters are generated and passed to the update method. One contains the original values, and the other contains the new values. The name of the parameter that contains the original values must be the same as the name of the parameter that contains the new values, preceded by the string that's specified by the OldValuesParameterFormatString property.

Requirements for the business class

- The class must provide a parameterless constructor.

- The class must have public properties with names that match the names of the bound fields that are passed to the object data source from the bound control.

- The public properties must have both get and set accessors.

Description

- To properly design an update, delete, or insert method, you must be aware of how the ObjectDataSource control generates the parameters passed to these methods.

Figure 17-10   How to create update, delete, and insert methods

Third, the property for each bound field must include both get and set accessors. The object data source uses the set accessors to set the values of the properties based on the values passed to it from the bound control. And the insert, update, and delete methods in the data access class use the get accessors to assign the values of the properties to parameters of command objects.

Once the ObjectDataSource control has determined what parameters need to be passed, it uses reflection to determine whether the data access class has a method that accepts the required parameters. If so, the method is called using these parameters. If not, an exception is thrown.

You should know that you don't have to use business objects as the parameters of insert, update, and delete methods. Instead, you can use a parameter for each bound field that's required by a method. This technique can be cumbersome, though, if more than just a few fields are required. In addition, it's more difficult to determine what parameters the object data source will generate. It's also more difficult to work with bound controls like the GridView control because you have to manually enter the name of each field you want to bind. That's because the fields are defined in the data access class and not directly in the data source. (When you use business objects, the business class is identified in the data source, and the properties of that class are made available to bound controls.) For these reasons, it's a best practice to use business objects whenever possible.

How to use attributes to mark a data access class

Figure 17-11 shows how you can use *C# attributes* to identify a data access class and its methods. In case you haven't worked with attributes before, they are simply a way to provide declarative information for classes, methods, properties, and so on. Although some of these attributes have meaning at runtime, the attributes in this figure are used at design time. In particular, the Configure Data Source wizard uses these attributes to determine which classes in the Models folder are data access classes and which methods in the data access class are select, insert, update, and delete methods.

Note, however, that you don't need to use these attributes. The only reason to use them is to help the Configure Data Source wizard recognize the data access classes and methods. If you haven't marked your data access classes with these attributes, you can still access them from the wizard by clearing the Show Only Data Components check box in the Choose a Business Object step of the wizard (see figure 17-4).

Whether or not you use the attributes shown here, you should know that the data access class and its attributes may not appear correctly in the Configure Data Source wizard. That's true if you just created the class or if you've made changes to it. In that case, you can build the solution as described in figure 17-4 so the class and methods will appear properly.

Attributes for marking data access classes

To mark an element as...	Use this attribute...
A data object class	`[DataObject(true)]`
A Select method	`[DataObjectMethod(DataObjectMethodType.Select)]`
An Insert method	`[DataObjectMethod(DataObjectMethodType.Insert)]`
An Update method	`[DataObjectMethod(DataObjectMethodType.Update)]`
A Delete method	`[DataObjectMethod(DataObjectMethodType.Delete)]`

A marked data access class

```
...
using System.Collections.Generic;
using System.Configuration;
using System.Data;
using System.Data.SqlClient;
using System.ComponentModel;


[DataObject(true)]
public static class CategoryDB
{
    [DataObjectMethod(DataObjectMethodType.Select)]
    public static List<Category> GetCategories()
    {
        List<Category> categoryList = new List<Category>();
        string sql = "SELECT CategoryID, ShortName, LongName "
            + "FROM Categories ORDER BY LongName";
        using (SqlConnection con = new SqlConnection(GetConnectionString())){
            using (SqlCommand cmd = new SqlCommand(sql, con)){
                con.Open();
                SqlDataReader dr = cmd.ExecuteReader();
                Category category;
                while (dr.Read()) {
                    category = new Category();
                    category.CategoryID = dr["CategoryID"].ToString();
                    category.ShortName = dr["ShortName"].ToString();
                    category.LongName = dr["LongName"].ToString();
                    categoryList.Add(category);
                }
                dr.Close();
            }
        }
        return categoryList;
    }
}
```

Description

- You can use DataObject and DataObjectMethod attributes to mark data access classes and methods. Visual Studio uses these attributes to determine which classes and methods to list in the drop-down lists of the Configure Data Source wizard.

- The DataObject and DataObjectMethod attributes are stored in the System. ComponentModel namespace.

Figure 17-11   How to use attributes to mark a data access class

A Category Maintenance application

To give you a better idea of how you can use an object data source to update, delete, and insert data, the following topics present an application that maintains the Categories table in the Halloween database. This application is a variation of the Category Maintenance application that was presented in chapter 14.

The design

Figure 17-12 presents the design for this version of the Category Maintenance application. It uses a GridView control to let the user update and delete category rows and a DetailsView control to insert new category rows. Both the GridView and DetailsView controls are bound to a single ObjectDataSource control. But the DetailsView control is used only in Insert mode, so it isn't used to display, update, or delete existing category rows.

The table in this figure shows the public methods that are provided by the CategoryDB class. These four methods provide the select, update, delete, and insert functions. Since all of these methods are defined as static, an instance of the CategoryDB class doesn't have to be created to access the database.

The aspx file

The two parts of figure 17-13 show the Default.aspx file for this application. In part 1, you can see the aspx code for the GridView control that displays the category rows. Its Columns collection includes three BoundField columns, named CategoryID, ShortName, and LongName.

In part 2, you can see the aspx code for the ObjectDataSource control. It names CategoryDB as the data access class and Category as the business class. It also provides the names of the select, insert, update, and delete methods that will be used to access the data. Notice that the ConflictDetection property is set to CompareAllValues so optimistic concurrency will be used. You'll see one way to implement optimistic concurrency with an object data source when you see the C# code for this application. Also notice that the OnUpdated and OnDeleted properties both point to the same method. You'll see what this method does when you see the C# code too.

As you can see, parameters are included only for the update method. These parameters are included because the update method requires two parameters: an object that contains the original values and an object that contains the new values. Because these parameters must be given appropriate names as explained earlier, the object data source must include parameters that specify these names. In contrast, the names of the parameters in the insert and delete methods can be anything you like, so they don't have to be defined by the object data source.

You can also see the aspx code for the DetailsView control in part 2. Here, the DefaultMode property is set to Insert so this control is always displayed in Insert mode.

The Category Maintenance application

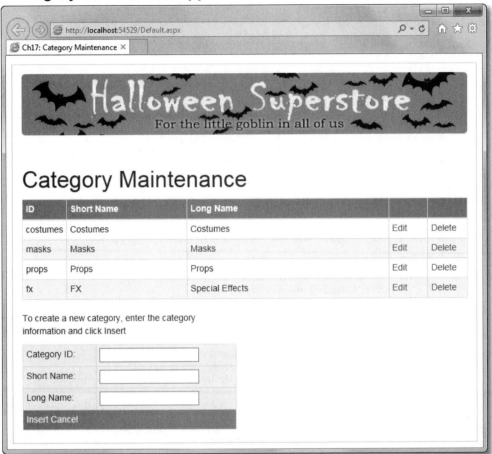

Methods of the CategoryDB class

Method type	Signature
Select	`public static List<Category> GetCategories()`
Update	`public static int UpdateCategory(` `        Category original_category, Category category)`
Delete	`public static int DeleteCategory(Category category)`
Insert	`public static int InsertCategory(Category category)`

Description

- This version of the Category Maintenance application uses a GridView control to update and delete rows and a DetailsView control to insert rows. These controls are bound to an ObjectDataSource control that accesses the Categories table of the Halloween database.

- The data access class named CategoryDB provides the select, insert, update, and delete methods.

Figure 17-12   The Category Maintenance application

The Default.aspx file

```
<%@ Page Language="C#" AutoEventWireup="true" CodeBehind="Default.aspx.cs"
Inherits="Ch17CategoryMaintenance.Default" %>

<!DOCTYPE html>

<html xmlns="http://www.w3.org/1999/xhtml">
<head runat="server">
    <title>Ch17: Category Maintenance</title>
    <meta name="viewport" content="width=device-width, initial-scale=1" />
    <link href="Content/bootstrap.min.css" rel="stylesheet" />
    <link href="Content/site.css" rel="stylesheet" />
    <script src="Scripts/jquery-1.9.1.min.js"></script>
    <script src="Scripts/bootstrap.min.js"></script>
</head>
<body>
<div class="container">
    <header class="jumbotron"><%-- image set in site.css --%></header>
    <main>
    <form id="form1" runat="server" class="form-horizontal">

        <div class="row">
            <div class="col-xs-12 table-responsive">
                <h1>Category Maintenance</h1>
                <asp:GridView ID="GridView1" runat="server"
                    AutoGenerateColumns="False" DataKeyNames="CategoryID"
                    DataSourceID="ObjectDataSource1"
                    OnPreRender="GridView1_PreRender"
                    OnRowDeleted="GridView1_RowDeleted"
                    OnRowUpdated="GridView1_RowUpdated"
                    CssClass="table table-bordered table-condensed">
                    <Columns>
                        <asp:BoundField DataField="CategoryID" HeaderText="ID"
                            ReadOnly="True">
                            <ItemStyle CssClass="col-xs-1" />
                        </asp:BoundField>
                        <asp:BoundField DataField="ShortName"
                            HeaderText="Short Name" SortExpression="ShortName">
                            <ItemStyle CssClass="col-xs-3" />
                        </asp:BoundField>
                        <asp:BoundField DataField="LongName"
                            HeaderText="Long Name" SortExpression="LongName">
                            <ItemStyle CssClass="col-xs-5" />
                        </asp:BoundField>
                        <asp:CommandField ButtonType="Link"
                            CausesValidation="false" ShowEditButton="true">
                            <ItemStyle CssClass="col-xs-1 text-danger" />
                        </asp:CommandField>
                        <asp:CommandField ButtonType="Link"
                            CausesValidation="false" ShowDeleteButton="true">
                            <ItemStyle CssClass="col-xs-1" />
                        </asp:CommandField>
                    </Columns>
                    <AlternatingRowStyle CssClass="altRow" />
                    <EditRowStyle CssClass="warning" />
                </asp:GridView>
```

Figure 17-13   The aspx file of the Category Maintenance application (part 1 of 2)

The Default.aspx file   **Page 2**

```
            <asp:ObjectDataSource runat="server" ID="ObjectDataSource1"
                DataObjectTypeName="Category"
                DeleteMethod="DeleteCategory"
                InsertMethod="InsertCategory"
                OldValuesParameterFormatString="original_{0}"
                SelectMethod="GetCategories" TypeName="CategoryDB"
                UpdateMethod="UpdateCategory"
                ConflictDetection="CompareAllValues"
                OnDeleted="ObjectDataSource1_GetAffectedRows"
                OnUpdated="ObjectDataSource1_GetAffectedRows">
                <UpdateParameters>
                    <asp:Parameter Name="original_Category"
                        Type="Object"></asp:Parameter>
                    <asp:Parameter Name="category"
                        Type="Object"></asp:Parameter>
                </UpdateParameters>
            </asp:ObjectDataSource>
        </div>
    </div>
    <div class="row">
        <div class="col-xs-6">
            <p>To create a new category, enter the category information
                and click Insert</p>
            <p><asp:Label ID="lblError" runat="server"
                    EnableViewState="false"
                    CssClass="text-danger"></asp:Label></p>

            <asp:DetailsView ID="DetailsView1" runat="server"
                AutoGenerateRows="false" DataSourceID="ObjectDataSource1"
                DefaultMode="Insert"
                OnItemInserted="DetailsView1_ItemInserted"
                CssClass="table table-bordered table-condensed">
                <Fields>
                    <asp:BoundField DataField="CategoryID"
                        HeaderText="Category ID:"></asp:BoundField>
                    <asp:BoundField DataField="ShortName"
                        HeaderText="Short Name:"></asp:BoundField>
                    <asp:BoundField DataField="LongName"
                        HeaderText="Long Name:"></asp:BoundField>
                    <asp:CommandField ButtonType="Link"
                        ShowInsertButton="true" />
                </Fields>
                <RowStyle CssClass="rowStyle" />
                <CommandRowStyle CssClass="commandRowStyle" />
            </asp:DetailsView>
        </div>
    </div>

    </form>
    </main>
</div>
</body>
</html>
```

Figure 17-13   The aspx file of the Category Maintenance application (part 2 of 2)

The code-behind file

Figure 17-14 shows the code-behind file for the Default.aspx page of the Category Maintenance application. This file consists of methods that handle the exceptions that might be raised and the concurrency errors that might occur when the object data source's update, delete, and insert methods are called.

The first method is executed after the data source is updated or deleted. This method retrieves the return value from the update or delete method using the ReturnValue property of the e argument and assigns it to the AffectedRows property of the e argument. This is necessary because the AffectedRows property isn't set automatically like it is for a SQL data source. For this to work, of course, the update and delete methods must return the number of rows that were affected. You'll see the code that accomplishes that in figure 17-15.

The second method is executed after a row in the GridView control is updated, which happens after the data source is updated. This method checks the Exception property of the e argument to determine if an exception has been thrown. If it has, an error message is displayed, the ExceptionHandled property is set to True to suppress the exception, and the KeepInEditMode property is set to True to leave the GridView control in Edit mode.

If an exception didn't occur, this method continues by checking the AffectedRows property of the e argument. The value of this property is passed forward from the AffectedRows property of the object data source's Updated event. If the value of this property is zero, the row was not updated, most likely due to the concurrency checking code that was added to the SQL UPDATE statement. As a result, an appropriate error message is displayed.

The third method is similar, except it handles the RowDeleted event of the GridView control. Like the RowUpdated event handler of the this control, the RowDeleted event handler checks for exceptions and concurrency errors.

The fourth method is executed after a row is inserted using the DetailsView control. It checks whether an exception has occurred and responds accordingly. Note that currency checking isn't necessary here because a concurrency error can't occur for an insert operation.

The last two methods create the error messages that are displayed if an error occurs. Notice that the first method checks the InnerException property of the current Exception object. That's because a system exception occurs when a database exception isn't caught by the CategoryDB class, so the InnerException property must be used to get the database exception.

By the way, this code illustrates just one way that you can provide for concurrency errors. Another way is to write the update and delete methods so they throw an exception if a concurrency error occurs. Then, the RowUpdated and RowDeleted event handlers can test the e.Exception property.

The Category class

Figure 17-14 also presents the Category business class. As required for business classes that are used by an object data source, each property is defined with both get and set accessors, and a parameterless constructor is created by default.

The Default.aspx.cs file

```
public partial class Default : System.Web.UI.Page
{
    protected void ObjectDataSource1_GetAffectedRows(object sender,
        ObjectDataSourceStatusEventArgs e)
    {
        e.AffectedRows = Convert.ToInt32(e.ReturnValue);
    }

    protected void GridView1_RowUpdated(object sender, GridViewUpdatedEventArgs e)
    {
        if (e.Exception != null) {
            lblError.Text = DatabaseErrorMessage(e.Exception);
            e.ExceptionHandled = true;
            e.KeepInEditMode = true;
        }
        else if (e.AffectedRows == 0)
            lblError.Text = ConcurrencyErrorMessage();
    }

    protected void GridView1_RowDeleted(object sender, GridViewDeletedEventArgs e)
    {
        if (e.Exception != null) {
            lblError.Text = DatabaseErrorMessage(e.Exception);
            e.ExceptionHandled = true;
        }
        else if (e.AffectedRows == 0)
            lblError.Text = ConcurrencyErrorMessage();
    }

    protected void DetailsView1_ItemInserted(object sender,
        DetailsViewInsertedEventArgs e)
    {
        if (e.Exception != null) {
            lblError.Text = DatabaseErrorMessage(e.Exception);
            e.ExceptionHandled = true;
        }
    }

    private string DatabaseErrorMessage(Exception ex)
    {
        string msg = $"<b>A database error has occurred:</b> {ex.Message}";
        if (ex.InnerException != null)
            msg += $"<br />Message: {ex.InnerException.Message}";
        return msg;
    }
    private string ConcurrencyErrorMessage() {
        return "Another user may have updated that category. Please try again";
    }

}
```

The Category.cs file

```
public class Category
{
    public string CategoryID { get; set; }
    public string ShortName { get; set; }
    public string LongName { get; set; }
}
```

Figure 17-14   The code-behind file and Category class

The CategoryDB class

The two parts of figure 17-15 present the CategoryDB class that's used as the data access class for this application. This class uses the DataObject and DataObjectMethod attributes to mark the class as a data object class and to mark the methods as data object methods.

The four public methods in this class provide for the select, insert, delete, and update operations performed by this application. These methods use standard ADO.NET code to access the database.

The GetCategories method retrieves all of the rows and columns from the Categories table in the Halloween database. Like the method you saw in figure 17-9, this data is stored in a List<Category> object. Then, this object is returned to the object data source, which uses it to populate the GridView control. Note that because List<Category> is a strongly-typed collection, bound fields are automatically generated for the properties in the Category class. If a strongly-typed collection wasn't returned by the method, the AutoGenerateColumns property of the GridView control would be set to True by default, and the bound fields wouldn't be generated until runtime. To change that, you'd have to set the AutoGenerateColumns property to False and then use the Fields dialog box to create the bound fields manually. You'll get a chance to do that in the exercise at the end of this chapter.

To get a connection to the Halloween database, the GetCategories method calls the private GetConnectionString method. This method gets the connection string from the Web.config file. The GetConnectionString method is also called by the other public methods in this class.

When the user clicks the Insert button in the DetailsView control, the object data source executes the InsertCategory method. This method is declared with a single parameter for a Category object. When the object data source executes this method, it passes the values that the user entered into the DetailsView control to this object. Then, the method assigns the CategoryID, ShortName, and LongName properties of that object to the parameters that are defined in the VALUES clause of the INSERT statement. When the INSERT statement is executed, a new row with these values is inserted into the Categories table.

One thing you should know is that, if you run an application that uses an object data source with debugging and an unhandled exception occurs, Visual Studio will enter break mode. That's true even if the code-behind file checks for database errors as shown in figure 17-14. When this happens, you can simply click the Continue button to execute the code in the code-behind file.

The CategoryDB.cs file   **Page 1**

```
...
using System.Collections.Generic;
using System.Configuration;
using System.Data;
using System.Data.SqlClient;
using System.ComponentModel;

[DataObject(true)]
public static class CategoryDB
{
    [DataObjectMethod(DataObjectMethodType.Select)]
    public static List<Category> GetCategories()
    {
        List<Category> categoryList = new List<Category>();
        string sql = "SELECT CategoryID, ShortName, LongName "
            + "FROM Categories ORDER BY LongName";
        using (SqlConnection con = new SqlConnection(GetConnectionString())) {
            using (SqlCommand cmd = new SqlCommand(sql, con)) {
                con.Open();
                SqlDataReader dr = cmd.ExecuteReader();
                Category category;
                while (dr.Read()){
                    category = new Category();
                    category.CategoryID = dr["CategoryID"].ToString();
                    category.ShortName = dr["ShortName"].ToString();
                    category.LongName = dr["LongName"].ToString();
                    categoryList.Add(category);
                }
                dr.Close();
            }
        }
        return categoryList;
    }

    private static string GetConnectionString()
    {
        return ConfigurationManager.ConnectionStrings
            ["HalloweenConnection"].ConnectionString;
    }

    [DataObjectMethod(DataObjectMethodType.Insert)]
    public static void InsertCategory(Category category)
    {
        string sql = "INSERT INTO Categories "
            + "(CategoryID, ShortName, LongName) "
            + "VALUES (@CategoryID, @ShortName, @LongName)";
        using (SqlConnection con = new SqlConnection(GetConnectionString())) {
            using (SqlCommand cmd = new SqlCommand(sql, con)) {
                cmd.Parameters.AddWithValue("CategoryID", category.CategoryID);
                cmd.Parameters.AddWithValue("ShortName", category.ShortName);
                cmd.Parameters.AddWithValue("LongName", category.LongName);
                con.Open();
                cmd.ExecuteNonQuery();
            }
        }
    }
```

Figure 17-15   The CategoryDB class for the Category Maintenance application (part 1 of 2)

When the user clicks the Delete button in the GridView control, the object data source executes the DeleteCategory method. This method also accepts a single parameter for a Category object. This object contains the values that were originally retrieved from the Categories table. The CategoryID, ShortName, and LongName properties of this object are assigned to the parameters that are defined in the WHERE clause of the DELETE statement.

Notice that this method returns an integer value. Then, when the command that contains the DELETE statement is executed, the result is stored in an integer variable, which is returned to the object data source. Because this value indicates the number of rows that were deleted, it can be used as shown in figure 17-14 to check for a concurrency error.

Note that you don't have to store the value that's returned by the ExecuteNonQuery method in a variable. Instead, you can just return this value directly to the object data source. You saw an example of that in figure 17-10. If you use a variable as shown here, though, your code can be easier to read.

The last method, UpdateCategory, is executed when the user clicks the Update button in the GridView control. It accepts two parameters for Category objects. The first one contains the values that were originally retrieved from the Categories table, and the second one contains the new values for the row. The CategoryID, ShortName, and LongName properties of the first object are assigned to the parameters that are defined in the WHERE clause of the UPDATE statement, and the ShortName and LongName properties of the second object are assigned to the properties that are defined in the SET clause of the UPDATE statement.

Like the DeleteCategory method, the UpdateCategory method returns an integer value that indicates the number of rows that were affected by the update operation. Then, this value can be used to check for a concurrency error.

The CategoryDB.cs file   **Page 2**

```csharp
[DataObjectMethod(DataObjectMethodType.Delete)]
public static int DeleteCategory(Category category)
{
    int deleteCount = 0;
    string sql = "DELETE FROM Categories "
        + "WHERE CategoryID = @CategoryID "
        + "AND ShortName = @ShortName "
        + "AND LongName = @LongName";
    using (SqlConnection con = new SqlConnection(GetConnectionString())) {
        using (SqlCommand cmd = new SqlCommand(sql, con)) {
            cmd.Parameters.AddWithValue("CategoryID", category.CategoryID);
            cmd.Parameters.AddWithValue("ShortName", category.ShortName);
            cmd.Parameters.AddWithValue("LongName", category.LongName);
            con.Open();
            deleteCount = cmd.ExecuteNonQuery();
        }
    }
    return deleteCount;
}

[DataObjectMethod(DataObjectMethodType.Update)]
public static int UpdateCategory(Category original_Category,
    Category category)
{
    int updateCount = 0;
    string sql = "UPDATE Categories "
        + "SET ShortName = @ShortName, "
        + "LongName = @LongName "
        + "WHERE CategoryID = @original_CategoryID "
        + "AND ShortName = @original_ShortName "
        + "AND LongName = @original_LongName";
    using (SqlConnection con = new SqlConnection(GetConnectionString())) {
        using (SqlCommand cmd = new SqlCommand(sql, con)) {
            cmd.Parameters.AddWithValue("ShortName", category.ShortName);
            cmd.Parameters.AddWithValue("LongName", category.LongName);
            cmd.Parameters.AddWithValue("original_CategoryID",
                original_Category.CategoryID);
            cmd.Parameters.AddWithValue("original_ShortName",
                original_Category.ShortName);
            cmd.Parameters.AddWithValue("original_LongName",
                original_Category.LongName);
            con.Open();
            updateCount = cmd.ExecuteNonQuery();
        }
    }
    return updateCount;
}

}
```

Figure 17-15   The CategoryDB class for the Category Maintenance application (part 2 of 2)

How to use paging and sorting with object data sources

When you use an object data source, you should know that it doesn't automatically provide for paging or sorting with controls like the GridView and ListView controls. Because of that, you have to set the properties of the object data source that provide for paging and sorting, and you have to provide for paging and sorting in the data access class. You can also make an adjustment to the code-behind file so the sorting works more smoothly.

How to configure an ObjectDataSource control for paging and sorting

To create an ObjectDataSource control that provides for paging, you set the first four properties shown in figure 17-16. When set to True, the EnablePaging property enables paging for the control. Then, the StartRowIndexParameterName and MaximumRowsParameterName properties specify the names of parameters that will be used by the select method in the data access class to determine which rows are returned by the method. You'll see an example of how that works in figure 17-18. For now, just realize that when you use a pager control to display another page of data in a bound control, the bound control passes the values that will be assigned to these two parameters to the ObjectDataSource control.

The fourth property, SelectCountMethod, names a method in the data access class that returns a count of the total number of rows that are retrieved by the select method. The control that's bound to the object data source uses this value to determine what pager controls to display. For example, if the bound control uses first, previous, next, and last pager controls, it will be able to determine when the first or last page is displayed so it can omit the first and previous or next and last pager controls. This is illustrated by the GridView control shown at the top of this figure. In this case, the first page is displayed so the first and previous pager controls aren't included.

The last property in this figure, SortParameterName, provides the name of the parameter in the select method that will be used to sort the data. When the user clicks on the column header of a column in a bound control that provides for sorting, this control passes the sort expression to the object data source. If the user clicks the ID header in the GridView control shown here, for example, the sort expression "ProductID" is passed to the object data source. And if the user clicks this column header again, the sort expression "ProductID DESC" is passed to the object data source. Then, the object data source passes the sort expression on to the select method.

By the way, if you use the wizard to create an ObjectDataSource control from a data access class that provides for paging or sorting, you should know that the wizard will ask you to define the parameters used by the select method. Because these parameters are identified by properties of the control, however, you can just click Finish when the Define Parameters step is displayed. Then, you'll need to delete the parameters that are generated by default.

A GridView control that provides for paging and sorting

ID	Name	Category	Unit Price	On Hand
pow01	Austin Powers	costumes	79.9900	25
bl01	Black Light	fx	19.9900	200
vader01	Darth Vader Mask	masks	19.9900	100
cat01	Deranged Cat	props	19.9900	45
bats01	Flying Bats	props	69.9900	25
fogj01	Fog Juice (1qt)	fx	9.9900	500
		> >>		

Properties of the ObjectDataSource control for paging and sorting

Property	Description
EnablePaging	True if the ObjectDataSource control supports paging.
StartRowIndexParameterName	The name of the parameter in the select method of the data access class that receives the index of the first row to be retrieved.
MaximumRowsParameterName	The name of the parameter in the select method of the data access class that receives the maximum number of rows to be retrieved.
SelectCountMethod	The name of a public method in the data access class that returns the total number of rows that are retrieved by the select method.
SortParameterName	The name of the parameter in the select method of the data access class that is used to sort the data.

How to configure a control for paging

- To use paging with a control like a GridView control that's bound to an object data source, you set the first four properties of the ObjectDataSource control shown above.

- When a pager control on a bound control is clicked, the index of the starting row to be displayed and the maximum number of rows to be displayed are passed to the ObjectDataSource control. The ObjectDataSource control then passes these values to the parameters of the select method specified by the StartRowIndexParameterName and MaximumRowsParameterName properties of the control.

- In addition to the select method that retrieves the rows to be displayed, the data access class must include a method that returns the total number of rows that are retrieved. This method is named on the SelectCountMethod property of the ObjectDataSource control, and it's used by the bound control to determine what pager controls to display.

How to configure a control for sorting

- To use sorting with a control that's bound to an object data source, you set the SortParameterName property of the ObjectDataSource control.

- When the column header for a column that provides for sorting on a bound control is clicked, the value of the SortExpression property for that column is passed to the ObjectDataSource control, which passes it to the parameter of the select method specified by the SortParameterName property.

Figure 17-16   How to configure an ObjectDataSource control for paging and sorting

The aspx file that provides for paging and sorting

Figure 17-17 presents the aspx code for the GridView control you saw in the previous figure, along with the ObjectDataSource control it's bound to. Here, you can see that both the AllowPaging and AllowSorting properties of the GridView control are set to True.

This GridView control also includes a SortExpression property for its product ID, name, and category ID columns. Notice that the sort expression for the category ID column includes the names of two columns. That way, this application will work just like the Product List application of chapter 14.

For the ObjectDataSource control to provide for paging, its EnablePaging property is set to True. In addition, its StartRowIndexParameterName, MaximumRowsParameterName, and SelectCountMethod properties are set to appropriate values. To provide for sorting, its SortParameterName property is also set.

The code-behind file that executes the initial sort

In many cases, the select method associated with an object data source will return the data in a sorted sequence. For example, the select method shown in figure 17-15 that retrieves the categories for the Category Maintenance application orders the categories by long name.

Unfortunately, the GridView control has no way of knowing that the data is already sorted. Because of that, the first time you click on a column header, it will assume that you want the column sorted in ascending order. If the data is already sorted by that column in that order, it will just sort it again. For instance, if the GridView control that displays products is already sorted by name in ascending order, the first time a user clicks on the Name column header, it will sort the products by name in ascending order again. Because of that, it will appear to the user as if nothing happened.

To fix this problem, you can remove the ORDER BY clause from the SELECT statement in the select method. Then, you can add code like that shown in figure 17-17 so the GridView control does the initial sort. Here, the Sort method of the GridView control is used to sort the products by the Name column in ascending order the first time the page is loaded. That way, the GridView control is aware of the initial sort order, and clicking on the Name header when the control is first displayed will sort the products by name in descending order.

The aspx code for the GridView and ObjectDataSource controls

```
<asp:GridView ID="GridView1" runat="server"
    AutoGenerateColumns="False" DataKeyNames="CategoryID"
    DataSourceID="ObjectDataSource1"
    AllowPaging="true" PageSize="6" AllowSorting="true"
    CssClass="table table-bordered table-striped table-condensed"
    OnPreRender="GridView1_PreRender">
    <Columns>
     <asp:BoundField DataField="ProductID" HeaderText="ID"
         SortExpression="ProductID">
         <ItemStyle CssClass="col-xs-1" />
     </asp:BoundField>
     <asp:BoundField DataField="Name" HeaderText="Name"
         SortExpression="Name">
         <ItemStyle CssClass="col-xs-4" />
     </asp:BoundField>
     <asp:BoundField DataField="CategoryID" HeaderText="Category"
         SortExpression="CategoryID, Name">
         <ItemStyle CssClass="col-xs-2" />
     </asp:BoundField>
     <asp:BoundField DataField="UnitPrice" HeaderText="Unit Price">
         <HeaderStyle CssClass="text-right" />
         <ItemStyle CssClass="col-xs-2 text-right" />
     </asp:BoundField>
     <asp:BoundField DataField="OnHand" HeaderText="On Hand">
         <HeaderStyle CssClass="text-right" />
         <ItemStyle CssClass="text-right" />
     </asp:BoundField>
    </Columns>
    <HeaderStyle CssClass="bg-halloween" />
    <PagerSettings Mode="NextPreviousFirstLast" />
    <PagerStyle CssClass="pagerStyle" BackColor="#8c8c8c"
        HorizontalAlign="Center" />
</asp:GridView>
<asp:ObjectDataSource runat="server" ID="ObjectDataSource1"
    SelectMethod="GetProducts" TypeName="ProductDB"
    EnablePaging="true" SelectCountMethod="SelectCount"
    StartRowIndexParameterName="start"
    MaximumRowsParameterName="rows"
    SortParameterName="sort">
</asp:ObjectDataSource>
```

The Default.aspx.cs file

```
public partial class Default : System.Web.UI.Page
{
    protected void Page_Load(object sender, EventArgs e)
    {
        // sort by Name on initial load
        if (!IsPostBack)
            GridView1.Sort("Name", SortDirection.Ascending);
    }
}
```

Figure 17-17   The aspx and code-behind files that provide for paging and sorting

How to create a data access class that provides for paging and sorting

Figure 17-18 shows the code for a data access class that's used by the object data source you saw in the last figure. This class includes three methods. GetProducts is a select method that returns the products for the requested page in the requested order. The method named LoadProductList, which isn't shown here, uses standard ADO.NET code to get all the products from the database and store them in the List<Product> object named productList that's declared at the class level. This method uses caching so the products only have to be retrieved from the database once. After that, they're retrieved from the cache. (Because the select method doesn't return a dataset, this can't be accomplished using the caching properties of the object data source.) Finally, the method named SelectCount returns a count of the products in the product list.

The body of the select method starts by calling the LoadProductList method. Then, it uses a switch statement to determine how the products should be sorted. To do that, the parameter that contains the sort expression, sort, is used as the switch expression. Then, the case labels implement the six possible sort orders: ascending and descending for each of the three sort columns.

Each case label uses LINQ extension methods to sort the products and return the products for the requested page. For example, if the user clicks the ID header in the GridView control when the web page is first displayed, the statement in the second case label is executed. This statement uses the OrderBy method to sort the products by the ProductID column. Then, it uses the Skip method to skip the number of items specified by the start parameter, and it uses the Take method to retrieve up to the number of products specified by the rows parameter. Finally, it uses the ToList method to convert the resulting IEnumerable object to a List<Product> object, and it returns the list to the object data source.

Note that the first time the select method is called, an empty string is passed to the sort parameter. Or, if you've added the code shown in the last figure that executes the initial sort, the string "Name" is passed. Either way, the statement in the default label is executed, which sorts the products by name in ascending order.

Now, take a look at the statements for the fourth and fifth case labels, which are executed when the user clicks the Category header in the GridView control. The first time this header is clicked, the statement in the fourth label sorts the products by category ID in ascending order, then by product name in ascending order. The second time it's clicked, the statement in the fifth label sorts the products by category ID in ascending order, then by product name in descending order.

Note that if the application didn't provide for sorting, the switch statement wouldn't be needed. Instead, you could provide for paging using a single statement like this that returns the rows for the requested page:

```
return productList.Skip(start).Take(rows).ToList();
```

The data access class used by the object data source

```
using System;
using System.Collections.Generic;
using System.Linq;
using System.Configuration;
using System.Data;
using System.Data.SqlClient;
using System.ComponentModel;

[DataObject(true)]
public static class ProductDB
{
    private static List<Product> productList;

    [DataObjectMethod(DataObjectMethodType.Select)]
    public static List<Product> GetProducts(int start, int rows, string sort)
    {
        LoadProductList();

        switch (sort)
        {
            case "Name DESC":
                return productList.OrderByDescending(p => p.Name)
                    .Skip(start).Take(rows).ToList();
            case "ProductID":
                return productList.OrderBy(p => p.ProductID)
                    .Skip(start).Take(rows).ToList();
            case "ProductID DESC":
                return productList.OrderByDescending(p => p.ProductID)
                    .Skip(start).Take(rows).ToList();
            case "CategoryID, Name":
                return productList.OrderBy(p => p.CategoryID)
                    .ThenBy(p => p.Name)
                    .Skip(start).Take(rows).ToList();
            case "CategoryID, Name DESC":
                return productList.OrderBy(p => p.CategoryID)
                    .ThenByDescending(p => p.Name)
                    .Skip(start).Take(rows).ToList();
            default:
                return productList.OrderBy(p => p.Name)
                    .Skip(start).Take(rows).ToList();
        }
    }

    public static int SelectCount()
    {
        return productList.Count;
    }

        .
        .
        .

}
```

Figure 17-18   A data access class that provides for paging and sorting

Perspective

In this chapter, you've learned how to use object data sources to build 3-layer web applications. As you've seen, object data sources take advantage of the data binding features of ASP.NET but still separate the presentation code from the data access code. Because of that, you may want to use object data sources instead of SQL data sources and thus build 3-layer applications.

If you decide that you do want to use object data sources in your applications, you will want to learn more about using ADO.NET code. For that, we recommend our ADO.NET book for C# programmers, which provides a complete course in ADO.NET database programming. Although this book covers ADO.NET 4, the only significant changes to more recent versions are to the Entity Framework, which you'll learn more about in the next chapter of this book. As you'll see in that chapter, the Entity Framework takes care of the ADO.NET code for you. Even then, though, it's a good idea to know how to use ADO.NET for those situations in which the Entity Framework doesn't do what you want.

Terms

3-layer architecture	data object class
presentation layer	data access class
middle layer	business object
business rules	data object
database layer	data component
object data source	reflection
ADO.NET (Active Data Objects)	C# attribute
business object class	

Summary

- In a *3-layer architecture*, the *presentation layer* consists of the web pages that define the user interface. The *middle layer* consists of the classes that implement the *business rules* for the application and manage the data access for the web pages. And the *database layer* consists of the database itself.

- One way to build 3-layer applications is to use *object data sources*. With this approach, you use the classes and members of *ADO.NET* to develop the *data access classes* that enforce the business rules and work with the database.

- Three of the ADO.NET classes that you can use with object data sources are the SqlConnection, SqlCommand, and SqlDataReader classes.

- The ObjectDataSource control specifies the name of the data access class and the names of the methods in the class that select, update, delete, and insert data. This control also determines the parameters that are passed to the methods.

- *Reflection* is a .NET feature that provides information about the compiled classes and methods at runtime.

- You can use the DataObject and DataObjectMethod *attributes* in the C# code for your data access classes to identify the classes and methods. These attributes determine what's in the drop-down lists in the Configure Data Source wizard.

- To provide paging and sorting for the data that's defined by an object data source, you have to configure the ObjectDataSource control and provide the C# code in the data access class that implements the paging and sorting.

Exercise 17-1   Create a Customer List application

In this exercise, you'll develop an application that uses two object data sources to display a list of customers in a selected state. To make that easier, you'll start from an application that contains the data access class that will be used by the object data sources, along with the starting page, the database, image, and style sheets used by the page, and a Web.config file that contains a connection string to the Halloween database.

Review the code in the data access class

1. Open the Ex17CustomerList application in the C:\aspnet46_cs directory.

2. Display the CustomerDB class in the Models folder, and notice that it contains three methods named GetAllStates, GetCustomersByState, and GetConnectionString. Also notice that the class is marked with a DataObject attribute and the GetAllStates and GetCustomersByState methods are marked with a DataObjectMethod attribute.

3. Review the code for the GetAllStates and GetCustomersByState methods to see that they both return an IEnumerable object. Specifically, the GetAllStates method returns a data reader object that contains the StateCode and StateName columns from the States table, and the GetCustomersByState method returns a data reader object that contains the LastName, FirstName, and PhoneNumber columns from the Customers table.

Add the drop-down list and its data source

4. Add a drop-down list to the div element that follows the label in the first form group. Then, display the page in Design view, and select the Choose Data Source command from the smart tag menu to display the first step of the Data Source Configuration Wizard.

5. Select the option for creating a new data source, select Object from the second step of the wizard, and click OK to display the first Configure Data Source dialog box.

6. Display the drop-down list in this dialog box. If it doesn't contain the CustomerDB class, cancel out of the wizard, build the solution, and then start the wizard again. This time, the list should contain the CustomerDB class. Now, select this class and then click Next to display the second Configure Data Source dialog box.

7. Display the drop-down list in this dialog box to see that that it contains both of the methods that are marked as select methods. Select the GetAllStates method and then click Finish to return to the first step of the Data Source Configuration Wizard.

8. Display the drop-down lists in the wizard to see that they're both empty. Then, enter "StateName" in the first drop-down list and "StateCode" in the second drop-down list.

9. Enable auto postback for the drop-down list you just created, and change the ID attribute to an appropriate value.

Add the GridView control and its data source

10. Add a GridView control to the div element in the second form group, and bind it to a new object data source that gets its data from the GetCustomersByState method of the CustomerDB class. This method should get the value of its parameter from the drop-down list.

11. Run the application, display customers from different states, and notice that the widths of the columns in the GridView change depending on the data they contain.

12. Return to Design view, display the Fields dialog box for the GridView control, and notice that the Auto-generate Fields option is selected.

13. Remove the check mark from the Auto-generate Fields option, and then add three bound fields for the three columns that are returned by the GetCustomersByState method. To do that, you'll need to manually enter the column name for the DataField property, and you'll need to add a column header for the HeaderText property.

14. Display the page in Source view, and add an ItemStyle element for each bound field that uses the CssClass property to set the width of the field to the Bootstrap col-xs-3 class.

15. Name the GridView control grdCustomers. Then, generate an event handler for the PreRender event of the GridView control, and add this statement to the event handler:

```
grdCustomers.HeaderRow.TableSection = TableRowSection.
TableHeader;
```

16. Run the application again to see how this looks. Then, close the browser window.

18

How to use model binding and the Entity Framework

Up until now, you've used data source controls to bind data from a database to a data control. Now you'll learn how to use the Entity Framework and model binding to bind data directly to a data control.

How to create an Entity Data Model

The *Entity Framework*, or just *EF*, is a component of ADO.NET that provides another way to work with the data in a database. Its goal is to address the mismatch that often exists between the tabular structure of a relational database and the objects used in an application. To resolve this problem, the Entity Framework uses an *Entity Data Model* that maps the objects used by an application to the relational model of the database. This model translates queries into a form that the database understands, and it translates the data that's returned from the database into the objects that are used by the application. It can also submit changes made to those objects to the database. In the topics that follow, you'll learn the basic skills for creating an Entity Data Model.

How to start an Entity Data Model with the Entity Data Model Wizard

The easiest way to create an Entity Data Model is to use the Entity Data Model Wizard as shown in figure 18-1. To start this wizard, you can use any of the standard techniques to display the Add New Item dialog box. Since you'll typically store the Entity Data Model in the Models folder, for example, you can display the Add New Item dialog box by right-clicking on this folder and selecting Add→New Item. Then, you can select the Data group, select the ADO.NET Entity Data Model template, and enter the name you want to use for the model.

When you click the Add button, the first step of the wizard is displayed. You can see this dialog box at the top of this figure. It lets you choose one of four ways to create the data model. The first option creates the data model from an existing database and then lets you work with it using the Entity Framework Designer. The second option creates an empty data model and then lets you use the designer to design it from scratch. The third option creates an empty data model and then lets you write the code for the model from scratch. And the fourth option creates a data model from an existing database and then lets you work with it using code. In this chapter, you'll learn how to use the first and last options.

The second step of the wizard that's shown in this figure lets you specify the database connection you want to use. If the connection already exists, you can select it from the drop-down list. In this example, the Halloween database file you've seen throughout this book is selected. As you can see, the connection string that's generated includes information EF needs, as well as information about the provider and the database to be accessed.

If the connection you need doesn't already exist, you can click the New Connection button and then use the Connection Properties dialog box that's displayed. This dialog box is identical to the dialog box that's displayed when you create a new connection from the Data Source Configuration Wizard, which you used in chapter 13.

The first two steps of the Entity Data Model Wizard

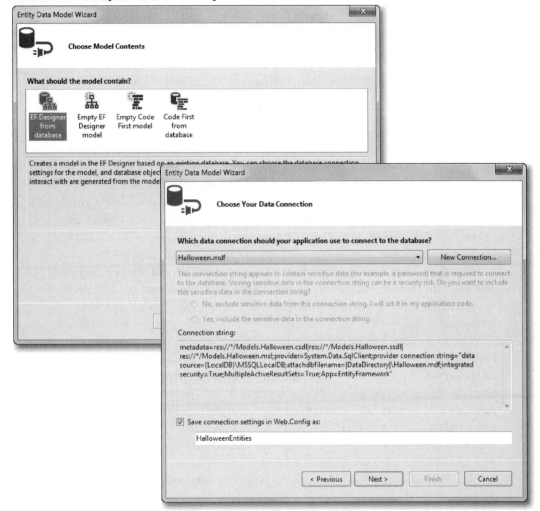

Description

- The *Entity Framework* (*EF*) provides an interface between the database used by an application and the objects used by an application. EF also provides for submitting changes made to those objects to the database.

- To use EF, you start by creating an *Entity Data Model* using the Entity Data Model Wizard. To start this wizard, display the Add New Item dialog box, select the Data group, select the ADO.NET Entity Data Model template, and enter a name for the model.

- In the Choose Model Contents step, you choose how you want EF to create the Entity Data Model.

- In the Choose Your Data Connection step, you choose or create the database connection the application needs and save the connection string. The default connection string name is the name of the database appended with the word "Entities".

Figure 18-1   How to start an Entity Data Model with the Entity Data Model Wizard

How to choose the version and data objects

The third and fourth steps of the Entity Data Model Wizard are shown in figure 18-2. The third step lets you select the version of the Entity Framework you want to use. By default, the Entity Framework 6.x option is selected, as shown at the top of this figure. With this option, the most current release of Entity Framework 6 will be used. This is the option this chapter uses, and this is the option you'll want to use for most new development.

If you want to use Entity Framework 5.0 instead, you can select that option. Or, you can click the link in the dialog box for this step to learn more about using an earlier version of the Entity Framework. Note that if you use a version before 6.0, some of the code that's shown in this chapter won't work.

The fourth step of the Entity Data Model Wizard lets you select the database objects that you want to include in the model. As you can see here, you can select any of the tables, views, stored procedures, and functions in the database. In this example, the Categories and Products tables are selected.

The dialog box for this step of the wizard doesn't let you select individual columns from tables and views. Instead, the entire table or view is included in the model. If that isn't what you want, you can edit the model after it's generated.

The first check box below the list of database objects affects the names that are given to the objects, or *entities*, in the model. When checked, the wizard will assign names that reflect whether an entity refers to a single item or multiple items. In this example, the entity that represents the Categories table will be renamed to Category because each entity object will represent a single Category. In contrast, collections of entities will be given pluralized names. Because this approach can reduce confusion, it's a good practice to use the default setting, which is to leave this check box checked.

The second check box allows entity properties that reflect the Foreign Key columns in the database tables to be created. This feature makes it easier to complete some tasks, such as data binding. As a result, it's a good practice to use the default setting for this also, which is to leave this check box checked.

The third check box determines whether any stored procedures and functions you select are imported into the Entity Data Model. Because you must import stored procedures and functions before you can work with them, you'll typically leave this check box checked. Alternatively, you can uncheck it and then import stored procedures and functions after the Entity Data Model is created. For more information on how to work with stored procedures and functions using the Entity Framework, see the Entity Framework documentation.

When you click on the Finish button from the fourth step of the wizard, you may see some Security Warning dialog boxes warning you that running a text template can potentially harm your computer. This is because of the .tt files that are created by the Entity Framework, which you'll learn about in a moment. You can click OK in any of these dialog boxes that appear.

The third and fourth steps of the Entity Data Model Wizard

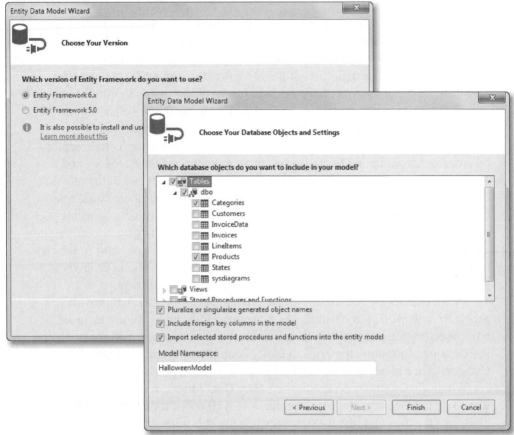

Description

- The Choose Your Version step of the wizard lets you choose the version of the Entity Framework you want to use. To use the most current version, select the 6.x option.

- The Choose Your Database Objects and Settings step of the wizard lets you choose the tables, views, stored procedures, and functions you want to include in the model.

- To include an object, expand the node that contains that object and select its check box. You can also select a node to include all the objects subordinate to that node.

- To change the name that's used for the model's namespace, enter a new name in the Model Namespace text box. By default, this is the name of the database that you've connected to appended with the word "Model".

- To disable the renaming of objects in the Entity Data Model, uncheck the Pluralize or Singularize Generated Object Names check box.

- To disable the generation of Foreign Key properties for entities, uncheck the Include Foreign Key Columns in the Model check box.

- To disable the importing of any stored procedures or functions you choose into the conceptual model, uncheck the Import Selected Stored Procedures and Functions check box.

Figure 18-2   How to choose the version and data objects

How to work with the Entity Data Model Designer

When you complete the Entity Data Model Wizard as described in the last figure, the Entity Data Model is displayed in the *Entity Data Model Designer*, or just *Entity Designer*, as shown in figure 18-3. This designer displays the model in graphical form. The definition of the model is stored in a file with the edmx extension. You can see this file in the Solution Explorer in this figure. Whenever you want to display the model in the Designer, you can double-click on this file.

Within the Entity Data Model, each table or view in the database is represented by an *entity class*, and each foreign key relationship is represented by an *association*. In this figure, for example, you can see the Category and Product entities and the association between the two. Here, the 1 at the left side of the connector that represents the association indicates that there is a single category for each product, and the asterisk at the right side of the connector indicates that there can be many products for a single category.

Each entity in the Entity Data Model contains one or more *scalar properties* that represent the columns in the associated table or view. A scalar property is a property that can hold a value, such as an integer value or a string.

If two entities are related, they have *navigation properties* that provide access to each other. For example, the Category entity in this figure includes a navigation property named Products that can be used to retrieve all the products in a category. Similarly, the Product entity contains a navigation property named Category that can be used to retrieve the category for a product.

When Visual Studio generates the Entity Data Model, it uses text template files to define the container for the entities as well as for the entities themselves. These are the files with the tt extensions that are subordinate to the edmx file. Then, the file with the Context.cs extension that's subordinate to the file with the Context.tt extension contains the generated code for the container. Similarly, the files with the cs extension that are subordinate to the file with the tt extension contain the generated code for the entities.

To update the Entity Data Model, you can use the Update Wizard. This lets you change the entity data model so it reflects any changes that have been made to the structure of the database after you first created the model. You can also use this wizard to select tables, views, stored procedures, and functions that you didn't select when you first created the model. To display this wizard, you can use the technique described in this figure.

This figure also describes some basic skills for using the Entity Data Model Designer. In general, the skills for using the designer are straightforward, so you can use normal Visual Studio techniques to work with it.

The Entity Framework Toolbox is also available when the Entity Designer is displayed. Although you can use the components in this toolbox to create new entities and associations, you may find it easier to do that by right-clicking on the designer and using the dialog boxes that are available from the shortcut menus.

The Entity Data Model in the Entity Data Model Designer

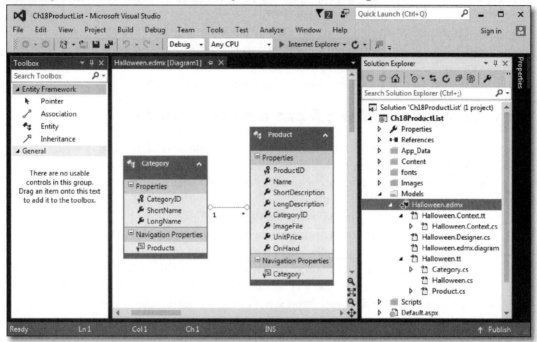

Description

- When you use the wizard to create an Entity Data Model, Visual Studio generates a file with the extension edmx that defines the model.

- Visual Studio also generates C# code that defines the classes that you use to work with the model, and it stores the connection string that you saw in figure 18-1 in the Web.config file.

- Each table or view that you add to an Entity Data Model is defined by an *entity class*. Each entity class contains *scalar properties* that map to the columns in the table or view.

- If any two tables that you add to an Entity Data Model are related by a foreign key, an *association* is defined between the entity classes based on that relationship.

- An association is defined by *navigation properties* in the entity classes. These properties let you refer to one class from the other class.

- To update the Entity Data Model, you can use the Update Wizard. To display this wizard, right-click anywhere in the Designer and then select Update Model from Database.

- To display the *Entity Data Model Designer* for an Entity Data Model, double-click the edmx file in the Solution Explorer.

- To change the properties of an entity or any of its individual properties, click the entity or property to display its settings in the Properties window.

- To delete an entity, property, or association, click on it and then press the Delete key.

Figure 18-3   How to work with the Entity Data Model Designer

How to use LINQ to Entities

Once you've created an Entity Data Model, you use *LINQ to Entities* to work with its classes, properties, and methods. In the topics that follow, you'll learn the basic skills for using LINQ to Entities to retrieve, update, insert, and delete data. You'll also learn how to provide for concurrency.

How to retrieve data from a single table

To use LINQ to Entities, you first create an instance of the *object context* for the Entity Data Model. This is illustrated by the first example in figure 18-4. Here, the statement creates an instance of the HalloweenEntities context and stores it in a variable named db.

Once you've done that, you can use the properties of this object to refer to the entity collections in the Entity Data Model that are mapped to tables in the database. For instance, in the second example, the query expression uses the Categories property of the object context to retrieve all the items in the Categories table. Then, the query is executed when its ToList method is called.

Similarly, the LINQ query expression in the third example also retrieves all the items from Categories table. In this case, though, the query uses the LINQ syntax to sort the categories by name. As before, the query isn't actually executed until the ToList method is called.

The fourth example shows how you can retrieve the first item with a column value that matches the specified value. In this case, the LINQ query retrieves the product whose productID column has the specified product ID. This query is executed when the FirstOrDefault method is called. This method returns the product if it exists or null if it doesn't.

How to load related objects

As you saw earlier in this chapter, if an entity is related to another entity in the Entity Data Model, it contains a navigation property that provides access to the related entity. It's important to understand, though, that related objects aren't automatically loaded into the object context when a query is executed. Rather, they're loaded when they're referred to in code. This is called *lazy loading*.

For example, when the query in the fourth example in figure 18-4 is used to load a Product object into the object context, the related Category object isn't loaded. Then, when the Category navigation property of the Product object is used to get the value of the LongName property of the category, as shown in the fifth example, a second query is executed to retrieve the Category object. That way, the Category object is only retrieved when it's needed.

You can also use a process called *eager loading* to load the objects that are related to another object when a query is executed. To do that, you use the Include method as shown in the last example in this figure. Here, the Include method is used to load the Category object at the same time as the Product object. Then, when the Category navigation property of the Product object is used to get the value of the LongName property of the category, no second database query is needed because the Category object has already been loaded.

A statement that creates an instance of the object context

```
HalloweenEntities db = new HalloweenEntities();
```

A LINQ query that gets data from the Categories table

The query expression

```
var categories = db.Categories;
```

The code that executes the query

```
ddlCategories.DataSource = categories.ToList();
ddlCategories.DataBind();
```

A LINQ query that gets and sorts data from the Categories table

The query expression

```
var categories = from c in db.Categories
                 orderby c.LongName
                 select c;
```

The code that executes the query

```
ddlCategories.DataSource = categories.ToList();
ddlCategories.DataBind();
```

A LINQ query that gets the product with the matching ID

```
var product = (from p in db.Products
               where p.ProductID == productID
               select p).FirstOrDefault();
```

Code that uses lazy loading to retrieve related objects

```
// executes a second database query to load the related object
lblCategoryName.Text = product.Category.LongName;
```

Code that uses eager loading to retrieve related objects

```
var product = (from p in db.Products.Include("Category")
               where p.ProductID == productID
               select p).FirstOrDefault();
// retrieves the data from the related object loaded by the query
lblCategoryName.Text = product.Category.LongName;
```

Description

- To work with the entities in an Entity Data Model, you create an instance of the object context for the model. You can then use LINQ to Entities to query the entities in the Entity Data Model.

- Only the entity objects that are specifically requested in a query are loaded into the object context. Related objects aren't loaded until they're used. This is called *lazy loading*.

- You can use the Include method to load related objects when the main query is executed. This is called *eager loading*. The Include method requires a *query path* that specifies the related entity objects to load in the object context.

Figure 18-4   How to retrieve data from a single table and load related objects

Note that the Include method accepts a *query path* as an argument. In most cases, the query path is the name of the navigation property that identifies the related objects to be loaded.

How to update an existing row

To modify the data in an existing row of a database, you use the techniques shown in figure 18-5. To start, you must retrieve the row you want to modify. For example, the LINQ query at the top of this figure retrieves the category with the specified category ID.

After you retrieve the row, you can modify the data in the entity object, as shown in the second example in this figure. This code simply assigns new values taken from text boxes to the ShortName and LongName properties of the Category object. Then, when the SaveChanges method of the context object is called, as in the third example in this figure, the changes are saved to the database.

How to delete an existing row

Figure 18-5 also shows how to delete an existing row from a database. To start, you retrieve the row you want to delete, just as you do when you modify a row. Then, you call the Remove method of the collection that contains the object, and you pass that object as an argument. This is illustrated in the fourth example. Here, the Category object that's retrieved by the query is marked for deletion. Finally, you call the SaveChanges method of the object context to actually delete the row.

In most cases, when you delete a row that has a one-to-many relationship with other rows in the database, you'll want to delete the related rows as well. If a foreign key relationship in the database provides for cascading the deletes to related rows, this is done automatically. Otherwise, you'll need to include code that deletes the related rows first. Since this can be a tedious task, the best solution is to add *cascading deletes* to the database.

How to provide for concurrency

By default, optimistic concurrency isn't used when you modify or delete a row from a database when you use EF. However, EF maintains the original values in the rows that you retrieve from the database, which means you can use optimistic concurrency if you need to. Figure 18-5 shows how this works.

To start, you need to identify the columns that you want to check for concurrency. To do that, you can use the Properties window in the Entity Designer to change the Concurrency Mode property for those columns from None to Fixed. Then, you code the SaveChanges method within the try block of a try-catch statement, as shown in the last example in this figure. In the catch block, you use the DbUpdateConcurrencyException class to catch any concurrency exceptions that occur.

Once you've caught the concurrency exception, you can reload the values in the database into the entity. That way, the user can make the changes again and resubmit them without a concurrency exception being thrown.

Code that retrieves a category row from the Halloween database

```
var category = (from c in db.Categories
                where c.CategoryID == ddlCategories.SelectedValue
                select c).FirstOrDefault();
```

Code that modifies the data in the category row

```
category.ShortName = txtShortName.Text;
category.LongName = txtLongName.Text;
```

A statement that saves the changes to the database

```
db.SaveChanges();
```

A statement that marks the Category object for deletion

```
db.Categories.Remove(category);
```

A try-catch statement that handles a concurrency exception

```
try {
    db.SaveChanges();
}
catch (DbUpdateConcurrencyException ex) {
    ex.Entries.Single().Reload();
    ...
}
```

Description

- Before you can modify or delete a row in the database, you must retrieve the row and store it in an object created from a class in the Entity Data Model.

- To modify a row, you assign new values to the properties of the object and then execute the SaveChanges method of the object context.

- To delete a row, you execute the Remove method of the collection that contains the object to mark the object for deletion. Then, you execute the SaveChanges method of the object context to confirm the deletion.

- If a foreign key relationship in a database provides for *cascading deletes*, the SaveChanges method deletes related rows in other tables.

- When you execute the SaveChanges method, the Entity Framework generates the appropriate SQL UPDATE or DELETE statement for each object to be updated or deleted, and then passes those statements to the database for processing.

- To check columns for concurrency, you can use the Properties window in the Entity Data Model Designer to set the Concurrency Mode property for those columns to Fixed.

- If an update or delete operation isn't performed because of a concurrency conflict, a DbUpdateConcurrencyException is thrown. To handle this exception, you code the SaveChanges method within the try block of a try-catch statement. Then, in the catch block, you can reload the current database values into the entity.

Figure 18-5   How to update and delete an existing row and provide for concurrency

To reload the database values, the Entries method of the exception is used to get the entity objects that couldn't be saved to the database. Because this method currently retrieves a single object for DbUpdateConcurrencyException, the Single method is needed to get that object. Then, the Reload method is used to reload the values in the database into the object.

It's important to note that the DbUpdateConcurrencyException class is a member of the System.Data.Entity.Infrastructure namespace. Because of that, you need to include a using directive for that namespace to work with this class.

How to add a new row

To add a new row to a database, you start by using standard techniques to create an object from an entity class. The first example in figure 18-6, for instance, starts by creating a new Category object. Then, it assigns values taken from text boxes to the properties of the Category object.

After you create a new object, you need to add it to the collection of objects in the object context. To do that, you use the Add method of the collection and pass it the object you want to add. In this example, the Add method is used to add the Category object to the Categories collection. Then, you call the SaveChanges method to update the database.

The second example in this figure shows how to add objects on the many side of a one-to-many relationship. Here, a product is added for the category created in the first example. In this case, the parent category has already been added to the Categories collection of the object context, and the category has been saved to the database.

Just as in the first example, once the Product object has been created, the Add method of the Products collection is used to add it to that collection. Then, the SaveChanges method is called to add the product to the database.

Another way to refer to the Products collection is through the navigation property of the new category. This is illustrated by the last statement in this example. This statement gets the collection of products for the new category and then uses the Add method to add the new product to that collection.

Code that creates a new Category object

```
var category = new Category();
category.CategoryID = txtCategoryID.Text;
category.ShortName = txtShortName.Text;
category.LongName = txtLongName.Text;
```

Code that adds the object to the Categories collection and updates the database

```
db.Categories.Add(category);
db.SaveChanges();
```

Code that creates a new Product object

```
var product = new Product() { ProductID = "yoda01", Name = "Yoda",
    CategoryID = category.CategoryID,
    ShortDescription = "Be the ultimate teacher of the Jedi way",
    LongDescription = "Luminous beings are we...not this crude matter.",
    ImageFile = "yoda1.png", UnitPrice = 89.99m, OnHand = 14 };
```

Code that adds the object to the Products collection and updates the database

```
db.Products.Add(product);
db.SaveChanges();
```

Another way to add the object to the Products collection

```
category.Products.Add(product);
```

Description

- To add a row to the database, you create an instance of an entity class and assign values to its properties. Then, you use the Add method for the collection of objects in the object context to add the object to the collection. Finally, you execute the SaveChanges method of the object context to save the changes to the database.

- If the value of a column is generated by the database, you can specify any value for that column when you create the object as long as it's unique. You can also omit this value.

- To insert a new object and add child objects that are related to the parent object, you can create and save the parent object first. The object context will then be aware of this new object, and you can create and insert new child objects that are related to the new parent.

- When you execute the SaveChanges method, the Entity Framework generates SQL INSERT statements for the new objects and then passes those statements to the database.

Figure 18-6   How to add a new row

How to use model binding to display data

Now that you've learned to work with the Entity Framework, you're ready to learn how to use the entity classes it generates to bind data directly to a data control like a GridView control. In the topics that follow, you'll see how to use this technique, called *model binding*, to retrieve and display data, filter data, and provide for sorting and paging.

How to select data

Up until now, you've used data source controls like the SqlDataSource and ObjectDataSource controls to bind data to a data control. Then, you've configured those controls with commands or methods that select, update, insert, or delete data. Now, you'll learn how to use model binding, which is a relatively new feature of ASP.NET, to bind entity classes like those generated by EF directly to a data control.

When you use model binding, you bind data controls directly to methods that select, update, insert, and delete data. The GridView control shown in figure 18-7 illustrates how this works. Here, you can see that the SelectMethod property of this control names the method that retrieves the category data. Then, in the code-behind file, this method starts by creating an object context from an Entity Data Model that includes the Category and Product entities. Next, a LINQ to Entities query is used to get the categories from the Categories table and load them into the object context. Note that this query uses the Include method to load the related product data as well.

Another feature of model binding in ASP.NET is that it allows you to make your data controls *strongly typed*. To do that, you set the control's ItemType property to the name of the entity object that the select method returns. In the aspx code shown here, for example, the ItemType property is set to the Category type that's returned by the select method in the code-behind file. Note that the value in the ItemType property uses the fully qualified name of the Category entity type. The code-behind file shown here, though, includes a using directive so it doesn't need to fully qualify the Category or HalloweenEntities types.

The main benefit of a strongly typed data control is that it makes it easier to work with the properties of the underlying type in templated fields. For example, the last column of the GridView control shown here displays a count of the number of products in each category. To do that, it uses the Item keyword to refer to the Category object. Then, it uses that object's Products navigation property to get the Product objects related to that category, and it uses the Count property to get the count of products.

Like the Eval method you learned about in chapter 13, the Item keyword provides for one-way binding. As you can see in this example, though, the Item keyword is more flexible than the Eval method. You can also use two-way binding like the Bind method provides for using the BindItem keyword. You'll see examples of that keyword later in this chapter.

A strongly typed GridView control that uses model binding

Categories			
ID	**Short Name**	**Long Name**	**Product Count**
costumes	Costumes	Costumes	6
masks	Masks	Masks	3
props	Props	Props	8
fx	FX	Special Effects	6

The aspx code

```
<asp:GridView ID="grdCategories" runat="server"
    AutoGenerateColumns="false" DataKeyNames="CategoryID"
    CssClass="table table-bordered table-striped table-condensed"
    OnPreRender="grdCategories_PreRender"
    ItemType="Ch18CategoryList.Models.Category"
    SelectMethod="grdCategories_GetData">
    <Columns>
        <asp:BoundField DataField="CategoryID" HeaderText="ID" />
        <asp:BoundField DataField="ShortName" HeaderText="Short Name" />
        <asp:BoundField DataField="LongName" HeaderText="Long Name" />
        <asp:TemplateField HeaderText="Product Count">
            <ItemTemplate>
                <asp:Label ID="Label1" runat="server"
                    Text='<%# Item.Products.Count %>'></asp:Label>
            </ItemTemplate>
        </asp:TemplateField>
    </Columns>
</asp:GridView>
```

The code in the code-behind file that retrieves the data

```
using Ch18CategoryList.Models;
public IQueryable<Category> grdCategories_GetData()
{
    HalloweenEntities db = new HalloweenEntities();
    return from c in db.Categories.Include("Products")
           orderby c.LongName
           select c;
}
```

Description

- ASP.NET *model binding* allows you to bind data directly to a data control rather than to a data source control like a SqlDataSource or ObjectDataSource control. To do that, you set the control's SelectMethod property to the name of a method that returns data.

- You can make a data control *strongly typed* by setting its ItemType property to the type returned by the select method. Then, you can use the Item and BindItem keywords to refer to the properties of that type, including its related objects, in templated fields.

- Like the Eval and Bind methods, the Item keyword is for one-way binding, while the BindItem keyword is for two-way binding. Figure 13-15 has more information about this.

Figure 18-7   An introduction to model binding

When you use model binding, you should know that the names of the properties in the entity objects aren't available from the designer for a data control, even if the control is strongly typed. Because of that, you have to enter the names of the properties manually. If you use the Fields dialog box to create the bound fields shown in the GridView control in figure 18-7, for example, you have to enter a name for the DataField and HeaderText properties shown here. If you use sorting as described later in this chapter, you'll also have to enter the name of the property to use for each sort expression. In addition, you have to enter the appropriate property or properties for the DataKeyNames property of the control.

How to use IntelliSense to work with model binding

Figure 18-8 presents three of the IntelliSense features that Visual Studio provides to make it easier to work with model binding. First, IntelliSense helps you select a value for the ItemType property of a data control. You can see how this works in the first example in this figure. Here, the Category and Product types that are included in the Entity Data Model, as well as the HalloweenEntities type that defines the object context, are included in the list.

Note that if you've just added or updated the edmx file, you may not see the types you want in this list. In that case, you'll need to build the solution first. Then, the types you need should be listed.

Next, Visual Studio provides IntelliSense to help you select a value for the SelectMethod property of the control as well as the UpdateMethod, InsertMethod, and DeleteMethod properties that you'll see later. If the code-behind file for the page already contains one or more methods that have the appropriate signature, those methods are included in the list that's displayed. This is illustrated in the second example in this figure. Here, a method named grdCategories_GetData is included in the list. As you saw in the previous figure, this method returns an IQueryable<Category> object.

The list that's displayed for the SelectMethod, UpdateMethod, InsertMethod, and DeleteMethod properties also include a <Create New Method> option. You can use this option to generate the starting code for the method, sometimes called a *method stub*. The starting code that Visual Studio generates for a select method is shown in this figure. Notice that this code uses fully qualified names by default, but you can add a using directive for the Models folder as shown in the previous figure to simplify these names. Also notice the comment at the beginning of this code. You'll learn more about what these comments are referring to shortly.

It's important to know that the order in which you select an item type and generate a method stub affects the code that's generated for the stub. If you select the item type first as shown here, the method stub will return a generic IQueryable object of the selected type. If you generate the method stub first, though, the method stub will return a non-generic IQueryable object. Then, if you don't change the return type to a generic object, the data control won't be strongly-typed, which means that you won't be able to work with its properties as shown in the previous figure. Because of that, you should always select an item type before generating a method stub.

How to set the ItemType property to an entity class

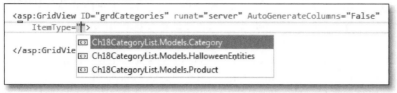

How to generate a method stub for the SelectMethod property

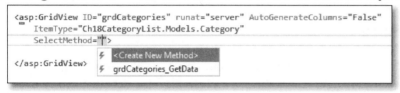

How to work with the properties of a type in a template

The starting code that's generated for a select method

```
// The return type can be changed to IEnumerable, however to support
// paging and sorting, the following parameters must be added:
//       int maximumRows
//       int startRowIndex
//       out int totalRowCount
//       string sortByExpression
public IQueryable<Ch18CategoryList.Models.Category> grdCategories_GetData()
{
    return null;
}
```

Description

- You can use IntelliSense to set the ItemType property to one of the entity classes created by EF. If these classes don't appear, you may need to build the solution.

- Once the ItemType property is set, you can use IntelliSense in templated fields to work with that type's properties.

- You can use IntelliSense to generate a *method stub* for the SelectMethod property in the code-behind file. You can also do this for a control's InsertMethod, UpdateMethod, and DeleteMethod properties.

- If you set the ItemType property before you set the SelectMethod property, the method stub that's generated by Visual Studio has a return type of an IQueryable object of that type. Otherwise, it has a return type of a non-generic IQueryable object.

Figure 18-8   How to use IntelliSense to work with model binding

Visual Studio also provides IntelliSense for working with the Item and BindItem keywords in templated fields. If you enter the Item keyword followed by the dot operator, for example, a list that includes the members of the underlying object is displayed. In the third example in figure 18-8, for instance, the Products navigation property of the Category object was selected. Then, after another dot operator was entered, the members of the Products collection were displayed. Note that for this to work, the ItemType property of the control must be set.

How to filter data

Just as you can with data source controls, you can use a value from sources like cookies, query strings, routes, or other controls to filter the data that's displayed in a data control that uses model binding. Instead of using parameter elements, however, you use the *model binding attributes* that are found in the System.Web.ModelBinding namespace. Some of these attributes are listed in the table in figure 18-9.

To do this kind of filtering with model binding, you add a parameter to the select method as shown in the first example in this figure. Then, you decorate that parameter with the appropriate attribute. In this case, a GridView control is filtered using the value of a drop-down list named ddlCategory. Because of that, the Control attribute is used, which tells the model binding framework that the source of the parameter's value is another control on the page. Notice that the parameter that's used has the same name as the control.

When you create a select method that accepts a parameter for filtering, it should provide for situations where the value of the parameter is null. In the first example shown here, for instance, the code returns all the products in the Products collection if the parameter is null. Otherwise, it uses the parameter to filter the products by category ID. In contrast, the select method in the second example assigns a default value to the parameter. In this case, the ID of the first category is assigned to the parameter. Then, that value is used to filter the products by category ID.

The third example in this figure shows the declaration for a method that uses a parameter name that's different from the name of the drop-down list. Here, the name of the control is coded on the Control attribute. This can make it clearer that you're referring to the value of the control rather than the control itself.

Attributes in the System.Web.ModelBinding namespace

Attribute	Description
`Control`	The value is provided by a control.
`Cookie`	The value is provided by a cookie.
`Form`	The value is provided by an HTML form field.
`Querystring`	The value is provided by a query string in the URL used to request the page.
`RouteData`	The value is provided by the route used to request the page.
`Session`	The value is provided by an item in session state.
`ViewState`	The value is provided by an item in view state.

A select method that accepts a value from a drop-down list

```
public IQueryable<Product> grdProducts_GetData([Control] string ddlCategory)
{
    HalloweenEntities db = new HalloweenEntities();
    if (ddlCategory == null) return db.Products;
    else
        return from p in db.Products
                where p.CategoryID == ddlCategory
                select p;
}
```

A select method that sets a default value

```
public IQueryable<Product> grdProducts_GetData([Control] string ddlCategory)
{
    HalloweenEntities db = new HalloweenEntities();
    if (ddlCategory == null)
        ddlCategory = db.Categories.FirstOrDefault().CategoryID;

    return from p in db.Products
            where p.CategoryID == ddlCategory
            select p;
}
```

A method declaration that uses a custom name for the parameter

```
public IQueryable<Product> grdProducts_GetData(
    [Control("ddlCategory")] string catID)
```

Description

- To filter the data that's returned by a select method, you add a parameter to the method's signature and decorate the parameter with a *model binding attribute* that indicates the source of its value.

- A select method that receives a parameter should provide for a null parameter. For example, it can return an entity collection or set a default value.

- You can give the parameter the same name as the source of the parameter's value, or you can give it a different name and then include the source name on the model binding attribute.

Figure 18-9   How to filter data

How to provide for sorting and paging

The technique you use to provide for sorting and paging when you use model binding depends on the return type of the select method that's used by the data control. If the select method returns an IQueryable type, for example, you can provide for paging and sorting using the standard techniques that you learned about in chapters 14, 15, and 16. This is illustrated in the first two examples in figure 18-10.

In the first example, you can see that the select method returns an IQueryable type that retrieves all of the products in the Products table, sorted by product name. It's important to note here that the query that's defined by this method isn't executed by the method. Instead, the query itself is returned by the method. Because of that, the data control that uses this method can further refine the query before executing it against the database. For instance, the GridView control in the second example in this figure refines this query by applying paging using the AllowPaging and PageSize properties and by applying sorting using the AllowSorting and SortExpression properties. These are the same properties that you learned about in chapter 14 for providing paging and sorting for a GridView control.

The third example in this figure shows a select method that returns an IEnumberable type instead of an IQueryable type. Because an IEnumerable type returns the collection of objects that's specified by the query rather than the query itself, the data control can't modify the query before it's executed. In that case, the select method must provide for the paging and sorting that's specified by the data control. To do that, it must include the maximumRows, startRowIndex, and totalRowCount parameters for paging and the sortExpression parameter for sorting as indicated by the comment that's generated for the select method. Then, it must include code similar to the code you use to implement paging and sorting with an object data source control. Since it's not usually necessary to use this technique, it's not presented in this book.

A select method with an IQueryable return type

```
public IQueryable<Product> grdProducts_GetData() {
    return from p in db.Products orderby p.Name select p;
}
```

A GridView control that provides for sorting and paging

```
<asp:GridView ID="grdProducts" runat="server"
    AutoGenerateColumns="False" DataKeyNames="ProductID"
    AllowSorting="True" AllowPaging="True" PageSize="4"
    ItemType="Ch18ProductList.Models.Product"
    SelectMethod="grdProducts_GetData">
    <Columns>
        <asp:BoundField DataField="ProductID"
            HeaderText="ID" /></asp:BoundField>
        <asp:BoundField HeaderText="Name" DataField="Name"
            SortExpression="Name"></asp:BoundField>
        <asp:BoundField HeaderText="Unit Price" DataField="UnitPrice"
            SortExpression="UnitPrice" DataFormatString="{0:C}">
        </asp:BoundField>
        <asp:BoundField HeaderText="On Hand" DataField="OnHand"
            SortExpression="OnHand">
        </asp:BoundField>
    </Columns>
    <PagerStyle CssClass="pagerStyle" />
</asp:GridView>
```

A select method with an IEnumerable return type

```
public IEnumerable<Product> grdProducts_GetData() {
    return (from p in db.Products orderby p.Name select p).ToList();
}
```

Description

- If a select method returns an IQueryable object, a data control that uses the select method can refine the query before it's executed against the database.

- To add paging to a data control that uses a select method with an IQueryable return type, you add the AllowPaging property. To add sorting, you add the AllowSorting property and then add a SortExpression property to each field that you want the user to be able to use for sorting.

- A select method with an IEnumerable return type returns the results of a query, so a data control can't refine the query before it's executed against the database. Because of that, the select method must provide for sorting and paging using the parameters listed in the comment that's generated for the method, as shown in figure 18-8. For more information on how to use these parameters, see the MSDN documentation.

- If you use a DynamicField control rather than a BoundField control, you don't need to set the SortExpression properties of the fields. To learn more about the DynamicField control, please see the MSDN documentation.

Figure 18-10   How to provide for sorting and paging

A Product List application

To illustrate the basics of working with EF and model binding, figure 18-11 presents a Product List application. This application is similar in appearance to the Product List applications that you saw in chapters 13 and 17. However, instead of using SqlDataSource controls or ObjectDataSource controls to retrieve the data, it uses classes generated by EF and it binds the data directly to the drop-down list and GridView control.

This application shows how to filter data in a GridView control based on the value of a drop-down list. It also shows how to provide for sorting and paging when you use model binding. Finally, it shows how to work with related data in a strongly typed GridView control.

The Product List application

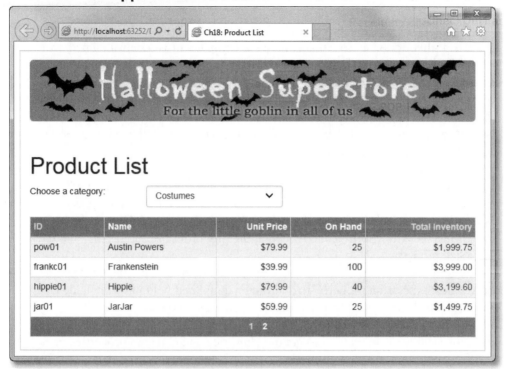

Description

- The Category drop-down list uses EF and model binding to retrieve and display a list of categories from the Categories table.
- The Products GridView control uses EF and model binding to retrieve and display a list of products from the Products table.
- The select method for the GridView control has a parameter with a Control attribute to filter the product data based on the value of the Category drop-down list.
- The select method for the GridView control has an IQueryable return type, so the control can provide for sorting and paging.
- The GridView control is strongly typed, so it can use the properties of the Product type in a templated field that shows a calculated inventory value.

Figure 18-11   The Product List application

The aspx file

Figure 18-12 presents the critical aspx code of the Product List application. It starts with a Bootstrap row that contains a DropDownList control named ddlCategory. This control's ItemType property indicates that it's bound to the Category entity type, and its SelectMethod property indicates that the data it displays is retrieved from a method in the code-behind file named ddlCategory_GetData. Note that IntelliSense doesn't always provide a completion list for the SelectMethod property of a drop-down list. In that case, you'll need to enter the value for this property manually.

The second Bootstrap row contains a GridView control named grdProducts. The ItemType property for this control indicates that it's bound to the Product entity type, and its SelectMethod property indicates that the data it displays is retrieved from a method named grdProducts_GetData. In addition to these properties, the AllowSorting and AllowPaging properties are set to True, and the PageSize property is set to 4.

Within the Columns element, you can see that three of the bound fields have a SortExpression property. In addition, a templated field has been added. Because the GridView control is strongly typed, this field can use the Item keyword to access the underlying Product object that the row is bound to. In this case, the Item keyword is used to get the UnitPrice and OnHand properties of the Product object and then multiplies them to get the total cost of inventory. The ToString method is then called on the result to format it as a currency value.

The critical code of the Default.aspx file

```
<div class="row">
    <div class="col-xs-12">
        <h1>Product List</h1>
        <div class="form-group">
            <label class="col-sm-3 text-left">Choose a category:</label>
            <div class="col-sm-4">
                <asp:DropDownList ID="ddlCategory" runat="server"
                    ItemType="Ch18ProductList.Models.Category"
                    SelectMethod="ddlCategory_GetData" AutoPostBack="True"
                    DataValueField="CategoryID" DataTextField="LongName"
                    CssClass="form-control"></asp:DropDownList>
            </div></div></div></div>

<div class="row">
    <div class="col-xs-12 table-responsive">
        <asp:GridView ID="grdProducts" runat="server"
            AutoGenerateColumns="False" DataKeyNames="ProductID"
            CssClass="table table-bordered table-striped table-condensed"
            OnPreRender="grdProducts_PreRender"
            AllowSorting="True" AllowPaging="True" PageSize="4"
            ItemType="Ch18ProductList.Models.Product"
            SelectMethod="grdProducts_GetData">
            <Columns>
                <asp:BoundField DataField="ProductID" HeaderText="ID">
                 <ItemStyle CssClass="col-xs-2" />
                </asp:BoundField>
                <asp:BoundField HeaderText="Name" DataField="Name"
                    SortExpression="Name">
                 <ItemStyle CssClass="col-xs-3" />
                </asp:BoundField>
                </asp:TemplateField>
                <asp:BoundField HeaderText="Unit Price" DataField="UnitPrice"
                    SortExpression="UnitPrice" DataFormatString="{0:C}">
                 <ItemStyle CssClass="col-xs-2 text-right" />
                 <HeaderStyle CssClass="text-right" />
                </asp:BoundField>
                <asp:BoundField HeaderText="On Hand" DataField="OnHand"
                    SortExpression="OnHand">
                 <ItemStyle CssClass="col-xs-2 text-right" />
                 <HeaderStyle CssClass="text-right" />
                </asp:BoundField>
                <asp:TemplateField HeaderText="Total Inventory">
                    <ItemTemplate>
                        <asp:Label ID="Label2" runat="server"
                            Text='<%# (Item.UnitPrice * Item.OnHand)
                                .ToString("c") %>'>
                        </asp:Label>
                    </ItemTemplate>
                    <ItemStyle CssClass="col-xs-3 text-right" />
                    <HeaderStyle CssClass="text-right" />
                </asp:TemplateField>
            </Columns>
            <PagerStyle CssClass="pagerStyle" />
        </asp:GridView>
    </div></div>
```

Figure 18-12   The aspx file for the Product List application

The code-behind file

Figure 18-13 presents the code-behind file for the Product List application. It starts with two using directives. These directives let you work with the entity classes in the Models folder and the model binding attributes without using fully qualified names.

The first statement within the class for the page declares a variable that stores a new instance of the HalloweenEntities object context. This variable is declared at the class level so it can be used by the select methods for both the drop-down list and the GridView control.

The first select method is for the Category drop-down list. It selects all of the categories from the Halloween database and sorts them by long name. The return type of this method is IQueryable. Note that you could change the return type to IEnumerable since the drop-down list doesn't use paging or sorting. In that case, though, you'd need to call the ToList method on the query to execute it so the query results were returned.

The second select method is for the Products GridView control. This method also has a return type of IQueryable to make it easy to provide for paging and sorting. This method accepts a string parameter that it gets from the drop-down list (ddlCategory). This method then checks the value of the parameter, and it assigns the ID of the first category in the Categories table to it if the parameter's value is null. After that, this method selects all the products that match the category ID and orders them by name.

Notice in this method that if the value of the drop-down list is null, the categories are sorted by long name just like they are in the select method for the drop-down list. That way, you can be sure that the FirstOrDefault method retrieves the same category that's displayed in the drop-down list when the page is first loaded.

Also notice that, because no category data is displayed in the GridView control, the query expression in this method doesn't use an Include method to retrieve the related category. If the GridView control did display category data, though, you'd want to use the Include method so the category data was loaded at the same time as the product data. Otherwise, you'd need to use a separate query to load the category data for each product. This would result in multiple database calls and could result in negative performance.

The final method in the code-behind file is an event handler for the PreRender event of the GridView control. You've seen code like this in previous chapters. It causes ASP.NET to include thead and tbody elements in the table that's rendered for the GridView control. That way, the Bootstrap table classes will produce the intended results.

The Default.aspx.cs file

```
...
using Ch18ProductList.Models;
using System.Web.ModelBinding;

public partial class Default : System.Web.UI.Page
{
    HalloweenEntities db = new HalloweenEntities();

    public IQueryable<Category> ddlCategory_GetData()
    {
        return from c in db.Categories
               orderby c.LongName
               select c;
    }

    public IQueryable<Product> grdProducts_GetData(
        [Control] string ddlCategory)
    {
        // get first category ID from database if nothing is passed in
        if (ddlCategory == null)
            ddlCategory = (from c in db.Categories
                           orderby c.LongName
                           select c).FirstOrDefault().CategoryID;

        // get the products for the selected category
        return from p in db.Products
               where p.CategoryID == ddlCategory
               orderby p.Name
               select p;
    }

    protected void grdProducts_PreRender(object sender, EventArgs e)
    {
        // to format the generated Bootstrap table
        grdProducts.HeaderRow.TableSection = TableRowSection.TableHeader;
    }
}
```

Description

- The using directives allow you to work with objects without having to use fully qualified names. The first one provides access to the object context and entity classes in the Models folder, and the second one contains the model binding attributes.

- Since more than one method will use the HalloweenEntities object context, the variable that holds it is declared at the class level.

- Both select methods have an IQueryable return type, which is what Visual Studio generates by default. This is what you want in most situations, and it lets you implement paging and sorting using standard techniques.

- If you're going to use objects that are related to another object in a data control, you should use eager loading. Otherwise, a separate query will be used to retrieve the related object from the database for each row.

Figure 18-13   The code-behind for the Product List application

How to use model binding to update, insert, and delete data

In addition to displaying data using model binding, you need to be able to update, insert, and delete data. That's what you'll learn in the topics that follow. You'll also learn how to check for concurrency and validation errors, and you'll learn how to create a data access class so you can separate your data access code from the code in the code-behind file.

How to provide for updates, inserts, and deletes

Figure 18-14 shows a GridView control that displays category data, along with a DetailsView control that displays the category that's selected in the GridView control. The DetailsView control lets the user update or delete the selected category. It also lets the user insert a new category, which is then displayed in the GridView control.

The aspx code for the DetailsView control is shown in this figure. Like the GridView control examples you've seen already in this chapter, the DetailsView control shown here has its SelectMethod set to the name of the method that selects the data it displays and its ItemType property set to the name of the entity type that the select method returns. Because this DetailsView control also handles updates, inserts, and deletes, though, it also has some additional properties set.

First, the DataKeyNames property contains the name of the primary key column, which in this case is the CategoryID column. Note that if this property isn't generated for you when you create the DetailsView control, you'll need to add it. That's because it's used by the update, insert, and delete methods that you'll see shortly.

Then, the UpdateMethod, InsertMethod, and DeleteMethod properties contain the names of the methods in the code-behind file that perform these operations. You can generate the starting code for these methods by creating method stubs as described in figure 18-8. You'll see this starting code next. Then, you'll see how to modify this code so it works the way you want.

A GridView control that displays data and a DetailsView control that provides for updates, inserts, and deletes

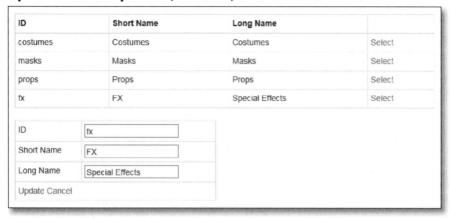

The aspx code for the DetailsView control

```
<asp:DetailsView ID="dvCategory" runat="server"
    AutoGenerateRows="false" DataKeyNames="CategoryID"
    CssClass="table table-bordered table-condensed"
    ItemType="Ch18ModelBinding.Models.Category"
    SelectMethod="dvCategory_GetItem"
    UpdateMethod="dvCategory_UpdateItem"
    InsertMethod="dvCategory_InsertItem"
    DeleteMethod="dvCategory_DeleteItem">
    <Fields>
        <asp:BoundField HeaderText="ID" DataField="CategoryID"
            ReadOnly="true" />
        <asp:BoundField HeaderText="Short Name" DataField="ShortName" />
        <asp:BoundField HeaderText="Long Name" DataField="LongName" />
        <asp:CommandField ShowInsertButton="True" ShowEditButton="true"
            ShowDeleteButton="true"></asp:CommandField>
    </Fields>
</asp:DetailsView>
```

Description

- To update an item, you specify the name of the update method on the UpdateMethod property of the bound control. This method should update the object in the object model and then update the database.

- To insert an item, you specify the name of the insert method on the InsertMethod property of the bound control. This method should add an object to the object model and then update the database.

- To delete an item, you specify the name of the delete method on the DeleteMethod property of the bound control. This method should mark the object for deletion and then update the database.

Figure 18-14   How to provide for updates, inserts, and deletes

The starting code that's generated for update, insert, and delete methods

Figure 18-15 presents the method stubs that Visual Studio generated for the update, insert, and delete methods of the DetailsView control you saw in the last figure. You should notice several things about this code.

First, the code for the update and insert methods use fully qualified names for the entity type, in this case, Category. If that's not what you want, you can add a using directive for the application's Models folder. You saw how that works in figure 18-13.

Second, both the update and delete methods are defined with a parameter that will receive the key value of the item to be updated or deleted. The comment at the beginning of these methods tells you that the parameter name should match the DataKeyNames value that's set on the control. For example, the DataKeyNames value for the DetailsView control in the previous figure is CategoryID. Because of that, you need to change the parameter name from "id" to "CategoryID". In addition, you may need to change the default data type of the parameter. In this case, because the CategoryID is defined as varchar(10), you need to change the data type from int to string.

Third, the code for the update and insert methods suggests patterns to use for updating and inserting an item. Specifically, the code for the update method suggests that you select the item to be updated, notify the user if the item doesn't exist, update the model if it does exist, and update the database if no errors occur when the model is updated. The code for the insert method suggests that you create a new item, add it to the model, and add it to the database if no errors occur. Although you aren't required to follow these patterns, it makes sense to do so.

To update the object model with a new or modified object, the code for the update and insert methods uses the TryUpdateModel method of the page. This method accepts an instance of a model object, such as a Category object. It then updates that object with the data from a data-bound control, such as a DetailsView control.

The code for the update and insert methods also uses a ModelStateDictionary object, which stores any errors that occur when the TryUpdateModel method is called. That includes errors such as null values or incorrect data types. You can use the ModelState property of the page to access the ModelStateDictionary object. The IsValid property of this object is used by both the update and insert methods to check for errors after the object model is updated. In addition, the AddModelError method of this object is used in the update method to add an error if the item with the key value that's passed to the method isn't found. This method can include two strings that specify the item's key and the error message.

Unlike the generated code for the update and insert methods, no pattern is suggested for the delete method. That's because you usually don't need to get user input for a delete operation, and you usually don't need to notify the user if the item they want to delete doesn't exist. However, since errors can occur if you try to call the Remove method on a null object, it's best to check for nulls before deleting. You'll see an example of this in the next figure.

The starting code that's generated for an update method

```
// The id parameter name should match the DataKeyNames value
// set on the control
public void dvCategory_UpdateItem(int id)
{
    Ch18CategoryMaintenance.Models.Category item = null;
    // Load the item here, e.g. item = MyDataLayer.Find(id);
    if (item == null) {
        // The item wasn't found
        ModelState.AddModelError("",
            String.Format("Item with id {0} was not found", id));
        return;
    }
    TryUpdateModel(item);
    if (ModelState.IsValid) {
        // Save changes here, e.g. MyDataLayer.SaveChanges();

    }
}
```

The starting code that's generated for an insert method

```
public void dvCategory_InsertItem()
{
    var item = new Ch18CategoryMaintenance.Models.Category();
    TryUpdateModel(item);
    if (ModelState.IsValid)
    {
        // Save changes here

    }
}
```

The starting code that's generated for a delete method

```
// The id parameter name should match the DataKeyNames value
// set on the control
public void dvCategory_DeleteItem(int id)
{
}
```

Description

- You can use the technique shown in figure 18-8 to generate method stubs for the update, insert, and delete methods.

- The ModelState property of a page gets a ModelStateDictionary object that contains a collection of errors for the model. That includes errors such as null values in fields that don't allow nulls and string values in int fields.

- You can add your own custom errors to the model using the AddModelError method.

- The TryUpdateModel method of a page updates the instance of the model object that's passed to it, using the values from a data-bound control. You can use the IsValid property of the ModelStateDictionary object to check if any errors occurred during this update.

Figure 18-15   The starting code for the update, insert, and delete methods

How to complete the methods for updating, inserting, and deleting data

Figure 18-16 shows how you can modify the generated code you saw in the last figure to complete the update, insert, and delete methods. Note that these methods assume a class variable named db that refers to an instance of the object context. It also assumes that a using directive has been added for the Models namespace for the application.

The update method shown here accepts a string parameter named CategoryID. As required, this parameter has the same name and data type as the key field specified by the DataKeyNames property of the DetailsView control. The update method uses the CategoryID value to retrieve the Category object to be updated from the object context.

Following the pattern recommended by the generated code, the update method then checks to see if the category exists in the database. If it doesn't, the method adds a message to the ModelStateDictionary object of the page and then returns control to the DetailsView control. Otherwise, it calls the TryUpdateModel method to update the Category object with the values in the DetailsView control. After that, it checks to see if the TryUpdateModel method generated any errors. If not, it calls the SaveChanges method of the object context to save the updated object to the database. Then, it binds the GridView control again so the updated values are displayed.

The insert method starts by creating a new Category object. Then it passes the Category object to the TryUpdateModel method, which gets the values for the object from the DetailsView control.

Next, the insert method checks to see if the TryUpdateModel method generated any errors. If not, it adds the new Category object to the Categories collection of the object context and then calls the SaveChanges method to insert the new category into the database. Finally, it binds the GridView control so the new Category is displayed.

The delete method accepts a string named CategoryID, which matches the name and data type of the key field specified by the DataKeyNames property of the DetailsView control. Then, it uses the CategoryID value to retrieve the Category object to be deleted from the object context. If the category is found, it calls the Remove method of the Categories collection to mark the object for deletion. Finally, it calls the SaveChanges method to delete the category from the database, and it binds the GridView control so the category is no longer displayed.

A method that updates a Category object

```
public void dvCategory_UpdateItem(string CategoryID)
{
    var item = (from c in db.Categories
                where c.CategoryID == CategoryID
                select c).FirstOrDefault();
    if (item == null) {
        ModelState.AddModelError("",
            $"Item with id {CategoryID} was not found");
        return;
    }
    TryUpdateModel(item);
    if (ModelState.IsValid) {
        db.SaveChanges();
        grdCategories.DataBind();
    }
}
```

A method that inserts a new Category object

```
public void dvCategory_InsertItem()
{
    var item = new Category();
    TryUpdateModel(item);
    if (ModelState.IsValid) {
        db.Categories.Add(item);
        db.SaveChanges();
        grdCategories.DataBind();
    }
}
```

A method that deletes a Category object

```
public void dvCategory_DeleteItem(string CategoryID)
{
    var item = (from c in db.Categories
                where c.CategoryID == CategoryID
                select c).FirstOrDefault();
    if (item != null) {
        db.Categories.Remove(item);
        db.SaveChanges();
        grdCategories.DataBind();
    }
}
```

Description

- The parameter for the update and delete methods must have the same name and data type as the field that's set as the DataKeyNames value on the bound control.

- If an entity object with the given value isn't found, the update method adds an error to the ModelStateDictionary object and then ends the method. Otherwise, the entity and database are updated using the values in the DetailsView control.

- The insert method creates a new entity object, assigns the values in the DetailsView control to that entity, adds the entity to the model, and then saves it to the database.

- The delete method retrieves the entity object to be deleted and, if it exists, marks it for deletion and removes it from the database.

Figure 18-16   How to complete the methods for updating, inserting, and deleting data

How to handle concurrency and data validation exceptions

As you know, you can handle concurrency exceptions when you use EF by coding the SaveChanges method of the object context in the try block of a try-catch statement and then reloading the new values from the database if an exception occurs. When you use model binding, you can also add the concurrency errors to the ModelStateDictionary object. Then, you can display these errors in a validation summary control. You can use a similar technique to catch and display the data validation exceptions that can occur when you use model binding. These exceptions include trying to save a null value to a field that doesn't allow nulls, or trying to save a value with the wrong data type.

Figure 18-17 shows a try-catch statement that catches both concurrency and data validation exceptions. To catch a concurrency exception, you use the DbUpdateConcurrencyException class in the System.Data.Entity.Infrastructure namespace. To catch a data validation exception, you use the DbEntityValidationException class in the System.Data.Entity.Validation namespace. If one of these exceptions occurs, it's passed to a method that handles the exception.

The method that handles concurrency exceptions simply reloads the data from the database and then adds an error to the ModelStateDictionary object. The method that handles data validation exceptions is somewhat more complicated because it's possible for more than one validation exception to occur. To start, a foreach statement is used to loop through the EntityValidationErrors collection of the exception object. Each object in this collection contains the validation results for a single entity. Then, within this loop, another foreach loop is used to get the validation exceptions for that entity. For each exception, an error that includes the ErrorMessage property of the exception is added to the ModelStateDictionary.

When you add errors to the ModelStateDictionary object, you can display them in a validation summary control as shown at the top of this figure. To do that, you simply set the control's ShowModelStateErrors property to true.

A validation summary control that displays data validation errors

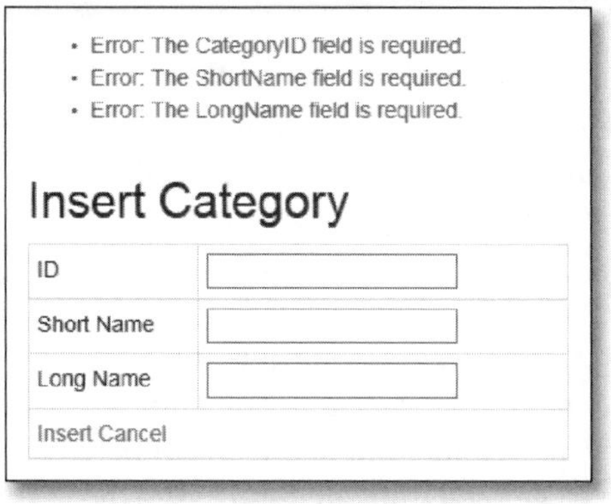

```
• Error: The CategoryID field is required.
• Error: The ShortName field is required.
• Error: The LongName field is required.
```

Insert Category

ID	
Short Name	
Long Name	

Insert Cancel

A try-catch statement that handles concurrency and validation errors

```
try { db.SaveChanges(); }
catch (DbUpdateConcurrencyException ex) { HandleConcurrencyError(ex); }
catch (DbEntityValidationException ex) { HandleValidationError(ex); }
```

A method that handles concurrency errors

```
private void HandleConcurrencyError(DbUpdateConcurrencyException ex)
{
    ex.Entries.Single().Reload();
    ModelState.AddModelError("",
        "Another user changed or deleted that category.");
}
```

A method that handles validation errors

```
private void HandleValidationError(DbEntityValidationException ex)
{
    foreach (var ve in ex.EntityValidationErrors) {
        foreach (var e in ve.ValidationErrors) {
            ModelState.AddModelError("", $"Error: {e.ErrorMessage}");
        }
    }
}
```

Description

- A DbUpdateConcurrencyException is thrown when a concurrency error occurs. This exception is in the System.Data.Entity.Infrastructure namespace.

- A DbEntityValidationException is thrown when a validation error occurs. This exception is in the System.Data.Entity.Validation namespace.

- You can loop through the EntityValidationErrors collection of the DbEntityValidationException, and then through the ValidationErrors collection of each EntityValidationErrors object to retrieve the specific validation errors.

- To display the errors in the ModelStateDictionary object in a validation summary control, you set the control's ShowModelStateErrors property to True.

Figure 18-17   How to handle concurrency and data validation exceptions

How to use a data access class with model binding

As you've seen, when you use Visual Studio to generate the starting code for the methods of a data control that uses model binding, the code is stored in the code-behind file for the page. As you learned in chapter 17, however, it's considered a best practice to put your data access code in a separate class. Figure 18-18 shows you how to do that when you use model binding.

The aspx code at the top of this figure shows a GridView control that uses a data access class with model binding. To make that work, this control includes an event handler for its CallingDataMethods event. Although it's not shown here, you should know that you can use IntelliSense to generate this method using the same technique for generating other methods that you saw earlier in this chapter.

Within the CallingDataMethods event handler, you create a new instance of your data access class and assign it to the DataMethodsObject property of the CallingDataMethodsEventArgs object that's passed to the event handler. That way, the bound control knows what class contains the methods it needs. In the event handler that's shown here, for example, a new instance of the CategoryDB class is created and assigned to the DataMethodsObject property.

The last example in this figure shows the code for the CategoryDB class. Notice that this class includes a class variable that will store an instance of the object context. Then, it includes a constructor that creates that object and stores it in the variable. This constructor is executed when an instance of the CategoryDB class is created by the CallingDataMethods event handler.

The code for the select and update methods shown here is similar to methods that you've already seen. In fact, the select method is identical to a method that you'd find in a code-behind file. However, the update method includes a ModelMethodContext object as its second parameter. This object is passed from the bound control to the update method and provides access to the ModelState property and the TryUpdateModel method of the page. That makes sense since the update method is no longer in the code-behind file for the page.

By the way, you should know that the ModelMethodContext object is also passed to the select, insert, and delete methods of a data access class. If it's not needed by a method, though, you can omit it from the method signature as illustrated by the select method in this example.

One final thing you should notice in this data access class are that the names of the select and update methods are different from the names that are used when you generate method stubs in the code-behind file. Although you can still generate method stubs and then cut and paste the methods into a data access class, you'll typically change the method names when you do that so they're like the names you'll find in other data access classes. If you do that, don't forget to change the values of the method properties of the bound control to the new names.

The aspx code for a GridView that uses a separate data access class

```
<asp:GridView ID="grdCategories" runat="server"
    AutoGenerateColumns="false" DataKeyNames="CategoryID"
    ItemType="Ch18CategoryMaintenance.Models.Category"
    OnCallingDataMethods="grdCategories_CallingDataMethods"
    SelectMethod="GetCategories" UpdateMethod="UpdateCategory">
    <Columns>...</Columns>
</asp:GridView>
```

An event handler that identifies the data access class

```
protected void grdCategories_CallingDataMethods(object sender,
    CallingDataMethodsEventArgs e)
{
    e.DataMethodsObject = new Ch18CategoryMaintenance.Models.CategoryDB();
}
```

The CategoryDB data access class in the Models folder

```
public class CategoryDB
{
    HalloweenEntities db;
    public CategoryDB() {
        db = new HalloweenEntities();
    }

    public IQueryable<Category> GetCategories() {
        return from c in db.Categories orderby c.LongName select c;
    }

    public void UpdateCategory(string CategoryID, ModelMethodContext cxt)
    {
        Category item = /* query to retrieve the category goes here */
        if (item == null) {
            cxt.ModelState.AddModelError("", "Category not found");
            return;
        }
        cxt.TryUpdateModel(item);
        if (cxt.ModelState.IsValid) {
            /* code to update the database goes here */
        }
    }
}
```

Description

- A data access class that's used with model binding needs an instance of the object context, as well as the required select, update, insert, and delete methods. In the code above, the object context is instantiated in a constructor.

- To use the data access class, you must include an event handler for the CallingDataMethods event of the bound control. This event handler should create an instance of the data access class and assign it to the DataMethodsObject property of the CallingDataMethodsEventArgs object that's passed to the event handler.

- You can access the ModelState property and TryUpdateModel method in any data access method using the ModelMethodContext object that's passed to these methods.

Figure 18-18   How to use a data access class with model binding

A Product Maintenance application

To give you a better idea of how you can use model binding to update, delete, and insert data, the topics that follow present an application that maintains the Products table in the Halloween database. This application works like the Product Maintenance application that you saw in chapter 15.

The operation of the application

Figure 18-19 shows the operation of the Product Maintenance application. This application uses a GridView control to list the products on the left side of the page. This control uses paging so the user can scroll through the entire Products table. It also uses sorting so the user can sort the products by ID or name.

When the user clicks the Select button for a product, the details for that product are displayed in the DetailsView control on the right side of the page. Then, the user can edit or delete the selected product. The user can also insert a new product.

The methods used for binding

Figure 18-19 also presents the signatures for the methods that are used for binding. These methods are stored in a data access class named ProductDB. The first select method is used to get the products that are displayed in the GridView control. The second select method is used to get the product that's selected in the GridView control and displayed in the DetailsView control. And the third select method is used to get the categories that are displayed in the drop-down list that's displayed in the DetailsView control when a user is updating or inserting a product. Finally, the update and delete methods are used to update and delete the product that's displayed in the DetailsView control, and the insert method is used to insert a new product using the DetailsView control.

Note that, unlike the methods in the data access class you saw in chapter 17, these methods aren't static. That way, an instance of the data access class can be created and passed to the GridView and DetailsView controls. Also notice that the update, insert, and delete methods include a parameter for the ModelMethodContext object as described in the previous figure.

The Product Maintenance application

Methods of the ProductDB class

Type	Signature

Select	`public IQueryable<Product> GetProducts()`
	`public Product GetProduct([Control] string grdProducts)`
	`public IQueryable<Category> GetCategories()`

Update	`public void UpdateProduct(string ProductID, ModelMethodContext cxt)`
Delete	`public void DeleteProduct(string ProductID, ModelMethodContext.cxt)`
Insert	`public void InsertProduct(ModelMethodContext cxt)`

Description

- This version of the Product Maintenance application uses a GridView control to display a list of products. When the user selects a product in this control, its details are displayed in a DetailsView control. Then, the user can use this control to Update or Delete the product or to add a new product.

- The GridView and DetailsView controls use model binding to access the Products and Categories tables of the Halloween database.

- A data access class named ProductDB provides the select, insert, update, and delete methods needed for model binding.

Figure 18-19   The operation and binding methods of the Product Maintenance application

The aspx file

The three parts of figure 18-20 show the code for the GridView, validation summary, and DetailsView controls in the Default.aspx file for this application. The GridView control is similar to the one you saw earlier in this chapter for the Product List application, except that it includes an event handler for the CallingDataMethods event. Because this event handler is also used by the DetailsView control, it's given a generic name of Control_CallingDataMethods.

After the GridView control is a validation summary control that will be used to display any errors that occur when the DetailsView control is used to insert, update, or delete a product. Notice that the ShowModelStateErrors property of the validation summary control is set to True. That way, it will display all the errors in the page's ModelStateDictionary object.

The DetailsView control includes the ItemType property, so it is strongly typed. That way, it can use the Item and BindItem keywords in its templates. You can see these templates in parts 2 and 3 of this figure. Here, the EditItem template for each of the fields except for product ID uses the BindItem keyword. That's because these templates pass data to the database when a product is updated. Because the product ID can't be updated, though, it uses the Item keyword instead.

In contrast to the EditItem templates, all of the InsertItem templates use the BindItem keyword. That's because all of these templates, including the one for the product ID field, pass data to the database when a product is inserted. On the other hand, all of the Item templates use the Item keyword, since no data is passed to the database when an item is displayed or deleted.

The EditItem and InsertItem templates also use a drop-down list for the category field. Like the GridView and DetailsView controls, the drop-down lists use model binding. In fact, they use the same event handler for the CallingDataMethods event as these controls do. You'll see that event handler and the data access class next.

The critical code of the Default.aspx file   **Page 1**

```
<div class="col-sm-6 table-responsive">
    <asp:GridView ID="grdProducts" runat="server"
        AutoGenerateColumns="False" DataKeyNames="ProductID"
        ItemType="Ch18ProductMaintenance.Models.Product"
        OnCallingDataMethods="Control_CallingDataMethods"
        SelectMethod="GetProducts" SelectedIndex="0"
        AllowSorting="True" AllowPaging="True" PageSize="8"
        CssClass="table table-bordered table-striped table-condensed"
        OnPreRender="grdProducts_PreRender">
        <Columns>
            <asp:BoundField DataField="ProductID" HeaderText="ID"
                ReadOnly="True" SortExpression="ProductID">
                <ItemStyle CssClass="col-xs-2" />
            </asp:BoundField>
            <asp:BoundField DataField="Name" HeaderText="Name"
                SortExpression="Name">
                <ItemStyle CssClass="col-xs-6" />
            </asp:BoundField>
            <asp:BoundField DataField="CategoryID" HeaderText="Category">
                <ItemStyle CssClass="col-xs-3" />
            </asp:BoundField>
            <asp:CommandField ButtonType="Link" ShowSelectButton="true">
                <ItemStyle CssClass="col-xs-1" />
            </asp:CommandField>
        </Columns>
        <HeaderStyle CssClass="bg-halloween" />
        <PagerSettings Mode="NumericFirstLast" />
        <PagerStyle CssClass="pagerStyle"
            BackColor="#8c8c8c" HorizontalAlign="Center" />
        <SelectedRowStyle CssClass="warning" />
    </asp:GridView>
</div>

<div class="col-sm-6">
    <asp:ValidationSummary ID="ValidationSummary1" runat="server"
        ShowModelStateErrors="true" CssClass="text-danger" />

    <asp:DetailsView ID="dvProduct" runat="server" DataKeyNames="ProductID"
        ItemType="Ch18ProductMaintenance.Models.Product"
        OnCallingDataMethods="Control_CallingDataMethods"
        SelectMethod="GetProduct" UpdateMethod="UpdateProduct"
        InsertMethod="InsertProduct" DeleteMethod="DeleteProduct"
        AutoGenerateRows="False" OnItemDeleted="dvProduct_ItemDeleted"
        OnItemInserted="dvProduct_ItemInserted"
        OnItemUpdated="dvProduct_ItemUpdated"
        CssClass="table table-bordered table-condensed">
```

Figure 18-20   The aspx file for the Product Maintenance application (part 1 of 3)

The critical code of the Default.aspx file   **Page 2**

```
<Fields>
    <asp:TemplateField HeaderText="Product ID:">
        <EditItemTemplate>
            <asp:Label runat="server" ID="lblProductID"
                Text='<%# Item.ProductID %>'></asp:Label>
        </EditItemTemplate>
        <InsertItemTemplate>
            <div class="col-xs-11 col-insert">
                <asp:TextBox runat="server" ID="txtProductID"
                    Text='<%# BindItem.ProductID %>' MaxLength="10"
                    CssClass="form-control"></asp:TextBox>
            </div>
        </InsertItemTemplate>
        <ItemTemplate>
            <asp:Label runat="server" ID="lblProductID"
                Text='<%# Item.ProductID %>'></asp:Label>
        </ItemTemplate>
        <HeaderStyle CssClass="col-xs-4" />
    </asp:TemplateField>
    <asp:TemplateField HeaderText="Name:">
        <EditItemTemplate>
            <div class="col-xs-11 col-edit">
                <asp:TextBox runat="server" ID="txtName"
                    Text='<%# BindItem.Name %>' MaxLength="50"
                    CssClass="form-control"></asp:TextBox>
            </div>
        </EditItemTemplate>
        <InsertItemTemplate>
            <div class="col-xs-11 col-insert">
                <asp:TextBox runat="server" ID="txtName"
                    Text='<%# BindItem.Name %>' MaxLength="50"
                    CssClass="form-control"></asp:TextBox>
            </div>
        </InsertItemTemplate>
        <ItemTemplate>
            <asp:Label runat="server" ID="lblName"
                Text='<%# Item.Name %>'></asp:Label>
        </ItemTemplate>
    </asp:TemplateField>
    .
    .
    <asp:TemplateField HeaderText="Category:">
        <EditItemTemplate>
            <div class="col-xs-11 col-edit">
                <asp:DropDownList runat="server" ID="ddlCategory"
                    OnCallingDataMethods="Control_CallingDataMethods"
                    SelectMethod="GetCategories"
                    DataTextField="LongName" DataValueField="CategoryID"
                    SelectedValue='<%# BindItem.CategoryID %>'
                    CssClass="form-control">
                </asp:DropDownList>
            </div>
        </EditItemTemplate>
```

Figure 18-20   The aspx file for the Product Maintenance application (part 2 of 3)

The Default.aspx file   **Page 3**

```
            <InsertItemTemplate>
                <div class="col-xs-11 col-insert">
                    <asp:DropDownList runat="server" ID="ddlCategory"
                    OnCallingDataMethods="Control_CallingDataMethods"
                    SelectMethod="GetCategories"
                    DataTextField="LongName" DataValueField="CategoryID"
                    SelectedValue='<%# BindItem.CategoryID %>'
                    CssClass="form-control"></asp:DropDownList>
                </div>
            </InsertItemTemplate>
            <ItemTemplate>
                <asp:Label runat="server" ID="lblCategory"
                    Text='<%# Item.CategoryID %>'></asp:Label>
            </ItemTemplate>
        </asp:TemplateField>
                .
                .
                .
        <asp:TemplateField HeaderText="On Hand:">
            <EditItemTemplate>
                <div class="col-xs-11 col-edit">
                    <asp:TextBox runat="server" ID="txtOnHand"
                        Text='<%# BindItem.OnHand %>'
                        CssClass="form-control"></asp:TextBox>
                </div>
            </EditItemTemplate>
            <InsertItemTemplate>
                <div class="col-xs-11 col-insert">
                    <asp:TextBox runat="server" ID="txtOnHand"
                        Text='<%# BindItem.OnHand %>'
                        CssClass="form-control"></asp:TextBox>
                </div>
            </InsertItemTemplate>
            <ItemTemplate>
                <asp:Label runat="server" ID="lblOnHand"
                    Text='<%# Item.OnHand %>'></asp:Label>
            </ItemTemplate>
        </asp:TemplateField>
        <asp:CommandField ButtonType="Link"
            ShowDeleteButton="true"
            ShowEditButton="true"
            ShowInsertButton="true" />
    </Fields>
    <RowStyle BackColor="#e7e7e7" />
    <CommandRowStyle BackColor="#8c8c8c" ForeColor="white" />
</asp:DetailsView>
</div>
```

Figure 18-20   The aspx file for the Product Maintenance application (part 3 of 3)

The code-behind file

Figure 18-21 shows the code-behind file for the Default.aspx page. The first event handler in this file is for the CallingDataMethods event of the GridView, DetailsView, and drop-down list controls. As you can see, this event handler creates an instance of the ProductDB data access class and then assigns it to the DataMethodsObject property of the CallingDataMethodsEventArgs object that's passed to the event handler. That way, the controls know where to find the select, update, delete, and insert methods they need.

The next three event handlers are for the ItemDeleted, ItemInserted, and ItemUpdated events of the DetailsView control. Each of these methods simply calls the DataBind method of the GridView control. That way, that control will always display the correct products.

The last event handler is one that you've seen throughout this section. It causes thead and tbody elements to be rendered for the GridView control so the Bootstrap classes can be applied properly.

The Default.aspx.cs file

```
public partial class Default : System.Web.UI.Page
{
    protected void Control_CallingDataMethods(
        object sender, CallingDataMethodsEventArgs e)
    {
        e.DataMethodsObject =
            new Ch18ProductMaintenance.Models.ProductDB();
    }

    protected void dvProduct_ItemDeleted(
        object sender, DetailsViewDeletedEventArgs e)
    {
        grdProducts.DataBind();
    }

    protected void dvProduct_ItemInserted(
        object sender, DetailsViewInsertedEventArgs e)
    {
        grdProducts.DataBind();
    }

    protected void dvProduct_ItemUpdated(
        object sender, DetailsViewUpdatedEventArgs e)
    {
        grdProducts.DataBind();
    }

    protected void grdProducts_PreRender(object sender, EventArgs e)
    {
        grdProducts.HeaderRow.TableSection = TableRowSection.TableHeader;
    }
}
```

Figure 18-21   The code-behind file for the Product Maintenance application

The ProductDB class

Figure 18-22 presents the ProductDB data access class that's used by this application. This class starts with the using directives that are needed to handle concurrency and data validation errors. Note that there's no using directive for the Models folder. That's because this file is in the Models folder, so it can access other classes in that folder without having to use fully-qualified names.

The ProductDB class has a private variable named db that stores a HalloweenEntities object context. This object context is instantiated in the constructor for the class. Then, this object is used by the six public methods in this class that provide for select, update, delete, and insert operations.

This class includes three select methods. The one named GetProducts is used to get the products that are displayed in the GridView control. Because this method returns an IQueryable object, it can implement paging and sorting as shown in figure 18-10.

The GetProduct method is used to get the product that's displayed in the DetailsView control. The product that's retrieved is determined by the product that's selected in the GridView control. This method starts by checking if the value that's passed from the GridView control is null, which happens the first time the page is loaded. Then, the method returns the first product after the products are ordered by name. Since the products in the GridView control are ordered by name by default, that means that the data for the first product in the GridView control is displayed.

If the value that's passed by the GridView control isn't null, the GetProduct method continues by calling the private GetProductById method. This method simply returns the product with the specified ID.

The GetCategories method returns the categories ordered by long name. These categories are displayed in the drop-down lists in the EditItem and InsertItem templates of the DetailsView control to make it easy for the user to select a category.

The InsertProduct method inserts a product into the Products table with the data the user enters in the DetailsView control. It accepts a ModelMethodContext object from the DetailsView control. Then, it uses this object to add a new product with the values from the DetailsView control to the model object and to check if any errors occurred during that operation. If no errors occurred, it then adds the product to the collection of objects in the object context and updates the database.

If a validation exception is thrown when the database is updated, a private method named HandleValidationError is called. If any other exception is thrown, a private method named HandleError is called. The signatures for these methods are shown at the end of this class. Note that the ModelMethodContext object is passed to both of these methods. That way, the methods can add an appropriate error message to the page's ModelStateDictionary object.

The ProductDB.cs file in the Models folder   **Page 1**

```
...
using System.Web.UI.WebControls;
using System.Data.Entity.Infrastructure;
using System.Data.Entity.Validation;

public class ProductDB
{
    HalloweenEntities db;
    public ProductDB()
    {
        db = new HalloweenEntities();
    }
    public IQueryable<Product> GetProducts()
    {
        return from p in db.Products
                orderby p.Name
                select p;
    }
    public Product GetProduct([Control] string grdProducts)
    {
        if (grdProducts == null)
            return (from p in db.Products
                    orderby p.Name
                    select p).FirstOrDefault();
        else
            return GetProductById(grdProducts);
    }
    private Product GetProductById(string id)
    {
        return (from p in db.Products
                where p.ProductID == id
                select p).FirstOrDefault();
    }
    public IQueryable<Category> GetCategories()
    {
        return from c in db.Categories
                orderby c.LongName
                select c;
    }
    public void InsertProduct(ModelMethodContext cxt)
    {
        var item = new Product();
        cxt.TryUpdateModel(item);
        if (cxt.ModelState.IsValid)
        {
            db.Products.Add(item);
            try {
                db.SaveChanges();
            }
            catch (DbEntityValidationException ex) {
                HandleValidationError(ex, cxt);
            }
            catch (Exception ex) {
                HandleError(ex, cxt);
            }
        }
    }
```

Figure 18-22   The ProductDB file for the Product Maintenance application (part 1 of 2)

The UpdateProduct method updates the selected product with the data the user enters in the DetailsView control. It accepts two parameters: a string that contains the product ID and a ModelMethodContext object. Both of these values are passed from the DetailsView control. Notice that the ProductID parameter has the same name and data type as the column that's identified by the DataKeyNames property of the control.

The update method uses the GetProductById method to retrieve the product to be updated. This is the same method that's used by the GetProduct method to get the product that's displayed in the DetailsView control. If this product isn't found, an error is added to the ModelStateDictionary object and the method ends. Otherwise, the TryUpdateModel method is used to update the model object with the data in the DetailsView control. If no errors occur, the updated product is saved to the database.

Like the insert method, the update method catches any exceptions that are thrown when the database is updated. That includes concurrency exceptions as well as validation exceptions and other exceptions. If a concurrency exception is thrown, a private method named HandleConcurrencyError is called. Notice that in addition to the Exception object and the ModelMethodContext object, this method accepts a Boolean value that indicates if a product is being updated or deleted. That way, a different message can be displayed for update and delete operations.

The DeleteProduct method deletes the product that's selected in the GridView control and displayed in the DetailsView control. It accepts a product ID and a ModelMethodContext object from the DetailsView control just like the update method. It also uses the GetProductById method to get the product to be deleted. If that product is found, it's marked for deletion and then deleted from the database.

Notice that nothing happens if the product isn't found. To understand why, you need to remember that an application ends after it generates a web page. Because of that, the object context is null when the user clicks the Delete button. Then, if the product isn't found in the database, nothing needs to be done because the product doesn't exist in the object context. If you wanted to, though, you could notify the user that the product has already been deleted, but that isn't usually necessary.

Also notice that this code catches concurrency exceptions. A concurrency exception can occur if the product is deleted by another user between the time it's retrieved at the beginning of the DeleteProduct method and the time the database is updated. Although that's unlikely to happen, you should still provide for this possibility.

The ProductDB.cs file in the Models folder   **Page 2**

```csharp
public void UpdateProduct(string ProductID, ModelMethodContext cxt)
{
    Product item = GetProductById(ProductID);
    if (item == null) {
        cxt.ModelState.AddModelError(
            "", $"Item with id {ProductID} was not found");
        return;
    }
    cxt.TryUpdateModel(item);
    if (cxt.ModelState.IsValid) {
        try {
            db.SaveChanges();
        }
        catch (DbUpdateConcurrencyException ex) {
            HandleConcurrencyError(ex, cxt, IsEdit: true);
        }
        catch (DbEntityValidationException ex) {
            HandleValidationError(ex, cxt);
        }
        catch (Exception ex) {
            HandleError(ex, cxt);
        }
    }
}
public void DeleteProduct(string ProductID, ModelMethodContext cxt)
{
    Product item = GetProductById(ProductID);
    if (item != null) {
        db.Products.Remove(item);
        try {
            db.SaveChanges();
        }
        catch (DbUpdateConcurrencyException ex) {
            HandleConcurrencyError(ex, cxt, IsEdit: false);
        }
        catch (Exception ex) {
            HandleError(ex, cxt);
        }
    }
}
private void HandleConcurrencyError(DbUpdateConcurrencyException ex,
    ModelMethodContext cxt, bool IsEdit)
{
    ...
}
private void HandleValidationError(DbEntityValidationException ex,
    ModelMethodContext cxt)
{
    ...
}
private void HandleError(Exception ex, ModelMethodContext cxt)
{
    ...
}
}
```

Figure 18-22   The ProductDB file for the Product Maintenance application (part 2 of 2)

How to use data annotations to validate data

Instead of creating an Entity Data Model that you can work with in the Entity Designer as you saw earlier in this chapter, you can create it using a feature of the Entity Framework called *Code First development*. When you use Code First development, you can work with the Entity Data Model only in the Code Editor. Many developers prefer this technique because it gives them more control over how the model works. It also makes it easier to understand how the Entity Framework enforces validation like you saw earlier in this chapter. Once you understand that, you can customize the validation so it works just the way you want. That's true whether you work with a model in the designer or in code.

In the topics that follow, you'll learn how to create an Entity Data Model from an existing database using Code First. Then, you'll learn how to use data annotations to add validation to your entity classes. Finally, you'll learn how to put your custom data annotations in separate class files.

How to create a Code First model from an existing database

Figure 18-23 shows how to create an Entity Data Model from an existing database using Code First. To do that, you select the Code First from Database option from the first step of the Entity Data Model Wizard. Then you select a connection and the database objects you want to use. Note, however, that you don't choose the version of the Entity Framework that you want to use. That's because Code First uses the most current release of Entity Framework 6 by default.

When you click the Finish button, the Entity Framework will create a C# class file for the object context, as well as individual C# class files for each database object that you selected. If you select the Categories and Products tables from the Halloween database as shown here, for example, the Entity Framework will create a file named Halloween.cs for the object context, a file named Category.cs for the Categories table, and a file named Product.cs for the Products table. The Category.cs and Product.cs files are like the business classes you've seen throughout this book, except that they include data annotations that provide for validation. You'll see how to work with data annotations next.

The Entity Data Model Wizard for Code First development

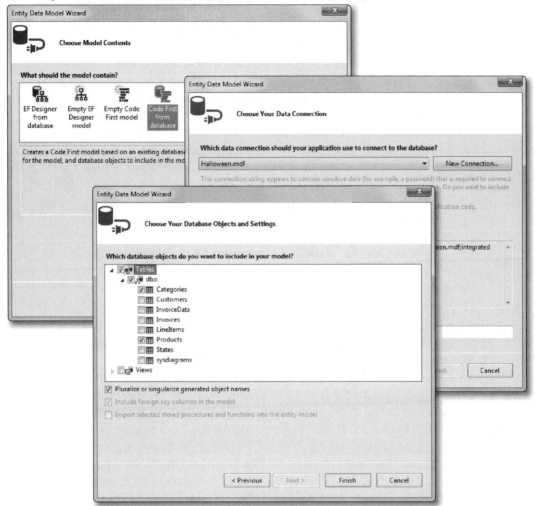

Description

- The Entity Framework's *Code First development* provides for creating an object model entirely in code rather than working in the Entity Data Model Designer.
- To create an Entity Data Model from an existing database using Code First, you select Code First from Database from the first step of the Entity Data Model Wizard. Then, you select a connection and the data objects you want to use.
- Foreign key columns are always included when you use Code First, and you can't include stored procedures and functions.
- When you click the Finish button in the last step, the Entity Framework creates a class file for the object context and opens it in the Code Editor. It also creates a class file for each of the database objects.

Figure 18-23   How to create a Code First model from an existing database

How to work with data annotations

The table in figure 18-24 shows some of the *data annotation attributes* that you can use to set validation rules for the properties in an entity class when you use Code First. The Entity Framework includes some of these data annotation attributes by default when you use Code First. For instance, the first code example in this figure shows the attributes that are added by default to the Name property of the Product class. The Required attribute is added because the database column doesn't accept null values, and the StringLength attribute is added to indicate the maximum number of characters that can be stored in the column. That way, if a user doesn't enter data in one of these columns or enters data that is longer than the specified length, a data validation error will be thrown. Then, that error will be caught and handled by the data validation code you saw in figure 18-17.

Note that the data validation attributes are stored in the System.ComponentModel.DataAnnotations namespace. Because of that, a using directive for this namespace is included in each entity class.

When you use Code First, you may see data annotations like this:

```
[System.Diagnostics.CodeAnalysis.SuppressMessage(...)]
```

These annotations are used by the code analysis feature of Team Foundation Server (TFS). If you're not using TFS, or you're not using its code analysis feature, you can delete these annotations if you'd like.

You can also customize the data annotation attributes that the Entity Framework generates, and you can add additional attributes. For instance, the second example in this figure shows how to add a custom error message to the Required attribute for the Name property, and the third example shows how to add a Range attribute to the OnHand property. Notice in the second example that the StringLength attribute has also been modified so it specifies a minimum length.

How to store data annotations in a separate file

When you use Code First, you can't update the model with changes made to the database like you can when you use the designer. However, you can achieve the same effect by deleting the generated class files and then following the steps in figure 18-23 to generate new class files based on the updated database. When you do that, though, you'll lose any changes and additions you made to the data annotations. One way to avoid that is to store these annotations in a separate class file, as shown in the last example in figure 18-24.

Here, two of the properties of the Product class that have custom data annotation attributes were stored in a new class named ProductMetadata. Then, a new class with the same name as the entity class was created. This class is defined as a partial class, so it's combined with the partial entity class. It also includes a MetadataType attribute that names the class that contains the custom attributes. Because this attribute is included in the System.ComponentModel.DataAnnotations namespace, you should include a using directive for this namespace in the class. Note that you can use this technique whether you're using Code First or the Entity Framework Designer.

Some of the data annotation attributes used for validation with Code First

Attribute	Description
Compare	Compares two properties.
ConcurrencyCheck	Specifies that a property participates in optimistic concurrency checks.
Key	One or more properties that uniquely identify an entity.
Range	Specifies numeric range constraints for the value of a property.
Required	Specifies that a property is required.
StringLength	Specifies the minimum and maximum number of characters allowed.

Data annotation attributes that are generated for the Name property of the Product entity class

```
[Required]
[StringLength(50)]
public string Name { get; set; }
```

How to add a custom error message and specify a minimum length

```
[Required(ErrorMessage = "You must enter a name for the product.")]
[StringLength(50, MinimumLength = 5)]
public string Name { get; set; }
```

How to check that a property's value is within a specified range

```
[Range(1, 50)]
public int OnHand { get; set; }
```

How to store data annotations in a separate class file

A class that contains data annotations for the Product entity class

```
public class ProductMetadata
{
    [Range(1.0, 499.99, ErrorMessage = "Unit Price must be between $1 and
    $499.99"))]
    public decimal UnitPrice { get; set; }

    [Range(1, 50, ErrorMessage = "On Hand must be between 1 and 50.")]
    public int OnHand { get; set; }
}
```

A partial class that allows the Product entity class to use the data annotations

```
[MetadataType(typeof(ProductMetadata))]
public partial class Product { }
```

Description

- When you use Code First, the Entity Framework generates classes that include *data annotation attributes* that provide for validation. You can customize these attributes, and you can store them in a separate class file so they're not overwritten if you regenerate the class files from the database.

- You can also add data annotation attributes to entity classes that you work with in the designer by storing them in a separate class file.

Figure 18-24   How to work with data annotations

Perspective

In this chapter, you've learned how to use model binding to build applications that separate the presentation code from the data access code. Unlike the applications in chapter 17 that used object data sources to separate the presentation and data access code, you can bind data directly to a data control when you use model binding. You can also create strongly typed data controls that give you more flexibility for working with the data that the control is bound to.

Although this chapter focused on using the Entity Framework to get the data that's used in model binding, you should know that model binding also works with standard ADO.NET data access techniques like the ones you learned in chapter 17. For more information on model binding, see the MSDN documentation. For more information on using the Entity Framework with ASP.NET, see this ASP.NET website: http://www.asp.net/entity-framework.

Terms

Entity Framework (EF)	lazy loading
Entity Data Model	eager loading
entity	query path
Entity Data Model Designer	cascading deletes
Entity Designer	model binding
entity class	strongly typed data control
association	method stub
scalar property	model binding attribute
navigation property	Code First development
LINQ to Entities	data annotation attribute
object context	

Summary

- The *Entity Framework* (*EF*) provides an interface between the database and the objects used by an application. It also provides for submitting changes to the database.

- To use EF, you create an *Entity Data Model* that includes the objects, or *entities*, you need. Then, you create an instance of the *object context* for that model, and you use *LINQ to Entities* to query the model.

- By default, LINQ to Entities uses *lazy loading*, which means that objects that are related to other objects you retrieve aren't loaded until they're referred to in code. To load related objects at the same time as the objects they're related to, you can use the Include method to do *eager loading*.

- You can bind the entity classes of an Entity Data Model directly to a data control using a technique called *model binding*. To make it easier to work with the properties of a data-bound object from the control, you set the ItemType property of the control to the type of objects it displays. This makes the control *strongly typed*.

- You specify the select, update, insert, and delete methods for a bound control on the SelectMethod, UpdateMethod, InsertMethod, and DeleteMethod properties of the control. You can generate *method stubs* for each of these methods using Visual Studio's IntelliSense.

- You can use *model binding attributes* to filter data. These attributes indicate the source of the value that's used for filtering.

- The select method that Visual Studio generates for a bound control has a return type of IQueryable, which makes it easy to enable sorting and paging for the control.

- The Page object has a TryUpdateModel method that retrieves values from a bound control and updates the model object with that data. It also has as a ModelState property that provides access to a ModelStateDictionary object that stores model errors. You can use this property to check for errors when the model object is updated.

- You can handle concurrency and data validation errors by placing code that inserts, updates, or deletes data within a try-catch statement.

- You can use a ValidationSummary control to display the error messages in the page's ModelStateDictionary object by setting the control's ShowModelStateErrors property to True.

- If you put the data access code for model binding in a separate class, you must code an event handler for the CallingDataMethods event of the bound control that creates an instance of the class.

- When you use a separate data access class, the bound control passes a ModelMethodContext object to the data access methods of the class. You can use this object to access the TryUpdateModel method and the ModelState property.

- If you create an Entity Data Model using *Code First*, the Entity Framework generates *data annotation attributes* that it uses to enforce data validation. You can customize these attributes and store them in a separate class file. You can also code data annotation attributes in a separate class when you use the designer.

Exercise 18-1   Create a Customer List application

In this exercise, you'll develop an application that uses an Entity Data Model and model binding to display a list of customers in a GridView control for the state that's selected from a drop-down list. To make that easier, you'll start from an application that contains the starting page, along with the database, image, and style sheets used by the page.

Review the code for the page
1. Open the Ex18CustomerList application in the C:\aspnet46_cs directory.
2. Review the code for the Default.aspx page, and notice that it already contains the drop-down list and GridView controls. However, no data sources are specified for these controls.

Create the Entity Data Model

3. Use the Entity Data Model Wizard as described in figures 18-1 and 18-2 to create an Entity Data Model named HalloweenModel that includes the Customers and States tables from the Halloween database in the App_Data folder. Be sure to add this model to the Models folder.

4. Review the entities in the Entity Data Model Designer. In particular, notice the navigation property that's defined for each table.

5. Build the project so the Entity Data Model is available as you bind the data controls.

Bind the drop-down list to the State entity type

6. Display the code-behind file for the page, and notice that it already contains the code for making the GridView control work with Bootstrap.

7. Declare a class-level variable that contains an instance of the HalloweenEntities object context.

8. Display the aspx code for the page. Then, add an ItemType property for the drop-down list and set its value to the State entity class. Now, add a SelectMethod property and notice that Visual Studio doesn't provide a completion list. Enter the name ddlStates_GetData for this property.

9. Return to the code-behind file, and add a using directive for the Models folder so you don't have to qualify the names of the entity classes.

10. Add a declaration for the ddlStates_GetData method. Code a LINQ to Entities query for this method that retrieves all the states ordered by state name, and return this query to the drop-down list.

Bind the GridView control to the Customer entity type

11. Return to the aspx code, add an ItemType property for the GridView control, and set its value to the Customer entity class. Then, add a SelectMethod property and select the Create New Method option when it's displayed.

12. Return to the code-behind file and simplify the declaration for the select method by removing the qualification from the Customer class.

13. Add a parameter to the select method so the state code for the customers to be displayed will be retrieved from the drop-down list.

14. Add code to the select method that checks if the parameter is null. If it is, get the first State object from the database after the states are sorted by state name, and assign the StateCode value for that state to the parameter.

15. Code a LINQ to Entities query that retrieves all the customers for the selected state ordered by last name, and return the query to the GridView control.

16. Run the application to see that Alabama is displayed in the drop-down list and the customers in Alabama are displayed in the GridView control. Select other states from the drop-down list to be sure this works. When you're done, close the browser window.

Section 4

Finishing an ASP.NET application

This section consists of four chapters that present ASP.NET skills that are often used in professional web applications. To start, chapter 19 shows you how to use a secure connection for an application, and chapter 20 shows you how to authenticate and authorize the users of an application. These are essential skills for e-commerce applications.

Next, chapter 21 shows you how to use email and custom error pages as well as how to deal with the problems that can occur when users click the Back buttons in their browsers. These are useful skills for most professional applications. Then, chapter 22 shows you how to deploy an application.

Because each of the chapters in this section is written as an independent module, you can read these chapters in whatever sequence you prefer. Eventually, though, you'll want to read all of these chapters because you should at least be aware of the capabilities that they describe.

19

How to secure a web application

Security is one of the most important concerns for any developer of e-commerce web applications. To secure a web application, you must make sure that the private data that's sent between the client and the server can't be deciphered. To accomplish that, this chapter shows you how to use an Internet protocol called TLS/SSL.

An introduction to TLS/SSL

To prevent others from reading data that's transmitted over the Internet, you use an Internet protocol that provides for encryption. The most current and most secure protocol is *Transport Layer Security*, or *TLS*. TLS replaces its predecessor, called *Secure Sockets Layer*, or *SSL*. Although SSL should no longer be used in new development, TLS is often referred to as SSL or in conjunction with SSL. In fact, as you'll see in figure 19-3, Visual Studio still uses the term SSL. To make it clear that you're using TLS, though, this chapter uses the term TLS/SSL. The topics that follow explain how TLS/SSL works and how you enable it for an application that uses IIS Express.

How secure connections work

Figure 19-1 shows a web page that uses TLS/SSL to transfer data between the server and the client over a *secure connection*. To determine if you're transmitting data over a secure connection, you can read the URL in the browser's address bar. If it starts with HTTPS rather than HTTP, then you're transmitting data over a secure connection.

With a regular HTTP connection, all data is sent as unencrypted text. As a result, if a hacker intercepts this data, it is easy to read. With a secure connection, though, all data that's transferred between the client and the server is encrypted. Although this data can still be intercepted, a hacker won't be able to read it without breaking the encryption code.

Notice here that a lock icon displays in the upper right of the browser's address bar. This is common to many browsers, and is another way to tell that you're on a secure connection.

A page that was requested with a secure connection

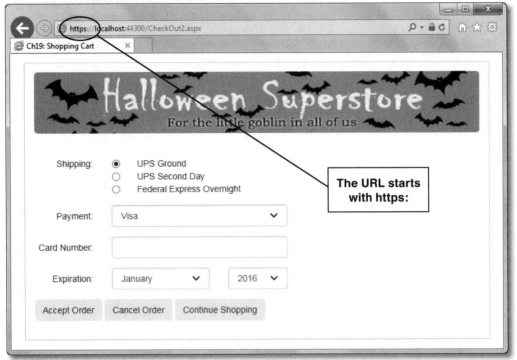

Description

- *Transport Layer Security*, or *TLS*, is the most current protocol used by the World Wide Web to allow clients and servers to communicate over a *secure connection*. TLS is the successor to the *Secure Sockets Layer*, or *SSL*,

- With TLS/SSL, the browser encrypts all data that's sent to the server and decrypts all data that's received from the server. Conversely, the server encrypts all data that's sent to the browser and decrypts all data that's received from the browser.

- TLS/SSL is able to determine if data has been tampered with during transit.

- TLS/SSL is also able to verify that a server or a client is who it claims to be.

- The URL for a secure connection starts with HTTPS instead of HTTP.

- With many browsers, a lock icon is displayed when a secure connection is being used.

Figure 19-1 How secure connections work

How digital secure certificates work

In the next figure, you'll learn how to use TLS/SSL with a project that uses IIS Express. When you do that, IIS Express generates a test certificate that you can use to test your application. When you deploy an application to a production server, though, you'll need to use a *digital secure certificate*. Figure 19-2 provides information about how these certificates work and where you get them.

Digital secure certificates serve two purposes. First, they establish the identity of the server or client. Second, they provide the information needed to encrypt data before it's transmitted.

By default, browsers are configured to accept certificates that come from trusted sources. If a browser doesn't recognize a certificate as coming from a trusted source, however, it informs the user and lets the user view the certificate. Then, the user can determine whether the certificate should be considered valid. If the user chooses to accept the certificate, a secure connection is established.

Sometimes, a server may want the client to authenticate itself with TLS/SSL *client authentication*. Although this isn't as common as TLS/SSL *server authentication*, it is used occasionally. For example, a bank might want to use client authentication to make sure it's sending sensitive information such as account numbers and balances to the correct person. To implement this type of authentication, a digital secure certificate must be installed on the client.

If you want to develop an ASP.NET application that uses TLS/SSL to secure client connections, you must first obtain a digital secure certificate from a trusted source such as those listed in this figure. These *certification authorities*, or *CAs*, verify that the person or company requesting the certificate is a valid person or company by checking with a *registration authority*, or *RA*. To obtain a digital secure certificate, you'll need to provide a registration authority with information about yourself or your company. Once the registration authority approves the request, the certification authority can issue the digital secure certificate.

A digital secure certificate from a trusted source isn't free, and the cost of the certificate will depend on a variety of factors including the level of security. As a result, when you purchase a digital certificate, you'll want one that fits the needs of your website. In particular, you'll need to decide what *TLS/SSL strength* you want the connection to support. TLS/SSL strength refers to the level of encryption that the secure connection uses when it transmits data.

Most certificates sold today provide for up to 256-bit TLS/SSL strength. It's nearly impossible to break the encryption code provided by this strength, but not all browsers support it. If a browser doesn't support it, however, the browser will use the maximum strength it does support.

Types of digital secure certificates

Certificate	Description
Server certificate	Issued to trusted servers so client computers can connect to them using secure connections.
Client certificate	Issued to trusted clients so server computers can confirm their identity.

Common certification authorities that issue digital secure certificates

```
www.symantec.com
www.geotrust.com
www.entrust.com
www.thawte.com
www.digicert.com
```

Concepts

- *Authentication* determines whether a server or client is who it claims to be.

- When a browser makes an initial attempt to communicate with a server over a secure connection that uses TLS/SSL, the server authenticates itself by sending its *digital secure certificate* to the browser.

- In some instances, the server may also request that a browser authenticate itself by presenting its own digital secure certificate. This is uncommon, however.

- To use TLS/SSL in your web applications, you must first purchase a digital secure certificate from a trusted *certification authority*, or *CA*. Once you obtain the certificate, you send it to the people who host your website so they can install it on the server.

- A certification authority is a company that issues and manages security credentials. To verify information provided by the requestor of the secure certificate, a CA must check with a *registration authority*, or *RA*. Once the registration authority verifies the requestor's information, the certification authority can issue a digital secure certificate.

- Since TLS/SSL is built into all major browsers and web servers, installing a digital secure certificate enables TLS/SSL.

- *TLS/SSL strength* refers to the length of the generated key that is created during the encryption process. The longer the key, the more difficult it is to break the encryption code.

- The TLS/SSL strength that's used depends on the strength provided by the certificate, the strength supported by the web server, and the strength supported by the browser. If a web server or browser isn't able to support the strength provided by the certificate, a lesser strength is used.

Note

- If IIS is installed on your local computer, you can use the IIS Management Console to request and install certificates. To display this console, display the Control Panel, click the Administrative Tools link, and then double-click on Internet Information Services (IIS) Manager. For information on installing IIS, see appendix A.

Figure 19-2 How digital secure certificates work

How to enable TLS/SSL for a project that uses IIS Express

When you create an application that runs under IIS Express, it's assigned a port number on the local server. You can see this port number in the address bar after the localhost keyword when you run the application. You can also see this port number in the URL property for the project, which is in the Properties pane.

To use TLS/SSL with an application that runs under IIS Express, you simply set the SSL Enabled property of the project to True. Then, the secure URL for the application is displayed in the SSL URL property. Usually this secure URL uses port 44300, which is the standard port for HTTPS when you use IIS Express.

The first time you run an application that has its SSL Enabled property set to True, the first dialog box in figure 19-3 is displayed. If you click the Yes button to trust the certificate that's generated by IIS Express, another dialog box is displayed warning you that Windows can't validate the certificate. If you click the Yes button in this dialog box, Internet Explorer will treat the certificate as trusted, and it will function just as if you have a digital secure certificate. Note, however, that browsers other than Internet Explorer might still treat the certificate as untrusted.

If you click the No button from either the first or second dialog box, the certificate will be treated by all browsers as untrusted. Then, in Internet Explorer, a page like the first one shown here will be displayed. This page tells you that there's a problem with the website's security certificate and lets you choose whether to go to the website. If you click the "Continue to this website" link, Internet Explorer loads the website on a secure connection but displays a Certificate Error message and gives the address bar a red background. The other major browsers provide similar warnings about untrusted certificates.

The dialog box that's displayed
when you run a TLS/SSL enabled application

The page that's displayed in IE if you choose not to trust the certificate

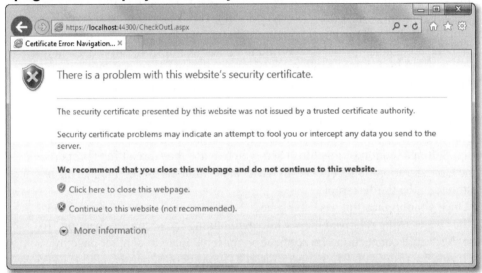

The address bar in IE if you continue to the website

Description

- To use TLS/SSL with a web application that's running under IIS Express, select the project in the Solution Explorer and then set its SSL Enabled property to True.

- The first time you run the application, you're asked if you want to trust the certificate that IIS Express generates. If you don't, you'll receive a warning that there's a problem with the website's security certificate. If you continue to the site, the address bar will indicate that there's an error with the certificate.

Figure 19-3   How to enable TLS/SSL for development in Visual Studio

How to use a secure connection

In the topics that follow, you'll first learn how to request secure connections for the pages of your applications. Then, you'll learn how to force a page to use a secure connection when a user bypasses your navigation features.

How to request a secure connection

Figure 19-4 shows how to request a secure connection in an ASP.NET application. To do that, you execute a Response.Redirect method with the URL for the HTTPS protocol rather than the URL for the HTTP protocol.

When you request a secure connection using HTTPS, you must use an absolute URL. If you're using IIS Express, that means that the URL must include the domain name and the port number. For example, the first URL in this figure specifies //localhost as the web server's domain name and 44300 as the port number. This is followed by the name of the page to be displayed.

Rather than including the domain name and port number in each URL, you may want to store this information in the Web.config file as shown in the second example in this figure. This information is stored as an element within the appSettings section of this file. Then, you can use the AppSettings property of the ConfigurationManager class to retrieve the value of this element. This is illustrated in the third example.

Once your application has established a secure connection, it can navigate to other pages using relative URLs while maintaining the secure connection. To close the secure connection, the application must navigate to another page by specifying an absolute URL that uses the HTTP protocol rather than the HTTPS protocol. This is illustrated in the last example in this figure. This example uses the second element in the appSettings section of the Web.config file, which specifies the HTTP protocol, localhost for the domain name, and 57035 for the port number, which is the port number that was assigned to this application.

A URL that requests a secure connection for IIS Express

```
https://localhost:44300/CheckOut1.aspx
```

A Web.config file that defines secure and unsecure path settings

```
<?xml version="1.0"?>
<configuration>
    <appSettings>
        <add key="SecurePath" value="https://localhost:44300/" />
        <add key="UnsecurePath" value="http://localhost:57035/" />
    </appSettings>
    .
    .
```

Code that retrieves the secure application path from the Web.config file

```
string url = ConfigurationManager.AppSettings["SecurePath"]
    + "CheckOut1.aspx";
Response.Redirect(url);
```

Code that returns to an unsecured connection

```
string url = ConfigurationManager.AppSettings["UnSecurePath"]
    + "Order.aspx";
Response.Redirect(url);
```

Description

- To request a secure connection, you must use an absolute URL that specifies HTTPS as the protocol. Once you establish a secure connection, you can use relative URLs to continue using the secure connection.

- To return to an unsecured connection after using a secure connection, you must code an absolute URL that specifies the HTTP protocol.

- Instead of including the application's path in each URL, you can store secure and unsecure paths in the appSettings section of the Web.config file. That way, if the paths change, you can change them in just one location.

- You can use the AppSettings property of the ConfigurationManager class within the application to access the elements in the appSettings section of the Web.config file. This class is in the System.Configuration namespace.

Figure 19-4   How to request a secure connection

How to force a page to use a secure connection

When you build a complete web application, you usually include navigation features such as menus or hyperlinks that guide the user from page to page. Unfortunately, users sometimes bypass your navigation features and access pages in your application directly. For example, a user might bookmark a page in your application and return to it later. Other users might simply type the URL of individual pages in your application into their browser's address bar. Some users do this innocently; others do it in an attempt to bypass your application's security features.

Because of that, a page that should use TLS/SSL to send or receive sensitive information shouldn't assume that a secure connection has been established. Instead, it should check for a secure connection and establish one if necessary. To do that, you can use the properties of the HttpRequest class shown in figure 19-5.

To check for a secure connection, you use the IsSecureConnection property. Then, if the connection isn't secure, you can switch to a secure connection as shown in the first example in this figure. This example uses the same technique that was shown in the previous figure, and it's appropriate if you're using IIS Express. Notice that you typically include this code at the beginning of the Load method for the page. That way, you can be sure that no other code is executed until a secure connection is established.

Note that this technique can be simplified if you're using a server other than IIS Express. If you're using IIS on your local computer, for example, no port number is required. Instead, you include the localhost domain name, followed by the application path like this:

```
https://localhost/aspnet_46/Ch19Cart/
```

In this case, you can use the technique shown in the second example. Here, the Url property is used to retrieve the URL for the page. Then, this URL is modified so it uses the HTTPS protocol. After you do that, you can use the Redirect method to redirect the browser using the new URL.

Properties of the HttpRequest class for working with secure connections

Property	Description
`IsSecureConnection`	Returns True if the current connection is secure. Otherwise, returns False.
`Url`	The URL of the current request.

A Page_Load method that forces the page to use a secure connection

```
protected void Page_Load(object sender, EventArgs e)
{
    if (!Request.IsSecureConnection)
    {
        string url = ConfigurationManager.AppSettings["SecurePath"]
            + "CheckOut1.aspx";
        Response.Redirect(url);
    }
}
```

A statement that replaces the HTTP protocol with the HTTPS protocol

```
string url = Request.Url.ToString().Replace("http:", "https:");
```

Description

- If a page requires the user to enter sensitive information, such as passwords or credit card data, it should make sure that it's operating on a secure connection. To do that, the page should check the IsSecureConnection property of the HttpRequest object in its Load event handler.

- If the page isn't using a secure connection, it should switch to a secure connection to protect the privacy of the user's data. To do that, it can replace the unsecure application path with a secure application path.

- If your application is using a server other than IIS Express, you can switch to a secure connection by replacing the HTTP protocol in the URL to HTTPS and then redirecting the browser to the new URL. To get the current URL, you can use the Url property of the HttpRequest object.

Figure 19-5   How to force a page to use a secure connection

A Shopping Cart application that uses TLS/SSL

To show how secure connections are used in a typical application, the next two topics present a version of the Shopping Cart application that uses TLS/SSL.

The operation of the Shopping Cart application

Figure 19-6 shows the five pages of the Shopping Cart application. As you can see, this application lets the user select products and display the shopping cart without establishing a secure connection. When the user clicks the Check Out button from the Cart page, however, a secure connection is established. The secure connection is then maintained while the two Check Out pages and the Confirmation page are displayed. When the user clicks the Return to Order Page button on the Confirmation page, however, the Order page is redisplayed with an unsecured connection.

The code for the Shopping Cart application

Figure 19-7 presents the code for using TLS/SSL in the Shopping Cart application. At the top of the first page of this figure, you can see the code for the Click event of the Check Out button on the Cart page. This code creates a URL that uses the value of the element with the SecurePath key that's specified in the appSettings section of the Web.config file. As you recall from figure 19-4, this value uses the HTTPS protocol. Then, the code redirects the browser to the first Check Out page using a secure connection.

In the code for the first Check Out page, you can see that the Load event handler checks if a secure connection has been established. If not, a URL with the SecurePath key is created. Then, the browser is redirected to that URL, which uses a secure connection.

If the user clicks the Continue Checkout button, a relative URL is used to display the second Check Out page, which means that the secure connection is maintained. If the user clicks the Cancel or Continue Shopping button, however, the browser is redirected to the Order page with an unsecured connection.

The code for the second Check Out page is shown in part 2 of this figure. Like the first Check Out page, its Load event handler makes sure that a secure connection is established before proceeding. In addition, if the user clicks the Cancel or Continue Shopping button, the Order page is redisplayed with an unsecured connection. If the user clicks the Accept Order button, however, the secure connection is maintained and the Confirmation page is displayed.

Some of the code for the Confirmation page is also shown in this figure. As you can see, if the user clicks the Return to Order Page button on this page, the Order page is redisplayed with an unsecured connection.

How security is used by the Shopping Cart application

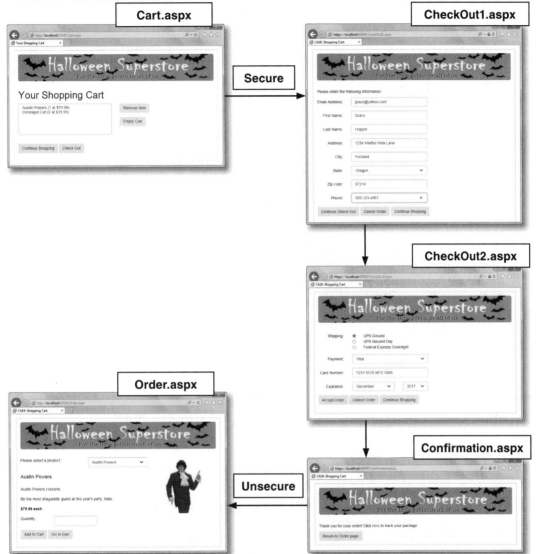

Description

- When the user clicks the Check Out button from the Cart page, the browser is redirected to the first Check Out page using a secure connection.

- When the user clicks the Continue Checkout button from the first Check Out page, the browser is redirected to the second Check Out page and remains in the secure connection.

- When the user clicks the Accept Order button from the second Check Out page, the browser is redirected to the Confirmation page and remains in the secure connection.

- When the user clicks the Return to Order Page button from the Confirmation page, the browser is redirected to the Order page in an unsecured connection.

Figure 19-6   The operation of the Shopping Cart application with TLS/SSL

Some of the C# code for the Cart page

```csharp
public partial class Cart : System.Web.UI.Page
{
    .
    .
    protected void btnCheckOut_Click(object sender, EventArgs e) {
        string url = ConfigurationManager.AppSettings["SecurePath"]
            + "CheckOut1.aspx";
        Response.Redirect(url);
    }
}
```

Some of the C# code for the first Check Out page

```csharp
public partial class CheckOut1 : System.Web.UI.Page
{
    .
    .
    protected void Page_Load(object sender, EventArgs e) {
        if (!Request.IsSecureConnection)
        {
            string url = ConfigurationManager.AppSettings["SecurePath"]
                + "CheckOut1.aspx";
            Response.Redirect(url);
        }
    }

    protected void btnCheckOut_Click(object sender, EventArgs e) {
        if (IsValid)
        {
            .
            .
            Response.Redirect("CheckOut2.aspx");
        }
    }

    protected void btnCancel_Click(object sender, EventArgs e) {
        Session.Remove("Cart");
        String url = ConfigurationManager.AppSettings["UnsecurePath"]
            + "Order.aspx";
        Response.Redirect(url);
    }

    protected void btnContinue_Click(object sender, EventArgs e) {
        string url = ConfigurationManager.AppSettings["UnsecurePath"]
            + "Order.aspx";
        Response.Redirect(url);
    }
}
```

Figure 19-7   The code for the Shopping Cart application (part 1 of 2)

Some of the C# code for the second Check Out page

```csharp
public partial class CheckOut2 : System.Web.UI.Page
{
    .
    .
    .
    protected void Page_Load(object sender, EventArgs e) {
        if (!Request.IsSecureConnection)
        {
            String url = ConfigurationManager.AppSettings["SecurePath"]
                + "CheckOut2.aspx";
            Response.Redirect(url);
        }
        .
        .
        .
    }

    protected void btnAccept_Click(object sender, EventArgs e) {
        if (IsValid)
        {
            .
            .
            .
            Response.Redirect("Confirmation.aspx");
        }
    }

    protected void btnCancel_Click(object sender, EventArgs e) {
        Session.Remove("Cart");
        String url = ConfigurationManager.AppSettings["UnsecurePath"]
            + "Order.aspx";
        Response.Redirect(url);
    }

    protected void btnContinue_Click(object sender, EventArgs e) {
        String url = ConfigurationManager.AppSettings["UnsecurePath"]
            + "Order.aspx";
        Response.Redirect(url);
    }
}
```

Some of the C# code for the Confirmation page

```csharp
public partial class Confirmation : System.Web.UI.Page
{
    .
    .
    .
    protected void btnReturn_Click(object sender, EventArgs e) {
        string url = ConfigurationManager.AppSettings["UnsecurePath"]
            + "Order.aspx";
        Response.Redirect(url);
    }
}
```

Figure 19-7   The code for the Shopping Cart application (part 2 of 2)

Perspective

Now that you've completed this chapter, you should be able to use TLS/SSL encryption to secure the data transmissions between client and server. That's one part of securing an application. The other part is making sure that only authorized users are able to use your application, and you'll learn how to provide for that in the next chapter.

By the way, if you're interested in seeing the rest of the code for the Shopping Cart application in this chapter, you should know that you can download all of the applications in this book from our website (www.murach.com). See appendix A for details.

Terms

Transport Layer Security (TLS)	client authentication
Secure Sockets Layer (SSL)	digital secure certificate
secure connection	certification authority (CA)
authentication	registration authority (RA)
server authentication	TLS/SSL strength

Summary

- To communicate over a *secure connection*, you use *Transport Layer Security*, or *TLS*. TLS is the successor to *Secure Sockets Layer*, or *SSL*. If you're using IIS Express, you can enable TLS/SSL by setting the SSL Enabled property of the project to True.

- When a browser uses TLS/SSL to communicate with a server, the server *authenticates* itself by sending its *digital secure certificate* to the browser. This is referred to as *server authentication*.

- A client can also use a digital secure certificate to authenticate itself using *client authentication*.

- You can obtain a digital secure certificate from a *certification authority* (*CA*), which checks with a *registration authority* (*RA*) to be sure that the request is from a valid person or company.

- When you purchase a digital certificate, you'll need to decide what *TLS/SSL strength* you need. The TLS/SSL strength determines the level of encryption that's used to transmit data over a secure connection.

- To request a secure connection, you use the absolute URL for the HTTPS protocol. Then, you can use relative URLs to maintain the secure connection. To close the secure connection, you use the absolute URL for the HTTP protocol.

- A page can use the IsSecureConnection property of the HttpRequest object to be sure that it's using a secure connection. It can also use the Url property of this object to get the URL of the current request.

20

How to authenticate and authorize users

In the last chapter, you learned how to secure the transmission of data between client and server. Now, you'll learn how to restrict access to some of the pages of an application, but let authorized users access those pages. To provide this functionality, you can use the new ASP.NET Identity system.

An introduction to authentication

If you want to limit access to all or part of your ASP.NET application to certain users, you can use *authentication* to verify each user's identity. Then, once you have authenticated the user, you can use *authorization* to check if the user has the appropriate privileges for accessing a page. That way, you can prevent unauthorized users from accessing pages that they shouldn't be able to access.

Three types of authentication

Figure 20-1 describes three types of authentication you can use in ASP.NET applications. The first, called *Windows-based authentication*, requires that you set up a Windows user account for each user. Then, you use standard Windows security features to restrict access to all or part of the application. When a user attempts to access the application, Windows displays a login dialog box that asks the user to supply the user name and password of the Windows account. This type of authentication is most appropriate for a local setting like a company intranet.

To use *individual user account authentication*, you have a login page that typically requires the user to enter a user name and password. Then, ASP.NET displays this page automatically when it needs to authenticate a user who's trying to access the application. ASP.NET automatically creates a database to store user data such as user names and passwords the first time a user registers with the application, and the Web Forms template that you learned about in chapter 2 includes a fully functional authentication system by default. That makes this type of authentication easy to use, and you'll see how this works as you progress through this chapter.

In recent years, authentication services offered by third parties such as Facebook or Google have also become popular. While this kind of authentication is beyond the scope of this book, the code that's generated by the Web Forms template includes sample code as well as links to more information about how to set up this type of authentication.

Windows-based authentication

- Causes the browser to display a login dialog box when the user attempts to access a restricted page.
- Is supported by most browsers.
- Is configured through the IIS management console.
- Uses Windows user accounts and directory rights to grant access to restricted pages.
- Is most appropriate for an intranet application.

Individual user account authentication

- Allows developers to code a login form that gets the user name and password.
- The user name and password entered by the user are encrypted if the login page uses a secure connection.
- Doesn't rely on Windows user accounts. Instead, the application determines how to authenticate users.

Third-party authentication services

- Provided by third parties using technologies like OpenID and OAuth. The Facebook, Google, and Twitter services are the most popular, but Microsoft also offers this kind of service.
- Allows users to use their existing logins, and frees developers from having to worry about the secure storage of user credentials.
- You can configure your ASP.NET applications to issue identities or accept identities from other web applications, and even access user data on other services.

Description

- *Authentication* refers to the process of validating the identity of a user so the user can be granted access to an application. A user must typically supply a user name and password to be authenticated.
- After a user is authenticated, the user must still be authorized to use the requested application. The process of granting user access to an application is called *authorization*.

Figure 20-1   Three types of authentication

How individual user account authentication works

To help you understand how individual user account authorization works, figure 20-2 shows a typical series of exchanges that occur between a web browser and a server when a user attempts to access a page that uses individual user accounts. The authentication process begins when a user requests the page. When the server receives the request, it checks to see if the user has already been authenticated. To do that, it looks for an *authentication cookie* in the request for the page. If it doesn't find the cookie, it redirects the browser to the login page.

Next, the user enters a user name and password and posts the login page back to the server. Then, if the user name and password are found in the database, which means they are valid, the server creates an authentication cookie and redirects the browser back to the original page. As a result, when the browser requests the original page, it sends the cookie back to the server. This time, the server sees that the user has been authenticated and the requested page is sent back to the browser.

By default, the authentication cookie is sent as a session cookie. In that case, the user is authenticated only for that session. However, you also can specify that the cookie be sent as a persistent cookie. Then, the user will be authenticated automatically for future sessions, until the cookie expires.

HTTP requests and responses with individual user account authentication

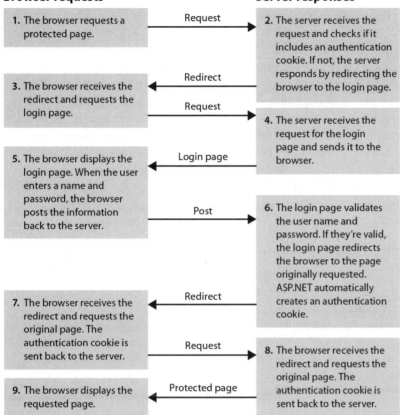

Browser requests

1. The browser requests a protected page.

    Request →

3. The browser receives the redirect and requests the login page.

    ← *Redirect*

    Request →

5. The browser displays the login page. When the user enters a name and password, the browser posts the information back to the server.

    ← *Login page*

    Post →

7. The browser receives the redirect and requests the original page. The authentication cookie is sent back to the server.

    ← *Redirect*

    Request →

9. The browser displays the requested page.

    ← *Protected page*

Server responses

2. The server receives the request and checks if it includes an authentication cookie. If not, the server responds by redirecting the browser to the login page.

4. The server receives the request for the login page and sends it to the browser.

6. The login page validates the user name and password. If they're valid, the login page redirects the browser to the page originally requested. ASP.NET automatically creates an authentication cookie.

8. The browser receives the redirect and requests the original page. The authentication cookie is sent back to the server.

Description

- When ASP.NET receives a request for a protected page from a user who has not been authenticated, the server redirects the user to the login page.
- To be authenticated, the user's computer must contain an *authentication cookie*. By default, this cookie is stored as a session cookie.
- ASP.NET automatically creates an authentication cookie when the application indicates that the user should be authenticated. ASP.NET checks for the presence of an authentication cookie any time it receives a request for a restricted page.
- The authentication cookie can be made persistent. Then, the user will be authenticated automatically in future sessions, until the cookie expires.

Figure 20-2   How individual user account authentication works

An introduction to ASP.NET Identity

In previous versions of ASP.NET, the Membership system provided authentication for ASP.NET applications. This was called forms-based authentication, and it had a Profile provider system and several server controls that let you easily work with the Membership system. In many instances, all you needed to do was put these server controls on a page and your application could register and log in users without you needing to set up a database or write any code.

However, it could be hard to customize the Membership database that stored user data or to work with custom Profile fields that were added to the database. In addition, it was hard or impossible to modify the Membership system to work with other data stores, to work with other devices, or to work with third-party social identity providers. In response to these issues, Microsoft replaced the old Membership system with the new ASP.NET Identity system. Figure 20-3 describes some of the main benefits of this new system.

To start, you can use it with all of the ASP.NET frameworks, including Web Forms and MVC. It's also easier to customize than the Membership system, it's easier to unit test, and it's easier to update because it's distributed as a NuGet package. It also supports claims-based authentication, which is a sophisticated form of authentication that can be more flexible than authorizing users based on the roles they belong to. (You'll learn more about roles later.)

Finally, it uses middleware called *OWIN*, or *Open Web Interface for .NET*. OWIN is an open source project that defines a standard interface between .NET web servers and web applications. The goal of OWIN is to create lightweight components with as few dependencies on other frameworks as possible.

In the topics that follow you'll see code that uses several of the objects of ASP.NET Identity, some of which are listed here. These objects are stored in a variety of namespaces, including Microsoft.AspNet.Identity, Microsoft.Owin, Owin, and System.Security. If you use the Web Forms template for development, the using directives for these namespaces will be generated for you.

Many of the code examples you'll see in this chapter start by retrieving the OwinContext object for the current request, which is built when a request is made. This figure shows two ways to do that. From a code-behind file, you use the Context property of the page to get the HttpContext object for the current request, and then call the GetOwinContext method of that object. From a non-page file, you have to use the Current property of the application's HttpContext object to get the HttpContext object for the current request.

The main objects used by ASP.NET Identity

Object	Description
OwinContext	The OWIN context for the current request.
IdentityDbContext	An Entity Framework DbContext object for working with the Users, Roles, Claims, and Logins of the ASP.NET Identity system.
IdentityUser	Represents an authenticated user.
UserStore	Works with users at the database level.
UserManager	Accepts a UserStore and works with users at the application level.
IdentityRole	Represents a role.
RoleStore	Works with roles at the database level.
RoleManager	Accepts a RoleStore and works with roles at the application level.
IdentityUserRole	Represents a user that belongs to a role.
SignInManager	Manages sign in operations for users.
SignInStatus	An enumeration whose values represent the results of a sign in attempt.
IdentityResult	Represents the result of an identity operation.
ClaimsIdentity	Represents a claims-based identity.

Some of the benefits of the new ASP.NET Identity system

- It can be used with all ASP.NET frameworks, including Web Forms, MVC, Web API, and SignalR to build web, phone, Windows Store, or hybrid applications.

- You have more control over the schema of the data store that holds user information, and it's easier to change the storage system from the default of SQL Server.

- It's modular, so it's easier to unit test.

- It supports claims-based authentication, which can be more flexible than using simple roles.

- It supports third party login providers like Microsoft, Google, Facebook, and Twitter.

- It's based on *OWIN (Open Web Interface for .NET)* middleware, which is an open source project that defines a standard interface between .NET web servers and web applications.

- It's distributed as a NuGet package, so Microsoft can deliver new features and bug fixes faster than before.

How to get the OwinContext object for the current request

In a code-behind file

```
var ctx = Context.GetOwinContext();
```

In a non-page file

```
var ctx = HttpContext.Current.GetOwinContext();
```

Description

- The ASP.NET Identity system replaces the Membership system and is used with all ASP.NET frameworks.

Figure 20-3   An introduction to ASP.NET Identity

How to create a web application that authenticates users

Although the new ASP.NET Identity system isn't as simple to work with as the old Membership system, you can still create a web application that can register and log in users without having to set up a database or write any code. To accomplish that, you can start your application from the Web Forms template, which contains a functional authentication system by default.

In the topics that follow, you'll learn how to use the Web Forms template with individual user accounts, and you'll see some of the code that this template generates for authentication. You should know, though, that this code can be complex. The good news is that you don't need to fully understand this code to use it. In fact, you could use the Web Forms template without even looking at this code, and you'd have a simple, functional authentication system for your web application. Because of that, you'll learn just the basics of how this code works.

How to start a web application from the Web Forms template

To start a web application from the Web Forms template, you display the New ASP.NET Project dialog box shown in figure 20-4 and then select the Web Forms template. When you do, Individual User Accounts authentication is selected by default. You can change this by clicking on the Change Authentication button and choosing a different authentication method. Most of the time, though, the default is what you want.

After you create a web application using the Web Forms template, it will contain the files and folders shown here. As you can see, the Account directory contains several aspx files that provide for things like registering users, logging users in, and managing user passwords. Some of these files, like the ones you'll see in the next few figures, are already fully functional. Others contain starter code or sample code with links to more information.

In addition to the Account directory, the App_Start and Models directories contain C# files that are used by the default authentication system. For example, the IdentityConfig.cs and Startup.Auth.cs files in the App_Start directory contain configuration code that determines the behavior of the authentication system. The IdentityModels.cs file in the Models directory, on the other hand, contains code that sets up objects that will be used to get user data into and out of a database. You'll see how to customize all three of these files later in this chapter.

Finally, the Startup.cs file in the root directory contains C# code that runs when the application first starts. The code in this file calls the code in the Startup_Auth.cs file to configure and start the application's authentication system.

The Web Forms template with Individual User Accounts authentication

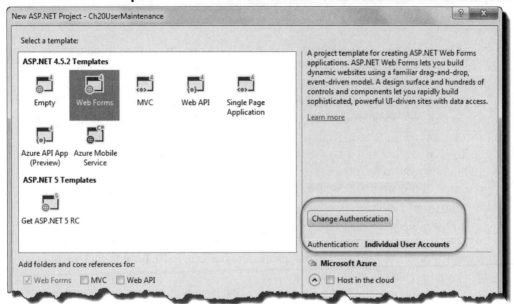

Files and folders of the root, Account, App_Start, and Models directories

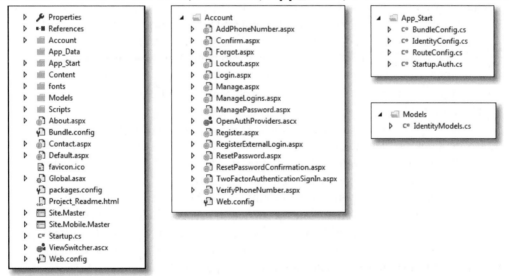

Description

- The Web Forms template uses Individual User Accounts authentication by default.
- The files in the Account, App_Start, and Models directories, along with the StartUp.cs file in the root directory, contain the code for a functioning authentication system.

Figure 20-4   How to start a web application from the Web Forms template

How to work with the LoginView and LoginStatus controls

When you start an application from the Web Forms template, it includes a master page with a Bootstrap navbar, as shown in figure 20-5. As you can see, this navbar looks different depending on whether the user is logged in. If the user isn't logged in, the navbar displays links that let the user register or log in. If the user has already logged in and been authenticated, though, the navbar displays a link that includes the user's name along with a link that lets the user log off.

To provide for these two views, the master page uses the LoginView and LoginStatus controls. You can see how this works in the aspx code that's presented in this figure. Note that this code, like the code you'll see in the next few figures, was generated automatically by the Web Forms template.

The LoginView control includes an AnonymousTemplate element and a LoggedInTemplate element. As their names imply, the AnonymousTemplate element is displayed to anonymous users, and the LoggedInTemplate element is displayed to authenticated users.

The AnonymousTemplate element shown here contains two <a> tags that link to the Register.aspx and Login.aspx pages in the Account directory. You'll see both of these pages shortly. Also, notice that the URLs for these pages don't include the .aspx file extension. That's because, by default, the Web Forms template uses the FriendlyUrls feature you learned about in chapter 11.

In contrast, the LoggedInTemplate element contains more complex code. It starts with an <a> tag that displays the user's name and links to the Manage.aspx page in the Account directory. Notice that this <a> tag uses declarative data binding with the <%# %> syntax to get the user's name from the User object of the page's HttpContext object. This data binding is similar to the data binding you saw in section 3 that uses the Eval method or the Item keyword.

The LoggedInTemplate also contains a LoginStatus control. This control can provide a link that lets authenticated users log off and a link that lets anonymous users log in. Since the control shown here is coded within a LoggedInTemplate element, though, it only provides a link for logging off.

The LogoutText property of the LoginStatus control specifies the text that's used for the logout link. Then, the LogoutAction property indicates that the user should be redirected to another page on log off, and the LogoutPageUrl property indicates the page to be displayed. In this case, the user will be redirected to the default.aspx page in the root directory, since no page is named.

The LoginStatus control shown here also handles the LoggingOut event, which fires when the user logs off. The code in the code-behind file starts by getting the OwinContext object. Then, it uses the Authentication property to access the authentication functionality of that object, and it uses the SignOut method to log the user off. Notice that the argument for this method indicates the type of authentication that's being used.

Although the LoginView and LoginStatus controls are included on the master page by default, you may occasionally want to add these controls to other pages. To do that, you can simply drag them from the Login group of the

The anonymous and logged in templates of the LoginView control

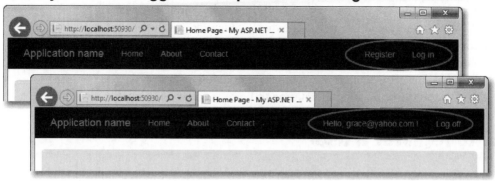

Some of the aspx code for the navbar in the master page

```
<div class="navbar-collapse collapse">
    <ul class="nav navbar-nav">
        <li><a runat="server" href="~/">Home</a></li>
        <li><a runat="server" href="~/About">About</a></li>
        <li><a runat="server" href="~/Contact">Contact</a></li></ul>
    <asp:LoginView runat="server" ViewStateMode="Disabled">
        <AnonymousTemplate>
            <ul class="nav navbar-nav navbar-right">
                <li><a runat="server" href="~/Account/Register">Register</a>
                </li>
                <li><a runat="server" href="~/Account/Login">Log in</a></li>
            </ul>
        </AnonymousTemplate>
        <LoggedInTemplate>
            <ul class="nav navbar-nav navbar-right">
                <li><a runat="server" href="~/Account/Manage"
                    title="Manage your account">Hello,
                    <%: Context.User.Identity.GetUserName()  %> !</a></li>
                <li>
                    <asp:LoginStatus runat="server" LogoutAction="Redirect"
                        LogoutText="Log off" LogoutPageUrl="~/"
                        OnLoggingOut="Unnamed_LoggingOut" /></li>
            </ul>
        </LoggedInTemplate>
    </asp:LoginView>
</div>
```

The code for the LoggingOut event of the LoginStatus control

```
protected void Unnamed_LoggingOut(object sender, LoginCancelEventArgs e) {
    Context.GetOwinContext().Authentication.SignOut(
        DefaultAuthenticationTypes.ApplicationCookie);
}
```

Description

- The master page includes a Bootstrap navbar that contains a LoginView control. This control displays links that let anonymous users register or log in. If a user is already authenticated, this control displays a link with the user's name and a log off link. The log off link uses the LoginStatus control.

Figure 20-5   How to work with the LoginView and LoginStatus controls

Toolbox. Note that most of the other Login controls are meant to be used with the membership system and not ASP.NET Identity, though.

When you look at the aspx code that's generated for the master page, you'll notice that it uses bundling to link to the CSS files, and it uses a ScriptManager control to refer to the JavaScript files. This is different than what you've seen up until now, but it's just another way to accomplish the same task. You can study the files and the online documentation to learn more about how this code works.

How to register a user

When the user clicks the Register link in the navbar, the Register.aspx page in the Account directory shown in figure 20-6 is displayed. Then, the user can use this page to create an account by entering an email address and a password, confirming the password, and clicking on the Register button. Because the aspx code for this page contains standard ASP.NET server controls and Bootstrap formatting, it isn't shown here. Note, though, that the Display property of all of the validation controls on this page have been set to Dynamic so they don't take up space unless an error message is displayed.

When the user clicks the Register button on this page, the event handler shown here is executed. This code starts by getting the ApplicationUserManager and ApplicationSignInManager objects from the OwinContext object. The classes that define these objects are coded in the IdentityConfig.cs file in the App_Start folder, which you'll learn about later. For now, you should just realize that the ApplicationUserManager class extends the UserManager class, and the ApplicationSignInManager class extends the SignInManager class.

Next, the code creates an ApplicationUser object, which extends the IdentityUser object. The class that defines this object is coded in the IdentityModels.cs file in the Models folder. You'll learn about this file later, too. When the ApplicationUser object is created, the value in the Email text box is set as the value of both the Email and UserName properties. This is where the user name that's displayed in the LoginView control comes from.

After the ApplicationUser object is created, it's passed to the Create method of the user manager, along with the password that the user entered. The Create method then adds the ApplicationUser object to the user manager's Users collection, and it inserts a new user into the authentication database. The result of this operation is stored in a variable named result that has a type of IdentityResult.

To determine if the user was created successfully, the code continues by checking if the Succeeded property of the result variable is equal to True. If it's not, an error message is displayed on the page. If it is, though, the code signs the user in by passing the User object to the SignIn method of the sign in manager. Then it calls the RedirectToReturnUrl method of the static IdentityHelper class to redirect the user.

Notice that the first argument that's passed to the RedirectToReturnUrl method tries to get the value of the ReturnUrl attribute from the query string for the page's URL. If you look back at the link to the Register page in the aspx

The Register.aspx page of the Web Forms template

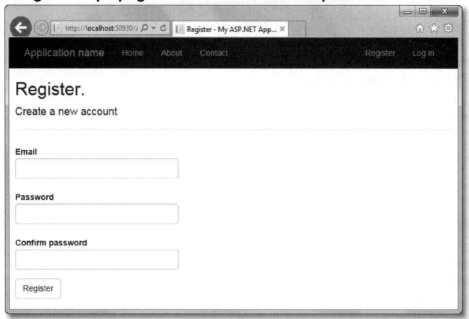

The code for the Click event of the Register button

```
protected void CreateUser_Click(object sender, EventArgs e)
{
    var manager =
        Context.GetOwinContext().GetUserManager<ApplicationUserManager>();
    var signInManager =
        Context.GetOwinContext().Get<ApplicationSignInManager>();
    var user = new ApplicationUser() { UserName = Email.Text,
        Email = Email.Text };
    IdentityResult result = manager.Create(user, Password.Text);
    if (result.Succeeded) {
        // For more information on how to enable account confirmation and
        // password reset please visit
        // http://go.microsoft.com/fwlink/?LinkID=320771
        // commented out sample code for how to handle an email confirmation

        signInManager.SignIn(
            user, isPersistent: false, rememberBrowser: false);
        IdentityHelper.RedirectToReturnUrl(
            Request.QueryString["ReturnUrl"], Response);
    }
    else {
        ErrorMessage.Text = result.Errors.FirstOrDefault();
    }
}
```

Description

- The register page creates a new user and signs them in to the application. It also includes commented out sample code with a link to more information.

- By default, the user is redirected to the home page when registration succeeds.

Figure 20-6   How to register a user

code for the master page in the previous figure, though, you'll see that it doesn't contain a query string. In addition, the code-behind file for the master page doesn't add a query string with this attribute dynamically. Because of that, the register page returns to the home page by default. To return to the original page, you can adjust the code-behind file for the master page so it adds a query string with a ReturnUrl attribute to the Register link.

The code that's generated by Visual Studio for a user that's created successfully also includes commented out starter code for enabling account confirmation and password reset functionality. This code isn't shown here due to space considerations, but the link to the article that contains more information is.

How to log in a user

To log in to an existing account, the user can use the Login.aspx page in the Account directory shown in figure 20-7. To log in, the user enters an email address and a password and then clicks on the Log In button. The user can also check the Remember Me check box to stay logged in even after the browser is closed. Finally, the user can display the Register page by clicking on the Register link below the Log In button. The aspx code for the Login page contains standard ASP.NET server controls and Bootstrap formatting.

Not shown here is the Use Another Service To Log In section that's displayed below the Register link by default. This section allows a user to log in with a service like Facebook or Twitter. By default, however, this section just contains text notifying the user that no external authentication services are configured. This text also contains a link to an article for details on setting up an ASP.NET application to log in with external services. You can remove this section from your application if you aren't using external services and you don't want users to see this section.

The code-behind file for the Login page contains a Page_Load event handler and an event handler for the Click event of the Log In button. The Page_Load event handler, not shown here, sets the URL for the page that will be displayed when the Register link is clicked. This URL includes a query string with the ReturnUrl attribute that was passed to the page, if there was one. You can use this code as a guide if you want to add code to the master page that adds a query string with a ReturnUrl to the URL for the link to the Register page.

The Load event handler also contains starter code that you can uncomment once you have account confirmation enabled for the password reset functionality. This commented out code sets the navigate URL for the Forgot Password link. Note that this link is also commented out by default in the aspx code, so you'd need to uncomment that aspx code as well to use this starter code.

The Click event for the Login button shown in this figure starts by checking whether the page is valid. That's because the page contains validation controls for the email and password. By the way, although the Register page also contains validation controls, it doesn't check whether the page is valid. So you should probably add code that does that.

If the page is valid, the code then gets the ApplicationUserManager and ApplicationSignInManager objects. Then, it signs the user in by calling the

The Login.aspx page of the Web Forms Template

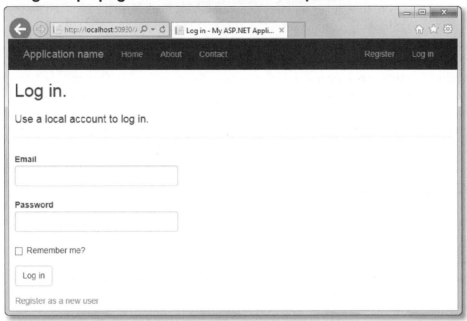

The code for the Click event of the Log In button

```
protected void LogIn(object sender, EventArgs e)
{
  if (IsValid) {
      var manager =
          Context.GetOwinContext().GetUserManager<ApplicationUserManager>();
      var signinManager =
          Context.GetOwinContext().GetUserManager<ApplicationSignInManager>();
      // This doesn't count login failures towards account lockout. To enable
      // password failures to trigger lockout, change to shouldLockout: true
      var result = signinManager.PasswordSignIn(Email.Text,
          Password.Text, RememberMe.Checked, shouldLockout: false);

      switch (result) {
          case SignInStatus.Success:
            IdentityHelper.RedirectToReturnUrl(
                Request.QueryString["ReturnUrl"], Response);
            break;
          case SignInStatus.LockedOut:
            Response.Redirect("/Account/Lockout");
            break;
          case SignInStatus.RequiresVerification:
            Response.Redirect(String.Format(
                "/Account/TwoFactorAuthenticationSignIn?ReturnUrl={0}&RememberMe={1}",
                Request.QueryString["ReturnUrl"], RememberMe.Checked), true);
            break;
          case SignInStatus.Failure:
          default:
            FailureText.Text = "Invalid login attempt";
            ErrorMessage.Visible = true;
            break;
      }
  }
}
```

Figure 20-7   How to log in a user

PasswordSignIn method of the sign in manager, passing it the values of the Email and Password text boxes and the RememberMe check box. It stores the value of the SignInStatus enumeration that this method returns in a variable named result.

Finally, the code checks the value of the result variable to determine if the login operation was successful. If the value is Success, LockedOut, or RequiresVerification, the code redirects to the appropriate page. Otherwise, it notifies the user that the login attempt failed. Note that LockedOut means that the user has attempted to log in too many times, and RequiresVerification means that additional verification is required. Both of these features are disabled by default.

How to change a user's password

Figure 20-8 shows the Manage.aspx and ManagePassword.aspx pages in the Account directory. Note that these pages are shown narrowed, so the Bootstrap navbar is collapsed. Because of that, the links in the LoginView control shown in figure 20-5 aren't visible. To display them, you can click on the Bootstrap menu icon in the upper right of the navbar.

To display the Manage page, the user clicks the first link in the LoggedInTemplate element of the LoginView control. Then, to display the ManagePassword page, the user clicks the Change link in the Password section of the Manage page. Here, you can see that to change a password, the user must enter the current password and the new password and then confirm the new password and click the Change Password button.

This figure also shows the event handler that's executed when the Change Password button is clicked. The code for this event handler starts by checking if the page is valid. If it is, the code continues by getting the ApplicationUserManager and ApplicationSignInManager objects using code like you've seen in previous figures. Next, it changes the password by calling the ChangePassword method of the user manager, passing it the ID of the current user and the values the user entered for the current password and new password. (The user ID is generated when the user is created.) Then, it stores the result of the operation in a variable named result that has a type of the IdentityResult.

To determine if the operation was successful, the code checks if the Succeeded property of the result variable is equal to True. If it isn't, an error message is displayed. Otherwise, the code gets the current user by passing the user ID to the FindById method of the user manager. Then, it signs the user in by passing the User object to the SignIn method of the sign in manager. Finally, it redirects to the Manage page using a URL with a query string value that will be used to notify the user that the password was changed.

Note that if a user doesn't have a password, the ManagePassword page will look different than what's shown here. Specifically, it will include two text boxes that let the user enter and confirm the password, along with a Set Password button. If the user clicks this button and the password is added successfully, the Manage page is redisplayed. Otherwise, an error message is displayed.

The Manage.aspx and ManagePassword.aspx pages of the Web Forms template

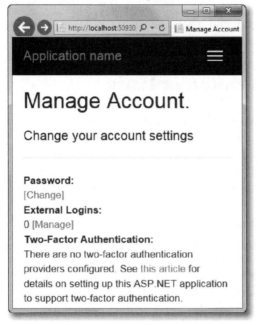 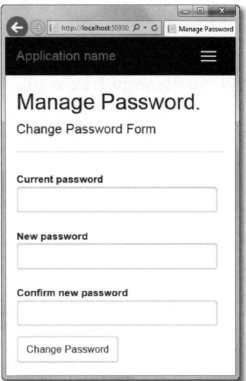

The code for the Click event of the Change Password button

```
protected void ChangePassword_Click(object sender, EventArgs e)
{
    if (IsValid)
    {
        var manager =
            Context.GetOwinContext().GetUserManager<ApplicationUserManager>();
        var signInManager =
            Context.GetOwinContext().Get<ApplicationSignInManager>();

        IdentityResult result = manager.ChangePassword(
            User.Identity.GetUserId(), CurrentPassword.Text,
            NewPassword.Text);

        if (result.Succeeded) {
            var user = manager.FindById(User.Identity.GetUserId());
            signInManager.SignIn(
                user, isPersistent: false, rememberBrowser: false);
            Response.Redirect("~/Account/Manage?m=ChangePwdSuccess");
        }
        else
            AddErrors(result);
    }
}
```

Figure 20-8   How to change a user's password

In addition to the code shown here, the ManagePassword page includes a Page_Load event handler and an event handler that's executed if the user clicks the Set Password button. Among other things, the Page_Load event handler determines if the current user has a password, and it sets the Visible property of some of the controls on the page depending on the result.

How to change basic configuration options

In the previous figures, you saw the pages and code-behind files for an authentication system that's generated by default by the Web Forms template. Although you can use this authentication system without making any changes to it, you'll typically want to make at least some minor changes. For example, you may want to change the password or lockout rules. Fortunately, it's easy to make these types of changes.

The IdentityConfig.cs file in the App_Start directory contains code that determines some of the authentication behavior of an application. This file defines the ApplicationUserManager class that you've seen used in previous figures. This class extends the UserManager class and has a static Create method that's shown in figure 20-9. This method is called when the OwinContext object for a request is built, and it creates and configures the ApplicationUserManager object that's used by the application. You'll learn more about how this works later.

As you can see, this Create method configures things like password length, types of characters required in a password, and how many login failures are allowed before a user is locked out. You can change the code in this method to adjust this functionality in an application.

The IdentityConfig.cs file also defines the ApplicationSignInManager class that you've seen used in previous figures. This class extends the SignInManager class and also has a static Create method that creates and configures the ApplicationSignInManager class that's used by the application. You won't typically need to edit this class, so it's not shown here.

Finally, the IdentityConfig.cs file contains starter code for EmailService and SmsService classes. You can add code to these classes to allow your authentication system to send emails or text messages as part of two-factor authentication functionality.

The static Create method in the IdentityConfig.cs file

```
public static ApplicationUserManager Create(
    IdentityFactoryOptions<ApplicationUserManager> options,
    IOwinContext context)
{
    var manager = new ApplicationUserManager(
        new UserStore<ApplicationUser>(context.Get<ApplicationDbContext>()));
    // Configure validation logic for usernames
    manager.UserValidator = new UserValidator<ApplicationUser>(manager) {
        AllowOnlyAlphanumericUserNames = false,
        RequireUniqueEmail = true
    };

    // Configure validation logic for passwords
    manager.PasswordValidator = new PasswordValidator {
        RequiredLength = 6,
        RequireNonLetterOrDigit = true,
        RequireDigit = true,
        RequireLowercase = true,
        RequireUppercase = true,
    };

    // Register two factor authentication providers. This application uses
    // Phone and Emails as a step of receiving a code for verifying the user
    // You can write your own provider and plug it in here.
    manager.RegisterTwoFactorProvider(
        "Phone Code", new PhoneNumberTokenProvider<ApplicationUser> {
        MessageFormat = "Your security code is {0}"
    });
    manager.RegisterTwoFactorProvider(
        "Email Code", new EmailTokenProvider<ApplicationUser> {
        Subject = "Security Code",
        BodyFormat = "Your security code is {0}"
    });

    // Configure user lockout defaults
    manager.UserLockoutEnabledByDefault = true;
    manager.DefaultAccountLockoutTimeSpan = TimeSpan.FromMinutes(5);
    manager.MaxFailedAccessAttemptsBeforeLockout = 5;

    manager.EmailService = new EmailService();
    manager.SmsService = new SmsService();
    var dataProtectionProvider = options.DataProtectionProvider;
    if (dataProtectionProvider != null) {
        manager.UserTokenProvider =
            new DataProtectorTokenProvider<ApplicationUser>(
            dataProtectionProvider.Create("ASP.NET Identity"));
    }
    return manager;
}
```

Description

- To adjust things like the password length and the number of login failures that are allowed, you can modify the code in the IdentityConfig.cs file.

Figure 20-9   How to change basic configuration options

How to authorize users

Now that you know how to authenticate users, you're ready to learn how to restrict access to one or more pages of an application to authorized users. To do that, you define access rules and roles as described in the topics that follow.

An introduction to access rules and roles

By default, all the pages of a web application can be accessed by all users, whether or not they're authenticated. As a result, if you want to restrict access to all or some of the pages of an application, you need to set up *access rules* for those parts of the application. An access rule indicates which users are allowed to access that page or group of pages.

Roles let you apply the same access rules to a group of users. Although roles are optional and aren't part of the Web Forms template by default, they make it easy to manage authentication. As a result, you'll typically use roles in your applications. In the next figure, you'll learn how to change the default configuration of the Web Forms template so you can use roles.

To understand how roles work, suppose you create a role named admin for all employees that will be administrators for the web application. Then, suppose you associate this role with multiple users. If you later want to give all users in the admin role additional permissions, you don't have to give the permissions to the users individually. Instead, you can just give the additional permissions to the admin role, and all users associated with that role will get the new permissions.

How to define access rules

Figure 20-10 shows how to define access rules for users and roles. To do that, you add code to one or more Web.config files as shown here. When you do, you can use the two wildcard characters shown in the table in this figure to refer to all users or all unauthenticated users.

The first two examples in this figure show how you code the allow and deny elements in a Web.config file. The first example lets all users access the files in the directory where the Web.config file is stored, as well as in any subdirectories of that directory. The second example lets only users in the Employees role access those files. To understand how this works, you need to realize that access rules are applied in order, and once a rule is applied, all further rules are skipped. In this example, then, if the rule that allows access to users in the Employees role is applied, the next rule that denies access to all users is skipped. Otherwise, the deny rule is applied.

In the next two examples, you can see that you code access rules within an authorization element, which is coded within the system.web element of the configuration element. You can also use the location element to limit rules to a specific directory or file, and you can code one or more location elements within a single Web.config file. Another way to limit rules to a specific directory is to add a Web.config file to that directory. Then, the rules in that file apply only to the pages in that directory and any subdirectories, and these rules override any rules in the Web.config file in the root directory.

Wildcard specifications in the users attribute

Wildcard	Description
*	All users, whether or not they have been authenticated.
?	All unauthenticated users.

An access rule that allows access to all users

```
<allow users="*" />
```

An access rule that allows access only to users in a specific role

```
<allow roles="Employees" />
<deny users="*" />
```

Two ways to allow only authenticated users access to the resources in a specific directory

In the root directory

```
<configuration>
  <location path="Maintenance">
    <system.web>
      <authorization>
        <deny users="?" />
      </authorization>
    </system.web>
  </location>
</configuration>
```

In the Maintenance directory

```
<configuration>
  <system.web>
    <authorization>
      <deny users="?" />
    </authorization>
  </system.web>
</configuration>
```

How to allow users in a specific role access to a specific page

```
<configuration>
  <location path="Admin.aspx">
    <system.web>
      <authorization>
        <allow roles="admin" />
        <deny users="*" />
      </authorization>
    </system.web>
  </location>
</configuration>
```

Description

- The authorization element in a Web.config file lets you code allow and deny elements that control which users or roles can access an application. You can let users access the entire application, the files in a specific directory, or an individual file.

- When a resource like an aspx page loads, the application iterates through the authorization rules in the Web.config files in the application, starting with the file that's closest to the resource and ending with the file in the root directory. As soon as a rule is found that fits the current user, that rule is applied and the iteration stops.

- To add a new Web.config file, display the Add New Item dialog box, select the Web Configuration File template, accept the default name, and click the Add button.

Figure 20-10 How to define access rules

How an application adds objects
to the OwinContext object

The Startup.Auth.cs file in the App_Start folder includes a class named Startup that contains a ConfigureAuth method. This method is called by the StartUp.cs file in the root directory at startup, and it makes sure there's only a single instance of certain objects per request.

Figure 20-11 shows some of the code in the ConfigureAuth method so you can see how this works. Here, the first three statements call the CreatePerOwinContext method and pass it static Create methods like the one you saw in figure 20-9. These statements are generated by the Web Forms template by default, and they will be used to create the ApplicationDbContext, ApplicationUserManager, and ApplicationSignInManager objects.

It's important to note that these Create methods aren't being executed here. Instead, they're being sent as callbacks to be executed later when the OwinContext object for the request is built. Then, these objects are stored in the OwinContext object throughout the life of the request. That's why you can use the Get methods of the OwinContext object to get these objects instead of having to instantiate them yourself. Note that you haven't seen the ApplicationDbContext class, but it's defined in the IdentityModels.cs file in the Models folder and it extends the IdentityDbContext class.

How to modify an application to use roles

To modify an application so it uses roles, you have to define an ApplicationRoleManager class that extends the RoleManager class. It's best to code this class in the IdentityConfig.cs class in the App_Start directory, along with the ApplicationUserManager and ApplicationSignInManager classes.

Figure 20-11 shows the code for an ApplicationRoleManager class. This class includes a constructor that accepts a RoleStore object and passes it to the base class constructor. It also includes a static Create method that accepts an IdentityFactoryOption object and an OwinContext object. Within the Create method, the class uses the OwinContext object to create a new RoleStore object, and passes this RoleStore object to the constructor of the new ApplicationRoleManager class that it returns.

After you code the ApplicationRoleManager class, you need to add a statement to the ConfigureAuth method of the Startup class that passes the Create method of the ApplicationRoleManager class. That way, this Create method will also be called when the OwinContext object is built.

Once you've added this code, you can use the Get method of the OwinContext object to retrieve the ApplicationRoleManager object. You can see how this works in the last example in this figure.

Some of the code in the ConfigAuth method

```
public partial class Startup {

    // For more information on configuring authentication, please
    // visit http://go.microsoft.com/fwlink/?LinkId=301883
    public void ConfigureAuth(IAppBuilder app)
    {
        // Configure the db context, user manager and signin manager to
        // use a single instance per request
        app.CreatePerOwinContext(ApplicationDbContext.Create);
        app.CreatePerOwinContext<ApplicationUserManager>(
            ApplicationUserManager.Create);
        app.CreatePerOwinContext<ApplicationSignInManager>(
            ApplicationSignInManager.Create);

        // Configure the role manager to use a single instance per request
        app.CreatePerOwinContext<ApplicationRoleManager>(
            ApplicationRoleManager.Create);
        ...
    }
}
```

The ApplicationRoleManager class

```
public class ApplicationRoleManager : RoleManager<IdentityRole>
{
    public ApplicationRoleManager(IRoleStore<IdentityRole, string> store)
    : base(store) {}

    public static ApplicationRoleManager Create(
        IdentityFactoryOptions<ApplicationRoleManager> options,
        IOwinContext context)
    {
        var roleStore = new RoleStore<IdentityRole>(
            context.Get<ApplicationDbContext>());
        return new ApplicationRoleManager(roleStore);
    }
}
```

Code that gets the ApplicationRoleManager object

```
ApplicationRoleManager roleMgr =
    Context.GetOwinContext().Get<ApplicationRoleManager>();
```

Description

- The Web Forms template creates ApplicationDbContext, ApplicationUserManager, and ApplicationSignInManager objects by default and adds a single instance of them to the OwinContext object of the current request. You can also add code to create an object for working with roles.

- To use roles with the Web Forms template, you create a new ApplicationRoleManager class in the IdentityConfig.cs file that extends the RoleManager class. Then, you add a statement to the ConfigureAuth method in the Startup.Auth.cs file that adds an instance of the ApplicationRoleManager class to the OwinContext object.

Figure 20-11   How to modify an application to use roles

How to work with the users and roles

The ApplicationUserManager class that's generated by the Web Forms template extends the UserManager class. Similarly, the ApplicationRoleManager class that you just saw extends the RoleManager class. Now you'll learn how to use the properties and methods of these classes to work with users and roles in your applications.

Figure 20-12 presents some of the properties and methods provided by the RoleManager and UserManager classes. All of the properties and methods presented here will be used by the User Maintenance application that you'll see next. Note that the code shown both here and in that application assumes that you have modified the application to use roles as shown in the previous figure.

As you can see in the first two tables in this figure, the RoleManager class includes methods that let you create, update, and delete roles. Similarly, the UserManager class includes methods that let you create, update, and delete users. All of these methods return an IdentityResult object that has the two properties shown in the third table in this figure. The Succeeded property returns a Boolean value that indicates if the operation was successful, and the Errors property returns a collection of error messages. Although you won't see an example of the Errors property here, it's a standard collection of strings so you can use standard collection and string methods to work with the error messages it contains.

The first code example in this figure shows how to create a new role. It starts by getting the ApplicationRoleManager object from the OwinContext object. Then, it creates a new IdentityRole object, assigns a value to the Name property of that object, and then passes the role to the Create method of the role manager. Then, it checks the Succeeded property of the IdentityResult object and takes some action based on its value. The second example is similar, except it creates a new user.

You should notice two things about these examples. First, you could easily add if blocks to the else statements that check the Succeeded property so they display the values in the Errors property. Second, you can see how adding the code for using an ApplicationRoleManager object makes it as easy to retrieve and work with that object.

The last example in this figure shows how to associate a user with a role. This code starts by calling the IsInRole method of the user manager to see if the user is already associated with the specified role. If it isn't, the code calls the AddToRole method of the user manager to add the user to the role. Both of these methods accept a string value that contains the ID of the user and a string value that contains the name of the role.

Some of the properties and methods of the RoleManager class

Property/Method	Description
`Roles`	Returns an IQueryable of application roles.
`Create(role)`	Creates a role and returns an IdentityResult object.
`Update(role)`	Updates a role and returns an IdentityResult object.
`Delete(role)`	Deletes a role and returns an IdentityResult object.

Some of the properties and methods of the UserManager class

Property/Method	Description
`Users`	Returns an IQueryable of application users.
`Create(user)`	Creates a user and returns an IdentityResult object.
`Update(user)`	Updates a user and returns an IdentityResult object.
`Delete(user)`	Deletes a user and returns an IdentityResult object.
`IsInRole(userID, role)`	Returns a Boolean value that indicates if the user is in the specified role.
`AddToRole(userID, role)`	Adds the user to the specified role and returns an IdentityResult object.
`RemoveFromRole(userID, role)`	Removes the user from the specified role and returns an IdentityResult object.

Two properties of the IdentityResult class

Property	Description
`Succeeded`	A Boolean value that indicates whether the operation was successful.
`Errors`	An IEnumerable collection of strings that contains error messages.

Code that creates a new role

```
ApplicationRoleManager roleMgr =
    Context.GetOwinContext().Get<ApplicationRoleManager>();
IdentityRole role = new IdentityRole();
role.Name = "Admin";
IdentityResult result = roleMgr.Create(role);
if (result.Succeeded) { ... }
```

Code that creates a new user

```
ApplicationUserManager userMgr =
    Context.GetOwinContext().GetUserManager<ApplicationUserManager>();
ApplicationUser user = new ApplicationUser();
user.UserName = "anne@murach.com";
IdentityResult result = userMgr.Create(user);
if (result.Succeeded) { ... }
```

Code that associates the new user with the new role

```
if (!userMgr.IsInRole(user.Id, role.Name))
    userMgr.AddToRole(user.Id, role.Name);
```

Figure 20-12   How to work with users and roles

A User Maintenance application

This topic presents part of a Halloween Store application that we'll refer to as the User Maintenance application. This application uses the default authentication system of the Web Forms template, but it customizes that system so roles can be used. It also restricts access to some pages to users who have created an account and logged in, and it restricts access to other pages to authenticated users that are associated with the admin role.

The user interface

Figure 20-13 presents two pages of the User Maintenance application. When the User Maintenance Application starts, the Home page is displayed. The three links on this page let the user order a product, edit their account, or maintain users and roles for the application. All users can access the Order page without being authenticated.

In contrast, a user must be authenticated to access the ManageAccount page that's displayed when the Edit My Account link is clicked. When the user clicks on this link, the system attempts to authenticate the user by checking if the browser has a valid authentication cookie. If a cookie is found, the user will be authenticated automatically and allowed to access the ManageAccount page. If not, the user will be redirected to the Login page. Once the user supplies a valid user name and password, the browser will be redirected to the ManageAccount page.

A user must also be authenticated to access the Maintenance page that's displayed when the Maintain Users and Roles link is clicked. In addition, the user must be associated with the admin role. If an authentication cookie isn't found when the user clicks this link, then, the Login page is displayed and the user must enter a user name and password for a user with admin privileges. Then, the browser is redirected to the Maintenance page.

From the Maintenance page, the user can edit and delete existing users and roles and insert new users and roles. To work with an existing user, the user clicks on the Select button in the first GridView control to display the email address for that user in the first DetailsView control. Then, the user can use the DetailsView control to edit or delete the selected user. Or, the user can click on the New button in the DetailsView control to insert a new user.

The user can use the second GridView and DetailsView controls in the same way to work with roles. The user can also use the drop-down list, list box, and button to associate one or more roles with a user. To do that, the user selects a user from the drop-down list, selects one or more roles from the list box, and clicks the Add Roles button. Then, the user is added to any selected roles and removed from any roles that aren't selected.

The Home and Maintenance pages of the User Maintenance application

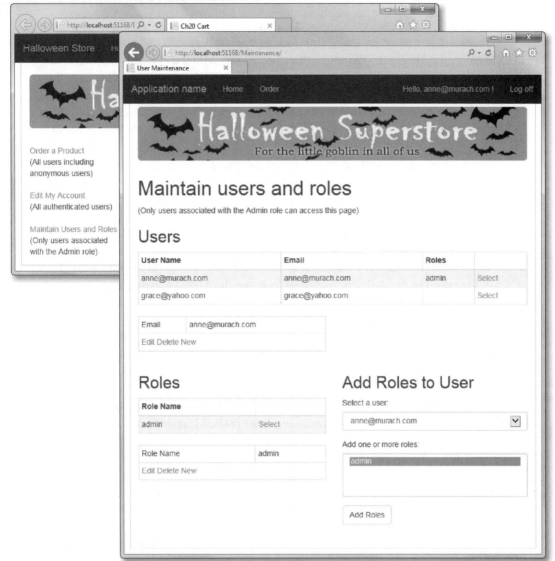

Description

- The User Maintenance application uses Web.config files to restrict some portions of the site to authenticated users or users associated with the admin role.

- The Home page contains three links. The first link lets all users access the Order page. The second link lets authenticated users access the Manage Account page. And the third link lets authenticated users in the admin role access the Maintenance page.

- The Login page is displayed if the user clicks on the second or third link and the browser doesn't contain a cookie that authenticates the user.

- The Maintenance page lets a user in the admin role insert, edit, and delete users and roles. It also lets an admin user select a user and associate them with one or more roles.

Figure 20-13   The user interface for the User Maintenance application

The Web.config files

The User Maintenance application has three Web.config files, two of which are added by default by the Web Forms template. Figure 20-14 shows these Web.config files in the directory structure, along with the contents of each file.

The Web.config files in the root directory and the Account directory are the ones that are added by default. Although the file in the root directory doesn't contain an authorization element, it does contain an authentication element. This element is used by the old Membership system, and its mode attribute is set to "None" by default. This means that the application isn't going to use the forms-based authentication of the old Membership system.

The Web.config file in the Account directory contains a location element that indicates that the access rules that follow apply to the Manage.aspx file in this directory. Then, the authorization element within the location element contains an access rule that denies access to unauthenticated users. This means that only logged in users can access the Manage.aspx page that you saw in figure 20-8. Note that if the location element was removed, this access rule would apply to all the pages in the Account directory, not just the Manage.aspx page.

The third Web.config file in this figure is in the Maintenance directory. This directory and the Web.config file were added after the application was started from the Web Forms template. The Web.config file contains an authorization element with two access rules. The first rule allows users in the admin role access to all the files in the Maintenance directory, and the second rule denies all users access to these files. Since access rules are applied in order, only users in the admin role can access the pages in the Maintenance directory. The Default.aspx page in the Maintenance folder is the Maintenance page that you saw in the last figure.

An interesting issue with this application is that no roles are added by default when you use the Web Forms template. To restrict access to files in the Maintenance directory to users that are associated with the admin role, then, you need to use the Maintenance page to add the admin role and associate a user with it. But, you can't access the Maintenance page unless you're in the admin role!

One way to work around this problem is to not add the Web.config file to the Maintenance folder to start. Then, you can run the application, register a user, navigate to the Maintenance page, create the admin role, and associate the user you just added with the admin role. After that, you can stop the application and then add the Web.config file.

If you've already added the Web.config file to the Maintenance folder, you can temporarily change the access rule in that file from deny all users (deny users="*") to deny unauthenticated users (deny users="?"). Then, you can register a user, create the admin role, and associate the user with the admin role as described above. Once that's done, you can change the Web.config file back to deny all users.

Another way to work around this problem is to use the Seed method that you'll learn about later in this chapter. You can use this method to add users and roles and to associate users with roles. But for now, the solutions described here are adequate.

The Web.config files for the User Maintenance application

For the root directory

```
<configuration>
  ...
  <system.web>
    <authentication mode="None"/>
    ...
  </system.web>
</configuration>
```

For the Account directory

```
<configuration>
  <location path="Manage.aspx">
    <system.web>
      <authorization>
        <deny users="?"/>
      </authorization>
    </system.web>
  </location>
</configuration>
```

For the Maintenance directory

```
<configuration>
  <system.web>
    <authorization>
      <allow roles="admin" />
      <deny users="*" />
    </authorization>
  </system.web>
</configuration>
```

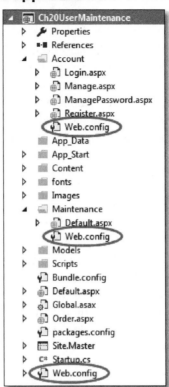

Description

- The Web.config file in the root directory doesn't apply any authorization rules. But it does include an authentication element with a mode attribute that's set to "None" by default when you use the Web Forms template. This indicates that the form-based authentication of the older Membership system is not being used.

- The Web.config file in the Account directory is also added by the Web Forms template. By default, it allows only authenticated users access to the Manage.aspx file within that directory.

- The Web.config file in the Maintenance directory applies to all the files in that directory. It allows only authenticated users associated with the admin role to access those files.

Figure 20-14   The Web.config files for the User Maintenance application

The aspx code for the users GridView control and the connection string for the application

Most of the aspx code in this application is similar to code you saw in section three of this book, so isn't presented here. For example, the GridView, DetailsView, DropDownList, and ListBox controls on the Maintenance page all use the model binding that you learned about in chapter 18 to work with the user and role data in the database. However, the code for the GridView control that lists the users has one difference that's worth pointing out.

Although you can't see it in figure 20-13, the Roles column contains a comma-separated list of the roles that are associated with each user. To get this information, the GridView control uses a templated field. This field gets its value from a method in the code-behind file named ListRoles. Here, the Roles collection of the data-bound ApplicationUser object, which is referred to using the Item keyword, is passed to this method.

Note that if you run this code using the authentication system and connection string that are generated by the Web Forms template by default, you'll get an error indicating that there's already an open DataReader associated with the command. (You'll need to look at the inner exception of the error to see this message.) That's because the connection string that's generated by the Web Forms template doesn't allow for the processing of multiple result sets on a single connection. To display the data for the users GridView control, for example, the application must retrieve data from both the table of users and the table of user roles. To provide for that, you can enable *Multiple Active Result Sets* (*MARS*) by setting the MultipleActiveResultSets value in the connection string to True as shown here. Note that in the application's Web.config file, the connectionString attribute should be all on one line.

Another way to fix this problem is to have the select method for the GridView return an IEnumerable object rather than an IQueryable object. However, as you learned in chapter 18, this can make it harder to add sorting and paging to a GridView. Because of that, it's usually better to enable multiple active result sets instead.

The GridView control that displays users and their roles

```
<asp:GridView ID="grdUsers" runat="server" DataKeyNames="Id"
    AutoGenerateColumns="false" SelectMethod="grdUsers_GetData"
    ItemType="Ch20UserMaintenance.Models.ApplicationUser"
    CssClass="table table-bordered table-striped table-condensed"
    OnPreRender="GridView_PreRender">
    <Columns>
        <asp:BoundField HeaderText="User Name" DataField="UserName" />
        <asp:BoundField HeaderText="Email" DataField="Email" />
        <asp:TemplateField HeaderText="Roles">
            <ItemTemplate>
                <asp:Label runat="server"
                    Text='<%# ListRoles(Item.Roles) %>'></asp:Label>
            </ItemTemplate>
        </asp:TemplateField>
        <asp:CommandField ShowSelectButton="true" />
    </Columns>
</asp:GridView>
```

The connection string for the User Maintenance application

```
<connectionStrings>
    <add name="DefaultConnection"
        connectionString="Data Source=(LocalDb)\MSSQLLocalDB;
        AttachDbFilename=|DataDirectory|\aspnet...mdf;
        Initial Catalog=aspnet-Ch20UserMaintenance-20160526022321;
        Integrated Security=True;
        MultipleActiveResultSets=True;"
        providerName="System.Data.SqlClient" />
</connectionStrings>
```

Description

- The GridView control that displays the list of users calls a method named ListRoles in the code-behind file that returns a comma-separated list of roles that are associated with each user.

- To get the list of roles for each user, you must add a property to the connection string so the database allows for multiple active result sets. This value isn't added to the connection string by default when you use the Web Forms template.

- Another way to make this work would be to have the GridView control's select method return an IEnumerable object rather than an IQueryable object.

Figure 20-15   The aspx code for the users GridView control and the connection string for the application

The code-behind file for the Maintenance page

Figure 20-16 shows some of the code in the code-behind file for the Default.aspx file in the Maintenance folder. For simplicity, this code doesn't do any data validation or concurrency checking. Also, as mentioned previously, this code assumes that the ApplicationRoleManager object that's described in figure 20-11 has been added.

This code starts by creating class variables for the ApplicationUserManager and ApplicationRoleManager objects. Then, in the page's Load event handler, the code uses the OwinContext object for the current request to retrieve the user manager and role manager and store them in these variables. These objects are then used in the model binding methods of the data controls on the page to handle selecting, inserting, updating, and deleting users and roles.

The first two methods after the Load event handler are the select methods that are used to select users. The first select method is used by the GridView control that displays the users. It returns the user manager's collection of ApplicationUser objects. The second select method is used by the DetailsView control that displays the user that's selected in the GridView control. This method returns the user in the Users collection of the application user manager that has the ID the selected user.

The next three methods are used by the DetailsView control for a user. The first method is used to update a user. It uses the ID that's passed to it to get the selected ApplicationUser object from the Users collection of the application user manager. Then, it updates the ApplicationUser object with the email address from the bound control using the TryUpdateModel method. Next, it assigns the value of the Email property to the value of the Username property, which is similar to what the code in the Register page in figure 20-6 does. After that, it passes the updated ApplicationUser object to the Update method of the application user manager, and it stores the result of the operation in an IdentityResult object. Finally, it checks if the update operation was successful. If it was, it calls the Reload method, which reloads the GridView controls, drop-down list, and list box so they contain current data.

The next method is used to insert a user. This method is similar to the update method. Instead of getting the selected user, though, it creates a new ApplicationUser object. And instead of using the Update method, it uses the Create method.

The last method on this page is used to delete a user. Like the update method, it uses the ID that's passed to it to get the selected user from the Users collection of the user manager. Then, it passes the user to the Delete method of the user manager, and it stores the result in an IdentityResult object. Finally, it checks the result of the operation and, if it was successful, it calls the Reload method.

After these methods are the methods that let the user select, update, insert, and delete roles. Because these methods work just like the methods for selecting, updating, inserting, and deleting users, they're not shown here.

The code-behind file for the Maintenance page   **Page 1**

```
public partial class Default : System.Web.UI.Page
{
    ApplicationUserManager userMgr;
    ApplicationRoleManager roleMgr;

    protected void Page_Load(object sender, EventArgs e)
    {
        userMgr =
            Context.GetOwinContext().GetUserManager<ApplicationUserManager>();
        roleMgr =
            Context.GetOwinContext().Get<ApplicationRoleManager>();
    }

    // Select users
    public IQueryable<ApplicationUser> grdUsers_GetData()
    {
        return userMgr.Users;
    }

    public Object dvUsers_GetItem([Control] string grdUsers)
    {
        if (grdUsers == null) return new ApplicationUser();
        return (from u in userMgr.Users
            where u.Id == grdUsers select u).SingleOrDefault();
    }

    // Update user
    public void dvUsers_UpdateItem(string Id)
    {
        ApplicationUser user = (from u in userMgr.Users
            where u.Id == Id select u).SingleOrDefault();
        TryUpdateModel(user);
        user.UserName = user.Email; // assign email to username
        IdentityResult result = userMgr.Update(user);
        if (result.Succeeded) Reload();
    }

    // Insert user
    public void dvUsers_InsertItem()
    {
        ApplicationUser user = new ApplicationUser();
        TryUpdateModel(user);
        user.UserName = user.Email; // assign email to username
        IdentityResult result = userMgr.Create(user);
        if (result.Succeeded) Reload();
    }

    // Delete user
    public void dvUsers_DeleteItem(string Id)
    {
        ApplicationUser user = (from u in userMgr.Users
            where u.Id == Id select u).SingleOrDefault();
        IdentityResult result = userMgr.Delete(user);
        if (result.Succeeded) Reload();
    }
```

Figure 20-16   The code-behind file (part 1 of 2)

The next method is the event handler for the Click event of the Add Roles button that's used to associate a user with one or more roles. This method starts by getting the ID of the user that's selected in the drop-down list of users. Next, the code loops through the roles in the list box. Then, if a role is selected, it calls the IsInRole method to check that the user isn't already associated with the role. If the user isn't associated with the role, the code continues by calling the AddToRole method to add the user to the role.

If a role isn't selected, the code checks if the selected user is associated with the selected role. If so, the code removes the user from that role. Note that the IsInRole, AddToRole, and RemoveFromRole methods all accept the user ID that's retrieved from the user drop-down list and the role name that's retrieved from the Text property of the current list item. Also note that this is just one way that you can maintain the roles that a user is associated with. Another way would be to have one button that adds a user to one or more roles and another button that deletes a user from one or more roles. These two functions have been combined here for simplicity.

The next two methods shown here are helper methods. The ListRoles method is the one you saw in figure 20-15 that's called by one of the columns in the users GridView control to create a comma-separated list of roles for each user. It accepts a collection of IdentityUserRole objects, which represent users that belong to roles. It gets this collection from the Roles collection of the data bound ApplicationUser object.

The first two statements of the ListRoles method instantiate a new IdentityRole object and a new list of strings. Then, the code loops through all the items in the collection of user roles. Within the loop, the code uses the role ID of the current IdentityUserRole object to get the related IdentityRole object from the role manager's Role collection. (Like a user, an ID is assigned to a role when it's created.) That's necessary because the IdentityUserRole object doesn't contain the role name. Instead, it contains just the ID of the role and the ID of the user that's associated with that role. Once the IdentityRole object is retrieved, the code adds the name of the role to the list of strings. Then, when the loop is complete, the code uses the Join method of the string object to convert the role names in the list of strings to a comma-separated value.

The second helper method updates the data that's displayed on the page by calling the DataBind method of the two GridView controls, the drop-down list, and the list box. As you saw in the first page of this listing, this method is called by the update, insert, and delete methods that are used by the users DetailsView control. It's also called by the update, insert, and delete methods that are used by the roles DetailsView control.

Finally, the code-behind file ends with the event handler for the PreRender event of both GridView controls. As you know, this code provides for the proper formatting of a GridView control that uses Bootstrap table classes. Note that since this event handler is used by both GridView controls, it starts by getting the control that caused the event to fire. Also note that this code checks that the HeaderRow property of the GridView control isn't null. That's necessary because both the GridView controls can be empty.

The code-behind file for the Maintenance page   Page 2

```
// Select, update, insert, and delete roles
    .
    .

// Add roles to users
protected void btnAddRoles_Click(object sender, EventArgs e)
{
    string userID = ddlUsers.SelectedValue;
    foreach (ListItem item in lstRoles.Items) {
        // if role is selected and user is not in it, add user to role
        if (item.Selected)
            if (!userMgr.IsInRole(userID, item.Text)) {
                userMgr.AddToRole(userID, item.Text);
            }
        }
        // if role isn't selected and user is in it, remove user from role
        else {
            if (userMgr.IsInRole(userID, item.Text)) {
                userMgr.RemoveFromRole(userID, item.Text);
            }
        }
    }
    grdUsers.DataBind();
}

// Helper methods
public string ListRoles(ICollection<IdentityUserRole> userRoles)
{
    IdentityRole role;
    var names = new List<string>();

    foreach (var ur in userRoles) {
        role = (from r in roleMgr.Roles
            where r.Id == ur.RoleId select r).SingleOrDefault();
        names.Add(role.Name);
    }
    return string.Join(", ", names);
}

private void Reload()
{
    grdUsers.DataBind();
    grdRoles.DataBind();
    ddlUsers.DataBind();
    lstRoles.DataBind();
}

// Provide for formatting GridView controls with Bootstrap
protected void GridView_PreRender(object sender, EventArgs e)
{
    GridView grd = (GridView)sender;
    if (grd.HeaderRow != null)
        grd.HeaderRow.TableSection = TableRowSection.TableHeader;
}
}
```

Figure 20-16   The code-behind file (part 2 of 2)

How to customize users

When you run an application that uses the Web Forms template, you can immediately start registering users and the application will remember these users so they can log in and out. That's because, behind the scenes, the application is using the Code First feature of the Entity Framework to create the authentication database the application needs to store and retrieve users. If your application provides for roles, this database can also store and retrieve roles. As you'll learn in the following topics, you can also use Code First to customize this database.

Before going on, you may be interested in knowing how you can look at the tables in the authentication database that's created by Code First. To do that, you can choose View→Server Explorer to display the Server Explorer. Then, you can expand the Data Connections, DefaultConnection, and Tables nodes to see a list of the tables. To see the columns for a table, you can expand the node for that table. And to view the data for a table, you can right-click on the table and select Show Table Data.

How to use Code First migrations

To customize a database with Code First, you use the *Package Manager Console (PMC)* to create and run *migration files*. These files contain C# code to do things like add and drop database tables and columns. Figure 20-17 shows what the PMC looks like and how to open it. Once you've opened the PMC, you can use the commands presented in the table to add custom user data.

This figure shows a procedure for adding a custom BirthDate property to the user data that's stored by an application. The first step is to register a user. Although this step is optional, it will cause the authentication database to be created. Then, when you enable migrations as described in the second step, an InitialCreate migration file that contains the code for creating the authentication database is created. This file can be useful when you're rolling back changes, as you'll see later.

Note that you only have to enable migrations once per application. After you do that, you'll have a Migrations directory with a Configuration.cs file and, optionally, an InitialCreate migration file.

The third step is to add a new property to the ApplicationUser class in the IdentityModels.cs file of the Models directory. An abbreviated version of this class is shown here. This class includes a new DateTime property named BirthDate.

The fourth step is to create a C# migration file by running the Add-Migration command. On this command, you code a name that identifies the data that you're adding. Then, a new migration file that creates a database column for the new property is added to the Migrations directory. Note that the name of this file will include a timestamp like this: 201605262145080_BirthDate.cs.

The fifth step is to update the database by running the Update-Database command. Note that the BirthDate column this step adds will accept null values. That's because the BirthDate property that was added to the ApplicationUser class is a nullable data type.

The Package Manager Console (PMC)

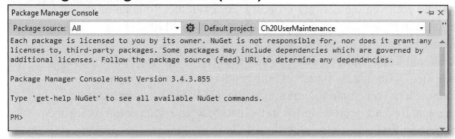

Some of the Code First migration commands

Command	Description
Enable-Migrations	Creates a Migrations folder and a Configuration.cs file. If an authentication database exists, also creates an InitialCreate file for that database.
Add-Migration "Name"	Adds a migration file with database changes to the Migrations folder.
Update-Database	Runs the migration files and updates the database schema.

How to open the Package Manager Console

* Choose the Tools→NuGet Package Manager→Package Manager Console command.

How to add a custom BirthDate property to the user data

1. Run the application and register at least one user. This step is optional.

2. Open the Package Manager Console, type Enable-Migrations at the command prompt, and press Enter. You only have to do this once per application.

3. Open the IdentityModels.cs file in the Models directory and find the code for the Application User class. Code a new DateTime property named BirthDate and then save the file.

4. Go back to the PMC, type Add-Migration "BirthDate" at the command prompt, and press Enter.

5. Still in the PMC, type Update-Database at the command prompt and press Enter.

The new property in the ApplicationUser class

```
public class ApplicationUser : IdentityUser
{
    public ClaimsIdentity GenerateUserIdentity ...
    public Task<ClaimsIdentity> GenerateUserIdentityAsync ...
    public DateTime? BirthDate { get; set; }
}
```

Description

* You can use *Code First migrations* to customize the authentication database. You use the *Package Manager Console* (*PMC*) to do this.

* For more information on working with Code First migrations, you can consult the MSDN documentation at this URL: https://msdn.microsoft.com/en-us/data/jj591621.aspx.

Figure 20-17   How to use Code First migrations to add custom user data

After you've completed this procedure, you can use the new property in code just like you would any other property. For example, you can modify the Register page in figure 20-6 to accept a date of birth in addition to a user name and password.

You should know that you can also add more than one property to a single migration file. To do that, you just add the properties to the ApplicationUser class. Then, when you create the migration file, Code First recognizes the properties that haven't been included in the database and adds columns for them in the migration file.

How to work with migration files

A migration file that's generated by the PMC contains a class that has the same name as the file (minus the timestamp). For instance, figure 20-18 shows some of the code in the InitialCreate migration file that you learned about in the last figure. As you can see, the InitialCreate class contains two methods named Up and Down. The Up method creates a number of tables, including the AspNetUsers table shown here, and the Down method drops these tables.

The code for the BirthDate class also contains Up and Down methods. In this case, though, the Up method simply adds the BirthDate column to the AspNetUsers table, and the Down method drops this column.

These Up and Down methods are called when you run the Update-Database method in the PMC. If you run this command as described in the last figure, the Up methods of all the migration files are called, and the database objects are created if they don't exist. If you include the -TargetMigration switch on the Update-Database command, though, only the Up methods in the migration files up to the one that's named on the switch will be called. Then, the Down methods of the migration files added after that will be called. This has the effect of rolling back changes made to the database.

The example in this figure illustrates how this works. Here, the InitialCreate migration is named on the -TargetMigration switch. When this command is executed, the Up method of the InitialCreate migration will be called. In contrast, the Down method of the BirthDate class will be called so the BirthDate column is dropped. Note that for this command to work, you must have registered a user before enabling migrations as described in the previous figure. Otherwise, the InitialCreate migration file won't be created.

As another example, suppose that after adding the BirthDate migration, you add another migration named Address that adds properties for a user's address. Then, you run the Update-Database command to add the address columns to the database. Now, suppose you decide that you don't want to include these columns. To remove the columns, you can run this command in the PMC:

```
Update-Database -TargetMigration: BirthDate
```

Then, the Up methods of the InitialCreate and BirthDate migrations are called, but the Down method of the Address migration is called, removing the columns added by that migration.

Some of the code in the Up and Down methods of the InitialCreate class

```
public partial class InitialCreate : DbMigration
{
    public override void Up() {
        ...
        CreateTable(
            "dbo.AspNetUsers",
            c => new {
                    Id = c.String(nullable: false, maxLength: 128),
                    Email = c.String(maxLength: 256),
                    EmailConfirmed = c.Boolean(nullable: false),
                    PasswordHash = c.String(),
                    SecurityStamp = c.String(),
                    PhoneNumber = c.String(),
                    PhoneNumberConfirmed = c.Boolean(nullable: false),
                    TwoFactorEnabled = c.Boolean(nullable: false),
                    LockoutEndDateUtc = c.DateTime(),
                    LockoutEnabled = c.Boolean(nullable: false),
                    AccessFailedCount = c.Int(nullable: false),
                    UserName = c.String(nullable: false, maxLength: 256),
                })
            .PrimaryKey(t => t.Id)
            .Index(t => t.UserName, unique: true, name: "UserNameIndex");
        ...
    }

    public override void Down() {
        ...
        DropTable("dbo.AspNetUsers");
        ...
    }
}
```

The Up and Down methods of the BirthDate class

```
public partial class BirthDate : DbMigration
{
    public override void Up() {
        AddColumn("dbo.AspNetUsers", "BirthDate", c => c.DateTime());
    }

    public override void Down() {
        DropColumn("dbo.AspNetUsers", "BirthDate");
    }
}
```

How to roll the database back to its initial state

```
PM> Update-Database -TargetMigration: InitialCreate
```

Description

- A migration file contains Up and Down methods. The Up method is called when a migration file is run by the Update-Database command, and the Down method is called when the -TargetMigration switch is included on this command to roll a database back to an earlier migration.

Figure 20-18   How to work with migration files

How to use the Seed method to add initial data to the database

The Seed method of the Configuration class in the Migrations directory is called every time the Update-Database command is run. This method is a good place to add test data or to add initial data like an admin user.

Figure 20-19 shows the commented out starter code that's generated by default for the Seed method. This code shows how to use the AddOrUpdate method of the DbSet object to add data to your application. As the comments note, this method lets you avoid creating duplicate data. That's because the AddOrUpdate method only adds a new row if the data doesn't exist. Otherwise, it updates the row.

For the first parameter of the AddOrUpdate method, you pass a lambda expression that tells the method what column to use to check for the row. In the starter code, the FullName property of the Person object will be used to see if that object is already in the People collection. For the second parameter, you send the objects you want to add or update. In the starter code, three instances of a Person object are passed.

The second example in this figure shows how to use the Seed method to add an admin user. It starts by adding two using directives for Identity namespaces. Then, it adds a using directive for the Models namespace so the code doesn't need to use fully qualified names. It also changes the name of the variable that holds the ApplicationDbContext object from "context" to "dbcontext" so you won't confuse this variable with the Context object you've seen in other code.

This Seed method uses the AddOrUpdate method described above to add a new role named "admin". However, it doesn't use this method to add a new user. That's because you want to make sure the password is hashed when you add a user. In this case, you also want to associate the user with the admin role.

To do that, the Seed method uses the Any method of the Users collection to see if the specified user is already in the collection. If it isn't, it creates a new application user manager and a new application user. Then, it uses the Create method of the user manager to add the user, and the AddToRole method of the user manager to add the user to the admin role.

Note that because the Seed method isn't run as part of an application request, you can't get the ApplicationUserManager object from the OwinContext object. Instead, you have to instantiate an ApplicationUserManager object directly as shown here. This code is similar to the code that's generated for the static Create method in the ApplicationUserManager class.

When you run the Update-Database command and an exception occurs in the Seed method, an error message and stack trace display in the PMC. Because the PMC doesn't provide any debugging tools, though, you'll need to provide any additional information you need from within Visual Studio. To do that, you can place the code for the Seed method within the try block of a try-catch statement. Then, in the catch block, you can create an error message that displays the values you need. Finally, you can create and throw a new ApplicationException object, and pass it your error message and the original exception. That way, both the original message and the custom message will be displayed in the PMC.

The Seed method with the starter code generated by Visual Studio

```
using System.Data.Entity;
using System.Data.Entity.Migrations;

protected override void Seed(
    Ch20UserMaintenance.Models.ApplicationDbContext context)
{
    //  This method will be called after migrating to the latest version.

    //  You can use the DbSet<T>.AddOrUpdate() helper extension method
    //  to avoid creating duplicate seed data. E.g.
    //
    //     context.People.AddOrUpdate(
    //       p => p.FullName,
    //       new Person { FullName = "Andrew Peters" },
    //       new Person { FullName = "Brice Lambson" },
    //       new Person { FullName = "Rowan Miller" }
    //     );
    //
}
```

A Seed method that adds an admin user

```
...
using Microsoft.AspNet.Identity;
using Microsoft.AspNet.Identity.EntityFramework;
using Ch20UserMaintenance.Models;

protected override void Seed(ApplicationDbContext dbcontext)
{
    // add the admin role
    dbcontext.Roles.AddOrUpdate(r => r.Name,
        new IdentityRole { Name = "admin" }
    );

    // use the ApplicationUserManager object to seed a user, rather than
    // the AddOrUpdate method, so its Create method creates a password
    // hash, and so the user can be associated with the new admin role
    if (!dbcontext.Users.Any(u => u.UserName == "anne@murach.com")) {
        var manager = new ApplicationUserManager(
            new UserStore<ApplicationUser>(dbcontext));
        var user = new ApplicationUser { UserName = "anne@murach.com",
            Email = "anne@murach.com" };

        manager.Create(user, "P@ssw0rd");
        manager.AddToRole(user.Id, "admin");
    }
}
```

Description

- The Seed method is called every time the Update-Database command is run. You can use this method to populate the database with test data or to provide default data.

- It's best to code the Seed method in a way that prevents duplicate data. One way to do this is to use the AddOrUpdate method.

Figure 20-19   How to use the Seed method to add initial data to the database

Perspective

This chapter has presented the basic skills for using the individual user accounts provided by ASP.NET Identity to authenticate users and restrict access to a web application. You should know, though, that there's a lot more that ASP.NET Identity can do. To learn about these additional features, you can start by reviewing the authentication files that are generated by the Web Forms template by default. The comments and links in these files will point you to web pages that provide more information.

Terms

authentication	role
authorization	access rule
Windows-based authentication	anonymous user
individual user accounts	authenticated user
third-party authentication	Multiple Active Result Sets (MARS)
authentication cookie	Package Manager Console (PMC)
ASP.NET Identity	migration file
OWIN (Open Web Interface for .NET)	

Summary

- *Authentication* is how you verify each user's identity. *Authorization* is how you determine what privileges a user has.

- *ASP.NET Identity* uses *individual user accounts* to add an *authentication cookie* when the user logs in, and then checks for the cookie on protected pages. If the cookie isn't found, the user is redirected to a login page. Identity is based on *OWIN (Open Web Interface for .NET)* middleware.

- You can use the Web Forms template to create a web application that has a fully functional authentication system by default.

- You can update the code in the IdentityConfig.cs and Start.Auth.cs files of the App_Start folder to change the default configuration of the authentication.

- *Access rules* restrict access to all or part of a web application. You can use *roles* to apply access rules to several users at once.

- You store access rules for an application in Web.config files. You can have rules for specific users and roles, and you can use wildcards to designate all users or unauthenticated users.

- You can use Code First *migrations* to customize the database that ASP.NET Identity uses. To do that, you make changes to the authentication code and then run commands in the *Package Manager Console*.

- You can use migration files to both add changes to a database and to roll them back. And you can use the Seed method to add test or initial data to the database.

21

How to use email, custom error pages, and back-button control

Once you've got an application working the way it's supposed to, you can add enhancements that make it work even better. In this chapter, you'll learn how to add three of the most useful enhancements. First, you'll learn how to send email from an ASP.NET application. Then, you'll learn how to create and use custom error pages. And last, you'll learn how to handle the problems that can occur when the user uses the Back button to access a page that's already been posted.

How to send email

When you create a web application, you often need to send email messages from the application. For instance, when a user makes a purchase from an e-commerce site, a web application usually sends the customer an email that confirms the order. Or, if a serious error occurs, the web application often sends the support staff an email message that documents the error. In the topics that follow, you'll learn how to send email from your ASP.NET applications.

An introduction to email

You're probably familiar with *mail client* software such as Microsoft Outlook or Outlook Express that allows you to send and retrieve email messages. This type of software communicates with a *mail server* that actually sends and retrieves your email messages. Most likely, your mail server software is provided by your Internet Service Provider (ISP) or through your company.

The diagram in figure 21-1 shows how this works. The two protocols that are commonly used to send email messages are *SMTP* and *POP*. When you send an email message, the message is first sent from the mail client software on your computer to your mail server using the SMTP protocol. Then, your mail server uses SMTP to send the mail to the recipient's mail server. Finally, the recipient's mail client uses the POP protocol to retrieve the mail from the recipient's mail server.

A third protocol you should know about is *MIME*, which stands for *Multipurpose Internet Mail Extension*. Unlike SMTP or POP, MIME isn't used to transfer email messages. Instead, it defines how the content of an email message and its attachments are formatted. In this chapter, you'll learn how to send messages that consist of simple text as well as messages that use HTML.

How email works

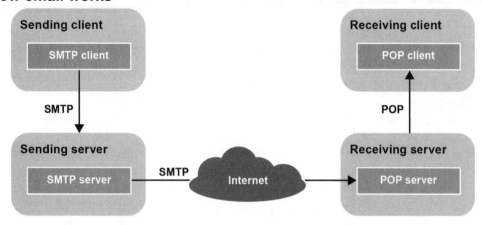

Three email protocols

Protocol	Description
SMTP	*Simple Mail Transfer Protocol* is used to send a message from one mail server to another.
POP	*Post Office Protocol* is used by mail clients to retrieve messages from mail servers. POP version 3, known as POP3, is the most widely-used version. A specification for POP version 4 exists but development hasn't progressed.
MIME	The *Multipurpose Internet Mail Extension* specifies the type of content that can be sent as a message or attachment.

Three common reasons for sending email from an ASP.NET application

- **To confirm receipt of an order.** When the user completes an order, the application can email a confirmation of the order to the user.

- **To remind a registered user of a forgotten password.** If the user forgets their password, the application can send an email that contains the user's password or a temporary new password to the email address that's on file for the user.

- **To notify support personnel of a problem.** If a problem like an unhandled exception occurs, the application can email a message that summarizes the problem to the appropriate support person.

Description

- When an email message is sent, it goes from the sender's *mail client* to the sender's *mail server* to the receiver's mail server to the receiver's mail client.

- *SMTP* and *POP* are the protocols that are commonly used for sending and retrieving email messages. *MIME* is the protocol for defining the format of an email message.

Figure 21-1   An introduction to email

How to use a third-party SMTP server

Out of the box, your ASP.NET applications won't be able to send email. This is true whether you're using IIS Express or the full version of IIS to host your applications. As a result, before you can test an ASP.NET application that sends email messages, you must install an SMTP server.

In previous versions of Windows, you could use the SMTP server that was built into IIS. Now, though, IIS doesn't include an SMTP server, so you'll need to get a separate one. Several SMTP servers can be downloaded for free from the Internet. One of these is called Papercut, and it's hosted on the Codeplex website. This SMTP server is designed for development environments.

Figure 21-2 describes how to download and use Papercut. It's a dummy SMTP server that works by intercepting emails sent from your application and displaying them in an inbox-like interface. No emails get sent, however, which means that you can send emails to and from any email address without worrying about cluttering up an actual inbox.

Once an email message is in the Papercut "inbox", you can use the options above the email message to view it. The Message option shows you how the email will look in an inbox as shown here. The Headers option shows you the email's headers, the Body option shows you the body of the email, and the Sections option lists the sections that make up an email. That includes the text and HTML in a multipart message, which you'll learn about shortly. Finally, the Raw option shows you the entire message, including headers, html, CSS, and anything else that's in the email.

When you close or minimize the user interface, it will be minimized to the system tray. This means that it will still be running, and when your application sends an email, you will get a notification in the lower right corner of your screen, as shown here. This is similar to the way that many mail clients work. Clicking on the notification will open the Papercut interface.

If you want to completely exit the Papercut application, you can click on the Exit button near the right side of the toolbar. You can also use the technique described in this figure to change the default behavior so the application exits on close rather than minimizing on close.

If you exit from Papercut completely, you should know that the code that sends the email will fail and the application will throw an exception. It's a good idea to do this during testing, though, so you can be sure that your application handles the exception appropriately.

The third-party Papercut SMTP server application interface

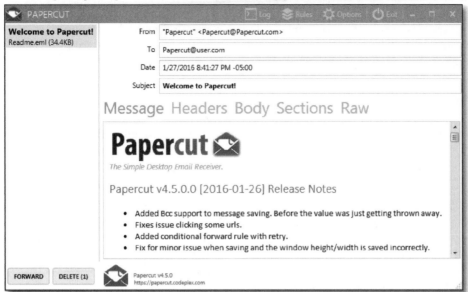

An email notification when Papercut is minimized in the system tray

How to install and work with Papercut

- At http://papercut.codeplex.com, click on Downloads and choose the ClickOnce Installer. Save the Papercut.application file to your downloads folder.

- Double-click the Papercut.application file and then click Install. When the installation is done, the interface will open with the Welcome to Papercut email shown above.

- When you click the close button at the right side of the toolbar, the Papercut application is minimized to the system tray. To display the application again, click on an email notification like the one shown above. Or, click the up arrow in the lower right corner of the task bar and then click on the Papercut icon.

- To completely exit Papercut, click the Exit button in the toolbar. If you'd like Papercut to exit on close, click on the Options button and uncheck the Minimize on Close check box.

- To open Papercut again, find the Papercut folder in the Start menu and click on the Papercut icon. This folder also has a link to the Codeplex website, which hosts Papercut.

Description

- Previous versions of Windows included an SMTP server with IIS, but now you must download a separate SMTP server even if you have the full version of IIS installed.

Figure 21-2   How use a third-party SMTP server

How to create an email message

Figure 21-3 shows the constructors and properties of the MailMessage class that you use to create email messages. It also shows the constructors of the MailAddress class. This class is used to create the addresses that are stored in the From, To, CC, and Bcc properties of a mail message. These classes are part of the System.Net.Mail namespace.

The first example in this figure illustrates how you can use these classes to create a mail message that includes a carbon copy (cc). Here, all of the values needed to create the email message are passed to the method as arguments. Then, the first three statements of the method create MailAddress objects for the from, to, and cc addresses. Notice that the MailAddress object for the from address includes both an email address and a display name. When a display name is included, it's displayed in the mail client's email list instead of the email address.

The fourth statement in this method creates a MailMessage object using the to and from MailAddress objects. Then, the next two statements set the Subject and Body properties of the message. Finally, the last statement adds the cc MailAddress object to the collection of objects in the CC property.

The second example in this figure shows how to create the same email as in the first example without setting the display name for the sender. To do that, you create the MailMessage object using the from and to addresses and the subject and body. This example also illustrates how you can create a MailAddress object for the carbon copy and add it to the collection of objects using a single statement.

Although the examples in this figure create messages that will be sent to a single recipient, you should realize that you can send a message to any number of recipients. To do that, you need to use the first constructor for the MailMessage class shown here to create an empty mail message. Then, you can create a MailAddress object for the sender and assign it to the From property of the message. And you can create a MailAddress object for each recipient and add it to the collection of MailAddress objects returned by the To property of the mail message. For example, to create a message that will be sent to two people, your code will look something like this:

```
MailMessage msg = new MailMessage();
msg.From = new MailAddress("anne@murach.com");
msg.To.Add(new MailAddress("mike@murach.com"));
msg.To.Add(new MailAddress("maryd@techknowsolve.com"));
```

Constructors and properties of the MailMessage class

Constructor	Description
`MailMessage()`	Creates an empty mail message.
`MailMessage(from, to)`	Creates a mail message with the to and from addresses specified as strings or MailAddress objects.
`MailMessage(from, to, subject, body)`	Creates a mail message with the to address, from address, subject, and body specified as strings.

Property	Description
`From`	A MailAddress object for the message sender.
`To`	A collection of MailAddress objects for the message recipients.
`CC`	A collection of MailAddress objects for the copy recipients.
`Bcc`	A collection of MailAddress objects for the blind copy recipients.
`Subject`	The subject line for the message.
`Body`	The body of the message.
`IsBodyHtml`	A Boolean value that indicates if the body of the message contains HTML. The default is False.
`Attachments`	A collection of Attachment objects.
`AlternateViews`	A collection of AlternateView objects for multipart emails.

Constructors of the MailAddress class

Constructor	Description
`MailAddress(address)`	Creates an email address with the specified address string.
`MailAddress(address, displayName)`	Creates an email address with the specified address and display strings.

Code that creates an email message with a carbon copy

```
private void SendTextMessageCC(string fromAddress, string fromName,
    string toAddress, string subject, string body, string ccAddress)
{
    MailAddress fromAdd = new MailAddress(fromAddress, fromName);
    MailAddress toAdd = new MailAddress(toAddress);
    MailAddress ccAdd = new MailAddress(ccAddress);
    MailMessage msg = new MailMessage(fromAdd, toAdd);
    msg.Subject = subject;
    msg.Body = body;
    msg.CC.Add(ccAdd);
}
```

Another way to create a message

```
MailMessage msg = new MailMessage(fromAddress, toAddress, subject, body);
msg.CC.Add(new MailAddress(ccAddress));
```

Figure 21-3   How to create an email message

How to send an email message

After you create an email message, you send it using the SmtpClient class shown in the table in figure 21-4. The technique you use to do that depends on the message you're sending and whether you have set the SMTP configuration settings for the application.

To set the SMTP configuration settings, you add code like that shown in the first example in this figure to the application's Web.config file. Here, the smtp element specifies the from address for the email. Then, the network element specifies the name of the host server and the port number to be used. It's important to note that the server name shown here, localhost, doesn't necessarily refer to IIS. Instead, it refers to the SMTP server that's installed on your local machine.

The second example in this figure shows how to send a message using settings in the Web.config file. When you use this technique, you don't have to specify the name or port for the SMTP server when you create the SmtpClient object. Instead, these settings are taken from the smtp element of the Web.config file.

The second example also illustrates how to send a message that's been stored in a MailMessage object. To do that, you simply name the MailMessage object on the Send method.

If you haven't set the SMTP configuration options, or if you want to override these options, you can specify the domain name of the server when you create the SmtpClient object. This is illustrated in the third example in this figure. Here, the name "localhost" is specified so the SMTP server on the local machine will be used. Notice that when you use the local server, you don't have to specify a port number. That's because the default port number is 25, which is also the default port for an SMTP server. If you use a server at a different port, though, you have to specify the port number.

The third example also illustrates how you can send a mail message without creating a MailMessage object. To do that, you just pass the from and to addresses and the subject and body text to the Send method. Then, the Send method creates the MailMessage object for you and sends it. You can use this format of the Send method if the message is in simple text format, you don't need to send the message to more than one person, you don't need to send copies of the message to anyone, and you don't need to send attachments with the message.

Constructors and methods of the SmtpClient class

Constructor	Description
`SmtpClient()`	Creates a client using the settings specified in the Web.config file.
`SmtpClient(name)`	Creates a client that can send email to the specified SMTP server.
`SmtpClient(name, port)`	Creates a client that can send email to the specified SMTP server and port.

Method	Description
`Send(message)`	Sends the specified MailMessage object.
`Send(from, to, subject, body)`	Creates and sends an email message using the specified from, to, subject, and body strings.

SMTP configuration settings in a Web.config file

```
<configuration>
    .
    .
    <system.net>
      <mailSettings>
        <smtp from="murachbooks@murach.com">
          <network host="localhost" port="25" />
        </smtp>
      </mailSettings>
    </system.net>
    .
    .
</configuration>
```

Code that sends a message using settings in the Web.config file

```
SmtpClient client = new SmtpClient();
client.Send(msg);
```

Code that creates and sends a message to a named server

```
SmtpClient client = new SmtpClient("localhost");
client.Send(fromAddress, toAddress, subject, body);
```

Description

- To send an email message, you use the SmtpClient class in the System.Net.Mail namespace.

- You can store the SMTP configuration settings that the SmtpClient class needs in the application's Web.config file, or you can specify these settings when you create an instance of the SmtpClient class.

Figure 21-4   How to send an email message

How to add an attachment to an email message

An *attachment* is a file that's sent along with an email message. The most common types of attachments are text files, word processing documents, spreadsheets, photos, and other media files such as sound and video files.

Figure 21-5 shows how you can create an attachment and add it to an email message. After you create an attachment object using the Attachment class, you add the object to the mail message's Attachments collection. Then, you can send the message.

Note that the code examples in this figure use the MapPath method of the HttpServerUtility object to get the file path of the document to attach. This is a good way to get file paths because it means you won't have to adjust this code when you move from a development to a production server and the file paths change.

Since SMTP protocol is designed to send text messages, not binary files, any email attachment for a binary file must be converted to text format before it can be sent. Then, the text attachment must be converted back to a binary file when it's received. Fortunately, ASP.NET handles this conversion for you.

The syntax for creating an attachment

```
new Attachment(fileName)
```

One way to create a new attachment and add it to a message

```
MailMessage msg = new MailMessage(fromAddress, toAddress, subject, body);
string fileName = Server.MapPath("Attachments/ReturnPolicy.docx");
Attachment attach = new Attachment(fileName);
msg.Attachments.Add(attach);
```

Another way to create a new attachment and add it to a message

```
MailMessage msg = new MailMessage(fromAddress, toAddress, subject, body);
string fileName = Server.MapPath("Attachments/ReturnPolicy.docx");
msg.Attachments.Add(new Attachment(fileName));
```

Description

- An *attachment* is a file that is sent along with an email message. When the recipient receives the email message, they can open or save the attachment.

- To add an attachment to an email message, you create the attachment using the Attachment class. Then, you add the attachment to the message using the Add method of the Attachments collection of the MailMessage class.

- If an email attachment contains a binary file, it must be converted to text before it can be sent, and it must be converted back to binary when it's received. ASP.NET handles this conversion automatically.

Figure 21-5   How to add an attachment to an email message

How to create an HTML message

By default, email messages consist of plain text with no formatting. However, you can also create a formatted message by using HTML. You should know, though, that it's a best practice to include a plain text message as well as an HTML message. You do this by creating a *multipart email message*.

The reason for sending multipart emails is that some people have their mail clients set to only show text, or to only show HTML from trusted senders and text from all others. Then, if you don't include a text version of your email, most mail clients will strip the HTML tags from your email message. This can cause words to run together and other formatting problems. Additionally, visually impaired people who use screen readers can have trouble with HTML messages.

Figure 21-6 shows a SendConfirmation method that creates a multipart email message. The method first creates a MailMessage object and adds a from address, a to address, and a subject. Then, it calls the GetConfirmationMessage method twice: once for the plain text version and once for the HTML version of the body of the message. The GetConfirmationMessage method uses basic HTML to create the HTML message, and carriage returns in the text message. Note that the messages include the customer's first and last names, which are retrieved from a customer object that contains the customer data.

An HTML email message can include links to your website. However, you should avoid sending HTML that includes scripts or web form controls. Many mail servers will reject them because that kind of content is often malicious.

After loading the plain text message in the Body property of the MailMessage object and the HTML message in a local variable called html, the method creates an AlternateView object. The AlternateView class of the System.Net.Mail namespace allows you to specify copies of an email message in different formats. Usually you will use the static CreateAlternateViewFromString method of the AlternateView class to create the alternate message. The first parameter of this method is the html message, the second is the encoding type, and the third is the media type.

After creating the AlternateView object for the HTML message, the method adds it to the MailMessage object's AlternateViews collection. It then creates an SmtpClient object and sends the email.

You can see the result as it appears in the Papercut application at the top of this figure. Here, the message is displayed in HTML format because Papercut provides for that format. If you look at the Sections option for the message, though, you can see that the message was received in both text and HTML formats.

A multipart email message with both text and HTML

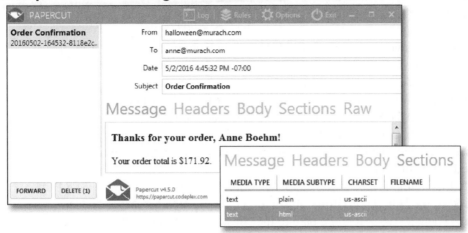

A method that sends a multipart email message

```
private void SendConfirmation(Customer customer, decimal total)
{
    MailMessage msg = new MailMessage(
        "halloween@murach.com", customer.EmailAddress);
    msg.Subject = "Order Confirmation";
    msg.Body = GetConfirmationMessage(customer, total, false);

    //create an alternate HTML view
    string html = GetConfirmationMessage(customer, total, true);
    AlternateView view = AlternateView
        .CreateAlternateViewFromString(html, null, "text/html");

    //add the HTML view to the message and send
    msg.AlternateViews.Add(view);
    SmtpClient client = new SmtpClient("localhost");
    client.Send(msg);
}

private string GetConfirmationMessage(Customer c, decimal total, bool isHtml)
{
    if (isHtml)
        return "<html><head><title>Order confirmation</title></head>"
            + "<body><h3>Thanks for your order, "
            + c.FirstName + " " + c.LastName + "!</h3>"
            + "<p>Your order total is " + total.ToString("c")
            + ".</p></body></html>";
    else
        return "Thanks for your order, "
            + c.FirstName + " " + c.LastName + "!\r\n"
            + "Your order total is " + total.ToString("c") + ".";
}
```

Description

- The AlternateView class of the System.Net.Mail namespace lets you include both text and HTML formats in an email, which is considered a best practice.

Figure 21-6   How to create an HTML message

How to create an HTML message
with an embedded image

Sometimes you will want your HTML to include images. These are called *embedded* images, and they're different than images that are attached to an email because embedded images appear in the HTML for the message.

Figure 21-7 shows how to embed an image in a multipart email message. This code uses the SendConfirmation method that you just saw, with two differences. First, the LinkedResource class of the System.Net.Mail namespace is used to contain the image. This class represents an external resource that is embedded in an email.

In this figure, for example, the SendConfirmation method uses the MapPath method of the HttpServerUtility object to get the file path for the embedded image. Then, it passes this file path to the constructor of the LinkedResource object. This creates an object named img that represents the embedded image. Last, it sets the img object's ContentId property to "logoImage". This last step is a crucial one, since this is the name that you will use to add the image to your HTML.

The other change in the code is in the GetConfirmationMessage method, where an image element is added to the HTML. The crucial step here is that the src attribute of the img element needs to point to the ContentID (cid) of the embedded image. In the example in this figure, the src attribute of the image tag is set to cid:logoImage, with no quotation marks.

An HTML email message with an embedded image

Subject | Order Confirmation

Message Headers Body Sections Raw

Thanks for your order, Anne Boehm!

Your order total is $171.92.

A method that sends a multipart email with an embedded image

```
private void SendConfirmation(Customer customer, decimal total)
{
    MailMessage msg = new MailMessage(
        "halloween@murach.com", customer.EmailAddress);
    msg.Subject = "Order Confirmation";
    msg.Body = GetConfirmationMessage(customer, total, false);

    //create an alternate HTML view
    string html = GetConfirmationMessage(customer, total, true);
    AlternateView view = AlternateView
        .CreateAlternateViewFromString(html, null, "text/html");

    //link and identify the image to embed
    string imgPath = Server.MapPath("Images/banner.jpg");
    LinkedResource img = new LinkedResource(imgPath);
    img.ContentId = "logoImage";

    //add the image to the HTML view, the view to the message, and send
    view.LinkedResources.Add(img);
    msg.AlternateViews.Add(view);
    SmtpClient client = new SmtpClient("localhost");
    client.Send(msg);
}
private string GetConfirmationMessage(Customer c, decimal total, bool isHtml)
{
    if (isHtml)
        return "<html><head><title>Order confirmation</title></head>"
            + "<body><img src=cid:logoImage>"
            + "<br /><br /><h3>Thanks for your order, "
            + c.FirstName + " " + c.LastName + "!</h3>"
            + "<p>Your order total is " + total.ToString("c")
            + ".</p></body></html>";
    ...
}
```

Description

- To embed an image as part of the HTML email, as opposed to including it as an attachment, you need to use the LinkedResource class of the System.Net.Mail namespace to hold the image and then refer to the image in the HTML code.

Figure 21-7   How to create an HTML message with an embedded image

How to use custom error handling

When an error occurs in an ASP.NET application, an exception is thrown. Then, if the exception isn't handled by the application, an ASP.NET Server Error page is displayed. This page includes an error message, a portion of the source code that threw the unhandled exception, and other debugging information. Since this type of error page usually isn't appropriate for the users of an application, you typically replace the generic error pages with your own custom error pages after you test the entire website but before you go live with it.

An introduction to custom error handling

Figure 21-8 describes four techniques you can use to display your own custom error pages. Depending on your application, you may need to use one or more of these techniques.

The first technique is to enclose code that might generate exceptions in a try block of a try-catch statement. Then, you can redirect to a custom error page if an exception does occur.

The second technique is to code a Page_Error method in the code-behind file for a page. This method is called whenever an unhandled exception occurs on the page. Then, in the Page_Error method, you redirect the user to a custom error page.

The third technique is to code an Application_Error method in the Global.asax file. This method is called whenever an unhandled exception occurs on a page that doesn't have a Page_Error method. Then, the Application_Error method can redirect the user to a custom error page.

The fourth technique is to use the customErrors element in the Web.config file to designate custom error pages. This technique is used to display custom error pages when common HTTP errors such as a 404 – Not Found error occur.

A custom error page in a browser

Four ways to display a custom error page when an exception occurs

- Use try-catch statements to catch exceptions as they occur, then redirect or transfer to a custom error page.
- Use the Page_Error method in a code-behind file to catch unhandled exceptions at the page level, then redirect or transfer to a custom error page.
- Use the Application_Error method in the Global.asax file to catch unhandled exceptions at the application level, then redirect or transfer to a custom error page.
- Use the customErrors element of the Web.config file to specify custom error pages that are displayed for specific types of HTTP errors.

Description

- If an unrecoverable error occurs, most applications display a custom error page to inform the user that a problem has occurred.
- Before the custom error page is displayed, the C# code will often do other processing, like recording the error in an error log or sending an email message to support staff that lets them know that a problem has occurred.

Figure 21-8   An introduction to custom error handling

How to get and use the Exception object for an error

Figure 21-9 shows how you can use the properties and methods of the Exception and HttpServerUtility classes to get and use the Exception object for an error. This is the object that contains information about the exception that has occurred. The examples in this figure show how this works.

The first example shows how you can use a try-catch statement to get the Exception object. Here, the catch block catches the Exception object if any of the statements in the try block throw an exception. You can use this technique in any method of a code-behind or class file.

The second example shows how to get the Exception object within the Page_Error method of a code-behind file or the Application_Error method of the Global.asax file. The Page_Error method is executed automatically if an exception isn't handled by the other methods of a code-behind file. And the Application_Error method is executed automatically if an exception isn't handled by any of the methods in the code-behind file, including the Page_Error method. In either case, you use the GetLastError method of the Server object, which you access using the Server property of the page or application.

The third example shows how to access the Server object in a file other than a code-behind file or the Global.asax file. In this case, you'll need to use the Server property of the HttpContext object for the current request to access the Server object.

In some cases, additional exceptions can be thrown after the original exception. In that case, a second Exception object is created that contains the original exception. For example, if an exception isn't handled by a try-catch statement or a Page_Error method, an HttpUnhandledException is thrown. Then, you can use the GetLastError method in the Application_Error method to get the HttpUnhandledException object, and you can use the InnerException property of that object to get the original Exception object. This is illustrated in the last example in this figure.

Common properties of the Exception class

Property	Description
Message	A message that describes the error.
Source	The name of the application or object that caused the error.
InnerException	The Exception object that caused the exception at the application level.

Methods of the HttpServerUtility class for working with exceptions

Method	Description
GetLastError()	Gets the most recent exception.
ClearError()	Clears the most recent exception.

Code that gets the last Exception object at the method level

```
try
{
    // statements that could throw an exception
}
catch (Exception ex)
{
    // statements that use the Exception object named ex
}
```

Code that gets the last Exception object at the page or application level

```
Exception ex = Server.GetLastError();
```

Code that gets the last Exception object in a non-page code file

```
Exception ex = HttpContext.Current.Server.GetLastError();
```

Code that gets the inner Exception object

```
Exception ex = Server.GetLastError().InnerException;
```

Description

- You can use a try-catch statement in any method of a code-behind or class file to get the Exception object for an error.

- The Page_Error method runs when an exception isn't handled by a try-catch statement. There, you can use the GetLastError method of the Server object to get the Exception object for the error.

- In some cases, such as when you don't handle an exception with a try-catch statement or a Page_Error method, the original exception is stored within another Exception object. Then, you'll need to use the InnerException property of the last exception to get the original Exception object.

- If your exception handling code isn't in a page or the Global.asax file, you can get the Server object from the current request.

- When you call the ClearError method to clear the error from the Server object, the ASP.NET Server Error page isn't displayed.

Figure 21-9   How to get and use the Exception object for an error

How to create a custom class for handling exceptions

As you just saw, code to handle exceptions can be used in many different places. Because of this, many developers create a custom error handling class that they can call from try-catch statements, page error handlers, and the Global. asax file. Another reason to use a custom error handling class is so you can process the exception as soon as it occurs, since the GetLastError method will return null once you redirect to an error page.

Figure 21-10 shows a custom error handling class. It contains a private variable named ex that can store an Exception object. An Exception object is assigned to this variable when an instance of the class is created.

The constructor that creates an instance of this class accepts an optional Exception object as a parameter. That way, if the exception has already been retrieved, as it would be in a catch block, it can be passed to the error handling class. The constructor starts by checking this parameter to see if it's null. If it is, the GetLastError method is used to get the Exception object, which is then assigned to the parameter. Notice that because this code isn't in a code-behind or Global.asax file, it uses the Current property of the HttpContext object to get the Server object.

Next, the constructor checks the Exception object to see if its InnerException property is null. If it is, the Exception object is assigned to the private variable. Otherwise, the inner exception is assigned to the private variable. Finally, the ClearError method is executed so the ASP.NET Server Error page isn't displayed.

This error handling class also has a method called SendEmail that uses the techniques you learned earlier in this chapter to send an email that contains the Message property of the Exception object to support staff. You should notice two things about this method. First, it places the code that sends the email in a try-catch statement. This is because code that sends email can fail, so you should plan for it in your code. Second, the try-catch statement returns string messages indicating the result of the send operation. That way, code that calls this method can be notified of the result and take appropriate action.

This figure also shows how the error handling class can be used in the Application_Error method in the Global.asax file. Here, the code creates a new ErrorHandler object from the ErrorHandler class, which stores the Exception object for the error in the private variable as described above. Next, the Application_Error method calls the SendEmail method, stores the result of the SendEmail operation in a local variable, appends the result to the URL as a query string, and redirects to the error page. The error page can then use the information in the query string to take further action, such as notifying the user whether or not the support team has been informed of the problem.

The reason that the code sends information to the error page in the query string of the URL is that this is the most reliable way to do it. If the error occurs at the beginning of a page's life cycle, information stored in session state or cookies might be lost.

A custom error handling class

```
using System.Net.Mail;

public class ErrorHandler
{
    private Exception ex;
    public ErrorHandler(Exception e = null)
    {
        if (e == null) e = HttpContext.Current.Server.GetLastError();
        if (e.InnerException == null) ex = e;
        else ex = e.InnerException;
        e.ClearError();
    }
    public string SendEmail()
    {
        string body = "An exception occurred at "
            + DateTime.Now.ToLongTimeString()
            + " on " + DateTime.Now.ToLongDateString()
            + "<br /> Error Message: " + ex.Message;
        MailMessage msg = new MailMessage(
            "halloween@murach.com", "support@murach.com");
        msg.Subject = "Exception in Halloween application";
        msg.Body = body;
        msg.IsBodyHtml = true;
        SmtpClient client = new SmtpClient("localhost");
        try {
            client.Send(msg);
            return "sent";
        }
        catch {
            return "notsent";
        }
    }
}
```

An Application_Error method in the Global.asax file that uses the error handling class and then redirects to a custom error page

```
void Application_Error(object sender, EventArgs e) {
    ErrorHandler handler = new ErrorHandler();
    string result = handler.SendEmail();
    Response.Redirect("ErrorPage.aspx?email=" + result);
}
```

Description

- You can use a custom error handling class in a try-catch statement, a Page_Error method, or an Application_Error method in the Global.asax file.

- The error handling class should process the exception before transferring to an error page. This is because after redirecting, the GetLastError method will return null.

- If you run an application with debugging and an unhandled exception occurs, Visual Studio enters break mode and displays a dialog box that describes the error and provides links you can use to get additional information on the error. To continue program execution when this dialog box is displayed, click the Continue button.

Figure 21-10   How to create a custom class for handling exceptions

How to handle HTTP errors
with the Web.config file

Not all unrecoverable errors cause ASP.NET to throw an exception. As figure 21-11 shows, some error conditions result in HTTP errors that are handled by the web server itself. For these errors, you can use the customErrors element in the Web.config file to specify custom error pages.

Although there are many different types of HTTP errors that can occur, the common types are listed in this figure. Of these, the most common is the 404 error. This error occurs when a user attempts to retrieve a page that doesn't exist. In some cases, a 404 error is caused by a missing page or a page that has been renamed. In other cases, a 404 error is caused by an error in your application's navigation controls, such as a hyperlink that uses an incorrect URL. Or the user may have typed an incorrect URL in to the browser's address bar.

As this figure shows, you include an error element in the Web.config file for each HTTP error that you want to redirect to a custom error page. In the example, this is done for two types of errors. The first error element specifies that the page named E404.aspx should be displayed if a 404 error occurs. The second element specifies that the page named E500.aspx should be displayed if a 500 error occurs.

You can also specify a default error page that's displayed if an HTTP error that isn't specifically listed in an error element occurs. In the example in this figure, the defaultRedirect attribute specifies that a page named DefaultError.aspx should be displayed if an HTTP error other than 404 or 500 occurs.

A customErrors element in the Web.config file for custom error pages

```
<configuration>
  <system.web>
    .
    .
    <customErrors mode="On" defaultRedirect="DefaultError.aspx">
        <error statusCode="404" redirect="E404.aspx" />
        <error statusCode="500" redirect="E500.aspx" />
    </customErrors>
    .
    .
  </system.web>
</configuration>
```

Common HTTP error codes

Code	Description
401	Unauthorized request. The client must be authorized to access the resource.
403	Forbidden request. The client is not allowed to access the resource.
404	File Not Found. The resource could not be located.
500	Internal Server Error. This is usually the result of an unhandled exception.

Description

- The customErrors element in the Web.config file lets you designate custom error pages that are automatically displayed when unrecoverable HTTP errors occur. You don't have to write any code to redirect or transfer to these pages.

- To enable custom error pages, add a customErrors element to the system.web element of the Web.config file. Then, set the mode attribute to On, and set the defaultRedirect attribute to the name of the generic error page.

- To associate a custom error page with an HTTP error, add an error element that specifies the HTTP error code in the statusCode attribute and the name of the custom error page in the redirect attribute.

Note

- You shouldn't use a customErrors element if you use the Application_Error method of the Global.asax file to handle errors. If you do, the customErrors element will be ignored.

Figure 21-11   How to handle HTTP errors with the Web.config file

How to handle the back-button problem

If the user clicks the Back button in the browser window to return to a previous ASP.NET form and then posts the form, the application's session state may be out of sync with that form. In some cases, this can result in a problem called the *back-button problem*. The topics that follow show you how to deal with this problem.

An introduction to the back-button problem

Figure 21-12 illustrates the back-button problem in a shopping cart application. Here, the contents of the user's shopping cart are stored in session state and displayed on the page. The user then deletes one of the two items, which changes the data in session state. At that point, the user changes their mind and clicks the Back button, which displays both items again, even though session state only includes one item.

If the user now proceeds to check out, the order is likely to show one item when the user thinks they have ordered two items. But that depends upon how the application is coded. In the worst cases, the back-button problem may cause an application to crash. In the best cases, clicking on the Back button won't cause a problem at all.

A similar problem occurs when the user clicks on the Refresh button for a page that has already been submitted. Although most browsers warn the user about resubmitting a page, this can still cause problems if the user ignores the warning.

In general, there are three ways to handle the back-button problem. The first is to try to prevent pages from being saved in the browser's cache by sending page cache settings with the HTTP response. Then, when the user clicks the Back button, the old page can't be retrieved and a new request for the page is sent to the server. There are several methods in ASP.NET for doing that, and you will find many examples online. However, these techniques don't work if the user's browser ignores the page cache settings that are sent with a response. Because of this, they aren't recommended and won't be covered in this chapter.

The second way is to use the *Post-Redirect-Get (PRG) pattern* to prevent pages that are posted to the server from being saved in the browser's cache. If the PRG pattern is used for the example in this figure, the user will be taken back to the Order page when they click the Back button. Then, when they navigate to the Cart page, they will see the correct cart information. As you'll see, the PRG pattern is easy to use, has only minor drawbacks, and also fixes the Refresh problem.

The third way is to code web forms so they detect when the user attempts to post a page that isn't current. To do that, a form can use timestamps or random numbers to track the use of pages. If timestamps are used for the example in this figure, the user will still see the incorrect data when they click the Back button in step 3. But if they try to resubmit the incorrect data, the application will detect that the data is incorrect and take appropriate action. This technique also fixes the Refresh problem.

A back-button problem in the Cart page of the Shopping Cart application

1. The user adds two products to the shopping cart. The shopping cart data is stored in session state and contains two items: one Deranged Cat at $19.99 and one Flying Bats at $69.99. The shopping cart displayed in the browser window looks like this:

2. The user selects the Deranged Cat product and clicks the Remove Item button to delete it. The product is deleted from the shopping cart in session state and the updated page is sent to the browser:

3. The user decides that they want to purchase the Deranged Cat after all and clicks the browser's Back button, thinking this will undo the Delete action. The browser retrieves the previous page from its local cache:

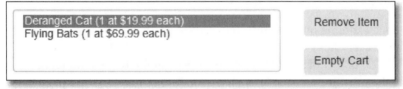

    Because the browser redisplayed this page directly from its cache, the Deranged Cat was not added back to the shopping cart in session state. As a result, session state contains only one item even though the web page displays two items.

Three ways to handle the back-button problem

*   Disable browser page caching for user input forms. Because this method is unreliable, it won't be covered in this chapter.
*   Use the *Post-Redirect-Get (PRG) pattern* to keep the posted page from being saved in the browser's cache.
*   Use timestamps or random numbers to track pages so you can detect when a page isn't current.

Description

*   When a user clicks the browser's Back button, the browser retrieves a locally cached copy of the previous page without notifying the server. As a result, the information stored in session state can become out of sync with the data displayed in the browser window.
*   Clicking the Refresh button can cause a similar problem, but the browser usually warns the user about re-submitting the page.

Figure 21-12   An introduction to the back-button problem

How to use the Post-Redirect-Get pattern

Figure 21-13 shows how to use the PRG pattern to solve the back-button problem. To start, this figure summarizes the normal postback pattern for a page. That is, the browser sends a POST request, the server handles the request, and the server returns a 200 HTTP response code with the HTML for the page. Then, the page is stored in the browser's cache.

The first code example in this figure shows the normal postback pattern in the Cart page. When the user clicks the Remove Item button, the selected item is removed from the Cart object in session state, and the HTML for displaying the updated Cart page is sent back to the browser. The problem is that by sending the page as a response to a POST request, the page is added to the browser's cache. Then, if the user clicks the Back button or the Refresh button to reload or resubmit this page, it can have serious consequences.

In contrast, the PRG pattern solves the back-button problem by splitting the posting of data and the retrieval of updated data into two separate roundtrips. More specifically, when the PRG pattern receives a POST request, it handles it and returns a 302 HTTP response code that tells the browser to redirect to the URL that's included with the response. Then, since no HTML is returned with the response, there's nothing for the browser to cache. Instead, the browser sends a GET request for the page and caches the page it receives in response to this second request.

The second code example in this figure shows the PRG pattern in the Cart page. When the user clicks the Remove Item button, the selected item is removed from the Cart object in session state, like it was in the first example. In this case, though, the next line of code tells the browser to redirect to the same page. Because of that, the updated data is stored in the browser's cache after the redirection. So, if the user clicks the Back button or the Refresh button to reload or resubmit the page, the browser will retrieve the updated data from the cache and the page won't be out of sync with the data on the server.

The normal postback pattern for a page

- The browser sends a POST request for a page.
- The server handles the request and returns a 200 HTTP response code (OK) and the HTML for the page, which is stored in the browser's cache.

The C# code for a method that uses the normal postback pattern

```
protected void btnRemove_Click(object sender, EventArgs e) {
    if (cart.Count > 0)       {
        if (lstCart.SelectedIndex > -1) {
            cart.RemoveAt(lstCart.SelectedIndex);
            this.DisplayCart();
        }
        else {
            lblMessage.Text = "Please select the item you want to remove.";
        }
    }
}
```

The Post-Redirect-Get (PRG) pattern for a page

- The browser sends a POST request for a page.
- The server handles the request and returns a 302 HTTP response code (Found) that tells the browser to redirect to the URL that's included in the response. Then, since no HTML is returned with the response, the page isn't stored in the browser's cache.
- The browser sends a GET request for the URL that was returned.
- The server returns a 200 HTTP response code (OK) and the HTML for the page, which is stored in the browser's cache.

The C# code for a method that uses the PRG pattern

```
protected void btnRemove_Click(object sender, EventArgs e) {
    if (cart.Count > 0)       {
        if (lstCart.SelectedIndex > -1) {
            cart.RemoveAt(lstCart.SelectedIndex);
            Response.Redirect("~/Cart.aspx");
        }
        else {
            lblMessage.Text = "Please select the item you want to remove.";
        }
    }
}
```

Description

- The PRG pattern works because a page isn't put into the browser's cache until after it has been updated.
- The PRG pattern is easy to implement, and it also fixes the Refresh button problem.
- The disadvantages of using the PRG pattern is that it requires two roundtrips instead of one and it doesn't preserve view state.

Figure 21-13   How to use the Post-Redirect-Get pattern

How to use timestamps

Figure 21-14 shows how to use timestamps, which is another reliable way to avoid the back-button problem. This technique also avoids the Refresh problem.

In this figure, you can see the code for a web page that uses timestamps to determine whether the posted page is current. The basic technique is to record a timestamp in two places when a page is posted: view state and session state. Then, the view state stamp is sent back to the browser and cached along with the rest of the information on the page, while the session state stamp is saved on the server.

Later, when the user posts a page for the second time, the Page_Load method calls a private method named IsExpired. This method retrieves the timestamps from view state and session state and compares them. If they're identical, the page is current and IsExpired returns False. But if they're different, it indicates that the user has posted a page that was retrieved from the browser's cache via the Back button. In that case, the IsExpired method returns True. Then, the Page_Load method redirects to a page named Expired.aspx, which in turn displays a message indicating that the page is out of date and can't be posted.

Notice that before comparing the timestamp items in session state and view state, the IsExpired method checks that both of these items exist. If not, the method returns False so current timestamps can be saved in both session state and view state.

For this to work, of course, the page must be posted back to the server. That means that you can't use the PostBackUrl property of a button to display another page if you first want to check that the current page hasn't expired. For example, suppose the user deletes an item from the cart and then uses the Back button to add it back as shown in figure 21-12. Then, if the user clicks either the Check Out button or the Continue Shopping button, you want the Expired page to be displayed so the user knows that the shopping cart isn't accurate. To do that, the Check Out and Continue Shopping buttons must post the Cart page back to the server, which doesn't happen if you use the PostBackUrl property.

A page that checks timestamps

```
public partial class Cart : System.Web.UI.Page
{
    private CartItemList cart;

    protected void Page_Load(object sender, EventArgs e)
    {
        if (IsExpired())
            Response.Redirect("Expired.aspx");
        else
            this.SaveTimeStamps();
        cart = CartItemList.GetCart();
        if (!IsPostBack)
            this.DisplayCart();
    }

    private bool IsExpired()
    {
        if (Session["Cart_TimeStamp"] == null)
            return false;
        else if (ViewState["TimeStamp"] == null)
            return false;
        else if (ViewState["TimeStamp"].ToString() ==
                    Session["Cart_TimeStamp"].ToString())
            return false;
        else
            return true;
    }

    private void SaveTimeStamps()
    {
        DateTime dtm = DateTime.Now;
        ViewState.Add("TimeStamp", dtm);
        Session.Add("Cart_TimeStamp", dtm);
    }
    .
    .
    .
}
```

Description

- When you use timestamps to solve the back-button problem, two copies of the timestamp for the page are saved: one in view state, the other in session state.

- The IsExpired method tests the view state and session state timestamps to make sure they are the same. If they aren't, the user has posted a page that has been retrieved from the browser's cache.

- This method also fixes the Refresh button problem.

- Some developers prefer to use random numbers rather than timestamps, but either technique will work.

Figure 21-14   How to use timestamps

Perspective

This chapter has presented three types of enhancements that you can add to an application after you have the basic functions working right. In practice, most applications use both email and custom error pages to make an application more user friendly and less error prone.

In contrast, many applications ignore the back-button problem on the theory that the users should be smart enough to avoid that problem themselves. As a result, clicking on the Back button and reposting a page will cause a problem on many e-commerce sites. That's why you may want to use the techniques in this chapter, especially the PRG pattern, to handle that problem on your website.

Terms

mail client	attachment
mail server	multipart email message
Simple Mail Transfer Protocol (SMTP)	embedded image
Post Office Protocol (POP)	back-button problem
Multipurpose Internet Mail Extension (MIME)	Post-Redirect-Get (PRG) pattern

Summary

- You can use the classes of the System.Net.Mail namespace to send email from your ASP.NET applications. The members in these classes let you send emails to multiple recipients, add carbon copies and blind carbon copies, add attachments, and format your emails with HTML that includes *embedded images*.

- The *Simple Mail Transfer Protocol (SMTP)* and *Post Office Protocol (POP)* are the protocols commonly used to send and receive emails. The *Multipurpose Internet Mail Extension (MIME)* protocol defines how the content of an email message is formatted.

- You will need to use a third-party SMTP server to send email with IIS or IIS Express. Several free servers that you can use for development are available online, including Papercut at the Codeplex website.

- When an error occurs in an ASP.NET application, you can handle it in a try-catch statement, in the page-level Page_Error method, in the application-level Application_Error method, or with customError elements in the Web.config file.

- When a user clicks the Back button in the browser window, it can cause the data in the browser's cache to become out of sync with the data on the server.

- The *Post-Redirect-Get (PRG) pattern* fixes the back-button problem by splitting the posting of data to the server and the retrieval of updated data from the server into two separate roundtrips to the server.

- The use of timestamps fixes the back-button problem by allowing the developer to detect when the user is posting a page from the browser's cache.

22

How to deploy ASP.NET web applications

Visual Studio provides a feature called one-click publish that you can use to deploy ASP.NET web applications. In this chapter, you'll learn the basics of using one-click publish. To start, you'll learn how to use the Publish Web wizard to create publish profiles and set file options. Then, you'll learn how to use two specific methods for publishing a web application.

How to work with Visual Studio's one-click publish feature

Deployment refers to the process of copying an ASP.NET web application from the development system to the production server where it can be accessed by users. An application can also be deployed to a test server so it can be tested in a different environment before it goes live. Visual Studio provides a *one-click publish* feature for deploying, or *publishing,* a web application. In the following topics, you'll get started with the Publish Web wizard that provides for one-click publishing.

How to work with the Publish Web wizard

The one-click publishing feature that's available in Visual Studio allows you to publish to various targets, such as a hosting provider, Microsoft Azure, or the local file system. It provides four methods for publishing to these targets, as summarized in figure 22-1. In this chapter, you'll learn how to use the File System and Web Deploy methods.

To use any of these methods, you start by displaying the Publish Web wizard as described in this figure. As you can see, this wizard includes four tabs named Profile, Connection, Settings, and Preview. You'll learn how to use these tabs as you progress through this chapter.

For now, you should know that the some of the tabs of the Publish Web wizard look different depending on which publish method you choose. In addition, you don't need to use all of these tabs for every method. In the next two topics, then, you'll learn how to use the Profile and Settings tabs with any method. Then, in the rest of this chapter, you'll see how to work with the other tabs and other options on the Settings tab when you use the File System and Web Deploy methods.

Another important thing to know is that the information that's presented here only covers basic deployment scenarios. You can actually make many more customizations when you use Visual Studio to deploy your web applications. For more information, you can start with the overview that's presented at the URL in this figure.

The Publish Web dialog box

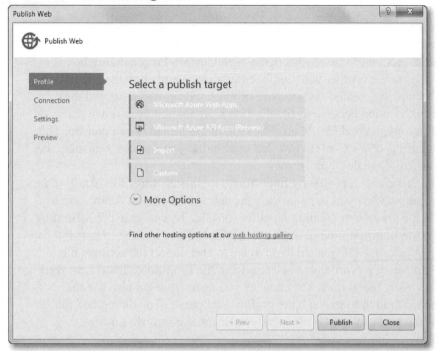

The four methods for publishing to a selected target

Method	Description
File System	Deploys files to a folder on the local file system so you can use your own FTP tool to copy them to a server.
FTP	Uses File Transfer Protocol (FTP) to deploy files to the target server over a network.
Web Deploy	Similar to FTP but has additional functionality like only copying files that have changed, deploying databases, and changing settings.
Web Deploy Package	Creates and deploys a .zip file that contains the files for the web application that can later be installed on the target server.

How to start the Publish Web wizard

- Select the project in the Solution Explorer and then choose the Build→Publish <project name> command. Or, right-click the project in the Solution Explorer and select Publish from the shortcut menu that's displayed.

Description

- When an application is complete, you'll need to *deploy* it to the server where it will be accessed by users. To do that, you can use Visual Studio's *one-click publish* feature.

- For an overview of web deployment with Visual Studio, you can go to this URL:
  https://msdn.microsoft.com/en-us/library/dd394698(v=vs.110).aspx

Figure 22-1   How to work with the Publish Web wizard

How to work with publish profiles

To create a *publish profile*, you use the Profile tab as shown in figure 22-2. One way to create a profile is to click on the Custom option in the Select a Publish Target section of the tab. Then, the New Custom Profile dialog box is displayed. To create a profile, you simply enter a name and click the OK button.

If you've already created one or more profiles, a drop-down list and the Manage Profiles button become available. In this figure, the drop-down list shows that a profile named Ch10Cart_FileSystem has already been created. This list also contains a <New Custom Profile> option that you can use to display the New Custom Profile dialog box.

You can also create a profile by importing a .publishsettings file. You'll often use this technique when you use a hosting provider or Microsoft Azure, and it can simplify the process of creating a publish profile. To import a .publishsettings file, click on the Import option in the list of options. Then, use the Import Publish Setting dialog box that's displayed to navigate to and import the settings file.

To edit an existing profile, you select it from the drop-down list. Then, you can navigate to any tab to make the changes you need. You can also use the Manage Profiles button to manage the profiles you create. The dialog box that's displayed when you click this button lets you rename or remove profiles.

The Profile tab of the Publish Web dialog box

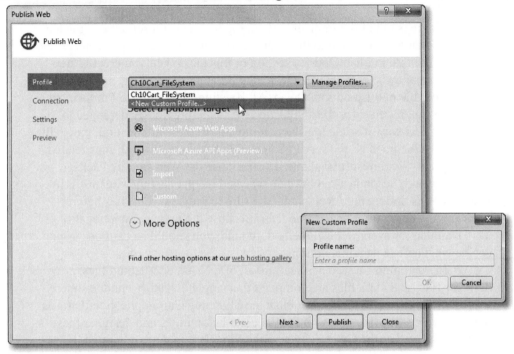

Description

- To add a new custom profile, click on the Custom option in the middle of the Profile tab. Then, enter a name in the New Custom Profile dialog box that's displayed.

- If you've already created one or more profiles, a drop-down list and the Manage Profiles button become available. Then, you can select <New Custom Profile> from the drop-down list to display the New Custom Profile dialog box.

- You can also create a profile by importing a .publishsettings file. To do that, click on the Import option in the middle of the Profile tab, and then use the Import Publish Settings dialog box that's displayed to navigate to the .publishsettings file.

- To edit an existing profile, select it from the drop-down list to display its options in the Publish Web wizard.

- To manage the profiles for an application, click on the Manage Profiles button. Then, a dialog box is displayed that lets you rename and remove existing profiles.

Figure 22-2   How to work with publish profiles

How to set the file publish options

The Settings tab of the Publish Web dialog box lets you set options related to the files that are published to the target server. In figure 22-3, you can see the options in the File Publish Options section of this tab. When you create a new profile, none of these options are selected by default.

The first file publish option, Delete All Existing Files Prior to Publish, lets you remove all the files for the application that were previously deployed to the server. That way, if some files were removed from the application, they will no longer be included on the server. You should be aware of two things related to this option. First, it isn't available if you choose the Web Deploy Package publish method. Second, it can have unexpected results in some situations. If you select this option, then, you should be sure to preview your files before publishing, which you'll learn to do later. Because the preview functionality isn't available for every publish method, though, you should be cautious as you decide whether to select this option.

When you publish a web application, all of the C# code-behind files, designer files, and class files are compiled to a single assembly and the source files aren't deployed. When you publish the Shopping Cart application that was presented in chapter 10, for example, the code-behind files and designer files for the pages as well as the C# class files in the Models folder are compiled. If you also want to include the C# code for any Global.asax files, the aspx files for any master pages, and the ascx files for any user controls in the assembly, you can select the Precompile During Publishing option.

The Configure link to the right of the Precompile During Publishing option also becomes available if you select this option. If you click this link, the Advanced Precompile Settings dialog box shown here is displayed. This dialog box lets you set additional options related to precompiled deployment. The option you're most likely to use is Allow Precompiled Site to be Updatable, which is selected by default. If this option is selected, all of the aspx files will be deployed with their original code, and you'll be able to make changes to that code even after the web application is deployed.

If you don't want the aspx code to be modifiable after it's deployed, you can remove the check mark from this option. Then, the aspx files will be compiled along with the other files. Although files with the same names as the aspx files will still be deployed, they will be used only as placeholders. In that case, instead of containing aspx code, each file will contain text that says that the file was generated by the precompile tool.

The last file publish option, Exclude Files From the App_Data Folder, determines whether the files in the App_Data folder are deployed. You might select this option if you include a database in the App_Data folder during development, but your deployed application uses a database on a database server.

In addition to the file publish options that are available from the Settings tab, this tab also includes database options. Since these options aren't available for every publish method, they're not shown here. But, you'll see them later when you learn how to use the Web Deploy method.

The file publish options in the Settings tab of the Publish Web dialog box

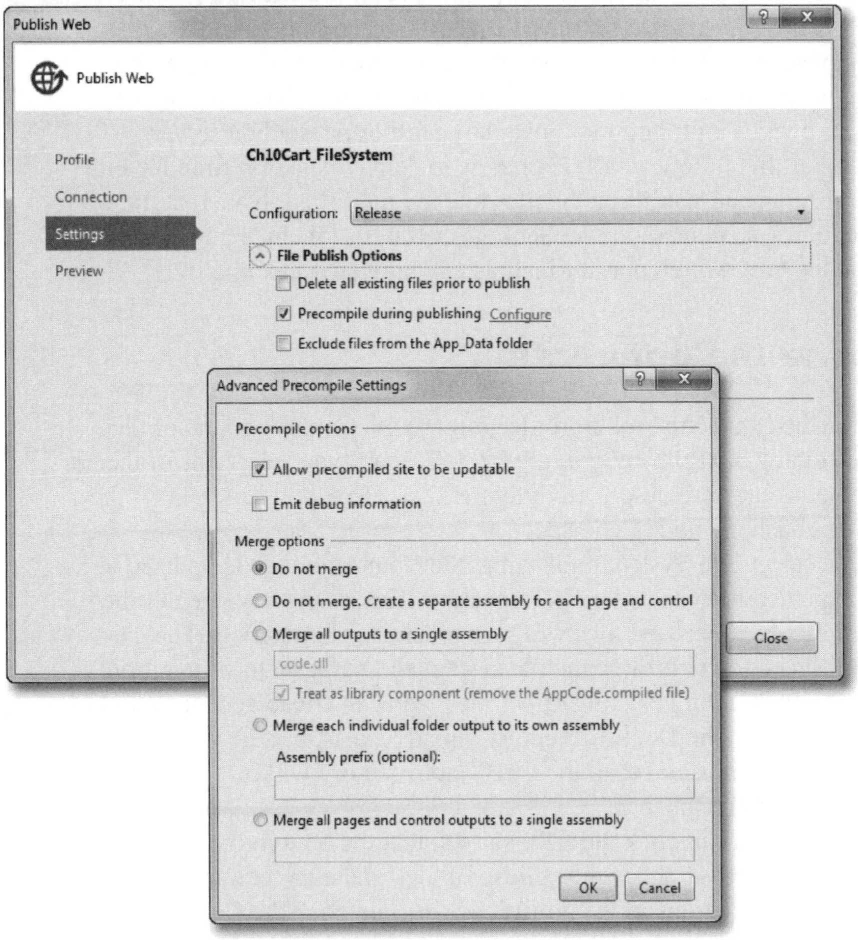

Description

- To remove files that were previously deployed for the application, select the Delete All Existing Files Prior to Publish option.

- The code files of a web application project are compiled whether or not you select the Precompile During Publishing option. If you select this option, though, any Global.asax files, aspx files for master pages, and ascx files for user controls are also compiled.

- If you select the Precompile During Publishing option, a Configure link becomes available that displays the Advanced Precompile Settings dialog box when clicked. One of the options in this dialog box lets you determine if the deployed files are updatable.

- If you don't want to deploy files in the App_Data folder, such as databases used for testing, select the Exclude Files From the App_Data Folder option.

Figure 22-3   How to set the file publish options

How to use the File System method

The simplest publish method is the File System method. You might choose this method when you want to precompile an application in a staging area and then use your own FTP program to move it to a test or production server.

In the topics that follow, you'll learn how to define the connection for File System publishing, and you'll see the files that are published. Note that the when you use the File System method, the Settings tab doesn't include any database options, and the Preview tab doesn't include any preview functionality.

How to define the connection

To define the connection for a profile, you use the Connection tab of the Publish Web dialog box, shown in figure 22-4. To start, you select one of the publish methods that were described in figure 22-1. Here, you can see that the File System publish method is selected.

Once you select File System publishing, the Connection tab is updated to display a single text box labeled Target Location. This is where you enter the path to the directory where the files will be published. Alternatively, you can click the ellipsis button to browse the file system and navigate to a directory.

In addition to selecting existing directories, you can create new ones. In this example, for instance, the Deploy directory already exists, but the Ch10Cart directory doesn't. Because of that, the Ch10Cart directory will be created when the web application is published.

At this point, you can click the Publish button at the bottom of the Publish Web dialog box to publish the web application files to the target location and save the deployment options in the profile. Or, you can click the Close button to save the profile without publishing the application. Then, when you're ready to deploy the application, you can open the Publish Web dialog box again, select the profile from the Profile tab, and click the Publish button.

The published files

Figure 22-4 also shows the structure of the C:\Deploy\Ch10Cart directory after the Shopping Cart application from chapter 10 was published to it using the File System publish method. As you can see, the Models directory has been omitted and a bin directory has been added. (Actually, the bin directory is always included in a web application, but you can't see it in the Solution Explorer unless you click the Show All Files button.) The bin directory includes .dll files for things like FriendlyUrls and the .NET compiler, along with a .dll file named Ch10Cart.dll. This is the assembly that contains the C# code in the code-behind files, the designer files, and the class files in the Models directory.

The publish profile that produced the files shown here used the default file publish options. That's why the Global.asax file and the aspx file for the master page are included rather than being precompiled. In addition, all of the published aspx files shown here contain their original aspx code.

The Connection tab of the Publish Web dialog box for the File System publish method

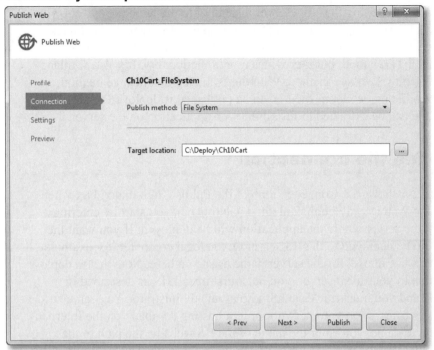

The published folders and files of the Shopping Cart application

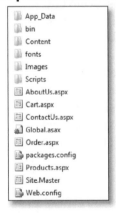

Description

- Select the File System option from the Publish method drop-down list of the Connection tab, enter the path for the directory to publish to in the Target Location text box, and click Publish. If the target location doesn't exist, it will be created.

Figure 22-4   How to define the connection and publish the files using the File System method

How to use the Web Deploy method

If you need to deploy files to a server instead of to the local file system, you can use the FTP, Web Deploy, or Web Deploy Package methods. In the topics that follow, you'll learn how to use the Web Deploy method. This method is similar to the FTP method, but it provides more functionality. It's also similar to the Web Deploy Package method. With the Web Deploy Package method, though, a .zip file that contains the files to be published is deployed to the server. Then, that file can be extracted to install the web application on the server.

How to define the connection

Figure 22-5 shows the Connection tab of the Publish Web dialog box when you select the Web Deploy publish method. On this tab, you start by entering the name of the server where the application will be deployed. If you want the application to be deployed to the IIS server on the local computer, for example, you can enter "localhost" for the server name as shown here. Note that to deploy an application to your local server, you must first install IIS as described in appendix A, and you must run Visual Studio as an administrator. You can also deploy to a web server on your network or to a hosting company on the Internet.

For the site name, you enter the name of the IIS website, the path to the IIS application, and the name of the application. In IIS, a website is simply a container for one or more applications. In this case, then, the name of the website is Default Web Site, which is the name of the website that's created by default when you install IIS, and Ch10Cart is the name of the application. Note that the website you specify must already exist. However, the path and application directory will be created if they don't exist.

If a user name and password are required to deploy to the server, you can enter that information as well. In addition, if you want to display the application in your default browser after it's deployed, you can enter the URL in the Destination URL text box as shown here. Finally, you can make sure that the settings on the Connection tab are valid by clicking the Validate Connection button.

The Connection tab of the Publish Web dialog box for the Web Deploy publish method

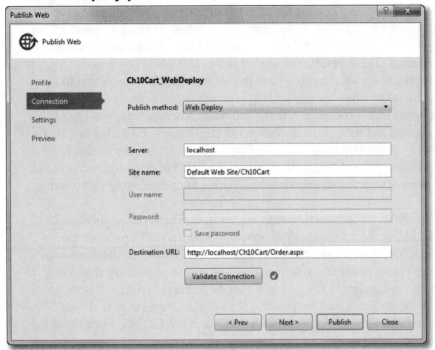

Description

- For the Web Deploy method, you must enter a server and a site name. You can also enter a destination URL to display the website after it's deployed.

- To be sure the connection is valid, click the Validate Connection button.

- To use the Web Deploy method to deploy a web application to your local computer, you'll need to install IIS as described in Appendix A, and you'll need to run Visual Studio as an administrator.

- To run Visual Studio as an administrator, right-click on its icon, select Run as Administrator, and click Yes in the dialog box that asks if you want to allow the program to make changes to your computer. For this to work, you need to have administrative privileges on your computer.

- Default Web Site is the name of the website that's created by default when you install IIS. The physical path to this website is C:\inetpub\wwwroot.

Figure 22-5   How to define the connection for the Web Deploy method

How to set the database options

As you saw in figure 22-3, the Settings tab of the Publish Web dialog box lets you set options related to the files that are published. When you use the Web Deploy method, it also lets you set options related to the databases that are used by the application. These options are shown in figure 22-6.

If the application uses a database and the information for connecting to that database will change when the application is deployed, you can enter the new connection string in the combo box that's provided. Alternatively, you can click the ellipsis button and then create a connection string using the dialog box that's displayed. This works much like the Add Connection dialog box you saw in chapter 13. When you're done, make sure that the Use This Connection String at Runtime option is selected so the connection string is updated in the Web.config file.

In this example, the connection string is set so the deployed application will use a Halloween database that's attached to SQL Server Express on the local machine. You can find out more about using the Halloween database with SQL Server Express in appendix A. For now, you just need to know that when you deploy an application to IIS, you can't use SQL Server Express LocalDB to work with the database files in the App_Data folder. Because of that, you won't need to deploy these files, so you should select the Exclude Files From the App_Data Folder option as shown here.

You can also deploy the database used by an application to the specified server. To do that, select the Update Database option. This deploys the database schema. To deploy the data, you'll need to write a SQL script and then add that script to the dialog box that's displayed when you click the Configure Database Updates link.

The database options in the Settings tab of the Publish Web dialog box

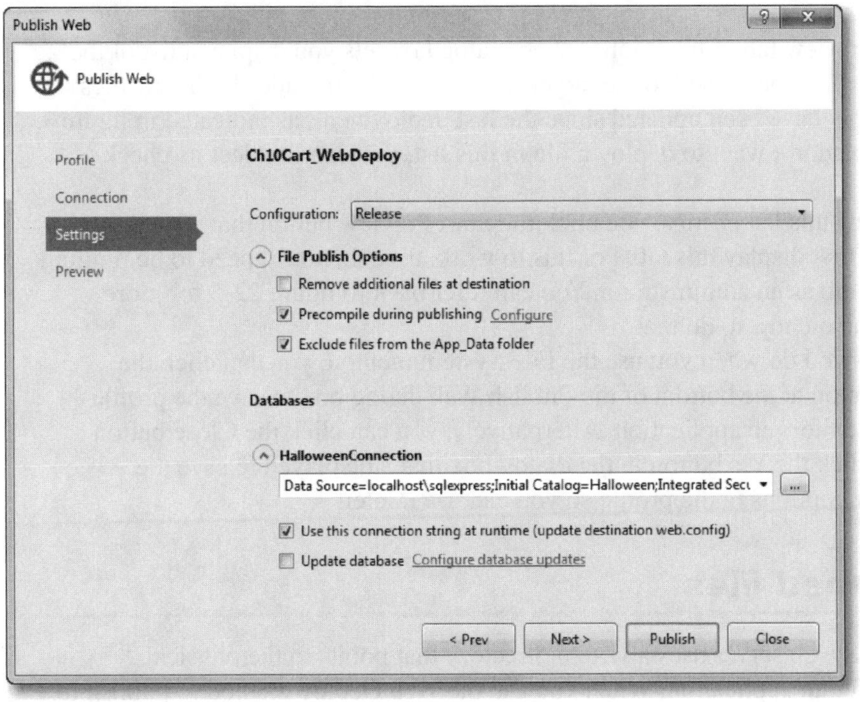

Description

- If the Web.config file defines one or more connection strings, the names of these strings will be displayed in the Databases portion of the Settings tab. Then, if the application will use a different connection string when it's deployed, you can enter that string or click the button with the ellipsis on it to display a dialog box that you can use to create the string.

- If you enter or create a new connection string, be sure the Use This Connection String at Runtime option is selected so the connection string in the Web.config file is updated.

- If you won't be using a database that's stored in the App_Data folder, you can select the Exclude Files From the App_Data Folder option.

- To create a database schema from a database that's used by the application, select the Update Database option. To add data to the database, create a custom SQL script, click the Configure Database Updates link, and add the script to the dialog box that's displayed.

Note

- When you use the Web Deploy method, the Delete All Existing Files Prior to Publish option changes to Remove Additional Files at Destination. This option causes files that were previously deployed and that are no longer included in the project to be removed from the server.

Figure 22-6   How to set the database options for the Web Deploy method

How to preview the files to be published

The Preview tab of the Publish Web dialog box lets you display a list of the files that will be published to the target server. This list includes both new files and files that have been updated since the last deployment, as indicated in figure 22-7. If you don't want to deploy a file in this list, you can deselect its check box.

To view this list of files, you click the Start Preview button that's available when you first display this tab. For this to work, though, you'll need to be running Visual Studio as an administrator. You can refer back to figure 22-5 for more information on how to do that.

Just as you do when you use the File System method, you can click the Publish button at the bottom of the Publish Web dialog box to save the profile and publish the web application. Alternatively, you can click the Close button and then click the Yes button in the dialog box that's displayed to save the deployment options in the profile so you can use it later.

The published files

The IIS web server uses a virtual directory that points to the physical directory for an application. When you use the Web Deploy method to publish to IIS, the files for an application are published to one of these physical directories. Then, you can navigate to that physical directory to view the published files.

Figure 22-7 shows the published files for the Shopping Cart application from chapter 10 after it was deployed using the Web Deploy method. The deployment options that were used are the ones that you saw in the last two figures. Because the files were deployed to the Default Web Site of the IIS server on the local computer, the files were published to the C:\inetpub\wwwroot\Ch10Cart directory.

Notice that the App_Data folder isn't included in this list. That's because the deployed application will use a SQL Server Express database, so files in the App_Data folder weren't deployed. Also notice that the Global.asax and SiteMaster.aspx files aren't included. That's because the option to precompile the application was selected.

In addition, the option that would allow the precompiled website to be updatable was deselected. Because of that, the aspx pages that are deployed don't contain any aspx code. Instead, they contain text like what's shown here for the Cart.aspx page.

The Preview tab of the Publish Web dialog box for the Web Deploy publish method

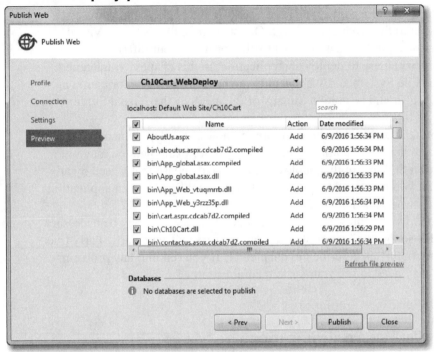

The published folders and files in the C:\inetpub\wwwroot\Ch10Cart directory

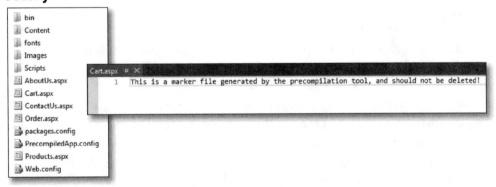

Description

- The Preview tab displays a list of new or updated files that will be published to the target server. You can deselect files that you don't want to deploy.

- For this to work, you need to run Visual Studio as an administrator, as described in figure 22-5.

Figure 22-7   How to preview the files to be published with the Web Deploy method

Perspective

To give the users of a web application access to the application, you need to deploy it to the production server. One way to do that is to use Visual Studio's click-once publish feature. This feature provides four different methods that you can use to deploy an application. In this chapter, you learned how to use the File System and Web Deploy methods. With this information as background, you should be able to use any of the methods that Visual Studio provides.

Keep in mind, though, that there's more to know about deployment than what's presented here. As mentioned in figure 22-6, for example, you may need to create an SQL script that deploys data to the database that's used by an application. Or, you may need to customize the Web.config file so an application works correctly when it's deployed.

In addition, if you deploy an application to an IIS server, it may be necessary to configure IIS so the application will run on that server. That's particularly true if you're using routing as described in chapter 11. If you run into any problems like this, you may need to see your system administrator.

Terms

deployment
one-click publishing

publish a web application
publish profile

Summary

- Visual Studio provides a *one-click publish* feature that lets you *deploy* your web application. This feature provides four publish methods: FTP, File System, Web Deploy, and Web Deploy Package.

- The Publish Web wizard lets you create one or more publish profiles that specify deployment options. You can use these profiles for initial deployment and to deploy updates and changes.

- A *publish profile* specifies where an application will be deployed, what files will be deployed, and whether the application will be precompiled. With some publish methods, it can also specify the connection strings for any databases used by the application, and it can publish the database.

Section 5

Going to the next level

This section consists of three chapters that present skills that will take you to the next level of professional web development. Chapter 23 shows you how to use ASP.NET Ajax in your applications. Chapter 24 shows you how to develop and use WCF and Web API services. And chapter 25 introduces you to ASP.NET MVC, which is an approach to web development that is dramatically different than using Web Forms. You can read these chapters in whatever sequence you prefer.

23

How to use ASP.NET Ajax

This chapter introduces you to the ASP.NET server controls that provide for building Ajax-enabled web pages. These controls let you develop web applications that are more responsive to users and that help reduce the load on the web server.

An introduction to Ajax

Over the years, websites have changed from collections of static web pages to dynamic, data-driven web applications. As web applications started performing many of the same functions as traditional desktop applications, users wanted their web applications to behave like desktop applications, too. Today, a *rich Internet application (RIA)* is a web application that provides users with an enhanced user interface, advanced functionality, and quick response times like desktop applications.

To build a RIA, you can use a framework like Java applets, Adobe Flash player, or Microsoft Silverlight. With these frameworks, though, the users must install plugins into their web browsers, and many mobile devices don't support these plugins. A better way to build a RIA, then, is to use *Asynchronous JavaScript and XML (Ajax)*, whose features are built into all modern web browsers and devices.

Examples of Ajax applications

Google's Auto Suggest feature, shown in figure 23-1, is a typical Ajax application. As you type the start of a search entry, Google uses Ajax to get the terms and links of items that match the characters that you have typed so far. Ajax does this without refreshing the page so the user doesn't experience any delays. This is sometimes called a "partial page refresh."

Because this Ajax technology is so powerful, it is used by many websites and applications. When you post a comment to a friend's Facebook page, for example, the comment just appears. And when you move the cursor over a movie on NetFlix, information about the movie appears in a popup. In both cases, Ajax is used to get the required data from a data store and update the page without reloading it.

Google's Auto Suggest feature

Netflix's popup feature

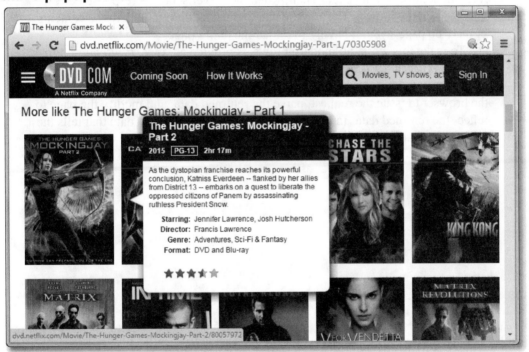

Description

- A *rich Internet application* (*RIA*) is an application that is displayed in a web browser, but has some of the features of a desktop application such as an enhanced user interface and quick response time.

- One way to build an RIA is to use *Asynchronous JavaScript and XML* (*Ajax*). Unlike normal HTTP requests, Ajax lets you receive data from a web server without reloading the page. This is sometimes known as a "partial page refresh."

Figure 23-1   Examples of Ajax applications

How Ajax works

When a web browser sends a normal HTTP request to a web server, the server returns an HTTP response that contains the content to be displayed for the page. Whether the page is static or dynamic, once the page is returned, the connection to the server is closed. Even if state is maintained with application variables, session variables, or cookies, a full HTTP request and response cycle must take place to update the web page. This is illustrated by the first diagram in figure 23-2.

By contrast, Ajax can update the web page after it's loaded without having to perform a full HTTP request and response cycle. This is illustrated by the second diagram in this figure. Here, the browser initiates a request that sends just the data that's needed by the server to respond to the request. That can include information about what event triggered the request, as well as the contents of the relevant controls on the page. Then, when the server sends its response back to the browser, the browser can use the data in the response to update the contents of the web page without having to reload the entire page.

To make this work, all modern browsers provide an *XMLHttpRequest object* (or *XHR object*) that is used to send an asynchronous request to the web server and to receive the returned data from the server. In addition, JavaScript is used in the browser to issue the request, parse the returned data, and modify the page to reflect the returned data. In many cases, a request will include data that tells the server what data to return.

How a normal HTTP request is processed

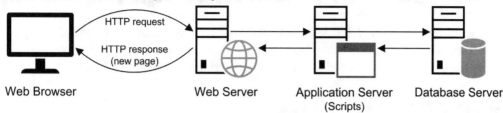

How an Ajax XMLHttpRequest is processed

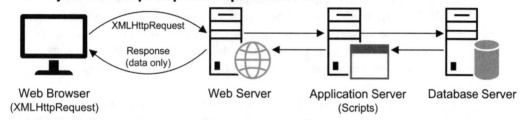

How Ajax updates the contents of a web page

1. An event happens on the web page, like moving the mouse, clicking a button, changing a field, or a timer going off. This event triggers the JavaScript code for the event.
2. JavaScript prepares a request and uses the XHR object to send it to the web server. This request contains information about the event and the current state of the controls on the web page.
3. The server receives the data, processes it, and sends a response back to the browser. The response contains the updated state of the controls on the web page.
4. JavaScript parses the response and uses the data it contains to update the contents of the web page. The browser then updates the user's screen.

Description

- Each time a standard HTTP request and response is performed, the entire page is returned from the server and the page is loaded into the browser. This type of request and response is required the first time a page is requested even if the page is Ajax-enabled.

- With an Ajax request, the browser can request just the information it needs to update the page. Then, the information that's returned from the server can be used to update the page without having to reload it.

- JavaScript is essential to the use of Ajax because JavaScript not only sends the requests but also processes the responses and updates the page with the new data.

- To send an Ajax request, JavaScript uses a browser object known as an *XMLHttpRequest object* (or just *XHR object*). This object can include data that tells the application server what data is being requested.

- An XHR object is often processed by server code that's written in PHP or C#. Then, the JavaScript has to be coordinated with the server code.

Figure 23-2   How Ajax works

An introduction to ASP.NET Ajax

Starting with ASP.NET 3.5 and Visual Studio 2008, Microsoft provided integrated support for building Ajax-enabled web applications using ASP.NET. The topics that follow introduce you to the components of *ASP.NET Ajax*.

How ASP.NET Ajax works

As you have seen, a standard HTTP request and response cycle that's triggered by an event in an ASP.NET web page is called a *postback*. When a postback occurs, the view state of the controls on the page is sent to the server as part of the request. Then, the server processes the request, updates the view state as necessary, and sends a response back to the browser that contains a new page with the new view state.

In contrast, ASP.NET Ajax enables a process known as an *asynchronous postback*. This is similar to a standard postback in that the view state of controls on the page is sent to the server in response to an event on the page. In an asynchronous postback, however, the XHR object is used to send the view state to the server. Then, the response that's returned by the server is used to update the controls on the page without having to reload the entire web page in the browser.

Figure 23-3 shows the three components of ASP.NET Ajax and illustrates how they work. The *ASP.NET Ajax client-side framework* is a JavaScript library that is loaded by the web browser when an Ajax-enabled ASP.NET page is displayed. It allows JavaScript code to interact with the ASP.NET application server through the XHR object it encapsulates.

ASP.NET Ajax also provides five server controls. They are used to Ajax-enable an ASP.NET web page so other ASP.NET server controls can be updated in the web browser without having to reload the page. These controls render JavaScript code as part of the web page just as other controls render HTML and CSS. The code they render uses the ASP.NET Ajax client-side framework to process events in the web page, manage and update controls in the web page, and trigger an asynchronous postback to interact with the server.

The ASP.NET Ajax client-side framework and the ASP.NET Ajax server controls are built into ASP.NET and Visual Studio. In contrast, the *ASP.NET Ajax Control Toolkit* is not. Instead, it's available as a separate download for Visual Studio. This toolkit consists of components and server control extensions that provide a variety of effects, animations, and interactive features.

The architecture of ASP.NET Ajax

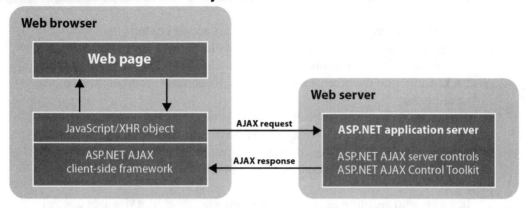

Components of ASP.NET Ajax

Component	Description
ASP.NET Ajax client-side framework	A JavaScript library that's loaded on the client to support the ASP.NET Ajax server controls.
ASP.NET Ajax server controls	Five server controls that encapsulate other ASP.NET controls on the web page to indicate that they will be controlled on the client by the ASP.NET Ajax client-side framework.
ASP.NET Ajax Control Toolkit	An open source project that provides more than 40 ASP.NET controls that you can use to build Ajax-enabled web applications.

Description

- An *asynchronous postback* is the process used by ASP.NET to perform a partial-page update. During an asynchronous postback, the view state of the web page is sent to the server, which processes the request and sends back the new view state of the controls being updated.

- The ASP.NET Ajax server controls enclose other ASP.NET server controls to make them Ajax-enabled. These controls can then be updated using an asynchronous postback.

- A single page can have one or more groups of Ajax-enabled controls that can be updated independently or simultaneously. Server controls that are not Ajax-enabled still trigger a full postback that causes the entire page to be reloaded.

- The *ASP.NET Ajax Control Toolkit* adds animation and effects to standard server controls. It started as a joint effort between Microsoft and the ASP.NET Ajax community, but is now maintained by DevExpress.

Figure 23-3   How ASP.NET Ajax works

The ASP.NET Ajax server controls

Figure 23-4 describes the five ASP.NET Ajax server controls that you can use to enable and manage asynchronous postbacks on a web page. These controls allow the other controls on the page to participate in an asynchronous postback. You'll find these controls in the Ajax Extensions group of the Toolbox in Visual Studio.

The ScriptManager control is the primary control that enables asynchronous postbacks, and it must be on a page for ASP.NET Ajax to work. It is often placed on a master page so all the pages that use the master page are Ajax-enabled. The other Ajax controls can then be placed on either the master page or content pages.

In addition to enabling asynchronous postbacks, the ScriptManager control provides for loading and managing additional JavaScript files. It also provides for registering *web services* so they can be accessed by JavaScript code on the client. Web services provide a way for one website to communicate with another website. You'll learn more about web services in the next chapter.

Note that you can have only one ScriptManager control on a page. If, for example, you add a ScriptManager control to a master page, you can't also add one to a content page that uses the master page. However, you can add a ScriptManagerProxy control to the content page. This control lets you load additional JavaScript files or register additional services needed by the content page but not by all the pages that use the master page.

In this context, a *proxy* is an object that's created on the client that you can use to access a service that's running on the server. When you use the ScriptManagerProxy control, it automatically creates the proxy for you.

After you add a ScriptManager control to a page, you can use the UpdatePanel control to enclose standard ASP.NET server controls. Then, the controls inside the UpdatePanel control are updated by Ajax when an asynchronous postback occurs. Note that you can have multiple UpdatePanel controls on a page. You can also have controls outside the UpdatePanel controls. If an event occurs on one of those controls, a full postback occurs on the web page, unless it has been designated as a trigger for an update panel.

Although an asynchronous postback is faster than a full postback, there may be times when an asynchronous postback takes more than a few seconds to perform. In that case, you may want to provide a visual indication that the postback is in progress. To do that, you can use the UpdateProgress control.

If you want to trigger an asynchronous postback at a set time interval, you can use the Timer control. This can be useful if you want to poll the server for any updates that need to be displayed. Keep in mind, however, that if an asynchronous postback is triggered too often, the load on the server can increase dramatically.

ASP.NET Ajax server controls

Control	Description
`ScriptManager`	Enables the use of the other ASP.NET Ajax controls, loads the ASP.NET Ajax client-side framework, and manages client-side JavaScript code.
`ScriptManagerProxy`	Extends the scripting services provided by a ScriptManager control.
`UpdatePanel`	Identifies a set of server controls to be updated using an asynchronous postback.
`UpdateProgress`	Provides visual feedback that an asynchronous postback is in progress.
`Timer`	Periodically triggers an asynchronous postback on an UpdatePanel control.

The ScriptManager control

- You can only have one ScriptManager control on a page. This includes master and content pages. If you put a ScriptManager control on a master page, you can't use one on a content page. If there is more than one ScriptManager control on a page, an Invalid Operation exception is generated.

- The ScriptManager control can also be used to load and manage additional JavaScript files and to register *web services* so they can be accessed by JavaScript code on the client. See figure 23-6 for details.

The ScriptManagerProxy control

- The ScriptManagerProxy control lets you load JavaScript files and register web services. It can be used in a content page if the master page contains a ScriptManager control.

The UpdatePanel control

- The UpdatePanel control is a container control that holds other server controls that will be updated during an asynchronous postback. All controls inside an UpdatePanel control will be updated at the same time. A page can contain multiple UpdatePanel controls, each containing a different set of controls.

The UpdateProgress control

- The UpdateProgress control provides a visual indication that an asynchronous postback is in progress. Then, the user will know to wait until the postback completes before doing anything else on the page.

The Timer control

- When one or more UpdatePanel controls need to be updated automatically, you can use the Timer control to trigger partial-page updates at a set time interval.

Figure 23-4   The ASP.NET Ajax server controls

The ASP.NET Ajax Control Toolkit

The ASP.NET Ajax Control Toolkit provides more dynamic, visually appealing user interface controls and control extensions. It is not a required component of ASP.NET Ajax and it is not built into Visual Studio. Instead, it's an open source project hosted at the DevExpress website that you can download and use for free. The URL for this website is shown in figure 23-5.

This figure also lists some of the most common controls and control extensions in the toolkit. The control extensions extend the functions of existing ASP.NET controls. For example, the Calendar extension extends the function of a TextBox control.

The toolkit currently contains over fifty controls and control extensions, and more are being added with every release. To view descriptions of these controls and extensions along with live examples, you can go to the website in this figure.

The toolkit is not an official part of ASP.NET. It is an open source project developed as a joint effort between Microsoft and the community at the Codeplex website and is now maintained by DevExpress. You should check the toolkit website often for new features, bug fixes, and security vulnerabilities.

The URL for the Ajax Control Toolkit

https://www.devexpress.com/Products/AJAX-Control-Toolkit/

Common controls and extensions in the ASP.NET Ajax Control Toolkit

Control/Extension	Description
`Accordion`	Contains multiple panes of content, but only displays one at a time.
`Animation`	Adds methods to change the position, size, opacity, and color of a control. They can be combined to create many dynamic effects.
`Calendar`	Shows a calendar in a pop-up window for easy date entry.
`CollapsiblePanel`	Provides a one-click, hide/show effect for a control.
`DragPanel`	Lets the user move a panel of content around on the page.
`HoverMenu`	Displays a menu when the user hovers over a control.
`ModalPopup`	A pop-up control that hides the page until the user selects an option.
`NumericUpDown`	Adds up and down arrows to a text box for changing the value.
`PopupControl`	Hides a set of controls until they are displayed in a pop-up window.
`RoundedCorners`	Adds rounded corners to a control.
`Slider`	Lets the user enter a value by dragging a slider.
`SlideShow`	Shows multiple images in one image tag. The images can change automatically or the user can manually scroll back and forth.
`TabContainer/` `TabPanel`	Shows multiple panes of content in a tabbed format.

Description

- The ASP.NET Ajax Control Toolkit provides a number of controls and control extensions that can make the user interface for an application look and work better.

- To install the ASP.NET Ajax Control Toolkit, download the installer file from the DevExpress website at the URL shown above. Then, run the installer file and accept the license agreement to add the toolkit to Visual Studio.

- The DevExpress website also includes documentation and live demonstrations of the controls and extensions in the ASP.NET Ajax Control Toolkit.

Figure 23-5   The ASP.NET Ajax Control Toolkit

How to use the ASP.NET Ajax server controls

The ASP.NET Ajax server controls can be added to almost any page to manage asynchronous postbacks. In the topics that follow, you'll learn the details of using each of the five controls.

How to use the ScriptManager control

As you have learned, you must add a ScriptManager control to a web page to enable asynchronous postbacks. Figure 23-6 presents some common properties of this control along with some code examples. Note that this code must be added inside a Form element before any other ASP.NET Ajax controls.

By default, all the JavaScript code for a page is loaded before the user interface is displayed. This ensures that the user interface is fully functional when it's displayed. In some cases, though, loading the scripts first makes the user interface take too long to display. Then, you should consider setting the LoadScriptsBeforeUI property to False so the user interface is displayed before the JavaScript is loaded. If you do that, keep in mind that the user interface may not be fully functional when it's first displayed.

The AsyncPostBackTimeout property determines how long the ASP.NET Ajax client-side framework waits for a response after triggering an asynchronous postback. If a response isn't received within the specified time period, an exception is raised and the postback is cancelled. If the value of this property is set to a time interval that's too short, users will see a larger number of errors. If it's set to a time interval that's too long, users will wait too long to find out that there's a problem with the request.

The IsInAsyncPostBack property is a read-only Boolean value that is set to True while an asynchronous postback is in progress. This property can be examined by either client-side or server-side code. In most cases, you'll use it in the Load event handler for a web page. Because this event handler is executed for full postbacks as well as asynchronous postbacks, you can use the IsInAsyncPostBack property to execute code depending on which type of postback is being performed. For example, code that initializes a control would not run during an asynchronous postback.

In addition to setting properties of the ScriptManager control, you can add Scripts and Services child elements. You use the Scripts element to load additional JavaScript code. Within this element, you code ScriptReference elements that identify the files that contain the code.

You use the Services element to create service proxies that allow the use of web services in client-side JavaScript code. Within this element, you code ServiceReference elements that specify the location of the svc file for each WCF service or the asmx file for each ASMX web service.

Common properties of the ScriptManager control

Property	Description
`AsyncPostBackTimeout`	Sets the time in seconds before an asynchronous postback times out if there is no response. The default is 90.
`EnablePageMethods`	Determines if static methods on an ASP.NET page that are marked as web methods can be called from client scripts as if they're part of a service. The default is False.
`EnableScriptLocalization`	Determines if the server looks for localized versions of script files and uses them if they exist. The default is True.
`IsInAsyncPostBack`	A read-only Boolean value that is True if the page is currently processing an asynchronous postback.
`LoadScriptsBeforeUI`	Determines if scripts are loaded before or after user interface elements. If False, the user interface may load more quickly but not be functional at first. The default is True.

The aspx code for a ScriptManager control

```
<asp:ScriptManager ID="ScriptManager1" runat="server">
</asp:ScriptManager>
```

The aspx code for a ScriptManager control that registers scripts

```
<asp:ScriptManager ID="ScriptManager1" runat="server">
    <Scripts>
        <asp:ScriptReference Path="~/Scripts/SampleScript.js" />
        <asp:ScriptReference Assembly="SampleAssembly"
            Name="SampleAssembly.SampleScript.js" />
    </Scripts>
</asp:ScriptManager>
```

The aspx code for a ScriptManager control
that registers two web services

```
<asp:ScriptManager ID="ScriptManager1" runat="server">
  <Services>
    <asp:ServiceReference
        Path="http://www.example.com/Services/SampleService.svc" />
        Path="~/Services/SampleService.asmx" />
  </Services>
</asp:ScriptManager>
```

Description

- The Scripts element of a ScriptManager control can contain ScriptReference elements that cause the ScriptManager control to load and manage additional scripts. The ScriptReference elements can load JavaScript code from a file using the Path property or from an assembly using the Assembly and Name properties.

- The Services element of a ScriptManager control can contain ServiceReference elements that cause the ScriptManager to create service proxies. To create a WCF service proxy, code a Path property that points to the svc file for the service. To create an ASMX web service proxy, code a Path property that points to the asmx file for the web service.

Figure 23-6   How to use the ScriptManager control

How to use the ScriptManagerProxy control

The ScriptManagerProxy control is used to extend the capabilities of a ScriptManager control. The most common scenario for using a ScriptManagerProxy control is when you use a ScriptManager control on a master page and you want to add either JavaScript code or a service proxy to a content page that uses that master page. This is illustrated in figure 23-7, which shows a content page that uses a master page that contains a ScriptManager control.

Unlike the ScriptManager control, you can have more than one ScriptManagerProxy control on a page. However, these controls can't be used to modify the properties of the ScriptManager control. They can only add additional ScriptReference and ServiceReference elements to a page. As you can see in the second and third examples in this figure, you code these elements just like you do a ScriptManager control.

A content page with a ScriptManagerProxy control

The aspx code for the ScriptManagerProxy control

```
<asp:ScriptManagerProxy ID="ScriptManagerProxy1" runat="server">
</asp:ScriptManagerProxy>
```

The aspx code for a ScriptManagerProxy control that registers scripts

```
<asp:ScriptManagerProxy ID="ScriptManager1" runat="server">
    <Scripts>
        <asp:ScriptReference Path="~/Scripts/SampleScript.js" />
        <asp:ScriptReference Assembly="SampleAssembly"
            Name="SampleAssembly.SampleScript.js" />
    </Scripts>
</asp:ScriptManagerProxy>
```

The aspx code for a ScriptManagerProxy control that registers a service

```
<asp:ScriptManagerProxy ID="ScriptManager1" runat="server">
    <Services>
        <asp:ServiceReference
            Path="http://www.example.com/Services/SampleService.svc" />
    </Services>
</asp:ScriptManagerProxy>
```

Description

- The ScriptManagerProxy control lets you extend the scripting services that are provided by a ScriptManager control. It's used most often on a content page whose master page contains a ScriptManager control.

- You can have multiple ScriptManagerProxy controls on a page. However, the ScriptManagerProxy controls can't override the properties of the ScriptManager control.

Figure 23-7   How to use the ScriptManagerProxy control

How to use the UpdatePanel control

The UpdatePanel control encloses other server controls that are updated during an asynchronous postback. These controls are placed inside the ContentTemplate element of the UpdatePanel control. Then, the controls within this element are updated as a group. Figure 23-8 shows how to use the UpdatePanel control.

When controls are added to an update panel, they are automatically made triggers for the panel. That means that if any of the controls cause an a synchronous postback, the panel is updated. In most cases, that's what you want. If you don't want the controls in an update panel to trigger an update, however, you can set the ChildrenAsTriggers property of the panel to False. Then, you'll need to identify the controls that trigger an update in the Triggers element of the UpdatePanel control. You'll learn about this element in just a minute.

As you have learned, you can have as many UpdatePanel controls on a page as you need. In addition, UpdatePanel controls can be nested inside each other. If you nest UpdatePanel controls, you should know that server controls in a child update panel won't trigger the update of the parent panel. That's true even if the ChildrenAsTriggers property of the panels is set to True.

By default, a panel is updated any time an asynchronous postback occurs on the page. This behavior is controlled by the UpdateMode property of the UpdatePanel control, which is set to Always by default. If you want a panel to be updated only when an asynchronous postback is caused by one of the panel's triggers, you can set the UpdateMode property to Conditional. Note that if an UpdatePanel control is nested inside another UpdatePanel control, it is always updated when its parent UpdatePanel control is updated. Also note that if you set the ChildrenAsTriggers property to False, you must set the UpdateMode property to Conditional or an exception will occur.

You can specify the controls that cause a panel to be updated in the Triggers element of the control, as illustrated in the second example in this figure. Here, the Triggers element includes two asp elements. The AsyncPostBackTrigger element identifies a control that causes an asynchronous postback to occur. In this case, the control is defined outside the update panel. However, you can also use this element for a control that's defined within an update panel. If necessary, you can use the EventName property to name the event that causes the postback. If this property is omitted, the postback occurs for the default event of the control.

The second element, PostBackTrigger, names a control inside the update panel that causes a full postback to occur rather than an asynchronous postback. In other words, instead of causing just the panel to be updated, it causes the entire page to be reloaded.

This figure also lists some compatibility issues you may encounter when you use certain controls and features with an UpdatePanel control. You'll want to be aware of these issues before you use the UpdatePanel control so you can avoid any potential problems.

Two properties of the UpdatePanel control

Property	Description
ChildrenAsTriggers	Determines if the controls in a panel trigger the content of the panel to be updated when a control causes a postback. The default is True.
UpdateMode	Determines when the content of a panel is updated. If set to Always, the panel is updated whenever a postback occurs. If set to Conditional, the panel is updated only when one if its own triggers causes a postback. A nested UpdatePanel control is always updated when its parent UpdatePanel control is updated. The default is Always.

The starting aspx code for an UpdatePanel control

```
<asp:UpdatePanel ID="UpdatePanel1" runat="server">
    <ContentTemplate>
    </ContentTemplate>
</asp:UpdatePanel>
```

The aspx code for an UpdatePanel control that specifies triggers

```
<asp:UpdatePanel ID="UpdatePanel1" runat="server">
    <ContentTemplate>
        <asp:Button ID="Button2" runat="server" Text="Add" />
    </ContentTemplate>
    <Triggers>
        <asp:AsyncPostBackTrigger ControlID="Button1" EventName="Click" />
        <asp:PostBackTrigger ControlID="Button2" />
    </Triggers>
</asp:UpdatePanel>
```

Compatibility issues with other controls

- The GridView and DetailsView controls can't be used in an update panel if you set their EnableSortingAndPagingCallbacks properties to True.

- A FileUpload control can only be used as a postback trigger for an update panel.

- An update panel may not function properly if the master or content page that contains the panel has its ControlIDMode property set to Static.

Description

- The ContentTemplate element of an UpdatePanel control contains the controls that are updated during an asynchronous postback. UpdatePanel controls can be nested.

- You can use the Triggers element to specify controls that cause the panel to be updated. The AsyncPostBackTrigger element identifies a control inside or outside of the UpdatePanel control that triggers an asynchronous postback. The PostBackTrigger element identifies a control inside the UpdatePanel control that triggers a full postback.

Figure 23-8   How to use the UpdatePanel control

How to use the Timer control

The Timer control triggers a periodic asynchronous postback. This control is typically placed inside the ContentTemplate element of the UpdatePanel control that's updated when the postback occurs. If it isn't placed inside an UpdatePanel control, it triggers a full postback of the entire page.

Figure 23-9 illustrates how the Timer control works. To start, you can determine how often an asynchronous postback occurs by setting the Interval property of the control. This property is measured in milliseconds. In the example in this figure, the Interval property is set to 10,000, or 10 seconds.

When you set the Interval property, you should be careful not to specify a value that's too small. If you do, it can cause a severe load on the server, particularly when many people have the page displayed. A value of 5,000 to 10,000 milliseconds is probably the smallest value you would want to use under most circumstances.

Also, you shouldn't expect the timer to be too accurate. That's because it's controlled by the timing mechanisms available to JavaScript in the web browser, and these mechanisms can be off by several hundred milliseconds.

If you need to, you can have two or more Timer controls on the same page. In most cases, you'll place these controls in different update panels. Then, you'll typically set the UpdateMode property of the UpdatePanel controls to Conditional so the Timer in one panel won't trigger the update of another panel.

Although you can use two or more Timer controls in the same update panel, there's usually no need to do that. Instead, if you need an update panel to refresh at different rates depending on what's happening in the web page, you can use a single Timer control and change its Interval property. If you want to use two or more Timer controls with preset intervals, however, you can use the Enabled property of the controls to determine which control is used at any given time.

A Timer control in Design view

Two properties of the Timer control

Property	Description
Interval	Determines how often in milliseconds the control triggers an asynchronous postback. The default value is 60,000 milliseconds (60 seconds).
Enabled	Determines whether a postback occurs when the time specified by the Interval property elapses. The default is True. You might set this property to False if you include more than one Timer control in the same panel, but you want only one to initiate a postback at any given time.

The aspx code for an UpdatePanel control with a Timer control

```
<asp:UpdatePanel ID="UpdatePanel1" runat="server">
    <ContentTemplate>
        <asp:Timer ID="Timer1" runat="server" Interval="10000">
        </asp:Timer>
    </ContentTemplate>
</asp:UpdatePanel>
```

Description

- The Timer control should be placed inside the ContentTemplate element of the UpdatePanel control that is updated when the timer triggers an asynchronous postback.

- Setting the value of the Interval property too small can cause an increase in the load on the web server and an increase in the amount of traffic to the web server.

- The accuracy of the Timer control is determined by the accuracy of the JavaScript implementation in the user's web browser.

Figure 23-9   How to use the Timer control

How to use the UpdateProgress control

The UpdateProgress control displays information to the user when an asynchronous postback is in progress. You code this information within the ProgressTemplate element of the control as shown in figure 23-10. Here, the information consists of text, but you can include images or controls as well. Note that this information is displayed only when an asynchronous postback is taking place. Otherwise, it's hidden.

The DynamicLayout property of the UpdateProgress control determines how space is allocated for the content of the control. By default, space is allocated only when the content is being displayed. That means that any elements on the page that appear after the UpdateProgress control are shifted down when the content is being displayed and shifted back up when the content is hidden again. If that's not what you want, you can allocate space for the content even when it isn't being displayed by setting the DynamicLayout property to False. It's up to the developer to determine which layout works best for the page.

In some cases, an asynchronous postback happens so quickly that the content of the UpdateProgress control flickers on the screen. To prevent that from happening, you can set the DisplayAfter property to determine how long the control should wait after the asynchronous postback starts to display its content. By default, this property is set to 0.5 seconds. Then, if the postback takes longer than that to complete, the content of the UpdateProgress control is displayed on the page.

In most cases, you'll code the UpdateProgress control within an UpdatePanel control as shown in this figure. Then, its content is displayed only when an asynchronous postback occurs on that panel. However, you can also code an UpdateProgress control outside an UpdatePanel control. Then, you can set its AssociatedUpdatePanelID property to the ID of the panel you want to use it with. Or, you can omit this property, in which case its content is displayed whenever any asynchronous postback occurs.

An UpdateProgress control in Design view

Three properties of the UpdateProgress control

Property	Description
`DynamicLayout`	Determines whether space for the content of the control is dynamically allocated on the page when the content is displayed. The default is True. If set to False, space is allocated for the content even when it is hidden.
`DisplayAfter`	Determines how long in milliseconds after the asynchronous postback has started to display the content. The default is 500 milliseconds (0.5 seconds). This value can prevent the content from flickering when the postback happens quickly.
`AssociatedUpdatePanelID`	The ID of the UpdatePanel control that the control is associated with.

The aspx code for an UpdatePanel control with an UpdateProgress control

```
<asp:UpdatePanel ID="UpdatePanel1" runat="server">
    <ContentTemplate>
        <asp:UpdateProgress ID="UpdateProgress1" runat="server">
            <ProgressTemplate>Updating...Please wait.</ProgressTemplate>
        </asp:UpdateProgress>
    </ContentTemplate>
</asp:UpdatePanel>
```

Description

- An UpdateProgress control must contain a ProgressTemplate element that defines the content of the control. This content is displayed only while an asynchronous postback is in progress. It is hidden after the asynchronous postback is complete.

Figure 23-10   How to use the UpdateProgress control

An application that uses ASP.NET Ajax

To illustrate how an application that uses Ajax works, the topics that follow present a page in the Shopping Cart application that displays information about the Halloween Store products and keeps track of how many times each product has been viewed.

The View Products page

Figure 23-11 presents the View Products page of the Shopping Cart application. To start, this page displays the products in a selected category in a GridView control. This part of the web page works like the Product List application you saw in chapter 13, but it's Ajax-enabled. This means that when the user selects a category in the drop-down list, the products for that category will be displayed in the GridView control without reloading the whole page.

Below the GridView control is a DetailsView control that displays product details when a user clicks the View link for a product. To the right of both of these controls is another GridView control that displays how many times each product has been viewed, and below this GridView control is an update progress control.

These controls are placed inside two UpdatePanel controls. The first one includes the GridView control for the products and the DetailsView control for the selected product. The second panel includes the GridView control for the most viewed products and the update progress control. This update progress control contains an animated "spinner" image and a "Loading…" message.

Although the Category drop-down list and the Clear Details button aren't inside an update panel, the drop-down list is set as a trigger for the first panel. This means that the drop-down list causes an asynchronous postback. In contrast, the button causes a regular postback.

As you'll see, the data for the most viewed products is stored in application state. If you wanted to have a permanent record of this data, you would need to save it in a persistent data store such as a database.

The View Products page

Description

- The View Products page is a variation of the Product List application you saw in chapter 13. It lets users view more details of a product, and also keeps track of how many times each product has been viewed. The product view information is stored in application state.

- This page uses two UpdatePanel controls. The first one contains a GridView control that displays the products and a DetailsView control that displays the selected product.

- The second UpdatePanel control contains a GridView control that displays the number of product views and an UpdateProgress control that displays an animated spinner image and a message while a selected product is being retrieved.

- The Category drop-down list and the Clear Details button aren't coded inside an UpdatePanel. However, the drop-down list is set as a trigger for the first panel, which causes an asynchronous postback. In contrast, the Clear Details button causes a regular postback.

- The second update panel is triggered by a change in the index of the GridView control that's in the first panel.

Figure 23-11   The View Products page

The ProductView class

Figure 23-12 presents the two classes that are used by this application. The ProductView class represents the data for one line in the GridView control for the most viewed products. This class consists of just four properties: ProductID, ProductName, CategoryID, and ViewCount.

The ProductViewList class

The ProductViewList class represents a list of ProductView objects. This class starts by declaring a private field named list that stores this list. Then, it includes two methods that are used to work with the list.

The public Add method uses the ProductID property of the ProductView object that's passed to it to see if that object is already in the list. It does this by attempting to retrieve an object with the same ProductID from the list. If the object it attempts to retrieve is null, the ProductView object isn't in the list yet, so the method adds it to the list. If the object isn't null, the method increments its ViewCount property by 1.

Note, however, that this method starts by executing the Sleep method of the current thread. This method is included just for testing purposes. It delays the Add method by two seconds to make sure that the update progress control is displayed. Otherwise, the page update may go so fast that the progress control is never displayed. You would of course remove this method after testing.

The other public method, the Display method, sorts the items in the list by the ViewCount property in descending order so the most viewed items will appear at the top of the grid when the list is displayed. Then, it sorts the items by the ProductName property so products with the same number of views will be displayed in alphabetical order.

The ProductView.cs file

```
public class ProductView
{
    public string ProductID { get; set; }
    public string ProductName { get; set; }
    public string CategoryID { get; set; }
    public int ViewCount { get; set; }
}
```

The ProductViewList.cs file

```
using System;
using System.Collections.Generic;
using System.Linq;
using System.Web;

public class ProductViewList
{
    private List<ProductView> list = new List<ProductView>();

    public void Add(ProductView newView) {
        System.Threading.Thread.Sleep(2000);
        string id = newView.ProductID;
        ProductView view = (from p in list
                            where p.ProductID == id
                            select p).SingleOrDefault();
        if (view == null) {
            list.Add(newView);
        }
        else {
            view.ViewCount += 1;
        }
    }

    public List<ProductView> Display() {
        return (from p in list
                orderby p.ViewCount descending, p.ProductName
                select p).ToList();
    }
}
```

Description

- The ProductView class is a data transfer object that holds information about the product and the number of times the product has been viewed.

- The ProductViewList class contains a private collection of ProductView objects, and exposes two methods.

- The Add method uses a LINQ query to check if the ProductView object that's passed to it is already in the collection. If it isn't, the object is added. If it is, the object's ViewCount property is incremented by one. This method also calls the Sleep method of the current Thread object to simulate a processing delay of two seconds.

- The Display method uses a LINQ query to return the collection of ProductView objects, sorted by the number of views in descending order and then by product name.

Figure 23-12   The ProductView and ProductViewList classes

The aspx file and the first UpdatePanel control

Figure 23-13 presents the form element in the aspx file for this application. This element starts with a ScriptManager control. That control is followed by the drop-down list for product categories and the Clear Details button. Neither of these controls is inside an update panel, and both call the Reset method when their default event occurs. The Reset method, as you'll see in the code-behind file, clears the selection from the GridView control for products. You'll come back to these controls in just a moment.

The drop-down list and button are followed by an update panel that contains the GridView control that displays the products and the DetailsView control that displays the data for the selected product. This update panel has a Trigger element that identifies the SelectedIndexChanged event of the Categories drop-down list as the trigger for an asynchronous postback. This means that when the user selects an item in the drop-down list, an asynchronous postback of the update panel is started, even though the drop-down list isn't inside the update panel. In contrast, when the Clear Details button is clicked, a regular postback occurs.

The form element in the Default.aspx file   **Page 1**

```
<form id="form1" runat="server" class="form-horizontal">
  <asp:ScriptManager ID="ScriptManager1" runat="server"></asp:ScriptManager>
  <div class="row">
    <div class="col-xs-12 table-responsive">
      <label id="lblCategory" for="ddlCategory"
          class="col-xs-3 control-label">Choose a category:</label>
      <div class="col-xs-3">
        <asp:DropDownList ID="ddlCategory" runat="server" AutoPostBack="True"
            CssClass="form-control" DataSourceID="SqlDataSource1"
            DataTextField="LongName" DataValueField="CategoryID"
            OnSelectedIndexChanged="Reset"></asp:DropDownList>
        <asp:SqlDataSource ID="SqlDataSource1" runat="server"
            ConnectionString="<%$ ConnectionStrings:HalloweenConnection %>"
            SelectCommand="SELECT [CategoryID], [LongName] FROM [Categories]
                      ORDER BY [LongName]">
        </asp:SqlDataSource>
      </div>
      <asp:Button ID="btnClear" runat="server" Text="Clear Details"
          OnClick="Reset" CssClass="btn" />
    </div>
    <div class="col-xs-7">
      <asp:UpdatePanel ID="pnlProducts" runat="server">
        <Triggers>
          <asp:AsyncPostBackTrigger ControlID="ddlCategory"
              EventName="SelectedIndexChanged" />
        </Triggers>
        <ContentTemplate>
          <asp:GridView ID="grdProducts" runat="server"
              DataSourceID="SqlDataSource2" DataKeyNames="ProductID"
              CssClass="table table-bordered table-striped table-condensed"
              AutoGenerateColumns="false" OnPreRender="GridView_PreRender">
              OnSelectedIndexChanged="grdProducts_SelectedIndexChanged"
              <Columns>
                <asp:CommandField ShowSelectButton="true" SelectText="View">
                    <ItemStyle CssClass="col-xs-1" /></asp:CommandField>
                <asp:BoundField DataField="ProductID" HeaderText="ID"
                    ReadOnly="True">
                    <ItemStyle CssClass="col-xs-2" /></asp:BoundField>
                ...
                <asp:BoundField DataField="OnHand" HeaderText="On Hand">
                    <ItemStyle CssClass="col-xs-2 text-right" />
                    <HeaderStyle CssClass="text-right" /></asp:BoundField>
              </Columns>
              <HeaderStyle CssClass="bg-halloween" />
          </asp:GridView>
          <asp:SqlDataSource ID="SqlDataSource2" runat="server"
              ConnectionString="<%$ ConnectionStrings:HalloweenConnection %>"
              SelectCommand="SELECT [ProductID], [Name], [UnitPrice], [OnHand]
                        FROM [Products]
                        WHERE ([CategoryID] = @CategoryID)
                        ORDER BY [ProductID]">
            <SelectParameters>
              <asp:ControlParameter Name="CategoryID" Type="String"
                  ControlID="ddlCategory" PropertyName="SelectedValue" />
            </SelectParameters>
          </asp:SqlDataSource>
```

Figure 23-13   The aspx file for the View Products page (part 1 of 2)

The second UpdatePanel control

The second update panel contains the GridView control that displays the number of times each product has been viewed. This update panel doesn't contain any controls that cause a postback. Instead, the data source for the GridView control is reset in code every time a product is viewed. You'll see this in the code-behind file in just a minute.

This means that the panel needs to be refreshed every time the user clicks on any View link in the products grid. Because the UpdateMode property of the update panel has been left at its default of Always, this happens automatically. In case this property is ever changed, though, a Triggers element is included in the update panel. This element triggers an asynchronous postback when the SelectedIndexChanged event for the GridView control fires.

This update panel also contains an UpdateProgress control. Because the DynamicLayout property of this control has been left at its default value of True, space is allocated for it on the page only when it's displayed. The content of this control includes an animated gif file and a text comment.

The form element in the Default.aspx file   **Page 2**

```
<h2>Product Details</h2>
<asp:DetailsView ID="dvwProduct" runat="server"
    AutoGenerateRows="False"
    DataKeyNames="ProductID" DataSourceID="SqlDataSource3"
    CssClass="table table-bordered table-condensed">
    <Fields>
      <asp:BoundField DataField="ProductID" HeaderText="ID"
          ReadOnly="True">
            <HeaderStyle CssClass="col-xs-4" /></asp:BoundField>
        ...
      <asp:BoundField DataField="CategoryID" HeaderText="Category ID" />
    </Fields>
    <RowStyle CssClass="dvRow" />
</asp:DetailsView>
<asp:SqlDataSource runat="server" ID="SqlDataSource3"
    ConnectionString="<%$ ConnectionStrings:HalloweenConnection %>"
    SelectCommand="SELECT [ProductID], [Name], [ShortDescription],
      [LongDescription], [CategoryID], [UnitPrice], [OnHand]
      FROM [Products] WHERE ([ProductID] = @ProductID)">
    <SelectParameters>
      <asp:ControlParameter ControlID="grdProducts" Type="String"
          PropertyName="SelectedValue" Name="ProductID" />
    </SelectParameters>
</asp:SqlDataSource>
</ContentTemplate>
</asp:UpdatePanel>
</div>
<div class="col-xs-5 table-responsive">
  <h2 id="most-viewed">Most viewed</h2>
  <asp:UpdatePanel ID="pnlViews" runat="server">
    <Triggers>
      <asp:AsyncPostBackTrigger ControlID="grdProducts"
          EventName="SelectedIndexChanged" />
    </Triggers>
    <ContentTemplate>
      <asp:GridView ID="grdViews" runat="server"
          AutoGenerateColumns="false" OnPreRender="GridView_PreRender"
          CssClass="table table-bordered table-condensed">
          <Columns>
            <asp:BoundField DataField="ProductName" HeaderText="Product">
              <ItemStyle CssClass="col-xs-5" /></asp:BoundField>
            <asp:BoundField DataField="ViewCount" HeaderText="Views">
              <ItemStyle CssClass="col-xs-3" /></asp:BoundField>
            <asp:BoundField DataField="CategoryID" HeaderText="Cat ID">
              <ItemStyle CssClass="col-xs-4" /></asp:BoundField>
          </Columns>
          <HeaderStyle CssClass="bg-halloween" />
      </asp:GridView>
      <asp:UpdateProgress ID="UpdateProgress1" runat="server">
        <ProgressTemplate>
          <div class="spinner"><img src="Images/spinner.gif"
              alt="Please Wait" />Loading...</div>
        </ProgressTemplate>
      </asp:UpdateProgress>
    </ContentTemplate>
  </asp:UpdatePanel>
</div>
  </div><%--end row--%>
</form>
```

Figure 23-13   The aspx file for the View Products page (part 2 of 2)

The code-behind file

Figure 23-14 presents the code-behind file for the page. This file consists of a private constant, a private helper method, and three event handlers.

The private constant is a string constant named APP_KEY. This will be used as the key value when working with the item in application state that holds the ProductViewList object. Using a constant in this way, rather than typing out "viewlist" each time you use the key, is a good way to reduce the chance of errors.

The private helper method is called BindViewGrid, and it accepts a list of ProductView objects as a parameter. As its name implies, this method gets the list, sets it as the data source for the GridView control that displays the number of product views, and calls that GridView control's DataBind method. This causes the product view information to show on the page. The BindViewGrid method is called when the page loads, and whenever a user views a product.

The first event handler is the Page_Load event handler. It starts by declaring a ProductViewList object named viewlist. Then, it checks application state to see if it contains an item with the same name as the APP_KEY constant value. If it doesn't, a new object is created from the ProductViewList class, and this object is added to application state. Otherwise, the item in application state is cast as a ProductViewList object and assigned to the viewlist variable. After the viewlist variable is loaded, its Display method is called to send a list of ProductView objects to the BindViewGrid method.

The second event handler handles the SelectedIndexChanged event of the products GridView control, which is fired whenever a user views a product. It starts by declaring a new ProductView object. Then, it loads the object's properties with data about the product that's been selected for viewing.

The ProductID property value comes from the SelectedValue property of the GridView control for the products. This is because the GridView control's DataKeyNames property is set to ProductID. In contrast, the ProductName property value has to come from the SelectedRow property of the GridView control. The CategoryID value comes from the SelectedValue property of the category
drop-down list, and the ViewCount property value is set to a default value of 1.

Next, this method locks application state so another user can't modify it at the same time. Then, it gets a reference to the ProductViewList item in application state, stores it in a variable named viewlist, adds the viewed product to the viewlist variable, and unlocks application state. Last, the viewlist's Display method is called to sort the list of ProductView objects, and the list is passed to the BindViewGrid method.

The third event handler is called Reset, and as you saw in the aspx code, it is called by both the Category drop-down list and the Clear Details button. It sets the SelectedIndex property of the products GridView control to -1, which clears the selected item in the GridView control. This also clears the data from the DetailsView control, since it gets the parameter value for its select method from the GridView control's SelectedValue property.

The Default.aspx.cs file

```
using System;
using System.Collections.Generic;
using System.Linq;
using System.Web;
using System.Web.UI;
using System.Web.UI.WebControls;

public partial class _Default : System.Web.UI.Page
{
    private const string APP_KEY = "viewlist";

    protected void Page_Load(object sender, EventArgs e) {
        ProductViewList viewlist;
        if (Application[APP_KEY] == null) {
            viewlist = new ProductViewList();
            Application.Add(APP_KEY, viewlist);
        }
        else {
            viewlist = (ProductViewList)Application[APP_KEY];
            BindViewGrid(viewlist.Display());
        }
    }

    protected void grdProducts_SelectedIndexChanged(object sender,
                                                    EventArgs e) {
        ProductView view = new ProductView();
        view.ProductID = grdProducts.SelectedValue.ToString();
        view.ProductName = grdProducts.SelectedRow.Cells[2].Text;
        view.CategoryID = ddlCategory.SelectedValue.ToString();
        view.ViewCount = 1;

        Application.Lock();
        ProductViewList viewlist = (ProductViewList)Application[APP_KEY];
        viewlist.Add(view);
        Application.UnLock();

        BindViewGrid(viewlist.Display());
    }

    protected void Reset(object sender, EventArgs e) {
        grdProducts.SelectedIndex = -1;
    }

    private void BindViewGrid(List<ProductView> views) {
        grdViews.DataSource = views;
        grdViews.DataBind();
    }
}
```

Description

- The code-behind file uses a ProductViewList object that's stored in application state to display and update the number of times each product has been viewed.

Figure 23-14   The code-behind file for the View Products page

Perspective

Now that you've completed this chapter, you should be able to use the ASP.NET Ajax server controls to develop Ajax-enabled web applications of your own. Of course, there's a lot more to learn about ASP.NET Ajax than what's presented here. You may also want to take a different approach to using Ajax and learn how to use jQuery to implement Ajax applications. For that, we recommend *Murach's jQuery*.

Terms

rich Internet application (RIA)
Asynchronous JavaScript and XML
  (Ajax)
XMLHttpRequest (XHR) object
ASP.NET Ajax
asynchronous postback

ASP.NET Ajax client-side framework
ASP.NET Ajax server controls
ASP.NET Ajax Control Toolkit
web service
proxy

Summary

- *Asynchronous JavaScript and XML (Ajax)* is a framework that allows you to develop *rich Internet applications (RIA)*. These are web applications that provide advanced functionality and quick response times. Unlike other RIA frameworks, Ajax uses just the features that are built into modern browsers.

- With a traditional web request, the browser sends an HTTP request to the web server, receives an HTTP response back, and reloads the page. With an Ajax request, portions of the page can be updated without having to perform a full HTTP request and response cycle, so the page doesn't have to be reloaded.

- Ajax works by using JavaScript and the browser's *XMLHttpRequest (XHR) object* to send an asynchronous request to the server. The server processes the request and sends back only the data needed to update the page. JavaScript then parses the data in the response and updates the page.

- *ASP.NET Ajax* is a framework that lets you build RIAs with standard server controls that are combined with Ajax server controls.

- The *ASP.NET Ajax client-side framework* is a JavaScript library that interacts with the ASP.NET application server through the XHR object. The *ASP.NET Ajax server controls* are server controls that Ajax-enable a page. The optional *ASP.NET Ajax Control Toolkit* is a collection of server controls and control extensions that add effects, animations, and interactive features to a page.

- The ScriptManager control enables *asynchronous postbacks* on a page. The UpdatePanel control encloses the standard server controls that are updated during an asynchronous postback.

- The Timer control triggers a periodic asynchronous postback. The UpdateProgress control displays information only while an asynchronous postback is in progress.

24

How to create and use WCF and Web API services

In earlier versions of ASP.NET, Microsoft offered ASMX web services. Then, Microsoft introduced WCF (Windows Communication Foundation) services, which provided more power and flexibility but were also more complex. Starting with ASP.NET 4.5, though, WCF services became easier. Because of that, they're often used in place of ASMX services.

In addition, ASP.NET 4.5 introduced Web API services, which have the goal of developing services that can be easily consumed by browsers and mobile devices. In this chapter, you'll learn the basic concepts and skills that you need to create and use both WCF and Web API services.

An introduction to web services

A *web service* is a class that resides on a web server and can be accessed via the Internet or an intranet. Web services provide a way to make useful functions available to clients on other platforms. For example, the website for the United States Postal Service offers web services that let you calculate shipping rates, correct addresses, and track packages.

Web services communicate with clients by using either SOAP or REST protocols. In general, WCF services use SOAP and Web API services use REST.

SOAP services

SOAP (*Simple Object Access Protocol*) uses XML to send data between host and client. SOAP can be used over many types of transport media and has many security options, but it can also be cumbersome to work with. Usually, some sort of proxy class is needed to work with a SOAP service. But, as you'll see later, WCF generates the proxy classes for you.

Figure 24-1 illustrates how WCF services work with SOAP. In this case, the service is offered by a website that's hosted by IIS, but WCF services can also be hosted by a Windows Forms application, a Console application, or a Windows service. This chapter, though, will focus on WCF services that are hosted by IIS.

As this figure shows, a WCF service exposes one or more *endpoints*. Then, the WCF client uses SOAP over HTTP to communicate with one of these endpoints. For this to work, both the client and the server must be running a version of the .NET Framework that supports WCF.

REST services

REST (*Representational State Transfer*) uses HTTP and URLs, rather than XML, so it is less cumbersome than SOAP. For example, proxy classes aren't needed with REST services. In fact, because REST services often return *JSON* (*JavaScript Object Notation*), they can be easily consumed by JavaScript with little or no transformation. This makes REST services popular for Ajax applications.

Figure 24-1 illustrates how Web API services work with REST. In this case, the client sends an HTTP request to a specified URL and receives a JSON or XML response. Also, the clients that consume Web API services don't need to have the .NET Framework installed. Although you can also build REST services with WCF, it requires much more configuration than with Web API services.

A WCF service that uses SOAP

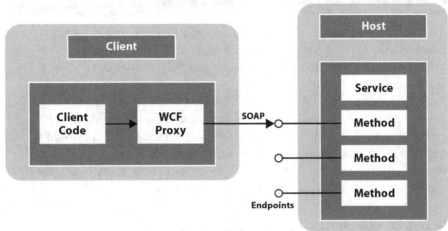

A Web API Service that uses REST

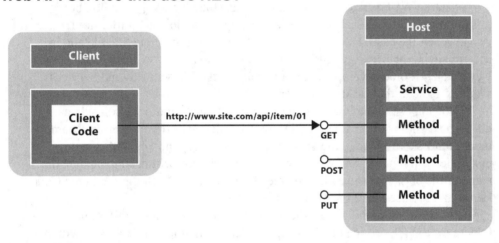

Advantages of SOAP

- Can be used over many transport media, such as TCP, MSMQ, and HTTP.
- Can create strict contracts between two parties and add security layers.

Advantages of REST

- Relies on the existing HTTP standard, so it's faster and easier to configure.
- Can return data in *JSON (JavaScript Object Notation)* or XML format.

Description

- A w*eb service* on a host server provides a service that can be *consumed* by clients on different platforms.
- Clients communicate with web services by using either *SOAP (Simple Object Access Protocol)* or *REST (Representational State Transfer)*.
- *WCF services* usually use SOAP to communicate with clients. *Web API services* always use REST.

Figure 24-1   An introduction to web services

How to create a WCF service

WCF (Windows Communication Foundation) was first released as part of
.NET Framework 3.0. Today, WCF unifies all older .NET Framework
communication technologies, including web services, advanced web service
specifications, and .NET Remoting.

With earlier versions of WCF, you had to create a WCF service library and
then create and configure an application to host your service library. Although
that approach offered a lot of flexibility, developers often found that they didn't
need the extra flexibility and were put off by the extra work. Now, you still have
the option of creating a separate library, but you can also create a WCF service
and host in one step by creating a *WCF service application.*

How to start a WCF service application

To start a WCF service application, you use the New Project dialog box
as shown in figure 24-2. This creates a project with a file named IService1.
cs. However, the easiest way to start a WCF service is to delete this file and its
accompanying Service1.svc file. Then, you can add a new WCF Service file.
Nevertheless, some developers prefer to rename the IService1.cs and Service1.
svc files and edit the starting code for those files.

If you choose to rename these default files, Visual Studio will display a
dialog box when you rename the IService1 file that asks if you want to rename
all references to this file in the project. You should respond Yes to this dialog
box. After you rename the Service.svc file, though, you will need to change the
name of the class that's used by this file. To do that, just open the file in the Code
Editor and replace the old name with the new name.

The procedure in this figure shows how to adjust the starting files and
folders for a WCF service named CategoryService that lets clients work with the
data in the Categories table of the Halloween database. In brief, you delete the
IService1.cs and Service1.svc files, and you add the folders and files that you
need for the Category service. The Solution Explorer in this figure shows the
folders and files of the service application after these adjustments are made.

In the Models folder, you can see a file named CategoryDB.cs. This file is
the same as the one used for the Category Maintenance application in the object
data sources chapter (figure 17-16). Similarly, the Halloween.mdf file is the same
database file that you've been using throughout this book.

The New Project dialog box and the files and folders after adjusting

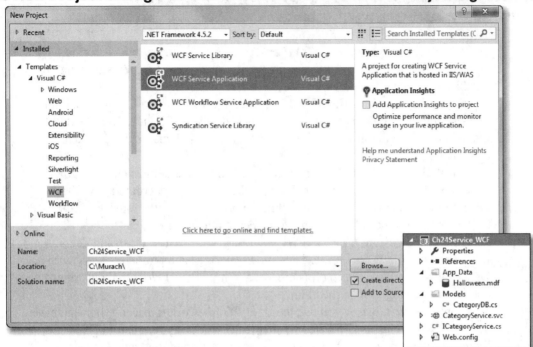

How to create a new WCF service application

- To start a *WCF service application*, select the File→New→Project command, select the WCF template group, and then select the WCF Service Application template.

- Enter a name and location for the service application and click OK.

How to set up the folders and files for a Category service

- Delete the files named IService1.cs and Service1.svc.

- Right click the project and select the Add→New Item command. In the Add New Item dialog box, select Visual C# and then select the WCF Service command (you might need to scroll to find it). Then, name the new service CategoryService, and click Add. This will add files called CategoryService.svc and ICategoryService.cs to the root directory.

- Right-click the App_Data folder and add the Halloween.mdf file.

- Right-click the project and add a new folder named Models. After adding the folder, right-click it and add a new class file named CategoryDB.cs. This is the data access class.

- Add a connection string for accessing the Halloween database to the <configuration> element of the Web.config file.

Description

- In this chapter, you'll learn how to create a Category service that lets a client work with the records in the Categories table of the Halloween database.

- The procedure in this figure shows how to set up the folders and files for this service.

Figure 24-2   How to start a WCF service application

How to code a service contract interface and a data contract class

To define the *operations* of a WCF service, you code a *service contract interface*. This interface defines the properties, methods, and events that classes for the service can implement.

Figure 24-3 presents the service contract interface for the Category service. To start, this code defines an interface named ICategoryService. To indicate that this interface defines a service, the statement that declares the interface is decorated with a ServiceContract attribute.

Similarly, to indicate that a method in this interface defines an operation for the service, the statement that declares the method is decorated with the OperationContract attribute. Notice that the operations in this interface either return a custom type called Category or accept it as a parameter.

To create a custom type for a WCF service, you create a class and decorate it with a DataContract attribute. Then, you decorate each public property with a DataMember attribute. Doing this creates a *data contract class* that describes the data to be exchanged with the client.

Note, however, that if you use the Entity Framework to access your database, you can use the classes generated by that framework as your custom types. Then, you don't have to create the custom classes or add the DataContract or DataMember attributes yourself.

The ICategoryService interface

```
using System;
using System.Collections.Generic;
using System.Linq;
using System.Runtime.Serialization;
using System.ServiceModel;
using System.Text;

namespace Ch24Service_WCF
{
    [ServiceContract]
    public interface ICategoryService
    {
        [OperationContract]
        List<Category> GetCategories();

        [OperationContract]
        Category GetCategoryById(string id);

        [OperationContract]
        int InsertCategory(Category c);

        [OperationContract]
        int UpdateCategory(Category c);

        [OperationContract]
        int DeleteCategory(Category c);
    }

    [DataContract]
    public class Category
    {
        [DataMember]
        public string CategoryID { get; set; }

        [DataMember]
        public string ShortName { get; set; }

        [DataMember]
        public string LongName { get; set; }
    }
}
```

Description

- To define the operations of a service, you code a *service contract interface* with the ServiceContract attribute. Then, you can code one or more methods with the OperationContract attribute.

- To define the data that's used by a service, you code a *data contract class* with the DataContract attribute. Then, you code one or more properties that have the DataMember attribute. If you're using classes generated by the Entity Framework, you can skip this step.

Figure 24-3   How to code a service contract interface and a data contract class

How to code a service contract class that implements the interface

Once you have a service contract interface in place, you write the *service contract class* that implements the interface's properties, methods, and events. Figure 24-4 presents the CategoryService.svc.cs file, which is the service contract class that implements the ICategoryService interface.

This CategoryService class starts by declaring a private CategoryDB object named data, which is initialized in the class's constructor. This is the data access class that will be used to interact with the database, and it is like the data access class that provides the methods for the object data source in chapter 17. The rest of the methods in the class implement the methods defined by the interface.

As the interface in the last figure specifies, the GetCategories method in the service contract class returns a list of Category objects. Similarly, the GetCategoryById method in the contract class returns one Category object based on the category ID that's passed to the method as a string.

In contrast, the InsertCategory, UpdateCategory, and DeleteCategory methods all return int types. This is because the data access class methods return the number of rows affected by the operation. By returning this value, these methods provide the clients that call these methods with a way of checking the results of the insert, update, and delete operations.

In some cases, you will also want to return information to the client if an error occurs. An easy way to do that is to return a specific value if the operation fails. In this figure, you can see that the InsertCategory method returns a value of -1 if the InsertCategory method of the data access class throws an exception. Although this has the benefit of being simple, the drawback is that the client will need to know what the return value means.

Another way to return error information to the client is through the use of *fault contracts*. To learn more, you can refer to the MSDN documentation.

The CategoryService class

```
using System;
using System.Collections.Generic;
using System.Linq;
using System.Runtime.Serialization;
using System.ServiceModel;
using System.Text;

namespace Ch24Service_WCF
{
    public class CategoryService : ICategoryService
    {
        private CategoryDB data;

        public CategoryService() {
            data = new CategoryDB();
        }

        public List<Category> GetCategories() {
            return data.GetCategories();
        }

        public Category GetCategoryById(string id) {
            return data.GetCategoryById(id);
        }

        public int InsertCategory(Category c) {
            try {
                return data.InsertCategory(c);
            }
            catch {
                return -1;
            }
        }

        public int UpdateCategory(Category c) {
            return data.UpdateCategory(c);
        }

        public int DeleteCategory(Category c) {
            return data.DeleteCategory(c);
        }
    }
}
```

Description

- To implement the operations of a service, you code a *service contract class* that implements the service contract interface.

- The service contract class can include members that aren't a part of the service interface, like the constructor and the private CategoryDB object above. This object gets and updates data in the Categories table in the Halloween database.

- The service contract class can also include data validation or error handling, as in the InsertCategory method above.

Figure 24-4   How to write the service contract class that implements the interface

How to view and test a WCF service

Figure 24-5 shows how to test a WCF service. In this figure, the GetCategoryById method was double-clicked and a value of "fx" was entered for the id parameter in the Request pane. In the Response pane, you can see that the WCF service returned a value of type Category. This is the custom type that was decorated with the DataContract attribute in figure 24-3. The Response pane also displays the individual properties of the Category type.

Although the response from the service is formatted in the Response pane, you can also look at the raw SOAP request and response by clicking on the XML tab in the lower left corner of the bottom pane. This shows the SOAP format that's required by WCF services.

When you create your service, WCF automatically creates asynchronous versions of each method. These methods have the same names as the synchronous methods, appended with "Async". Although you can see the asynchronous method in the left pane of the WCF Test Client window, this window hasn't been updated to handle the Task return type that the asynchronous methods use. Because of that, all of these methods have red error icons next to their names, and nothing happens if you double-click on them.

This figure also shows how to view information about a service in a Service page in the web browser. The Service page includes basic information about how to use the service, including some C# and Visual Basic code that you can use to consume the service from a client application. You'll learn more about consuming a service next.

The WCF Test Client window

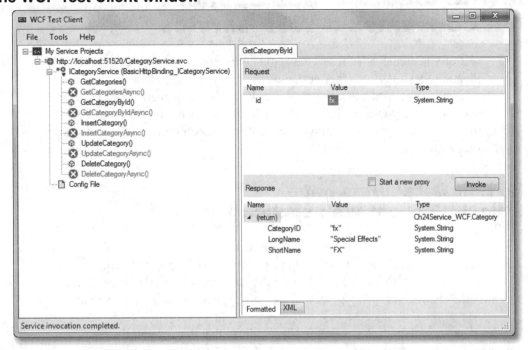

How to test a WCF service

- Start by setting the .svc file for the service as the start page for the application. Then, click the browser name in the Standard toolbar or press F5. That causes Visual Studio to display the WCF Test Client window for the service.

- To test a service operation, double-click on the operation in the left pane of the window to display a tab for the operation in the right pane of the window. Then, enter any required parameters for the operation in the Request section of the tab and click the Invoke button. If you get a security warning, click OK. The Response pane will then show the data that's returned by the operation.

- You can view the XML for the response by clicking on the XML tab in the lower left corner of the right pane of the WCF Test Client window

How to view information about a WCF service in a browser

- Right-click the .svc file for the service and select View in Browser, or open a browser and type the URL shown at the top of the left pane of the Test Client window, just below My Service Projects. Either way, a Service page is displayed.

Description

- WCF automatically exposes an asynchronous version of each of your methods. However, the WCF Test Client hasn't been updated to allow you to test them.

Figure 24-5   How to view and test a WCF service

How to create a web application that consumes a WCF service

After you create a WCF service application, you can create a client web application that consumes the service. Because any web application can be a client application, you can use any of the skills you've learned in this book to develop it. Then, you can add a reference for the service you want the client application to use, and you can write code or use server controls that consume that service.

The Edit Categories page of the WCF client web application

Figure 24-6 shows two views of the Edit Categories page that will consume the WCF Category web service. This page consists of two server controls. The first one is a drop-down list that lists all the categories in the database. Since its AutoPostBack property is set to True, this page posts back to the server whenever the user selects a new category.

The second control is a DetailsView control that displays all the data for the category that's selected in the drop-down list. In the first screen in this figure, you can see that the Costumes category is selected and the CategoryID, LongName, and ShortName fields of that category are displayed.

This DetailsView control is also configured to let a user edit and delete existing categories, as well as insert new ones. As a result, link buttons that allow for these operations are displayed in the bottom row of the control.

The second screen in this figure shows the DetailsView control after the New link is clicked and the control is in Insert mode. In this mode, the user can enter the data for a new category and click the Insert link to insert the category or the Cancel link to cancel the insert operation.

The Edit Categories page of the WCF client web application

The Edit Categories page in Insert mode

Description

- The Edit Categories page consists of a drop-down list that displays the categories, and a DetailsView control that displays the details of the category selected by the drop-down list.

- In default mode, the DetailsView control displays the data in the selected category. But the links in the bottom row let the user edit, delete, and insert a category.

- In Insert mode, the user can enter the data for a new category and then click on the Insert or Cancel link to complete the operation.

Figure 24-6   The Edit Categories page of the WCF client web application

How to add a WCF service reference to a client web application

To make a WCF service available to a client web application, you add a reference to the service in the client application by using the Add Service Reference dialog box, as shown in figure 24-7. If your client web application is in the same solution as your WCF web service, you can just click the Discover button. Otherwise, you'll need to enter the URL of the service. The easiest way to get that URL is to copy it from a web browser that's displaying the service, or to copy it from the Test Client window you saw in figure 24-5.

It's important to note that in order to add a reference like this, the web service must be running. That's why this figure describes two ways that you can have your web service and your client running at the same time. The easiest way is to put them both in the same solution. However, having each in its own solution is almost as easy, and it provides a more "real world" feel of the web service and the client being in different places.

Once you click Discover or enter the URL and click Go, the service will be displayed in the Services list. Then, you can expand this service to see the service contract, service interface, and operations of the interface, although you don't need to do that to add the reference. Finally, you enter the name you want to use for the service's namespace and click the OK button. In this example, that name is CategoryService.

When you add a reference to a WCF service to a web application, Visual Studio creates a *proxy* class that provides access to the operations and data types that are defined by the service, and it creates a folder for the service reference named Service References in the Solution Explorer. Inside this folder is a file that has the name that you entered for the namespace in the Add Service Reference dialog box. If you double-click on this file, an Object Browser window comes up in Visual Studio. You can use this Object Browser to view information about the web service, including its methods and return types.

Before going on, you should know that you'll need to make an adjustment to the client application for this chapter after you download it from our website before it will work. That's because the client application and web service for this chapter use IIS Express, which means that their URLs contain port numbers. And, because the port number on your computer will be different than the port number on the computer where our applications were developed, you'll need to change the service reference for the WCF web service so it has the correct port number. To do that, you need to delete the file for the service reference from the Service References folder in the client application. Then, you need to view the web service in a browser as described in figure 24-5 and use its URL to add a service reference back to the client web application.

The Add Service Reference dialog box

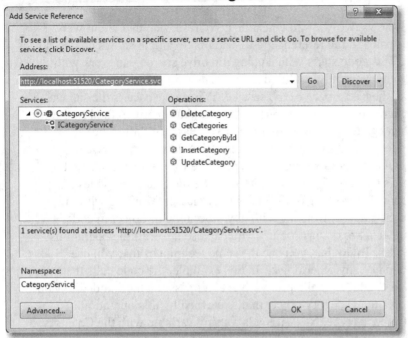

Two ways to have a client and service run simultaneously in IIS Express

- Add the client web application to the same solution as the service using the File→Add→New Project command. Or, if the web application already exists, use the File→Add→Existing Project command to add it. After the web application is added, right-click it and select Set as StartUp Project.
- Open and run the service in Visual Studio. Then, open another instance of Visual Studio to create and run the client web application.

How to add a web service reference to a web application

- With the web service running, use the Project→Add Service Reference command, or right-click the project and select Add→Service Reference. That displays the Add Service Reference dialog box.
- If the web application is in the same solution as the service, click the Discover button. Otherwise, paste the URL for the service into the Address text box and click the Go button. Then, enter a namespace for the service and click OK. Visual Studio will create a folder named Service References in the Solution Explorer and add a file for the service to that folder.

Description

- When you add a service reference to a client, the service must be running. Then, Visual Studio creates a *proxy* class that provides access to the operations and data types that are defined by the service.

Figure 24-7   How to add a WCF service reference to a client web application

How to consume a WCF service

Figure 24-8 shows two ways to consume a WCF service in a client web application after you add the reference to it. The first example shows how to do it with C# code. This code starts with a using directive so you can work with the service without using fully qualified names. The using directive includes the project name and the namespace of the service. This namespace is the same as the name you entered in the Add Service Reference dialog box in the last figure.

The code then creates an instance of the proxy class for the service. The proxy class consists of the name of the class that defines the service, appended with "Client". For example, the type name for the service named CategoryService is CategoryServiceClient. Since Visual Studio provides IntelliSense support for working with WCF proxy classes, working with the proxy in code is the same as working with any other type of object in code.

Once you create a proxy class object, you can use it to call the operations the service provides. To do that, you use the same techniques that you use to execute a method of any other object. In this example, the code calls the GetCategoryById operation of the proxy object and passes a hard-coded id value to it. Then, it stores the Category object that's returned by this operation in a variable of the Category type. Next, it loads a string variable with the Category object's LongName property. Finally, it closes the proxy object because it's a best practice to always close the proxy object when you're done with it.

The second way to consume a WCF service from a client web application is with data sources and data-bound controls. The second example in this figure shows the aspx code for the drop-down list and DetailsView controls of the Edit Categories page that you saw in figure 24-6. These server controls are bound to ObjectDataSource controls, and the data source controls use fully-qualified type names. Then, the data source controls use the operations, or methods, of the proxy for their select, insert, update, and delete methods.

You configure an ObjectDataSource control to work with a WCF proxy class in the same way that you do for any other data access object, by clicking on the smart tag and then choosing Configure Data Source. However, you may need to uncheck the Show Only Data Components check box to see the WCF proxy class in the drop-down list. Remember that you want to choose the object whose name ends with "Client".

In this example, the aspx code for the DetailsView control has event handlers set up for its OnItemDeleted, OnItemInserted, and OnItemUpdated events. This, however, isn't required for working with a WCF service. Rather, it's particular to this application. All three of these event handlers just call the DataBind() method of the drop-down list control to reload the data for the list. That way, for example, if a category is deleted, the dvCategory_ItemDeleted method of the code-behind file is called, which reloads the data for the drop-down list so the deleted category won't show any more.

C# code to use the WCF service

```
using Ch24CategoryMaint_WCF.CategoryService;

CategoryServiceClient svc = new CategoryServiceClient();
Category category = svc.GetCategoryById("fx");
string name = category.LongName;
svc.Close();
```

The data source and data-bound controls from the Edit Categories aspx file

```
<asp:DropDownList ID="ddlCategories" runat="server" AutoPostBack="True"
    DataSourceID="ddlDataSource" DataTextField="LongName"
    DataValueField="CategoryID" CssClass="form-control">
</asp:DropDownList>
<asp:ObjectDataSource runat="server" ID="ddlDataSource"
    SelectMethod="GetCategories"
    TypeName="Ch24CategoryMaint_WCF.CategoryService.CategoryServiceClient">
</asp:ObjectDataSource>

<asp:DetailsView ID="dvCategory" runat="server" DataKeyNames="CategoryID"
    CssClass="table table-bordered table-condensed"
    AutoGenerateRows="False" DataSourceID="detailsDataSource"
    OnItemDeleted="dvCategory_ItemDeleted"
    OnItemInserted="dvCategory_ItemInserted"
    OnItemUpdated="dvCategory_ItemUpdated">
    <Fields>
        <asp:BoundField DataField="CategoryID" HeaderText="CategoryID"
            ReadOnly="true" />
        <asp:BoundField DataField="ShortName" HeaderText="ShortName" />
        <asp:BoundField DataField="LongName" HeaderText="LongName" />
        <asp:CommandField ShowInsertButton="True" ShowEditButton="True"
            ShowDeleteButton="True" />
    </Fields>
</asp:DetailsView>
<asp:ObjectDataSource runat="server" ID="detailsDataSource"
    TypeName="Ch24CategoryMaint_WCF.CategoryService.CategoryServiceClient"
    DataObjectTypeName="Ch24CategoryMaint_WCF.CategoryService.Category"
    SelectMethod="GetCategoryById" UpdateMethod="UpdateCategory"
    InsertMethod="InsertCategory" DeleteMethod="DeleteCategory">
    <SelectParameters>
        <asp:ControlParameter ControlID="ddlCategories"
            PropertyName="SelectedValue" Name="id" Type="String" />
    </SelectParameters>
</asp:ObjectDataSource>
```

Description

- You can work with the service proxy classes in code or with data source and data-bound controls.
- You can use the DataObjectTypeName property of the ObjectDataSource control to set the name of the class the control uses for a parameter in update, insert, or delete operations.

Figure 24-8   How to consume a WCF service

How to create a Web API service

As more websites and mobile devices use Ajax to communicate with web services, two main problems with SOAP-based web services have been exposed. First, SOAP requests and responses are verbose, leading to slower network speeds for large requests or responses. Second, the XML returned by a SOAP service must be parsed before it can be used.

REST-based web services address these concerns in two ways. First, because the requests are made using the HTTP protocol, the requests and data are in the URL and HTTP request body, just like any other HTTP request made by a browser. Second, the response to a REST service is usually in JSON format, which is more compact than XML. If, for example, you look at the XML of the SOAP response as described in figure 24-5, you'll see a response that is several lines long, even though the equivalent JSON response is one line. Beyond that, a JSON response is a JavaScript object, which means that it can be consumed by JavaScript with little or no parsing.

Now, you can use Web API (Application Programming Interface) to create and consume *Web API services*. This feature uses the ASP.NET MVC framework to create REST web services that can return either JSON or XML to a client. In the next chapter, you'll learn more about ASP.NET MVC so what follows is just an introduction to how it can be used to develop Web API services.

How to start a Web API service

To start a Web API service, you use the procedure in figure 24-9. This is the same procedure you use to create any ASP.NET Web Application, except you choose the Web API template from the New ASP.NET dialog box. After you create the service application, the Project_Readme.html file is displayed. This page provides information about the service and includes links for getting additional information.

When you create a Web API service this way, numerous files and folders are created by default. In most cases, though, you'll only work with the App_Data, Models, and Controllers folders. As a result, you will usually want to adjust the starting files and folders. This figure, for example, shows you how to adjust the folders and files for a Categories service that's like the WCF service you just studied. After you add the database and C# files to the application, you will want to develop the *controller* in the Controllers folder. This file will provide the methods for your service.

One way to start the controller is to use the Rename command to rename the ValuesController file so its name is more appropriate. The benefit of this is that you can use the default methods that it provides as a guide to coding your own methods. The other way to develop the controller is to add a new controller. Then, you can copy and paste the default action methods from the ValuesController file into the new file and then delete the ValuesController file.

The New ASP.NET Project dialog box

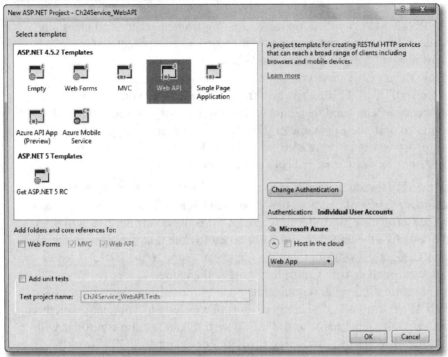

How to start a new Web API service

- Select the File→New→Project command, select the Web template group, and select the ASP.NET Web Application template. Then, enter a name and location for the service application, and click OK.
- In the New ASP.NET Project dialog box, select the Web API template and click OK.

How to adjust the initial files and folders for the Edit Categories page

- Right-click the App_Data folder and add the Halloween.mdf file.
- Right-click the Models folder and add class files named Category.cs and CategoryDB.cs. The Category class is similar to the Category class in the WCF example, but it doesn't need to have any DataContract or DataMember attributes. The CategoryDB class is the data access class.
- To add a new controller file to the Controllers folder, right-click the folder and select Add→Controller. In the Add Controller dialog box, name your controller, select Empty API controller in the Template drop-down list, and click Add.
- Add a connection string for the Halloween database to the Web.config file.

Description

- The Web API template adds numerous files and folders to the project, but in most cases you will only be concerned with the App_Data, Models, and Controllers folders.
- When adding a *controller*, be sure its name ends with the word "Controller".

Figure 24-9   How to start a Web API service

How to write a web service controller

An ASP.NET MVC application uses a *routing framework* to send incoming HTTP requests to the appropriate controller according to a predefined *route pattern*. For now, all you need to know is that this routing is set up for you automatically when you create your application, and that the default pattern is "api/{controller}/{id}". This means that any URL request to your service must start with the term "api", and then contain the name of the controller that will handle it and an optional id parameter. For example, a request to get information about a category whose id is "masks" would look like this:

`http://www.domain.com/api/categories/masks`

Once the HTTP request is routed to the controller, the controller determines which *action method* will handle it based on the HTTP verb of the request. For instance, the CategoriesController in figure 24-10 is the controller that will handle requests like the one above. It's important to note that the name of the file and class is CategoriesController, but the controller name in the URLs is lower case and doesn't include the "Controller" part of the name.

This CategoriesController demonstrates one of the naming conventions used by the Web API framework. The convention is that as long as your action method name starts with the same name as the HTTP verb it handles, the controller will route that kind of request to that action method. For example, POST (insert) requests are routed to the method named PostCategory, and PUT (update) requests are routed to the method named PutCategory. The comments above the methods in this figure show what action the HTTP verb is associated with and what a URL request for that method would look like.

Note that you can have more than one action method for a specific HTTP verb. For instance, the CategoriesController in this figure has three methods that handle GET requests. If there is more than one method for a verb, the controller uses the method signature and the default route pattern to select the correct one.

For example, the GetCategories method has no parameters, so GET requests with no URL parameter are routed there. In contrast, GET requests with a parameter get routed to the GetCategoryById or GetCategoriesByShortName method. The controller decides which one based on the name of the parameter in the URL. If the parameter name is specified, as in "categories/?name=Masks", the controller looks for a method with that same parameter name. If the parameter name isn't specified, as in "categories/masks", the controller looks for a method with a parameter with the default name of "id".

The Web API framework expects to retrieve simple parameter types like ints or strings from the URL and complex parameter types like a Category object from the body of the HTTP request. To make it clear that a parameter is retrieved from the body of a request, the default ValuesController file uses the [FromBody] attribute, as shown in the PostCategory and PutCategory methods. For a complex type like this, the Web API framework converts the JSON object that's in the body of a POST or PUT request to a .NET object. Later you'll see how to set up your client application to make this work.

The CategoriesController.cs file

```
namespace Ch24Service_WebAPI.Controllers
{
    public class CategoriesController : ApiController
    {
        CategoryDB data;
        public CategoriesController() {
            this.data = new CategoryDB();
        }
        // GET: api/categories
        public IEnumerable<Category> GetCategories() {
            //System.Threading.Thread.Sleep(3000); // 3 seconds
            return data.GetCategories();
        }
        // GET: api/categories/masks
        public Category GetCategoryById(string id) {
            return data.GetCategoryById(id);
        }
        // GET: api/categories/?name=Masks
        public IEnumerable<Category> GetCategoriesByShortName(string name)
        {
            return data.GetCategoriesByShortName(name);
        }
        // POST(Insert): api/categories
        public int PostCategory([FromBody]Category value) {
            return data.InsertCategory(value);
        }
        // PUT(Update): api/categories/masks
        public int PutCategory(string id, [FromBody]Category value) {
            value.CategoryID = id;
            return data.UpdateCategory(value);
        }
        // DELETE: api/categories/masks
        public int DeleteCategory(string id) {
            Category value = new Category() { CategoryID = id };
            return data.DeleteCategory(value);
        }
    }
}
```

Description

- The controller for a service needs to end with the word "Controller" and be in the Controllers folder.

- As long as the names for the *action methods* in the controller begin with the right HTTP verbs, the *routing framework* will route HTTP requests to them correctly.

- You can use the System.Threading namespace to simulate service delays for testing.

Figure 24-10   How to write a web service controller

As you can see in figure 24-10, the PostCategories method retrieves all the Category properties from the request body, while the PutCategories method retrieves the id property from the URL and the rest from the request body. That's because most update operations don't allow the user to change the primary key property. Because of that, the value of that property will usually be in the URL and not in the body of the request.

The controller in this figure also includes a commented-out call to the Sleep method of the current Thread. This can be a useful way to simulate service delays when you're testing the client web application that consumes this service.

How to view and test a Web API service

Although Visual Studio doesn't provide a test mechanism for Web API services like it does for WCF services, remember that REST services are accessed by using regular HTTP requests. This means that you can test the GET methods by using a browser.

The table in figure 24-11 shows the HTTP verbs, action methods, and URLs for the Web API Categories service, as well as a procedure for testing the GET methods in a browser. Because the web service response is sent as JSON rather than HTML, the test won't automatically display the data in your browser if you're using Internet Explorer. Rather, you'll get a message asking if you want to open or save the JSON file. For instance, this figure shows the response for this GET request

```
http://localhost:<portnumber>/api/categories
```

after clicking the Open button. In this case, the response is displayed in Visual Studio and consists of a JSON array of all the categories in the database. In contrast, if you enter the URL above in Chrome or Firefox, the categories data is displayed as XML in the browser window.

You can also display information about a Web API service in a web browser, as described in this figure. Then, a Help page is displayed that displays the methods of the service. This Help page is actually a NuGet package called AspNet.WebApi.HelpPage, and its code files are located in the Areas/HelpPage folder.

By default, the Help page for a Web API service displays minimal information, but you can enhance that if you want to. To learn more about that, you can search for "ASP.NET Web API Help Page." Note, however, that the Help page uses ASP.NET MVC, so you'll probably want to read the MVC chapter in this book before trying to enhance the Help page.

You can also test the HTTP verbs for a Web API service by using a third-party proxy tool. For instance, Fiddler is a popular freeware tool, and Charles is a popular paid tool.

HTTP verbs and corresponding methods and URLs in the Category service

Verb	Action method	URL
GET	GetCategories()	/api/categories
GET	GetCategoryById(string id)	/api/categories/masks
GET	GetCategoriesByShortName(string name)	/api/categories/?name=Masks
POST	PostCategory(Category value)	/api/categories
PUT	PutCategory(string id, Category value)	/api/categories/masks
DELETE	DeleteCategory(string id)	/api/categories/masks

Testing the GET methods in a browser

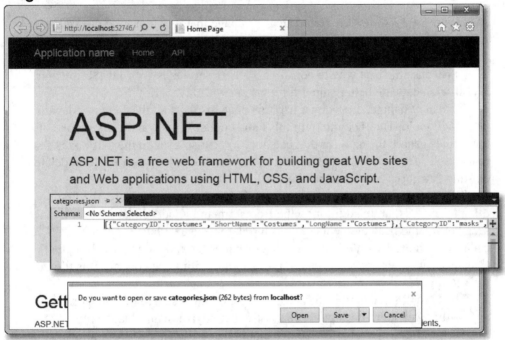

How to test the GET methods of a Web API service

- In Visual Studio, click the browser name in the Standard toolbar or press F5. Then, a home page like the one above is displayed in the browser.

- Add one of the GET URLs shown in the table above to the URL in the address bar of the browser and press Enter.

- In IE, click the Open button to see the JSON response from the server in Visual Studio. Or, click the Save button to download the JSON and then view it in any text editor.

- In Chrome or Firefox, the response from the server displays as XML in the browser.

How to view information about a Web API service

- Click the "API" link at the top right of the home page shown above. This will display a Help page that lists basic information about your service.

Figure 24-11   How to view and test a Web API service

How to create a web application that consumes a Web API service

After you create a Web API service, you can create a client web application that consumes it. Since this client is a regular web application, you can use any of the skills you've learned in this book to develop it. In contrast to the way you work with WCF services, though, you don't need to add any references.

The Edit Categories page of the Web API client web application

Figure 24-12 shows the Edit Categories page that will consume the Web API Categories web service. In contrast to the client page for consuming a WCF service, this page uses HTML elements instead of ASP.NET server controls. That's because the best way to consume a REST service is with JavaScript, and HTML elements are better suited for working with JavaScript.

Instead of using a drop-down list, this page displays all the category data in an HTML table. The ID column in this table contains links, and clicking one of these links causes the data for that category to be displayed in the text boxes next to the table. The buttons at the bottom of the text boxes let a user edit and delete existing categories and insert new ones.

This figure also presents some of the HTML for the page. Here, the first thing to note is that, in addition to the Bootstrap and jQuery links you've seen before, the head element contains a link to a custom JavaScript file called webapi.js. This file is the one that provides the functions for calling the Categories web service. You'll learn more about writing the code for this file in the next figure.

The HTML table that displays the category data has an id of "categories", and its tbody element is empty because it will be dynamically loaded by JavaScript. Below the table is a span element that will display information about the current operation. For instance, when the page first loads, it says "Loading…" until the categories are loaded. This is a good idea since there are often network latencies when dealing with a web service.

The input elements next to the HTML table are for the text boxes that display the data items for a category, and each of these input elements has both an id and a name attribute. The id attribute is used for CSS styling and by the JavaScript code that works with each element. The name attribute is used by jQuery to retrieve the value from the element for POST and PUT requests.

When coding these name attributes, the values must be the same as the property names of the Category object. This is so the Web API framework can correctly retrieve the property values from the JSON object that will be sent in the body of the POST and PUT requests, as you saw in figure 24-10. So, the name attribute must be "CategoryID" for the id text box, "ShortName" for the short name text box, and "LongName" for the long name text box. You can find the property names the Web API service requires on the Help page described in figure 24-11.

A Categories page when jQuery is used to consume the Web API service

The head element and the column divs that contain the category data

```
<head id="Head1" runat="server">
    <!-- Bootstrap and jQuery link and script tags here -->
    <script src="Scripts/webapi.js"></script>
</head>

<div class="col-sm-6 table-responsive">
  <h1>Edit Categories</h1>
  <table id="categories" class="table table-bordered table-striped">
    <thead><tr><th>ID</th><th>Short Name</th><th>Long Name</th></tr></thead>
    <tbody></tbody>
  </table>
  <span id="message">Loading...</span>
</div>
<div id="details" class="col-sm-6">
  <div class="form-group">
    <label class="control-label">ID</label>
    <input type="text" id="id" name="CategoryID" class="form-control" />
  </div>
  <div class="form-group">
    <label class="control-label">Short Name</label>
    <input type="text" id="short" name="ShortName" class="form-control" />
  </div>
  <div class="form-group">
    <label class="control-label">Long Name</label>
    <input type="text" id="long" name="LongName" class="form-control" />
  </div>
  <div class="form-group">
    <input type="button" value="Insert" class="btn" onclick="insertCat();" />
    <input type="button" value="Update" class="btn" onclick="updateCat();" />
    <input type="button" value="Delete" class="btn" onclick="deleteCat();" />
    <input type="button" value="Clear" class="btn" onclick="clearAll();" />
  </div>
</div>
```

Figure 24-12   The Edit Categories page of the Web API client web application

Finally, the input button elements below the text boxes handle the insert, update, delete, and clear operations. They each have an onclick attribute that identifies the JavaScript function that will be called when the button is clicked.

How to consume a Web API service using jQuery

Most of the time, you'll want to use jQuery to consume a Web API service. That's because you can make asynchronous Ajax requests with jQuery, which can improve response times. To illustrate the use of jQuery, figure 24-13 presents some of the JavaScript and jQuery code that's in the webapi.js file for the web application that consumes this Web API service. This JavaScript code is loaded automatically when the page is requested by a browser, it runs in the browser without server calls, and it can respond to user events like clicking on a link.

If you know how to use jQuery, you should be able to follow most of this code. If you don't know how to use jQuery, this example shows how important JavaScript and jQuery have become to the modern web developer. In either case, here's a description of what's going on.

The first line of JavaScript code loads the base URL of the web service in a variable called api. This is a good practice because if the URL of the web service changes, you only have to change it in one place.

The first function in this figure is the jQuery ready function that runs when the web page is ready but before it's displayed. This function calls a helper function named displayCategories that uses the jQuery $.getJSON function to retrieve the category data from the web service. Then, it uses the jQuery $.each function to put the JSON data into an array of rows, one row at a time, including a link for the ID column. The href attribute for each link is the value of the api variable plus the category's id. Last, this function puts the rows of the array into the body of the table in the HTML for the form and calls the clearAll function. This function clears the text boxes and the "Loading…" message below the table, and makes sure that the category id text box is enabled. At that point, the web page looks like the one in the previous figure.

The next line of code in the ready function wires an event handler to the click event of each of the links in the ID column that were created by the displayCategories function. This click event handler prevents the default redirect behavior of the link, and then calls the findCategory function and passes the value of the link's href attribute to it.

The findCategory function first provides information about what operation is occurring. Then, it uses the $.getJSON method to make a request to the web service. The first parameter for this method is the URL of the web service method, which was passed in from the link's href attribute. The second parameter is an embedded function whose data parameter contains the JSON response from the web service. Within the embedded function, the values of the text elements are loaded, the category id text box is disabled, and the message label is cleared.

The next three functions are the insert, update, and delete functions, and they function similarly to each other. First, they provide information about the operation. Then, they call the jQuery $.ajax method. In the insertCat function, for example, the $.ajax method sets the request verb to POST, provides the URL

The JavaScript and jQuery in the webapi.js file for the Edit Categories page

```javascript
var api = "http://localhost:52746/api/categories/";

$(document).ready(function () {
    displayCategories();
    $(document.body).on('click', 'a', function (e) {
        e.preventDefault();
        findCategory($(this).attr("href"));
    });
});
function displayCategories() {
    $.getJSON(api, function (data) {
        var rows = "";
        $.each(data, function (key, val) {
            rows += "<tr><td><a href=" + api + val.CategoryID + ">"
                    + val.CategoryID + "</a></td>";
            rows += "<td>" + val.ShortName + "</td>";
            rows += "<td>" + val.LongName + "</td></tr>";
        });
        $('#categories > tbody tr').remove();
        $('#categories > tbody').append(rows);
        clearAll();
    })
    .fail(showError);
}
function findCategory(href) {
    $('#message').html("Finding...");
    $.getJSON(href, function (data) {
        $('#id').val(data.CategoryID);
        $("#id").attr("disabled", "disabled");
        $('#short').val(data.ShortName);
        $('#long').val(data.LongName);
        $('#message').text("");
    })
    .fail(showError);
}
function insertCat() {
    $('#message').text("Inserting...");
    $.ajax({
        type: 'POST',
        url: api,
        data: $('#form1').serialize(),
        dataType: "json",
        success: displayCategories,
        error: showError
    });
} // the updateCat, deleteCat, showError and clearAll functions follow
```

Description

- When you use jQuery to consume a Web API service, Ajax is used to get and update the data with asynchronous requests. This is generally considered to be the best way to consume Web API services.

- This again shows how important JavaScript and jQuery are to the web developer. To learn more, you can use our books, *Murach's JavaScript* and *Murach's jQuery*.

Figure 24-13   How to consume a Web API service using jQuery for the web service, gets the form values by using the serialize function, sets the data type as JSON, and sets the functions to be called on success and on error.

These three functions set the HTTP verbs for an insert, update, or delete operation, and they use different URLs for the web service. The insert method uses just the base URL, while the update and delete methods append the category id to the URL. That way, the HTTP verbs, the data in the URL, and the data in the body of the request will match what the web service methods you saw in figure 24-10 expect.

This should give you an idea of how jQuery can be used to consume a Web API service. To learn more, please refer to our JavaScript and jQuery books.

How to consume a Web API service using C# code

As you've just learned, you will usually want to use jQuery to consume Web API services because jQuery can make asynchronous Ajax requests from the browser. However, you can also consume a Web API service synchronously using C# code. In figure 24-14, for example, you can see a web page that uses a GridView control and a C# code-behind file to display the category data that's returned by the Categories web service.

When a web application consumes a Web API service, the data can be returned as JSON or XML data. Although there are native and third-party .NET classes for working with JSON, the .NET XML classes and the LINQ to XML functionality make XML a good choice when you're using C# code to consume a Web API service.

To illustrate, the code in this figure uses the HttpWebRequest object of the System.Net namespace to make a GET request. Here, the ContentType property of the request object specifies XML as the return type. Next, the GetResponse method is used to load the response from the web service in a WebResponse object, and the data in that object is converted into a Stream object of the System.IO namespace.

Once the web service response has been serialized to a stream, it can be read into a DataSet object of the System.Data namespace. In this example, the categories data will be the only table in the dataset, so you set the first table in the dataset as the GridView's data source and then bind it to the GridView control. Incidentally, the code in this figure will also work in a Windows Forms application.

A Categories page when C# is used to consume the Web API service

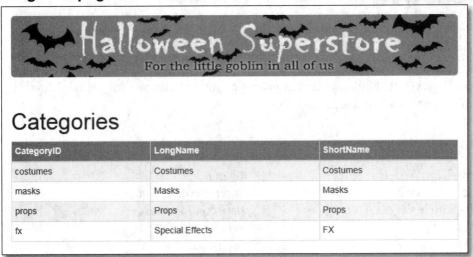

CategoryID	LongName	ShortName
costumes	Costumes	Costumes
masks	Masks	Masks
props	Props	Props
fx	Special Effects	FX

The code-behind file for the page

```
...
using System.Net;
using System.IO;
using System.Data;

public partial class ServerSide : System.Web.UI.Page
{
    protected void Page_Load(object sender, EventArgs e)
    {
        //configure web request object
        string url = "http://localhost:52746/api/categories/";
        HttpWebRequest request = (HttpWebRequest)WebRequest.Create(url);
        request.Method = "GET";
        request.ContentType = "text/xml; encoding='utf-8'";

        //send request, get xml response and convert to stream
        WebResponse response = request.GetResponse();
        Stream stream = response.GetResponseStream();

        //read stream into a dataset
        DataSet ds = new DataSet();
        ds.ReadXml(stream);

        //bind dataset to gridview
        grdCategories.DataSource = ds.Tables[0];
        grdCategories.DataBind();
    }
}
```

Description

- When you consume a Web API service with C#, normal HTTP requests are made.

Figure 24-14   How to consume a Web API service using C# code

Perspective

In this chapter, you've learned the basic skills for creating and consuming WCF services, and you've been introduced to Web API services. Of course, there's a lot more to learn, starting with the next chapter on ASP.NET MVC. We hope, however, that this chapter has given you the foundation that you need for learning more on your own.

Terms

web service	operation
consume a service	service contract interface
SOAP (Simple Object Access Protocol)	data contract class
	service contract class
endpoint	proxy
REST (Representational State Transfer)	Web API service
	controller
JSON (JavaScript Object Notation)	routing framework
WCF (Windows Communication Foundation) service	route pattern
	action method
WCF service application	

Summary

- A *web service* is a class that resides on a web server and can be *consumed* by clients. Web services communicate with clients using *SOAP* or *REST*.

- ASP.NET 4.5 provides two primary web service technologies: *WCF (Windows Communication Foundation)* and *Web API (Application Programming Interface)*. WCF services usually use SOAP, and Web API services always use REST.

- To create a *WCF service*, you write a *service contract interface* that defines the service's *operations*. This interface and its properties, methods, and events must be decorated with the correct attributes. Then, you write a *service contract class* that implements the operations defined in the interface.

- With some WCF services, you must also write a *data contract class* that describes the data to be exchanged between service and client. To do that, you write a class and decorate it and its properties with the correct data attributes.

- To consume a WCF service from a client, you first add a service reference, which generates a *proxy* class. Then, you work with the proxy class.

- To create a *Web API service*, you create an ASP.NET MVC application from the Web API template. Then, you write a *controller* that contains the *action methods* that handle HTTP requests.

- To consume a Web API service from a client, you usually use jQuery methods to communicate with the service and parse the JSON data that's returned from it. But you can also use ASP.NET server controls and C# to consume the service.

An introduction to ASP.NET MVC

In recent years, ASP.NET MVC has gotten more attention as a web development tool. That's because it facilitates unit testing, uses naming and structure conventions for configuration, and works directly with HTTP requests. Sometimes, you'll even see ASP.NET MVC touted as a replacement for ASP.NET Web Forms, but that isn't the case.

Rather, you should see ASP.NET MVC as a complement to Web Forms, because each has its own strengths. Web Forms are typically used for intranet web applications and websites that need to use state or complex server controls. MVC is typically used for websites with high traffic and a need for search engine optimization and good performance.

In this chapter, you'll learn the basic concepts and skills for working with ASP.NET MVC web applications. Then, you can decide whether ASP.NET MVC is something you want to learn more about.

An introduction to MVC

Web Forms applications often combine code that accesses databases with HTML code, as with SqlDataSource controls. Also, the code-behind files in Web Forms applications are tightly coupled with their aspx files, which makes it hard for one person to work on an aspx file while another works on its code-behind file. Shortcomings like that can make it difficult to code, test, debug, and maintain large applications. That's why the developers of large websites often use the *MVC (Model-View-Controller) design pattern.*

The MVC design pattern

The MVC pattern works by breaking an application into component parts. Figure 25-1 presents a diagram that shows the components of the MVC pattern and how they work together.

The *model* is in charge of data. Specifically, it gets and updates the data in a data store. It applies business rules to that data. And it validates data entered by the user.

The *view* is in charge of the user interface. Specifically, it creates the HTML that the application will send to the browser in response to the browser's HTTP request.

The *controller* is in charge of coordinating the model and the view. Specifically, it receives the HTTP request from the browser, decides what data to get from the model, and then sends the data from the model to the appropriate view.

The *view model* is an optional component in charge of transferring the data retrieved by the controller to the view. View models are usually data transfer objects that consist only of properties. Although view models aren't required, they're widely used in ASP.NET MVC applications because they facilitate some of the data binding. You'll see how this works later in the chapter.

It's important to note that each component should stick to its own area of concern and be as independent as possible. For example, the model should retrieve and validate data but it shouldn't have anything to do with displaying it. Similarly, the controller should move data between the model and the view but it shouldn't apply any business rules to it. Setting up the components this way makes them more testable, and it makes it easier to change a component without affecting other components.

This figure also lists the main benefits of the MVC design pattern. In brief, breaking an application into separate parts makes it easier to have different team members work on different parts, to swap out parts, and to test individual components. MVC also produces applications that work better with the stateless HTTP protocol.

The MVC design pattern

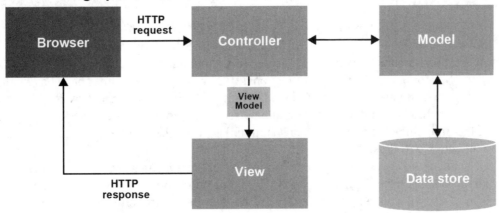

The MVC Components

- The *Model-View-Controller (MVC) design pattern* breaks web applications into their component parts so they are easier to code, test, and maintain.
- The *model* consists of the files that contain data access code, business logic code, and data validation code.
- The *view* consists of the files that create the HTML for the user interface and return a response to the user.
- The *controller* consists of the files that receive requests from the user, get the appropriate data from the model, and provide that data to the view.
- The *view model* is an optional component that consists of files whose only job is to transfer data from the controller to the view. Technically, this isn't part of the MVC pattern, but view models are often used with ASP.NET MVC.

The benefits of MVC

- The MVC structure leads to better *separation of concerns*. For instance, the designers can work with the views and the developers can work with the controllers.
- Even if you are both designer and developer, with MVC you can more easily make changes. For example, if you change your data store from SQL Server to Oracle, you only have to change the model.
- The MVC structure can be more complex, because everything is broken into pieces. But if you follow specific conventions regarding what to name the pieces and where to put them, MVC frameworks will hook everything up for you. This means less code to write, and fewer configuration files to edit.
- The HTML produced by MVC frameworks is concise, which makes it easier to integrate with JavaScript libraries and can also improve page load performance.
- MVC works with the stateless nature of the web, so there's less overhead trying to replicate state. This can also improve performance.

Figure 25-1   An introduction to MVC

The Shopping Cart as an MVC application

This chapter will introduce you to the basic ASP.NET MVC concepts and skills by showing examples from an MVC version of the Shopping Cart application that this book has been using. To keep things simple, though, the MVC Shopping Cart has limited functionality. For example, the Order page has an Add to Cart button but not a Go to Cart button. And the Cart page displays what's in the cart but doesn't do anything else. Figure 25-2 shows one page of the Shopping Cart application and summarizes what the four pages of the application will illustrate.

This figure also gives a general procedure for creating an MVC application. First, you create the application itself. Then, you add a model. After your model is in place, you create a controller for it. And after the controller is in place, you use the controller to create one or more views.

You repeat steps 2 through 4 of this procedure many times as you build an MVC application. For instance, when working on the Contact Us page, you'll first create the model that provides the contact information for the page. Next, you'll create the controller that retrieves the contact information in response to an HTTP request. Finally, you'll create the view that displays the contact information in the browser.

As you read this chapter, don't worry if you find yourself struggling to follow some of the examples. Since an ASP.NET MVC application is so different from a Web Forms application, it takes time to grasp the concepts. What you should have by the end of the chapter is some exposure to the basics, some code examples to refer to, and a jumping off point for further study.

The Shopping Cart as an MVC application

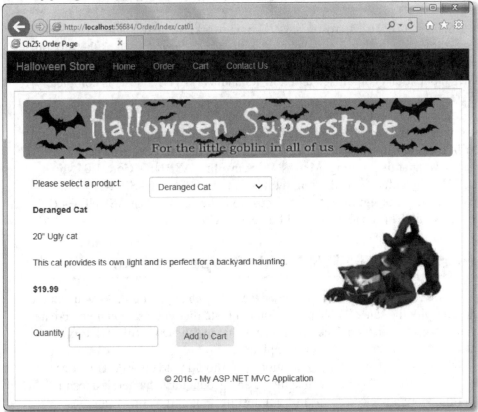

The pages in the Cart application and the concepts they illustrate

Page	Illustrates
Home	A simple controller and a simple view.
Contact Us	A controller that uses a view model and a strongly-typed view.
Order	Controls in a view, controllers that handle both GET and POST requests, and how to work with the data posted to the server.
Cart	Models and view models, and how to work with model binding.

A procedure for creating an MVC application

1. Create the application.
2. Create a model.
3. Create a controller.
4. Create a view.

Description

- This chapter uses an MVC version of the Shopping Cart application to illustrate ASP.NET MVC. This is a simplified version of the Web Forms application that has been used throughout this book.

Figure 25-2   The Shopping Cart as an MVC application

An introduction to ASP.NET MVC

ASP.NET MVC is Microsoft's MVC framework. Since it's built on ASP.NET, many of the objects that you've worked with in Web Forms, such as the session state object and the response object, are also available in MVC. But how an MVC application is organized and how it handles HTTP requests is completely different.

In the topics that follow, you'll learn to start a new MVC application and work with its files and folders. You'll learn about view engines and routing. And you'll learn how to add models, views, and controllers to your project.

Note that at this writing, Microsoft is unveiling ASP.NET Core 1.0, which uses MVC by default. In addition, the version of MVC that ASP.NET Core uses (MVC6) has some significant differences from the version that ASP.NET 4.6 uses (MVC5). This chapter only addresses MVC5.

How to start an ASP.NET MVC application

Figure 25-3 shows how to start a new MVC web application. As you can see, you start with the same Web Application template that you use when you create a Web Forms application. The difference is that in the New ASP.NET Project dialog box, you choose the MVC template.

When you start an MVC application, you should note the Add Unit Tests check box in the dialog box. Since this is an introductory chapter, it doesn't cover the more advanced subject of unit testing. But unit testing is an important advantage of the MVC framework, so you'll want to learn more about it later. When you're ready, the MSDN documentation contains several tutorials about creating unit tests for ASP.NET MVC applications and is a good overall resource.

The New ASP.NET Project dialog box for starting an ASP.NET MVC application

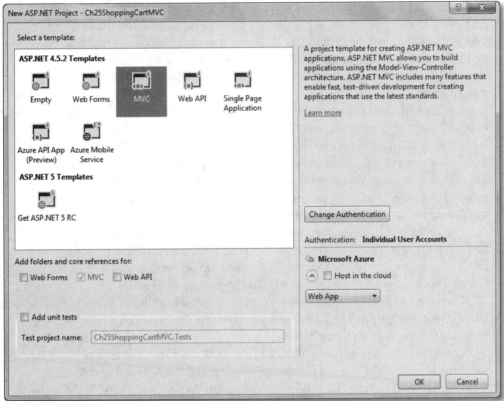

How to start an MVC application

- Select the File→New→Project command, select the Web template group, and select the ASP.NET Web Application template. Then, enter a name and location for the project, and click OK.

- In the New ASP.NET Project dialog box, select the MVC template and click OK.

Description

- To start an MVC application, you use the same procedure you use to create a Web Forms application, except you choose the MVC template from the New ASP.NET Project dialog box.

Figure 25-3   How to start an ASP.NET MVC application

The folders and files for a new MVC application

Figure 25-4 shows the folders and files that are produced when you start an ASP.NET MVC application. Although the number of folders and files can seem overwhelming at first, you should realize that the large number of folders has to do with the structure of an MVC application. Since an MVC application is broken into components, there needs to be separate folders and files for these components.

You should also realize that you usually won't need to touch most of these files or folders. For example, the Global.asax file automatically contains the Application_Start code that an MVC application requires, and the App_Start folder automatically contains the code that the Application_Start code calls. So, unless you want to work with bundling or adjust routes, you won't need to do anything here. Similarly, the various .config files are already set up, so you usually won't need to make any changes to them.

The table in this figure describes some of these folders and files in more detail. You'll spend most of your time working with the Models, Controllers and Views folders. And, of course, you'll want to put your style sheets in the Content folder and your JavaScript files in the Scripts folder.

One thing to note about the Models, Views, and Controllers folders is that they contain several files and subfolders by default. That's because, like the Web Forms template, the MVC template has a fully functional authentication system by default. So, the Account and Manage folders in the Views folder, the Account and Manage controllers in the Controllers folder, and the Account and Manage view models and the Identity model in the Models folder contain the HTML and code for this system.

As you've seen throughout this book, the Scripts and Content folders are used by Bootstrap, which the MVC template adds by default. The Scripts folder also contains some other JavaScript files, such as modernizr.js, which detects which HTML5 and CSS3 features a browser supports, and respond.js, which enables responsive web design in browsers that don't support CSS3 Media Queries.

Like the Web Forms template you saw in detail in chapter 20, the MVC template uses a *bundling framework* to add scripts and style sheets to your application. This framework bundles the files together, and serves them to the browser as one file. The BundleConfig.cs file in the App_Start folder contains the instructions that specify which files to include in a bundle.

You can add your own scripts and style sheets to the bundling instructions, or you can use traditional script and link elements. Although this chapter doesn't show how to work with the BundleConfig.cs file, you should be able to figure out how to add your own scripts and style sheets to it by studying the default instructions.

The initial folders and files produced by the MVC template

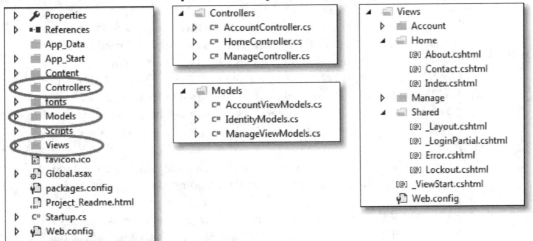

Some of the folders and files that are created by default

Folder/File	Contains
App_Data folder	Data files such as database or XML files.
App_Start folder	The code called on application startup. By default, it contains code that initializes an error handling filter, bundles the default JavaScript and CSS files, and sets up routing and authentication.
Content folder	The style sheet files and images.
Controllers folder	The controller files.
Models folder	The model and view model files.
Scripts folder	The JavaScript files.
Views folder	The view files.
Global.asax file	The application-level event handlers. By default, its Application_Start method calls code in the App_Start folder.
Startup.cs file	A C# class file that calls configuration code for the authentication system at startup.
.config files	The configuration files for NuGet packages and the application.

Description

- Most of the time, you will only need to work with the files in the Models, Views, and Controllers folders.

- The MVC template starts with several files in each of those folders. Some of these files are for the default authentication system that you learned about in chapter 20. Others are for a default home, about, and contact page.

- You can adjust these default files as needed to make your own MVC application. You can also use the HTML and code in the default files as examples.

Figure 25-4   The folders and files produced by the MVC template

The Razor view engine and syntax

When you're working with a dynamic web application, you need some way to combine dynamic data with the static HTML of the page and render it all to the browser. The mechanism that does this is called the *view engine*.

ASP.NET Web Forms applications use the *ASPX view engine*. This engine uses HTML, server controls, and *inline data binding* that looks like this:

```
<h3>Hello <%=name %>, the year is <%= DateTime.Now.Year %></h3>
```

The ASPX view engine then puts it all together and sends it to the browser as HTML.

When ASP.NET MVC first came out, it also used the ASPX view engine. However, many developers found its inline data binding syntax cumbersome and hard to read.

In response, Microsoft came out with the *Razor view engine*, which has a simpler data binding syntax. For example, the Razor version of the ASPX data binding example above looks like this:

```
<h3>Hello @name, the year is @DateTime.Now.Year</h3>
```

Figure 25-5 contains several examples of the Razor data binding syntax.

How to work with routing

Figure 25-5 also presents the RegisterRoutes method of the RouteConfig.cs file. This file is located in the App_Start folder, and it's created by default when you start a new ASP.NET MVC web application. Usually, this is all that you need, so you won't have to create your own routes. But here's what's going on in the RegisterRoutes method.

The first line of the RegisterRoutes method tells the *routing framework* to ignore requests for .axd files. This is to keep routing from interfering with the features of ASP.NET that use .axd extensions.

The next line of the RegisterRoutes method calls the MapRoute method to set up the default route for the application. This method has three parameters, and the name parameter simply names the route.

The url parameter sets the *route pattern* of {controller}/{action}/{id}. This parameter tells the routing framework that when it sees a URL like http://halloweenstore.com/Order/Index/rat01, "Order" is the name of the controller, "Index" is the name of the controller's action method, and "rat01" is a URL parameter named "id". The routing framework will then look in the Controllers folder for a controller called OrderController, and pass it the request.

The defaults parameter sets default values for the route. The default values in this example mean that a URL of http://halloweenstore.com will be sent to the Index action method of the HomeController controller, and that the id parameter is optional.

ASP.NET MVC view engines

- *View engines* are modules that take the data sent by the controller, combine it with the HTML in the view, and render it to the browser. Since the view engine for ASP.NET MVC is designed to be easily replaced, third-party view engines are available, and some developers create custom view engines.

- The default view engine for ASP.NET MVC used to be the same as for ASP.NET Web Forms.

The Razor view engine

- In 2010, Microsoft developed a new view engine called Razor, which is now the default view engine for ASP.NET MVC. The *Razor view engine* has a simple syntax that allows developers to easily *bind* data from the controller to the HTML in the view.

Razor syntax examples

```
<p id="copyright">&copy; @DateTime.Now.Year</p>

@*This is a comment in the markup*@
<p>@foreach (string url in Model.SocialMediaUrls) {
        <a href="@url" target="_blank">@url</a><br />
    }
</p>

@{
    //And this is a comment inside a code block
    ViewBag.Title = "Shopping Cart";
    string day = DateTime.Now.DayOfWeek.ToString();
}
```

The default RegisterRoutes method in the RouteConfig.cs file

```
public static void RegisterRoutes(RouteCollection routes)
{
    routes.IgnoreRoute("{resource}.axd/{*pathInfo}");

    routes.MapRoute(
        name: "Default",
        url: "{controller}/{action}/{id}",
        defaults: new { controller = "Home", action = "Index",
            id = UrlParameter.Optional }
    );
}
```

Description

- The Razor view engine and the default *routing* are available when you create an ASP.NET MVC application, with no configuration necessary.

- The Razor view engine provides IntelliSense support, and web files that use Razor have a .cshtml file extension, rather than .aspx.

Figure 25-5   The Razor view engine and routing in ASP.NET MVC

How to create a model

A *model* contains the code that deals with data. To illustrate, figure 25-6 shows the expanded Models folder for the Shopping Cart MVC application. It has a Data folder that contains an Entity Data Model that was created with the Entity Framework. You should know, though, that the data access class could also use regular C# code. In addition, the Models folder has a ViewModels folder that contains several view model files. Note that some of the files in the Models and ViewModels folders were generated by the MVC template, and some are new files that were added for the shopping cart.

The model for an application has three main tasks. First, it gets and updates the data in the data store. Second, it applies business rules to the data. And third, it applies validation rules to the data.

Because a model can do so much, model files can get large. Then, it can be a good idea to break the files into smaller areas of responsibility. For example, in the Cart model shown in this figure, you could move the data access method to a separate file called CartData.cs in the Data folder.

The model files themselves are regular class files that use regular C# code. In fact, most of the code in the Cart model (not shown here) is similar to the data access code you've seen in the Web Forms versions of the shopping cart application.

The *view model* files in the ViewModels folder are light-weight objects used to transfer data to the view. As mentioned earlier, these aren't required, but they're a good idea because they make many MVC tasks easier. This figure shows the complete Cart view model object, which consists of one property.

Keep in mind that you don't need to have a one-to-one relationship between models and view models. For example, the Cart and Order pages each have a model and a view model, but the Contact page has a view model only. You also don't need to have a one-to-one relationship between the models or view models and the pages in the application. For example, there is a Product view model but there isn't a Products page.

Instead, you set up the model files in a way that makes sense for the data you're working with. In this application, for instance, both the Cart page and the Order page work with products, so it makes sense to have a Products view model that can be sent to their respective views.

Conversely, the Contact Us page displays data that doesn't change over time, so the application doesn't keep the data in a data store. Rather, it hard codes the data in a view model that contains read-only properties like Email and Phone. Because there's no need to retrieve Contact data from a data store, there's no need for a Contact model.

The Models folder of the Shopping Cart application

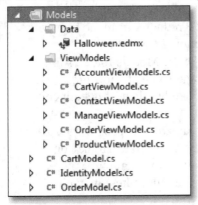

How to add a model

- Right-click the Models folder and select Add→Class to display the Add New Item dialog box. Then, enter a name and click Add.

The Cart model

```
namespace Ch25Cart.Models {
    public class CartModel {
        public CartViewModel GetCart() {...}
        public void AddToCart(OrderViewModel order) {...}

        //Data Access method
        private List<ProductViewModel> GetCartFromDataStore() {...}
    }
}
```

The Cart view model

```
namespace Ch25Cart.Models {
    public class CartViewModel {
        public List<ProductViewModel> CartItems { get; set; }
    }
}
```

Description

- The *model* contains the code that deals with data.
- A model is composed of regular class files. Generally, you'll follow some kind of naming convention for these files, as shown above, but this isn't required.
- You can use as many class files in your model as you need, and you can divide your model into smaller sections, such as sections for data access code and view models.
- View models aren't required, but if you use them, they should contain only what is needed by the view.

Figure 25-6   How to create a model

How to create a controller

A *controller* contains the code that handles HTTP requests from the browser. Figure 25-7 shows the Controllers folder for the Shopping Cart MVC application and how to add a new controller to it. Like the Models folder, some of these files were generated by the MVC template, and some are new files. And one, the Home controller, was generated by the template but then its default code was overwritten.

The MVC framework expects a controller to be named in a specific way. It should start with the name you want to appear in the URL, like "Home" or "Cart", and it should end with "Controller". If you follow this naming convention, your controllers will be hooked up to the default routes shown in figure 25-5 without any further effort.

A controller has three main tasks when it receives an HTTP request. First, it identifies the type of HTTP request it has received. Second, it gets the data needed for the request. And third, it sends that data to the appropriate view.

A controller accomplishes these tasks with *action methods*. For instance, the Home controller in this figure contains two action methods, Index and Contact. Each of these methods handles HTTP GET requests. The Index method loads hard-coded data, and the Contact method gets data from a view model.

Action methods are regular class methods that return objects derived from the ActionResult base class. For example, the Index and Contact methods each return a ViewResult object. The MVC framework knows that an action method that returns a ViewResult object is going to send data to a view. Similarly, it knows that an action method that returns a RedirectToRouteResult object is going to redirect to another controller. The MVC framework uses the data in these objects to do the appropriate action.

It's important to note that you don't have to have a controller file for every page. In the Shopping Cart MVC application, for instance, there are four pages but only three controllers. This is because the Home controller handles requests for both the Home page and the Contact Us page. The Home page is handled by the Index action method, and the Contact Us page is handled by the Contact action method.

It's also common to have two action methods in a controller with the same name, such as two Index action methods. When this happens, you need to add an ActionMethodSelectorAttribute, like [HttpGet] or [HttpPost], to each method. This tells the controller which action method to use when the page loads for the first time, and which one to use when the page posts back. This is similar to a Page.IsPostBack test in Web Forms. Although you don't have to use ActionMethodSelectorAttributes on all action methods, it's a good idea to use them anyway to reduce the chance of error.

Last, it's important to know that controllers are only in charge of coordinating and transferring. They shouldn't apply any business or validation logic. A common phrase that can help you keep this in mind is that you should have "fat" models and "skinny" controllers.

The Controllers folder of the Shopping Cart application and the Add Scaffold dialog box

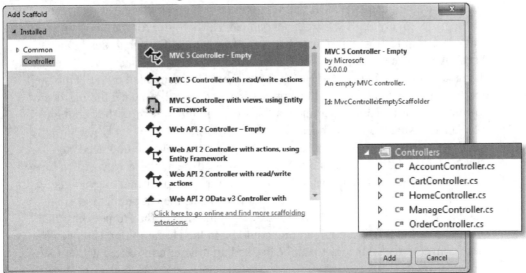

How to add a controller

- Right-click the Controllers folder and select Add→Controller to display the Add Scaffold dialog box. Select a controller template and click Add. Then, enter a name for the controller in the Add Controller dialog box that's displayed and click Add.

The Home controller

```
namespace Ch25Cart.Controllers {
    public class HomeController : Controller
    {
        [HttpGet]
        public ViewResult Index() {
            ViewBag.HeaderText = "Welcome to the Halloween Store";
            ViewData["FooterText"] = "Where every day is Halloween!";
            return View();
        }
        [HttpGet]
        public ViewResult Contact() {
            ContactViewModel model = new ContactViewModel();
            return View(model);
        }
    }
}
```

Description

- *Controllers* follow a naming convention, so you must name them carefully. The part of the name before "Controller" is what will appear in your friendly URLs.

- Controllers contain *action methods* that perform actions in response to HTTP requests. The names of the actions also appear in your URLs.

- Controllers pass data to the view with the ViewData or ViewBag objects, or with the View method.

Figure 25-7   How to create a controller

How to create a view

A *view* contains the HTML and Razor code that creates the user interface for the page. Figure 25-8 shows the expanded Views folder for the Shopping Cart MVC application and how to add a new view to it. The view files in the Account and Manage folders were generated by the template and haven't been changed. The view files in the Home folder were also generated by the template, but they've been modified for this application, and the About view file has been deleted. In contrast, the Order and Cart folders and the view files they contain were added using the method described in this figure.

Every action method in a controller that calls the View method needs to have a corresponding view. The MVC framework expects these views to be in a folder with the same name as the first part of the controller that the view is associated with. It should also have the same name as the action method it is associated with. So, a view for the Index action method of the HomeController should be called Index.cshtml, and it should be in the Home folder. If you follow these conventions, your views will be hooked up to your controllers without any further effort.

In the Views folder in this figure, for instance, you can see that the Home folder contains files called Contact.cshtml and Index.cshtml. These correspond to the Contact and Index action methods of the HomeController that you saw in the last figure. Although there are several ways to add views to the Views folder, the easiest way to make sure your views follow the proper conventions is to use the procedure in this figure.

The Views folder in this figure also contains a _ViewStart.cshtml file and a Web.config file, which were added by the MVC template by default. You'll learn more about working with the _ViewStart view and the contents of the Shared folder later. All you need to know for now is that the Web.config file contains configuration information related to the MVC framework, and you probably won't need to edit it.

When you create a view, you can create a regular view or a strongly-typed view. Strongly-typed views let you take advantage of IntelliSense when working with data sent from the controller, and you'll learn more about them in a minute.

You can also choose different templates or create a partial view. Although neither of these options is covered in this chapter, you might want to experiment with them, particularly the different template options.

The Views folder of the Shopping Cart application and the Add View dialog box

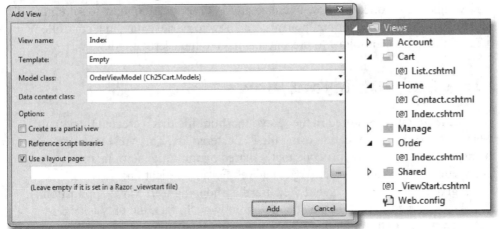

How to add a view to an application

- Right-click an action method in a controller, like the Index method in the previous figure, and select Add View.

- In the Add View dialog box, make sure that the view name matches the action method name, and that the Use a Layout Page option is checked.

- If you want to create a strongly-typed view, change the Template drop-down from Empty (without model) to Empty. Then, select a type from the Model Class drop-down list. (If the object you want isn't there, build the solution and try again.)

- Click Add. Then, Visual Studio will create a new view and place it in a subfolder of the Views folder that has the same name as the controller name. If the subfolder doesn't exist, it will create it.

Description

- You need to create a *view* for each controller action method that calls the View method. If you name the view correctly and put it in the right spot, the MVC framework will automatically hook it up to the action method.

- If you use the procedure above to create the view, Visual Studio takes care of the naming and placement for you.

- The other options in the Template drop-down let Visual Studio create pre-designed views for specific purposes, such as views that list items. This chapter doesn't cover these other templates, but you might want to experiment with them.

Figure 25-8   How to create a view

How to work with views

At this point, you know how to create an MVC application, how to set up the model, view, and controller components, and how to retrieve data in a controller. The next step is to learn how to present that data to the user with views.

How to work with layout views

The *layout view* is stored in the _Layout.cshtml file that's created by default when you create an application using the MVC template. This view is in the Shared folder, and it contains code that's shared by multiple views in an application, similar to a master page in a Web Forms application.

Figure 25-9 shows the layout view for the Shopping Cart MVC application. This layout view is based on the default layout view. In fact, the only changes this view makes to the default are the names and routes of the links and the order of some of the HTML5 elements. The areas that are highlighted here were all part of the layout view by default.

The _ViewStart.cshtml file is also created by default when you use the MVC template to create an application. It contains a single line of code that tells any view that you create with the Use a Layout Page option checked to use _Layout.cshtml as its layout view.

The layout view in this figure contains RenderBody and RenderSection methods. These are similar to the content placeholders of a master page. The RenderBody method in the main element renders the HTML for the view.

The RenderSection method in the footer element renders anything in the view that is within an @section footer{} block. The RenderSection method below the footer element works the same way. You should know, though, that any view that uses this layout view isn't required to have these code blocks. That's because the required parameter of each RenderSection method is set to false.

The layout view also contains Styles.Render and Scripts.Render methods that link style sheets and JavaScript files. They call the bundled scripts and styles that you learned about in figure 25-4. If you wanted to, you could also add traditional script and link elements to this view.

You'll notice that the Scripts.Render method appears at both the top of the page in the head element, and at the bottom of the page just after the closing footer tag. This is because it's good to place JavaScript files at the bottom of a page so they don't block rendering of the HTML. However, the modernizr library needs to be loaded in the head element for it to work properly with IE8.

The layout view uses HTML helpers to render the menu links for the Bootstrap navbar. You'll learn about these helpers shortly. And finally, the layout view uses a partial view named _LoginPartial to render the Register and Login links used by the default authentication system. Since the shopping cart application doesn't use authentication, though, the Razor code for this is commented out here.

The _Layout.cshtml file

```
<html><head>
    <meta charset="utf-8" />
    <meta name="viewport" content="width=device-width, initial-scale=1.0">
    <title>Ch25: @ViewBag.Title</title>
    @Styles.Render("~/Content/css")
    @Scripts.Render("~/bundles/modernizr")
</head>
<body>
    <nav class="navbar navbar-inverse navbar-fixed-top">
        <div class="container-fluid">
            <div class="navbar-header">
                <button type="button" class="navbar-toggle"
                    data-toggle="collapse" data-target=".navbar-collapse">
                    <span class="icon-bar"></span>
                    <span class="icon-bar"></span>
                    <span class="icon-bar"></span>
                </button>
                @Html.ActionLink("Halloween Store", "Index", "Home",
                    new { area = "" }, new { @class = "navbar-brand" })
            </div>
            <div class="navbar-collapse collapse">
                <ul class="nav navbar-nav">
                    <li>@Html.ActionLink("Home", "Index", "Home")</li>
                    <li>@Html.ActionLink("Order", "Index", "Order")</li>
                    <li>@Html.ActionLink("Cart", "List", "Cart")</li>
                    <li>@Html.ActionLink("Contact", "Contact", "Home")</li>
                </ul>
                @*@Html.Partial("_LoginPartial")*@
            </div>
        </div>
    </nav>
    <div class="container">
        <header class="jumbotron"></header>
        <main>@RenderBody()</main>
        <footer class="text-center">
            @RenderSection("footer", required: false)
            <p>&copy; @DateTime.Now.Year - My ASP.NET MVC Application</p>
        </footer>
    </div>
    @Scripts.Render("~/bundles/jquery")
    @Scripts.Render("~/bundles/bootstrap")
    @RenderSection("scripts", required: false)
</body></html>
```

Description

- The *layout view* is in the _Layout.cshtml file in the Shared view folder. This view is similar to a master page.
- The _ViewStart.cshtml file is in the Views folder. This file is similar to setting the master page for the application in the Web.config file.
- The RenderBody and RenderSection Razor methods are similar to master page content placeholders.
- The Styles.Render and Scripts.Render methods render style and script elements.

Figure 25-9   How to work with layout views

How to work with regular views

Figure 25-10 shows the Home page of the Shopping Cart MVC application, along with the controller action method and view that produced it.

The Index action method in this figure returns a ViewResult object in response to an HTTP GET request. Because there are no other action methods named Index in the controller, you don't have to add the HttpGet attribute to the method. Including it, though, makes it clear when this action method will be called.

This action method loads string data into the ViewBag and ViewData objects. The ViewData object is a dictionary collection that stores data as key/value pairs. The key is a string data type and the value is stored as an object data type. The ViewBag object, by contrast, is a dynamic object. This means that you add properties to it on the fly, and it dynamically adds the properties and determines their data types. Under the covers, this object stores these properties in the ViewData dictionary and handles the type casting.

One thing to note about the Index action method is that it loads hard-coded strings as data. This is to keep the example simple, but in real life you wouldn't want to hard code data in a controller like this.

The Index.cshtml view file in this figure is located in the Home subfolder of the Views folder. That's because it's associated with the Index action method of the Home controller. As you learned earlier, naming the view this way and placing it in this location allows the MVC framework to hook it up with its controller.

This view starts with a block of Razor code that contains a ViewBag.Title property assignment. This code block and assignment are added by default when you create the view. The value you add to the ViewBag.Title property will be displayed in the title element of the layout view.

You can also add any other code that you might use in your view to this code block. For instance, this example creates a string variable named day that holds the name of the current day of the week.

Next, this view works with the data sent by the action method of the controller and with the variable declared in the opening block. First, it adds the HeaderText property of the ViewBag object inside the h1 element. Then, it adds the day variable to the text in a div element using Razor's inline data binding.

Finally, it adds the FooterText property of the ViewData collection to the footer of the page. It does this by using a Razor @section block. As you may recall from the last figure, anything within an @section code block will be rendered by the RenderSection method in the layout view that has the same name.

Note that the data from the ViewData object needs to be cast, but the data from the ViewBag object doesn't. You should also know that you won't have IntelliSense support for either object.

A regular view: Home/Index

The HomeController Index action method

```
[HttpGet]
public ViewResult Index() {
    ViewBag.HeaderText = "Welcome to the Halloween Store";
    ViewData["FooterText"] = "Where every day is Halloween!";
    return View();
}
```

The Home/Index.cshtml view

```
@{
    ViewBag.Title = "Shopping Cart";
    string day = DateTime.Now.DayOfWeek.ToString();
}
<h1>@ViewBag.HeaderText</h1>
<div>Thank you for visiting us this beautiful @day!</div>
@section footer {
    <p>@ViewData["FooterText"].ToString()</p>
}
```

Description

- The text you place in the ViewBag.Title object is added to the layout view's title element.
- Data in the ViewData object must be typecast. Data in the ViewBag object is dynamically typed and doesn't need to be cast. Neither has IntelliSense support.
- A Razor @section code block is rendered by a RenderSection method in the layout view that has the same name.

Figure 25-10   How to work with regular views

How to work with strongly-typed views

Figure 25-11 shows the Contact Us page of the Shopping Cart MVC application, along with the controller action method and view that produced it. Like the Index action method in the previous figure, the Contact action method in this figure returns a ViewResult object in response to an HTTP GET request. Unlike the Index action method, though, the Contact action method doesn't use the ViewBag or ViewData objects to send data to the view.

Instead, the action method creates an instance of the ContactViewModel object. You may remember from the figure on models that the Contact view model contains contact information that's hard-coded in read-only properties like Email and Phone. If you need to work with hard-coded data like this, putting the data in a view model is better than hard coding it in the controller.

Once the action method has retrieved the data, it sends the data to the view by passing the Contact view model as a parameter to the View method. Objects that are passed in this way are available to the view through the view's Model property.

The Contact.cshtml view file in this figure is located in the Home subfolder of the Views folder because it is associated with the Contact action method of the Home controller. Again, this naming and placement is necessary for the MVC framework to hook the view up with its controller.

As mentioned above, the view's Model property contains the ContactViewModel object that is passed to the View method in the Contact action method. In a regular view, the Model property works like the ViewBag object in that you don't have to typecast its properties. However, you also don't get IntelliSense support.

What makes a *strongly-typed view* like this one different from a regular view is the @model directive you see here at the top of the view file. This directive identifies the type of object in the Model property, which is what allows Visual Studio to provide IntelliSense support.

Most of the time, you'll make a view strongly-typed when you create it by following the procedure described in figure 25-8. But you can also make a regular view strongly-typed by manually adding the @model directive. If you add the directive manually, though, be sure it's fully qualified as shown in this figure.

This view uses inline Razor data binding to add the properties of the ContactViewModel to the user interface. One of the read-only properties of the ContactViewModel is a collection of URLs for the Halloween store's social media sites. To display these, the view uses a block of Razor code and the foreach syntax to loop through the collection and display each URL within an anchor element.

A strongly-typed view: Home/Contact

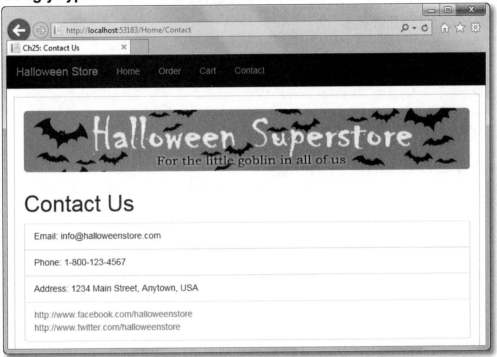

The HomeController Contact action method

```
[HttpGet]
public ViewResult Contact() {
    ContactViewModel model = new ContactViewModel();
    return View(model);
}
```

The Home/Contact.cshtml view

```
@model Ch25Cart.Models.ContactViewModel
@{
    ViewBag.Title = "Contact Us";
}
<h1>Contact Us</h1>
<ul class="list-group">
    <li class="list-group-item">Email: @Model.Email</li>
    <li class="list-group-item">Phone: @Model.Phone</li>
    <li class="list-group-item">Address: @Model.Address</li>
    <li class="list-group-item">
        @foreach (string url in Model.SocialMediaUrls) {
            <a href="@url" target="_blank">@url</a><br />
        }
    </li>
</ul>
```

Description

- The Model property contains the object that was passed to the View method. A *strongly-typed view* uses an @model directive to add IntelliSense support.

Figure 25-11   How to work with strongly-typed views

How to work with controls and postbacks

Now you know how to send data from a controller to a view, and how to work with the data once it gets to the view. But the simple views you've seen so far only display data. In a real world MVC application, you also need to interact with users through controls on a form, and you need to be able to work with the form data once the page is posted to the server.

How to work with controls

In a Web Forms application, you use server controls to interact with users. But server controls aren't available in ASP.NET MVC. Instead, you can use HTML and Razor to add input or select fields. Or, you can use some of the MVC *HTML helpers* that are summarized in the table in figure 25-12. These helpers are similar to server controls. Each of the helpers has several overloaded methods, and most have a second For version. The HTML For helpers are used with model binding and you'll see how they work later.

To see how to use both HTML with Razor and the MVC HTML helpers, you can review the examples shown here. Note that these examples are from the view that produces the Order page you saw in figure 25-2.

The first two examples show how to add a form element with a drop-down list to a page. If you want the values entered in an HTML element to post back to the server, you need to place that element inside a form. But unlike Web Forms, with MVC you can have more than one form element on a page. For example, the view for the Order page has two forms. The first one, shown here, posts to the Index action method of the Order controller when a product is selected from the drop-down list. The second one, not shown here, posts to the List action method of the Cart controller when the Add to Cart button is clicked.

As you can see, the first example uses a traditional form element. Note, though, that the action attribute is a friendly URL that contains the name of the controller and action method to post to. The second example, by contrast, uses the Html.BeginForm helper method. The first two parameters in this method are the controller name and the action method name. The third parameter is the post method, and the fourth is an optional object that contains HTML attributes like id or class. Note that either way, you don't include the "Controller" part of the controller's name.

The first two examples also show how to create the products drop-down list. To do this using HTML, you code a select element and use Razor syntax to create the list items inside a foreach loop. To do this with an HTML helper method, you pass the id of the select element, the collection of items to display, and another optional HTML attributes collection.

The last two examples show how to create the quantity text box and product id hidden field. If you followed the code in the first two examples, you should be able to follow this code.

Common HTML helpers

HTML Helpers	Corresponding HTML
`Html.ActionLink`	`<a href="">Text</a>`
`Html.BeginForm`	`<form action="" method=""></form>`
`Html.Checkbox[For]`	`<input type="checkbox" />`
`Html.DropDownList[For]`	`<select></select>`
`Html.Hidden[For]`	`<input type="hidden" />`
`Html.Label[For]`	`<label for="" />`
`Html.Password[For]`	`<input type="password" />`
`Html.RadioButton[For]`	`<input type="radio" />`
`Html.TextArea[For]`	`<textarea></textarea>`
`Html.TextBox[For]`	`<input type="text" />`

A form element with a drop-down list using traditional HTML and Razor

```
<form id="frmDropDown" action="/Order/Index" method="post">
    <select id="ddlProducts" name="ddlProducts" class="autoPostBack">
        @foreach (var item in @Model.ProductsList){
            <option value="@item.Value" selected="@item.Selected">
                @item.Text
            </option>
        }
    </select>
</form>
```

The same form element and drop-down list using HTML helpers

```
@using (Html.BeginForm("Order", "Index", FormMethod.Post,
    new { id = "frmDropDown" }))
{
    @Html.DropDownList("ddlProducts", Model.ProductsList,
        new { @class = "autoPostBack" })
}
```

A text box and a hidden field using traditional HTML and Razor

```
<input id="txtQuantity" name="txtQuantity" type="text"
    value="@product.Quantity" class="form-control" />
<input type="hidden" name="hdnId" value="@product.ProductID" />
```

The same text box and hidden field using HTML helpers

```
@Html.TextBox("txtQuantity", @product.Quantity,
    new { @class = "form-control" })
@Html.Hidden("hdnId", @product.ProductID)
```

Description

- The MVC *HTML helpers* are similar to server controls in Web Forms.
- Most HTML helpers have a second For version. This version is used in model binding, which you'll see at the end of this chapter.

Figure 25-12   How to work with controls

How to work with redirection

If your web application has more than one page, you'll need to add navigation links to your pages. You'll also need to redirect in code, such as after processing a postback.

To provide navigation links, you can use traditional HTML anchor elements or the Html.ActionLink helper shown in figure 25-13. A benefit of using the helper is that you don't need to worry about getting the relative URL right. Instead, you provide the name of the controller and the name of the action method and the MVC routing framework takes care of the rest. This is also a benefit of using the Html.BeginForm helper you saw in the last figure.

This figure shows how to create a navigation link using the Html.ActionLink method, and it provides comments that explain each of the parameters sent to the method. The route arguments parameter is where you include any URL parameters. The parameter in this figure is adding a value for the id part of the default routing pattern.

The htmlArguments parameter is how you can add attributes to the anchor element that the Html.ActionLink helper produces. The parameter in this figure is adding a class="link" attribute.

To redirect in code, you use one of the Redirect methods shown in the table in this figure. This is similar to using the Response.Redirect method in a Web Forms application, and, in fact, the MVC methods use the Response.Redirect method under the covers. Each of the MVC methods has two versions. The Redirect version returns a response status code of 302 Found to the browser, and the RedirectPermanent version returns a status code of 301 Moved Permanently.

For redirecting between controllers, you'll use the RedirectToAction method most of the time. The parameter for the controller name is optional if you are redirecting to an action method in the same controller, but it's usually best to include it so it's clear what the code is doing.

When a form is submitted, ASP.NET MVC applications commonly use the *PRG (Post-Redirect-Get) pattern*. This is to avoid the back-button and refresh problems described in chapter 21, and to separate the POST responsibility of sending data to the server from the GET responsibility of retrieving data from the server.

This figure shows an example of the PRG pattern in the Cart controller. Here, the POST List action method adds an item to the cart and then redirects to the GET List action method to display the cart. Since the POST method retrieves the cart object as part of its processing, it sends it along to the GET method in the TempData object. This is similar to using session state, and the TempData object actually uses session state under the covers. The difference is that the data in the TempData object is only stored until the next request is received.

Redirection in a view using the Html.ActionLink helper method

```
@Html.ActionLink(Model.Name,              // link text
    "Index",                              // action method
    "Order",                              // controller name
    new { id = Model.ProductID },         // route arguments
    new { @class = "link" }               // htmlArguments...if none, use null
)
```

Redirection in a controller using the Redirect methods

Method	Description
`Redirect[Permanent]()`	Requires a full URL. Most often used for external URLs.
`RedirectToRoute[Permanent]()`	Requires a full RouteDictionary object.
`RedirectToAction[Permanent]()`	Requires an action method name. Has overloads.

Three examples of redirection in controllers

```
[HttpGet]
public RedirectResult Index() {
    return Redirect ("http://www.murach.com");
}
[HttpPost]
public RedirectToRouteResult Index(OrderViewModel order) {
    return RedirectToRoute(
        Url.RouteUrl(new { controller = "Order", action = "Index" }));
}
[HttpGet]
public ActionResult Index(string id) {
    if (id == null)
        return RedirectToAction("Index", "Order");
    else {
        //code to get product by id goes here
        return View(product);
    }
}
```

The Post-Redirect-Get pattern in a controller

```
[HttpGet]
public ViewResult List() {
    CartViewModel cart = (CartViewModel)TempData["cart"];
    Return View(cart);
}
[HttpPost]
public RedirectToRouteResult List(OrderViewModel order) {
    //code to add order and get cart goes here
    TempData["cart"] = cart;
    return RedirectToAction("List", "Cart");
}
```

Description

- The *PRG (Post-Redirect-Get) pattern* is recommended with ASP.NET MVC. You can pass data from the POST action to the GET action using the TempData object.

Figure 25-13   How to work with redirection

How to add AutoPostBack functionality with jQuery

A handy feature of ASP.NET Web Forms is that you can set the AutoPostBack attribute of controls like drop-down lists and check boxes to True. That makes those controls initiate a postback when their value changes. Although this functionality isn't available with ASP.NET MVC, it's easy to add it using the jQuery shown in figure 25-14. With this code in place, all you need to do to add AutoPostBack functionality to your controls is add a class attribute with its value set to "autoPostBack". An example is shown here, and you also saw this in the select element in figure 25-12.

How to work with the FormCollection object

To help you work with the data that's posted back to the server, ASP.NET MVC stores the data in a FormCollection object. This is a NameValueCollection object that stores values as key/value pairs. The key for each key/value pair is the element's name.

To illustrate how to work with the FormCollection object, figure 25-14 shows the Order controller. This controller has two Index action methods, one that handles POST requests and one that handles GET requests. As you saw earlier, the corresponding Order view contains a form that posts to Order/Index. Within the form is a select element with a name attribute of "ddlProducts" and a class attribute of "autoPostBack". This means that the form posts to the server each time the value of the select element changes, and the selected value is included in the FormCollection object.

In this example, the POST Index action method retrieves the selected value from the FormCollection object, which is returned as a string. Then, it initiates the PRG pattern by redirecting to the GET Index action. To do that, it uses the RedirectToAction method and passes it the name of the action method, the name of the controller, and the select value as the id URL parameter.

Although it doesn't use the FormCollection object, it's worth taking a minute to look at how the GET Index action method works. First, it checks the TempData object for a SelectList object called products. If it's not there, it gets a list of products from the Order model and creates a new SelectList object by sending in the list, the name of the value field, the name of the display field, and the id of the selected product.

Then, it checks for the id URL parameter. If there isn't one, it gets the id of the first item in the SelectList object, saves the SelectList object in the TempData object so it doesn't have to build it again, and then redirects to itself using the RedirectToAction method and the first item's id.

If there is an id parameter, it creates a new Order view model and passes it and the id to the Order model, which loads the view model with product data for that id. It then adds the products list to the view model and sends the view model to the view. Note that the return type for this action method is the base ActionResult. That way, the method can return either a ViewResult or a RedirectToRouteResult object.

How to add AutoPostback functionality with jQuery

In your Javascript file

```javascript
$(document).ready(function () {
    $('.autoPostBack').change(function () {
        $(this).closest('form').submit();
    });
});
```

In your view

```html
<select id="ddlProducts" name="ddlProducts" class="autoPostBack">
```

Working with the FormCollection object in the Order controller

```csharp
namespace Ch25Cart.Controllers {
    public class OrderController : Controller
    {
        [HttpGet]
        public ActionResult Index(string id) {
            OrderModel orderData = new OrderModel();

            // get list for drop-down from temp data or model
            SelectList products = (SelectList)TempData["products"];
            if (products == null) {
                var list = orderData.GetProductsList();
                products = new SelectList(
                    list, "ProductId", "Name", id);
            }
            // if no URL parameter, get first product and reload page
            if (string.IsNullOrEmpty(id)) {
                id = products.ElementAt(0).Value;
                TempData["products"] = products;
                return RedirectToAction("Index", "Order", new { id });
            }
            else { // get selected product and pass it to the view
                OrderViewModel order = new OrderViewModel();
                orderData.LoadOrder(order, id);
                order.ProductsList = products;
                return View(order);
            }
        }
        [HttpPost] // post back - get selected ddl value and reload page
        public RedirectToRouteResult Index(FormCollection form)
        {
            string pID = form["ddlProducts"];
            return RedirectToAction("Index", "Order", new { id = pID });
        }
    }
}
```

Description

- The FormCollection object is a name/value collection object. It contains the string values of the elements of a form that has been posted to the server. To be in the FormCollection object, an element must have a name attribute.

Figure 25-14   How to add AutoPostBack functionality and work with the FormCollection object

How to work with model binding

In the last figure, you learned how to work with data posted to the server by retrieving it from the FormCollection object. But there are two problems with that approach. First, you have to remember the names of the controls in the view and manually type the names in the controller. This requires switching between the two files and can also introduce errors. Second, it means your controller needs to know details about your view, which makes them more tightly coupled than you want.

The solution to these problems is to use *model binding*. You can think of model binding as making your controller's POST action method strongly-typed. Here's how to set it up.

First, in your view, you bind the controls to the model using Html For helpers. For instance, figure 25-15 shows the Quantity text box and the ProductID hidden field of the Order/Index view, rewritten to use the Html.TextBoxFor and Html.HiddenFor helpers.

Unfortunately, the syntax for a For helper can be hard to follow because the first parameter is a Lambda expression. In the Lambda expressions in this example, "m" represents the view's Model property. So, the expression is telling the helper which property of the model to bind to. This means that the Html.TextBoxFor helper is binding the textbox to the Quantity property of the Model's SelectedProduct property, and the Html.HiddenFor helper is binding the hidden field to the ProductID property of the SelectedProduct property.

Then, in the POST action method in the controller, you change the object passed to the method from the FormCollection object to the type of the view's Model property. In this example, the Cart controller uses the POST List action method to accept an OrderViewModel object rather than a FormCollection object.

Making these two adjustments means that when your form posts to the server, the action method is passed a strongly-typed object, and you can use IntelliSense to work with the data sent from the form.

Once again, it's worth taking the time to look at the rest of the Cart controller. Here, the POST List action method receives data posted from the form, uses it to add a product to the cart, and then implements the PRG pattern by redirecting to the GET List action method. But first, it stores the cart in the TempData object.

The GET List action method first checks the TempData object for a CartViewModel object called cart. If it isn't there, it uses the Cart model to retrieve the cart view model object. Then, it sends the cart view model to the view.

There is also a GET Index action method that does nothing but redirect to the GET List action method. This is because the main GET action method for this controller is called List instead of Index. Although this name was chosen to make the URL more descriptive (Cart/List), if users navigate to just Cart/, they will get 404 File Not Found errors. However, adding an Index action method that redirects to List fixes this problem.

The Quantity textbox and ProductID hidden field of the Order/Index view, after it has been revised for model binding

```
@Html.TextBoxFor(m => m.SelectedProduct.Quantity,
    new { id = "txtQuantity" , @class = "form-control" })
@Html.HiddenFor(m => m.SelectedProduct.ProductID)
```

Working with model binding in the Cart controller

```
namespace Ch25Cart.Controllers {
    public class CartController : Controller
    {
        private CartModel cartData = new CartModel();

        [HttpGet]
        public RedirectToRouteResult Index() {
            return RedirectToAction("List/");
        }

        [HttpGet]
        public ViewResult List()
        {
            CartViewModel cart = (CartViewModel)TempData["cart"];
            if (cart == null) cart = cartData.GetCart();
            return View(cart);
        }

        [HttpPost]
        public RedirectToRouteResult List(OrderViewModel order)
        {
            cartData.AddToCart(order);
            TempData["cart"] = cartData.GetCart();
            return RedirectToAction("List", "Cart");
        }
    }
}
```

Description

- When working with the FormCollection object, you need to remember the names of the view's controls. This can lead to typos and other errors.

- *Model binding* lets you post the view model of a strongly-typed view directly to the controller and then work with the view model instead.

- Model binding provides IntelliSense support when working with data posted from the view, and it also keeps your controller from having to know anything about how your view is constructed.

- The easiest way to set up model binding is to use the Html For helpers in your view. In the example above, the Html.TextBoxFor and Html.HiddenFor helpers replace the last two examples shown in figure 24-12.

- Both the textbox and the hidden field will have the name attributes generated by the HTML helpers. You can view the page source code in the browser to see the HTML produced by these helpers.

Figure 25-15   How to work with model binding

Perspective

Now that you've completed this chapter, you can start to appreciate the striking differences between Web Forms and MVC development. If you experiment with the downloadable application for this chapter, you will get an even better idea of how MVC works. Then, you can decide whether you want to learn more about MVC and maybe use it for your own applications.

Terms

MVC (Model-View-Controller) design pattern	inline data binding
model	Razor view engine
view	routing framework
controller	action method
view model	layout view
bundling framework	strongly-typed view
ASP.NET MVC	HTML helper
view engine	PRG (Post-Redirect-Get) pattern
	model binding

Summary

- The *MVC (Model-View-Controller) design pattern* provides a modular structure that makes applications easier to test and maintain.

- The *model* handles data, the *view* handles the user interface, and the *controller* handles HTTP requests and coordinates the model and the view. The optional *view model* transfers data from the controller to the view and is widely used in ASP.NET MVC applications.

- ASP.NET MVC uses the *Razor view engine* to add dynamic data to the static HMTL in a view, and it uses a *routing framework* to direct HTTP requests to the correct controller.

- The files in the Models and Controllers folders are regular class files. The model files handle data, including applying business and validation rules. The controller files handle HTTP requests by using *action methods*. The goal is to have "fat" models and "skinny" controllers.

- The files in the Views folder produce the HTML for the pages. These files should have the same name as their associated action method, should be in a folder with the same name as their associated controller, and can be *strongly-typed*. The *layout view* functions as a master page for other views.

- *HTML helpers* are used to add controls to a view. Controls must have a name attribute and be in a form element. You can work with data posted to the server through the FormCollection object or with *model binding*.

- ASP.NET MVC applications commonly implement the *PRG (Post-Redirect-Get) pattern* when handling postbacks.

Appendix A

How to install and use the software and downloadable files

To develop ASP.NET 4.6 applications, you need to have Visual Studio 2015 or Visual Studio 2015 Community Edition on your PC. Both of these products include an edition of IIS called IIS Express that you can use to run and test your applications. They also include an edition of SQL Server called SQL Server Express LocalDB that you can use with databases on your local computer.

This appendix describes how to install Visual Studio 2015 or Visual Studio 2015 Community Edition. In addition, it describes what you need to do to use the database for this book, and it describes how to set up IIS on your local computer in case you want to deploy your applications to that server. But first, it describes the files for this book that are available for download from our website and shows you how to download, install, and use them.

Please note that if you just want to develop and test ASP.NET applications on your own computer, you only need to install Visual Studio 2015 or Visual Studio 2015 Community Edition, along with our downloadable files. You don't need to do separate installs for SQL Server Express or IIS.

How to download and install the files for this book

Throughout this book, you'll see complete applications that illustrate the material presented in each chapter. To help you understand how these applications work, you can download the source code and database for these applications from our website at www.murach.com. Then, you can open and run them in Visual Studio. These files come in a single download, as summarized in figure A-1. This figure also describes how you download and install these files.

When you download the single setup file and execute it, it will install all of the files for this book in the Murach\aspnet46_cs directory on your C drive. Within this directory, you'll find a directory named book_applications that contains all the applications in this book. You can open these applications in Visual Studio and run them as described in this figure.

The download also includes the files for the Halloween database that's used throughout the book. You can use these files with SQL Server 2014 Express LocalDB, which comes with Visual Studio 2015. If you want to use SQL Server Express instead of LocalDB, you'll need to install SQL Server Express on your computer, and you'll need to create the Halloween database. You'll learn how to do that in figure A-3.

To help you practice the skills you'll learn in this book, we've included exercises at the ends of most of the chapters. We also provide starting points for many of these exercises in the C:\Murach\aspnet46_cs\exercises directory. When you execute the setup file, the contents of this directory are copied to the C:\aspnet46_cs directory (creating this directory if necessary). This makes it easy to locate the exercise starts as you work through the exercises.

We also provide the solutions to the exercises in the C:\Murach\aspnet46_cs\ solutions directory. If you have trouble doing the exercises, you can use Visual Studio to open these applications. Then, you can compare the solutions to your applications to solve any problems that you encountered while attempting to do the exercises.

If you aren't able to download the setup file that we provide, you should know that we also provide a zip file that you can download. If you download this file, you will need to extract its files into the C:\Murach\aspnet46_cs directory. Then, if you'll be doing the exercises for this book, you'll need to create the C:\aspnet46_cs directory and copy the exercise_starts subdirectory of the C:\Murach\aspnet46_cs directory into the new directory.

What the downloadable files for this book contain

- The source code for all of the applications presented in this book
- The starting points for the exercises in this book
- The solutions for the exercises in this book
- The Halloween database used by the applications and exercises

How to download and install the files for this book

1. Go to www.murach.com, and go to the page for *Murach's ASP.NET 4.6 Web Programming with C# 2015*.
2. Click on the "FREE Downloads" tab and scroll to the "Book Applications and Exercises" section.
3. Click on the "DOWNLOAD NOW" button for the exe file. This will download a setup file named ac46_allfiles.exe to your computer.
4. Use Windows Explorer to find the setup file on your computer. Then, double-click on this file and respond to the dialog boxes that follow. This installs the files in directories that start with C:\Murach\aspnet46_cs.

How your system is prepared for doing the exercises

- Some of the exercises have you start from existing applications. The source code for these applications is in the C:\Murach\aspnet46_cs\exercises directory. After the setup file installs the files in the download, it runs a batch file named exercise_starts_setup.bat that copies the contents of the exercises directory to the C:\aspnet46_cs directory. Then, you can find all of the starting points for the exercises in directories like C:\aspnet46_cs\Ex01FutureValue and C:\aspnet46_cs\Ex04Cart.

How to view the source code for the applications

- The source code for the applications presented in this book can be found in the C:\Murach\aspnet46_cs\book_applications directory. You can view this source code by opening the solution in the appropriate directory.

How to view the solutions to the exercises

- The exercise solutions can be found in the C:\Murach\aspnet46_cs\solutions directory. You can view these applications by opening the solution in the appropriate directory.

How to prepare your system for using the SQL Server database

- If you will be using SQL Server 2014 Express LocalDB, no preparation is required. The files for the Halloween database are included in the App_Data folder of each application that uses the database.
- If you will be using SQL Server 2014 Express, you will need to install and configure this product as described in figure A-3.

Figure A-1   How to download and install the files for this book

How to install Visual Studio 2015

If you've installed Windows applications before, you shouldn't have any trouble installing Visual Studio 2015. If you purchased a DVD, you simply insert it and the setup program starts automatically. If you downloaded a disc image of Visual Studio, you can just mount that image using a program for that purpose and then run the setup program. For more information on programs for work with disc images, you can search the Internet for "mount disc image".

When the setup program runs, it will lead you through the steps for installing Visual Studio as summarized in figure A-2. To start, you select whether you want to install the default features or the custom features. Then, after reviewing the license terms and privacy statement, you click the Install button that's displayed if you selected the Default option or the Next button that's displayed if you selected the Custom option.

If you selected the Custom option, the program then lets you select the optional features you want to install. This includes features like LightSwitch, developer tools for Microsoft Office, and data tools for Microsoft SQL Server. If you're sure you won't need some of the features that are selected by default, you can uncheck them. Then, when you click the Next button, a list of the custom features you selected is displayed. If this list is correct, you can click the Install button to install Visual Studio.

Note that the .NET Framework 4.6, IIS Express, and SQL Server 2014 Express LocalDB are installed along with Visual Studio, regardless of whether you select the Default or Custom option. Also note that Microsoft changes the setup program from time to time, so it may look or work differently from what's described here.

If you want to install Visual Studio 2015 Community Edition, you can do that using a similar technique. Because this edition is free, though, it must be downloaded from Microsoft's website, and it's typically installed using a web installer so you don't have to mount a disc image. In addition, if you select the Custom option when you run the setup program, you'll notice that not all the same options are available.

The Visual Studio 2015 Setup program

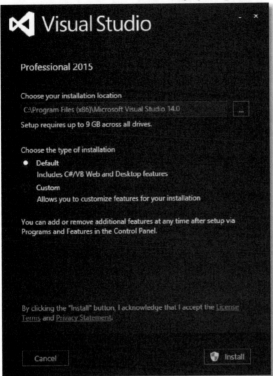

How to install Visual Studio 2015

1. Insert the Visual Studio DVD and the setup program will start automatically. Or, mount a downloaded disc image of Visual Studio and then run the setup program.

2. To install the default features for desktop and web development with C# and VB, select the Default option. To customize the features that are installed, select the Custom option.

3. Review the license terms and privacy statement, and then click the Install button (Default) or Next button (Custom).

4. If you selected the Custom option, you can add or delete features from the next page that's displayed.

5. When the Setup Complete page is displayed, you can click the Restart Now button to restart your computer and finish the installation.

Visual Studio 2015 Community Edition differences

1. Since this edition is free, it can only be downloaded from Microsoft's website.

2. Not all of the same custom features are available for this edition.

Note

-   The Visual Studio 2015 setup programs install not only Visual Studio, but also .NET Framework 4.6, IIS Express, and SQL Server 2014 Express LocalDB.

Figure A-2   How to install Visual Studio 2015

How to use the Halloween database

In section 3 of this book, you will learn how to develop applications that work with the data in a database. The book applications in that section use a database named Halloween with an edition of SQL Server 2014 called SQL Server 2014 Express LocalDB. This edition of SQL Server is designed specifically for developers and doesn't require any management. It lets you create applications that automatically start the database engine and attach the database to the server when an application is run. In addition, it is automatically installed with Visual Studio 2015.

Figure A-3 summarizes the techniques for using the Halloween database with SQL Server Express LocalDB. To do that, you can simply add the Halloween.mdf file to the App_Data folder of a project. Then, you can create a SQL data source that uses this database as described in chapter 13. Alternatively, you can use an object data source with the database as described in chapter 17, or an Entity Data Model and model binding as described in chapter 18.

Of course, you can also use the Halloween database with other editions of SQL Server 2014. If you deploy an application to IIS on your local computer as described in chapter 22, for example, you won't be able to use SQL Server Express LocalDB with the application. In that case, you may want to install and use SQL Server 2014 Express as described in this figure. This edition of SQL Server is free, and it provides all of the features of the full editions of SQL Server.

Although you don't need to know much about how SQL Server Express works to use it, you should know that when you run the setup program, it creates an instance of SQL Server with the same name as your computer appended with SQLEXPRESS. For example, the copy of SQL Server on my system is named Anne-PC\SQLEXPRESS. After this server is installed and started, you can create databases that are managed by the server. Then, you can connect to those databases from your C# applications using the generated server name or the name localhost\SqlExpress. Here, *localhost* indicates that the database server is running on the same computer as the application.

To create the Halloween database, you can run the batch file named create_database.bat that's stored in the C:\Murach\aspnet46_cs\Database directory when you download and install the files for this book as described in figure A-1. This batch file runs a SQL Server script named create_database.sql that creates the Halloween database and attaches it to the SQL Server Express database server that's running on your computer.

Note, however, that if the database server on your system has a name other than the computer name appended with SQLEXPRESS, the batch file we provide won't work. But you can easily change it so it will work. To do that, just open the file in a text editor such as NotePad. When you do, you'll see a single command with this server specification:

```
sqlcmd -S localhost\SqlExpress -E /i create_database.sql
```

Then, you can just change this specification to the name of your server.

How to use the database with SQL Server 2014 Express LocalDB

- The Halloween database files (Halloween.mdf and Halloween_Log.ldf) are included in the App_Data folder of each application for this book that uses this database.

- To use the Halloween database in your own applications, you can add the Halloween.mdf file to the App_Data folder of your project. This will automatically add the Halloween_Log.ldf file. Then, you can work with the database using a SQL data source as described in chapter 13, an object data source as described in chapter 17, or an Entity Data Model and model binding as described in chapter 18.

How to use the database with SQL Server 2014 Express

- To use the Halloween database with SQL Server Express, you must first create it. To do that, you can use Windows Explorer to navigate to the C:\Murach\aspnet46_cs\ Database directory and double-click the create_database.bat file. This runs the create_database.sql file that creates the database objects and inserts the rows into each table.

- The create_database.sql file starts by deleting the Halloween database if it already exists. That way, you can use it to recreate the database and restore the original data if you ever need to do that.

- When you create the database, the Halloween.mdf and Halloween_Log.ldf files are created and stored in the default data directory for your instance of SQL Server. For SQL Server 2014, that directory is C:\Program files\Microsoft SQL Server\ MSSQL12.SQLEXPRESS\ MSSQL\DATA for the 64-bit version of SQL Server. If you're using the 32-bit version instead, they'll be stored in the Program files (x86) directory.

- To define a connection to the Halloween database, you can use the server name localhost\SqlExpress or a name that consists of your computer name followed by \SqlExpress.

How to install and work with SQL Server 2014 Express

- To install SQL Server 2014 Express, you can download its setup file from Microsoft's website for free and then run that file.

- After you install SQL Server Express, it will start automatically each time you start your PC. To start or stop this service or change its start mode, start the SQL Server Configuration Manager, select the server in the right pane, and use the buttons in the toolbar.

- To start the Configuration Manager from Windows 7 or Windows 10, use the Start→All Programs→Microsoft SQL Server 2014→Configuration Tools→SQL Server Configuration Manager command. From Windows 8, enter SQL Server Configuration Manager in the Search bar and then double-click the shortcut when it's displayed.

Notes

- SQL Server 2014 Express LocalDB is automatically installed with Visual Studio 2015, so no setup is required to use it.

- If you're using Windows 8 or later, you can also install and use SQL Server 2016 Express. The procedures for doing that are similar to those shown above.

Figure A-3   How to use the Halloween database

How to set up IIS on your local computer

In addition to IIS Express, which comes with Visual Studio 2015, Windows comes with the full edition of IIS. For the purposes of this book, you won't need to use the full edition unless you want to deploy an application to IIS on your local computer. Then, you'll need to know how to set up IIS. Figure A-4 shows you how.

To start, you need to install IIS. To do that, you display the Windows Features dialog box as described here. This dialog box lists all the available Windows features. If all of the features of a component are installed, the check box in front of the component will have a check mark in it. If only some of the features are installed, the check box will be shaded.

To install the default features of IIS, you simply check its box and then click the OK button. If you want to install features other than the defaults, you can expand the Internet Information Services node and any of its subordinate nodes to select the features you want. For example, you may want to select the IIS Management Console feature to use this program to work with IIS.

If you know that you're going to deploy your applications to IIS, you should install IIS before you install Visual Studio. That way, Visual Studio can register ASP.NET with IIS. Otherwise, you'll need to use the aspnet_regiis program to do that as described in this figure.

First, you'll need to open a command prompt as an administrator. To do that in Windows 7 or Windows 10, select Start→All Programs→Accessories. Then, right-click the Command Prompt shortcut, select Run as administrator, and respond yes to the dialog box that asks if you want to allow changes to the computer. In Windows 8, you can enter "Command Prompt" in the Search bar, right-click the shortcut when it's displayed, and respond yes to the dialog box.

To find the latest build number of .NET that you need to run this program, you can first enter a cd\ command at a command prompt to return to the root directory of the C drive. Then, you can run this command to identify the Windows root directory:

```
C:\>cd %systemroot%\Microsoft.NET\Framework
C:\Windows\Microsoft.NET\Framework>
```

This shows you what the root directory is so you can use Windows Explorer to find the latest build number in the Framework directory. To complete the registration, you can run these commands (assuming the build number is 30319):

```
C:\Windows\Microsoft.NET\Framework>cd v4.0.30319
C:\Windows\Microsoft.NET\Framework\v4.0.30319>aspnet_regiis -i
```

If the web application you're deploying uses the Halloween database, you'll also need to grant ASP.NET access to that database. To do that, you can use the grant_access.bat file as described in this figure. This file runs a script named grant_access.sql, which actually grants access to the DefaultAppPool application pool. Application pools are used by IIS to separate the processing of various applications. The DefaultAppPool application pool is the one that your ASP.NET 4.6 applications will run in by default if you run them under IIS.

The Windows Features dialog box

How to install IIS

1. Display the Control Panel and click the Programs link. Then, click the Turn Windows Features On or Off link in the Programs and Features category to display the Windows Features dialog box.

2. Select Internet Information Services from the list of features that are displayed. Then, if you want to be able to use any features that aren't selected by default, like the IIS Management Console, you can expand the nodes until you see that feature and then select it.

3. Click the OK button to complete the installation.

How to register ASP.NET with IIS

- If you know that you're going to use IIS, you should install it before you install Visual Studio. Otherwise, you'll need to register ASP.NET with IIS.

- To register ASP.NET with IIS, open a command prompt as an administrator and use the cd command to change the directory to %systemroot%Microsoft.NET\ Framework\ v4.0.xxxxx, where %systemroot% is the root directory for Windows and xxxxx is the latest .NET build number. Then, enter the command aspnet_regiis -i.

How to grant ASP.NET access to the Halloween database

- Run the grant_access.bat file in the C:\Murach\apsnet46_cs\Database directory, which runs the grant_access.sql file.

Figure A-4   How to set up IIS on your local computer

Index

X

If you need to refresh your C# skills

Murach's C# 2015 delivers the core skills you need for ASP.NET web programming. So it's great to have on hand whenever you need to learn a new C# skill or brush up on an old one.

Books for .NET developers

Murach's C# 2015	$57.50
Murach's ASP.NET 4.6 Web Programming with C# 2015	59.50
Murach's Visual Basic 2015	57.50

Books for database developers

Murach's SQL Server 2016 for Developers	$57.50
Murach's MySQL (2nd Ed.)	54.50
Murach's Oracle SQL and PL/SQL for Developers (2nd Ed.)	54.50

Books for Java and Python developers

Murach's Python Programming	$57.50
Murach's Java Servlets and JSP (3rd Ed.)	57.50
Murach's Beginning Java with NetBeans	57.50
Murach's Beginning Java with Eclipse	57.50
Murach's Java Programming (5th Ed.)	59.50

Books for web developers

Murach's HTML5 and CSS3 (3rd Ed.)	$54.50
Murach's JavaScript and jQuery (3rd Ed.)	57.50
Murach's PHP and MySQL (3rd Ed.)	57.50

Prices and availability are subject to change. Please visit our website or call for current information.

We want to hear from you

Do you have any comments, questions, or compliments to pass on to us? It would be great to hear from you! Please share your feedback in whatever way works best.

 www.murach.com

 twitter.com/MurachBooks

 1-800-221-5528
(Weekdays, 8 am to 4 pm Pacific Time)

 facebook.com/murachbooks

 murachbooks@murach.com

 linkedin.com/company/
mike-murach-&-associates

What software you need for this book

- Any of the full editions of Microsoft Visual Studio 2015 or Visual Studio 2015 Community Edition.
- These editions include everything you need for developing ASP.NET 4.6 applications, including .NET Framework 4.6, ASP.NET 4.6, C# 2015, a scaled-back version of IIS called IIS Express, and a scaled-back version of SQL Server called SQL Server Express LocalDB.
- If you want to store databases on your own PC and you don't want to use SQL Server 2014 Express LocalDB, you can install SQL Server 2014 Express.
- If you want to use IIS (Internet Information Services) on your own computer to test the deployment of an application, you'll need to be sure it's installed and set up properly.
- For information about installing these products, please see appendix A.

The downloadable files for this book

- The source code for all of the applications presented in this book.
- Starting points for the exercises in this book so you can get more practice in less time.
- Solutions for all of the exercises in this book so you can check your work on the exercises.
- The files for the Halloween database that's used by this book, along with files for creating this database if you're using an edition of SQL Server 2014 other than SQL Server 2014 Express LocalDB.
- Files for granting ASP.NET access to the Halloween database if you're running an application under IIS instead of IIS Express.
- For information about downloading and installing these applications and files, please see appendix A.

www.murach.com